An Eerdmans Reader in
Contemporary Political Theology

An Eerdmans Reader in Contemporary Political Theology

Edited by

William T. Cavanaugh,
Jeffrey W. Bailey &
Craig Hovey

WILLIAM B. EERDMANS PUBLISHING COMPANY
GRAND RAPIDS, MICHIGAN / CAMBRIDGE, U.K.

© 2012 William B. Eerdmans Publishing Company
All rights reserved

Published 2012 by
Wm. B. Eerdmans Publishing Co.
2140 Oak Industrial Drive N.E., Grand Rapids, Michigan 49505 /
P.O. Box 163, Cambridge CB3 9PU U.K.

Printed in the United States of America

17 16 15 14 13 12   7 6 5 4 3 2 1

Library of Congress Cataloging-in-Publication Data

An Eerdmans reader in contemporary political theology /
     edited by William T. Cavanaugh, Jeffrey W. Bailey & Craig Hovey.
          p.   cm.
     Includes bibliographical references.
     ISBN 978-0-8028-6440-6 (pbk.: alk. paper)
     1. Political theology.   I. Cavanaugh, William T., 1962-
     II. Bailey, Jeffrey W.   III. Hovey, Craig, 1974-

     BT83.59.E47   2012
     261.7 — dc23

                                                        2011025648

www.eerdmans.com

Contents

IV. America and the Church

V. In the Shadow of Auschwitz

VIII. Postcolonial Challenges

IX. Church-Based Politics

Acknowledgments

The editors and publisher gratefully acknowledge permission granted by the following publishers to reprint these copyrighted works. Works are numbered as they appear in this volume.

1. Christopher Rowland, "The Foundation and Form of Liberation Exegesis." In Christopher Rowland and Mark Corner, eds., *Liberating Exegesis: The Challenge of Third World Liberation Theology to the World of Biblical Studies.* © 1989 Westminster John Knox Press. Used by permission of Westminster John Knox Press.

2. Richard Bauckham, *The Bible in Politics: How to Read the Bible Politically.* © 1989 Richard J. Bauckham. Used by permission of Westminster John Knox Press.

3. R. S. Sugirtharajah, *Postcolonial Reconfigurations: An Alternative Way of Reading the Bible and Doing Theology* (2003). Used courtesy of Chalice Press, St. Louis.

4. Néstor Míguez, "Latin American Readings of the Bible: Experiences, Challenges, and Its Practice," *Expository Times* 18.3, pp. 120-129. Used by permission.

5. A. Maria Arul Raja, S.J., "Some Reflections on a Dalit Reading of the Bible." In V. Devasahayam, ed., *Frontiers of Dalit Theology* (London: SPCK, 1997). Used by permission.

6. Ernesto Cardenal, "Song of Mary: Luke 1:46-55." In Ernesto Cardenal, *The Gospel in Solentiname,* trans. Donald D. Walsh (Maryknoll: Orbis, 1982). Used by permission.

7. Virgil Michel, "Liturgy the basis of social regeneration," *Orate Fratres* (Nov 1935). Used by permission.

8. Excerpted from *For the Life of the World: Sacraments and Orthodoxy* by Alexander Schmemann. Copyright 1973 by Saint Vladimir's Seminary Press. Reproduced with permission of Saint Vladimir's Seminary Press in the format Textbook via Copyright Clearance Center.

9. Rafael Avila, *Worship and Politics,* trans. Alan Neely (Maryknoll: Orbis, 1981). Used by permission.

10. Catherine Pickstock, "Liturgy and Modernity," *Telos* 113 (Fall 1998). Used by permission.

11. Walter Rauschenbusch, *A Theology for the Social Gospel* (New York: Macmillan, 1917). (Public domain.)

12. Gustavo Gutiérrez, "Option for the Poor." Trans. Robert R. Barr. In Ignacio Ellacuria, Jon Sobrino, and Robert R. Barr, eds., *Mysterium Liberationis: Fundamental Concepts of Liberation Theology* (Maryknoll: Orbis, 2004). Used by permission.

13. Jon Sobrino, "The Central Position of the Reign of God in Liberation Theology." Trans. Robert R. Barr. In Ignacio Ellacuria, Jon Sobrino, and Robert R. Barr, eds., *Mysterium Liberationis: Fundamental Concepts of Liberation Theology* (Maryknoll: Orbis, 2004). Used by permission.

14. Reinhold Niebuhr, "Augustine's Political Realism." In Robert MacAfee Brown, ed., *The Essential Reinhold Niebuhr: Selected Essays and Addresses* (New Haven: Yale University Press, 1986). Reprinted by permission of the Estate of Reinhold Niebuhr.

15. John Courtney Murray, S.J. *We Hold These Truths: Catholic Reflections on the American Proposition* (Lanham: Rowman & Littlefield, 2005). Used by permission.

16. Copyright © 1932 by the *Christian Century.* "The Grace of Doing Nothing" by H. Richard Niebuhr is reprinted by permission from the March 23, 1932, issue of the *Christian Century.*

17. Copyright © 1932 by the *Christian Century.* "Must we do nothing?" by Reinhold Niebuhr is reprinted by permission from the March 30, 1932, issue of the *Christian Century.*

18. Copyright © 1932 by the *Christian Century.* "The only way into the kingdom of God" by H. Richard Niebuhr is reprinted by permission from the April 6, 1932, issue of the *Christian Century.*

19. Carl Schmitt, *Political Theology: Four Chapters on the Concept of Sovereignty,* trans. George Schwab (Cambridge, MA: MIT Press, 1986). Used by permission.

20. Dietrich Bonhoeffer, *Ethics,* trans. Neville Horton Smith (New York: Touchstone, 1995). Used by permission.

21. Karl Barth, *Ethics,* trans. Geoffrey W. Bromiley (New York: Seabury, 1981). Used by permission.

22. Johann Baptist Metz, "Theology in the New Paradigm: Political Theology." In Hans Küng, ed., *Paradigm Change in Theology* (New York: Crossroad, 1989). Used by permission.

23. Dorothee Sölle, *The Window of Vulnerability: A Political Spirituality,* trans. Linda M. Maloney (Minneapolis: Augsburg Fortress, 1990). Used by permission.

24. Dorothy Day, "We Are Un-American: We Are Catholics," *The Catholic Worker* (April 1948). Used by permission.

25. René Girard, "Violence and the Lamb Slain: An Interview with René Girard by Brian McDonald." The original version of this essay appeared in the December 2003 issue of *Touchstone: A Journal of Mere Christianity* (www.touchstonemag.com). Used by permission.

26. Walter Wink, *The Powers That Be: Theology for a New Millennium* (New York: Morehouse, 1999). Used by permission.

27. Rosemary Radford Ruether, *Sexism and God-Talk: Toward a Feminist Theology* (Boston: Beacon Press, 1984). Used by permission.

28. Anon. Conference Statement from the 1987 Asian Women's Theology Consultation. Used by permission.

29. Delores S. Williams, "The Color of Feminism: Or Speaking the Black Woman's Tongue." In Lois K. Daly, ed., *Feminist Theological Ethics: A Reader Library of Theological Ethics.* © 1994 Westminster John Knox Press. Used by permission of Westminster John Knox Press.

30. Ada María Isasi-Díaz, *Mujerista Theology: A Theology for the Twenty-First Century* (Maryknoll: Orbis, 1996). Used by permission.

31. James H. Cone, "Looking Back, Going Forward: Black Theology as Public Theology." In Dwight N. Hopkins, ed., *Black Faith and Public Talk: Critical Essays on James H. Cone's Black Theology and Black Power* (Maryknoll: Orbis, 1999). Used by permission.

32. J. Kameron Carter, *Race: A Theological Account* (New York: Oxford University Press, 2008). Used by permission.

33. Desmond Tutu, *No Future without Forgiveness,* reprint ed. (New York: Doubleday, 2000). Used by permission.

34. Emmanuel Katongole, "Postmodern Illusions and the Challenges of African Theology: The Ecclesial Tactics of Resistance," *Modern Theology* 16.2 (April 2000): 237-254. Used by permission.

35. Kim Yong-Bock, "Messiah and Minjung: Discerning Messianic Politics over against Political Messianism." In Commission on Theological Concerns of the Christian Conference of Asia, ed., *Minjung Theology: People as the Subjects of History* (Maryknoll: Orbis, 1981). Used by permission.

36. Arvind Nirmal, "Towards a Christian Dalit Theology." In James Massey, ed., *Indigenous People: Dalits: Dalit Issues in Today's Theological Debate* (Delhi: ISPCK, 1994). Used by permission.

37. Kosuke Koyama, *Mount Fuji and Mount Sinai: A Critique of Idols* (Maryknoll: Orbis, 1985). Used by permission.

38. Rafiq Khoury, "Die theologischen Implikationen der aktuellen Situation im Heiligen Land. Aus der Sicht eines christlichen Palästinensers." Trans. Michael Hollerich. In Harald Suerman, ed., *Zwischen Halbmond und Davidstern: Christliche Theologie in Palästina Heute* (Freiburg: Herder, 2001). Used by permission.

39. Musa W. Dube, "Toward a Post-Colonial Feminist Interpretation of the Bible," *Semeia* 78 (1997): 11-26. Used by permission.

40. Kwok Pui-lan, "Theology and Social Theory." In Kwok Pui-lan, Don H. Compier, and Joerg Rieger, eds., *Empire and the Christian Tradition: New Readings of Classical Theologians* (Minneapolis: Fortress, 2007). Used by permission.

41. Excerpted from Mark Lewis Taylor, "Spirit and Liberation: Achieving Postcolonial Theology in the United States." In Catherine Keller, Michael Nausner, and Mayra Rivera, eds., *Postcolonial Theologies: Divinity and Empire.* Copyright 2004 by Christian Board of Publication. Reproduced with permission of Christian Board of Publication in the format Textbook via Copyright Clearance Center.

42. John Howard Yoder, "Sacrament as Social Process: Christ the Transformer of Culture," *Theology Today,* 48.1 (April 1991): 33-44. Used by permission.

43. Stanley Hauerwas, *After Christendom?* (Nashville: Abingdon Press, 1991). Used by permission.

44. John Milbank, "The Last of the Last: Theology, Authority, and Democracy," *Telos* 123 (Spring 2002). Used by permission.

45. Oliver O'Donovan, "Government as Judgment," in Oliver O'Donovan and Joan Lockwood O'Donovan, *Bonds of Imperfection: Christian Politics, Past and Present* (Grand Rapids: Eerdmans, 2004). First published in *First Things* 92 (1999): 35-44. Used by permission.

46. Rowan Williams, "The Politics of the Soul: A Reading of the City of God," *Milltown Studies* 19/20 (1987): 55-72. Used by permission.

47. Elsa Tamez, "Justicia Infinita, Injusticia sin Fin," *Pasos* 98 (November-December 2001): 9-17. Used by permission. Trans. William T. Cavanaugh.
48. George Weigel, "Moral Clarity in a Time of War," *First Things* (January 2003). Used by permission.
49. Rowan Williams and George Weigel, "War and Statecraft: An Exchange," *First Things* (March 2004). Used by permission.

Introduction

Why This Volume?

It may be hard to believe now, but it was only a decade ago that *The Economist* magazine ran a headline-grabbing obituary for God. "The Almighty," it editorialized, "after a lengthy career, has passed into history."[1]

Such a judgment reflected longstanding assumptions for many in the West. Throughout the latter half of the twentieth century, the disappearance of God from public life was increasingly taken for granted. Not only the popular media, but much of academia followed the eminent sociologist Peter Berger's confident "secularization thesis" predicting that as cultures became more modern they would increasingly throw off the yoke of faith. To be modern, they assumed, was to be secular.

The paradigmatic example of this was Europe. Europe was once the seedbed for Western Christendom, but now churchgoing had become the preserve of a mere remnant of the European population. America, which remained both modern and pious, was simply viewed as the quirky exception. Europe embodied the understanding that history, as Max Weber told us, was marching inevitably toward "the disenchantment of the world." And by the mid-twentieth century it appeared that the example of Europe was, indeed, spreading elsewhere: Kemal Atatürk had instituted a secular government in Turkey; Jawaharlal Nehru tried to make a "clean sweep" of institutionalized religion in India; the Pahlavi shahs of Iran argued that

1. *The Economist*, 23 December 1999, p. 43.

modernity was in opposition to the Mosque. Even the oddity that was America appeared to be catching up: by 1960, with evangelical Christians in full retreat, John F. Kennedy assured the electorate that his Catholicism would not affect his politics, and a 1966 cover of *Time* magazine could ask "Is God Dead?" Atheism became the new intellectual vanguard, and by the early 1990s Francis Fukuyama would affirm the triumph of secular liberalism with his book *The End of History and the Last Man.* It appeared that faith had been permanently exiled to a peripheral, or at least privatized, sphere.

Few believe that anymore. Today atheism is in retreat in former communist regimes: unregulated practices like Falun Gong flourish in China, while former KGB heavyweight Vladimir Putin is busily reclaiming Christianity for the state, conspicuously wearing his baptismal cross, visiting churches, and publicly maintaining a small chapel next to his office in the Kremlin. We witness clashes in North Africa between evangelical Christians in the north and fundamentalist Muslims in the south. In Sri Lanka, Buddhist monks appear locked in ongoing conflict with Hindu Tamils. Conflict in the Middle East has, in comparison with earlier decades, increasingly adopted theological language. Atatürk's Turkey is now ruled by an Islamist political party, and increasing numbers of Turkey's educated, elite women have taken to wearing the headscarf. In America, of course, the return of evangelicals to the public square has been amply documented: President George W. Bush opened each cabinet meeting in prayer, Vice-Presidential candidate Sarah Palin was an unabashed Pentecostal, and President Barack Obama wrote freely of his adult conversion to Christianity and his appreciation for the political theology of Reinhold Niebuhr. Even in Europe, the loosening of church-state connections appears to be creating space for religious life to once again flourish in embryonic ways: Pentecostalism is the fastest-growing branch of religion in France, for example, while British Prime Minister Tony Blair, notably open about his Christian commitments in comparison with most European leaders, started a high-profile Faith Foundation within months of leaving office. In addition, the arrival of millions of Muslims throughout Europe is forcing Europeans to grapple with questions of religious identity in new and profound ways, while arguments over the membership of new states in the European Union is leading Europe's leaders to debate their Christian heritage in unexpected ways.

Thus it should perhaps not be surprising that in 2009 the Editor in Chief of *The Economist* would pen a bestselling book contritely titled *God Is*

Back,[2] or that Peter Berger would begin rattling the world of sociology with frequent and public renunciations of his earlier theories of secularization (it is Europe, he now asserts, not America, that should be viewed as the exception in the world).

What is perhaps most interesting, however, is that it is not some deracinated, abstract category called "religion" that is back; it is committed faith, in all of its messy particularity and with its distinctly theological ways of speaking, that is back in the public realm. As the intellectual historian Mark Lilla wrote in a front-page article for the *New York Times* magazine in 2008, "We in the West find it incomprehensible that theological ideas still inflame the minds of men . . . we had assumed that this was no longer possible, that human beings had learned to separate religious questions from political ones, that political theology died in 16th-century Europe. We were wrong. It is *we* who are the fragile exception."[3] Of course, to say theology is "back" does not quite capture it. Perhaps it is more accurate to say that theology, despite the hopes of some, never really went away; it simply masqueraded in other guises throughout modernity. But that time is past. Theology is learning to speak to the public realm in its own voice once again.

It is with an awareness of this shift that we put this collection of essays together. For both in the media and across various disciplines in the academy, it is being increasingly recognized that debates about faith in public life, if they are to be conversations of any substance, are debates about *theology*, about the way a tradition has reasoned about God and God's relationship with the world. To engage in such debates, however, requires that one become theologically literate and develop the knowledge and skills to enter into a conversation that has been taking place across a diversity of contexts for generations.

This volume aims to contribute to that conversation by bringing together some of its most important voices from the recent past, with selections of writing that capture central trajectories of thought. In that respect, we are attempting to extend those projects which have brought together some of the most important voices from earlier eras; a prime example is the wonderful volume edited by Oliver O'Donovan and Joan Lockwood O'Donovan, *From Irenaeus to Grotius: A Sourcebook in Christian Political Thought* (Eerdmans, 2000). We believe that a similar type of volume is

2. John Micklethwait and Adrian Wooldridge, *God Is Back: How the Global Revival of Faith Is Changing the World* (New York: Penguin Press, 2009), p. 24.

3. Mark Lilla, "The Politics of God," *The New York Times Magazine,* 19 August 2007.

needed to bring together key voices from the contemporary period, roughly from the twentieth century (though we have included some texts that predate this slightly) to the present. Hence we draw on leading essays that explore everything from "Reading the Bible Politically" to "After 9/11."

We also engaged in this project convinced that, with the locus of Christianity shifting to the global South, we needed to include voices that were not always in the "standard" accounts of political theology. Thus, in addition to important texts within the Western canon of contemporary political theology, we have sought to include key voices from Africa, Asia, Latin America, and elsewhere. We know that theological voices from these parts of the world will only increase in importance, and hope that their inclusion here will function as something of a foretaste, however inadequate, of more to come in future editions.

We have also put this collection together as teachers, as those who introduce political theology to students often encountering the topic for the first time, who would profit from having in one place key texts that we have deemed of sufficient importance, provocation, and, in some cases, difficulty in locating. We have done this in close consultations with colleagues around the globe.[4] We have not followed everyone's advice on every occasion, but the selections that follow are the result of collegial conversations that have taken place over the last several years, and for which we are very grateful.

In the process of putting this volume together, we were also struck by the need to make careful use of limited space, in the hope that important elements would not be sacrificed in pursuit of clarity and ease of use. We have not been able to include everything we would have liked to. Despite our consultation with others in putting together the final reading list, we remain responsible for its inevitable shortcomings.

The thematic, rather than chronological, arrangement of this book was made partly to enable us to invite contemporary experts to provide short introductions to each group of essays. Our hope is that a dialogue between certain classic writings and some of the most interesting contemporary voices in political theology will prove stimulating to the ongoing conversations that are central to the task of theology. The responses are not meant to provide the final word on any subject, but to draw attention to important

---

4. We are especially grateful for input from Jeffrey Stout, Rusty Reno, Kwok Pui-Lan, Duncan Forrester, Emmanuel Katongole, Jennifer Herdt, Dan Bell, Scott Bader-Saye, Craig Carter, and Michael Northcott.

motifs, alternative readings, and potential questions, in hopes that readers might be inspired to make the task of political theology their own.

What Is Political Theology?

For many years, one of us lived within walking distance of a neoclassical, city amphitheater where members of the community would gather on summer evenings for free, local entertainment. Above the cypress-flanked stage, in faux Latin lettering, was inscribed an eminently political slogan taken from Proverbs 29:18: "Without Vision a People Perish." It is a striking phrase. In some ways it frames some of the key loci for thinking about political theology in a contemporary context, which the readings we have compiled here aim to show.

Vision

In response to an advisor's counsel to concentrate not on particular issues but on a broader political vision, the first President Bush was reported to have said dismissively, "Oh. The vision thing." (He was not reelected.)

Decisions in any community — such as how much space for parks should be protected, or if it is right to go to war in a particular situation — depend upon a prior vision of what constitutes that community, and what goods it believes it should be pursuing. H. Richard Niebuhr once reminded Christian thinkers that a narrow focus on the question "What should we do?" can be answered only in the wake of a more basic question, "What is going on?" Being able to see reality clearly is crucial to the ethical questions that are at the heart of political theology. For Christians, seeing reality clearly begins with reflection on God. What kind of God do we serve? What is the nature of the human person who has been created by God? What is the end of human history? What is the relationship of divine and human authority? From a Christian point of view, fundamental issues such as these shape the way in which tangible questions about the political arrangement of human communities will be answered.

There are those, however, who will object that such questions should be kept out of politics. The vision that united the Hebrew people was, for the writer of the proverb, the revelation of the God of Israel and his prophetic word, which sustained Israel in faithfulness to this God's covenant. But surely this vision of a community is too particular to bring together a people who think of themselves primarily as a civic body. Despite the fact that Mark Lilla, mentioned above, recognized the ongoing role that political theology has played throughout history, he doesn't think this is a good thing; Lilla argues that what makes politics in the contemporary situation so dangerous is precisely the introduction of theological questions into the political. In this view, the modern separation of politics and theology is the salutary, but fragile, achievement of the modern West. Political philosophy can perhaps provide a circumscribed vision of limited goods that a secular, democratic polity should pursue. But a fairly loose and ambiguous political rhetoric is in fact what unites a people who, perhaps subconsciously, fear that their commonalities would dissipate should they begin to deliberate over a robust vision of the good life. It was by design that the framers of secular society sought ways of uniting citizens around things other than orthodox Christianity. Some suggest that, for a nation like America, religion is summarily pushed into the private sphere by maintaining a public expression that is acceptable only so long as it serves civic aims conceived on secular terms.

Part of the problem is captured by the double meaning of the word "vision." On the one hand, it denotes a clear view of reality, a taking stock of what really is, which provides a sound basis for action in the world. On the other hand, "vision" is not about what is, but about what could be. Vision is about seeing into a future that is often hidden from the ordinary gaze. Indeed, visions are had by people whose sanity is sometimes questioned. John, the seer of Patmos, had visions of dragons, and of horses with serpents for tails. Some might ask, do we really want these kinds of visions welcomed in our politics?

As some of the essays in this volume make clear, however, there are those who not only believe that political theology is possible and worthwhile but also question the very idea that politics could exist *without* a theological vision. The ambitious revolutionary projects of the twentieth century have, of course, been widely viewed as thinly veiled theological eschatologies. Carl Schmitt, for example, sees *all* modern theories of the state as theologies in disguise, as evidenced in battles over the "desecration" of the national flag. This is what sociologist Robert Bellah, in 1967, called "American civil religion." Every society, nation, and people must either be able to point to those things which unify them or else risk disastrous and poisonous fracture. In America, which started with such denominational pluralism, it could not be a distinct theological vision that unified; yet in its absence a covertly theological "faith in America" quickly filled the void, allowing notions of sacred election to elide from Israel and the Church to the nation-state of America. It was a profoundly theological vision masquerading as political policy, in other words — an implicit doctrine of election — that supported the politics of "Manifest Destiny." Such arguments suggest, therefore, that when theology is banished from the public realm, it simply reasserts itself in other guises.

People

Who is "a people" that is the subject of political vision? Since the Westphalian solution in the seventeenth century, politics has been focused on states and nations. Christian churches melded seamlessly with the new reality, creating new forms of Christendom. In late modernity, however, such models of "a people" have been challenged from within and without. From within, a late-capitalist economy and social world produces individuals whose idea of freedom is expressed in terms of a take-it-or-leave-it relationship to the traditions that produce them. Charles Taylor contends that what makes the contemporary world different from previous cultures is the optional nature of faith traditions. Many relate to the feeling of standing neutrally before a set of options even while remaining distant enough from all of them to preserve the ability to take flight at any moment. What constitutes "a people" under such circumstances is sometimes little more than a collection of individuals united by common self-interest.

From without, the Westphalian focus has been challenged by globalization and the increasing way that capital, people, and identities overflow national borders. For Christians in particular, being a people has been enhanced and challenged by a keener awareness in the twenty-first century that the faith is global and is spoken and represented by a host of disparate voices. For Christians in Europe and North America, who had grown accustomed to being the center of gravity for all things Christian in the world, the global reality can be perceived as a shift, or even as something new. In truth, centuries of colonialism in various forms have obscured Christianity's long history in places like Japan, India, South America, and Africa. For those in the global south, who live in those regions which are becoming Christianity's center of gravity, the urgent need to bring their faith to bear on their political and social realities often means doing theology as a stark counterpart to Christendom.

What have been emerging are often radical alternatives to the long-established ways of thinking about peoplehood and sovereignty. Produced in a situation where bending the ear of politicians or ascending the ranks of government is impossible, Christian political thought in the Two-Thirds World takes seriously the ways in which popular forms of organization — such as base ecclesial communities in Latin America — are themselves political even apart from the levers of sovereign power. In situations such as Africa, where various states exercise only a weak form of sovereignty, churches have stepped into an organizational vacuum and provided spaces for non-state forms of politics to emerge. The West, on the other hand, has a long tradition of viewing sovereign power as the only legitimate source of political organization. (As Michel Foucault once put it, "the West has yet to cut off the king's head.") Whatever one's assessment of the ongoing power of the nation-state, however, globalization has clearly contributed to the sense that politics is no longer exclusively tied to territorial sovereignty.

The meaning of "people" has, in this setting, prompted many thinkers to reconsider what it means to be the church. Benedict Anderson famously applied his term "imagined communities" to the modern nation-state, which relies strongly on the power of a people's imagination to police invisible borders or to fight for invisible collective loyalties and contingent ties. But this imagination is only as strong as the alternatives to it are weak. For many, the Christian alternative — an international, "catholic" people who are materially constituted as a people through baptism as one body in Christ — asserts a political significance once again. Some of the readings in this volume exemplify the shifting currents that have made such thinking possible. It can no longer be taken for granted that sovereign definitions of "people" are straightforward and unproblematic.

Perish

The current resurgence of interest in political theology can be attributed in part to the explosion, both figurative and literal, of militant Islam. Terrorism has raised the stakes on all sides, and one's vision does indeed seem relevant to one's ability to survive. For Osama bin Laden, it is precisely secularism's lack of vision, its attempt to quarantine Islam from public life, that appears as a mortal threat. In a videotape from October 7, 2001, Osama bin Laden referred to the "humiliation and disgrace" that Islam had been experiencing for "more than eighty years." But as Bernard Lewis observes, most people in the West did not know what he was talking about. Bin Laden was referring to the 1918 defeat of the Ottoman sultanate and its subsequent abolition by the new, nationalistic Turkish government in 1922. The sultan was also the recognized caliph, head of Sunni Islam, a leader whose lineage could be traced all the way back to the death of Mohammed in 632 CE. For bin Laden, the ascendancy of the secular disgraces Islam and does not sit well for a faith that countenances much less easily the secular settlement reached within the Christian West.

This raises new challenges for Islam. Though we are beginning to hear emerging Muslim voices calling for new political theologies suited to contexts in which Islam is not the religious majority, it is still early days. For the West, the mortal threat that militant Islam poses raises more than military and diplomatic questions. Defenders of the West must ask, Do we have a kind of vision that can match the vision of Islam? Are we, in some sense, a theologically inspired social order, a Judeo-Christian country in our roots? Can a non-theological secularism on its own provide the principles necessary to survive?

Despite the attention that the clash between militant Islam and the West has brought to political theology, the field of political theology is much broader and deeper. As a self-conscious scholarly field of inquiry, political theology in the twentieth century originally took shape in the wake of European wars, but quickly spread beyond the West. In the Two-Thirds World, the clash of civilizations is of less importance than the daily perishing of people from poverty. Vision seems less urgent than food when it comes to what causes people to perish, but the question for political theology in many contexts is, What kind of vision is required to *see* those who die invisibly and quietly, not in spectacular explosions but in silent deprivation of the basic necessities of life? Politics is defined not only by the concerns of those within the Beltway but also by the daily, material concerns that threaten to disintegrate both individual bodies and communal bodies of people. It is our hope that this volume can help nourish robust responses, in both theory and practice, to such suffering.

WILLIAM T. CAVANAUGH,
JEFFREY W. BAILEY &
CRAIG HOVEY

I. Reading the Bible Politically

Introduction

Walter Brueggemann

A cynical form of "the Golden Rule" goes like this: "The one with the *gold* makes the *rules*." Transposed into our topic, the dictum is, "The one with *power* determines the mode of *interpretation*." Both slogans acknowledge the way in which power controls (or seeks to control) the categories of knowledge and imposes a particular shape on truth. This has certainly been the case in the modern world in which Euro-American interests have completely dominated and determined modes of scriptural interpretation that have been everywhere accepted as not only legitimate but normative. For much of the modern period, for over two centuries, the dominant mode of interpretation has been "historical critical," an approach that sought to interpret texts within their own proper "historical context."

The practical effect of this dominant approach, without for now suggesting this was the intent, was to accommodate the biblical text to the requirements of Enlightenment rationality. This entailed a preoccupation with historical questions, and a derivative distancing of the text from any whiff of contemporaneity with the interpreter or the community of the interpreter. It resulted, moreover, in making texts plain and unambiguous, and so dispelling the play of contradiction, ambiguity, or irony that pervaded the text and that in an artful way summoned the reader beyond any taken-for-granted world. A commitment to historical explanation led inexorably to the elimination of an active God who could be taken seriously as a *character and agent* in the world of the text. This in turn eventuated in a "history of religions" approach whereby any articulation of God is regarded simply as construction or projection, without any potential for the revela-

3

tory. Thus the text no longer offered much that constituted "an inconvenient truth," because everything that might be rationally objectionable was explained away.

This sort of critical perspective was taken, in good modernist fashion, to be objective and interpretively neutral. In retrospect, however, it is easy enough to see that such interpretation served an important political agenda, namely, leaving the world safely in the hands of human reason; any portrayal of God in the text that violated that reason could be situated in a past world that had no pertinence to present-tense interpretation. The presentation of an active, transformative agent, moreover, was reduced to a benign memory in a way that readily served a religious and therefore a political-economic status quo.

To be sure, many practitioners of such criticism were theologically serious and intended better than that. Consequently such modernist criticism was often linked to a vigorous theological enterprise, but it was a linkage that was sustained only by a lack of clarity. That passion for serious theological-ethical work did not in fact derive from such critical practice with the text, but was offered in spite of such critical perspective.

Given such an understanding and practice of "the critical project," the title of this section of essays, "Reading the Bible Politically," is something of a misnomer. It is a misnomer because all reading of the Bible is political, that is, read with dimensions of power and vested interest operative in the interpretive process. The Bible is supple enough that it can be read from and toward almost any socio-political agenda. A case can be made that historical criticism came to be a prominent and persuasive method precisely in order to resist the reductionist claims of church orthodoxy, and so to serve a more-or-less "liberal agenda." But it was a liberal agenda that had no great bite to it and reflected a bourgeoisie concern of establishment types in both church and academy. It was a "liberalism" that accorded with Enlightenment rationality that had little patience with much of the testimony of the text itself. As a result, historical criticism came to serve particular interests through the categories that were imposed upon the text.

The big news of the last half century, reflected in these essays, has been the remarkable process through which interpretive voices from outside the Euro-American hegemony of historical criticism have gained a hearing and have begun to reflect the faith and the interests that are not committed to the assumptions of hegemonic interpretation. These "outside voices" of interpretation arose first of all in Central America in the 1960s and 1970s, accompanied especially in the United States by feminist interpreters and more recently womanist interpreters; since that time there has been a broad emergence of Asian and African voices of interpretation of those who have worked both within the historical critical consensus and against it as well.[1]

Thus we may say that all interpretation of the Bible is political and that it is not objective but, either knowingly or unwittingly, explicitly or implicitly, is a voice of advocacy. Given the generic meaning of the term "political reading," the essays in this section do not serve "political reading" of a generic kind, but refer to a quite specific political agenda and advocacy. While I do not suggest that all of these voices speak in the same way or toward the same end, it is evident that there is a shared core conviction among them that was classically articulated by Central American Roman Catholic bishops as "God's preferential option for the poor." That claim can be given nuance in many variations. Taken as a core conviction, it is the epitome of the essays represented here, namely, that the God of the Bible is not an even-handed God with an indifferent agenda, nor an ally of established power as the church has often attested in its practice, but is a passionate partisan who is deeply committed precisely to those who have been excluded from the material and political gains of the modern world. Political reading of the Bible in this sense begins in the recognition that God has taken sides in history and is the sponsor and agent of revolutionary transformation of the world. This revolutionary impetus, moreover, makes possible a new socioeconomic arrangement that is of peculiar benefit to those presently denied access to the material resources that make for well-being. It goes without saying that some biblical texts serve this interpretive perspective better than others. Thus it is the case that this particular political theology (better termed "liberation theology," for the dominant interpretation is also a political theology of another ilk), like every interpretive program, prefers some texts to others. It is for that reason urgent that the exposition of the *Magnificat* by Ernesto Cardenal is included in this set of essays (as the only text-specific one among these essays), so that Mary's song may be taken as the "National Anthem" of this interpretive movement, an anticipation of a messianic time when there is a radical moral inversion with material implications. No wonder Cardenal can have Mary sing:

---

1. For helpful bibliographical summaries of more recent post-colonial interpretation, see Leo Perdue, *Reconstructing Old Testament Theology: After the Collapse of History*, Overtures to Biblical Theology (Minneapolis: Fortress Press, 2005), pp. 280-339, and Leo G. Perdue et al., *Biblical Theology: Introducing the Conversation* (Nashville: Abingdon Press, 2009), pp. 91-97, 176-85.

> He has filled the hungry with good things,
> And sent the rich empty away. (Luke 1:53)

Such a liberationist perspective is not usually much preoccupied with the negative of the rich being sent empty away; but the implication is clear enough. That exposition of Cardenal identifies the way in which wealth and power are linked to "pride." Characteristically, the spiritual condition of pride draws close to the material, for pride belongs with wealth and power.

A more recent variation on this particular "political theology" is the articulation of post-colonial theology that pays primary attention to the specific interpretive context and condition of those who have been kept in a dependent colonial status. The background of such post-colonial reading is a refusal to continue to read "colonially," that is, in deference to the (critical?) interpretive assumptions of empire.[2] It is the way of empire to assume that its own privileged socioeconomic status is normative, and therefore readings congruent with that status are readily taken to be immediately and everywhere normative. The contextual specificity of the post-colonial is the firm insistence that empire has no legitimate right to impose its own preferred reading on others so that it is everywhere normative. For what now determines what is normative in interpretation is the experience of the interpreting community. This contention is at the heart of every liberation hermeneutic, for hegemonic interpretation always pretends to be contextless, but is in fact congruent with the interpretive interests of those who occupy hegemonic space. Thus the interpretive revolution of the last half century is the gaining of leverage by other interpretive voices who could claim no legitimacy in the empire or in the critical establishment of academic study. The outcome is pluralistic interpretation, readings that arise from and serve many contexts and therefore many interests. Such an array of interpretive offers is a vexation to those accustomed to a single reading, but pluralism is the inescapable condition of interpretation that honors many voices in many contexts, every voice to be taken seriously and valorized in the very act of interpretation.

Such a pluralism, as pluralistic as the many voices of interpretation that insist upon being heard, poses two kinds of problems. On the one hand, such pluralism may strike "old authority" as hopelessly relativistic. On the

---

2. For an assessment of the deep grip that "imperial" assumptions have on conventional scriptural interpretation, see Elisabeth Schüssler Fiorenza, *The Power of the Word: Scripture and the Rhetoric of Empire* (Minneapolis: Fortress Press, 2007).

other hand, such openness to new interpretation permits or even invites readings that are manifestly silly and not to be taken seriously. The task, in such a rich and problematic context, is to develop criteria that exclude such silliness and that recognize the broad possibility of faithful reading, without return to an orthodoxy that is excessively exclusionary. The process of the last half century will remind us that every effort at exclusion contains both a bid for truthfulness and a more-or-less self-serving agenda. Sorting out faithfulness in such a process is never easy or obvious; nor is it likely to be sustained for very long unless the self-serving aspect of the enterprise is acknowledged.

The essays themselves invite the reader into this interpretive revolution on which there is no going back. No insistence of church orthodoxy or of guild objectivity will silence the voices. No authority can say "silencio" with any effect. The silencers have been at work forever, but the new voices make a claim out of suffering, marginality, and vulnerability that finds a warrant for speaking without waiting for any external validation.

Christopher Rowland traces the rise of "grassroots" reading through the experience of oppression, poverty, hunger, and the "death of God" to an awareness that the old objectivity would never contain in its reading. The old objectivity presented the reader as silent before the text as a recipient. Now we know better!

Richard Bauckham considers the complex issue of the relation between the Testaments (old and new "dispensations") and arrives at "canonical context" as a frame of reference that allows freedom in interpretation, but as a task that requires "qualities of insight, imagination, critical judgment, and expert knowledge of the contemporary world."

R. S. Sugirtharajah considers the misguided, silly, and trivial uses to which the Bible can be put in popular reading. Such "poaching" is accountable to no reading community and proceeds by taking texts out of context and imposing meanings on texts that are clearly against the grain of the text. He notices, moreover, that such exploitative practices regularly appeal to the King James Version of the Bible, a translation that has now become a totem and "an eccentric cultural artifact sans religious authority or theological clout."

Néstor Míguez traces, in more specificity than does Rowland, the rise of a new hermeneutical sensibility in Latin American reading. Of special note is the crucial impact of Vatican II and the new reading that celebrates God's poor as a revelatory factor in history. I note in passing that among the many writers whom he mentions in his survey, Míguez does not include José

Miranda; I take the liberty of mentioning him because Miranda, in his book of 1973, was my own access point into this interpretive perspective.

A. Maria Arul Raja writes of what will be for many readers a quite fresh field of interpretation, the Dalit communities of the poor in India who are "unlettered" but who, out of their lived experience, have grasped the revelatory power of the biblical text. Such a venue for interpretation exposes the ideology of much conventional reading and draws us back to the dangerous specificity of the text.

It is fitting that the concluding pages of this section, containing the *Magnificat* (to which I have already referred), are placed in the volume just after the essay on the Dalit. The Dalit are a community about which Mary sings, among the hungry who will be fed with good things. The juxtaposition of the Song of Mary and this people of need calls attention to the way in which the text is good news that generates new worldly possibilities, the possibilities that settled imperial readings never want us to dream of. We may risk a new dictum that arises out of these several studies: "Those with emancipated imagination, rooted in suffering, may coin new *rules* that outflank and confound old truth practiced by the ones with the *gold.*"

1 The Foundation and Form of Liberation Exegesis

Christopher Rowland

The Biblical Perspective of the Poor:
The Challenge of Grassroots Exegesis

Most faculties of theology and religious studies have not moved too far from the well-trodden paths of the historical-critical method, with its painstaking quest for the text's original meaning and context. The hegemony of this interpretative approach is firmly rooted in theological education and the churches. Indeed, successive generations of ministers have been taught to read the Bible using the historical-critical method.[1] In the process of acquiring the tools of historical scholarship we have all been enabled to catch a fascinating glimpse of the ancient world as it has been reconstructed for us by two hundred years of a biblical scholarship of increasing sophistication. But all too often our devotion to the quest for the original meaning of a Pauline text or a dominical saying has left us floundering when we are asked to relate our journey into ancient history to the world in which we live and work.

---

1. On the problems of the historical-critical method, see, for example, W. Wink, *Transforming Bible Study* (London: SCM Press, 1981), ch. 7, and (in more detail) *The Bible in Human Transformation: Toward a New Paradigm for Biblical Study* (Philadelphia: Fortress Press, 1973), ch. 1. On the relations between First and Third World exegesis, see C. E. Gudorf, "Liberation Theology's Use of Scripture: A Response to First World Critics," *Interpretation* 41 (1987): 5-18, but note also the robust defense of the First World approach in J. Barr, *Holy Scripture: Canon, Authority, Criticism,* The Sprunt Lectures 1982 (Oxford: Oxford University Press, 1983), and J. Barton, *People of the Book? The Authority of the Bible in Christianity,* The Bampton Lectures 1988 (London: SPCK, 1988).

While the journey into the past has offered us insights aplenty, our historical preoccupations have left us with the feeling that the biblical world we have constructed is alien to us. So the biblical text, instead of being a means of life, can become a stumbling-block in the way of our contemporary discipleship. When we use the Bible in wrestling with the contemporary problems of Christian discipleship we find that our exegetical efforts frequently have not been matched with the skills necessary for the provision of illumination from the Bible on the exploration of those questions which our generation is asking.

There is a deep divide among contemporary interpreters of Scripture. On the one hand there are those who think that the original meaning of the text is not only retrievable but also clearly recognizable, and that it should be the criterion by which all interpretations should be judged. On the other hand there are those who argue either that the quest for the original meaning of the text is a waste of time or that, even if it is possible to ascertain what the original author intended, this should not be determinative of the way in which we read the text. It believes that whatever the *conscious* intention of the original author, different levels of meaning can become apparent to later interpreters, granted that the text is free from the shackles of the author's control and has a life of its own in the world of the reader.

Understandably, the first group is worried that the freedom implied in the second approach might lead to exegetical anarchy.[2] It wants some kind of control over interpretation, and where better to find it than in the original meaning of the text? No doubt most biblical exegetes would chafe at the imposition of any kind of hermeneutical control on their endeavors, yet there is today a "magisterium of the historical-critical method" in the Church. The magisterium of the Holy Office has been replaced by the critical consensus of the biblical exegetes, preoccupied as most of them are with the original meaning of the text and its controlling role in the quest for meaning of the Scriptures.[3] As part of that quest, the search goes on for "history," whether it be that of Jesus, the mind of the evangelist or Paul, or the situation of the early Christian communities. But history is such an elusive quarry. Not only is it never directly accessible to us, but our involvement in the search casts such a shadow over the whole process that the significance of

2. See, for example, J. D. G. Dunn's inaugural lecture, "Testing the Foundations: Current Trends in New Testament Study" (University of Durham, 1984), p. 23.

3. Cf. M. Kahler, *The So-Called Historical Jesus and the Historic Biblical Christ* (Philadelphia: Fortress Press, 1984).

our investment in time and effort itself demands an explanation. Frederic Jameson reminds us that

> History is *not* a text, not a narrative, master or otherwise, but that, as an absent cause, it is inaccessible to us except in textual form, and that our approach to it and to the real itself necessarily passes through its prior textualization, its narrativization in the political unconscious.[4]

Of course, that political unconscious has been at work in the multifarious attempts to get at the real meaning of the text during the last two hundred years (though all too frequently it has remained unrecognized). That said, the *quest* for the original context (or for better contexts of the biblical texts, since many of them show signs of being part of an ongoing community of interpretation) is necessary as a component of any historical approach to the reading of texts. It is part of the history of the interpretation of a text. But the starting-place is the way in which and the place in which the texts are being used in the contemporary world, whether by millions of ordinary Christians or the sophisticated researchers of the First World academic institutions.

But it is not just *ancient* history that is important. Recently, the application of sociological theory to the study of early Christianity has enabled us to look at familiar issues in a new light.[5] The new insights which the sociological approach affords, however, present a challenge to a preoccupation with the original meaning of the text. Sociology of the New Testament must involve a penetrating analysis of the social formation of the contemporary reader too.

Of course, the truly historical method will also attend to the specific historical situation of the various interpretations on offer. But it must be conceded that we have been singularly negligent over the application of historical criticism to our world, and to ourselves as interpreters. We may want to suppose that the exegetical enterprise is an autonomous one, to be kept distinct from the various ways in which the text is being *used*. Nevertheless, we

---

4. F. Jameson, *The Political Unconscious: Narrative as a Socially Symbolic Act* (London: Methuen, 1981), p. 35.

5. See, for example, G. Theissen, *The First Followers of Jesus: A Sociological Analysis of the Earliest Christianity* (London: SCM Press, 1978), W. Meeks, *The First Urban Christians: The Social World of the Apostle Paul* (New Haven/London: Yale University Press, 1983), and the concise survey in D. Tidball, *An Introduction to the Sociology of the New Testament* (Exeter: Paternoster Press, 1983).

have to accept the fact that the historical-exegetical project owes everything to the interpreter and the interpretative culture of which he or she is a part. The reconstruction of that past world in which the texts originated can therefore enable the contemporary reader to view present prejudices in a fresh light.[6] The world of the New Testament is, after all, *our* creation from the fragments, both textual and otherwise, that have come down to us. The sort of people we are and the kind of interests that we have must necessarily determine, or at least affect, the biblical world we create.

There is an unease among many biblical readers about the way in which the Bible has been studied. Those who use the Bible as part of Christian ministry wonder at the enormous investment in biblical interpretation which seems to enable so little fruitful use of the foundation documents of the Christian religion. Something similar is said about the crisis facing biblical interpretation by Carlos Mesters as he writes from the perspective of one whose work has involved him in interpreting the Bible with the poor of Brazil.[7]

Mesters points out the indebtedness of liberation theology to Enlightenment methods and contrasts its original vitality with the weariness which characterizes its contemporary use. He regrets the way in which the "scientific" study of Scripture has had the effect of distancing the Bible from the lives of ordinary people, so that its study has become an arcane enterprise reserved for a properly equipped academic elite. In its early career the historical-critical method had the power and courage to contribute greatly to the revival of interest in the Bible. Its historical concern played a major part in the critique of the ideology of ecclesiastical dogma. But that negative function, now so well established, has not been matched by the positive encouragement of methods of reading which would enable the people of God to respond to the needs which the life of faith in a changing world is placing upon them.

Mesters points out that the same weariness was also to be found in Brazilian biblical study, with the growth of learned works on exegesis which had little appeal or relevance for the millions seeking to survive in situations of injustice and poverty. In that situation, however, a new way of reading the text has arisen, not among the exegetical elite of the seminaries and universities but at the grassroots. Its emphasis is on the threefold method: *see* (start-

---

6. See W. Meeks, *The Moral World of the First Christians* (London: SPCK, 1987), and J. Stambaugh and D. Balch, *The Social World of the First Christians* (London: SPCK, 1986).

7. C. Mesters, "Como se faz Teologia hoje no Brasil?" *Estudos Biblicos* 1 (1985): 1ff.

ing where one is with one's experience, which for the majority in Latin America means an experience of poverty), *judge* (understanding the reasons for that kind of existence and relating them to the story of the deliverance from oppression in the Bible), and *act*. Ordinary people have taken the Bible into their own hands and begun to read the word of God not only in the circumstances of their existence but also in comparison with the stories of the people of God in other times and other places. Millions of men and women abandoned by government and Church have discovered an ally in the story of the people of God in the Scriptures.

This new biblical theology in the Basic Christian Communities is an oral theology in which story, experience, and biblical reflection are intertwined with the community's life of sorrow and joy. That experience of celebration, worship, varied stories and recollections, in drama and festival, is, according to Mesters, exactly what lies behind the written words of Scripture itself. That is the written deposit which bears witness to the story of a people, oppressed, bewildered and longing for deliverance. While exegete, priest, and religious may have their part to play in the life of the community, the reading is basically uninfluenced by excessive clericalism and individualistic piety. It is a reading which is emphatically communitarian, in which reflection on the story of a people can indeed lead to an appreciation of the *sensus ecclesiae* and a movement towards liberative action. So revelation is very much a present phenomenon: "God speaks in the midst of the circumstances of today." In contrast, the vision of many priests is of a revelation that is entirely past, in the deposit of faith — something to be preserved, defended, and transmitted to the people by its guardians.

So for Mesters the Bible is not just about past history only. It is also a mirror to be held up to reflect the story of today and lend it a new perspective. Mesters argues that what is happening in this new way of reading the Bible is in fact a rediscovery of the patristic method of interpretation which stresses the priority of the spirit of the word rather than its letter. God speaks through life; but that word is one that is illuminated by the Bible: "the principal objective of reading the Bible is not to interpret the Bible but to interpret life with the help of the Bible."[8] The major preoccupation is not the quest for the meaning of the text in itself but the direction which the Bible is suggesting to the people of God within the specific circumstances in which they find themselves. The popular reading of the Bible in Brazil is directed to contemporary practice and the transformation of a situation of injustice. That situation per-

8. Mesters, "Como se faz Teologia hoje no Brasil?" p. 10.

mits the poor to discover meaning which can so easily elude the technically better equipped exegete. Where one is determines to a large extent how a book is read. This is a reading which does not pretend to be neutral, and it questions whether any other reading can claim that either. It is committed to the struggle of the poor for justice, and the resonances that are to be found with the biblical story suggest that it may not be unfaithful to the commitments and partiality which the Scriptures themselves demand.

Of course, Mesters recognizes the difficulties of this approach.[9] He expresses his unease about the way in which the biblical story can become so identified with the experiences of the poor that any other meaning, past or present, can be excluded. So the story of the deliverance of God's people from oppression in Egypt can become for the poor *our* story, its message being directed solely to the outcast and impoverished. Mesters' emphasis on the importance of a historical dimension of scriptural study in a quest for the original meaning is a remedy against this kind of tendency. It can remind readers that the text has been the property of many who have read it in many different situations. The original readers would not have had identical concerns with the contemporary poor, whatever else they may have had in common.[10]

Mesters asks us to judge the effectiveness of the reading by its fruits: is it "a sign of the arrival of the reign of God . . . when the blind see, lepers are clean, the dead rise and the poor have the good news preached to them"? The experience of poverty and oppression is for the liberation exegete as important a text as the text of Scripture itself. The poor are blessed because they can read Scripture from a perspective different from most of the rich and find in it a message which can so easily elude those of us who are not poor. The God who identified with slaves in Egypt and promised that he would be found among the poor, sick and suffering demands that there is another text to be read as well as that contained between the covers of the Bible: God's word is to be found in the literary memory of the people of God.

9. See C. Mesters' comments in his essay "The Use of the Bible in Christian Comments of the Common People," in N. K. Gottwald, ed., *The Bible and Liberation: Political and Social Hermeneutics* (Maryknoll, NY: Orbis Books, 1984), and "The Use of the Bible in Christian Communities of the Common People," in S. Torres and J. Eagleson, eds., *The Challenge of Basic Christian Communities: Papers from the International Ecumenical Congress of Theology 1980* (Maryknoll, NY: Orbis Books, 1984), pp. 197-210.

10. Such a reminder is continually offered by Ernesto Cardenal in his contributions to *The Gospel in Solentiname*, where a historical perspective is injected into the contemporary discussion by the *campesinos;* see E. Cardenal, ed., *The Gospel in Solentiname*, 4 vols. (Maryknoll, NY: Orbis Books, 1977-84).

But that is a continuing story, and is to be heard and discerned in the contemporary world, among those people with whom God has chosen to be identified.

The biblical text is therefore not a strange world which can come alive only by re-creating the circumstances of the past. The situation of the people of God reflected in many of its pages is the situation of the poor. What such biblical interpretation dramatically reminds us of is that the pressing issues for any critical exegesis must be the rigorous analysis of the complex production of meaning, the contexts in which that production takes place, and the social and economic interests which an interpretation is serving. There must be a continuous dialogue between that present story told by the poor of oppression and injustice and the ancient stories they read in the Bible. Indeed, the knowledge of that past story is an important antidote to the kind of unrestrained fantasy which then binds the text as firmly to the world of the immediate present and its context as historical-critical exegesis bound it to the ancient world. That twofold aspect is well brought out by Carlos Mesters:

> the emphasis is not placed on the text's meaning in itself but rather on the meaning the text has for the people reading it. At the start the people tend to draw any and every sort of meaning, however well or ill founded, from the text. . . . [T]he common people are also eliminating the alleged "neutrality" of scholarly exegesis. . . . [T]he common people are putting the Bible in its proper place, the place where God intended it to be. They are putting it in second place. Life takes first place! In so doing, the people are showing us the enormous importance of the Bible, and at the same time, its relative value — relative to life.[11]

This understanding of theology as a second-order task (viz., one of critical reflection on life and practice) is not new to Christian theology. That subtle dialectic between the "text" of life, viewed in the light of the recognition and non-acceptance of unjust social arrangements, and the other "text" of Scripture and tradition is the kernel of a lively theological, or for that matter any, interpretative enterprise.[12] The world of the poor, as well as their imagination, provides shafts of light which can often throw into the sharpest possible relief the poverty of much First World interpretation.

11. Mesters, "Use of The Bible," in Gottwald, ed., *Bible and Liberation*, p. 122.
12. See J. Libanio's succinct summary in his contribution to D. Winter, ed., *Putting Theology to Work* (London: British Council of Churches, 1981), pp. 77ff.

A similar point is made about the contribution of liberation theology by Charles Elliott in his 1985 Heslington Lecture:

> Liberation theology is about a fundamental change in the way in which persons, personal relationships and therefore political relationships are conceived and structured. . . . Why is liberation theology so important intellectually? . . . Firstly, it is true to elements . . . of the biblical tradition which were long neglected by the colonialist church. . . . Neither a colonialist church nor an established church can bear to think that the biblical tradition is actually about challenging power: but, if you see the essence of the nature of God as being to free the oppressed from their oppression, then you are necessarily engaged in a challenge to power. . . . Secondly it marks a quite different theological method . . . what liberation theologians are saying is . . . the only way you will derive theological truth is by starting where people are, because it is where poor and particularly oppressed people are that you will find God. Now that stands on its head sixteen hundred years of philosophical tradition in Christendom. From the third century, Christians have thought the way to establish theological truth has been to try to derive consistent propositions, that is to say propositions that are consistent with the facts of the tradition as revealed primarily in the Bible. . . . What the liberation theologians are saying . . . is that this will not do as a way of doing theology. If you want to do theology, you have to start where people are, particularly the people that the Bible is primarily concerned with, who are dispossessed, the widow, the orphan, the stranger, the prostitute, the pimp and the tax collector. Find out what they are saying, thinking and feeling, and that is the stuff out of which the glimpses of God will emerge. Thirdly . . . this method of thinking about God solves the problem of verification. . . . It has always been a puzzle to theologians to know how you test for truth any proposition you want to make about God. The fundamentalist Protestants still say "It's fine. The Bible will tell you whether it is true or not." . . . The sophisticated liberal theologian will say "Test it against the tradition, against the mind of the church, against other propositions and see if it is coherent with those." . . . The liberation theologians will say very simply "the test for truth is the effect it has on people's lives. Is this proposition . . . actually liberating people or enslaving them?"[13]

13. C. Elliott, "Is There a Liberation Theology for the UK?" Heslington Lecture, the University of York, 1985, p. 11.

A New Way of Doing Theology?

Most exegetes who are influenced by liberation theology would not want to claim that they have *the* hermeneutical key to the reading of Scripture (though there *are* some who think the perspective of the poor is *the* criterion for a true reading of Scripture). They are insistent that the immediacy of the relationship between the biblical narratives and the situation and experiences of the poor has enabled them to glimpse interpretative insights which have so often eluded the sophisticated, cerebral approach of First World biblical exegesis.

The evangelical and popular roots of liberation theology need to be recognized. It is known in this country as a result of the translations which have been made of many of the writings of the leading liberation theologians from Latin America. The Boff brothers from Brazil, Sobrino from El Salvador, Pixley from Mexico and Nicaragua, Segundo from Uruguay, and Miguez Bonino from Argentina have become leading spirits of that theology.[14] The form which liberation theology takes is normally not unfamiliar to the sophisticated theological readership of the First World. Often buttressed with footnotes, and demonstrating a wide knowledge of the philosophical and cultural tradition of European thought, these books seem to offer an alternative (but no less sophisticated) approach to the theological task which uses the familiar language of conventional theological discourse. It is a façade which needs to be pierced in order to understand more clearly what precisely energizes these writers.

At the heart of the theology of liberation is the twofold belief that in the experience of oppression, poverty, hunger, and death, God is speaking to all people today and that God's presence among the millions unknown and unloved by humanity but blessed in the eyes of God is confirmed by the witness of the Christian tradition, particularly the Scriptures themselves.[15] It is this dual conviction, nurtured by the thousands of Basic Christian Communities, which is the dynamic behind liberation theology. Liberation theology would not exist in any meaningful sense without it and the corresponding

14. There are useful introductions to the thought of the leading proponents of liberation theology in P. Berryman, *Liberation Theology: Essential Facts about the Revolutionary Movement in Latin America and Beyond* (London: I. B. Tauris, 1987), C. and L. Boff, *Introducing Liberation Theology* (London: Burns & Oates, 1988), and T. Witvliet, *A Place in the Sun: An Introduction to Liberation Theology in the Third World* (London: SCM Press, 1985).

15. A point well made in G. Gutiérrez, *The Power of the Poor in History* (London: SCM Press, 1983), pp. 65-66.

preferential option for the poor. It is, as Derek Winter has remarked, "theological reflection that arises at sundown, after the heat of the day when Christians have dirtied their hands and their reputations in the struggle of the poor for justice, for land, for bread, for very survival."[16]

Liberation theologians have themselves drunk deep at the well of European biblical scholarship, and are grateful for it. Nevertheless, their method of work differs from what is customary in this country. Many spend a significant part of each week working with grassroots communities in the shanty towns on the periphery of large cities or in rural communities. As part of their pastoral work they listen to the poor and facilitate the process of reflection on the Bible which is going on in the grassroots communities. Unlike many European and North American theologians, their writing has not taken place in the context of academic institutions which have rendered them immune from the personal and social pressures of the countries in which they live. Thus Leonardo and Clodovis Boff are closely identified with grassroots activities among the poor and marginalized in various parts of Brazil. Jon Sobrino has known what it is like to be a target of death squads in El Salvador and to have seen his dear friend Archbishop Oscar Romero assassinated. It is that experience of identification with the poor and involvement in the injustices of their environment which is the motivating force driving the liberation theologians' theology and the spirit which fills an apparently European edifice with insight and power.

Thus those involved in liberation theology stress the importance of the wisdom and insight of the poor as the focal point of theology. They gain insights from listening to the poor, as they read and use Scripture in the whole process of development and social change. The exegetes find that this process of listening and learning has given them a stimulus to their exegesis and, more importantly, has opened up new vistas and questions in the interpretative enterprise. This grassroots biblical interpretation provides a basis for the more sophisticated theological edifices the liberation theologians wish to build. Yet it is clear that the different experiences and the worldview of the poor offer an unusually direct connection with the biblical text. This approach, whatever its shortcomings in terms of exegetical refinement, has proved enormously fruitful as far as the life of the Christian Church is concerned. The liberation theologians are what Antonio Gramsci, the distinguished Italian Marxist theoretician, described as "or-

---

16. Quoted from his study pack on Basic Christian Communities published by Christian Aid, 1988.

ganic intellectuals,"[17] something that is brought out in this description of the theological task by Leonardo Boff:

> Obviously this recapturing of the original import of Christianity entails a break with hegemonic religious traditions. Normally it is up to the *intellectual of the religious organism* to sew a new seam when the rupture takes place. On the one side, through their links with the oppressed classes these intellectuals help them to perceive, systematize, and express their great yearnings for liberation. On the other side, they take up these aspirations within a religious (theological) project, pointing up their coherence with the fundamental ideas of Jesus and the apostles. Thanks to this breaking of the ice, important segments of the ecclesiastical institution can ally themselves with the oppressed classes and make possible the emergence of a people's church with characteristics of the common people.[18]

Rooted in the Basic Christian Communities, an agenda is being set for liberation theology which is firmly based in the struggles of millions for recognition and justice. The text becomes a catalyst in the exploration of pressing contemporary issues relevant to the community; it offers a language so that the voice of the voiceless may be heard. There is an immediacy in the way in which the text is used because resonances are found with the experiences set out in the stories of biblical characters which seem remote from the world of affluent Europe and North America.

The Bible offers a typology which can be identified with and at the same time be a means by which the present difficulties can be shown to be surmountable in the life of faith and community commitment. To enable the poor to read the Bible has involved a program of education which teaches the contents of the biblical material so that it can be a resource for thousands who are illiterate. In such programs the value of the primary text, experience of life, is fully recognized. Therefore, the poor are shown that they have riches in plenty to equip them for exegesis. This is balanced with the basic need to communicate solid information about the stories within the Bible themselves, of which many remain ignorant.

---

17. This was the way in which Frei Betto, a Brazilian Dominican, described the work of the liberation theologian in a lecture delivered in Cambridge in December 1987. For Gramsci's ideas, see Q. Hoare and G. N. Smith, eds., *Selections from the Prison Notebooks* (London: Lawrence and Wishart, 1971), pp. 10ff., 60, 330ff.

18. L. Boff, "Theological Characteristics of a Grassroots Church," in Torres and Eagleson, eds., *Challenge of Basic Christian Communities,* p. 133.

So when we talk of the theology of liberation we are not just speaking of the works of the theologians but of a theological approach which gains its inspiration from the activities of the Basic Christian Communities in many countries in Latin America. The Bible is being used as part of the reflection by the poor on their circumstances as they seek to work out appropriate forms of response and action. In that process the reading of Scripture is often by-passing the dominant methods of the First World. To those of us brought up on the historical-critical method the interpretations can often appear cavalier. They frequently have little regard for the historical circumstances of the text, its writer, and its characters. There is often a direct identification by the poor with biblical characters and their circumstances, with little concern for the hermeneutical niceties which are invoked in applying the text to their own circumstances. In their use of Scripture the resources of the text are used from their perspective of poverty and oppression, and a variety of meanings are conjured up in a way reminiscent of early Christian and ancient Jewish exegesis.

The perspective of the poor and the marginalized offers another story, an alternative to that told by the wielders of economic power whose story becomes the "normal" account. The story of Latin America is a story of conquest. It is *Latin* America, a continent whose story begins only with the arrival of the Europeans. The quest for Mayan and Aztec cultures in Central America and the much more recent attempts to uncover the buried story of the hidden millions of Nicaragua since 1979 are examples of a necessary challenge to the normal story which is portrayed as a European one. Liberation theology has its contribution to make to these projects. Of course, its complicity as part of the ideology imposed on the indigenous peoples of the sub-continent as the European conquerors swept previous cultures aside puts Christianity, in however progressive a form, in a rather difficult position. Yet its encouragement of the study of popular religion, whether Christian, Indian, or Afro-American, must be part of its project to enable the story of the "little people" of the sub-continent to be heard. In addition, it has championed the recovery of the religion of those within the Christian tradition who resisted the practice of conquest and despoliation, like Bartolomé de Las Casas and Antonio Valdivieso, whose prophetic ministry stands alongside those whom the conquerors would prefer to forget. The familiar story of the wars of kings and princes, which all too easily becomes the staple fare of a normal view of life, is challenged as the horizons are expanded by attention to the voices drowned out by the noise of the mighty. It is part of the task suggested in Walter Benjamin's words: "In every era the attempt must be made anew to wrest tradition away from a conformism that is about to overpower it."[19] Those who have suffered humiliation and persecution of a kind which must never be repeated should resist the temptation to use the power they obtain to play the part of the oppressor.

The Hermeneutical Key: God Sides with the Poor

The experience of siding with the majority of an oppressed and impoverished region has sent Christian ministers and theologians back to the pages of Scripture to think again about the demand of God. One of the leading figures in the implementation of liberation theology in the pastoral practice of the Brazilian Catholic Church, Helder Camara, explains how the Church arrived at its "preferential option for the poor":

> We men [sic] of the church have been so preoccupied in maintaining authority and the social order that we didn't suspect that the social order masks a terrible disorder, a stratified disorder. For centuries, we were concerned with a very passive presentation of Christianity. We preached patience, obedience, respect for authority; we finished up by saying (this was the opium of the people!) that the sufferings here on earth are so ephemeral, and eternal happiness so great, that all this would be forgotten in a flash. But gradually it became clear that we couldn't go on preaching Christianity like this. Social injustice was becoming ever more blatant; so much so, that at Medellín in Colombia in 1968, at the conference of Latin American bishops, we denounced the presence in Latin America of an internal colonialism. It's not just foreign colonialists who come to exploit our people, but the privileged of the continent who maintain their wealth at the expense of penury — of millions of their fellow citizens.[20]

The poor are privileged in the eyes of God, and therefore should be the particular concern of those who are committed to the ways of God. While this divine preference is seen in the legal prescriptions of the Torah and in the condemnations of the canonical prophets of Israel's social arrangements, it is affirmed particularly in the life of Jesus of Nazareth, in whom Christians find the key to reading the text of Scripture as well as life:

19. Walter Benjamin, *Illuminations*, ed. H. Arendt (New York: Schocken, 1978), p. 255.

20. Quoted in Derek Winter's study pack on Basic Christian Communities published by Christian Aid, 1988.

Jesus affirms the privilege of the poor, since He proclaims that they are to inherit the Kingdom. God, who undertakes to correct human mistakes, will give the keys of the Kingdom to the poor, for in the Kingdom justice will reign. It is natural that the victims of injustice and exploitation should be the first to receive the privilege of the Kingdom. Moreover, in Jesus we find a model of the way of life of the poor man who is also a "servant of Yahweh"; he is not resigned to his poverty, but practises the hope which kindles hope in others too.[21]

If one examines the way in which the Beatitudes are treated in the writings of some liberation theologians, we can see that poverty is not glamorized. Indeed, poverty, which means a lack of resources necessary for life, is regarded as evil. Rather, the Beatitudes reveal the character of God, who identifies with the poor and marginalized: "the kingdom of God comes first and foremost for those who, by virtue of their situation, have most need of it: the poor, the afflicted, the hungry of this world."[22] God is therefore to be known by virtue of identity with the poor:

> The kingdom . . . comes to change the situation of the poor, to put an end to it. As the first Beatitude tells us, the poor possess the kingdom of God. That is not due to any merit of theirs, much less any value that poverty may have. On the contrary, the kingdom is theirs because of the inhuman nature of their situation as poor people. The kingdom is coming because God is humane, because God cannot tolerate that situation and is coming to make sure that the divine will is done on earth. Poverty must cease to wreak destructive havoc on humanity.[23]

Jesus' identification, whether in his divine self-emptying (Phil. 2:6ff.) or in the character of the relationships he established during his mission, demonstrates solidarity with those on the margins. Theologians like Gutiérrez recognize the difference which is to be found between the Lucan ("Blessed are you poor," Luke 6:20) and Matthean ("Blessed are the poor in spirit," Matt.

---

21. J. de Santa Ana, *Good News to the Poor: The Challenge of the Poor in the History of the Church* (Maryknoll, NY: Orbis Books, 1979), p. 95. See further J. Parr, "Jesus and the Salvation of the Poor: The Use of the Bible in Latin American Liberation Theology," unpublished PhD thesis, Sheffield University, 1989. We are indebted to John Parr for help with this section.

22. J. L. Segundo, *Jesus of Nazareth Yesterday and Today,* vol. 2: *The Historical Jesus of the Synoptics* (London: Sheed & Ward, 1985), p. 62.

23. G. Gutiérrez, *A Theology of Liberation* (London: SCM Press, 1974), p. 107.

5:3) Beatitudes. Instead of preferring one to the other, Gutiérrez stresses that both reflect the appropriate attitudes. Matthew's emphasis on spiritual poverty depicts an attitude of openness to God. Luke's more material emphasis demands a commitment by which one assumes the conditions of the needy of this world in order to bear witness to the evil which makes most poor and the minority rich.

Another passage which is used as part of the elaboration of the option for the poor is the parable of the sheep and the goats in Matthew 25. Here the Son of Man judges on the basis of practical responses to the poor and outcast. This Son of Man, according to the Gospel of Matthew, is none other than the figure who had nowhere to lay his head, went up to Jerusalem, was executed, and rose again. Finally, he is to appear to his disciples as the Danielic Son of Man to whom all power had been given (Matt. 28:18; cf. Dan. 7:14). He promises that he will be with them always. That presence may seem most naturally to be found in the circle of disciples ("where two or three are gathered in my name," Matt. 18:20). But the last judgment makes it clear that the hidden presence of the risen and glorified Son of Man comes in unexpected persons. Not even the righteous were aware that they had met the glorious Son of Man ("Lord, when did we see thee hungry?" etc.). Liberation theologians would accept Jürgen Moltmann's point, on the basis of Matthew 25:31ff., that the wretched "are the latent presence of the coming Saviour and Judge in the world, the touchstone which determines salvation and damnation."[24] The poor are a reminder of that transcendent God in our midst. That is a significant role, and it gives a clue to the important hermeneutical implications which are derived from this conviction. As the poor are particularly close to God in whom one meets the risen Christ, that must be the place from which to view the world and its injustices.

> Oppressed persons are the mediation of God because, first of all, they break down the normal self-interest with which human beings approach other human beings. Merely by being there the oppressed call into question those who approach, challenging their being human, and this radical questioning of what it means to be a human being serves as the historical mediation of our questioning of what "being God" means. That is why those who approach the oppressed get the real feeling that it is they who are being evangelized and converted rather than those to whom they seek

24. J. Moltmann, *The Church in the Power of the Spirit: A Contribution to Messianic Ecclesiology* (London: SCM Press, 1977), p. 127.

to render service. What we are saying here . . . is what comes across in the famous gospel passage about the Last Judgment: Going to God means going to the poor. The surprise felt by human beings on hearing that the Son of Man was incarnated in the poor is the surprise we must feel to comprehend the divinity of God on the cross.[25]

As we can see, what some of these writers are claiming is that the vantage-point of the poor is particularly and especially the vantage-point of God. As such it acts as a criterion for all theological reflection and exegesis. In addition, it has ecclesiological implications, for, according to Sobrino,[26] the church must "be formed on the basis of the poor" and "as the 'center' of the whole":

> [the poor] are therefore structural channels for finding the truth of the Church and the direction and content of its mission.
>
> The Church of the poor is not automatically the agent of truth and grace because the poor are in it; rather the poor in the Church are the structural source that assures the Church of being really the agent of truth and justice. In the final analysis, I am speaking of what Jesus refers to in Matthew 25 as the place where the Lord is to be found.[27]

Sobrino does not suggest that "the Church of the poor" is going to be something alongside mainstream Christianity. In asserting that the mark of the true Church is going to be its acceptance of the perspective of the poor he is clearly rejecting the claims of opponents of the theology of liberation that it has been attempting to create a parallel "popular" Church alongside the institution. Sobrino explicitly rejects this:

> When we say that the Church of the poor is the true Church we are not speaking of "another" Church alongside the Catholic Church or the various Protestant Churches. Nor are we saying that where this Church of the poor exists it exists in a pure form, uncontaminated by sin and error, nor that it is coextensive with the Church of faith. What we are saying is that the Church of the poor is in its structure the true way of being a Church in Jesus; that it provides the structural means of approximating ever more closely to the Church of faith; and that it is more perfectly the historical sacrament of liberation.

---

25. J. Sobrino, *The True Church and the Church of the Poor* (London: SCM Press, 1985), p. 222.

26. Sobrino, *The True Church and the Church of the Poor*, p. 93.

27. Sobrino, *The True Church and the Church of the Poor*, p. 95.

If all this is the case and if it is happening in Latin America, it is because Christ has willed to show himself not in any place whatsoever, nor even in the structure, good in principle, which he established, but in the poor. We must describe this new phenomenon of the Church of the poor as representing on the one hand a conversion of the historical Church and on the other its resurrection.[28]

In the light of criticism of the so-called "Popular Church," theologians like Leonardo Boff have been at pains to stress the deep roots of the Basic Christian Communities within the life of the Catholic Church. Certainly they may offer a new perspective and are (in the words of Cardinal Joseph Ratzinger) a sign of hope for the renewal of the Church. But Boff makes it quite plain that he does not conceive of the Basic Christian Communities as comprising an embryonic sect, however much some of their critics may like to portray them as such. Rather, he argues that they are the leaven in the lump, a remnant within the people of God:

> The new church will have to remain faithful to its path. It will have to remain loyally disobedient. It will have to seek a profound loyalty to the demands of the gospels. Critically reflecting upon these questions and convinced of its path it must have the courage to be disobedient to the demands of the centre, without anger or complaint, in deep adherence to the desire to be faithful to the Lord, the gospels, and the Spirit — the same desire that is presumed to motivate the institutional church.[29]

We note here the repeated emphasis on Jesus and the Gospels as the central criterion of obedience. The question of selectivity will be touched on elsewhere, but its place in the understanding of the option for the poor must be noted here. The idea of a "canon within the canon" has always been an important exegetical device for Christians. Criticism of the selectivity of the liberation theologians' option for the poor cannot disguise the way in which other passages and ethical outlooks have been preferred by those who have construed Christian discipleship in an equally partisan and controversial manner. What needs to be stressed, of course, is that the theme of concern for the poor and outcast does not exhaust all the material related to social ethics in the Bible. The entry of more and more rich people into the Church

---

28. Sobrino, *The True Church and the Church of the Poor,* pp. 123-4.

29. L. Boff, *Ecclesiogenesis: The Base Communities Reinvent the Church* (Maryknoll, NY: Orbis Books/London: Collins Flame, 1986), p. 63.

led to a rather more accepting attitude towards the status quo, and to a compromise over wealth and with the society in which ordinary Christians had to live. This point is noted, for example, by Julio de Santa Ana:

> . . . there are at least two levels at which the community of faith responds to the challenge of poverty: while some Christians live as ordinary believers and in one way or another come to a compromise between the demands of faith and the styles of life around them, others attempt a more radical response, with no concessions to context, thus trying to maintain the fundamental demands of faith. As a result, we have on the one hand "ordinary" Christians, and, on the other, those who choose a monastic life; on the one hand those who believe they could continue to have property and wealth, and on the other, those who abandon everything in their eagerness to be absolutely faithful to the demands of the gospel. This we believe was the result of the synthesis which took place in the second century between the problem of the presence of the rich in the church, and the challenge presented to it by the poor and poverty. The two extremes came together in a compromise concerning the way in which brotherly charity should be practiced.[30]

The point at issue between the liberation theologians and their conservative critics is the meaning of these passages and the question whether in fact the references to the poor in the Jesus tradition can actually bear the weight of the interpretation of the option for the poor which also involves an *active* struggle against injustice. Much will depend on the interpretation of the eschatological material. The argument is widely used that the earliest Christians, including Jesus himself, did not concern themselves with changing society because they believed that God was going to do that in the near future when the Kingdom of God was brought in. Thus it may be possible to repudiate the idea that a tension ever existed between the radical practitioners of the Jesus ethic and those who sought to work out a compromise with the existing order. Recent study, however, suggests that already in the New Testament a tension such as is outlined by de Santa Ana was being felt.[31] They have recalled us to the Jesus of the synoptic Gospels as a crucial hermeneutical key in understanding the heart of the response of Christian discipleship: "as you did it to one of the least of these my brethren, you did it to me" (Matt. 25:40). . . .

30. De Santa Ana, *Good News*, p. 62.
31. See, for example, Theissen, *First Followers*.

Conclusion

In his *Theology and the Church,* a response to the Vatican document published in September 1984, *Instruction on Certain Aspects of the Theology of Liberation,* Juan Luis Segundo declares that "a theology of liberation correctly understood constitutes an invitation to theologians to deepen certain essential biblical themes with a concern for the grave and urgent questions which the contemporary yearning for liberation and those movements which more or less faithfully echo it pose for the church."[32] . . .

The exegetical approach of the liberation theologian maintains the dialectic between text and interpreter. It neither allows the interpreter free rein at the expense of the text, with a license to make of it what he or she wants, nor the text free rein at the expense of the interpreter, as in those "objectivist" approaches which think that the situation of the reader is irrelevant to the exegetical task. It is an approach which seeks to be faithful to the long hermeneutical process by which, within the Judeo-Christian tradition itself, the texts themselves emerged as commentary upon the changing political situation of their own times.

In a profound study of the sociology of knowledge, *Knowledge and Human Interests,* Jürgen Habermas wrote as follows:

> Whether dealing with contemporary objectivations or historical traditions, the interpreter cannot abstractly free himself from his hermeneutic point of departure. He cannot simply jump over the open horizon of his own life activity. . . . An interpretation can only grasp its object and penetrate it in a relation in which the interpreter reflects on the object and himself at the same time as moments of an objective structure that likewise encompasses both and makes them possible.[33]

The fact that the interpreter cannot jump out of his or her cognitive skin is not a denial of objectivity. It does not mean drowning truth in a bath of relativism. It means understanding that the possibility of objectivity exists only in the relation between object and interpreter, as Habermas argues here. Concepts of truth and objectivity are not made redundant by the approach which, in common with others, liberation theology makes to the text, aware of the crucial significance of the present horizon of the interpreter to exege-

32. J. L. Segundo, *Theology and the Church: A Response to Cardinal Ratzinger and a Warning to the Whole Church* (London: Geoffrey Chapman, 1985), p. 172.

33. Jürgen Habermas, *Knowledge and Human Interests* (London: Heineman, 1972), p. 181.

sis. But, as Habermas says, the "objective structure" which is employed here must encompass both object and subject. The truth of which liberation exegesis speaks as much as any other method of exegesis must be recognized as dialectical. It is a dialogue between past and present, in which neither can displace the other. If there is a danger of the past being displaced by liberation theologians who adopt the Bible as an additional weapon with which to mount a pre-determined campaign, there is a danger of the present being displaced in the approach to the text of much academic scholarship. It may therefore be that liberation exegesis has an important contribution to make to biblical interpretation.

2 Reading the Bible Politically

Richard Bauckham

Many Christians have recently been rediscovering the political dimension of the message of the Bible. This is really a return to normality, since the notion that biblical Christianity has nothing to do with politics is little more than a modern Western Christian aberration, which would not have been entertained by the Church in most periods and places of its history. But political interpretation of the Bible has many pitfalls for the unwary. It is all too easy to read our own prejudices into the Bible, while it is not at all easy to move intelligently, without anachronism, between the political societies of biblical times and the very different societies of today. The aim here is to help the reader towards an understanding of the political relevance of the Bible which will be both more disciplined and more imaginative than some current attempts to read the Bible politically. It offers neither a summary of the political teaching of the Bible nor a program for Christian political action, but a prerequisite for those things: a course in political hermeneutics. In other words — lest the word *hermeneutics* put some people off — it is for those who want to know how to interpret the Bible politically. Along the way we may reach particular conclusions about the teaching of the Bible and its relevance to modern political issues, but these are essentially illustrations of a method which readers are encouraged to pursue for themselves. Although they cover quite a lot of biblical and political ground, they are a representative sample, not an exhaustive survey.

A book-long treatment of this topic would need to consider several elements in the argument. The first element would be methodological: an introduction to hermeneutical issues and principles which would need to be illustrated in practice. Biblical interpretation is more of an art than an exact science. Like all art it has its rules and requires considerable discipline, but good interpretation is much more than a matter of following rules which can be learned in advance.

The next element would be to involve the reader in the practice of hermeneutics by considering political exegesis of specific biblical passages, representing different types of biblical literature and relating to a fairly broad range of political issues. And, since the hermeneutical approach pursued here is to interpret texts not in isolation but in relation to the rest of Scripture, discussion would necessarily range further than the passages to which they are anchored. The focus, however, must always be rooted in the detailed exegesis of particular texts, without which any biblical interpretation is bound to be shoddy and insecure.

A different, equally necessary approach to the biblical material would be to consider the way in which a particular theme is traced through the whole Bible and the broad contours of its treatment in the Bible are delineated and developed. The aim would be to show how a creative encounter between biblical texts — even texts not normally expected to invite political readings — and modern realities can generate fresh insight, and so how the Bible can prove itself relevant in quite novel as well as well-tried ways. For it to do so is quite essential if a political hermeneutic is to be at all adequate to the needs of political praxis in the contemporary world. Readers should try not to prejudge the political relevance of the various parts of the Bible. Open-minded readers of Scripture will always have challenging and stimulating surprises in store for them.

Issues in Interpretation

Here we discuss some of the most important hermeneutical issues that arise in applying the Bible to politics and formulate some principles for reading the Bible politically. We begin with one of the most crucial hermeneutical issues, which accounts for many differences between Christians on political matters: the relation between the Old and New Testaments.

Varieties of Biblical Politics

Most readers of the Bible notice an obvious difference between the Old Testament and the New Testament in their treatment of political matters. On a superficial view, at least, the Old Testament seems to have much to say about politics, the New Testament rather little. However, this may be a misleading way of stating the difference, since it ignores the extent to which New Testament material which is not very explicitly political may nevertheless have political implications. It is not so easy to be non-political as some people think. The difference between the testaments might be better expressed in terms of a difference of political context. Much of the Old Testament is addressed to a people of God which was a political entity and for much of its history had at least some degree of political autonomy. The Old Testament is therefore directly concerned with the ordering of Israel's political life, the conduct of political affairs, the formulation of policies, the responsibilities of rulers as well as subjects, and so on. The New Testament is addressed to a politically powerless minority in the Roman Empire. Its overtly political material therefore largely concerns the responsibilities of citizens and subjects who, though they might occasionally hope to impress the governing authorities by prophetic witness (Matt. 10:18), had no ordinary means of political influence. Their only conceivable (though scarcely practical) route to political power would have been that of armed revolt, an option which they seem to have rejected.

This difference between the testaments explains why, from the time of Constantine onwards, whenever the political situation of Christians has moved towards more direct political influence and responsibility, the Old Testament has tended to play a larger part in Christian political thinking than the New Testament. This has been the case not only in the classic "Christendom" situation of much of Western Christian history, where the confessedly Christian society bore an obvious resemblance to political Israel. It can also quite often be seen in situations where Christians have supported revolutionary movements and in modern pluralistic democracies. In the course of Christian history Old Testament law and precedent have been used to support an extraordinary variety of political institutions and policies: such as divine-right monarchy, crusades, redistribution of wealth, use of the death penalty, aid for the Third World, and royal authority over national churches. The Old Testament has been used to argue both the admissibility and the inadmissibility of female rulers, slavery, and political assassination.

The Problem of Selectivity

One of the problems which the history of Christian political use of the Old Testament highlights is that of selectivity. Clearly Christians have always se-

31

lected those elements of Old Testament teaching which they consider to have contemporary political relevance, and in different times and places they have selected different elements. The problem here is that this selection has all too often been governed by expedience rather than by any hermeneutical principle, and it has therefore been in danger of being an ideological manipulation of Scripture to support current principles and programs. It can be very salutary for modern Christians to compare their own selective use of Old Testament material with that of their predecessors, and to ask whether they have any principles which justify the one over against the other. How many of those who freely quote the prophets' demands for social justice in favor of the poor and oppressed, while ignoring, for example, the prophets' demand, sometimes in the same breath (Ezek. 22:7-8; Amos 8:4-6), for sabbath observance, do so in the light of a hermeneutical principle? For nineteenth-century sabbatarians, support for legislation to enforce national sabbath observance had the same significance — in being a crucial issue of Christian obedience in the political sphere — as concern for the unemployed or the Third World has for many Christians today. In Old Testament terms, at least, they had a point.

Dispensational Differences

When Christians are asked to explain why an Old Testament political provision should not, in their view, be applied to present-day political circumstances, they most often make one of two types of response. One is an appeal to a difference of cultural context: what made political sense in ancient Israelite society may not do so in modern technological society. This is a consideration which applies equally to the relevance of New Testament teaching and will be discussed later in the chapter. Alternatively, however, appeal may be made to a difference of "dispensational" context: in other words, to the pre-Christian character of the Old Testament. It is here that the relation between the two testaments becomes a vital issue. In fact, this appeal can itself take two rather different forms:

1. It can be argued that New Testament ethics, say in the Sermon on the Mount, are an advance on Old Testament ethical teaching, which therefore becomes to some extent obsolete.
2. It can be argued that Old Testament Israel was in the unique position of being a theocratic state, and cannot therefore provide a political model

for the New Testament era, in which God's people are not a political entity but scattered throughout the nations. (In passing, it may be noted that in fact the Old Testament itself faced the political issues of a diaspora people of God, and provided not only some guidance for Jewish subjects of pagan states [Jer. 29], but also examples of Jews exercising political authority or influence in pagan states: Joseph, Daniel and his friends, and Esther and Mordecai.)

Both these forms of argument are used, for example, to render Old Testament wars inapplicable as political precedents. On the basis of the first argument, Old Testament teaching on war is often said to be replaced by Jesus' ethic "of non-violence." On the basis of the second, Israel's wars were holy wars, waged by God against his enemies, but modern states cannot claim such divine sanction for their wars.

We need to be clear that, though they both depend on the dispensational position of the Old Testament, these are two quite different arguments. Both may have their place in a consideration of the biblical teaching on war. It is also worth noticing that both arguments involve us in another issue which we shall shortly take up: the relation between the people of God and the world. In the case of the first, if the argument is valid, we still need to know whether Jesus' ethic prohibits war only for Christian believers, or for secular states also. In the case of the second, we need to consider how far it is true that God governed his own people Israel on principles quite different from those he expects of other nations. Clearly the question of the modern relevance of Old Testament political material is a complex hermeneutical issue.

Using the Old Testament Today

In view of this complexity, some may be tempted to dismiss the political relevance of the Old Testament altogether. But there is a good reason for not doing so. God and his purposes for human life remain the same in both testaments, and it is primarily the character of God and his purposes for human life which are expressed in the political material of the Old Testament. They are expressed in forms appropriate to the specific conditions of Old Testament Israel: both the specific cultural context (or contexts) of a nation living in that time and place, and also the specific salvation-historical context of the national people of God in the period before the coming of Christ. This means that, while the law and the prophets cannot be *instructions* for our political life, they can be *instructive* for our political life: We cannot apply their teaching directly to ourselves, but from the way in which God expressed his character and purposes in the political life of Israel we may learn something of how they should be expressed in political life today.

This means that our first concern should not be to select those parts of the Old Testament which still apply today. None of it applies directly to us, as *instructions*, but all of it is relevant to us, as *instructive* (cf. 2 Tim. 3:16). Various aspects of Old Testament politics will prove instructive in different ways, as we consider both the differences and the similarities between their context, both cultural and salvation-historical, and ours. Not only analogous but also contrasting situations can be instructive. In every case we shall have to consider the salvation-historical context and relate the Old Testament material to the New Testament. The fundamental point about the relation between the testaments is not that in some cases Old Testament provisions are superseded by the New Testament, while in other cases they are left unchanged. The fundamental point is that Jesus *fulfilled* the whole of the law and the prophets. None of the Old Testament can be unaffected by its fulfillment in Christ, but all of it, as fulfilled in Christ, remains instructive. We should not force this fulfillment in Christ into some artificial scheme (such as the traditional claim that Christ abrogated the civil and ceremonial law, but left the moral law in force), but should consider each part and aspect of the Old Testament in the light of Christ. The effect of doing this will take a wide variety of forms. We should also not forget that, just as we read the Old Testament in the light of its fulfillment in the New, so we must also read the New Testament against the background of the Old Testament, which it presupposes. In their political teaching, as in other matters, the two testaments supplement and inform each other.

Personal and Political Ethics

In addition to the question of the relation between the testaments, there are at least three other hermeneutical issues which constantly arise in considering the Bible's relevance to politics. These all affect our judgment about the extent of the biblical material that is relevant to modern politics. Has this or that passage something to say to our political life? "No, because it is about personal ethics, not politics," we sometimes say. Or: "No, because it is about the social life of the Church, and cannot be applied to society outside the Church." Or: "No, because it applied to the particular cultural conditions of that time and cannot apply to our very different kind of society." We need to look rather closely at these three sets of distinctions before we can decide what is and what is not politically relevant.

We begin with a hermeneutical principle which can be and has been used to render much biblical — especially New Testament — teaching irrelevant to political issues: the principle of a radical distinction between the ethical principles which apply to immediate personal relations and those which apply to political institutions and activities. According to this principle, the Sermon on the Mount would apply to a politician in her private life, but not in her public activity *qua* politician. An influential form of this view, though not its most extreme form, was held by Martin Luther. He pointed out, for example, that a judge who in his private life is obliged to forgive personal injuries against himself and not to demand reparation is equally obliged in his public capacity as a judge to pass sentence on criminals and not to let them off without punishment.

Luther did not make the mistake of arguing that *wholly* different ethical principles apply in the private and the public spheres. He did not, for example, distinguish love as the principle of personal ethics from justice as the ethical principle of public life — a distinction not to be found in the Bible. On the contrary, Luther recognized that the command to love one's neighbor (on which, according to Matt. 22:40, the *political* requirements of the law and prophets depend) was the ethical principle of government as well as of private life. But love must take different forms in public and private life.

To some extent he had a valid point. When Jesus' ethical teaching becomes specific it is most often with reference to personal life. Matthew 5:38-42, for example, is not addressed to judges as judges, but to private individuals. But it is doubtful whether any sharp distinction can be drawn between public and private life in the way that Luther's principle seems to require. The individual is obliged to forgive personal injuries against himself, but this principle will not be enough to guide him in situations where the interests of several people are involved, where other people have been injured or need protection, or where (as a parent, for example) he has a responsibility for the moral education of the person who has done wrong. In such situations forgiveness becomes one duty of love among others. But then no radical difference occurs when we move into political situations. The principle of forgiveness does not become inapplicable, but needs to take appropriate forms in conjunction with other principles of love.

Thus we have the ordinary Christian ethical task of applying the principles of Jesus' teaching to all the varying situations of life, including the political ones. Of course they will not all apply in all situations (Matt. 5:27-28 will have little relevance to, say, the problem of the arms race), but they must simply be allowed to apply where they do apply. There should be no hermeneutical rule which excludes them from the political sphere.

Ethics for the Church and for the World

Another way of limiting the application of New Testament ethics can also be illustrated from the sixteenth century. Whereas Luther drew a sharp distinction between the private and the public roles of the Christian, the Anabaptists drew a sharp distinction between Christians and others, the Church and the world. The ethics of the Sermon on the Mount, they claimed, govern the whole life of the Christian community but are irreconcilable with the tasks of governing a state, so Christians may not hold public office in the state. Political activity must be left to non-Christians, to whom the Sermon on the Mount is not addressed and of whom a different ethical standard is required. It should be noticed that the extent to which all citizens are implicated in the activities of government, for example by paying taxes, raised problems for this view even in the sixteenth century. In modern democracies the difficulties are greater.

It is one thing to say that Christians should have both the motivation and the spiritual resources to live better lives than others (cf. Matt. 5:46-48) and to realize the intentions of God for human community more perfectly in the Church than elsewhere. It is another thing to say that differing ethical principles apply to Christians and to others. It is hard to find biblical support for the latter.

This being so, it not only follows that the Sermon on the Mount requires political as well as other forms of implementation. It also follows that fundamental New Testament principles for life in the Christian community extend in principle to life in human community as such, and therefore have political relevance. This applies, for example, to Jesus' revolutionary principle of authority as service (Mark 10:42-45), Paul's principle of sexual and racial equality (Gal. 3:28), his effective abolition of the status of slave (Philem. 16), and his principle of equality of material possessions (2 Cor. 8:14). It is to the great credit of the early Anabaptists that they took some of these principles more seriously in their primary application to the Christian community than their Protestant contemporaries did, and they were able to do this because they maintained a clear distinction between the Church and the world.

But such principles, once recognized, cannot be confined to the Church. This was seen, for example, by the nineteenth-century Evangelicals who worked to abolish slavery not only as a status within the Church but also as a condition sanctioned by the state. It is seen by South African Christians who realize that if apartheid is unjustifiable in the Church it is unjustifiable in the state and society too.

In extending New Testament principles of Christian community beyond the Church to political society we must take full account of the differences. Politics cannot do what the gospel and the Spirit can do, and politics cannot do in all societies what it can do in a society deeply influenced by Christian or other religious-ethical values. This is why the realization of those principles in the Church's life as a witness to the world must always be the Church's priority. But we should also remember that in some cases, such as sexual and material equality, the Church has had to be reminded of biblical principles by other people's witness to them.

Permanent Norms and Cultural Relativity

If the fundamentals of the human situation have not changed since biblical times, the conditions and forms of human society have — drastically. In modern society, whether democratic or totalitarian, industrialized or already moving towards the coming post-industrialized situation, government is a very different business from what it was for Deborah, Hezekiah, or Pontius Pilate. Both its methods and its functions have necessarily changed and continue to change. This must be kept at the forefront of our minds in all attempts to make political use of the Bible. Otherwise naive absurdities will result. To argue, for example, that since education in biblical times was not a government responsibility it should nowadays be left purely to parental responsibility, as it was then, makes no more sense than to argue that in accordance with biblical precedent governments should not legislate for road safety. The functions of government are much more extensive now than in biblical times, not because governments have overstepped the biblically defined limits of their authority, but because of the vastly increased complexity of modern society. This at the same time makes different, more democratic forms of government both more practicable and more desirable than in ancient societies.

We need, therefore, to take a thoroughly historical attitude to this matter. The functions and forms of government are highly changeable features of human life (by their very nature they must be), and the Bible cannot therefore provide rigid norms for political institutions and methods in all periods of history. Moreover, a recognition of this is not foreign to the Bible's own view of government. Genesis does not, as we might expect, trace the exercise of political authority back to creation or the Fall, but describes its emergence in the course of the historical development of human culture. Just as cities (Gen. 4:17), music (Gen. 4:21), and viticulture (Gen. 9:20) did not descend from heaven, but had thoroughly human origins, so government, in its most common Old Testament form of kingship, emerged with Nimrod: "the first on earth to be a mighty man" (Gen. 10:8).[1] The portrayal of Nimrod as a hunter (Gen. 10:9), and as ruling an empire formed not by conquest but by colonization (Gen. 10:10-12), is significant, since it links Nimrod's rule with the human task of dominion on earth as given by God, after the Flood, to Noah (Gen. 9:1-7). This task was not in itself necessarily political, but took political form in Nimrod, who as a hunter protected his people from wild animals (cf. Gen. 9:2, 5) and as founder of a colonial empire fulfilled the command to fill the earth (Gen. 9:1). Thus according to Genesis, kingship, the rule of one man over a whole society, originated as a way of fulfilling these God-given human tasks, even if, as the beginning of Nimrod's empire in Babel indicates (Gen. 10:10; cf. 11:1-9), it may not have been an ideal way of fulfilling them. But it is then very important to notice that the functions of Nimrod's rule, which account for the origin of kingship, were not the functions of government as Old Testament Israel knew government in later periods. Nimrod's fame as a hunter (Gen. 10:9) preserves a memory of a very early period of human society, when one of the special duties of a king was to ward off and destroy the wild animals threatening his community. In the historical period of the Old Testament this original function of kingship was preserved in a purely conventional form: hunting was the favorite sport of kings in Egypt and Mesopotamia. But the king's hunting no longer had the vital, practical function of preserving the life of the community. Nor was the colonizing of uninhabited land a major function of government in the time of Old Testament Israel. Thus the functions of Nimrod's kingship were no longer the functions of kingship when Genesis was written. By describing in this form the origins of government, Genesis recognizes the thoroughly historical character of human government, how its functions must change and develop in relation to the changes and development of human society. Legitimate government must always re-

1. See C. Westermann, *Genesis 1–11: A Commentary* (London: SPCK, 1984), pp. 514-18.

flect God's will for human life, as Nimrod's did the divine command to Noah, and the Bible's account of God's will for human life will therefore always be relevant to it, but *how* it reflects God's will for human life, and what aspects of that will can appropriately be furthered by political institutions and methods, must change and can be discerned only in each new historical situation.

So we need to recognize that the political material in the Bible consists largely of stories about and instructions addressed to political societies very different from our own. I have sometimes wondered whether this is not part of the reason for the relatively modern tendency for many Christians to disengage from political and social reality. The adaptations needed to transfer biblical teaching on personal morality from its cultural situation to ours are comparatively easily made, but a more imaginative and creative hermeneutic is necessary for the Bible to speak to modern political life. Even when superficial parallels do strike us they can be highly problematic, as I discovered when leading studies on Joshua in a church house group at the time of the Israeli invasion of Lebanon.

The dilemma with which cultural relativity presents us is that the more specific the biblical material is in its application to its own historical context, the less relevant it seems to be in our context. Must we then look in the Bible only for permanent norms of a highly generalized character? This would be foreign to the nature of the Bible and would leave a great deal of it unusable, since the Bible is God's message in, to, and through very particular historical situations. Its universality must be found *in* and *through* its particularity, not by peeling its particularity away until only a hard core of universality remains. So the appropriate method seems to be that of appreciating the biblical material first of all in its own culturally specific uniqueness, and then seeing it as a "paradigm" (as Chris Wright suggests)[2] or an "analogy" (as André Dumas suggests)[3] for our own time. In other words, the Bible provides models of God's purposes at work in particular political situations which can help us to discover and to implement his purposes in other situations. Such models, *because* they are highly specific, can often stimulate our thinking and imagination more effectively than very general principles can. For example, the law of gleaning in Leviticus 19:9-10 was appropriate only for a

2. C. J. H. Wright, *Living as the People of God: The Relevance of Old Testament Ethics* (Leicester: Inter-Varsity Press, 1983), pp. 40-45.

3. A. Dumas, *Political Theology and the Life of the Church* (London: SCM Press, 1978), pp. 68-69.

simple, agrarian society, but by observing how very appropriate it was as a means of provision for the poor in that society, we can be stimulated to think about forms of social legislation appropriate to our society. Of course we need always to consider such models in conjunction with the general principles that the Bible also provides.

However, the principles are fairly general and the models cannot be blueprints. In a sense they leave us considerable freedom to work out for ourselves, under the guidance of the Spirit, how God's purposes for human life can be realized in our political life. But that is rather a negative way of putting it. Positively, they can *inspire* our own creative thinking about politics today.

That the Bible's teaching is culturally specific, in the sense that it addresses specific situations in ancient history, will be generally acknowledged. Rather more controversial is the claim that the Bible's political teaching is in some degree *conditioned* by the social and political context in which it arose. But it seems to me we must recognize this as part of the real humanity of Scripture. For example, the political wisdom of the book of Proverbs, with its emphasis on the stability of a fixed social order (Prov. 19:10; 30:21-3) and its sometimes deferentially uncritical attitude to the monarchy (Prov. 16:10-15; 25:3), reflects the outlook of the court circles from which it derives. This makes it not a mistaken but a *limited* viewpoint, and therefore one which needs to be balanced by other aspects of biblical teaching. In this case at least, the relativizing effect of its cultural background coincides with the relativizing effect of its occupying its particular place in the whole canon of Scripture. We shall have more to say about the hermeneutical significance of the canon shortly.

Text and Context

Finally, we turn to the principles involved in reading a biblical text within the relevant contexts for its correct understanding. Inevitably we shall be mainly concerned with general principles that apply to all biblical interpretation, but we shall bear in mind the particular needs of political interpretation.

The meaning of a text is dependent on its context. This is the key to all responsible interpretation of biblical texts. But "context" has a variety of aspects:

1. There is *the linguistic context* of accepted meanings of words and idioms in the linguistic milieu in which the text was written and first read.

2. There is *the immediate literary context* of the literary unit in which the text belongs. (The unit will often be the biblical book of which the text is now part, e.g. Mark's Gospel, but it may sometimes be a smaller unit, e.g. a psalm, and sometimes a larger unit, e.g. 1-2 Chronicles.)

3. There is *the wider literary context* of literary genre, conventions, allusions and so on, within the tradition of literature to which the text belongs.

4. There is *the cultural context* of the kind of society — political, social, economic, religious — in which the text originated.

5. There is *the broad historical context* of current events which may be relevant to understanding the text.

6. There is *the immediate historical context* in the life of the writer or his circle which occasioned the text.

All these aspects belong to the "original" context in which the text was written. But a text which goes on being read and valued long after it was written acquires new contexts. In the case of a biblical text, its original literary unit has been incorporated into several larger literary contexts. A psalm, for example, which may originally have been an isolated literary unit, became part of one of the smaller collections of psalms which were then put together to make our psalter. In the process it may have been edited, to make it suitable for use in the temple when the collection was made, and may have been given a title. Then the psalter itself became part of the Hebrew canon of Scripture, and that in turn part of the Christian Bible, in which the psalm may be quoted and interpreted by New Testament writers. Each of these broader literary contexts must affect its meaning.

Then there are the constantly changing historical, cultural, liturgical, and theological contexts within which the psalm has been read and understood down to the present day, some of which still affect our reading of it. Its meaning for us depends, then, on its original context (so far as we may be aware of it), on its wider literary contexts in the canon (so far as we take these into account), on traditional contexts (such as its interpretation in a particular theological tradition or its traditional place in a liturgy) which may influence our understanding of it, and on the contemporary context within which we read it. What this contemporary context amounts to depends, of course, on the interpreter's particular relationships to the world in which he lives.

Evidently the meaning of a text must change as it is read in these various new contexts. It will lose dimensions of meaning which it had in its original context (since aspects of that context have been lost or forgotten) and it will gain new dimensions of meaning as it acquires new contexts. Nevertheless

41

the task of interpretation must presuppose that a constant (or at least recoverable) core of meaning persists and generates, in interaction with its new contexts, these new dimensions of meaning. Those who argue that the original context is irrelevant to a text's meaning for us should, logically, abandon the use of dictionaries and treat the Hebrew and Greek texts as mere meaningless marks on the page, to which they can give any meaning the shapes suggest to them! The historical nature of language itself requires us to give the original context a determinative role in the text's meaning for us. On the other hand, those who claim that a biblical text can legitimately mean only what it meant to its first readers need to be reminded of the way in which all great literature constantly transcends its original context and achieves fresh relevance to new situations.

Expanding Meaning

A brief example (not irrelevant to politics) may illustrate the way a biblical text can acquire new dimensions of meaning. Humanity's God-given dominion over the rest of the animals (Gen. 1:26, 28) must, for its first readers, have had a fairly restricted meaning, referring to their taming, hunting, and farming of animals. In fact in Old Testament times the language of Genesis 1:26, which speaks of human dominion over all animals, must have seemed hyperbolic to anyone who thought about it, since many animals were not, in any realistic sense, under human dominion. (The writer of Job 39:2-12 certainly realized this.) In the context of its own literary unit, the book of Genesis, the text receives a kind of exposition in the account of Noah's relations with the animals, which again suggests a more far-reaching dominion than was the actual experience of Old Testament people. Then in the context of the Hebrew Bible, the thought of Genesis 1:26 is made, in Psalm 8:4-8, the basis for praise of God ("What is man that thou art mindful of him? . . . Yet thou hast made him little less than God"), with the implication that human dominion over the animals is to be exercised to the glory of God. The New Testament passage Hebrews 2:8 then gives the idea a Christological significance, seeing Jesus as the man who will fully realize the ideal of human dominion over creation.

Both of these inner-canonical interpretations are relevant to the fresh extension of meaning which Genesis 1:26 has gained in our own time, when humanity has become so dominant as to threaten the very survival of much of the animal creation. Applying the text to this new situation, which could not have been envisaged by its author, is not a distortion, but a natural extension, of the text's "core" meaning. Indeed, the open-ended language of the text really comes into its own only in modern times, when at last it is literally true that scarcely a species on earth can escape the effects of human activities. In this new situation it is clear that humanity, in its dominance on earth, incurs new responsibilities, such as the preservation of endangered species, which the first readers of Genesis 1:26, because of the restricted realization of their dominion, did not have. But precisely in this new situation, continuity with the original meaning of the text gains fresh importance, since this ensures that "dominion" refers to responsible, not exploitative, rule, on the model of God's own care for his creation. I am surprised that Noah has not become, as he deserves to be, a model for Christian conservationists!

If a biblical text is not to mean whatever we want it to mean, we must pay disciplined attention to its original and canonical contexts. But if it is to mean something for us, we must pay equally disciplined attention to the contemporary context in which we interpret it.

Pre-Canonical Contexts

The term "pre-canonical contexts" is really preferable to "original context," because, as the example of a psalm (given above) illustrates, many biblical passages in fact passed through a series of historical contexts before entering the canon. Much biblical material existed first as oral tradition and/or passed through several stages of written compilation and editing before reaching its present form. The "original" context is not always discoverable nor always the most important for our understanding of the text. To understand a psalm as originally composed may be less important than to understand it as part of the collection of temple hymns. A good rule of thumb (not to be applied without exceptions) is to take the present form of a biblical book as the primary context for exegesis, but to take account of the previous history of the materials contained in it in so far as these earlier contexts remain significant for understanding the material in the context of the biblical book. For example, the prophetic books of the Old Testament are edited collections of prophetic oracles, intended as such not for the prophet's contemporaries but for later readers. But the relevance of the original context of these oracles is preserved within their later context, because the very nature of the oracles, which are often dated and address identifiable historical situations at the time of utterance, makes it impossible to ignore their original context.

To interpret the text in its pre-canonical contexts, the well-known methods of historical exegesis apply and must be rigorously applied. No exceptions must be allowed to the principle that the historical meaning of the text must be a meaning which readers at that time could perceive. Since the "core meaning" of the text, which persists in all new contexts, must be contained in this historical meaning, this principle gives the task of achieving relative objectivity in historical exegesis a key role in preserving all interpretation from uncontrolled subjectivity. All new dimensions of meaning which a text may later acquire must be intelligibly continuous with a meaning accessible to readers of the text in its pre-canonical contexts.

Thus, for example, the medieval political exegesis of Luke 22:38, according to which the two swords represent the ecclesiastical and civil authorities of Christendom, is unacceptable because it has no basis in a meaning which could have been discovered by the first readers of the text.

The Canonical Context

The final context which is *authoritative* for the meaning of a biblical text is the complete canon of Scripture. We cannot be content to read a text as its pre-canonical readers read it, but must also read it in the context of the whole biblical story of God's dealings with his people and the overriding theological and moral themes of the Bible. This does not mean a harmonistic leveling out of the diversity and distinctiveness of the various parts of Scripture, because the canonical context is not a substitute for, but is additional to the pre-canonical contexts. It does mean that we must think about the relative significance of the various parts of the canon, and recognize that some viewpoints within Scripture are relativized or even corrected by others. It means appreciating that the unity of the canon sometimes emerges in dialectical fashion from the diversity of the canon. It involves us in constant interaction between understanding particular texts in their primary contexts and attempting a biblical theology which does justice to the whole canon.

The Contemporary Context

There are several dangers involved in the task of interpreting the text in the context of our contemporary world. One is the danger of manipulating the text to support our preconceived attitudes and projects. This is an often unconscious temptation in the political use of the Bible, since biblical authority can sometimes be a very useful source of justification for political policies and since we often find it difficult to be self-critical about our own political attitudes. To allow the Bible to challenge and change our political attitudes is harder than we perhaps realize.

Disciplined listening to the text in its original and canonical contexts is one protection against this danger. Of course, historical exegesis is never *wholly* objective, but the rigorous attempt at historical objectivity can liberate us from all kinds of misuse of the text. So can serious attention to the place of the text within the canon. Ideological abuse of Romans 13:1-7 to support the status quo can be corrected by reference to passages critical of unjust government. Study of the history of interpretation can also be helpful, since historical distance enables us to appreciate what was going on in the Church's political use of the Bible in the past more easily than we can in the present. For example, the nineteenth-century use of the Bible to justify slavery, even by so eminent a theologian as Charles Hodge,[4] is a salutary warning, which needs to be heeded especially where the interests of the interpreter's own class or nation are at stake in the interpretation of Scripture.

The peril of blindness to the influence of our interests on interpretation can also be countered by attention to the work of interpreters whose political and economic circumstances are different from our own. American black slaves read the Bible very differently from the way their masters read it. Today it is important that we listen to the liberation theologians of the Third World and that we try to hear how the Bible sounds to Christians persecuted by oppressive regimes. Of course we must recognize that revolutionary interpretations of Scripture can be as ideological as interpretations by those in power, just as feminist interpretations can be as ideological as patriarchal interpretations. But we have a duty to listen to anyone who claims that the Bible has been misused against them and to anyone whose interpretation of Scripture goes hand in hand with costly discipleship of Christ.

All this reminds us that in the end the task of contextualizing Scripture today is the task of the whole Church, and must take place in the dialogue between Christians whose varied cultures, conditions, and Christian traditions can alert them to aspects of Scripture which others may miss. Much discussion of contextualization has been about the different forms which Christianity should take within particular cultures today, and of course this is important. But at a time when the most urgent political issues are the in-

---

4. There is a useful discussion in W. M. Swartley, *Slavery, Sabbath, War, and Women* (Scottdale, Penn.: Herald, 1983), chap. 1.

ternational ones affecting all parts of the world, our political use of the Bible needs to reflect the thinking of the universal Church.

Another danger in relating the Bible to contemporary situations is that of too simplistic application. There are two antidotes to this. One is, again, careful study of the texts in their historical context, which will alert us to the real differences between that context and the modern one. Second, the more we realize how biblical texts relate to the actual social structures and economic conditions of their time, the more we shall see the need to engage in serious analysis of our contemporary world if we are to specify the Bible's relevance to it. Too often Christians concerned about social justice have imagined that Amos's critique of eighth-century Israel needs only a little adjustment to apply to our own society. But this is often cheap relevance, which evades the need for proper analysis of and prophetic insight into the actual evils of our society.

This last observation prompts us to notice, finally, that the Bible's meaning for today cannot result automatically from the correct use of a set of hermeneutical principles. It requires in the interpreters qualities of insight, imagination, critical judgment, and expert knowledge of the contemporary world. It also requires the guidance of the Holy Spirit, who inspired not the mere text but the contextual meaning of the text, and therefore remains active at the interface between the text and its changing contexts.

3 Loitering with Intent:
Biblical Texts in Public Places

R. S. Sugirtharajah

The Bible is useful for doing the Alexander Technique. I always use it, in hotels.

Boy George[1]

My old man was a farmer. The only books we had in the house were the Sears catalog and the Bible, and all he ever used the Bible for was to hit me on the head.

James Hynes[2]

Let me begin by citing two news items reported in the English daily, *The Guardian,* where there were references to the Bible. The first one had to do with the Rwandan crisis. It was a letter written by Tutsi pastors to their church president, a Hutu. It was written on April 15, 1994 — the day before they were to be massacred. It went like this:

Our dear leader, Pastor Elizaphan Ntakirutimana, How are you! We wish you to be strong in all these problems we are facing. We wish to inform you that we have heard that tomorrow we will be killed with our families. We therefore request you to intervene on our behalf and talk with the

1. Boy George, "This Much I Know," *The Observer Magazine,* 18 August 2002, p. 18.
2. James Hynes, *The Lecturer's Tale* (New York: Picador, 2001), p. 18.

mayor. We believe that, with the help of God, who entrusted you the leadership of this flock, which is going to be destroyed, your intervention will be highly appreciated, the same way as the Jews were saved by Esther. We give honour to you.[3]

The second item was about the fateful United Airlines flight 93 from Newark to San Francisco on September 11, 2001. Todd Beamer, from New Jersey, was one of the doomed passengers on board. He was a religious man and had a Lord's Prayer bookmark in the Tom Clancy novel which he was carrying with him. Now the flight was being rerouted to Washington by the hijackers, and, not wanting unnecessarily to upset his pregnant wife, Beamer called the GTE phone company, the company which provided telephone services for United Airlines, and had an unusual talk with a telephone switchboard operator called Lisa Jefferson who was on the ground in one of the suburbs of Chicago. He and Lisa conversed for 13 minutes and during this time they recited together Psalm 23: "Though I walk through the valley of the shadow of death I will fear no evil; for thou art with me; thy rod and thy staff they comfort me."[4]

I cite these dramatic incidents as a starting point to exploring how biblical texts are employed in the popular press. In this exploratory piece my intention is very simple — to use this reportage to raise hermeneutical issues such as how biblical texts are used in popular newspapers, the nature of texts, the interface between popular and professional reading, the role of the common reader as postillator. In looking at these issues, I draw chiefly upon *The Guardian* but occasionally bring in citations from other popular newspapers as well.

The Text Tells Them So

In looking at these textual appearances, one gets the impression that the biblical text can be used to justify virtually any extra-biblical cause. The texts are activated to perform functions which are not even remotely connected with the authorial intention. For instance, house arrest as imposed by the Afrikaner regime during the apartheid days in South Africa was supported by biblical claims. Brigadier Neels Du Plooy explained that a lot of security

3. Philip Gourevitch, "The Beautiful Land of Death," *The Guardian Saturday Review*, 6 March 1999, pp. 1-3.

4. Ed Vulliamy, "Let's Roll," *The Observer Magazine*, 2 December 2001, pp. 15-16.

legislation during that oppressive period was based on biblical teaching. For example, house arrest was justified by 1 Kings 2:36: "The king sent and called for Shimei and said unto him, Build thee an house in Jerusalem, and dwell there, and go not forth thence any whither."[5] In another case, the owner of the confectionery Logia Foods claimed that his firm marketed only foods prescribed by the Bible. He professed that his product, Bible Bar, was made according to the nutritional guidance provided in Holy Writ: "A land of wheat and barley, of vines and fig trees and pomegranates; a land of olives, oil and honey" (Deut. 8:8).[6] Even cloning a human embryo has a direct biblical source. Severino Antinori, who was in the thick of controversy over human cloning and human reproduction, remarked that it was his "fascination with the Old Testament story of Abraham's aged wife Sara which led to his world-wide fame and notoriety."[7] These textual citations illustrate that there is no way biblical writers could have anticipated all these contexts in which their texts have been put to use.

Secondly, biblical texts play a part in a new kind of celebrity activism. At a time when celebrities champion worthy causes, they marshal the Bible if it is profitable to promote their case. One such occasion was when the pop idol Bono met the fearsomely right-wing evangelical Christian Jesse Helms, the US senator whose election campaign routinely exploited racial and sexual prejudices. The singer-turned-political-activist told this supposedly religious person that nearly 2,103 verses of the Bible were concerned with the status of the poor and that Jesus spoke of judgment only once and then it was not about being gay or about sexual behavior but about social morality. When Bono quoted the verse in Matthew 25: "I was naked and you clothed me," the senator was really moved and in tears.[8] Another celebrity example is provided by anti-globalization activists. One of the organizers, Kevin Danaher, in justifying the protest against the financial houses of the world, cited the temple incident where Jesus for the one and only time ever used violence. Danaher went on to claim that the violence was aimed not at the Roman soldiers, or the tax collectors, but at a specific target — the bankers.[9]

Thirdly, biblical texts are also employed to expose the insincerity of pol-

---

5. Paul Erasmus, "Confessions of an Apartheid Killer," *The Tiddler: The Observer's Little Bit Extra*, 6 October 1996, p. 5.

6. Boxed item: "Is nothing Sacred?" *New York Times*, Week in Review, 15 April 2001, p. 2.

7. *The Guardian*, 8 August 2001, p. 3.

8. Madeline Bunting and Oliver Burkeman, "Pro Bono," *The Guardian*, G2, 18 March 2002, p. 3.

9. Kevin Danaher, "Power to the People," *The Observer*, 4 October 2001, p. 25.

iticians and their feigned piety and in the process to puncture their sancti-
monious postures. During the Iraq crisis, when President Bush talked about
his vision for Iraq after the successful overthrow of Saddam Hussein, a letter
writer to *The Guardian* reminded Bush, a devout and Bible-reading Christian: "Let not him that girdeth on his armour boast himself as he that
putteth it off" (1 Kings 20:11).[10] When the British government introduced a
fine of £2,000 per person for carriers which fly illegal immigrants into the
country, the Immigration Advisory Service cited Matthew 2:13-15 as a way of
exposing the un-Christian nature of the rule, a rule which would have put
the Holy Family's case in jeopardy as they did not have proper papers. In the
Matthean verse, Joseph was warned by an angel in a dream to fly to Egypt
because King Herod was intending to kill children under the age of two. In a
clever use of the text during the Christmas season, the Immigration Advisory Service pointed out that, though Joseph, Mary, and Jesus would have
had a case under 1951 Geneva Convention rules to claim refugee status had
they flown into Britain, they would have been detained at Orpington detention center because their claims would have been treated as baseless and fabricated. Israel under Herod would not have been deemed to be a country under persecution. The angel would have found itself in serious trouble for
aiding and abetting Joseph and his family's entry into Britain. What is more,
the angel could have been fined £2,000 for bringing in each economic mi-
grant from Bethlehem.[11] Still on asylum, when the Archbishop of Canterbury waded into controversy by suggesting that asylum seekers should be
put in secure accommodation while their cases were being heard, Joe
Philips, a professing atheist, wrote: "The guy Dr. Williams claims to follow
said: I was hungry and you gave me meat, I was thirsty and you gave me
drink, I was a stranger and you took me in."[12] When President Bush challenged the world after September 11 with the words, "Are you for us or for
our enemies?" a *Guardian* columnist placed this verse in its narrative context. He reminded the American president that these words were first uttered
by Joshua (5:13-15) when he was confronted by the commander of the Lord's
army holding a sword. The latter replied "neither." On hearing this unexpected reply, Joshua knelt in humility.[13] Similarly, in mocking vein, David
Ward from Cumbria, in a letter to *The Guardian*, reminded the hawkish

10. *The Guardian*, 8 February 2003, p. 23.

11. "Christmas without Christ," *India Today International*, 15 January 2001, p. 24h.

12. *The Guardian*, 4 February 2003, p. 17.

13. Geraint ap Iorwerth, "In Search of a Gentle God," *The Guardian*, 7 December 2001, p. 21.

world leaders, President Bush and Prime Minister Blair, apparently eager to attack Iraq whatever the outcome of the UN inspectors' investigations, to return to their well-thumbed Bibles and turn to the book of Jonah. Ward wrote: "Jonah was sent against his will to inform the people of Nineveh (in what is now northern Iraq) that unless they repented, they would be destroyed. To his annoyance they repented. He was furious with God because God asked: 'And should not I have pity on Nineveh, that great city wherein are more than six score thousand persons — and also much cattle?'"[14] This was a telling reminder by an ordinary reader to a Bible-lover such as Bush of the danger of uncontextualized use of texts.

Fourthly, the serious tone of the Bible is punctuated with humor and playfulness. During the height of football hooliganism in England, Vincent Hanna in his column referred to a Bible-quoting football fanatic, Greg, a Scot, who had taken to reciting Deuteronomy 28:35, claiming that it was relevant to a forthcoming game: "The Lord shall smite you in the knees and in the legs with a sore botch that cannot be healed." When Paul Gascoigne had a poor game for Rangers (associated with Scottish Protestant tribalism) in a Scottish league match, the same Greg, obviously a Protestant, told Hanna that "He (Gascoigne) should remember what God said to the other St Paul, 'It is hard for thee to kick against the pricks' (Acts 9:5)."[15] Even the ritualized form of football results aired after the matches was traced to the Hebrew Bible. Matthew Engel, an erstwhile cricket correspondent to *The Guardian*, cites one:

> And these are the kings of the land whom Joshua and the children of Israel smote beyond Jordan westwards . . .
> The king of Jericho, one; the king of Ai, which is beside Bethel, one;
> The king of Jerusalem, one, the king of Hebron, one;
> The king of Jarmuth, one; the king of Lachish, one;
> The king of Eglon, one; the king of Gezer, one.
> The king of Debir, one; the king of Geder, one. (Joshua 12:9ff.)[16]

This kind of playfulness is not confined to football. The motor industry also has its share of scriptural teasing. For example: "God drove Adam and Eve from the garden of Eden in a Fury." Biblical precedents are also found for

14. David Ward, letter to *The Guardian*, 19 September 2002, p. 23.
15. Vincent Hanna, "And Over to Deuteronomy," *The Guardian*, 6 June 1996, p. 26.
16. Matthew Engel, "Dark Escort," *The Guardian*. I am unable to provide the date and page number. My guess is circa middle-1990s.

the British motorbike: "Joshua's Triumph was heard throughout the land, and the roar of Moses' Triumph is heard in the hills." Jesus' embarrassment at the Honda Accord was deduced from his saying, "For I did not speak of my own Accord," but this did not prevent the same Gospel recording that "the apostles were in one Accord." Such a statement is also seen for its additional significance — the earliest historical evidence for car pooling.[17]

In keeping with this tongue-in-cheek textual burlesque, one could say that such textual usage was akin to Imelda Marcos's method of shoe selection — looking for something that fits.

Finally, disputes are sometimes conducted by brandishing biblical texts one against the other. Using irony and parody, these disputes can reveal real confidence in handling texts. Sometimes this is done with wit and charm. Two examples stand out. One is related to the gay and lesbian issue, and the other is about corporal punishment. Simon Hoggart reported a delicious example in his Saturday Diary column of how to unsettle bigotry with humor. When the daytime TV host Laura Schlesinger, who is known for her blatant bigotry towards homosexuals, cited the notorious verse Leviticus 18:22, which states that homosexuality is an abomination, a Steve Turner culled texts from the very same Leviticus in order to poke fun at her and expose the ineffectualness of using texts in too literal a way. In a reply which took the form of an epistle, Turner wrote:

> Dear Laura, when I burn a bull on the altar as a sacrifice I know it creates a pleasing odour for the Lord (Lev. 1:9). The problem is that my neighbours complain that the odour is not pleasing to them. Should I smite them? . . . Lev. 25:44 states that I may indeed possess slaves, both male and female, provided they are purchased from neighbouring nations. A friend of mine says this applies to Mexicans but not Canadians. Can you clarify? Why can't I own Canadians? . . . Lev. 21:20 states that I may not approach the altar of God if I have a defect in my sight. I admit that I wear reading glasses. Does my vision have to be 20/20 or is there some wiggle room here? My uncle has a farm. He violates Lev. 19:19 by planting two different crops in the same field, as does his wife by wearing garments made of two different kinds of thread (cotton/polyester blend). He also tends to blaspheme a lot. Is it really necessary that we go to all the trouble of getting the whole town together to stone them (Lev. 24:10-16)? Couldn't we just burn them to death at a private family affair like we do with people who

17. All these examples come from Giles Smith, "And the Lord Said, Let There Be Space," *The Guardian*, G2, 4 March 2003, p. 17.

sleep with our in-laws? Thanks again for reminding us that God's word is eternal and unchanging. Your devoted disciple and adoring fan.[18]

Another textually disputed area is the question of caning children. Those who support corporal punishment often invoke passages from Proverbs which extol the value of smacking children. When principals, teachers, and parents of Christian Independent Schools challenged the banning on the grounds that it breached both biblical teaching and human rights, their lawyer, John Friel, in his petition to the courts, quoted from the book of Proverbs 23:13 and 14: "The rod of correction imparts wisdom, but the child left to itself disgraces its mother. Do not withhold discipline from a child; if you punish him with the rod, he will not die. Punish him with a rod and save his soul from death." In a letter to the editor, a reader wrote: "I was surprised that the schools' representatives did not touch on Matthew 5:39, 'but whosoever shall smite thee on thy right cheek, turn to him the other also.'" In a somewhat related case in Southern California when the parents cited the text from Proverbs, the judge in passing his sentence, with his legal tongue firmly in his cheek, complimented the parents for not meting out the more rigorous form of punishment prescribed for an unruly child in Deuteronomy 21:21: "Stone him with stones, that he die." It is fortunate that the parents of these children were Protestants and they were unaware of the Catholic canon, which contains a deutero-canonical book — Ecclesiasticus. There, chapter 30 decrees a severe form of chastisement as a good way of bringing up young children.

Speaking of caning, Phil Williamson, the head teacher of the Christian Fellowship School in Liverpool who campaigned for a judicial review of the outright government ban on parents' right to exercise physical discipline, declared that his school would not cane children but "would smack them on the hand or leg using the teacher's hand." Stressing his long experience in administering physical punishment, Williamson went on to say: "With the older pupils, girls would be strapped on the hand by a lady teacher, and boys would be smacked on the backside with something akin to a ruler, but wider."[19] Alan Halden from Hemel Hempstead, poking fun at Williamson's medieval brutality, pointed out that he failed to pass the Bible's literal test: "The Bible distinctly says 'rod,' and not paddle or strap. A cane narrows and accentuates the area of pain, thus improving the beneficial effect upon the

18. Simon Hoggart, "Simon Hoggart's Diary," *The Guardian Saturday Review*, 16 September 2000, p. 12.

19. Tania Branigan, "Christian Schools Ask for Right to Hit Pupils," *The Guardian*, 3 November 2001, p. 2.

recipient. Any attempt to alleviate this undermines the fundamentalist Christian reliance on the Word."[20] Those who support physical punishment do not confine themselves to that overused passage from Proverbs. They draw profitably on the New Testament too. When the twelve-year-old daughter of Larry and Constance Slack failed to find her mother's coat quickly enough for them to go out on time, Laree was beaten to death with an electric rod five-feet long and one-inch thick. They claimed that they had beaten her in accordance with Deuteronomy 25:1-3 prescribing 40 lashes minus one as authorized by the Jewish tradition. They were zealously reproducing St. Paul's punishment by multiplying it by three times.[21]

Going Public

At a time when biblical texts, biblical allusions, and imagery are disappearing from the cultural consciousness of the West, the occasional appearance of biblical texts in the popular press is an indication that they still have hermeneutical purchase, especially when one tries to make sense of international conflict, sexual orientation, law and order, and bringing up children. Obviously newspapers are not littered with biblical quotations, but what do we make of the modicum of biblical quotations and allusions we find in them? These textual citations disclose an ambivalent attitude to the Bible. From the use of these quotations it is sometimes difficult to assess whether the sacred text of Christians is held in veneration or being mocked. For those who believe that every word of the Bible is true, the Bible is not an object consisting of printed paper and ink but a venerable and awesome artifact. Like the sightseers at the Taj Mahal, such readers come to discover and marvel, not to dissent. The text's meaning for them has been determined once and for all by the will of the author, God. In such cases, the reader is looking for enlightenment in the text. But others see texts used as forms of sacred parody. For them, it furnishes resources to ridicule and puncture the smugness of those in power.

Not all letter-writers to the press and journalists are Christians. Nonetheless, Christian texts creep into their writings. Their appropriation of texts and use of quotations could be likened to the way some medieval writers used texts from the Christian tradition as, in Bakhtin's words, a kind of

---

20. Letter to *The Guardian,* 5 November 2001, p. 19.

21. Stephen Bates, "Witness on the Watchtower," *The Guardian,* 26 January 2002, p. 22.

"parodic-travestying."[22] In this process of parodying "the entire Bible, the entire gospel was as it were cut up into little scraps, and these scraps were then arranged. . . . In this work a correspondence of all details to the Sacred Writ is strictly and precisely observed but at the same time the entire Sacred Writ is transformed into carnival."[23] It is a complex and complicated act in which the other's word is simultaneously respected and ridiculed, accepted and teased. In such usages, one is often baffled as to whether the Sacred Word is held in reverence or taken for its comic value.

In looking at the usage of texts, there are two things obvious at the outset. I shall mention one now and come back to the other at the end of the chapter. What is apparent is that texts here function at a micro level — the narratives are broken into neat, pithy texts, and reassembled, activated, and invoked to elucidate a point. It is not the Bible *in toto* or even individual books which go to constitute the Bible but sliced-up textual pieces. It is the fragmented text which makes its way into the public arena. Those raised with the notion of a grand narrative of the Bible holding together the various parts will find the citing of isolated, split, and individual texts forced out of their immediate contexts unattractive, and in some cases even detestable. For the users of these texts, the question of the wholeness of Scripture unified by a biblical theme may be not only foreign but also puzzling. They are unlikely to look for such an integrated purposive whole. They may not see a need for this. Moreover, the question about the wholeness of the Bible is not easily settled, as ecclesiastical history over the centuries has shown.

This kind of plucking-out of texts could be termed, to use Michel de Certeau's suggestion, "poaching." He describes readers as travelers moving "across land belonging to someone else, like nomads poaching their way across the fields they did not write, despoiling the wealth of Egypt to enjoy it themselves."[24] Poaching is thus a hermeneutical device employed by common readers who shred texts into small, simplified, and specific forms, to make sense of their existential needs, piecing them together in the way that best suits their practical needs. In a sense, common people's reading is about "tactics and games played with the texts."[25]

Before I expand on reading as poaching, a brief note on the history of

22. M. M. Bakhtin, *The Dialogic Imagination: Four Essays,* trans. Caryl Emerson and Michael Holquist, ed. Michael Holquist (Austin: University of Texas Press, 2000), p. 69.

23. Bakhtin, *The Dialogic Imagination,* p. 70.

24. Michel de Certeau, *The Practice of Everyday Life,* trans. Steven Rendall (Berkeley: University of California Press, 1988), p. 174.

25. Certeau, *The Practice of Everyday Life,* p. 175.

breaking of the biblical narrative into numbered verses. This goes back to the Puritans and their Geneva Bible, which paved the way for text-twisting as an art form. The early English Bibles were in paragraph form without any numbering of individual verses or chapter divisions. The first English edition to introduce verse and chapter divisions was Whittingham's New Testament published in 1557. He followed Stephanus's Latin Bible, which was the first to use divisions in both testaments. In his preface, Whittingham states: "Furthermore, that the reader might by all means be profited, I have divided the text into verses and sections, according to the best editions in the other languages."[26] This new literary device made it possible for preachers to point out the specific location of a particular passage, instead of introducing a hermeneutical point with prefatory statements such as "Mark said" or "Paul wrote in his epistle." This enabled a congregation to follow a text more closely. Besides making the texts easier on the eye, easily identifiable verses from the various parts of the Bible could be summoned not only to clinch a theological argument but also to authenticate it as authoritative. The truth which was once believed to reside in revelation, vision, sacraments, sacred sites was now understood to reside exclusively in texts or documents. It was something independently verifiable.

Reading as Poaching

Reading as poaching is a solitary activity which becomes a natural and easy act to an individual. The interaction with the text becomes a private and a Protestant and capitalist affair in which each individual has an encounter alone with the text. The mood seems to be that the Bible is all I need. I do not want notes or criticisms or explanations about the authorship or origin, or the mediation of clerics and academics. Solitary reading of texts is often controlled by practical interests. More than doctrinal speculation, interpretation is application-oriented. Private readings convey personal and idiosyncratic insights, and often simplify and remythicize the biblical texts. In such readings, Scripture is taken in its plain, natural, and obvious meaning. There is a desire to dispense with complicated textual nuances and find unambiguous and simple meanings of texts.

26. Alfred W. Pollard, ed., *Records of the English Bible: The Documents Relating to the Translation and Publication of the Bible in English, 1525-1611* (London: Oxford University Press, 1911), p. 276.

Readers as poachers continue to highlight the ongoing struggle between manufacturers of meaning and consumers. Poaching is the common reader's self-assertion through the text. It is the overturning of the control exercised by the managers of the texts, namely church and academy, who determine what parts should be read and who employ interpreters who determine, monitor, and dispense the correct meanings of a given text. More significantly, reading as poaching does not mean just disconnecting texts from their immediate habitat. Poachers can also build connections between texts, as Steve Turner has made playful use of the Leviticus texts in his amusing riposte to Laura Schlesinger.

Readers as poachers open up a great gap between popular and professional modes of interpretation. Reading as poaching further weakens the authority of the text and the meaning imposed by clerics and academics and becomes a personal choice based on personal beliefs and contextual needs. In such cases, readers freely pick and mix the content and meaning of the text, and operate on a private "canon within the canon" which suits them, rather than be restricted by church diktats, commentarial tradition, or creedal statements. It liberates the text from the control of ecclesiastical and scholastic authority. Those raised in the Enlightenment mode of interpretation will find such reading overtly literalistic, legalistic, and totally careless with historical details. Scholarly practitioners have been cautioning that texts set certain limits to the way one reads them and that readers are not free to produce any meanings they like from texts, and that the possession of an interpretative history prevents any indulgence of subjective readings. However much academics tend to protect the text and guard against "wayward readings," readers and texts are nimble and agile enough to undermine such protectiveness and are capable of producing totally unforeseen readings. The incidents I quoted at the beginning of this article are striking cases in point — the Tutsis' invoking of Esther, and Todd Beamer and Lisa Jefferson reciting Psalm 23. Academics may be appalled at these easy identifications. But for the Tutsis and Beamer and Jefferson, texts become a mirror in which they read their hope and despair. For them and countless people, the impetus to interpret stems from the need to make sense of their lives, and in this respect the hermeneutics of poaching is an existential impulse. Hence, there is the attempt by people to invoke clearly identifiable typological models located within the Bible and apply them directly to their current psychological, political, and spiritual quagmires. In such circumstances, texts settle the readers' current existential dilemma and offer them succor.

Finally, reading as poaching raises the question: Who has the power — the reader or the text? If readers wield power, the text becomes an empty slate on which the readers can write any meaning. On the other hand, if power is invested in the text, then readers would have to surrender and comply with whatever the text says. The trouble with such a polarized position is that it is extremely reductionist, and views readers and texts as separate entities having lives of their own and continuing separate during the act of reading. In reality, the formation of meaning is achieved through a mutual interaction between a number of ingredients — text, context of the text, reader, and his or her context.

What poaching indicates is that texts and their meanings are not final but that the texts derive their meaning in their encounter with context and reader. They are like sojourners who hardly ever go back to the habitat they left behind. Texts in essence are molded by the context in which they are located. Because they are malleable and accommodative, they are vulnerable. Ultimately, what reading as poaching indicates is that it is not possible to finalize a text, or restrict it to one context, or predetermine its meaning.

Postcolonial Postscript

During the Middle Ages under the influence of ecclesiastical authorities the Bible was installed with intrinsic power and had a recognizable identity. Access to it was limited. In the current context, the Bible is marketed as a consumable commodity and made available to all. As a religious package, in an open market, it has to vie for attention with countless other texts. Its authority, identity, and meaning are clarified in connection with other texts which arise out of different theological and secular needs. In a sense, texts are always in transit between contexts, and like nomads they do not have a fixed abode or a steady identity. Their transitory attachment to contexts, their indeterminate nature, and their potential to generate meanings in manifold ways, are all well exploited by readers. In such a hermeneutical scenario, to chutnify what Ecclesiastes said: "Of producing meaning there will be no end."

Let me come back to the second striking feature of the usage of texts, which I promised to do in the middle of the chapter. What is conspicuous is that almost all the citations in the popular press come from the King James Version. At the height of the British Empire, Anderson cockily proclaimed that this was "the only version in existence on which the Sun never sets."[27] Now, to use Homi Bhabha's words, "the holiest of books — the Bible — bearing both the standard of the cross and the standard of empire, finds itself dismembered."[28] The founding totem of the Western world has now ended up in the popular press as "an erratic" and "an eccentric" cultural artifact sans religious authority or theological clout.

27. Christopher Anderson, *The Annals of the English Bible,* vol. 1 (London: William Pickering, 1845), p. xi.

28. Homi K. Bhabha, *The Location of Culture* (London: Routledge, 1994), p. 92.

4 Latin American Readings of the Bible: Experiences, Challenges, and Its Practice

Néstor O. Míguez

This short account of the emergence and practice of a liberationist hermeneutics, also called "popular reading of the Bible" in Latin America, is more an essay than the report of a full-blown investigation. When this began I was in my early teens, and as I grew in age I got caught in the process, until I became fully engaged and a "professional" Bible scholar. So this narrative mixes the reviewing of part of the available publications, data from some more academic circles, but also other things gathered in very informal ways, some personal memories, the accounts of my own teachers and friends. I know of no other specific report. Perhaps it is the most representative way to talk about our subject because that is the texture of this particular hermeneutics, the ways it is built — a blending together of knowledge and experience, of everyday life and critical thinking, of suffering and hope, of fear and imperfect love in the light of the Scriptural witness and faith in the coming Reign of God.

An Unpretentious Historical Survey

It is impossible to offer an accurate date for the beginning of what we call "popular reading of the Bible" in Latin America. The experience began to

Previously published in the *Journal of Latin American Hermeneutics* 1 (2004). Accessible at www.isedet.edu.ar.

grow in the 1960s. In order to look for its first developments we should consider what we understand to be the two main trends of this particular Latin American Christian movement. They are at the origins of what is known as Latin American liberation theology, that is, the popular base communities and the youth and student Christian groups (like ULAJE and WCSF,[1] or the JUC-MIEC and the JOC[2] in the Roman Catholic lay movement). In rather informal ways, they began to read the Bible and share Bible studies as part of their regular meetings, and new insights grew as the biblical texts were related to the other issues involved in the discussions. The content and results of those first experiences are probably mostly lost for someone in search of written records.[3] An expert historian might rescue, here and there, some

1. ULAJE (Latin American Union of Evangelical Youth) was the first continental ecumenical youth group. Born in the 1940s as an interdenominational Protestant youth gathering, in 1970 the "E" in the name changed from Evangelical to Ecumenical. Looking for the background of these movements, the work of Valdo Galland, a Waldensian from Uruguay who was the Latin American secretary of the WCSF during the fifties, must be noted. He gave great impetus to Bible studies in student groups. He found an able support for this task in the New Testament German scholar R. Obermüller, who came from Germany before World War II as the pastor of a German congregation in Buenos Aires and was invited as a visiting professor in the Facultad Evangélica de Teología (today part of ISEDET). He and his family finally decided to stay in Argentina. To provide material for these activities, the Latin American section of the WCSF published a first booklet on the Sermon on the Mount that appeared in 1955, under the title of "El Nuevo Mundo de Dios" (God's New World). The author was José Míguez Bonino, then a newly appointed theological professor. Though still far from anything we might call today "popular reading of the Bible," some suggestions on method, questions for debate, and bypassing observations already point in that direction. Many of the university students that were part of these activities became afterwards leaders in the ecumenical, political, and cultural movements in Latin America, and also at world level.

2. MIEC was the Movimiento Internacional de Estudiantes Católicos (International Movement of Catholic Students, mostly oriented towards high school students), and the JUC, the specific branch for university students (Juventud Universitaria Católica). The JOC, Juventud Obrera Católica (Young Catholic Workers) was the organization for working youth. They were all born out of and related to the Catholic Action, but soon they made their own way, taking distance from the theological and political conception of the adult counterpart. In the JOC two tendencies were manifested: one, close to the Italian model, more in line with the Christian Democratic Party. The other was inspired in the French experience of the "prete-ouvrier," with its orientation closer to socialism. In Latin America this second one was to prevail. According to Carlos Mesters this is the origin of the typical methods for scriptural hermeneutics: *to see, to judge, to act* ("Como se Faz Teologia Biblica Hoje no Brasil," *Estudos Biblicos* 1 (ed. Vozes, Brasil, 1984, pp. 7-19). The article is dated November 1982.

3. Carlos Mesters, "Como se Faz Teologia Biblica Hoje no Brasil," writes: "At that time,

"mimeo" copies, the memories of some of the first base communities in Panama or Brazil, or a bulletin or booklet of some student group, that could be an example of what was done at the time. Some songs from that time, the way Psalms were adapted for popular faith celebrations, and some poetic expressions could also give us a clue of the "popular hermeneutics" at that time.

An Active Social and Cultural Background

But this cannot be considered the outburst of some spontaneously generated phenomena, developed exclusively within the religious realm. We must take into account some important secular facts (among many others) that are at the origins of these developments, the soil that allowed it to grow, that nourished its roots, events that brought long-time concealed forces in Latin American societies up to public consideration and influence. In the sociopolitical realm, the triumph of the Cuban revolution was read in Latin America as the emergence of the possibility of overcoming imperialistic policies, as a victory of the people over the powers of the established ruling oppressive minorities and of the future of liberation movements. A change in the system is possible, was the message, and the people clung to it with hope. Latin America experienced, therefore, although not for the first time, a period of social uneasiness and political struggle. Whether through guerrilla warfare or non-violent methods, entering in the discussion of the validity of democratic forms or rejecting them absolutely, more Marxist-oriented or with a populist nationalistic inclination, the whole continent was shaken by popular restlessness. The atmosphere of change was so strong that by the beginning of the 1970s almost all Latin American countries had very strong popular movements, some ready to seize power. A Catholic priest, Camilo Torres, joined a guerrilla movement in Colombia, and though he was murdered, the movement continues until today (but the practice and ideology of the movement have changed greatly since). The Marxist socialist Allende was elected President in Chile, and the left wing of the Peronist party fought

---

it was an almost entirely spoken theology. Weak and strong, like the spoken word. It is not written. It is transmitted in different ways than those of written science. Not through published books, but through oral tradition, through celebrations and *benditos* (procession prayer songs), stories and drama, poems and songs, meetings, workshops and courses, visits, popular assemblies and feasts. Exactly like the Word of God itself, before receiving its written form."

for places in the Argentinean government. The Frente Amplio and the Tupamaros were steadily growing in Uruguay. Peru, Panama, and Bolivia experienced the rule of more popular nationalistic military regimes. In Central America guerrillas were active, and eventually took power in Nicaragua, or dominated almost half the territory of El Salvador. Brazil had a brief time with a more leftist government that attempted a much-needed land reform, and was the first country to suffer a strong military *coup d'état* and repression (1964), but resistance and the quest for change were nevertheless much alive in that country and specially within the Brazilian Catholic Church. But that activity of the powers for change met a blunt reaction of the conservative forces, and by the late seventies almost all of these countries were again under very oppressive military regimes, or the strong pressure of the international financial powers that inhibited any attempt for deep social change.

Important changes occurred also at a cultural level during the 1960s. Latin America experienced a strong urbanization, and that brought in close contact groups that were clearly differentiated, and gave entrance to the political and socio-cultural scenario of sections of society that had previously been marginalized and ignored. A rebirth of folk-lore music and art, of aboriginal artisanship and traditional crafts occurred even in urban spaces, and together with the more traditional thrust, the emergence of new movements in the arts, especially at the level of popular theater and music, was experienced. Sometimes both converged in creative ways. It coincided with the massive use of the new communications media, and a "Latin American media culture" was created. A boom of new trends in literature made some Latin American writers well known beyond the continental limits. The idea that Latin Americans could be creative and develop our own *intelligentsia* gave new impulse to the research of philosophy, social sciences, and studies in native cultures.

Another important event in the religious sphere, outside Latin America but with huge impact on our continent, is Vatican Council II, and, for our particular concern, the Conciliar Constitution *Dei Verbum*. The reception and consequences of the conciliar spirit in Latin America were formalized in the Latin American Bishops' Conference of Medellín in 1968. In a continent with a vast majority of Roman Catholics, and a very influential church, the renewal of the religious and theological momentum did not go unnoticed. Some (at those times young) theologians were bringing in the results of their training in other parts of the world, mostly of the most progressive European theology of that time, or from the United States. They reflected in new ways on what was happening, showed their affinity with popular causes, and some of them became actively involved in the peoples' struggles. Some bishops, Dom Elder Camera the most noted, clearly promoted the involvement of the Church with the masses of the poor, partaking in that liberationist thrust. So, a renewed and progressive theological thinking and biblical scholarship met with the requirements of a society (or better, "societies") in change, struggling for justice, with strong popular movements. A new theology and a new way of reading and interpreting the Bible were due to be born out of this encounter.

The influence and dynamics of the ecumenical movement also played a significant part. If Vatican Council II brought to the fore some trends that were at work in the Roman Catholic Church, the Conference on Church and Society (Geneva, 1966) of the World Council of Churches made visible similar movements that were already active in many Protestant churches. The Latin American delegation performed an important role in that conference. Ecumenical lay movements were created or reshaped in that period, having a shared understanding of reality and envisioning social change as the place and way of Christian witness.

If we point to this ample horizon of political, cultural, and ecclesial developments in this sketch of the history of biblical interpretation in Latin America, it is because we can affirm that biblical science and biblical interpretation are not done in a separate, self-sustained, and self-centered unpolluted scholarly (or even ecclesiastical) environment. Biblical scholarship is not unilineal, always growing out of itself in the same direction. It is the outcome of, and is in constant interface with, scientific progress in the fields of history and related knowledge. It also needs to be aware of new trends in the study of linguistics, and of new paradigms in hermeneutics. It has to deal with interdisciplinary efforts also in contact with the social and anthropological sciences, and with studies in the fields of culture, gender, and similar areas. But it is also to be placed in the larger scenario of social, religious, and political developments that affect the "reading community." We share the same things with all the scholar community throughout the world. But the context shades the whole enterprise of biblical interpretation in such a way that even those dimensions that we share are considered in different ways and modified by a different praxis in the diverse reading locations.

Reading the Bible with Other Eyes

At the beginning, the quest for a "popular" reading of the Bible more consciously and critically engaged with the social and cultural reality was mostly, as already stated, oral tradition, spontaneous commenting on the text, and, it must be said, certainly plagued with wishful revolutionary thinking and naïve expressions, not totally free of "sloganism." The use of some more advanced literature and the resource of biblical scholarship (historical criticism was at the top in those days) brought about, on one hand, a certain consciousness of the need for a more rigorous approach, but on the other hand the possibility of going beyond the traditional doctrinally loaded interpretations to which the people had been mostly exposed.[4] "El Evangelio en Solentiname," the comments on the Gospels of a *campesino* (rural) community of Nicaragua compiled by Ernesto Cardenal, is a witness to this experience. In its introduction, Cardenal regrets the fact that many valuable comments are lost because of the lack of any record of many of the meetings. Though the first edition is rather late for our historic approach (1978), it is a good example of what had been going on in the continent for the last fifteen years or so.

At the beginning of the seventies all these movements began to be made more visible at a systematic and academic level. The *Teología de la Liberación* by Gustavo Gutiérrez, the touchstone of that movement, was published in 1971. It is not the first theological reflection on the social and political reality of Latin America, but it became its emblematic book and provided the characteristic name for the whole movement. Two years later the first publication in this line by a well-trained biblical scholar, *Liberación y Libertad* by José Severino Croatto,[5] appeared. That small book (translated into English with the less appealing title of *Exodus*) was, to our best knowledge, the first major study explicitly approaching the experience of political liberation as the key for biblical hermeneutics. It took the image and experience of Exodus, already used in the Medellín Documents (Introduction, 6) as the image of a people moving from "less human to more human conditions of life," and interpreted its meaning in the light of Latin American liberation struggles. In some more learned circles the books by the Mexican José Porfirio Miranda, *Marx y la Biblia* and *El ser y el Mesías*,[6] though not specific biblical hermeneutics, became influential in the hermeneutical approach. *The Materialistic Reading of Mark,* the doctoral dissertation by the Portuguese Catholic priest Fernando Belo, and his more simplified version, *Political Reading of*

---

4. René Krüger, "La Biblia en los procesos recientes de América Latina," *Cuadernos de Teología* 13, 1 (1993): 75-92.

5. Ediciones Mundo Nuevo, Buenos Aires, 1973.

6. Both from Ediciones Sígueme, Salamanca, 1972 and 1973.

the Gospel, also circulated in some circles, in Portuguese, Italian, and French, though the Spanish translation (that circulated in informal ways) had to wait to be published till the end of military dictatorships; it came out in 1984.

Croatto himself was not without partners. He was among a number of open-minded ecumenical biblical scholars, both Protestant and Roman Catholic, who were highly trained and were renewing biblical scholarship in Latin America, through new Bible translations, publications, and joint study groups.[7] It must be noted, however, that this group of people unfortunately split between those who desired to maintain a more "pure" biblical scholarship and those who joined a politically and socially involved hermeneutics. Ecclesiastical politics also played a heavy hand in the differences.

But the experience of the people reading the Bible, as well as the scholars together with the people, surely continued and grew, notwithstanding the severe conditions of repression under the black years of military dictatorships. Some scholars and many lay leaders were forced into exile, or suffered torture, prison, and even death. This experience also was integrated into the reading of the Bible. I recall meeting with an ecumenical bunch of students and social workers of a parish in a very poor neighborhood (about ten in all, we never dared a higher number), once a week, by night, in the living room of the parsonage of the church I was serving as a Methodist pastor in the city of Rosario. I shared the co-ordination of the group with a former Catholic priest, a very able scholar, who once was a New Testament professor at the local Catholic Seminary, but had been ousted by a very conservative bishop. He was now making his living as helper with a soda delivery truck and part-time bricklayer. We never met on the same day of the week. All windows were closed. We never entered or left the house in groups larger than three. And each of the participants had to phone when arriving home to make sure no one had disappeared on the way back. But this group met under those

7. A Roman Catholic scholar, Msgr. Juan Straubinger (a German refugee), founded the first Latin American journal focused on the Bible, *Revista Bíblica,* in Buenos Aires in 1939. He also published a new translation of the Bible into Spanish, and that was a courageous and very progressive move at the time. (Note that it foreruns by four years *Divino Afflante Spiritu,* the encyclical letter through which Pius XII opens the possibility of biblical scholarship in the Catholic Church.) The journal, which is still being published, was "refounded" with an ecumenical approach after the Second Vatican Council. The publication gives place to biblical scholarship with pastoral and social interest, but carefully staying within the limits of the *magisterium* of the Roman Church. Many scholars fully involved in a liberationist approach still publish more "technical" articles in *Revista Bíblica.*

conditions through four full years. We knew of several other similar groups in the city, in the neighborhoods and in the poor villages of the outskirts of the city. But no one could, or dared, keep any record of what we were doing. In other dioceses, with more open Catholic bishops, they could move a little more freely under the umbrella of parochial activities. Summer camps were a privileged opportunity to introduce the younger generation to this approach to the Bible. Nevertheless, police control and fear were always at hand. I recall receiving the "visit" of the police three times during a five-day Church camp with teenagers. They thought that something "fishy" was going on and they were not mistaken. In the Bible studies that were part of the regular camp activities, we were discovering "The life in the Spirit" (Romans 8) as a life of liberty. But the only book they could find in the backpacks of the participants was the Bible. But reading the Bible together in those circumstances was part of a liberating experience, even in the midst of terror. Reading the Bible together was part of the experience of some people while fighting in the Sandinista Front, even of people in jail.[8] This is also part of the story of biblical interpretation in Latin America. But, once again, we will find very few written records of those experiences.

In some countries, where the situation was less oppressive, it was possible to publish some things that brought to the surface what in other places was clandestine. So, in 1979 Elsa Tamez published *La Biblia de los Oprimidos: La Opresión en la Teología Bíblica* (San José, Costa Rica: DEI, 1979). It is dedicated "to the Christians of the Frente Sandinista de Liberación Nacional and to all the people who fought the Nicaraguan popular revolution." That dedication is a hermeneutical principle in itself, and announces the approach we are to find in that small but anticipatory book. Juan Luis Segundo had developed a systematic approach to this new hermeneutical circle as a theological breakthrough in a sketch, in the first chapter of his *Liberación de la Teología*.[9] A more detailed work entirely devoted to this approach in biblical scholarship had to wait for the military period to pass. It was also authored by Croatto: *Hermenéutica Bíblica*,[10] a first edition in 1984. In the meantime, Carlos Mesters, in Brazil, had also worked out and published some approaches to the Bible from the perspective of the poor, and short commentaries to help the base communities in their reading of the Bible. J. Pixley

8. But in Uruguay the military regime even prohibited political prisoners from having a Bible to read in their cells.

9. Carlos Lohlé, Buenos Aires, 1975.

10. Tierra Nueva — La Aurora, Buenos Aires. The book has known since several translations and has been considerably enlarged in successive new editions.

and Pablo Richard are also to be mentioned in that line, as major references in Central America.

One of the signs that, in spite of the harsh repression, work was continuing is the fact that during those days two of the leading and most resourceful ecumenical seminaries in South America, ISEDET[11] in Buenos Aires, Argentina, and the joint effort of the Faculdade Luterana de Teologia in São Leopoldo with the Programa Ecumênico de Pós-Graduaçâo em Ciencias da Religiâo of the Methodist University in São Paolo, Brazil, were able to create their post-graduate programs in theology, for the first time in Latin America.[12] And it is interesting to note that the first doctorates granted by those houses were in the field of biblical studies. Latin America was ready to create its own scholars in the biblical field.

As time went on and the military regimes yielded to formal democratic rule, the rather covert developments quickly gained open skies, and multiplied in publications and journals. *Estudos Biblicos,* issued as a supplement to *Revista Eclesiastica Brasilera,*[13] was probably the first major journal entirely devoted to this new emergent hermeneutical approach. The journal began its publication early in 1984. The thematic title of its first volume is also revealing: *A Bíblia como Memória dos Pobres* (The Bible as Memory of the Poor). That first issue brings together articles from C. Mesters, Pablo Richard, and Milton Schwantes, among others. The second volume is not less explicit: *Caminho da Libertaçâo* (The Way of Liberation).

The multiplicity of the experiences, the growing number of scholars who joined this new approach, and the emergence of new subjects needed many local small publications, textbooks, bulletins, and the like. Parochial groups, workshops, popular organizations, and ecumenical centers were all engaged in publishing what they were doing at the time. The *Bibliografía Teológica Comentada*[14] and the *Bibliografía Bíblica Latinoameri-*

11. Instituto Superior Evangélico de Estudios Teológicos (Higher Evangelical Institute for Theological Studies).

12. Some Catholic universities also have post-graduate studies in theology. But in most cases they are under the supervision of the Pontifical University of Rome.

13. Vozes, Petropolis, Brasil, 1984. It was published within the journal, but also distributed under separate cover.

14. Published by ISEDET, Buenos Aires, 1973-91. It lists, classifies, and provides abstracts of all major and most medium publications (including articles in journals) issued in the "iberoamerica" (Latin America and Spain and Portugal) concerned with theology and related sciences (including social sciences when related to religion). It has a very important section on Bible. Croatto was its first director. It was discontinued because of financial cut-

cana[15] are witnesses to that explosion. But it also needed a more systematic and embracing publication of continental range. So, in 1989 the *Revista de Interpretación Bíblica Latino Americana* (RIBLA)[16] was launched. All the above-mentioned names, and many others, were involved in the initiative. In the first year the emphasis was mostly directed to the methodological questions and the theological and hermeneutical basis of the experiences of "popular reading of the Bible." But, more and more, the articles reflect the advances in biblical scholarship achieved through these approaches. In the following years the journal concentrated on thematic issues, which related to relevant topics in Latin American society the experience of the biblical witnesses: militarism, poverty and debt, violence, citizenship, ecology, and economy. Others have recorded different readings brought by different subjects: feminist, aboriginal, or African slave descendants in Latin America. They were bringing in their own concerns and approaches to the biblical text, to challenge not only the classical biblical knowledge but also the previous views of Latin American liberationist hermeneutics. In the last four years some issues have been devoted to serve as introductory textbooks for certain scriptural books or sections (Matthew's and John's Gospels, James, Philemon, Paul, the Prophets, the Pentateuch), or to exploring Christian origins. It is amazing how the reading location and the departure point brought by reading with the people at the grassroots and their specific concerns can offer a new perspective on what seems to be rather classical and technical themes.

Changing Hermeneutics

We cannot expect that, during all this time, things were always the same way. The context, the theology, the methodological approaches, the emphasis, the interpretations, and results were modified. It would take a whole other research and articles (or perhaps books) to point out the trajectories made in

---

backs, but it can be accessed through the Internet: www.ISEDET.edu.ar. The Library of ISEDET (Biblioteca) is working to update the bibliography.

15. Programa Ecumenico de Pós-Graduacao em Ciencias da Religiao, São Paolo, Brasil. The first volume is 1988. Milton Schwantes coordinates it, and its purpose is to list all publications in the field of Bible studies, including, when accessible, local leaflets, bulletins, and the like.

16. It is published three times a year, in Portuguese, by Vozes (Petropolis, Brasil) and Editora Sinodal (São Leopoldo, Brasil) and in Spanish by RECU (Quito, Ecuador).

the popular reading of the Bible in the last forty years. It is not always convenient to talk in general terms, because there are always exceptions to be
made, shades and differences to be noted. But running the risk of being unfair to those shades and exceptions, I will make some comments on the development of the practice of reading the Bible from a Latin American liberationist perspective. I will limit myself to mark some of the main points to be
considered in my view.

From "Leftist Fundamentalism" to a More Complex Reading

It can be said that, at the beginning, there was, to some degree, what we can
call a "fundamentalism of the left." It is true that you will not find that in the
more elaborated books and more careful scholars, but in the "popular" reading you could hear a kind of fundamentalist approach, but now used to assert some revolutionary positions. Take, for example, Matthew 11:25: "At that
time Jesus said, 'I thank you, Father, Lord of heaven and earth, because you
have hidden these things from the wise and the intelligent and have revealed
them to infants.'" Once and again it was said that the Word of God is only
available to the poor and simple, that truth dwells with the more culturally
and economically deprived people. So, any critical study of the Bible that did
not confirm or comply with popular religion or folk beliefs should be dismissed as "the scholar's conceit." The Bible was "the memory of the poor"; it
was considered as coming totally from below, from the experience of the
destitute, where God dwells. So, the texts could only be interpreted in that
sense, and many biblical passages were forced to talk in that direction. The
Bible was entirely the "book of the people," ideologically captured by the
powerful and conquerors, but now the poor and powerless were recovering
their own heritage, and bringing back the true meaning of the text.

   It took a certain time, and especially the critique of feminist hermeneutics, to realize that, even though that was true in great measure, it could not
be affirmed without certain caveats. From both ends: on one hand, the Bible
was a more complex memory, with diverse trajectories in itself, with internal
diversity and even contradictions. The memories had been reshaped in different hands and generations; scribes who wrote the people's traditions were
not innocent and without their own vested interests, and the patriarchalism
of the culture became inscribed in the text. Thus, the hegemonic function of
religion and the biases inscribed in popular culture, previously ignored,
turned to be more evident. And on the second hand: what is "popular" had

to be redefined. The ambiguity of cultures called for a more careful and close vigilance of the prejudices, inequalities, bias, and concealed interests in the Bible itself as well as in the readers, even the "poor and simple." Different situations of diverse "subjects" (African descendants, aboriginal peoples, mestizos, women, campesinos, etc., and the crisscrossing of these categories) showed that there is no "simple poor," but a complexity of reading locations that could not be ignored. A liberating interpretation of Scriptures could not be fundamentalist of any one given location, or naïve in its appropriation of the text. A liberationist hermeneutics must also be self-critical, give account of the complexities and contradictions within the text as well as in the reading community.

From a "Liberationist Canon" to a "Canonical Liberation"

A second development that took place throughout these years is related to the need to be "canonical." At the beginning there was a selection of "liberating texts" that were quoted over and over: Exodus, excerpts of the Deuteronomistic history, some prophets like Amos, Isaiah, a selection of Psalms, the synoptic Gospels and the first chapters of Acts, James, and, occasionally, Revelation read as an anti-imperialistic manifesto. These became the "canon within the canon." When you look at the standing remains of the first years, or in the memory of the participants, the intensive resource to those texts and the almost total absence of others become evident, at a bird's sight.

But as time passed, new experiences and groups joined and situations changed. The mere repetition of the "liberationist creed" was not enough. People knew certain texts and explanations by heart, and new insights had to be brought in to keep the dynamics. As stated before, even those familiar texts showed class ambiguities, traces of dominant cultures and of a patriarchal underground. In the dialogue with other groups, and in the debate within the Church, we were called to render also an alternative reading of "less friendly" texts, in which ethnic discrimination, racist prejudices, sexism, religious intolerance, and other forms of oppression are to be found. It was not enough to quote a handful of favoring passages or create a verse artillery for argument. The "enemy" could do that just as well. A new way of dealing with the whole Bible was needed, and other texts had to be examined as well. The people, as they read the Bible, not with the assigned selection but also in other parts, came many times with the question, "But what about this?" or "Look at what it says here!" The growth of Pentecostal and neo-pentecostal groups in Latin America in the last ten years also brought discussion about the Bible within the neighborhood and the family, and those discussions were afterward reflected in the reading in the base community.

A new "canonical" approach was needed. Not because of a scholarly fad, though the scholarly canonical approach could help, but because of the people's need to consider the whole of the Bible, to have a comprehensive approach to less familiar texts, to deal with those passages that seemed hostile. That meant that also the concept of Scripture and canon had to be modified. Two things began to happen. Communities became engaged in reading other texts. Some issues of RIBLA show that experience, when "textbooks" that deal with the Gospel of John or with the Pauline corpus come out of that enterprise.

Aboriginal communities brought new critical insights to some texts, but gave new meaning to others. Gender issues forced the communities to become critical of their own previous selections, and also to revise their understanding of "the authority of the Bible." Afrobrasilian and Afro-Caribbean cults influenced the reading of certain texts, and promoted a new approach to "syncretism." So Scripture became a concept larger than the Bible, and "canon" had to become not a closed concept but a flexible tool able to deal with a variety of experiences. Working through the diversity of Christian origins, and the fact that that diversity did not hinder the possibility of a unified account in a common canon, was one of the ways of dealing with that plurality. RIBLA also provides some resources in that line. In that sense, the fact that the Bible itself does not have "only one, all embracing and coherent message" but that there are a diversity of experiences, situations, and expressions, linked to specific cultural backgrounds and historical circumstances, and not totally free of the one-sidedness of the authors, far from eroding the liberating thrust of its testimonies, became in itself liberating. Canonical reading became reading the whole of the Bible and trying to overcome a "canon within the canon" approach. Also there was the need to put side by side texts that a selective reading, or historical criticism and other analytical methods, had torn apart or disqualified. But more than that, it also meant the need to open the canon to the new experiences of the communities (we will come back to that *ad infra*), to the plurality of interpreting subjects, and also to the frontiers of faiths. Canonical, then, is not the close measure of doctrinal purity, but a point of comparison that allows us to enter into a liberating dialogue with others. Canon is opened by interpretation. But interpretation is not only an intellectual exercise; it is also a liberating experience of overcoming injustice, a living experience of loving others.

Some Things about Challenges, Frustration, and Compassion

We would turn the world upside down! It was clear that, at the turn of history, and the sooner the better, a new society was at hand. We were building the Reign of God, and things could go only one way, the one we expected them to go. A positive mechanicism was not to be excluded. "The oppressed people are the Lord of History" was a theological expression of what seemed the necessary outcome of liberation struggles. A particular concept of salvation history, and salvation within history, was at the roots of many wishful intentions, certainly held with good will. A good will, it should be said, that was coherent with and sustained by people's own life, in many cases.

In that atmosphere, the Bible was read as a book of challenges. We were "doing theology in a revolutionary context," and the reading of the Bible had to be part of that chore. We were called to confront injustice, and the strong Word of the Lord, resounding in the text, was the revolutionary program. The message was received and passed as the request of the militant. We were ready to take into our own hands the responsibility of giving flesh to the Spirit of change. God's love involved us in God's project for a better humanity. As we read the text we were called to action, and realized that the text could only be read by praxis. Many were ready to lose their own life, and, unfortunately, that did happen.

But changes did not come about as hoped. Repression won the upper hand, and instead of changing, Latin America was plunged into a very difficult historical time from the point of view of human rights and economic exploitation. We cannot bring here an account of that period, but the results are at hand. We have hundreds of thousands of tortured, disappeared, and killed. But that was necessary for the dominant forces, in order to assure the continuance of the inequalities of the economic system, to do away with political, worker's union, or youth movements opposition and to create the framework to impose the most savage measures of financial capitalism, which we endure today. Challenge became frustration, and the reading of the Bible as a permanent challenge to "do all things new" needed to be reframed in that aftermath of the revolution that did not come to be.

A "theology of exile" came along with the theology of liberation. The experience of grief had to be read not only as the provisional situation in the midst of the struggle, but as a more permanent condition that has no visible end in the short time, in the life span of the generation that in the sixties had dreamed about a new social and just order. Far from that, a growing awareness of the complexities of world politics in the era of globalization, of the many forms of victimizing children and women, of the ecological dangers that affect our people, of the constraints of the financial devices of international powers, forced us to realize that the Bible could not only have a word of challenge through which we were empowered for struggle, but also a word of comfort, an empowerment for endurance and resistance, when the hope of liberation turned out to be a hope of survival. The title of the last book by Elsa Tamez, *Cuando los horizontes se cierran*[17] (When horizons are closed), is enlightening in this sense.

The Emergence of a Plurality of Subjects and the Need for an Inclusive Vision

The struggle for liberation also brought along a more complex understanding of society. At the beginning it was considered that the all-embracing category of "social class" could explain all the causes and mechanisms of oppression. The "poor" was taken as a self-explicative concept. Gender, ethnic, rural conditions were comprised as internal and not always important subcategories. This generated many discussions, within Latin America and also in the dialogue with partners of other parts of the world. We had to learn from that discussion, which came from "below," from those communities (aboriginal, African descendants) and from people within the communities that demanded that their particular situations and claims could not be melted away in a general and unspecific proposition.

So, within the popular reading of the Bible a more varied approach began to appear. A Latin American feminist reading of the Bible gained its space. A whole movement that reached its climax in 1992 (the fifth centennial of European invasion of the Americas) developed in the aboriginal communities (which are a majority or in great numbers in many countries). Even within that movement there were diverse approaches. Some refused Christianity and the Bible as an imposition of the conquerors, claiming that it was time to recover the ancient religions and ways of perceiving the cosmos. Others thought a bridge with the white culture had to be kept and that alternative readings in the Bible could offer that bridge. In some countries strong peasant movements expressed in base communities and local Pentecostal and Protestant congregations (Peru, Bolivia, Colombia, Ecuador) also

17. *Cuando los horizontes se cierran. Relectura del libro de Eclesiastés o Qohelet* (San José, Costa Rica: DEI, 1998).

74

offered their own readings of the Bible. In the North of Brazil and the Caribbean a strong presence of African descendants created its own approach. Consideration for the situation of children, youth, and people of different abilities was brought in as a part of the needed concerns. I realize I am being unfair in just mentioning these, without entering into a more detailed explanation of their characteristic features, identities, and contributions. But that would take many more pages, and this is still an unpretentious essay. Once again, a view of the RIBLA indexes can show how these themes and readings gained an important space in Latin American hermeneutics.

But also new religious expressions developed, within and outside Christianity. The "base community" and the "catholic popular religiosity" were not any more the only manifestations of faith in popular quarters. Pentecostals, Catholic Charismatics, healing ministries, esoteric cults are also present. How are we to deal with this more diverse and multiform reality, with experiences that do not conform to our predisposition? Are we to exclude them as "not popular," because we have already defined what is popular and liberating from an ideological point of view? Are not many of these and similar phenomena also included in biblical narratives and books? Take, for example, the book of Revelation, read in Latin American hermeneutics in its beginning (and still today in many circles) mostly as an anti-imperialistic manifesto. Afterwards some consideration to the book as endurance and resistance in the midst of persecutions was also integrated in the reading. But what about the dimensions of the book as vision, of experience "in the Spirit," of prophecy? What does it say about anthropological dimensions of power, magic, the mystic dimensions of faith? Those kind of considerations are also being made now. RIBLA 34 (*Apocalipsis de Juan y la mística del milenio*, 1999) is a first attempt to gather also these kind of experiences, which are also related to the different cultural milieu in which hermeneutics take place.

But I want also to bring in some concern that we find in many biblical circles and communities about this diversity. Because, on the one hand, it has to be considered and honored, but on the other hand it endangers the need of an inclusive view. It risks shattering people in so many pieces that it inhibits solidarity, that fragmentation becomes a hindrance to joint action, that partial vindications are played by dominant powers, one against the other. Poor against poor: we are seeing that already. A new challenge is open for our popular reading of the Bible: the need to identify the different subjects and build identities and the dignity of each, but at the same time, find the links that permit the body to keep coordinated, the unity to be kept, and the network of social solidarity to be rebuilt.

The Context of Globalization and Exclusion
and the Recovery of Everyday Life

The context of globalization has been, at large, bad news for Latin America, as for the vast majority of the Third World. We enjoy very little of its technological advances, and suffer a lot by the accumulation of wealth and power that it is bringing about, because it is the result of the exploitation and exclusion of many. The word in the agenda is "exclusion." People previously called "marginal," that is, on the borders of social structures of production and distribution, are today "excluded," which means, they are totally outside of the system. There is no place for them, even on the margins. There is no chance for them to be taken into consideration by market forces or world policy makers. Many of our "popular Bible readers" are now in this frightening new category.

It is also impossible to try to go into any detail of what globalization is and means. But we have to respond to the fact of globalization, of the overarching structures that run the major decisions in world economy and politics. At the same time we still have to recognize that globalization has not simply erased the variegated spectrum of people's life, of cultures, of ways of relating and enjoying, of religious feelings and sensitivities.

The idolatry of the market, exclusion, and "one way thinking" are the bloodthirsty powers that are shaping our world today. People do not matter, only commodities. Not even real commodities, but financial commodities that set the pace of life. How long can this go on without provoking a human shock, a total crisis? Is there a way out that can avoid hurting once again the weak, the eternal victims of injustice? How can hope, love, and faith be kept in situations of exclusion and denial of the humanity of the victims? How can real everyday life be found meaningful in a context of stress, of bare survival, of increasing structural, criminal, and spontaneous violence? We have no clear answer. Once again we will go to our biblical narratives with hope and anguish.

Perhaps our "reading" of the Bible in popular context has to become more and more a "hearing" of the narratives of the people, of the life stories, of their endurance, anguish, and faith. How people understand their own life, what symbols of survival they are building, how they come across their wounds and pains. The small narratives of the people as they go on in the quest for a little bit of happiness, friendliness, joy, in the midst of aggression and competence. How we cling to hope on the edge of despair. "Liberation" must not then be a big ideological word, but the refreshing experience of a little bit of dignity. Obviously, we cannot take refuge in the small world of intimacy and forget that much of the suffering is located in the macro structures of injustice, and that as long as those stay put as they are, little can be done to overcome the oppression that damages human and all life on the planet. So the small narratives of everyday life are to be joined in the big narrative of a new possible promise. As in the Bible. This, as said before, is also a new "canonical corpus" that allows interpretation.

So reading the Bible becomes once again hearing the story and telling the story, the little life stories of the lesser people scattered as sheep without a shepherd, and how they met with the Lord who gave them the bread of life. But also the big story of God's faithfulness and love, of God's keeping of the Promise, of the Resurrection of the discarded carpenter of Nazareth. For interpretation is about texts, but it is also about meaning. And meaning occurs in life.

5 Some Reflections on a Dalit Reading of the Bible

A. Maria Arul Raja, S.J.

Orientations

Dalit reading of the Bible is a transformative/pragmatic approach which focuses not on the author/redactor and his/her intention nor on the deep structures of the external architecture of the text, but on the flesh-and-blood persons of the Dalit community hearing/reading the text.[1] This reading experience is defined by the intimate conversation between the totality of the history, context, social relationships, horizon, and worldview of the Dalitness and that of the biblical text. The significance of the "biases and prejudices" of the (Dalit) interpreters in shaping their unique interpretation of the Bible is favorably considered in the place of the fiction of so-called "objective" scholarship. These hermeneutical rustlings are due to the growing awareness of the oppressed people like the Dalits and the influence of the recent intellectual movements such as sociology of knowledge, deconstruction, and depth psychology.[2]

With this backdrop, our attempt here in this brief article is to propose a few reflections on effective reading strategies in reading the Bible from a Dalit perspective.[3]

1. The Dalit reading does not seek the meaning behind the text which creates a distance but the meaning in front of the text which demands involvement. Cf. E. V. McKnight, *The Bible and the Reader: An Introduction to Literary Criticism* (Philadelphia: Fortress Press, 1985), p. xviii.

2. Cf. M. A. Tolbert, "Defining the Problem: The Bible and Feminist Hermeneutics," *Semeia* 28 (1983): 114.

3. For some introductory reflections on this topic, Cf. A. M. A. Raja, "Towards a Dalit Reading of the Bible: Some Hermeneutical Reflections," *Jeevadhara* 26, 151 (1996): 29-34.

Written Text for Unlettered Dalits

First of all, it is an irony to think of a Dalit interpretation of the written text of the Bible, when a vast majority of them are kept as illiterates. The cultural realm of the Dalits is not predominantly text-bound or logocentric. Rather it functions, by and large, on the plane of oral discourses. And hence, the meaningfulness evoked by the Bible should be carefully uncoded from the written text and re-encoded in the form of oral Dalit discourses.[4] In this responsible task, the intermediary role of the learned "experts," I am afraid, may cause a serious handicap[5] (though, perhaps, inevitable) while seeking to enable both the "oral" Dalits and the "written" Bible to vibrate harmoniously with each other.

Also, today more than ever before, all are under the grip of the global networks of the mass-media communication world. The audio-video "discourses" are the new modes of relating ourselves to everyone and everything, including our roots and foundations. In this post-literate stage, the unwritten "discourses" play a significant role in decoding the meaning/meaningfulness of the written text of the Bible.

The Dalits too are no strangers to this new culture of post-literate "discourses," though a vast majority of them have not passed through the so-called literate stage and are still within the stage of the pre-literate "discourses." Any reading genuinely involved in the liberation of the Dalits today should necessarily assume the form of "discourses" (whatever be its label as pre-literate or post-literate or both). Our objective is to do justice, both to the liberation of the unlettered Dalits and to the written text of the Bible in our context.

---

4. For a brilliant discussion on the significance of orality, cf. W. J. Ong, "Text as Interpretation: Mark and After," *Semeia* 39 (1987): 7-26, and esp. 9. "In so far as a text is static, fixed, 'out there,' it is not utterance but a visual design. It can be made into an utterance only by a code that is existing and functioning in a living person's mind. When a person knowing the appropriate code moves through the visual structure and converts it into a temporal sequence of sound, aloud or in the imagination, directly or indirectly — that is, when someone reads the text — only then does the text become an utterance and only then does the suspended discourse continue, and with its verbalized meaning. Texts have meaning only insofar as they emerge from and are converted into the extratextual. All text is pretext."

5. We agree when the "experts" are said to "have emphasized the cognitive significance of gospel texts at the neglect of their affective and acoustic quality." Cf. W. H. Kelber, "Biblical Hermeneutics and the Ancient Art of Communication: A Response," *Semeia* 39 (1987): 99. Enough with any further deployment of knowledge (and thus the hegemony of the symbolic universe) as a means of social control upon the Dalits by the "elites and experts"!

Beyond "Windows" and "Mirrors"

Behind the Text

The historical criticism seeks to reach behind the development of the various strata of the traditions, to reconstruct the *Sitz im Leben* of the successive interpreting communities and even that of the actual biblical events. The primary focus here is, not the text, but the historical data behind the text. Along the same line, the sociological criticism looks for social indicators and correlations sedimented within the text. Using the recent sociological models, it attempts to reconstruct the social world behind the text. In these diachronic approaches, the treatment of the text as a mere "window" does not establish a direct relationship between the reader and the text.

Into the Text

The literary criticism, instead of delving deep behind the text, looks at/into the text as a well-knit narrative "mirror," which reflects an autonomous complex system of its own life and integrity. The meaning elicited from this synchronic approach is not with its reference to the historical situations, but with the modes of functioning of various formal literary elements found in the text.

In Front of the Text

"If historical criticism betrays the narrative integrity of the text, literary criticism betrays its historical integrity."[6] When these are judiciously synthesized, the combination of both the extrinsic criticism (economic and social factors as ideological conditions) and intrinsic criticism (genre, structure, and narrative content as ideological strategies), the paradigms of biblical response to the past socio-cultural context could be delineated. The complex whole of these paradigms is the dialogue partner with the questions emerging from the context of today's Dalit reader.

---

6. C. Myers, *Binding the Strong Man: A Political Reading of Mark's Story of Jesus* (Maryknoll, NY: Orbis, 1990), p. 25.

Performative and Bodily Religiosity

Dalits, as non-persons and sons/daughters of the soil, are the interlocutors between their experience of dehumanization and the world of the biblical text. Their ethos is born out of their close association with sweat and soil, dirt and tears, corpse and blood. And their perception is marked with an intuitive component with an emphasis on an empirical mode of experiencing reality.

The raw realities of the day-to-day life with its joys and sorrows, the physical performances in the actual, the ritual and the symbolic world, and the essential needs for a dignified life are the very stuff Dalit religiosity is made of. Hence, Dalit hermeneutics is basically of the performative order.[7]

Precisely because of this, the Dalit reading of the Bible does not take place from the "idealist site of inferiority" but rather from the "bodily site of exteriority."[8] And this explains why the Dalits are rooted in and accustomed to rich interpretations of the down-to-earth myths and symbols.

Attraction Towards Apocalyptic Tradition

One has to take into serious account the significant affinity of the Dalits towards the world of apocalyptic literature, though apparently it is the frightening part of the canon. This observation reiterates that the Dalit epistemological plane is enriched with imageries and symbols.

The abundant symbolism of evil, immediacy of the divine intervention, irreconcilable dualism between good and the evil, inevitability of the suffering of the marginalized for bearing testimony to compassion, the subversive elements shaking up the dominant powers, groaning silence, dissatisfaction with the present order, hope of historical consummation in the future era of equality-justice, etc., are some of the special attractions for the Dalits found in the apocalyptic traditions.

The social death of the Dalits repeatedly thrust upon them by the caste

7. For an excellent treatment of the subaltern hermeneutics, cf. F. Wilfred, "Towards a Subaltern Hermeneutics: Beyond the Contemporary Polarities in the Interpretation of Religious Traditions," *Vaiharai* 1, 1 (1996): 61-81, esp. 77-80 for emphasizing the primacy of the oral and the performative dimensions of the subaltern interpretation.

8. Dalits being the impoverished working class in India, the critical view on the bourgeois exegesis and its theological ideology by Belo will be appropriate here. Cf. F. Belo, *A Materialist Reading of the Gospel of Mark* (Maryknoll, NY: Orbis, 1981), p. 256.

system forces them to nurse new hopes one after another. These Dalit hopes, while being rooted in the soil of the raw material of history, ramify even towards the eschatological horizons. Very often, they offer immediate and unambiguous answers to many contemporary problems. It is with these hopes that new alternatives are generated, critiquing the existing order, promulgated by the present-day "demons" and "beasts."

A note of caution, however, has to be made here. When these hopes are individualized and transcendentalized, the magical/false consciousness overpowers the collective historical commitment of the Dalits. This flight from reality is basically inimical to Dalit liberation. Responsible pastors and Bible scholars should be very careful in rightly locating the genuine liberative reading of the Bible and especially the apocalyptic literature, while engaged in Dalit liberation.

Beyond the Logic and Language of Classical Theism

The language of classical theism fails to capture the Dalit imagination. In the place of the image of an omniscient, omnipotent, and omnipresent Father God, a new blend of a plurality of (apparently even contradictory) images of the vulnerable-strong, mother-father, suffering-enjoying, immanent-transcendent, material-spiritual deity is to be ushered in. This deity is to be also immediate, in directly responding to the cries of the Dalits repeatedly crushed under the oppressive hands. After all, an "omnipotent" God is required to redeem those who experience the complete "impotence" of the helpless human deity crying out "Why have you forsaken me?"

The existential religious stream of the Dalits, by and large, does not tally with the belief systems — well-defined creed, code, and cult — of the official/classical religions they externally belong to. Abstract theological concepts as faith expressions are not the leading principles defining their religiosity. Any concrete symbols through the intermediary of which the battered Dalit mind and heart experience the transcendent will be accommodated into their symbolic universe. If the objection arises that such accommodation borders on eclecticism of idol worship or violation against monotheism, it is from the quarters of the religions or the systems of the elite seeking to fence themselves.

The reading of the Bible from a Dalit location need not be obsessed with such probable or even actual objections raised by those trained in the idealist site, "proudly owning refined dogmas classically formulated and carefully promulgated."[9]

Creativity and Celebration

The matrix of the tribal hermeneutics is enriched with the orientation of egalitarianism and that of the feminist hermeneutics with the promotion and sustenance of life. The Dalit hermeneutics seems to be actively vibrant with the life-stream in terms of creativity and celebration of life.[10]

In spite of the denial of human dignity on a par with the co-humans and thus divided and defaced, the Dalits refuse to be cowed down by the high-handed measures of the repression of the caste hierarchy. The rhythmic beauty and the aesthetic expressions in-built in the Dalit consciousness are spontaneously and creatively at play, even if a minimum of space is created. The eloquent expressions of the celebration of life to the maximum, with noise, illumination, and corporate activities in open space, even with limited availability of minimal resources, are commonly witnessed in the lives of the Dalits.

Having in mind this Dalit ethos as the background, one can understand why the Dalits feel out of place when the Bible is read from the milieu of privatist piety, of individualistic perfection with an exclusive insistence on personal conversion alone, of contemplative exercises within a guru-centered or an ashramic set-up, of the dialogue culture of the leisurely class, of the academia claiming to have systematic and scientific approaches, etc.

In contrast with these elements, one has to locate the milieu and the moments of the communal celebrations with creative expressions as the most conducive for a meaningful Dalit reading of the Bible.

Critical Function

The raw experience of the Dalits being painfully discriminated against leads them to seek to critically view — and rightly so — everything given: be it

9. For this opinion of mine, I depend much on my observations made of the Dalits during my service as a pastor in charge at Kelampakkam (1993-96), the sub-station of Kovalam parish in the Catholic Archdiocese of Madras-Mylapore.

10. For further elucidation on this point cf. also J. T. Appavoo, "Dalit Religion," and D. Carr, "A Biblical Basis for Dalit Theology," in J. Massey, ed., *Indigenous People: Dalits — Dalit Issues in Today's Theological Dehate* (Delhi: ISPCK, 1994), pp. 111-21 and 231-49.

context, text, history, ideology, conquest, defeat, etc. This critical conscious-ness of the Dalits is to be further sharpened by the critical cognitive tools of the social sciences, made palatable to the simple minds of the Dalits by those "organic intellectuals" already evangelized by the Dalits.[11] The constant dia-logue between the unlettered Dalits (a majority indeed!) and the above type of intellectuals will help both the sectors to de-idealize the presuppositions behind the biblical texts, the process of redaction and canonization, and the cognitive tools employed for interpretation.[12] In this process, the Dalit read-ers will be much helped to hermeneutize even the apparently anti-Dalit texts. The following categorization may help us in locating the required tasks to be undertaken, while encountering the "problematic texts" in the engage-ment of a Dalit liberative hermeneutics:[13]

Texts
1. Whose redaction and canonization erased the voice of the oppressed.
2. Giving voice to the dominant group.
3. With ambiguous messages for the rulers and the ruled.

Tasks
1. Recovery of the probable past through suspicion.
2. Ideology — critique.
3. Assessment of power distribution/false consciousness.

Dalit Assertion and Kenosis

Can a slave be liberated by another slave? Can the enslaved Dalits[14] be re-stored to human dignity by the self-abasement of the Crucified Servant or the Silent Sufferer or the Humiliated Deity?

11. J. L. Segundo, "The Shift Within Latin American Theology," *Journal of Theology of South Africa* 52 (1985): 23-28.

12. G. West and J. Draper, "The Bible and Social Transformation in South Africa: A Work-in-Progress Report on the Institute for the Study of the Bible," *SBL Seminar* (1991): 376-82.

13. Cf. S. Briggs, "Can an Enslaved God Liberate? Hermeneutical Reflections on Philippians 2:6-11," *Semeia* 47 (1989): 137-39.

14. Patterson's description of the social death of a slave throws light on the Dalit situa-tion also. "The slave is violently uprooted from his milieu. He is desocialized and depersonal-ized. This process of social negation constitutes the first, essentially the external, phase of en-slavement. The next phase involves the introduction of the slave into the community of his master, but involves the paradox of introducing him as non-being." O. Patterson, *Slavery and Social Death: A Comparative Study* (Cambridge, MA: Harvard University Press, 1982), p. 38.

When the honor of the oppressing non-Dalits is supposed to be upheld, insofar as the Dalits are made to be shameful creatures and kept as innocent sufferers, the biblical God revolts. As an expression of this revolt, (s)he determines to become Emmanuel; the mighty logos becomes the vulnerable sarx in order to pitch his/her tent with us; the son of God makes the loud cry of *eloi, eloi, lama sabachthani;* the *morphē theou* takes up *morphē doulou;* the one who knew no sin is made to be sin.

The innocent and the righteous sufferer of the wisdom literature (perhaps, the suffering prophets also) undergoes the suffering as an inevitable reality; but the state in which Christ found himself was a conscious choice made on the human plane *(heauton auton)*[15] to empty himself.

This deliberate decision of self-abasement of Jesus unto death has the twin dimension of (1) the obedience to God (2) whose heartbeat is the absolute solidarity with the innocent sufferers. In other words, the slave-deity has to undergo the salvific suffering as the divine necessity *(dei)* in order to alleviate the dehumanizing suffering in the act of his absolute solidarity. As the result of this human decision of Jesus, he was highly exalted to be the Lord of the universe.

In line with this paradigm of "a slave liberating another slave," the Dalits are challenged

1. to obey the God of Jesus, in order to disobey the idol of caste-hierarchy,
2. and to decide to empty themselves further, in order to be in deep solidarity with the co-Dalits.

With this decision towards the solidarity with the suffering co-Dalits and God, the Dalits are certainly to be highly exalted.

Conclusion

Every Dalit reading of the Bible openly claims an approach to the text with its typical pre-understanding not divested of the pain and "prejudices" of being discriminated against. The critical consciousness of the Dalits needs to be sharpened by those intellectuals whose expertise is constantly ready to be evangelized by the ongoing Dalit struggle. The active solidarity between the

---

15. J. Murphy-O'Connor, "Christological Anthropology in Phil. II, 6-11," *Revue biblique* 83 (1976): 41.

Dalits and the "Dalitized" experts will educate both the sectors to evolve new tools to delve deep into the realities of Dalitness and the God who speaks to the Dalits through the Bible.

The typical Dalit ethos — comprised of oral discourse, in-built creativity and exuberance in the celebration of life, performative order of hope, and natural affinity towards the rich apocalyptic world of symbolism and conflict — is to be looked into for evolving effective reading strategies for Dalit liberation. These attempts, we hope, will create a conducive atmosphere for an engaged conversation between the horizons of the unlettered Dalits and the written Bible.

All our attempts at a Dalit hermeneutics of the Bible could be genuine only when our solidarity with the Dalits enthuse them to decide on their own to fight a pitched battle with relentless hope, till the end, against all the forces upholding the caste-hierarchy.

6 The Song of Mary (Luke 1:46-55)

Ernesto Cardenal

We came to the Song of Mary; the *Magnificat*, traditionally known by that name because it is the first word in the Latin. It is said that this passage of the Gospel terrified the Russian Czars, and Maurras was very right in talking about the "revolutionary germ" of the *Magnificat*.

The pregnant Mary had gone to visit her cousin Elizabeth, who also was pregnant. Elizabeth congratulated her because she would be the mother of the Messiah, and Mary broke out singing that song. It is a song to the poor. The people of Nicaragua have been very fond of reciting it. It is the favorite prayer of the poor, and superstitious *campesinos* often carry it as an amulet. In the time of old Somoza when the *campesinos* were required always to carry with them proof they had voted for him, the people jokingly called that document the *Magnificat*.

Now young ESPERANZA read this poem, and the women began to comment on it.

> My soul praises the Lord,
> my heart rejoices in God my Savior,
> because he has noticed his slave.

"She praises God because the Messiah is going to be born, and that's a great event for the people."

"She calls God 'Savior' because she knows that the Son that he has given her is going to bring liberation."

"She's full of joy. Us women must also be that way, because in our community the Messiah is born too, the liberator."

"She recognizes liberation. . . . We have to do the same thing. Liberation is from sin, that is, from selfishness, from injustice, from misery, from ignorance — from everything that's oppressive. That liberation is in our wombs too, it seems to me . . ."

The last speaker was ANDREA, a young married woman, and now ÓSCAR, her young husband, breaks in: "God is selfish because he wants us to be his slaves. He wants our submission. Just him. I don't see why Mary has to call herself a slave. We should be free! Why just him? That's selfishness."

ALEJANDRO, who is a bachelor: "We have to be slaves of God, not of men."

Another young man: "God is love. To be a slave of love is to be free because God doesn't make slaves. He's the only thing we should be slaves of, love. And then we don't make slaves of others."

ALEJANDRO'S MOTHER says: "To be a slave of God is to serve others. That slavery is liberation." I said that it's true that this selfish God Oscar spoke about does exist. And it's a God invented by people. People have often invented a god in their own image and likeness — not the true God, but idols, and those religions are alienating, an opium of the people. But the God of the Bible does not teach religion, but rather he urges Moses to take Israel out of Egypt, where the Jews were working as slaves. He led them from colonialism to liberty. And later God ordered that among those people no one could hold another as a slave, because they had been freed by him and they belonged only to him, which means they were free.

And TERESITA, William's wife: "We have to keep in mind that at the time when Mary said she was a slave, slavery existed. It exists today too, but with a different name. Now the slaves are the proletariat or the *campesinos*. When she called herself a slave, Mary brought herself closer to the oppressed, I think. Today she could have called herself a proletarian or a *campesina* of Solentiname."

And WILLIAM: "But she says she's a slave of the Lord (who is the Liberator, who is the one who brought freedom from the Egyptian slavery). It's as if she said she was a slave of the liberation. Or as if she said that she was a proletarian or a revolutionary *campesina*."

Another of the girls: "She says she's poor, and she says that God took into account 'the poverty of his slave,' that is, that God chose her because she was poor. He didn't choose a queen or a lady of high society but a woman from the people. Yes, because God has preferred us poor people. Those are the 'great things' that God has done, as Mary says."

And from now on all generations will call me happy,
for Mighty God has done great things for me.
His name is holy,
and his love reaches his faithful ones from generation to generation.

One of the ladies: "She says that people will call her happy. . . . She feels happy because she is the mother of Jesus the Liberator, and because she also is a liberator like her son, because she understood her son and did not oppose his mission. She didn't oppose him, unlike other mothers of young people who are messiahs, liberators of their communities. That was her great merit, I say."

And another: "She says that God is holy, and that means 'just.' The just person who doesn't offend anybody, the one who doesn't commit any injustices. God is like this and we should be like him." I said that was a perfect biblical definition of the holiness of God. And then I asked what a holy society would be.

"The one we are seeking," LAUREANO answered at once. He is a young man who talks of the Revolution or revolutionaries almost every time he comments on the Bible. After a brief pause he added: "The one that revolutionaries want to build, all the revolutionaries of the world."

He has shown the strength of his arm;
he conquers those with proud hearts.

Old TOMÁS, who can't read but who always talks with great wisdom: "They are the rich, because they think they are above us and they look down on us. Since they have the money. . . . And a poor person comes to their house and they won't even turn around to look at him. They don't have anything more than we do, except money. Only money and pride, that's all they have that we don't."

ÁNGEL says: "I don't believe that's true. There are humble rich people and there are proud poor people. If we weren't proud we wouldn't be divided, and us poor are divided."

LAUREANO: "We're divided because the rich divide us. Or because a poor person often wants to be like a rich one. He yearns to be rich, and then he's an exploiter in his heart, that is, the poor person has the mentality of the exploiter."

OLIVIA: "That's why Mary talks about people with proud hearts. It's not a matter of having money or not, but of having the mentality of an exploiter or not."

I said that nevertheless it cannot be denied that in general the rich person is a proud man, not the poor one.

And TOMÁS said: "Yes, because the poor person doesn't have anything. What has he got to be proud of? That's why I said that the rich are proud, because they have the money. But that's the only thing they have we don't have, money and the pride that goes with having money."

> He pulls down the mighty from their thrones and raises up
>   the humble.
> He fills the hungry with good things and he leaves the rich
>   with nothing.

One said: "The mighty is the same as the rich. The mighty are rich and the rich are mighty."

And another: "The same as proud, because the mighty and the rich are proud."

TERESITA: "Mary says that God raised up the humble. That's what he did to Mary."

And MARIÍTA: "And what he did to Jesus who was poor and to Mary, and to all the others who followed Jesus, who were poor."

I asked what they thought Herod would have said if he had known that a woman of the people had sung that God had pulled down the mighty and raised up the humble, filled the hungry with good things and left the rich with nothing.

NATALIA laughed and said: "He'd say she was crazy."

ROSITA: "That she was a communist."

LAUREANO: "The point isn't that they would just *say* the Virgin was a communist. She *was* a communist."

"And what would they say in Nicaragua if they heard what we're saying here in Solentiname?"

Several voices: "That we're communists."

Someone asked: "That part about filling the hungry with good things?"

A young man answered: "The hungry are going to eat."

And another: "The Revolution."

LAUREANO: "That is the Revolution. The rich person or the mighty is brought down and the poor person, the one who was down, is raised up."

Still another: "If God is against the mighty, then he has to be on the side of the poor."

ANDREA, Óscar's wife, asked: "That promise that the poor would have those good things, was it for then, for Mary's time, or would it happen in our time? I ask because I don't know."

One of the young people answered: "She spoke for the future, it seems to me, because we are just barely beginning to see the liberation she announces."

> He helps the nation of Israel his servant, in remembrance of his love;
> as he had promised to our fathers, to Abraham, and to his
> > descendants forever.

ALEJANDRO: "That nation of Israel that she speaks about is the new people that Jesus formed, and we are this people."

WILLIAM: "It's the people who will be liberated, like before the other people were liberated from the dictatorship of Egypt, where they were treated like shit, changed into cheap hand labor. But the people can't be liberated by others. They must liberate themselves. God can show the way to the Promised Land, but the people themselves must begin the journey."

ÓSCAR asked: "Can you take riches from the rich by force? Christ didn't force the rich young man. He said to him: 'If you wish . . .'"

I thought for a while before answering. I said hesitantly: "You might let him go to another country . . ."

WILLIAM: "But not let him take his wealth with him."

FELIPE: "Yes, let him take it."

The last remark was from MARIÍTA: "Mary sang here about equality. A society with no social classes. Everyone alike."

II. Liturgy and Politics

Introduction

Bernd Wannenwetsch

New Awareness

The twentieth century witnessed a new awareness in theology of the political dimension of the liturgy and of the liturgical dimension of politics. The Benedictine monk Virgil Michel of St. John's in Collegeville, Minnesota, stands for the generation that initiated this trend in connection with the liturgical revival movement that influenced various ecumenical churches in the first third of the century. In this first phase, inspiration was drawn from intensified historical liturgical study, which alerted the churches to the richness of liturgical practices and theologies of the past, and in particular of the early Church and the patristic age. Attention to ancient rites such as the offertory, which implied a fine-tuned pattern of participatory politics, served as a reminder of why public worship had been named *leitourgia,* "work of the people," in the first place.

The second "wave," which began in the last third of the bygone century, was inspired more by trends in political philosophy and political theology. In this context, the liturgy could be understood either as an expression of or means for political change (liberation theology) or as the intensified representation of a communal ethos — the complex of rituals, narratives, and constitutive practices that underlies political formation, political identity, and political action.

The theologians who contributed to this discussion have been conscious of the fact that liturgy never happens in a vacuum or in a parallel world. Each liturgical act is reflecting and reacting to the particularities of the historical situation of the celebration, whether it be the post-industrial "social question" to which the tradition of papal social encyclicals responded (Michel), the struggles for liberation in Latin America (Avila), or the peculiar temptations that Christians face in late capitalist societies of the West (Schmemann, Pickstock).

Critical Power

In any such context, a perception common to all of the authors represented in the chapters in this section has been that the liturgy is not only a constitutive basis for "reconstructing the social order," a resourcing for that Christian spirit which keeps the balance necessary to avoid the social ills of individualism and collectivism (Michel), but at the same time a dangerous undertaking that challenges the status quo socially and politically (Avila). As has been widely acknowledged in this debate, the political dimension of the liturgy is a reality that cannot be evaded, but only denied or suppressed. The call, therefore, is not for a politicization of the liturgy but rather for a rediscovery (Schmemann), an awakening of its participants to the inherent political nature of public worship (Avila). By emphasizing the intrinsic political dimension of the liturgy, one also acknowledges that the Eucharist cannot be subjected to dichotomies that are otherwise taken for granted, such as between public and private, sacred and profane, immanent and transcendent.[1] But this is not to say that there is uniformity among the authors in this section. On investigation, it is clear that different authors emphasize different ways in which the liturgy's critical power is brought to bear. While it appears uncontroversial that "authentic" or "non-conformist" worship counts as a practice whose participatory, inclusive, and truth-oriented nature must be at odds with any form of complicity with sin — whether individual or structural — one controversial question that liberationist accounts in particular have provoked is whether the Eucharist can be adequately and sufficiently described as a means for overcoming social ills that exist "outside" of it, that is, social realities that can be described pre-liturgically, say, in sociological fashion.

---

1. Cf. Bernd Wannenwetsch, *Political Worship* (Oxford: Oxford University Press, 2004).

Revelatory Power

Or are we rather to assume a certain epistemological quality of the Eucharist, in that we expect it to reveal something to the world that the world cannot see otherwise — not only about the "other" world of spiritual things, but about the world's own actual ways and its true nature? Schmemann's and Pickstock's contributions are particularly interested in the revelatory function of the liturgy. For both authors, it is only in the light of authentic liturgy that the anti-liturgies of our time become transparent for what they are. In this vein, Schmemann describes secularism as a "negation of worship," and Pickstock speaks of modernity as characterized by the "refusal of liturgy" that cannot but engender "parodies of the liturgical." In her view, modern culture has systematically suppressed the liturgical ordering of space and time, as evident in modern city planning that does without the centering that cathedrals used to offer, and in eating habits that no longer encourage the setting aside of certain times for shared meals. She detects similar tendencies in the development of modern languages where the increasing employment of *asyndeton* or syntax devoid of conjunctions and clausal hierarchies impresses an atomized worldview on learners and speakers, and in the replacement of liturgical bonds with a civility or good manners in which style is worshiped for its own sake. The tendencies that Pickstock names may appear a random collection of mutually unrelated observations. Their hidden commonality becomes visible only when these tendencies are contrasted with the nature of genuine liturgy, which Pickstock characterizes in terms of the fusion of the ethical and aesthetic, and as "occupying a mediating position between art and politics."

For the Russian Orthodox theologian Alexander Schmemann, who lived and taught in the West (Paris, New York), the revelatory power of worship is given specifically with regards to the "sacramental character" of the universe that exists from, in, and towards God, and which can therefore be described as a divine epiphany. When, for example, the sacraments of baptism and Eucharist "deal" with the elements of water, bread, and wine, what happens there is not the expression of a spiritual meaning with the help of a visible sign, but nothing less than the revelation of the true meaning of matter as such. Thus, for Schmemann, the liturgy reveals the true nature of modern secularism, which is very different from what mainstream accounts of the "secularization thesis" point out in terms of the diminishing role of religion in modern societies. What secularism actually denies is not the existence of God or the importance of religious belief and religiously grounded morality.

Secularist thought, in Schmemann's view, might even be keen on "ritual" and liturgy. Yet, the way this interest develops reveals the nature of the underlying denial: denied is the sacramentality of humankind and world, insofar as the world, instead of being itself an epiphany of God, is assumed to carry meaning *within itself*. What secularist liturgism, occupied as it is with the expression or gestation of psychological states of mind or with a symbolic promotion of social and political values, overlooks is that *leitourgia* is not simply one instance of the generic concept of "worship." If Christ is the *telos* and fulfillment of natural worship, every act of Christian liturgy is to be a *new* beginning and radical *new* worship.

Transformative Power

The way in which the Orthodox theologian describes secularist interest in liturgy as one that emphasizes the promotion of certain preconceived social and political values raises the question as to whether some accounts of the role of the liturgy in Latin American liberation theology would also fall under this verdict. What does it mean in this context to suggest that one must seek to "realign, harmonize the liturgy with the aspirations of our continent," as the Colombian sociologist and theologian Rafael Avila does? Are his ideas for the design of a Eucharist that celebrates the history of Latin American people and their struggle for liberation, "just as Jesus himself celebrated his history and self-giving for the people," but one more example of the sort of liturgical secularism that Schmemann loathed? Are sufficiently clear distinctions drawn among agents of liberation — God, the people, and the Church — as well as among types of means of liberation?

Any attempt at answering these questions should begin by paying attention to the theological context in which Avila situates his discussion of the "centrifugal character" of the Eucharist. The Church, he insists, does not own the Eucharist as private property; what happens in the body of Christ is destined to eventually include the whole of humanity. Why then is the sociological analysis of the brokenness of the body (in political and economic terms) so important to the liberation theologian? Here Avila points to the offertory rite, an ancient moment in Eucharistic celebration that he wants to see reintroduced in its full scope, in that every communicant brings his or her own gifts to the table from which the Eucharistic elements are taken. In accord with the logic of this rite, Avila understands the bread presented for the Eucharist as representing the very lives of those who bring it — hence his very legitimate interest in giving a non-euphemistic account of its status that does not gloss over its messiness and brokenness.

Acknowledging the importance of this first moment of identification (of the elements with the people), we must ask, though, whether Avila is perhaps less aware of a second such moment of identification in the Eucharistic process: the identification of Christ with the elements, when the latter (representing the believers and their messy world) are taken up into his unique sacrifice and transformed into a new existence. Does Avila's rhetorical question, "How could Christ consecrate the fruit of despoliation?", betray a misunderstanding of the concept of consecration, with a mistaken emphasis on "legitimizing" over "transforming"? Is it not precisely the *inextricable* mix of good creaturely work and exploiting features involved in the production process that goes into the baking of the bread that humans bring to the altar and that is to become the element of the Eucharist, ready to be taken up and transformed into the newness of Christ's body? While Avila is certainly right in emphasizing the importance of what people bring to the Eucharist, and that they know what it is (themselves!), he appears to turn this importance into a moral prerequisite for participation itself. The following quotation seems to underline this point: "Therefore the only persons qualified to participate in this celebration are those working for liberation. . . . To assume that the church can be a 'place of worship for all' is to confuse the church with the kingdom of God and paralyze the movement of history toward the kingdom."

Although we certainly notice the temptation of superimposing moral criteria on the Eucharist in this context, it should also be noted that to speak of a moralizing of the Eucharist with a view to restricting "participation rights" comes especially easily to a Christianity that has long abandoned the ancient practice of public penance. What if the liberation theologian's interest in the liturgy as a prophetic sign is primarily a way of reminding the Church of the challenge of its own liturgical tradition, when participating in the Eucharist was an occasion of the community's serious moral self-reflection?

Loss of Power

In the light of the confidently thick account of the liturgy as key to social and political resistance and renewal that Schmemann and Pickstock in particular present, it should not be overlooked that, in both cases, the authors do not confine themselves to a simple juxtaposition of liturgy and modern secularism, in which the former exclusively appears as a remedy for the latter. Both Schmemann and Pickstock point out that there were defective developments in liturgical practices and concomitant theological reflection that have paved the way for the various pseudo-, substitute-, and anti-liturgies that dominate the modern arena. While Pickstock merely hints at the problematic trend in the late medieval age — when liturgy became ever more centralized, regulated, and a matter of theatrical spectacles to sustain order — Schmemann offers a challenging account of the demise of Eucharistic theology from the twelfth century onwards, which contributed to liturgical degeneration in the West and which also affected the Christian East. In his view, the First Lateran Council induced a deplorable development when it condemned the claim of Berengarius of Tours that the presence of Christ in the elements was "mystical" or "symbolic," and hence not "real," by simply reversing the formula: real, hence not symbolic or mystical. On Schmemann's reading, Western theology began to collapse the notion of *mysterion* by driving a wedge between reality and symbol, and it was this theological development that prepared the way for the secularist stressing of the world's autonomy and self-sufficiency, and also impacted the theology of worship by encouraging neat distinctions between sacred and profane, natural and supernatural, pure and impure. Essentially, for Schmemann, this development replaced sacramentality by sacrality, and this needs to be reversed in order to awaken the people anew to the genuine character of Christian *leitourgia*.

The impact that such criticism of theological and liturgical developments might have on our understanding and practicing of politics may not be immediately obvious to everyone, and further work in this area is certainly needed. But without a renewed alertness to the theological and liturgical underpinnings of the political that the authors represented in this section seek to further, without a revived sense of its inseparability from questions about and celebrations of the nature, destiny, and truth of human sociality, what else do we have to prevent the political from shrinking to mere pragmatics of power?

7 Liturgy the Basis of Social Regeneration

Virgil Michel, O.S.B.

At the mention of the subject of this article one might be inclined to ask: What has the liturgy to do with social reconstruction or the social question? Can the liturgy help to give jobs or raise wages? Can there be any connection between the liturgy and the social problem?

The moment we deal with the problem of social regeneration, we shall do well to have recourse to the classic Catholic text on the question, the encyclical *Quadragesimo Anno* of the present Holy Father "On Reconstructing the Social Order."

The very idea of social regeneration or reconstruction implies that there is something very much awry with our present social order. Pius XI refers to this fact in the following brief sentence: "Nowadays, as more than once in the history of the Church, we are confronted with a world which in large measure has almost fallen back into paganism." In analyzing conditions the Pontiff speaks of a double danger. This is how he expresses it when he discusses the particular question of private property: "There is, therefore, a double danger to be avoided. On the one hand, if the social and public aspect of ownership be denied or minimized, the logical consequence is Individualism, as it is called; on the other hand, the rejection or diminution of its private and individual character necessarily leads to some form of Collectivism (e.g., communism). To disregard these dangers would be to rush headlong into the quicksands of Modernism."

These, then, are the two dangers the Holy Father warns us to avoid if society is to be regenerated: they are the products of an un-Christian view of life and are therefore pagan at heart; and they are both current symptoms of a diseased social order.

Now this renewal of human society, which must needs bring about a harmonious relation between men, one of cooperation and mutual aid and not one of mutual strife and cut-throat competition, must have its origin and inspiration in religion. The Holy Father quotes his great predecessor Leo XIII to that effect: "For the foundation of social laws being thus laid in religion, it is not hard to establish the relations of members one to another, in order that they may live together in concord and achieve prosperity."

Renewal of Christian Spirit Needed

He is indeed very emphatic on this point: "If we examine matters diligently and thoroughly we shall perceive clearly that this longed-for social reconstruction must be preceded by a profound renewal of the Christian spirit, from which multitudes engaged in industry in every country have unhappily departed. Otherwise, all our endeavors will be futile, and our social edifice will be built, not upon a rock, but upon shifting sand."

Now the question logically arises: Where are we to find this Christian spirit that is essential to the successful regeneration of the social order? The answer was given long ago by the saintly Pius X in a statement that many of you have undoubtedly heard repeated time and again. He first of all expressed it as his keenest desire "that the true Christian spirit flourish again and become more firmly grounded in all the faithful." Then he pointed out the great need "of deriving this spirit from its primary and indispensable source, which is active participation in the sacred mysteries and the public and solemn prayers of the Church."

With this we have come to the liturgy. For the liturgy is nothing else than the solemn and public worship of the Church, her official prayers and blessings, the sacraments, and above all the holy Sacrifice of Christ, the Mass. Pius X not only called this liturgy the indispensable source of the true Christian spirit, but added that the faithful must derive this spirit from the Church's worship by active participation; therefore, not by passive bodily presence, but by being present in such a manner that mind and heart are actively joined to the official worship and take intelligent part in the holy action.

There is no time here to dwell on the meaning of active participation, nor to analyze further the nature of the elements that make up the Church's liturgy. I shall proceed at once to the question: What is the basic idea of this liturgy?

It is that of the Mystical Body of Christ — a concept that was not only well known to the early Christians but also a primary inspiration for all their conduct and life. It was constantly preached by the Church Fathers and taught by the Church down to our own day, but it has often, among the faithful of all ranks, been left in the background, even quite forgotten, especially since the growing dominance of an un-Christian individualism.

The doctrine of the Mystical Body was explained by Christ under the example of the vine and the branches and by St. Paul under the picture of the human body composed of head and members. When through the liturgical initiation of Baptism we enter the Church, by that same fact we become intimately united with Christ as members of the Mystical Body of which he is the Head. Christ is then most truly and supernaturally our Brother, we are all children of God in a very special and sublime manner, we are all brethren together who are intimately united in the one Christ. In this holy fellowship we find a harmonious combination of the two complementary factors of humankind, that is, organic fellowship coupled with full respect for human personality and individual responsibility.

Similarly the liturgy of the Church not only makes and keeps us members of this fellowship, but it always puts the idea of fellowship in Christ into full practice. Just in so far as we participate in the liturgy is so truly the primary and indispensable source of the true Christian spirit; it not only teaches us what this spirit is but also has us live this spirit in all its enactments. In the liturgy the teaching is inseparable from the putting into practice.

This, then, is the true Christian spirit and first and last the supreme lesson of the liturgy as the official worship and life of the Mystical Body of Christ. And this spirit must needs be the source of all further extension and application of the principles of solidarity and fellowship in our common life and civilization.

So it is pointed out by the Holy Father himself. For him this mutual supernatural relationship of men united in Christ is the model towards which all social regeneration must strive. Speaking of the proper economic relations between men he says, for instance: "Where this harmonious proportion is kept, man's various economic activities combine and unite into one single organism and become as members of a common body, lending each other mutual help and service." Again: "Then only will it be possible to unite all in a harmonious striving for the common good, when all sections of society have the intimate conviction that they are members of a single family and children of the same heavenly Father, and further, that they are one body in Christ and everyone members one of another."

In conclusion, I may summarize in what happens to take on the form of a logical syllogism:

- Pius X tells that the liturgy is the indispensable source of the true Christian spirit;
- Pius XI says that the true Christian spirit is indispensable for social regeneration.
- Hence the conclusion: The liturgy is the indispensable basis of Christian social regeneration.

Liturgy: Font of Life in the Body of Christ

This then is the sublime function of the liturgy of the Church: to assimilate us unto Christ, to make us partakers of the Christ-life, of the eternal life of God. We attain God through the mediatorship of Christ who lives and acts in his Church. The life of the Church is this continuing life of Christ. Hence we must seek God first of all in this life of the Church, that is, in her liturgy. Without the latter it is impossible to attain union with Christ. To be in the Church, to be a living member of the Church and of Christ, means precisely to be in living union with the divine Godhead of the Trinity. And so the Church, which has been characterized as the continuation of Christ on earth, is constituted not only of those who by special transmission from the apostles exercise the priestly and missionary office of Christ in an official way, but of all those who by participation in the liturgical life of the Church also live the life of Christ.

Thence arises the beautiful idea of the Church as the Mystical Body of Christ, all the faithful being the members that make up this body, with Christ as the head; and again the idea of the faithful as the branches of the vine which is Christ. "I am the vine; you the branches: he that abideth in me, and I in him, the same beareth much fruit: for without me you can do nothing." The members of the Church of Christ are all engrafted upon him as the vine. They are not an accidental agglomerate or aggregate, like a heap of stone, no matter how close these may be together, but a unified organism. The Church is thus a common fellowship of souls in Christ, a fellowship that extends to all who have been incorporated in Christ. It therefore embraces also the souls of the blessed in heaven — a doctrine which Christian tradition expresses by the term "communion of saints."

8 Worship in a Secular Age

Alexander Schmemann

1

To put together — in order to relate them to one another — the terms *worship* and *secular age* seems to presuppose that we have a clear understanding of both of them, that we know the realities they denote, and that we thus operate on solid and thoroughly explored grounds. But is this really the case? I begin my paper with a question mainly because I am convinced that in spite of today's generalized preoccupation with "semantics," there is a great deal of confusion about the exact meaning of the very terms we use in this discussion.

Not only among Christians in general, but even among the Orthodox themselves there exists in fact no consensus, no commonly accepted frame of reference concerning either *worship* or *secularism,* and thus *a fortiori* the problem of their interrelation. Therefore my paper is an attempt not so much to solve the problem as to clarify it, and to do this if possible within a consistent Orthodox perspective. In my opinion, the Orthodox, when discussing the problems stemming from our present "situations," accept them much too easily in their Western formulations. They do not seem to realize that the Orthodox tradition provides above all a possibility, and thus a necessity, of reformulating these very problems, of placing them in a context whose absence or deformation in the Western religious mind may have been the root of so many of our modern "impasses." And as I see it, nowhere is this task more urgently needed than in the range of problems related to *secularism* and proper to our so-called *secular age.*

2

Secularism has been analyzed, described, and defined in these recent years in a great variety of ways, but to the best of my knowledge none of these descriptions has stressed a point which I consider to be essential and which reveals indeed better than anything else the true nature of secularism, and thus can give our discussion its proper orientation.

Secularism, I submit, is above all *a negation of worship.* I stress — not of God's existence, not of some kind of transcendence and therefore of some kind of religion. If secularism in theological terms is a heresy, it is primarily a heresy about man. It is the negation of man as a worshiping being, as *homo adorans:* the one for whom worship is the essential act which both "posits" his humanity and fulfills it. It is the rejection as ontologically and epistemologically "decisive," of the words which "always, everywhere, and for all" were the true "epiphany" of man's relation to God, to the world, and to himself: "It is meet and right to sing of Thee, to bless Thee, to praise Thee, to give thanks to Thee, and to worship Thee in every place of Thy dominion. . . ."

This definition of secularism most certainly needs explanation. For obviously it cannot be accepted by those, quite numerous today, who consciously or unconsciously reduce Christianity to either intellectual ("future of belief") or socio-ethical ("Christian service to the world") categories, and who therefore think that it must be possible to find not only some kind of accommodation, but even a deeper harmony between our "secular age" on the one hand, and worship on the other hand. If the proponents of what basically is nothing else but the Christian acceptance of secularism are right, then of course our whole problem is only that of finding or inventing a worship more acceptable, more "relevant" to the modern man's secular worldview. And such indeed is the direction taken today by the great majority of liturgical reformers. What they seek is worship whose forms and content would "reflect" the needs and aspirations of the secular man, or even better, of secularism itself. For once more, secularism is by no means identical with atheism, and paradoxical as it may seem, can be shown to have always had a peculiar longing for a "liturgical" expression. If, however, my definition is right, then this whole search is a hopeless dead end, if not outright nonsense. Then the very formulation of our theme — "worship in a secular age" — reveals, first of all, an inner contradiction in terms, a contradiction which requires a radical reappraisal of the entire problem and its drastic reformulation.

3

To prove that my definition of secularism ("negation of worship") is correct, I must prove two points. One concerning worship: it must be proven that the very notion of worship implies a certain idea of man's relationship not only to God, but also to the world. And one concerning secularism: it must be proven that it is precisely this idea of worship that secularism explicitly or implicitly rejects.

First let us consider worship. It is ironic but also quite revealing, it seems to me, of the present state of our theology, that the main "proof" here will be supplied not by theologians but by the *"Religionswissenschaft,"* that history and phenomenology of religions whose scientific study of worship, of both its forms and content, has been indeed virtually ignored by theologians. Yet even in its formative stage, when it had a strong anti-Christian bias, this *Religionswissenschaft* seems to have known more about the nature and meaning of worship than the theologians who kept reducing sacraments to the categories of "form" and "matter," "causality," and "validity," and who in fact excluded the liturgical tradition from their theological speculations.

There can be no doubt, however, that if, in the light of this by now methodologically mature phenomenology of religion, we consider worship in general and the Christian *leitourgia* in particular, we are bound to admit that the very principle on which they are built, and which determined and shaped their development, is that of the *sacramental* character of the world and of man's place in the world.

The term "sacramental" means here that the basic and primordial intuition which not only expresses itself in worship, but of which the entire worship is indeed the "phenomenon" — both effect and experience — is that the world, be it in its totality as cosmos, or in its life and becoming as time and history, is an *epiphany* of God, a means of His revelation, presence, and power. In other words, it not only "posits" the idea of God as a rationally acceptable cause of its existence, but truly "speaks" of Him and is in itself an essential means both of knowledge of God and communion with Him, and to be so is its true nature and its ultimate destiny. But then worship is truly an essential act, and man an essentially worshiping being, for it is *only* in worship that man has the source and the possibility of that knowledge which is communion, and of that communion which fulfills itself as true knowledge: knowledge of God and therefore knowledge of the world-communion with God and therefore communion with all that exists. Thus the very notion of worship is based on an intuition and experience of the world as an "epiphany" of God, thus the world — in worship — is revealed in its true nature and vocation as "sacrament."

And indeed, do I have to remind you of those realities, so humble, so "taken for granted" that they are hardly even mentioned in our highly sophisticated theological epistemologies and totally ignored in discussions about "hermeneutics," and on which nevertheless simply depends our very existence as Church, as *new creation,* as people of God and temple of the Holy Spirit? We *need* water and oil, bread and wine in order to be in communion with God and to know Him. Yet conversely — and such is the teaching, if not of our modern theological manuals, at least of the liturgy itself — it is this communion with God by means of "matter" that reveals the true meaning of "matter," i.e., of the world itself. We can only worship in time, yet it is worship that ultimately not only reveals the meaning of time, but truly "renews" time itself. There is no worship without the participation of the body, without words and silence, light and darkness, movement and stillness — yet it is in and through worship that all these essential expressions of man in his relation to the world are given their ultimate "term" of reference, revealed in their highest and deepest meaning.

Thus the term "sacramental" means that for the world to be means of worship and means of grace is not accidental, but the revelation of its meaning, the restoration of its essence, the fulfillment of its destiny. It is the "natural sacramentality" of the world that finds its expression in worship and makes the latter the essential ἔργον of man, the foundation and the spring of his life and activities as man. Being the epiphany of God, worship is thus the epiphany of the world; being communion with God, it is the only true communion with the world; being knowledge of God, it is the ultimate fulfillment of all human knowledge.

4

At this point, and before I come to my second point — secularism as negation of worship — one remark is necessary. If earlier I mentioned *Religionswissenschaft,* it is because this discipline establishes at its own level and according to its own methodology that such indeed is the nature and the meaning not only of Christian worship, but of worship "in general," of worship as a primordial and universal phenomenon. A Christian theologian, however, ought to concede, it seems to me, that this is especially true of the Christian *leitourgia* whose uniqueness lies in its stemming from the faith in the Incarnation, from the great and all-embracing mystery of the "Logos made flesh." It is indeed extremely important for us to remember that the uniqueness, the *newness* of Christian worship is not that it has no *continuity* with worship "in general," as some overly zealous apologists tried to prove at the time when *Religionswissenschaft* simply reduced Christianity and its worship to pagan mystery-cults, but that in Christ this very continuity is fulfilled, receives its ultimate and truly new significance so as to truly bring all "natural" worship to an end. Christ is the fulfillment of worship as adoration and prayer, thanksgiving and sacrifice, communion and knowledge, because He is the ultimate "epiphany" of man as worshiping being, the fullness of God's manifestation and presence by means of the world. He is the true and full Sacrament because He is the fulfillment of the world's essential "sacramentality."

If, however, this "continuity" of the Christian *leitourgia* with the whole of man's worship includes in itself an equally essential principle of *discontinuity,* if Christian worship being the fulfillment and the end of all worship is at the same time a *beginning,* a radically *new* worship, it is not because of any ontological impossibility for the world to be the sacrament of Christ. No, it is because the world rejected Christ by killing Him, and by doing so rejected its own destiny and fulfillment. Therefore, if the basis of all Christian worship is the Incarnation, its true content is always the Cross and the Resurrection. Through these events the new life in Christ, the Incarnate Lord, is "hid with Christ in God," and made into a life "not of this world." The world which rejected Christ must itself die in man if it is to become again means of communion, means of participation in the life which shone forth from the grave, in the Kingdom which is not "of this world," and which in terms of this world is still to come.

And thus the bread and wine — the food, the matter, the very symbol of this world and therefore the very content of our *prosphora* to God, to be changed into the Body and Blood of Christ and become the communion to His Kingdom — must in the *anaphora* be "lifted up," taken out of "this world." And it is only when the Church in the Eucharist leaves this world and ascends to Christ's table at His Kingdom, that she truly sees and proclaims heaven and earth to be full of His glory and God as having "filled all things with Himself." Yet, once more this "discontinuity," this vision of all things as new, is possible only because at first there is continuity and not negation, because the Holy Spirit makes "all things new" and not "new things." It is because all Christian worship is always *remembrance* of Christ "in the flesh" that it can also be remembrance, i.e., expectation and anticipation, of His

Kingdom. It is only because the Church's *leitourgia* is always cosmic, i.e., assumes into Christ all creation, and is always historical, i.e., assumes into Christ all time, that it can therefore also be eschatological, i.e., make us true participants of the Kingdom to come.

Such then is the idea of man's relation to the world implied in the very notion of worship. Worship is by definition and act a reality with cosmic, historical, and eschatological dimensions, the expression thus not merely of "piety," but of an all-embracing "worldview." And those few who have taken upon themselves the pain of studying worship in general, and Christian worship in particular, would certainly agree that on the levels of history and phenomenology at least, this notion of worship is objectively verifiable. Therefore, if today what people call worship are activities, projects, and undertakings having in reality nothing to do with this notion of worship, the responsibility for this lies with the deep semantic confusion typical of our confused time.

5

We can now come to my second point. Secularism, I said, is above all a negation of worship. And indeed, if what we have said about worship is true, is it not equally true that secularism consists in the rejection, explicit or implicit, of precisely that idea of man and world which it is the very purpose of worship to express and communicate?

This rejection, moreover, is at the very foundation of secularism and constitutes its inner criterion, but as I have already said, secularism is by no means identical to atheism. A modern secularist quite often accepts the idea of God. What, however, he emphatically negates is precisely the sacramentality of man and world. A secularist views the world as containing within itself its meaning and the principles of knowledge and action. He may deduce meaning from God and ascribe to God the origin of the world and the laws which govern it. He may even admit without difficulty the possibility of God's intervention in the world's existence. He may believe in survival after death and the immortality of the soul. He may relate to God his ultimate aspirations, such as a just society and the freedom and equality of all men. In other words, he may "refer" his secularism to God and make it "religious" — the object of ecclesiastical programs and ecumenical projects, the theme of Church assemblies and the subject matter of "theology." All this changes nothing in the fundamental "secularity" of his vision of man and world, in

the world being understood, experienced, and acted upon in its own immanent terms and for its own immanent sake. All this changes nothing in his
fundamental rejection of "epiphany": the primordial intuition that everything in this world and the world itself not only have *elsewhere* the cause and
principle of their existence, but are *themselves* the manifestation and presence of that *elsewhere,* and that this is indeed the life of their life, so that dis-
connected from that "epiphany" all is only darkness, absurdity, and death.

And nowhere is this essence of secularism as negation of worship better
revealed than in the secularist's dealing with worship. For paradoxical as it
may sound, the secularist in a way is truly obsessed with worship. The
"acme" of religious secularism in the West — Masonry — is made up almost
entirely of highly elaborated ceremonies saturated with "symbolism." The
recent prophet of the "secular city," Harvey Cox, felt the need to follow up
his first best-seller with a book on "celebration." Celebration is in fact very
fashionable today. The reasons for this seemingly peculiar phenomenon are
in reality quite simple. They not only do not invalidate, but on the contrary
confirm my point. For on the one hand, this phenomenon proves that whatever the degree of his secularism or even atheism, man remains essentially a
"worshiping being," forever nostalgic for rites and rituals no matter how
empty and artificial is the ersatz offered to him. And on the other hand, by
proving the inability of secularism to create genuine worship, this phenomenon reveals secularism's ultimate and tragic incompatibility with the essential Christian worldview.

Such inability can be seen, in the first place, in the secularist's very approach to worship, in his naive conviction that worship, as everything else in
the world, can be a rational construction, the result of planning, "exchange
of views," and discussions. Quite typical of this are the very fashionable discussions of new symbols, as if symbols could be, so to speak, "manufactured," brought into existence through committee deliberations. But the
whole point here is that the secularist is constitutionally unable to see in
symbols anything but "audio-visual aids" for communicating ideas. Last
winter a group of students and teachers of a well-known seminary spent a
semester "working" on "liturgy" centered on the following "themes": the
S.S.T. [Supersonic Transport], ecology, and the flood in Pakistan. No doubt
they "meant well." It is their presuppositions which are wrong: that the traditional worship can have no "relevance" to these themes and has nothing to
reveal about them, and that unless a "theme" is somehow clearly spelled out
in the liturgy, or made into its "focus," it is obviously outside the spiritual
reach of liturgical experience. The secularist is very fond today of terms such

as "symbolism," "sacrament," "transformation," "celebration," and of the entire panoply of cultic terminology. What he does not realize, however, is that the use he makes of them reveals, in fact, the death of symbols and the decomposition of the sacrament. And he does not realize this because in his rejection of the world's and man's sacramentality he is reduced to viewing symbols as indeed mere illustrations of ideas and concepts, which they emphatically are not. There can be no celebration of ideas and concepts, be they "peace," "justice," or even "God." The Eucharist is not a symbol of friendship, togetherness, or any other state of activity however desirable. Vigils and fasts are, to be sure, "symbolic": they always express, manifest, fulfill the Church as expectation; they are themselves that expectation and preparation. To make them into "symbols" of political protest or ideological affirmation, to use them as means to that which is not their "end," to think that the liturgical symbols can be used arbitrarily — is to signify the death of worship, and this in spite of the obvious success and popularity of all these "experiments."

To anyone who has had, be it only once, the true experience of worship, all this is revealed immediately as the ersatz that it is. He knows that the secularist's worship of relevance is simply incompatible with the true relevance of worship. And it is here, in this miserable liturgical failure, whose appalling results we are only beginning to see, that secularism reveals its ultimate religious emptiness and, I will not hesitate to say, its utterly anti-Christian essence.

6

Does all this mean a simple dismissal of our very theme: "worship in a secular age"? Does this mean that there is nothing we, as Orthodox, can do in this secular age except to perform on Sunday our "ancient and colorful" rites, and to live from Monday until Saturday a perfectly "secularized" life, sharing in a worldview which is in no way related to these rites?

To this question my answer is an emphatic *No.* I am convinced that to accept this "coexistence,"[1] as is advocated today by many seemingly well-

---

1. Nowhere better seen than in the classical argument of the partisans of the "old calendar": on December 25th we can fully share in the "secularized" Western Christmas with its Christmas trees, family reunions, and exchange of gifts, and then on January 7th we have the "true" — religious — Christmas. The tenants of this view do not realize, of course, that had the early Church shared in such an understanding of her relation to the world, she would have never instituted Christmas, whose purpose was precisely to "exorcize," transform, and Christianize an existing pagan festival.

intentioned Christians, would not only mean a betrayal of our own faith, but that sooner or later, and probably sooner than later, it would lead to the disintegration of precisely that which we want to preserve and perpetuate. I am convinced, moreover, that such a disintegration has already begun and is concealed only by the grace-proof walls of our ecclesiastical "establishments" (busy as they are in defending their ancient rights and privileges and primacies and condemning one another as "noncanonical"), peaceful rectories, and self-righteous pieties. To this latter we shall return a little later.

What we have to understand first of all is that the problem under discussion is complicated by something our well-intentioned "conservatives" do not comprehend, in spite of all their denouncing and condemning of secularism. It is the fact of the very real connection between secularism — its origin and its development — and Christianity. Secularism — we must again and again stress this — is a "stepchild" of Christianity, as are, in the last analysis, all secular ideologies which today dominate the world — not, as it is claimed by the Western apostles of a Christian acceptance of secularism, a legitimate child, but *a heresy*. Heresy, however, is always the distortion, the exaggeration, and therefore the mutilation of something true, the affirmation of one "choice" (*hairesis* means choice in Greek), one element at the expense of the others, the breaking up of the catholicity of Truth. But then heresy is also always a question addressed to the Church, and which requires, in order to be answered, an effort of Christian thought and conscience. To condemn a heresy is relatively easy. What is much more difficult is to *detect* the question it implies, and to give this question an adequate answer. Such, however, was always the Church's dealing with "heresies" — they always provoked an effort of creativity within the Church so that the condemnation became ultimately a widening and deepening of Christian faith itself. To fight Arianism St. Athanasius advocated the term *consubstantial*, which earlier, and within a different theological context, was condemned as heretical. Because of this he was violently opposed, not only by Arians but by "conservatives," who saw in him an innovator and a "modernist." Ultimately, however, it became clear that it was he who saved Orthodoxy, and that the blind "conservatives" consciously or unconsciously helped the Arians. Thus, if secularism is, as I am convinced, the great *heresy* of our own time, it requires from the Church not mere anathemas, and certainly not compromises, but above all an effort of understanding so it may ultimately be overcome by truth.

The uniqueness of secularism, its difference from the great heresies of the patristic age, is that the latter were provoked by the encounter of Christianity with Hellenism, whereas the former is the result of a "breakdown" within Christianity itself, of its own deep metamorphosis. The lack of time prevents me from dealing with this point in detail. I shall limit myself therefore to one "symbolic" example directly related to our theme. At the end of the twelfth century a Latin theologian, Berengarius of Tours, was condemned for his teaching on the Eucharist. He maintained that because the presence of Christ in the Eucharistic elements is "mystical" or "symbolic," it is not *real*. The Lateran Council which condemned him — and here is for me the crux of the matter — simply reversed the formula. It proclaimed that since Christ's presence in the Eucharist is *real*, it is not "mystical." What is truly decisive here is precisely the disconnection and the opposition of the two terms *verum* and *mystice*, the acceptance, on both sides, that they are mutually exclusive. Western theology thus declared that that which is "mystical" or "symbolic" is not real, whereas that which is "real" is not symbolic. This was, in fact, the collapse of the fundamental Christian *mysterion*, the antinomical "holding together" of the reality of the symbol and of the symbolism of reality. It was the collapse of the fundamental Christian understanding of creation in terms of its ontological *sacramentality*. And since then, Christian thought, in Scholasticism and beyond it, never ceased to oppose these terms, to reject, implicitly or explicitly, the "symbolic realism" and the "realistic symbolism" of the Christian worldview. "As if God did not exist" — this formula originated not with Bonhoeffer or any modern apostle of "religionless Christianity." It is indeed implied already in Thomism, with its basic epistemological distinction between *causa prima* and *causae secundae*. Here is the real cause of *secularism*, which is ultimately nothing else but the affirmation of the world's autonomy, of its self-sufficiency in terms of reason, knowledge, and action. The downfall of Christian symbolism led to the dichotomy of the "natural" and the "supernatural" as the only framework of Christian thought and experience. And whether the "natural" and the "supernatural" are somehow related to one another by *analogia entis*, as in Latin theology, or whether this analogy is totally rejected, as in Barthianism, ultimately makes no difference. In both views the world ceases to be the "natural" sacrament of God, and the supernatural sacrament to have any "continuity" with the world.

Let us not be mistaken, however. This Western theological framework was in fact accepted by the Orthodox East also, and since the end of the patristic age our theology has been indeed much more "Western" than "Eastern." If secularism can be properly termed a Western heresy, the very fruit of the basic Western "deviation," our own scholastic theology has also been permeated with it for centuries, and this in spite of violent denunciations of Rome and papism. And it is indeed ironic, but not at all accidental, that psychologically the most "Western" among the Orthodox today are precisely the ultra-conservative "Super-Orthodox," whose whole frame of mind is legalistic and syllogistic on the one hand, and is made up, on the other hand, of those very "dichotomies" whose introduction into Christian thought is the "original sin" of the West. Once these dichotomies are accepted, it does not matter, theologically speaking, whether one "accepts" the world, as in the case of the Western enthusiast of "secular Christianity," or "rejects" it, as in the case of the "Super-Orthodox" prophet of apocalyptic doom. The optimistic positivism of the one and the pessimistic negativism of the other are, in fact, two sides of the same coin. Both, by denying the world its natural "sacramentality" and radically opposing the "natural" to the "supernatural," make the world *grace-proof*, and ultimately lead to *secularism*. And it is here, within this spiritual and psychological context, that the problem of worship in relation to modern secularism acquires its real significance.

7

For it is clear that this deeply "Westernized" theology has had a very serious impact on worship, or rather, on the experience and comprehension of worship, on that which elsewhere I have defined as liturgical piety.[2] And it has had this impact because it satisfied a deep desire of man for a legalistic religion that would fulfill his need for both the "sacred" — a divine sanction and guarantee — and the "profane," i.e., a natural and secular life protected, as it were, from the constant challenge and absolute demands of God. It was a relapse into that religion which assures, by means of orderly transactions with the "sacred," security and clean conscience in this life, as well as reasonable rights to the "other world," a religion which Christ denounced by every word of His teaching, and which ultimately crucified Him. It is indeed much easier to live and to breathe within neat distinctions between the sacred and the profane, the natural and the supernatural, the pure and the impure, to understand religion in terms of sacred "taboos," legal prescriptions and obligations, of ritual rectitude and canonical "validity." It is much more difficult to realize that such a religion not only does not constitute any threat to "secularism," but on the contrary, is its paradoxical ally.

2. See my *Introduction to Liturgical Theology* (London: Faith Press, 1966).

And yet this is exactly what happened to our "liturgical piety," and not to worship as such — to its forms and structures, which were too traditional, too much a part of the Church's life to be altered in any substantial degree — but to our "comprehension" of these forms, to what *we* expect and therefore receive from worship. If worship as shaped by the liturgical tradition, the *lex orandi* of the Church, remained the same, its "comprehension" by the faithful became more and more determined by those very categories which the Orthodox liturgical tradition explicitly and implicitly rejects by its every word, by its entire "ethos." And the deep tragedy here is that the imposition of these categories is accepted today to such an extent that any attempt to denounce them, to show their incompatibility with the true spirit and meaning of the *leitourgia,* is met by accusations of *modernism* and other mortal sins. And yet this is not a superficial verbal quarrel, not one of those academic storms which more often than not leave the Church undisturbed. This is truly a matter of life and death, because it is here and only here that the frightening heresy of secularism can find its proper Christian diagnosis and be defeated.

Lack of time compels me to limit myself to one example to show that the "dichotomies" mentioned above, which without any doubt have determined the deep metamorphosis of our liturgical piety, not only do not "connect" and relate one to another God, man, and the world, uniting them in one consistent worldview, but on the contrary, abolish all "communications" and "correspondences" between them.

Thus, for example, to bless water, making it "holy water," may have two entirely different meanings. It may mean, on the one hand, the transformation of something *profane,* and thus religiously void or neutral, into something *sacred,* in which case the main religious meaning of "holy water" is precisely that it is no longer "mere" water, and is in fact opposed to it — as the sacred is to the profane. Here the act of blessing reveals nothing about water, and thus about matter or world, but on the contrary makes them irrelevant to the new function of water as "holy water." The sacred posits the profane as precisely profane, i.e., religiously meaningless.

On the other hand, the same act of blessing may mean the revelation of the true "nature" and "destiny" of water, and thus of the world — it may be the epiphany and the fulfillment of their "sacramentality." By being restored through the blessing to its proper function, the "holy water" is revealed as the true, full, adequate water, and matter becomes again means of communion with and knowledge of God.

Now anyone who is acquainted with the content and the text of the great prayer of blessing of water — at Baptism and Epiphany — knows without any doubt that they belong to the second of the two meanings mentioned above, that their term of reference is not the dichotomy of the sacred and the profane, but the "sacramental" potentiality of creation in its totality, as well as in each of its elements. Yet anyone who is acquainted with our liturgical piety — in this case the "comprehension" by the immense majority of the faithful of the meaning of "holy water" — knows equally well that it is the first meaning which triumphs here to the virtual exclusion of the second one. And the same analysis can be applied, with the same results, to practically every aspect of worship: to sacraments, to the liturgy of time, to heortology, etc. "Sacramentality" has been replaced everywhere by "sacrality," "epiphany" by an almost magical incrustation into time and matter (the "natural"), by the "supernatural."

What is truly disturbing here is that such liturgical piety, such understanding and experience of worship, not only is in no way a challenge to secularism, but is in fact one of its very sources. For it leaves the world profane, i.e., precisely *secular*, in the deepest sense of this term: as totally incapable of any real communication with the Divine, of any real transformation and transfiguration. Having nothing to reveal about world and matter, about time and nature, this idea and this experience of worship "disturb" nothing, question nothing, challenge nothing, are indeed "applicable" to nothing. They can therefore peacefully "coexist" with any secular ideology, any form of secularism. And there is virtually no difference here between liturgical "rigorists," i.e., those who stress long services, compliance with rubrics and the Typicon, and liturgical "liberals," always ready and anxious to shorten, adapt, and adjust. For in both cases what is denied is simply the *continuity* between "religion" and "life," the very function of worship as power of transformation, judgment, and change. Again, paradoxically and tragically, this type of approach towards worship and this kind of liturgical experience are indeed the source and the support of secularism.

8

And this at a time when secularism begins to "crack" from inside! If my reading of the great confusion of our time is correct, this confusion is, first of all, a deep crisis of secularism. And it is truly ironic, in my opinion, that so many Christians are seeking some accommodation with secularism precisely at the moment when it is revealing itself to be an untenable spiritual position. More and more signs point toward one fact of paramount importance: the famous "modern man" is already looking for a path beyond secularism, is again thirsty and hungry for "something else." Much too often this thirst and hunger are satisfied not only by food of doubtful quality, but by artificial substitutes of all kinds. The spiritual confusion is at its peak. But is it not because the Church, because Christians themselves, have given up so easily that unique gift which they alone — and no one else! — could have given to the spiritually thirsty and hungry world of ours? Is it not because Christians, more than any others today, defend secularism and adjust to it their very faith? Is it not because, having access to the true *mysterion* of Christ, we prefer to offer to the world vague and second-rate "social" and "political" advice? The world is desperate in its need for Sacrament and Epiphany, while Christians embrace empty and foolish worldly utopias.

My conclusions are simple. No, we do not need any *new* worship that would somehow be more adequate to our new secular world. What we need is a rediscovery of the true meaning and power of worship, and this means of its cosmic, ecclesiological, and eschatological dimensions and content. This, to be sure, implies much work, much "cleaning up." It implies study, education, and effort. It implies giving up much of that dead wood which we carry with us, seeing in it much too often the very essence of our "traditions" and "customs." But once we discover the true *lex orandi*, the genuine meaning and power of our *leitourgia*, once it becomes again the source of an all-embracing worldview and the power of living up to it — then and only then the unique antidote to "secularism" shall be found. And there is nothing more urgent today than this rediscovery, and this return not to the past — but to the light and life, to the truth and grace that are eternally fulfilled by the Church when she becomes — in her *leitourgia* — that which she is.

9 Elements for the Design of a Eucharist (A Reinterpretive Essay)

Rafael Avila

The Eucharist: A Particular Example of Church-World Relations

If on the one hand the Eucharist is a condensed epistemological moment that the church recovers or recaptures in order to rethink and revise its mission in and with the world, and if on the other hand the gathered church is not supra-humanity, nor parallel-humanity, nor even anti-humanity, but humanity *reflexively* "Christified,"[1] humanity distinguished by "a difference in the level of consciousness," then Latin Americans who celebrate the Eucharist are not — and this we must emphasize — themselves supra–Latin Americans, or parallel–Latin Americans, or even anti–Latin Americans, but simply Latin Americans. They are Latin Americans who, *conscious of the paschal rhythm of their history,* recover this history (and in this sense recover themselves) to celebrate its paschal and eschatological meaning, recovering anew in the process the purpose of their historical thrust. They imagine by and in this "parable in action" not only their history, but also the unexplored universe of their own potentials.

According to Harvey Cox, rites are to society what fantasy is to the individual.[2] Eucharist is therefore collective imagination that creatively fantasizes our history.

---

1. See Rafael Avila, *Teologiá, evangelización y liberación* (Bogotá: Paulinas, 1973), pp. 74ff.

2. Cited by Bernard Besert, *Tomorrow a New Church,* trans. Matthew J. O'Connell (New York: Paulist, 1973), p. 92.

We would assert that if "the church does not signify the church but signifies humanity,"[3] then the relation of church to humanity is the same as that of sign to content. And the Latin American Eucharist, the "moment in which the church is most perfectly itself,"[4] is — or should be — to the history of Latin America what the sign is to the content. Visualize it in the following formula:

$$\text{If} \ldots \quad \frac{\text{Church}}{\text{World (or History)}} = \frac{\text{Sign}}{\text{Content}}$$

$$\text{Then} \ldots \quad \frac{\text{Latin American Eucharist}}{\text{Latin American History}} = \frac{\text{Sign}}{\text{Content}}$$

To put it even more clearly: *the content of the Latin American Eucharist is (or should be) the history of Latin America.*

It should memorialize, therefore, the Latin American liberation in which Christ has been actively present[5] and it should be a prognostic sign of the liberations that should be achieved in order to realize eschatological fulfillment.[6] Latin Americans, therefore, do not celebrate another history, but their own history, and they are not committed to another history but to their own history, just as Jesus himself celebrated his history and self-giving for the people.

It is possible that at this point readers are somewhat surprised or even scandalized, and that there is floating around in their minds questions such as the following: Have you not reduced the Eucharist to nothing more than a secular event or patriotic celebration? Have you not Latin-Americanized the Eucharist to the extent that you have emptied it of its sacred content? And have you not therefore disqualified it as a sacred sign? Where then are Christ and his paschal mystery? Is this not a typical case of historical and secular reductionism? Even more, how can you even call this the Eucharist?

I will begin by repeating what I have said before. "All national history is

---

3. See *Catequesis Latinoamericana*, No. 16, p. 345.

4. Medellín, "Liturgy," 3. Introduction to the Final Document, 5. English translation, CELAM, *The Church in the Present-Day Transformation of Latin America in the Light of the Council*, vol. 2, *Conclusions* (Washington, D.C.: Latin American Bureau, USCC, 1968), cited hereafter as Medellin.

5. Medellín, "Liturgy," 3. Introduction to the Final Document, 5.

6. Avila, *Elementos para una evangelización liberadora* (Salamanca: Ediciones Sígueme, 1971), p. 138.

also sacred history, and for that reason it is preparation for the coming of Christ. God speaks to us in all local histories."[7] The paschal mystery of Jesus Christ is not the private property of Israel or of the church. Rather it includes and affects the entire history of humanity and the eschatological meaning that this history has in itself and in all its parts.

Approximately one hundred fifty years ago we were able to free ourselves from Spanish domination, and we would say that we moved from "conditions of life that were less human to conditions of life that were more human."[8] In this way our country began its paschal mystery, much as Israel began its paschal mystery when it was liberated from Egyptian oppression. And given the fact that "all liberation is an anticipation of the complete redemption of Christ,"[9] that achievement of independence from a foreign power moved us effectively toward the kingdom of liberty. The past, nevertheless, should not divert us, and we cannot live merely by remembering a partial liberation. Today we are committed to the future.

The true battle for independence has not even been fought, and all of us Latin Americans are combatants in this new struggle. The terrible night of battle has *not yet* passed, and the sublime liberty has *not yet* radiated its beams of invincible light. All human beings who remain in chains *have not yet* understood the words of him who died on the cross.[10]

To those who believe that we have emptied the Eucharist of its sacred character, we respond by saying that the history of Latin America, as already suggested, and the content of this history are also the history of salvation, a *locus theologicus,* and a theological word. I must make, however, one other comment. The terms "sacred" and "secular" verbalize or imply a dualistic concept that pits the sacred against the secular. To assert that the Eucharist can be reduced to a mere secular act or to a simple patriotic celebration is once again to be the victim of a dualism alien to Judeo-Christian theology. Moreover, does it make sense to continue talking about patriotic celebrations and religious celebrations? Would it not be better to work out the deeper sense of the former?

I am not attempting here to secularize the sacred, or sacralize the secular. History — the only one we have — is neither sacred nor secular. It has one meaning, and it moves toward one end — namely, the fulfillment of its

---

7. VII Semana Internacional de Catequesis, Comisión 4, No. 3.
8. Paul VI, *Populorum progressio,* 20.
9. Medellin, "Education," 4, 9.
10. Avila, *La Liberación* (Bogotá: Voluntad, 1970), p. 177.

purpose. Nor do we mean to imply that the secular history of Latin America is related to sacred history in a kind of "intimate" unity and that the Eucharist is a celebration of this "deeper" unity. In a unitary vision of history, the problem consists in relating a *part* (the history of Latin America) with the *whole* (the history of humankind), both of which have the same goal, the Parousia. The Latin American Eucharist celebrates the history of Latin America *and* it celebrates its incorporation into the general history of all humankind. From this it derives its paschal and eschatological meaning, for the paschal mystery of Christ has taken place in it.

It is a Eucharist jealous of its particularity, but "not so as to seal itself off from, but . . . open itself to union with the rest of the world, giving and receiving in a spirit of solidarity."[11]

Apolitical Faith?

The "apolitical" nature of the church is an ideological illusion similar to that of the Prophet Jonah, who dreamed that he was riding a whale when in reality he was wallowing around in its entrails.[12]

To discuss, therefore, whether the eucharistic "moment in which the church is most perfectly itself"[13] is or is not a political act has no meaning. This "moment" has from the beginning been political. The real question is whether the church is exercising its critical political function or is legitimizing the existing political system. Consequently this is not an attempt to suggest a politicizing of the liturgy — given the fact, we repeat, that it has always been politicized. What we are attempting to do is to awaken ourselves to the political character of confirming or reorienting the direction of our political conduct and of making the readjustments necessary in order to do so consciously and effectively.

The Eucharist:

- Is political *in itself* as a result of its own context.
- Is political because it occurs necessarily *in a political context.*
- Is political because, lest it betray its prophetic mission, it has *to confront* its own context with the faith.

11. Medellín (Message to the People of Latin America), p. 42 in English edition.
12. G. Gimenez, "La dimensión socio-política de la practica de la fe," *Contacto* 1 (1973): 37.
13. Medellín, "Liturgy," 3.

- Is political because each of the members who participates *has a line* of political conduct.
- Is political although the political lines of the participants may be *different*.
- Is political although the celebrants are *not aware* of the kind of politics in which they are involved.
- Is political because it *radicalizes* and *energizes* politics.
- Is political because it promotes personalization, socialization, and liberation.
- Is political because it celebrates the utopia *awakened* by creative imagination.
- Is political because it inescapably sows seeds of *nonconformity*.
- Is political because here the real *authenticity* of the faith is measured by political commitment.
- Is political because political commitment demands that the faith *do the truth* (verify) and not merely *preach* the truth (verbalize).
- Is political because it *relativizes* every political scheme no matter how appealing it might appear.

As Besert puts it:

To the degree that the celebration of the Eucharist is authentic prophecy of a new world, to the degree that all those who celebrate it are sufficiently removed from their habitual situation, to the degree that the Eucharist is celebrated as a true fiesta, the church injects in all its members seeds of protest.

If they believe that they are hopelessly bound to certain servitudes, it is here that they glimpse that this order of things is not inevitable. If they accept with resignation society as it is or as it has been forced upon them, the creative imagination, awakened by the celebration of the utopia, reveals to them that there are other possible schemes and designs for society.

The Eucharist can be an anesthetic or an evasion. But it can also be the seed of revolution that awakens the mind to what is possible, to what is not yet achieved, to what has not yet even been contemplated by the creative imagination. It is no accident that the celebration of the passover was preceded in Israel many times by political rebellions against foreign occupation.[14]

14. Besert, *Tomorrow a New Church*, pp. 148-49.

The eucharistic gesture, as we have said, takes place necessarily in a political context and cannot avoid a confrontation with faith. When St. Ambrose of Milan communicated to Emperor Theodosius that he could not celebrate the Mass in the Emperor's presence because of his brutal slaughter of innocent persons in Thessalonica, when Pope Vigilius brought to the very heart of the liturgical celebration the siege of Rome (A.D. 537), when in Bolivia protest Masses are celebrated because of unjust repressions, when in Colombia the same thing is done in order to raise questions about the social system — all these examples manifest the deep conviction that the *Eucharist must not* take place without relationship to the political context, and that it cannot be celebrated without judging the political context.

One case can be cited that needs little comment. The archbishop of Asunción, Paraguay, Ismael Rolón, refused to celebrate the traditional Te Deum of thanksgiving on the day of national independence *"as a clear and calculated protest against the state of violence to which the Christian community was being subjected."* Archbishop Rolón explained the reasons for his refusal:

> When the freedom and rights that are linked to the community are systematically violated; when liberation is no more than a word; when the Christian community and its church are openly suffocated in the exercise of their life and evangelical mission of liberation, a liturgical celebration of thanksgiving referring to the heroic deeds of national independence would be meaningless.[15]

The truth is that the refusal to celebrate the Te Deum was a most articulate liturgy, for it expressed very clearly the *prophetic* word directed against the "lords" of Paraguay.

In the "moment in which the church is most perfectly itself," it cannot renounce its prophetic mission. It is not possible to present the body of the Lord in its eucharistic *kerygma* in a den of thieves or in a cave of cowards who want no part of being involved in the problems of the people; that would be to abandon Jesus' commitment to humanity.

We may certainly assume that any liturgical celebration will inevitably take place within a political context, and that this context will not be without a religious significance.[16] The Eucharist is contextualized, not celebrated *in*

15. Cited in *Revista de Equipos Docentes para América Latina* 24 (December 1973): 23. Italics added.
16. Bertrand de Clercq, "Political Commitment and Liturgical Celebration," in *Political*

vacuo, and we should have the courage to recognize it. Better said, the meaning of reality cannot be separated from the vicissitudes of history.

For this reason those who attend the Eucharist have already — or at least should have — their directions of political commitment, though usually they are different and even at times opposed. What should we do in view of this fact? Flee from this intra-ecclesial conflictual situation? No, quite the contrary. It should be confronted. Those who come together, if they are truly Christians, and if in fact they are convinced of their common destiny, should not only be able to come together but also should be able to debate in turn the political means conducive for reaching their stated goals. They should confront their political theses with their faith and should be disposed to the Christian community's judging the quality of their political action together with the eventual compatibility or lack of compatibility with the politics of the gospel. In this way the Eucharist will become a kind of workshop of faith and a laboratory of history. De Clercq expresses it thus:

> It should also be possible for part of this liturgy to consist of a discussion of political points of view so long as there is a strict adherence to the principle that those representing each side in this political debate make their religious motivations clear and are ready to pray together.[17]

In this way faith would not only question political commitment, but this questioning by the faith would demand authenticity and concrete acts. Both would make their mutual demands and both would achieve something by them. Those unaware of the political stakes would also be awakened from their apolitical sleep and be forced to implement their faith with an effective political praxis. In summary, there would be an awakening of the consciousness of one's historical responsibility beyond the intimate relationship between God and me, and the privatized relationship between you and me.

We believe that the politicizing of the liturgy (namely, an awareness of its political character) is not an attempt to popularize the liturgy, nor a simple therapy against boredom among the faithful, and certainly not a calculated design to attract Christians who have withdrawn from the church. It is, we believe, a gesture of responsibility against implicit support of political programs which Christians explicitly do not want to support. Nothing is more dangerous, we repeat, than unrecognized power. One must ask, therefore, is it

---

Commitment and Christian Community, ed. Alois Muller and Norbert Greinacher, Concilium 84 (New York: Herder and Herder, 1973), p. 113.

17. De Clercq, "Political Commitment and Liturgical Celebration," p. 116.

not possible that the depoliticization of the liturgy is the fundamental reason why the Eucharist has little or no attraction for the majority of males?

The Eucharist as the Cultural Objectification of History

In the first part of this work we saw that one of the peculiarities of Israel consisted in its having produced a new ritualistic form, converting religious rites into a system of objectifying their historical exploits. Is it possible also for the Eucharist to objectify our history (the diachronic aspect) and also our sociological structure (the synchronic)?

One may respond in two ways. Above all we should keep in mind that the church is a structural sign in which the messages in their totality can be different from their parts.[18] The command of Jesus, "Do this" — which refers primarily to his giving of himself for the people, and secondarily to the ritualistic commemoration of this giving — binds the protagonist of the event to the gestures, the words, and the elements that were utilized in the celebration to predict it.

"This," therefore, is the community that celebrates Christ's giving of himself for the people, but also the natural elements that were not in their "native" state but were the "fruit of human labor." This may be diagramed as follows:

Sign: Human Beings (subject) — the ecclesial community

Elements (object) — bread and wine, fruit of human labor.

Content: Our own history as the Body of Christ in gestation of the *Total* Christ mediating the dialectic of death (oppression) and resurrection (liberation).

When, therefore, we affirm that the Eucharist is (or should be) the objectification of our history, *we understand that the objectification is an action* (acted out by the ecclesial community) and not a thing (bread and wine). These are the elements utilized in an objectifying action, but they are not the objectification itself. They derive their significance from the general

18. The concept of structure is not easily expressed, but we can attempt a tentative definition. Structure is "a system that presents laws and properties of a totality. These laws of totality are therefore different from the laws or properties of the parts of the system." See Jean Piaget, "Genesís y estructura, en la sicología de la inteligencia," *Seis estudios de sicología* (Barcelona: Seix Barral, 1971), p. 205.

context of the eucharistic action. The community, therefore, does not objectify the history in the elements (bread and wine) but in the total eucharistic *act* that comprehends these gestures, words, and elements. The significance cannot be monopolized by one single component of objectifying action, and one who "reads" the sign cannot decompose it (chemically) in order to retain only the significance of one of these elements (bread and wine). It is the total act that has significance, not the parts.

But someone will ask, "Is it not the church that is objectified in the eucharistic action? Furthermore, is it not the history of all the Latin American church that we should be celebrating and not the history of one particular people?" What is it, therefore, that the church objectifies in the Eucharist? Its own mystery or that of humanity?

We must remember that the church does not possess its own private mystery. What is particular to the church is its awareness of the mystery — and from this it derives its responsibility.

The forward thrust of the Parousia is not something "owned" by the church: it belongs to humanity as such; it is humankind's forward thrust. It follows from this that the church does not have its own future course. The only future projection that the church can assume is that of humankind. And if the church joins forces with humanity in this venture, it is not for the purpose of superimposing the church's future on that of humankind. The church can only *participate* in the unique forward thrust of history. Its own future depends on it.[19]

Inasmuch as the Eucharist is that "moment in which the church is most perfectly itself," it cannot be an act of narcissistic self-contemplation contradicting its purpose for being in the world. The Eucharist is fundamentally *an act in which the church measures its centrifugal character,* aware that it is celebrating a venture that is not its own private property but is simply the expression of humanity moving toward its own final destiny.

When humanity, here represented by the church, proclaims, "This is my Body," it is affirming itself — and "the fruit of human labor" (concretized in the bread and the wine) — to be the Body of Christ, the Total Christ. But the church is not only this, for with the eyes of faith and the tools of social analysis we understand that this Body is broken; it is torn and divided between exploiters and exploited.[20] Therefore, if we are asked what it is that we present

19. See Avila, "La profecía en América Latina," Seminario de Teología Latinoamericana, Bogotá, September 1973, manuscript.

20. Works dealing specifically with the relation between social classes and Christianity

to the Father as the Body of Christ, the answer is that we present the Body as we have discovered it with socio-analytical tools as the broken and divided Body. The "bread of offertory" actually presents to humanity a Body that is torn and broken, the same Body that is presented to the Father. "This is my Body" becomes "This is my Body divided among exploiters and exploited." Those who see Christ in this way cannot avoid sensing the challenge to break down the ignominious "wall of separation" in order to create from the two a single new humanity (Eph. 2:15).

That Christ is *also* in the bread and in the wine implies that he is not only human, but also "the fruit of human labor," by which human beings humanize nature and also humanize themselves. This implies further that the process of elaboration of this fruit of labor is not alien to the process of christogenesis, and that in it Christ places (offers, proposes) himself before us as the fruit of our "gestation," *obligating us to evaluate our offering and the human process that precedes and defines the offering — that is, the social relationships of production hidden under the appearances of bread and wine.* The real is not only the material (a piece of bread), but also what is produced. The source of the bread (as a cultural product) is human labor.[21]

It remains therefore that the bread and the wine are not objectified in the Eucharist as part of a material, reified cosmos, but as a product of a properly social phenomenon of sharing a meal, of taking together. Nor are the bread and wine to be "swallowed as is"; they are to be examined and judged (critically, as in a *krisis*) before being eaten, with a view to righting the social relationships of production that precede and shape the fruit of human labor. Communicants, emulating their teacher Jesus Christ, will focus their attention not only on the thing presented (offered, proposed), but also on the human action that precedes and defines it.[22]

---

are Giulio Girardi, "Cristianismo y lucha de clases," a lecture given at the University of Deusto, 1969; Noel Olaya, *Unidad cristiana y lucha de clases* (Montevideo: Tierra Nueva, 1972), pp. 57-67; Gustavo Gutiérrez, *A Theology of Liberation* (Maryknoll, NY: Orbis, 1973), pp. 340-49; and Benoit Dumas, *Los dos rostros alienados de la Iglesia una* (Buenos Aires: Latinoamérica Libros, 1971).

21. Enrique Dussel says essentially the same thing in a different context: *Historia de la fe cristiana y cambio social en América Latina* (Salamanca: Sígueme, 1973), p. 75. He cites Marx: "The principal error of all materialisms until now (including that of Feuerbach) consists in making the object the reality; the objective being of sensibility has been understood only under the form of an object, or of an intuition, but not as a tangible human fact, as praxis."

22. See Chapter 3, "Camilo Torres and Priorities," in Rafael Avila, *Worship and Politics* (Maryknoll, NY: Orbis, 1981).

The bread and the wine are not there simply as themselves, nor simply as something material, much less as something magical. They are there as products of the community that celebrates its labor, its results, and its manner of production.

The question is not so analogical as it may appear, for it deals with a "collective organism" (the Total Christ) that should reevaluate continually the way it produces the fruit of its labor (bread and wine, although not necessarily these things alone) in order to establish whether it is diverting or blocking the autogestation of the Parousia of humankind. It is a question of ontogenesis, of anthropogenesis, of christogenesis.

For this reason, when the fruit of human labor is being exploited by a minority, the Parousia — the full possession and enjoyment of this fruit — is blocked by those who are depriving the community of its increase in value. In order to prevent this anomaly, the church celebrating the Eucharist should despoil the exploiters in order to recover the fruit of labor (the Body of Christ) for the whole community. In this way the Body of Christ will not be appropriated by a few.

Objectification of Our Structural Center

We have already said that the experience of the exodus was "the central event around which the Hebrews organized their total perception of reality" (Harvey Cox). On the other hand, we have seen that they objectified this principle of organization and interpretation of reality, and that in doing so they favored (or determined) the characterization of themselves as a people and of the permanent source of the nourishment of their faith. Here they learned and reviewed the history of their community and the liberating acts of Yahweh.

What is the "structuring center" around which we should organize our basic perception of reality? It would appear to be *our first independence,* because it is in reference to it that we discover our "personality" as offspring of the "prepotent Hispanic father" and of the indigenous violated mother.[23] It is here in the confluence of these two genetic and cultural sources (one Eu-

23. The mythical image is that of Enrique Dussel. He writes: "Bartolomé [de las Casas] said of the Indian, referring to the alienation of the indigenous woman, that the mother of Latin America cohabitated with the prepotent Hispanic father, who in turn killed the woman's husband — the Indian — and had children (the *mestizo,* the Latin American) who became the servants." See Dussel's work cited in note 21, pp. 67, 85.

ropean and the other of Asiatic origin) that we begin to recognize our past and also our historical identity, even though with many lacunae. The first rebellion was the self-affirmation of our personality and existence (I rebel, therefore I exist, as Albert Camus would say).

Our historical memory goes back to the traumatic fact that an aggressive and voracious "father" violated (he did not seduce) an unsuspecting and naive "servant." Herein began our history as children of a slave and not as free persons; we were dependent from the beginning. This is the reason why the feats of our first independence — as imperfect as they might have been — are an indication of our emancipative possibilities, a reminder of the self-affirmation of our own "personality" confronting colonizers, and a harbinger of our complete liberation. For this reason we need to objectify our first liberation in the paschal celebration not only to connect it to its own plenitude, but also to nourish our faith, review our own emancipative attempts, and finally define ourselves as a people. Only in this way can the consciousness of our historical destiny be awakened.

How can we recognize ourselves in a Eucharist in which "the structuring center" of our own corporate "personality" is not the center of our celebration? Would a liturgy be authentically Latin American in which the characteristic features of our own "countenance" were only peripheral and secondary?

How, therefore, can we incorporate into the Eucharist this "structuring center" without displacing the other center who is Christ? Someone will ask, "Is Christ the center of the Eucharist, or are the events of independence the center?" "Will it be christocentric, or anthropocentric, or temporal?"

It would appear, in the first place, that Christians without knowing it transfer to their Christology the circular and spherical scheme of the Hegelian concept of society and of history. For Hegel a historical formalization densifies into a determined form or essence, unifying and totalizing it, and refracting it into all its categories or spheres. Each historical epoch was characterized by a determined formalization. (Rome, for example, was "formed" by its exaltation of law.) This form was the "circle of circles," the "sphere of spheres." It radiated into all the others; it was ubiquitous and all-pervasive.[24]

When this conceptualization is transferred to the church, it is verbalized in such expressions as Christocentric, Christocentricity, Christ the center, Christ the keystone, around whom all things "revolve." In this, as in all topical metaphors, a theological datum is represented by a geometrical figure — the circle, the sphere. We do not reject the need our knowledge has of these

---

24. Eugenio Trías, *Teoría de las ideologías* (Barcelona: Península, 1970), p. 53.

topical images, which moreover are not exclusive to theology. Marx, for example, also spoke of infra- and super-structures, thus utilizing an architectural image of human society.

What we want to emphasize is that this circular scheme emasculates Christology, making us human beings the irrelevant periphery, irrelevant to the Total Christ. It is as if we were the Christological surplus. At the hermeneutical level this signifies that only the biblical word (Christ included) is the center and that all others are in the world of shadows, incapable of speaking their word. Such a theology can only be applied, adapted, or accommodated to the Latin American reality but in no way reinterpreted by the word that God speaks to us from within our continent.

A Christ without his "members" is not the Total Christ. Without a body there is no head, and without the head the body is decapitated. St. Augustine, faithfully interpreting St. Paul, said that we are the Total Christ: "There are many human beings and they are one thing; there are many Christians and they are one Christ. Christians with their head who ascended into heaven are the one Christ: not that he is one and we are many, but that we many are one in him. There is therefore one man-Christ, head and body."[25]

If a geometric image is necessary, we propose an elliptic Christology, an elliptic evangelization, an elliptic hermeneutic, and an elliptic Eucharist. In all of these the outstanding feature would be the *dialectical* articulation of the two "centers": Christ and the Latin American in the first place, the situation of Christ and our situation in the second place, the biblical word and the word from Latin America in the third place, the paschal deed and our own liberating deeds in the fourth place. The circle, having a single center, does not appear therefore to be adequate to "geometrize" the dialectical bipolarity of these two variants. The ellipse, on the other hand, with its two "centers," ably does so.

The Eucharist so understood would establish for us a more adequate relationship with Christian tradition because it would be the *kerygmatic* proclamation of the paschal deed of Jesus Christ, the radical liberation of the entire person and of all persons, the basic act that suggests the possibility and the meaning of our own liberation. Remember that "the Risen Christ . . . is the goal that the designs of God set for the development of humankind, so that 'we may all reach the stature of the integral person.'"[26] This would guarantee us *continuity*.

---

25. St. Augustine, *Enarratio in Ps. CXXVII*, No. 3, P.L. 37, 1678.
26. Medellín, "Education," 9.

On the other hand, to celebrate our historical deeds and to become aware of the social relationships of production hidden in the appearances of bread and wine, we would reevaluate our incipient independence as the "anticipation of complete redemption in Christ," and it would implant in us the conviction that "all 'growth in humanity' brings us closer to 'reproducing the image of the Son so that he will be the firstborn among many brothers and sisters.'"[27] In contrast, it would force us to revise the Christogenetic process that precedes and defines "the fruit of human labor." In this there would be a fundamental *discontinuity*.

The Affirming Context of the Eucharist

We earlier emphasized that in Old Testament times there were religious festivals that tended to readjust social inequalities. This was possible within the socio-cultural framework of Israel because their laws and organization were at one and the same time religious and juridico-political. Today, however, the church does not have the power to declare laws as was done in ancient times when debts were pardoned, slaves were liberated, and deprived owners reclaimed their properties. Moreover, even if the church could do this today, it is doubtful whether there would be a periodic attempt to enact laws that would readjust social inequalities. The problem consists rather in struggling for the creation of *objective conditions* that will make fellowship, justice, and peace possible.

We believe that at this historical moment *the only legitimate context for the Eucharist — a Eucharist such as we have proposed — is one in solidarity with the movement for the liberation of our continent*, and more concretely with the exploited classes of our society. Any declared alliance with the dominant classes will create an emasculated context for the Eucharist, given the fact that such a tactic eliminates with the "right hand" all that the "left hand" accomplishes.

A community celebration of the Eucharist solemnly commits all Christians to struggle actively against everything that discriminates against and disintegrates humanity. It is a sacrilege, according to St. Paul, when a Christian community, after having received the same bread and the same wine, continues to maintain social, economic, and cultural differences under the pretext that a mystical unity has been established. If church assemblies are,

27. Medellín, "Education," 9.

to the observers of the contemporary world, signs of separation that emphasize class differences and the retention of privileges, at that moment the church automatically ceases to be the church because it is not a productive sign of the unity of the human genus.[28]

It cannot be otherwise if the total language of the institutional church is contradicted by the eucharistic word we proclaim. Even though we shout loudly and clearly something different, there would still exist a contradictory gap. Instead of this anomaly, the Eucharist should be the socio-political reactivator and the occasion of confrontation in which the church judges its commitment to the interests of the socially exploited class. The church's option therefore must be clear and sharp. Any accommodation will reduce its role to that of being a lubricant of the social system, and "this mode of approaching the problem moves easily to an ideology of unity without conflict"[29] and ignores and disparages the real conditions of the paschal dynamic in which only a church that dares to "drink his cup" can expect Christ's resurrection.

To opt for the poor does not mean only a vocation of poverty. It implies also supporting the cause of the poor, identifying openly with them against those who oppress and burden them. For this reason the class struggle should not be left aside, for the goal is not the *"reduction of tensions" but the overcoming of them,* creating better conditions of life for those who — until now — have lived with rejection, ignominy, and oppression. To manifest solidarity with the poor in the class struggle presupposes a radical reorientation of the community of faith. It will no longer be the pillar of the established order (as during the time when the church supported the Constantinian government), but an element that challenges the established order. From being an instrument of preservation the church will become an agent of transformation, and rather than defending decrepit orders of creation (which in itself, because of the transformations it undergoes, is always decrepit and renewing itself at the same time) the church will try to implement the order of the announced new creation. Here the disadvantaged will be the privileged, and the last will be first.[30]

When Christians celebrate the Eucharist and are really committed to the interests and struggles of the oppressed, this solidarity (conviction and op-

28. J. M. González Ruiz, in *Víspera 6* (1970): 28.

29. Hugo Assmann, *Opresión-Liberación, desafío a los cristianos* (Montevideo: Tierra Nueva, 1971), p. 166.

30. Julio de Santa Ana, "Notas para una ética de liberación a partir de la Biblia," *Pueblo Oprimido, Señor de la Historia* (Montevideo, 1972), pp. 129-130.

tion) cannot but affect the general structure of eucharistic action. In the first place it will affect eucharistic action by means of a deserved respect for its forms of expression, its festivities, and its rites, and in the second place by the relationship (incarnation) of the Eucharist with its cultural world. The Old Testament prophets, rather than attacking the agricultural celebrations of the Canaanites, connected these rites to the exodus and gave them a historical meaning that removed them from idolatry. The prophets of today will know how to relate the agricultural festivities of our *campesinos* and the rites of our workers with the paschal deed of the Eucharist in which, as we have already said, there will also be included our emancipative deeds. What the *campesinos* and agricultural workers need to understand — inclined by the nature of their work to begin again what is already begun — is that they have a history, a past, a relation with the whole social system of production, and that they have a destiny. There is no other occasion more propitious for awakening our people to structural contradictions than when they celebrate the "maternity" of nature, which, made fertile by human effort, gives birth to the fruit of labor, labor that can be laid bare in eucharistic action in order to discern its Christogenetic inner nature.

To contextualize these festivities in the general framework of a history that moves toward its fulfillment is to relativize and temporalize them. But we can thus eliminate the idolatrous dangers inherent in cosmological rites and also free them from the recidivistic scheme of the eternal return, which from the sociological point of view is the sacralization of intra-systemic fatalism. Or to put it another way, it is the absolutization of the impossibility of an act that would be really trans-systemic.[31]

Koinonia of the Word, of the Bread, and of Possessions

Of the Word. How many times have we heard Christians complain of the loneliness that they experience when participating in the Eucharist? "We go every Sunday," they say, "and we see faces, *but we don't know who they are.*" Those present do not know each other either in the Greek or in the biblical sense. How can they reach out to each other, communicate, share their problems, their anxieties, their doubts, their questions, if there is no opportunity

---

31. The masses express this fatalism in statements such as: "Nothing can be done"; "It's the same old story" or "the same old thing"; "All is lost. . . ." It is even more difficult today to convince the people that something can be done when repressive powers are seen as the very embodiment of the apocalyptic beasts.

to share the word? It is not only the biblical word that should be spoken in the assembly; it is also the everyday word, the word of our common experience, in order that from sharing there will emerge the demands of *the Word*. Only by establishing these kinds of conditions can the everyday word be shared and thus will it be possible to practice the communion of communication. This would break down many walls of isolation and permit persons to reveal themselves and speak *their* word.

Why all this verticalism of the word? Because we have made the celebration of our sacrament or Passover so sophisticated that we have "packaged" it, we have filled it with formalism to such a degree that no one dares to speak. Silence is more a symbol of fear than an indication of praise. No one dares to speak because they fear being "out of place," and it would appear that the average believer therefore has neither voice nor vote and that their daily experiences are really of no importance. Faith and daily life are permanently severed.

Why not welcome in the Eucharist the voice of those without voice, the prophetic voice, the contesting voice, the voice of the poor who have no access to any other means of communication? Is it not the responsibility of the church to make the voice of the silenced and suppressed resonant in the eucharistic environment?

Don't we say that the poor are the visible face of Christ in the world? And that the oppressed masses are suffering even now his passion? And that through them Christ is now speaking his word? And if we do not hear them, are we not turning our backs on Christ? And if we refuse to hear them, are we not refusing to hear him?

Of the Bread. Sharing the word will prepare for the communion of the bread, of the wine, and of the food. All those participating in the celebration should bring their contribution to the Lord's supper, for only in this way can they share the bread. In reality, we repeat, those who do not practice the *koinonia* of food (of the bread) do not discern that *though many, we are one Body, because we share the one bread,* and they do not discern the ecclesial Body of Christ.

In other words, they do not see the church in the multitude of Christians who gather for the sacrament. Even less do they see Christ in the plurality of his members. They do not see the church or Christ as the sources of universal communion. Nor do they feel challenged by the economic, political, and cultural differences. If the bread, as we have said, is the fruit of labor, to share the bread is to share the results of our labor, and it can be the grounds for discovering our labor as collaboration.

No one, therefore, who is monopolizing the fruit of labor can celebrate the Eucharist with a clear conscience. How could Christ consecrate the fruit of despoliation? Who could share the fruits of work without discovering that this bread is the result of co-labor and co-elaboration? Who can share the fruit of labor who has not participated in its production? Even more, can the church share the fruit of labor in a society divided between exploiters and exploited? Can the church consecrate the fruit of labor (bread and wine) without "consecrating" the social relationships of production that make work possible? Or is this bread come down from heaven not incarnated in the bread that is offered up from the earth?

Of Possessions. What is said here is implicit in what has been said above. The Eucharist should promote the creation of human communities with an original form of economico-communitarian infrastructure that will shore up communion-union in the faith. At the same time, and to the degree possible within the system, it should demonstrate the practicability of utopia by heralding a universal communion to which one cannot come without committing oneself to the creation of the objective infrastructural conditions necessary. The sharing of possessions should have no other meaning.

Great doses of hidden Manichaeism anesthetize the conscience of many Christians who prefer "mystical" or merely religious community to human community.

A Eucharist in which this genuine threefold *koinonia* is practiced will be an authentic protest against the monologue of individualism, against the monopolization of the fruit of human labor, and against the atomization and division of humankind between exploiters and exploited. This would be a true cultural revolution.

Conclusion

To conclude, we want to point out that the interests of contemporary humanity move progressively and increasingly toward the political. To attempt an ostensibly apolitical liturgy in a world essentially political is absurd — unless one wants to banish the Eucharist from history. In this case a policy of withdrawal from the world has been adopted. And if withdrawal is effected consciously, we can only suspect that it is being done to separate the people from their concern with this world.

On the other hand, it appears that today it is impossible for the church to be composed of members whose political interests are antagonistic (not merely different), and with good reason, because the Eucharist cannot be celebrated by persons who are radically divergent in regard to their political designs. Participation in the same Mass by persons of opposing social classes has been possible only by the anonymity that frequently characterizes the composition of the church.[32] A hypothesis that consciously attempts to reconcile antagonistic classes means that there has been acceptance of a Eucharist put at the service of a divided society. It consequently opposes the movement for the elimination of classes. It is therefore a Eucharist consciously at the service of the status quo.

For a conciliationist ecclesiology *the subjects of a eucharistic celebration* can be the members of all social classes. But for an ecclesiology that sees itself affected by the division of classes, the subjects of the eucharistic celebration can be only the members of the socially exploited class and their effective allies, including converts coming from the exploiting class.

We confirm therefore from another point of view what we stated earlier, that the only legitimate context for the Eucharist is one of ecclesial solidarity with the undertaking of the liberation of the oppressed, because the poor and the oppressed cannot be isolated abstractly from the social class to which they belong. This implies solidarity with the exploited class and conflict with the exploiting class. Therefore the only persons qualified to participate in this celebration are those working for liberation, with the understanding that this implies the suppression of the objective conditions that make it possible for some to be exploited and others to be exploiters.

Unity is the final goal and not the point of departure, and to reach it, it is necessary to embrace the essential conflict in order to destroy the real causes of division. To assume that the church can be a "place of worship for all" is to confuse the church with the kingdom of God and paralyze the movement of history toward the kingdom. The Eucharist retains therefore the same ambiguity and conflict inherent in history, and only those who truly accompany Christ in his work of the paschalization of society can truly participate. Excluding one or more social sectors is not done with the malicious intention of excluding them from the kingdom, but precisely the opposite, in the hope that they can eventually become a part of the kingdom.

In this way the Eucharist is not reduced to a mere positivist reflection of the class society, but rather becomes the prophetic judgment not only on the celebration itself, but also on the restriction of participation. That only one

32. Jean Guichard, *Iglesia, lucha de clases y estrategias políticas* (Salamanca: Sígueme, 1973), p. 45.

social segment can celebrate the Eucharist is a prophetic and challenging judgment.

We conclude by stating explicitly that the Eucharist and the liturgy in general appear to be *a kind of symbolico-structural exegesis of history.* As interpretation, it should utilize socio-analytic instruments, and it cannot avoid the ambiguity of all interpretation. As symbolic, it should utilize the same symbols that the people utilize to celebrate their history. As exegesis of *history,* the content of that exegesis should be history. The Eucharist will be in this way a hermeneutical variant of history, celebrative and evaluative of the historical process. It will be a hermeneutic that is in a certain sense imitative, in a certain sense dramatic, but always in constitutive reference to the historical event.

10 Liturgy and Modernity

Catherine Pickstock

Efforts to find alternatives to liberal individualism and, in particular, problems relating to social fragmentation and the construction of the self have generated interest in a liturgical critique of modernity. The deployment of liturgy as a political category, however, needs to be examined carefully. First, liturgy is a special case of ritual behavior. In addition to designating the commitment of individuals or communities to particular traditions, liturgy occupies a unique mediating position between art and politics, which ensures that the political can transcend its own immediate ends and, at the same time, prevent the artistic from lapsing into a "magic circle" of compensatory realities and merely negative or utopian critiques of politics. Second, modernity has produced a parody of the liturgical, a sort of anti-liturgical liturgy that confirms the dominance of politics and art without liturgy. Third, there are serious problems with any purely secular concepts of liturgy and, in order to develop a political critique of modernity, liturgy needs to be seen as a theological as much as a political category.

Why should the term "liturgical" be preferred over "ritual"? For two reasons. First, as Talal Asad has pointed out, since the nineteenth century "ritual" has come to indicate a specific activity within a delimited sphere, rather than a pattern of social action.[1] Liturgy does not have this freight of questionable, Western scientific assumptions about a distinctive religious category occupying an isolated superstructural sphere. Second, ritual may denote merely me-

---

1. Talal Asad, *Genealogies of Religion: Discipline and Reasons of Power in Christianity and Islam* (Baltimore: The Johns Hopkins University Press, 1993), pp. 55-79.

chanical repetitions divorced from any informing narrative. Consequently, questions arise as to the relation of rite to myth. "Liturgy," however, rejects any myth-rite dualism, because it assumes that as a signifying system a rite is always possible only in terms of its organization around some privileged transcendent signifier, even if this remains mysterious and open to interpretation. Of course, this assumed transcendent can be metaphysically immanent. In this essay, however, since purely neutral descriptions are not possible, "liturgy" is used as much as an evaluative as an empirical term. While all cultures necessarily manifest the liturgical, those cultures positing something metaphysically transcendent fulfill the liturgical best.

Liturgy as a Political Category

In Plato's *Laws*, the city of the Magnesians is described as more possible than the *Kallipolis* of the *Republic*.[2] This has led many readers to believe that it is a "second best," but more practicable city. As Zdravko Planinc and others have shown, however, such is not the case.[3] The city of the Magnesians is more ideal than the *Kallipolis*, because it is based on the sharing of goods among all citizens,[4] whereas in the *Republic* this is true only of the guardian-class. The highest aspiration of the rest of the population is to mind its own business. How can the "more ideal" also be the more "realizable"? The answer lies in the fact that, whereas the goodness of the *Kallipolis* relies on the philosophers' contemplation of the Forms, in the Magnesian city it is a function of participation in the unity of the cosmos. In turn, the latter reflects the unity of the realm of the Forms and is mediated to each citizen collectively via the continual performance of liturgy. In the Magnesian city, every day of the year has its own specific festival. Thus, the everyday constantly reaches beyond itself in worship. The city is bound together by an extraordinary rhythmic pattern: "the whole city can utter one and the same word," and all citizens "are strung together on a thread of song and dance."[5] At the same time, this rhythm refers the Beyond to nature and to the eternal.[6]

2. Plato, *Laws*, 702c-e, 739c-e, 968b-69d, contrasted to the *Kallipolis* as a *paradeigma* laid up in heaven, *Republic*, 592b.
3. Zdravko Planinc, *Plato's Political Philosophy: Prudence in the Republic and the Laws* (London: Gerald Duckworth and Co Ltd, 1991), pp. 157, 262 and 297 n. 1.
4. *Laws*, 942c.
5. *Laws*, 664a and 653c, respectively.
6. See Planinc, *Plato's Political Philosophy: Prudence*, pp. 164 and 261-62; on the city of

These opening remarks about the *Laws* already contain an important clue about liturgy as a political category. The liturgical fuses the most realistic with the most ideal. It is realistic in that all reflective conceptual behavior and thought is grounded in a *Lebenswelt,* which one would have to characterize at least partially in terms of certain repeated rhythms that make reasoning possible and that are themselves without rational foundations. It immediately follows that this reality, presupposed by everything else, has also an *ideal aspect,* for these original patterns privilege certain formations, shapes, and sounds over others. Here lies the origin of unquestioned value or transcendence on which all else depends, even if, metaphysically, this transcendence lies within the immanent realm. It is impossible for human culture to avoid this starting point. In other words, the ideal aspect of human life is not an optional extra, but something essential to specifically human action. To say that human life has a fundamentally liturgical character is a way of recognizing that even the most pragmatic actions exceed themselves by pointing to the unquestioned and the transcendent, which is the horizon within which they operate.

Specifically, *human* existence is liturgical in the same way it is linguistic and social. All cultures begin in liturgy, which fuses the repetition of ideal value with physical inscription upon bodies, places, times and motions. This fusion results in several further characteristics of all human cultures — characteristics modern Western society seems in danger of losing. The liturgical relativizes the everyday without denying its value. Personal joys are not allowed to become over-inflated, because they are placed within the context of communal enjoyment and are seen as but specific manifestations of a continuous communal celebration. Inversely, personal sorrows are shared with others and are viewed in the context of cosmic patterns including such tragic eventualities. In various ways, the pattern itself will allow the individual to see his sorrow as redeemed and transfigured. By contrast, a modern individual may alternate between seeking refuge from public misery in private delight, and escaping personal sorrow through absorption in the impersonal world of the media. In neither case, however, do the public and the private mediate each other in a liturgical fashion: they remain *dirempted.* This

the *Laws* as based on the One and on cosmic patterns, see *Laws,* 945d-e, and especially Book X; see also Jacob Klein, *Greek Mathematical Thought and the Origin of Algebra,* trans. E. Brann (Cambridge, MA: MIT Press, 1968); Hans Joachim Kramer, *Plato and the Foundations of Metaphysics: A Work on the Theory of the Principles and Unwritten Doctrines of Plato with a Collection of the Fundamental Documents,* trans. John Catan (Albany: State University of New York Press, 1990); Harold Fredrick Cherniss, *The Riddle of the Early Academy* (Berkeley: University of California Press, 1945).

situation inevitably gives way to various pathologies. People cannot live with themselves and in public simultaneously. But this co-dwelling is exactly what liturgy makes possible.

If liturgy is able to situate people within a meaningful cosmos, it is also not complacent. On the contrary, because liturgy refers a society to something beyond itself, it can generate an immanent critique of that society in the sense that it does not introduce the wholly new and extraneous. Yet, it is *more* than immanent, in that it allows for the disclosure of something different from the transcendent. By contrast, modernity tends to assume that "critique" can come only from the margins and the semi-excluded. This has made many traditional situations almost incomprehensible, such as where the monarch was accompanied by a priest-figure who performed the role of his critical conscience, and yet could not be dispensed with, because he was a channel for the monarch's authority.

Another set of consequences concerns the self within the liturgical order. Characteristically, this self is "middle voiced."[7] He is not purely active, since his liturgical performances are made possible by divine forces. Nor is he wholly passive, since his creative subjectivity is necessary to mediate those forces. As Carl Schmitt puts it, he is *a representative* subject, not first and foremost of himself, not self-directed and self-governed. He is first and foremost constituted as a subject by his symbolic, mediating, and channeling role.[8] In this way, the self is distanced from himself. It is constituted by a certain openness, since he never perfectly fulfills the role, which nonetheless defines him. This is not the randomly indeterminate openness of the postmodern subject, which is not a really inhabited self but a self-made, perpetually ironic self. To the contrary, the liturgical subject sees himself as having achieved a certain measure of true identity, while what remains indeterminate in his character can be regarded as the ever-open promise of further development, which cannot be anticipated in advance.[9]

---

7. The middle voice is a grammatical category known to ancient Indo-European languages. It was employed to denote action of a verb that is neither active nor passive. There is some evidence to suggest that its use was not simply to cast an action as either reciprocal or reflexive, but to express the mediation of divine by human action. See Jan Gonda, "Reflections on the Indo-European Medium," Part I, in *Lingua* 9 (March 1960): 30-67, Part II, in *Lingua* 9 (June 1960): 175-93.

8. Carl Schmitt, *Roman Catholicism and Political Form*, trans. G. L. Ulmen (Westport, CT: Greenwood Press, 1996), pp. 18-19, 21, and 31-33.

9. Catherine Pickstock, *After Writing: On the Liturgical Consummation of Philosophy* (Oxford: Blackwell Publishers, 1997), pp. 198-213ff.

The possibility of non-ironic openness suggests yet another way of characterizing the liturgical. This concerns the fusing together of "real life" with "art" or "fiction." From the liturgical viewpoint, this approaches things backwards. The very categories "real life" and "art" are the result of the wreckage of the liturgical. Since, however, this dualism is part of today's predicament, the liturgical can be approached only by unthinking this dualistic legacy. Whereas art posits "the imaginary" in opposition to "the given," liturgy imagines, e.g., a world of angels seen as more real than the given, a world that holds out the *telos* to which the given aspires and alone defines what the "given" is.[10] The fusion of life and art also ensures that there is no rupture between work and enjoyment.

Etymologically, "liturgy" means "work of the people" and, in a fully liturgical culture, all activities are brought to some degree within the scope of liturgical enactment, just as originally art was not a privileged domain, but referred to a skill or something well made. In theory, this ensures that nothing is merely instrumental, and that every act exceeds itself, since every act becomes an ecstatic celebratory offering.[11] Conversely, all enjoyment is interpersonal and *measured;* it results neither in private disaffection, nor in disillusioned disappointment once the rapture has taken place. Liturgical enjoyment is sustainable enjoyment — one that must be worked at, because it involves certain efforts, disciplines, and renunciations. By contrast, in today's society work and enjoyment have been separated in such a way that, very often, work is not a sphere of self-fulfillment and enjoyment is sought in escape in uncontrolled and unmediated self-expression. This situation was captured by Horkheimer and Adorno in their reading of the story of Odysseus and the Sirens. Odysseus, strapped to the mast, listens voyeuristically to the sirens' voices of ancient myth and ritual — liturgy — enjoying them for a time with sublime pain, like modern art or a drug, while the workers rowing the boat have their ears plugged to keep out any experience other than that of functionality. The implication is that, unlike Hegel's slaves, they are no more capable of emancipatory consciousness than is their

10. See, e.g., Eric Gill, *Beauty Looks After Herself* (London: Sheed and Ward, 1933); *A Holy Tradition of Working* (Suffolk: Golgonooza Press, 1983); *It All Goes Together: Selected Essays* (New York: The Devin-Adair Company, 1944); David Jones, "Art and Sacrament," in his *Epoch and Artist* (London: Faber and Faber, 1959), pp. 143-79; Franz Rosenzweig, *The Star of Redemption*, trans. William W. Hallo (London: Routledge and Kegan Paul, 1971), pp. 147, 243, 244, 332, 340, 352, 355, and 360ff.

11. Jean-Yves Lacoste, "De la Technique à la Liturgie: Un Pas ou Deux Hors de la Modernité," *Communio* 11, no. 2 (1984): 26-37.

master, Odysseus. There is no remedy either in bourgeois art or in capitalist labor, because only the liturgical offers a vision of an alternative that nonetheless can be regarded as a *real* possibility.

When liturgy imagines something beyond everyday life, this is not an imaginary sphere one enters into and then leaves behind, like a dramatic performance ironically bracketed. On the contrary, within the logic of Catholic liturgy, if one goes to the altar, which prefigures the altar set in the middle of the heavenly Jerusalem, then one does so as *oneself*. In fact, one *only becomes oneself* in doing so. Indeed, in doing this, one really does go up to the heavenly Jerusalem. Perhaps it was in order to articulate such an ontologically constitutive liturgical synthesis of the aesthetic and the ethical that in the *Laws* Plato pronounced the liturgical city of the Magnesians to be the site of "the true tragedy." Far from being an exclusion of art, this was a call for there to be nothing *but* art, meaning *a sincere* art or liturgy.[12] To insist on art being liturgical is not to insist that there should be only liturgy and no art. Rather, it is to elevate all modes of art or the category of things made, as Eric Gill defined it. To achieve this is to close the gap between art and life.

The protocols of a liturgical ethic tend to prevent accumulation of a capitalist surplus because, as Georges Bataille has pointed out, surplus wealth is expended in public festivals. Yet, Bataille had no real grasp of liturgy, since he postulated the purest liturgy as being a nihilist riot of pure dereliction or wastage, which only interrupted accumulation because it also interrupted work and life.[13] But authentic liturgy is not opposed to work. Therefore, Bataille's analysis only takes the secular refusal of liturgy to a nihilistic extreme. The sacrificial expenditure involved in liturgy is merely one aspect; equally important is the intensification and renewal of those rhythms on which social and economic life depend. The offerings and exchanges to and with the divine that occur in liturgy are the prototypical models for all actions and exchanges between people in a liturgical society. In such a society, work is a gift-offering to someone else or to the community, leading to some counter-gift, some benefit to workers as well. Here patterns of work and exchange tend to move in cycles in accord with the liturgical cycle. Thus, in the High Middle Ages, feasting, the economy, and acts of charity were all closely related. Bands of craftsmen put their upholding of

12. Plato, *Laws*, 817b; Helmut Kuhn, "The True Tragedy: On the Relationship between Greek Tragedy and Plato," Part 1, *Harvard Studies in Classical Philology* 52 (1941): 1-40; Part 2, 53 (1942): 37-88.

13. Georges Bataille, *Theory of Religion*, trans. Robert Hurley (New York: Zone Books, 1992).

standards under the patronage of saints, and often upheld certain liturgical celebrations. This helped to return the economic surplus to the liturgical cycle. Moreover, the endowment of charitable works and hospitals gave rise to institutions that further promoted ritual circulation. All groups for charitable purposes were also groups for liturgical purposes. This tended to ensure that the bonds of charity bore a ritual weight. This does not mean anything formalistic or impersonal, but rather the reverse. Charity was seen as a holy event, a sacred state of being that had to involve a real exchange and intimacy between the participants. Here it was impossible for charity to be a remote and bureaucratic transaction. If anything, the problem medieval charity did resolve was the lack of fraternal bonds that impaired the life of the potential benefactor as much as that of the recipient. Because the problem of a lack of charity was spiritual rather than material, it could be resolved only in an immediate, highly physical and familial fashion. Restoring charity meant literally the re-establishment of a kinship bond, since all were regarded as the children of Adam.[14]

The Refusal of Liturgy

Modernity is characterized most of all by the refusal of liturgy, which is another way of saying that secularization is the pre-condition for a capitalist, bureaucratic, and technocratic order, however much this issue may be evaded. Despite the fact that, in some ways, religion survives much more in the U.S. than in Europe, American public space appears to be the most unliturgical. Its cities, with few exceptions, are not centered on cathedrals (thus, in a sense, are not cities at all). People tend to eat at any time; shops are open all night; and every week lacks a Sunday. To be nonliturgical means to have discarded the differentiations of time and space, and to live in a perpetual virtual space of identical repetition.[15] Without the closing down of

14. John Bossy, *Christianity in the West, 1400-1700* (Oxford: Oxford University Press, 1985), pp. 57-59; R. N. Swanson, *Religion and Devotion in Europe c. 1215–c. 1515* (Cambridge: Cambridge University Press, 1995), pp. 206-34; J. J. Jusserand, *English Wayfaring Life in the Middle Ages* (London: Methuen, 1889), pp. 20-23; W. K. Jordan, *Philanthropy in England, 1480-1660* (London: George Allen and Unwin Ltd, 1954), p. 54; Antony Black, *Guilds and Civil Society in European Thought from the Twelfth Century to the Present* (London: Methuen, 1984); Eamon Duffy, *The Stripping of the Altars: Traditional Religion in England, 1400-1580* (New Haven: Yale University Press, 1992), pp. 141-54.

15. See, Rosenzweig, *The Star of Redemption*, pp. 420ff.

diurnal activity at dusk, there is no interval before sleep for the descent of angels, no time to relativize man's dominion, just as the red sky of the city hides the stars from our view.

This rejection of liturgy is tantamount to denying the priority of the *Lebenswelt*. Yet, this is impossible, since the *Lebenswelt* is itself the ground of possibility for realizing human subjectivity. There is a sense in which, to cite Bruno Latour, one can never be modern, because modernity must live off the capital of what it denies. In order to recover the *lebensweltliche* base of true subjectivity, modernity has to resort to *artificial negativity* or to the simulation of anti-bureaucratic opposition. In the end, however, this artifice will not be enough. Modernity is locked in a cultural contradiction whereby it requires the very subjectivity it erodes. Thus, the collapse of enlightened centralized states in the East is paralleled by the decentralization of economies in the West, and both foreshadow the end of liberal enlightened despotism.

Doubts about the cultural contradictions of capitalism revolve around the idea that modernity has invented a sustainable pseudo-liturgy. Other characteristics of this pseudo-liturgy should be mentioned. First, a genuine transcendence has been displaced in modernity by the fixity of *space*. This is evidenced in several different ways: in the baroque era, in the new sacrality accorded to the monarch and to sovereign power, and also in the emergence of the New Science, with the attempt to force all knowledge into the grid of a spatial *mathesis* in which all the essences of things have a fixed and perpetual place.[16] It is also shown in the structures of modern language, especially in the increasing tendency to substitute static nouns or nominalizations for verbs. These new linguistic patterns are good examples of how, later, uniform spatial power can achieve a much more successful sway through strategic dispersal. If everyone uses certain linguistic forms that assume the absence of time, personhood, and government by the same impersonal forces, then policing by an absolute monarch becomes unnecessary, for everyone is now an unwitting delegate of a dispersed, but no less central power.

The same applies to the increasing use of *asyndeton* or syntax devoid of conjunctions and clausal hierarchies, for this gives the impression that the world is composed entirely of discontinuous items without value hierarchies or traditional continuities through time, but which are mere playthings of the forces enshrined in nominalizations. Asyndeton is a good example of sustainable pseudo-liturgy, because the notion of a world of discontinuous items is an unlivable illusion. Yet, this illusion becomes an original reality,

---

16. Pickstock, *After Writing*, chapter 2.

because it is instilled through a single remaining continuity and value, i.e., the asyndetic rhythm of speech. Thus, children will take an atomized view of the world for granted, because their *Lebenswelt* is already constituted by asyndetic and nominalized rhythms. One must *historicize* the notion of a *Lebenswelt*, and insist that the appeal to genuine liturgy is not an appeal to the transcendentally inescapable, but to the morally and aesthetically superior. Of course, this superiority can be grasped only by one who has achieved liturgical subjectivity.

In addition to spatialization, another feature of modern pseudo-liturgy is the substitution of civility for ritual, as traced by Norbert Elias, Talal Asad, John Bossy, Stephen Shapin, *et al.* Once the common ritual basis in which the symbolic order is mediated has collapsed, one must do something to prevent misunderstandings and conflicts. Instead of liturgical bonds, which presupposed a shared horizon of substantive conviction, one must substitute codes of civility or good manners that assume only a formal agreement about accepted protocols. Manners are a kind of *method*, and it is no accident that the more pluralistic U.S. is a far more polite place than, e.g., Great Britain, and that peoples' reactions are generally more predictable in the U.S. than in Europe. Alexis de Tocqueville already noted this. A crucial difference between liturgy and civility is that liturgy cannot possibly deceive. If the priest at the Mass secretly denies what he is doing, it does not matter. He has performed his representative function and the truth of the Mass remains. With the emergence of civility in the Renaissance, however, the pervasive problem of dissembling had already become evident. A symbol had ceased to be an unalterable *event* and had turned into a sign that might or might not be reliable.

Whereas previously one could put one's faith in the Mass, which disclosed God's trustworthiness, now it became imperative to put one's faith in other people, even though this trust was by no means guaranteed by the kinds of signs they offered. The only recourse was to protocols of behavior, including binding contracts and signs whose consequences one could predict. Thus, whereas genuine liturgy leads one back beyond oneself, the new pseudo-liturgy of civility is its own transcendence and guarantor. One starts to worship style and gentility for their own sake. Shapin has shown how this was supremely true in seventeenth-century England, and how, if there was anything persisting beyond civility, it was now a supposed realm of given *fact*. The New Science depended on trusting the procedures and reports of gentlemen too modest to impose their own theories, but reliable as passive witnesses. Thus, one had an immanentized pseudo-liturgy. Whereas previously the worshiper participated in the truth before which he bowed down, now the scientific inquirer does not participate in the truth he witnesses. There is an absolute contraposition of objective truth and subjectivity. Shapin has shown how this contraposition could be established only through the acceptance of certain ritual codes of behavior. From the viewpoint of genuine liturgy, such codes may appear impoverished and ethically menacing, yet as rituals they constitute a new and sustainable mode of human existence before nature and in society.[17]

The final characteristic of modern pseudo-liturgy is the use of spectacles to sustain order, from the baroque era to the present. Such spectacles can vary from carnival compensations for the drabness of the everyday, to the turning of the everyday into a spectacle. Another reason why capitalism may not suffer cultural contradictions is that it no longer needs a work ethic as it once did, for work itself, as Marcuse noted, can be suffused with token elements of play and eroticism. Thus, although the non-liturgical world tends to separate work and enjoyment to produce purely functional work and purely fictional private enjoyment, today it tends to collapse both. This is not the same as the fusion of work and enjoyment in genuine liturgy, because what it is fusing is a drained, functionalized work with a drained, virtualized, and reductively aestheticized enjoyment. Thus, connecting the two does not restore teleology to work, nor worship to enjoyment. Rather, it reinforces the cycling of both around an abyss of recycled immanent spatiality.

Today, the diversion of the spectacle is everywhere. But it is no return to the "true tragedy" of Plato's Magnetic city. Rather, a process initiated within genuine liturgy has been brought to its ultimate conclusion. In the Late Middle Ages and in the baroque era liturgy became increasingly centralized and regulated. At the same time, it turned into a theatrical display. In this way, the liturgical world had already begun to misunderstand itself and become a necessary precondition of the pseudo-liturgical.

Why Catholic Liturgy?

Clearly, there are unresolved problems concerning the pure communitarian celebration of the resistance exercised by local organic communities. First, how does one distinguish it from a kind of heightened liberalism in which

17. Steven Shapin, *The Social History of Truth: Civility and Science in Seventeenth Century England* (Chicago: University of Chicago Press, 1994).

freely choosing subjects are not individuals, but organic collectivities? Second, while these organic localities may be characterized by teleological practices, it is difficult to see how this will be true for a confederation of such groups. Will not their collectively agreed-upon goals be minimal and, given the degree of divergence, will not the only binding glue be pragmatist and contractual in character? If one deploys the principle of subsidiarity, this does not matter, but if the only common language is liberal, then the universalism intrinsic to liberalism will tend to reassert itself and will press once more toward centralization, even if this remains concealed.

This leads to a third problem: if one appeals to organicity from a neutral standpoint, uncommitted to any specific organic community, one's celebration of organicity is perforce merely ironic, i.e., another variant of liberalism in which one merely tolerates the other without wanting to enter into substantive and harmonious association with him.

This variant of liberalism readily blends with a postmodern nihilism. The only way out of this nihilism is either to embrace some particular local belief-system or to make some claims about a universal truth. Clearly, the latter course is suspect. Most conservative revisions of natural law are not traditional, because they seek to derive universal norms from purely immanent considerations. If one takes this course, natural law will be just a kind of functionalism or pragmatism. Ever since Ernst Troeltsch, scholars have pointed out that medieval notions of natural law were not like this, since they did not try to deduce norms from universal observable facts, but saw natural law as natural equity grounded in a transcendent eternal law, discernible by *practical* reason that involved a good disposition of the will. Here natural law involved an intimation of transcendence mediated through specific communities rooted in narrative traditions.

Yet, lingering worries that mere celebrations of pluralist localisms do not go beyond liberalism also appear well-founded. Apparently, this is an irresolvable dilemma. Both Roman Law and Catholicism, however, may be able to combine the universal and the particular. Unlike the Byzantine East, in the barbarian West the Church had to provide a legal framework from the very beginning. Yet, up until the twelfth or thirteenth century, the juridical remained subordinate to the sacramental and to the processes of substantive reconciliation exceeding the formality of law.[18] From then on, canon law *itself* started to move from legitimacy to legality, because it had to adopt merely formal contractual norms to mediate various boundary disputes.

18. Judith Herrin, *The Formation of Christendom* (Oxford: Basil Blackwell, 1987).

Catholicism is superlatively liturgical, because it extends the liturgical tension between the ideal and the real to a new extreme, yet still holds them together. Thus, it links the most remote unknowable and unpredictable transcendence with the most immediate and particular sacramental presentation. It is just this combination that allows the universal and the particular to be brought together. Where the universal is not an immanent and fully grasped, but rather a remote, dimly intimated principle, it becomes possible to allow an unlimited variety of different intimations of the transcendent truth in space and time, even though these intimations are not discontinuous with one another. Concomitantly, they must be woven to form a complex tradition.

As such, Catholicism is much more tolerant than liberalism. In this schema, each difference is fully tolerated precisely because it is *more* than tolerated, since each difference is a figural repetition of the other differences. Thus, Catholicism has allowed many local rites and variations, and has sheltered much traditional folk narrative and practice. It has been able to reconstrue pre-Christian myths and rituals as figurative anticipations of Catholicism. This may seem like an imperialist gesture, but this figurative reading enriches the sense of Catholicism. Thus, in the legends of the Holy Grail, Celtic ideas of inspirational cauldrons are read eucharistically. This also discloses new dimensions in eucharistic understanding.

There is another way in which Catholic universalism is unlike liberal universalism. The latter is constituted by abstract beliefs which may tolerate earlier narratives and rituals, but are not continuous with them. In a sense, Catholic universal language is a series of narratives and rites that can be linked to local tradition without any abrupt rupture. What is it about Catholic liturgy that makes it universal as well as specific in character? The Catholic rite is free from any exclusions. Simply by virtue of their common humanity, all are admitted to the Body of Christ, without obliterating their differences. The qualification to enter, i.e., baptism, which is open to all, leaves no trace of specific difference, such as circumcision (though that was already *a hidden* trace). After baptism, the water washes away, leaving an invisible transfiguration. The person is irrevocably changed, but only to what one already was. It makes the person *more* himself, rather than setting a barrier between the previously impure self and the new initiated self.

This lack of fetishized boundaries is also shown in a certain removal from sacralized space. Since the Catholic's place is to be before God, and God as transcendent endlessly recedes, this space is one of journeying now coterminous with time. The journey, however, is not an undifferentiated nihilistic flow without articulation, because it is undertaken only with others, and this polyphony brings back a synchronic space, albeit not a static un-changing synchrony. Within such a space, one can again celebrate sacred sites, but these are no longer exclusive. The proper attitude toward them, as Jean-Yves Lacoste has said, is neither one of fetishized triumph, nor of no-madic denial or dispossession, but rather of pilgrimage, which links the sites as beads along a thread.[19] Here, there is no Holy Land, no Mecca, and yet one can find everywhere new and specific hills of epiphany, new and specific Jerusalems: Mont San Michel, where angels roost like birds; Glastonbury, where the sacred vessel was brought for safe-keeping; Iona, where paradise was restored in a Celtic isle of the blessed.

In a sense, the subject of the Mass is at once universal and particular. Similarly, Catholic liturgical space is universal without suppressing regional difference. Within this space, there are protocols that tend to *advert* to a common center only to divert it. Again, this is because God, who is "placed" at the top of the hierarchy, is not really seen as the "highest thing," but is be-yond all "things," and so is equally proximate to every step of the hierarchy. There is a hierarchy of priesthood, diaconate, and people, or bishop, priest, and deacon. At any rate, hierarchy can never be abolished entirely. If a soci-ety is built, as it must, on certain values, some people and sites will embody these values more than others. Since modernity respects power and wealth, hierarchy is legitimated by the mere possession of power. Within the Catho-lic concept of hierarchy, however, authority is tolerable, because it represents a superior degree of something to which temporally subordinated people can aspire and attain. Moreover, at the top of the hierarchy is not a *person*, as it came to be for juridically debased early modern Catholicism, but rather a sign that represents the highest value.

As Nicholas of Cusa emphasized, above the clergy stands the Eucharist it-self. This means that the Church is only the Body of Christ insofar as it receives the Body of Christ, i.e., receives *itself* from the Eucharist.[20] Thus, authority is not a person, but a sign. Since *all* receive this sign, all receive the Eucharist. The hierarchical principle is balanced by a democratic one, because the necessary expertise of priests and theologians, which guides the laity, must defer to that more inchoate and yet profound sense of incorporated truth residing in the Church as a whole — an ancient Catholic principle revived by Newman and

---

19. Jean-Yves Lacoste, *Experience et Absolu* (Paris: P.U.F., 1994), pp. 7-25, 28-48; and "En Marge du Monde et de la Terre: l'Aisle," *Revue de Metaphysique et de Monde* 2 (1985): 185-200.

20. Nicholas of Cusa, *The Catholic Concordance*, trans. Paul E. Sigmund (Cambridge: Cambridge University Press, 1991).

others in the nineteenth century.[21] In this way, the notion of the in-dwelling of the Spirit in the Church, of the Church as infallible, helped to nurture the democratic idea, but in a non-sophistic version. In this view, truth does not follow the majority. Yet, within an authentic tradition and under authentic guidance, the majority ultimately tends to attract the truth.

To some extent, this same qualification of hierarchy in the direction of popular dispersal can also be seen in the very process of the sacrificial offering in the Mass. Normally, in space, sacrifice is linked to rigid divisions and exclusions: parts of the sacrificed animal are given to all, while the smoke alone ascends to heaven to appease the gods, never to return. To the contrary, in time, sacrifice is linked to abandonment of the less-valued, in order to gain the more-valued possession. It could be argued that this logic actually intrudes an element of the theatrical into the liturgical, because the lack of full participation necessarily reduces a sizable number of the participants to mere spectators. The eucharistic process, however, denies this logic and removes altogether the pagan element of theater. This is another reason why one can think of Catholicism as superlatively liturgical: by removing the element of theater that lurks even in most primitive rites, it fuses the symbolic and the ordinary. Bread and wine are offered to God, yet they return from heaven differently, as divinized, and then are consumed in their entirety. The *whole* of this sacrifice, God Himself, is eaten by every single individual without any exclusion and distinction.

Although the Eucharist can be seen as having universal and democratic aspects, it is not a collective event in the sense of some task in which everyone has a part. On the contrary, each individual receives unreservedly Christ's whole body and blood. This is another reminder of dispersal: for Christianity, there is no immanent universal. Instead, the universal is accessible only through the various, specific, time-bound traditional and customary paths. By cleaving to particularity, one can participate in the true universal, which is transcendent and inaccessible. Whereas if one seeks to encompass the universal through an abstracted theory or practice, in disdain of particularity, one irrevocably loses the universal, along with the diversity of the particular.[22]

Just as the Church exists only through its relation to the Body of Christ

21. John Henry Newman, *On Consulting the Faithful in Matters of Doctrine,* ed. John Coulson (London: Collins, 1986). See also Nicholas Lash, *Newman on Development: The Search for an Explanation in History* (London: Sheed and Ward, 1975).

22. Augustine, *De Libero Arbitrio,* trans. Thomas Williams (Indianapolis: Hackett Publishing Company, 1993), pp. 49-50 and 67; and *Against the Academicians,* trans. Peter King (Indianapolis: Hackett Publishing Company, 1995), pp. 167-69.

it receives, so, in general, a community founded on transcendence is paradoxically preceded by its relation to something else — the *arrival* of something else. Moreover, since the transcendent is grasped only imperfectly, it cannot be grasped once and for all, but can only be renewed continually. This imposes an openness to the stranger at the community's very core: not an uncritical openness, nor a readiness to receive anyone on formalistic grounds, but an openness nonetheless. It must maintain this openness in order to be true to itself, because it knows it has not yet become fully itself. Thus, the Hebrew Bible enjoins a specific respect for the sojourner. The founding figure of the *Torah*, Moses, was culturally an Egyptian, i.e., external to the community he refounded.

This priority of relations and openness to new arrivals in a given organic totality suggests a different way of looking at the issue of confederation. Maybe one should not think of federation as something superimposed on pre-constituted localities, as artificial contracts superimposed on natural units. Rather, one should start from the point that communities already exist within complex relational chains, within the overlapping and intertwining of different groups, within fundamental borrowings and integrations of other communal norms, whether present or past. This concept is not the same as that of the liberal nation-state, nor of liberal pluralism, nor of a tolerance of anything whatsoever. Rather, community consists not just in organic solidarity, but also in a specific harmonious blending of differences. This blending is the substance of what occurs within a community. Yet, it is continuous with blendings between communities. Indeed, from this relational perspective, the difference between within and without is relativized.

In this light, the aim of politics should be both to follow and to promote these relational continuities that constantly interweave a common substantive perspective. Of course, there are conflicts between irreconcilable visions of the true, the good, and the beautiful — and other visions could be put forward besides the Catholic one, e.g., Judaic, Islamic, and pagan Platonic. But to posit these transcendent realities at all is to deny any ontological and ultimate status to conflicts of human difference, and to presuppose the possibility that they can be modified and integrated in such a way as to be united in a continuous liturgical cycle through space and time. Here there would be respect for localities, but confederation also would have to speak a specific and concrete, if also richly complex, language. Confederation would have to pursue specific liturgical — not liberal, abstract, and quasi-liturgical — goals. Is not *this* political project the West's very *telos*?

Finally, there are two crucial points that need to be emphasized. First, the notion of the liturgical as a theological category (and not as an exotic word for traditionalism) provides the only real alternative to the anti-liturgy liturgy of modern times. Second, the ideal type presented by Catholicism offers at least one example of the logic of liturgy taken to an extreme, which turns out to be equidistant from the modern and the merely local and organic. Especially in its more extreme form, liturgy manages to reconcile two different things that do not readily seem to go together. First, it collapses dualities of life and art, practice and representation, to produce a seamless whole. The trouble with such a totality is that it can easily assume an organic and immanent form that completely disqualifies any self-critique. In this way, it becomes a pure power-structure, be it on a primitive magical model or a modern technical model. Second, liturgy in its superlative form not only negates the duality of practice and representation, but achieves this negation only by referring the entire social order to a principle beyond itself that continuously re-creates this social order in ever different ways. This may seem to erect a new sort of duality. But it does not, because the transcendent here is not the "higher aspect," but rather a mysterious source of that same social reality. There is no fixed boundary between the source and society. Instead, society comes about as a continuously renewed participation in this source. This suggests that participation in the metaphysical sense is the key to making participation in the social sense possible. Where a community arises by first receiving itself, it is constituted originally as gratitude for a gift of love. Thus, it cannot be seen as a totalized given, or solely as a vehicle of power, for in receiving itself it continuously dispossesses itself, but neither in a nihilistic way, nor in favor of an alien code of rules.

This might sound all rather mystical. But it has a distinct practical embodiment. It suggests that, in addition to the non-duality of art and life, one also overcomes the duality of *law* and life, because here order is not seen as imposed as a grid on a given reality, but as mediated through all the different runnels of personal elective affinities that are not closed-off, but always looking to extend themselves. Thus, the social and the authoritative, the real and the ideal are established together only because the social is not seen as a given, but as a gift that arrives from the source of both life and authority. Consequently, all affective social bonds carry within themselves the sovereign power of the principles of legitimation. Without in any way idealizing the High Middle Ages, it is possible to argue that to some degree they did continue to instantiate such a fusion of love and power.[23] By contrast, in

---

23. Bossy, *Christianity in the West, 1400-1700*, p. 75.

later Western history, with the decline of liturgical order and the rise of legal positivism and formalized civility, power has been defined increasingly as a realm alien to love. Concomitantly, love has been relegated to a private sphere, where it has been sentimentalized and confined to the realm of arbitrary affection and whims of taste. What liturgy may provide is a way of aligning oneself with social order, not through alienation toward an abstract law or an organic whole, but rather through the natural turning toward the series of human others.

III. Kingdom Come

Introduction

Peter Manley Scott

"Thy Kingdom come" — so Christians pray daily all around the world and thereby claim to be repeating words given by the son of a carpenter, an untutored rabbi living in an unremarkable part of the Roman Empire in the first century of the common era. Yet these three words announce the arrival of a Kingdom that is not from this world.

This then is the most political of Christianity's doctrines. From the apocalypse of John to postcolonial theologies, whenever Christianity seeks to challenge the powers and principalities, there is reference to this Kingdom. Moreover, central to the development of European theology through the twentieth century has been a turn to eschatology.[1] Of course, Christianity cannot be reduced to politics. Yet it is this refusal to be reduced to politics that makes reference to a Kingdom so powerful. For this Kingdom exceeds all earthly kingdoms. Despite efforts to establish thousand-year reichs and unending empires, it is the community of the carpenter, with its announcement of the approach of a Kingdom, that endures.

The political unruliness of this Kingdom does not lie, as some critics claim, in the politicizing of Christianity but in the fact that this Kingdom exceeds or surpasses all other kingdoms. It is precisely in presenting the politics of God that the Kingdom is, in a significant way, anti-political. In the Gospel of John, Pilate fails to see this. In declaring Christ to be the King of

---

1. Christoph Schwöbel, "Last Things First? The Century of Eschatology in Retrospect," in D. Fergusson and M. Sarot, eds., *The Future as God's Gift: Explorations in Christian Eschatology* (Edinburgh: T&T Clark, 2000), pp. 217-41.

the Jews he unwittingly acknowledges YHWH's reign but fails to see that such acknowledgment identifies his own rule, and the rule of the Roman Empire, as that of a "failed state." This is Jesus' raspberry to a powerful ruler: "I'm sorry, Pilate, but in the dispensation that I bear witness to and that is present in my body, you have little standing."

Contexts

The three excerpts presented in this section on eschatology are written in two different contexts and are separated by some seventy years. A fine example of work from the Protestant Social Gospel movement in the United States, the essay by Rauschenbusch was published in 1917. The essays by Gutiérrez and Sobrino, part of a mainly Catholic movement called liberation theology, are written from Latin America and were first published in 1990 (in Spanish; Gutiérrez is Peruvian, Sobrino from El Salvador).

Selecting texts only from the Americas is a little misleading in that the renewal of eschatology has been developed most strongly in this period by European — especially German — theology. Indeed, the influence of nineteenth-century Protestant, German theology on Rauschenbusch is clear: between 1891 and 1892, he returned to Germany to study the tradition of liberal theology associated with Schleiermacher, Ritschl, and Harnack; it is at this point that he realized that the "Kingdom of God" provided the organizing theological principle he had been seeking.[2] For liberation theology, there has been some acknowledgment — usually in criticism — of the work on eschatology by German theologians such as Jürgen Moltmann and Johann Baptist Metz. When Sobrino writes in his essay about modern theology "having rediscovered the dimension of the future on the metaphysical level, hope on the anthropological level, and promise on the level of revelation," the resonances with Moltmann's early theology are evident.

Social Gospel

Alongside Washington Gladden and Shailer Mathews, Walter Rauschenbusch (1861-1918) is now regarded as the leading exponent of the movement

2. Gary Dorrien, *Reconstructing the Common Good* (Maryknoll, NY: Orbis, 1990), pp. 22-23.

known as the Social Gospel. Yet it is today difficult to grasp the radicality of the movement's theology in that the reception of the Social Gospel has been strongly determined by its rejection by Reinhold Niebuhr (U.S. ethicist and theologian, 1892-1971) and his self-styled Christian Realism. For Niebuhr, the Social Gospel was too optimistic — although it is disputed as to whether the charge can be made to stick. Moreover, in the U.S. the period after Niebuhr saw the dominance of Paul Tillich's "answering" or therapeutic theology and later the emergence of strongly particularizing theologies (black, feminist, etc.), which in turn made the theology of the Social Gospel appear both anemic and insufficiently contextual. The partial triumph of post-liberal theology in American seminaries over the last two decades has probably not aided a careful consideration of the theologies of the Social Gospel.

One root of the movement is, as I have already noted, to be found in the German liberal theological tradition. Another is the social and economic developments occurring in North American society in the late nineteenth century in the midst of which the churches were required to provide an effective ministry. Important for the emergence of Rauschenbusch's theology of the social gospel was his pastorate in New York, which he began in 1886, and which caused him to rethink the social mission of the church. (Similarly, Reinhold Niebuhr's theological development began in a pastorate, in Bethel, Detroit, some thirty years later.) The Social Gospel is thereby a distinctively American, Protestant, and pastoral movement.

On his own report, Rauschenbusch proposes the Kingdom of God as the organizing principle of his theology. (There is an overlap here with liberation theology: in his essay reprinted below, Sobrino maintains a similar position.) Although it is likely that Rauschenbusch had already come to this conclusion on the centrality of the Kingdom of God by the time of his return from his theological studies in Germany in 1892, the essay reprinted here, from the 1917 book *A Theology of the Social Gospel,* clearly presents this centrality. By drawing on the Kingdom of God, Rauschenbusch promotes a type of doubled "Protestant principle": the Kingdom of God is not the property of the church and needs to be freed from ecclesiastical control for the good of society (the social gospel); the Kingdom of God is properly grounded in and learned from the mind and ethical principles of Jesus (salvation and morality cannot be separated).

Yet the political force of the Social Gospel is not found in this double relativizing but in the theological-political implications of the restoration of the Kingdom of God to its proper place. Thus, toward the end of the essay we are treated to the moral solidarity of humankind, an ethical voluntarism, a moral progressivism, and, perhaps, a sort of natural moral law. It is easy to trace these emphases to Kantian and post-Kantian themes in the development of a continental-European liberal theology. Moreover, it is here that critics have concentrated their fire by arguing that we have not so much the restoration of the Kingdom of God as its reconstruction. Yet, it is a testament to the enduring influence of the Social Gospel that what Ernst Troeltsch called "the social question" has not since fallen off the theological agenda. Indeed, eschatology has become increasingly influential in political theology — challenged only perhaps by certain theologies of the environment and a strand of feminist theology. However, unlike liberation theology, there are few exponents of the Social Gospel today, nor can it be said with any confidence that its influence extended much beyond the United States.[3]

Liberation Theology

Gustavo Gutiérrez and Jon Sobrino are leading representatives of this movement, which is ecclesial and theological and originates in Latin America. Although the movement's influence has spread widely through theology in the South and North, it emerged from the Catholic Church's sense of responsibility in the face of widespread and chronic poverty throughout Latin America. Liberation theology is a Catholic phenomenon also in the sense that it emerges out of the response by Latin American Catholicism to the Second Vatican Council (1962-65).

Approaching liberation theology is not straightforward in that as a movement of ecclesiastical renewal it has encountered resistance, not least from the Vatican. (One of the principal objectors was the present pope, Benedict XVI, who, as Joseph Cardinal Ratzinger, led the attacks on liberation theology from his position as Prefect of the Sacred Congregation for the Doctrine of the Faith.[4]) Among liberation theology's major themes are the preferential option for the poor, God as liberator, the poor Jesus who is the suffering Christ, and the liberating Reign of God. The primary task of theol-

3. Gary Dorrien, *Social Ethics in the Making: Interpreting an American Tradition* (Oxford: Wiley/Blackwell, 2008), argues for the relevance of ideas from the Social Gospel as part of a distinctively American contribution to Christian social ethics.

4. Ratzinger was named Prefect in 1981; see especially *Libertatis Nuntius: On Certain Aspects of the "Theology of Liberation"* (1984). Available at: http://www.vatican.va/roman_curia/congregations/cfaith/documents/rc_con_cfaith_doc_19840806_theology-liberation_en.html [accessed on 3 September 2009].

ogy is to offer theological reflection on the concrete praxis by the church of love against injustice.

Moreover, we should note that the two essays presented here are part of the second wave of liberation theological writing and so need to be understood as refinements and clarifications of earlier work in liberation theology — of which, the first edition of Gutiérrez's *A Theology of Liberation* (Spanish 1971, English 1973) is the outstanding example.[5] These essays, then, are responses to criticisms and responses to a debate. Some of that debate has occurred within the Catholic Church in Latin America, especially at the episcopal meetings held at Medellín (1968) and Puebla (1979).

The point to be made forcefully here is that liberation theology maintains the preferential option for the poor and affirms the central position of the Reign of God for *theological* reasons. "Because God is God" is a phrase you will find in Gutiérrez's and Sobrino's essays. Of course, no appeal to the Godness of God is definitive. In other words, it remains contested whether the liberation positions presented here are adequately theological. Yet, by their own understanding, the preferential option for the poor and the affirmation of the Kingdom are presented not on sociological but on theological grounds. It is vital to grasp this both in order to explore the radicality of liberation theology (see, for example, the tracing of the preferential option for the poor in scriptural revelation and the history of the church) and in order to appreciate that in these essays Gutiérrez and Sobrino seek to show that their positions are properly theological (see, for example, the self-conscious references to papal writings).

Thus, although he speaks of the preferential option for the poor as a way of identifying the "situatedness" of the poor — as marginalized and yet as historical subjects — Gutiérrez explores also and at some length "both the universality of God's love and the divine predilection for 'history's last.'" Those who argue that it should not be part of theology's task to draw on "secular" disciplines to account for the situatedness of the poor miss what is of greater concern to the movement: the theological identification of the poor by way of "God's gratuitous love."

The reference to God's love enables us to make the link between the preferential option for the poor and the Reign of God. Such a preferential option is, Gutiérrez contends, at the heart of Jesus' proclamation of a Kingdom. I do not think that Gutiérrez means that to make such an option is to

---

5. Gustavo Gutiérrez, *A Theology of Liberation: History, Politics, and Salvation,* trans. and ed. Sister Caridad Inda and John Eagleson (Maryknoll, NY: Orbis, 1973).

opt for the God of Jesus Christ, as if in making the option for the poor one opts — anonymously, so to speak — for God. Instead, although it must be said that his presentation is not straightforward, Gutiérrez intends that the two options are linked: the preferential option for the poor occurs — for faith — within the love of God for the poor as proclaimed in Jesus' discourse of the Kingdom.

For Sobrino, liberation theology finds the Reign of God attractive because here theology struggles with the fulfillment of history and fulfillment in history. (Sobrino and Gutiérrez speak of "Reign" rather than "Kingdom" in order to avoid the monarchical and hierarchical associations of the latter term.) The Reign of God is liberation theology's teleology — as it also is for Rauschenbusch. Moreover, this history is to be interpreted as a history of human beings as social; the Reign of God thereby identifies pointers toward a historical praxis for social human beings. The Reign of God thereby introduces a *utopian* concentration within human history. In his essay, Sobrino draws a contrast between history and transcendence to make this point. Moreover, we can detect a change of tone in his essay when compared with earlier writings in liberation theology. Previously, liberation theology had stressed utopia as one way of exploring the human work of justice as a contribution to the Kingdom of God. Here the tone is more downbeat: transcendence identifies that which is the negation of God's Reign: sins, personal and collective.

Liberation theology has had an international impact. In truth, this impact is not associated so much with either the preferential option for the poor or its reinterpretation of the Reign of God. Rather, its international influence is associated with its method: a stress on praxis for justice, and theology as a reflection on that praxis; "[t]heology is always a second act, within and in the presence of a reality," as Sobrino notes. Yet we may also say that the preferential option for the poor and the liberation emphasis on the Reign of God have had a more diffuse impact. The former presses the question as to which political — in a broad sense — interests a theology serves; if no theory is "neutral," which master does theology serve? The latter presses the question of the significance of political action, including revolutionary action. In an anti-bourgeois moment, liberation theology argues that utopian longings transfer "subjectivity" from the individual to the collective and enable and encourage historical transcendence in the "more" of social praxis.

11 The Kingdom of God

Walter Rauschenbusch

If theology is to offer an adequate doctrinal basis for the social gospel, it must not only make room for the doctrine of the Kingdom of God, but give it a central place and revise all other doctrines so that they will articulate organically with it.

This doctrine is itself the social gospel. Without it, the idea of redeeming the social order will be but an annex to the orthodox conception of the scheme of salvation. It will live like a negro servant family in a detached cabin back of the white man's house in the South. If this doctrine gets the place which has always been its legitimate right, the practical proclamation and application of social morality will have a firm footing.

To those whose minds live in the social gospel, the Kingdom of God is a dear truth, the marrow of the gospel, just as the incarnation was to Athanasius, justification by faith alone to Luther, and the sovereignty of God to Jonathan Edwards. It was just as dear to Jesus. He too lived in it, and from it looked out on the world and the work he had to do.

Jesus always spoke of the Kingdom of God. Only two of his reported sayings contain the word "Church," and both passages are of questionable authenticity. It is safe to say that he never thought of founding the kind of institution which afterward claimed to be acting for him.

Yet immediately after his death, groups of disciples joined and consolidated by inward necessity. Each local group knew that it was part of a divinely founded fellowship mysteriously spreading through humanity, and awaiting the return of the Lord and the establishing of his Kingdom. This universal Church was loved with the same religious faith and reverence with which Jesus had loved the Kingdom of God. It was the partial and earthly realization of the divine Society, and at the Parousia the Church and the Kingdom would merge.

But the Kingdom was merely a hope, the Church a present reality. The chief interest and affection flowed toward the Church. Soon, through a combination of causes, the name and idea of "the Kingdom" began to be displaced by the name and idea of "the Church" in the preaching, literature, and theological thought of the Church. Augustine completed this process in his *De Civitate Dei.* The Kingdom of God which has, throughout human history, opposed the Kingdom of Sin, is today embodied in the Church. The millennium began when the Church was founded. This practically substituted the actual, not the ideal Church for the Kingdom of God. The beloved ideal of Jesus became a vague phrase which kept intruding from the New Testament. Like Cinderella in the kitchen, it saw the other great dogmas furbished up for the ball, but no prince of theology restored it to its rightful place. The Reformation, too, brought no renascence of the doctrine of the Kingdom; it had only eschatological value, or was defined in blurred phrases borrowed from the Church. The present revival of the Kingdom idea is due to the combined influence of the historical study of the Bible and of the social gospel.

When the doctrine of the Kingdom of God shriveled to an undeveloped and pathetic remnant in Christian thought, this loss was bound to have far-reaching consequences. We are told that the loss of a single tooth from the arch of the mouth in childhood may spoil the symmetrical development of the skull and produce malformations affecting the mind and character. The atrophy of that idea which had occupied the chief place in the mind of Jesus, necessarily affected the conception of Christianity, the life of the Church, the progress of humanity, and the structure of theology. I shall briefly enumerate some of the consequences affecting theology. This list, however, is by no means complete.

1. Theology lost its contact with the synoptic thought of Jesus. Its problems were not at all the same which had occupied his mind. It lost his point of view and became to some extent incapable of understanding him. His ideas had to be rediscovered in our time. Traditional theology and the mind of Jesus Christ became incommensurable quantities. It claimed to regard his revelation and the substance of his thought as divine, and yet did not learn to think like him. The loss of the Kingdom idea is one key to this situation.

2. The distinctive ethical principles of Jesus were the direct outgrowth of

his conception of the Kingdom of God. When the latter disappeared from theology, the former disappeared from ethics. Only persons having the substance of the Kingdom ideal in their minds, seem to be able to get relish out of the ethics of Jesus. Only those church bodies which have been in opposition to organized society and have looked for a better city with its foundations in heaven, have taken the Sermon on the Mount seriously.

3. The Church is primarily a fellowship for worship; the Kingdom is a fellowship of righteousness. When the latter was neglected in theology, the ethical force of Christianity was weakened; when the former was emphasized in theology, the importance of worship was exaggerated. The prophets and Jesus had cried down sacrifices and ceremonial performances, and cried up righteousness, mercy, solidarity. Theology now reversed this, and by its theoretical discussions did its best to stimulate sacramental actions and priestly importance. Thus the religious energy and enthusiasm which might have saved mankind from its great sins, were used up in hearing and endowing masses, or in maintaining competitive church organizations, while mankind is still stuck in the mud. There are nations in which the ethical condition of the masses is the reverse of the frequency of the masses in the churches.

4. When the Kingdom ceased to be the dominating religious reality, the Church moved up into the position of the supreme good. To promote the power of the Church and its control over all rival political forces was equivalent to promoting the supreme ends of Christianity. This increased the arrogance of churchmen and took the moral check off their policies. For the Kingdom of God can never be promoted by lies, craft, crime, or war, but the wealth and power of the Church have often been promoted by these means. The medieval ideal of the supremacy of the Church over the State was the logical consequence of making the Church the highest good with no superior ethical standard by which to test it. The medieval doctrines concerning the Church and the Papacy were the direct theological outcome of the struggles for Church supremacy, and were meant to be weapons in that struggle.

5. The Kingdom ideal is the test and corrective of the influence of the Church. When the Kingdom ideal disappeared, the conscience of the Church was muffled. It became possible for the missionary expansion of Christianity to halt for centuries without creating any sense of shortcoming. It became possible for the most unjust social conditions to fasten themselves on Christian nations without awakening any consciousness that the purpose of Christ was being defied and beaten back. The practical undertakings of the Church remained within narrow lines, and the theological thought of

the Church was necessarily confined in a similar way. The claims of the Church were allowed to stand in theology with no conditions and obligations to test and balance them. If the Kingdom had stood as the purpose for which the Church exists, the Church could not have fallen into such corruption and sloth. Theology bears part of the guilt for the pride, the greed, and the ambition of the Church.

6. The Kingdom ideal contains the revolutionary force of Christianity. When this ideal faded out of the systematic thought of the Church, it became a conservative social influence and increased the weight of the other stationary forces in society. If the Kingdom of God had remained part of the theological and Christian consciousness, the Church could not, down to our times, have been salaried by autocratic class governments to keep the democratic and economic impulses of the people under check.

7. Reversely, the movements for democracy and social justice were left without a religious backing for lack of the Kingdom idea. The Kingdom of God as the fellowship of righteousness would be advanced by the abolition of industrial slavery and the disappearance of the slums of civilization; the Church would only indirectly gain through such social changes. Even today many Christians can not see any religious importance in social justice and fraternity because it does not increase the number of conversions nor fill the churches. Thus the practical conception of salvation, which is the effective theology of the common man and minister, has been cut back and crippled for lack of the Kingdom ideal.

8. Secular life is belittled as compared with church life. Services rendered to the Church get a higher religious rating than services rendered to the community.[1] Thus the religious value is taken out of the activities of the common man and the prophetic services to society. Wherever the Kingdom of God is a living reality in Christian thought, any advance of social righteousness is seen as a part of redemption and arouses inward joy and the triumphant sense of salvation. When the Church absorbs interest, a subtle asceticism creeps back into our theology and the world looks different.

9. When the doctrine of the Kingdom of God is lacking in theology, the salvation of the individual is seen in its relation to the Church and to the future life, but not in its relation to the task of saving the social order. Theology has left this important point in a condition so hazy and muddled that it

---

1. After the death of Susan B. Anthony a minister commented on her life, regretting that she was not orthodox in her beliefs. In the same address he spoke glowingly about a new linoleum laid in the church kitchen.

has taken us almost a generation to see that the salvation of the individual and the redemption of the social order are closely related, and how.

10. Finally, theology has been deprived of the inspiration of great ideas contained in the idea of the Kingdom and in labor for it. The Kingdom of God breeds prophets; the Church breeds priests and theologians. The Church runs to tradition and dogma; the Kingdom of God rejoices in forecasts and boundless horizons. The men who have contributed the most fruitful impulses to Christian thought have been men of prophetic vision, and their theology has proved most effective for future times where it has been most concerned with past history, with present social problems, and with the future of human society. The Kingdom of God is to theology what outdoor color and light are to art. It is impossible to estimate what inspirational impulses have been lost to theology and to the Church, because it did not develop the doctrine of the Kingdom of God and see the world and its redemption from that point of view.

These are some of the historical effects which the loss of the doctrine of the Kingdom of God has inflicted on systematic theology. The chief contribution which the social gospel has made and will make to theology is to give new vitality and importance to that doctrine. In doing so it will be a reformatory force of the highest importance in the field of doctrinal theology, for any systematic conception of Christianity must be not only defective but incorrect if the idea of the Kingdom of God does not govern it.

The restoration of the doctrine of the Kingdom has already made progress. Some of the ablest and most voluminous works of the old theology in their thousands of pages gave the Kingdom of God but a scanty mention, usually in connection with eschatology, and saw no connection between it and the Calvinistic doctrines of personal redemption. The newer manuals not only make constant reference to it in connection with various doctrines, but they arrange their entire subject matter so that the Kingdom of God becomes the governing idea.[2]

---

2. William Adams Brown, *Christian Theology in Outline* (New York: Scribner, 1906), p. 192: "We are witnessing to-day a reaction against this exaggerated individualism (of Reformation theology). It has become an axiom of modern thought that the government of God has social as well as individual significance, and the conception of the Kingdom of God — obscured in the earlier Protestantism — is coming again into the forefront of theological thought." See the discussion on "The View of the Kingdom in Modern Thought" which follows [later in Rauschenbusch's book].

Albrecht Ritschl, in his great monograph on Justification and Reconciliation, begins

In the following brief propositions I should like to offer a few suggestions, on behalf of the social gospel, for the theological formulation of the doctrine of the Kingdom. Something like this is needed to give us "a theology for the social gospel."

1. The Kingdom of God is divine in its origin, progress, and consummation. It was initiated by Jesus Christ, in whom the prophetic spirit came to its consummation, it is sustained by the Holy Spirit, and it will be brought to its fulfillment by the power of God in his own time. The passive and active resistance of the Kingdom of Evil at every stage of its advance is so great, and the human resources of the Kingdom of God so slender, that no explanation can satisfy a religious mind which does not see the power of God in its movements. The Kingdom of God, therefore, is miraculous all the way, and is the continuous revelation of the power, the righteousness, and the love of God. The establishment of a community of righteousness in mankind is just as much a saving act of God as the salvation of an individual from his natural selfishness and moral inability. The Kingdom of God, therefore, is not merely ethical, but has a rightful place in theology. This doctrine is absolutely necessary to establish that organic union between religion and morality, between theology and ethics, which is one of the characteristics of the Christian religion. When our moral actions are consciously related to the Kingdom of God they gain religious quality. Without this doctrine we shall have expositions of schemes of redemption and we shall have systems of ethics, but we shall not have a true exposition of Christianity. The first step to the reform of the Churches is the restoration of the doctrine of the Kingdom of God.

---

the discussion of his own views in Volume III (§ 2) by insisting that personal salvation must be organically connected with the Kingdom of God. He says ("Rechtfertigung und Versöhnung," III, p. iii): "Theology has taken a very unequal interest in the two chief characteristics of Christianity. Everything pertaining to its character as the redemption of men has been made the subject of the most minute consideration; consequently redemption by Christ has been taken as the center of all Christian knowledge and life, whereas the ethical conception of Christianity contained in the idea of the Kingdom of God has been slighted. . . . It has been fatal for Protestantism that the Reformers did not cleanse the idea of the ethical Kingdom of God or Christ from its hierarchical corruption (i.e. the idea that the visible Church is identical with the Kingdom), but worked out the idea only in an academic and unpractical form." Kant first recognized the importance of the Kingdom of God for ethics. Schleiermacher first applied the teleological quality of Christianity to the definition of its nature, but he still treated now of personal redemption and now of the Kingdom of God, without adequately working out their connection. Ritschl has done more than any one else to put the idea to the front in German theology, but he does not get beyond a few great general ideas. He was born too early to get sociological ideas.

2. The Kingdom of God contains the teleology of the Christian religion. It translates theology from the static to the dynamic. It sees, not doctrines or rites to be conserved and perpetuated, but resistance to be overcome and great ends to be achieved. Since the Kingdom of God is the supreme purpose of God, we shall understand the Kingdom so far as we understand God, and we shall understand God so far as we understand his Kingdom. As long as organized sin is in the world, the Kingdom of God is characterized by conflict with evil. But if there were no evil, or after evil has been overcome, the Kingdom of God will still be the end to which God is lifting the race. It is realized not only by redemption, but also by the education of mankind and the revelation of his life within it.

3. Since God is in it, the Kingdom of God is always both present and future. Like God it is in all tenses, eternal in the midst of time. It is the energy of God realizing itself in human life. Its future lies among the mysteries of God. It invites and justifies prophecy, but all prophecy is fallible; it is valuable in so far as it grows out of action for the Kingdom and impels action. No theories about the future of the Kingdom of God are likely to be valuable or true which paralyze or postpone redemptive action on our part. To those who postpone, it is a theory and not a reality. It is for us to see the Kingdom of God as always coming, always pressing in on the present, always big with possibility, and always inviting immediate action. We walk by faith. Every human life is so placed that it can share with God in the creation of the Kingdom, or can resist and retard its progress. The Kingdom is for each of us the supreme task and the supreme gift of God. By accepting it as a task, we experience it as a gift. By laboring for it we enter into the joy and peace of the Kingdom as our divine fatherland and habitation.

4. Even before Christ, men of God saw the Kingdom of God as the great end to which all divine leadings were pointing. Every idealistic interpretation of the world, religious or philosophical, needs some such conception. Within the Christian religion the idea of the Kingdom gets its distinctive interpretation from Christ. (a) Jesus emancipated the idea of the Kingdom from previous nationalistic limitations and from the debasement of lower religious tendencies, and made it world-wide and spiritual. (b) He made the purpose of salvation essential in it. (c) He imposed his own mind, his personality, his love and holy will on the idea of the Kingdom. (d) He not only foretold it but initiated it by his life and work. As humanity more and more develops a racial consciousness in modern life, idealistic interpretations of the destiny of humanity will become more influential and important. Unless theology has a solidaristic vision higher and fuller than any other, it can not

maintain the spiritual leadership of mankind, but will be outdistanced. Its business is to infuse the distinctive qualities of Jesus Christ into its teachings about the Kingdom, and this will be a fresh competitive test of his continued headship of humanity.

5. The Kingdom of God is humanity organized according to the will of God. Interpreting it through the consciousness of Jesus we may affirm these convictions about the ethical relations within the Kingdom: (a) Since Christ revealed the divine worth of life and personality, and since his salvation seeks the restoration and fulfillment of even the least, it follows that the Kingdom of God, at every stage of human development, tends toward a social order which will best guarantee to all personalities their freest and highest development. This involves the redemption of social life from the cramping influence of religious bigotry, from the repression of self-assertion in the relation of upper and lower classes, and from all forms of slavery in which human beings are treated as mere means to serve the ends of others. (b) Since love is the supreme law of Christ, the Kingdom of God implies a progressive reign of love in human affairs. We can see its advance wherever the free will of love supersedes the use of force and legal coercion as a regulative of the social order. This involves the redemption of society from political autocracies and economic oligarchies; the substitution of redemptive for vindictive penology; the abolition of constraint through hunger as part of the industrial system; and the abolition of war as the supreme expression of hate and the completest cessation of freedom. (c) The highest expression of love is the free surrender of what is truly our own, life, property, and rights. A much lower but perhaps more decisive expression of love is the surrender of any opportunity to exploit men. No social group or organization can claim to be clearly within the Kingdom of God which drains others for its own ease, and resists the effort to abate this fundamental evil. This involves the redemption of society from private property in the natural resources of the earth, and from any condition in industry which makes monopoly profits possible. (d) The reign of love tends toward the progressive unity of mankind, but with the maintenance of individual liberty and the opportunity of nations to work out their own national peculiarities and ideals.

6. Since the Kingdom is the supreme end of God, it must be the purpose for which the Church exists. The measure in which it fulfills this purpose is also the measure of its spiritual authority and honor. The institutions of the Church, its activities, its worship, and its theology must in the long run be tested by its effectiveness in creating the Kingdom of God. For the Church to see itself apart from the Kingdom, and to find its aims in itself, is the same

sin of selfish detachment as when an individual selfishly separates himself from the common good. The Church has the power to save in so far as the Kingdom of God is present in it. If the Church is not living for the Kingdom, its institutions are part of the "world." In that case it is not the power of redemption but its object. It may even become an anti-Christian power. If any form of church organization which formerly aided the Kingdom now impedes it, the reason for its existence is gone.

7. Since the Kingdom is the supreme end, all problems of personal salvation must be reconsidered from the point of view of the Kingdom. It is not sufficient to set the two aims of Christianity side by side. There must be a synthesis, and theology must explain how the two react on each other. The entire redemptive work of Christ must also be reconsidered under this orientation. Early Greek theology saw salvation chiefly as the redemption from ignorance by the revelation of God and from earthliness by the impartation of immortality. It interpreted the work of Christ accordingly, and laid stress on his incarnation and resurrection. Western theology saw salvation mainly as forgiveness of guilt and freedom from punishment. It interpreted the work of Christ accordingly, and laid stress on the death and atonement. If the Kingdom of God was the guiding idea and chief end of Jesus — as we now know it was — we may be sure that every step in His life, including His death, was related to that aim and its realization, and when the idea of the Kingdom of God takes its due place in theology, the work of Christ will have to be interpreted afresh.

8. The Kingdom of God is not confined within the limits of the Church and its activities. It embraces the whole of human life. It is the Christian transfiguration of the social order. The Church is one social institution alongside of the family, the industrial organization of society, and the State. The Kingdom of God is in all these, and realizes itself through them all. During the Middle Ages all society was ruled and guided by the Church. Few of us would want modern life to return to such a condition. Functions which the Church used to perform have now far outgrown its capacities. The Church is indispensable to the religious education of humanity and to the conservation of religion, but the greatest future awaits religion in the public life of humanity.

12 Option for the Poor

Gustavo Gutiérrez

The poor occupy a central position in the reflection that we call the theology of liberation theology. Only theological method and a concern for evangelization need be added in order to have the original — and still valid — core of this effort in understanding of the faith. From the outset, liberation theology has posited a distinction, adopted by Medellín in its "Document on Poverty," among three notions of poverty: real poverty, as an *evil* (that is, as not desired by God); spiritual poverty, as *availability* to the will of the Lord; and *solidarity* with the poor, as well as with the situation they suffer.

The importance of this point is proclaimed by biblical revelation itself. A preferential commitment to the poor is at the very heart of Jesus' preaching of the Reign of God (and we shall take up this matter in part II). The Reign of God is a free gift, which makes demands on those who receive it in the spirit of children and in community (as we shall see in part III). Real poverty has therefore been a challenge to the church throughout history, but due to certain contemporary factors it has acquired fresh currency among us (the subject of part I).

I. A New Presence

Our days bear the mark of a vast historical event: the *irruption of the poor.* We refer to the new presence of those who had actually been absent in our

Translated by Robert R. Barr.

society and in the church. By *absent* we mean of little or no significance, as well as being without the opportunity to manifest their sufferings, solidarities, projects, and hopes.

As the result of a long historical process, this situation has begun to change in recent decades in Latin America. Of course the same change has been occurring in Africa, with the new nations; in Asia, with the independence of old nations; among the racial minorities of wealthy nations as well as poor ones. Another important movement, taking many forms, has also gotten under way: the new presence of woman, regarded by Puebla as "doubly oppressed and marginalized" (Puebla Final Document, no. 1135, n.) among the poor of Latin America.

The poor, then, have gradually become active agents of their own destiny, initiating the solid process that is altering the condition of this world's poor and despoiled. The theology of liberation — an expression of the right of the poor to "think their faith" — is not the automatic result of this situation and its incarnations. It is an attempt to read these signs of the times — in response to the invitation issued by John XXIII and Vatican Council II — by engaging in a critical reflection in the light of the word of God. That word should lead us to make a serious effort to discern the values and limitations of this event, which read from the standpoint of faith, also represents an irruption of God into our lives.

1. The World of the Poor

Expressions like "dominated peoples," "exploited social classes," "despised races," and "marginalized cultures" — along with the reference to that constant, coextensive phenomenon, "discrimination against women" — have become common formulations in a framework of the theology of liberation for the unjust situation of the poor. The purpose of these formulations is to call attention to the fact that the poor — who constitute a de facto social collectivity — live in a situation of "inhuman misery" (Medellin, "Document on Poverty," no. 1) and "anti-evangelical poverty" (Puebla Final Document, no. 1159).

Furthermore, a great and constantly growing commitment to the poor has afforded us a better perception of the enormous complexity of their world. We are dealing with a veritable universe, in which the socioeconomic aspect of poverty, while fundamental, is not the only aspect. Ultimately, poverty means *death*. Food shortages, housing shortages, the impossibility of attending adequately to health and educational needs, the exploitation of labor, chronic unemployment, disrespect for human worth and dignity, unjust restrictions on freedom of expression (in politics and religion alike) are the daily plight of the poor. The lot of the poor, in a word, is suffering. Theirs is a situation that destroys peoples, families, and individuals; Medellín and Puebla call it "institutionalized violence." Equally unacceptable are the terrorism and repressive violence with which they are surrounded.

At the same time — and it is important to remember this — to be poor is a way of life. It is a way of thinking, of loving, of praying, of believing and hoping, of spending free time, of struggling for a livelihood. Being poor today also means being involved in the battle for justice and peace, defending one's life and liberty, seeking a greater democratic participation in the decisions of society, "organizing to live one's faith in an integral way" (Puebla Final Document, no. 1137), and committing oneself to the liberation of every human person.

Again — by way of a convergent phenomenon — we have seen during this same period the emergence of a more acute awareness of the racial problem among us. One of our social lies is that there is no racism in Latin America. There may be no racist laws, such as prevail in other lands, but we do have racist customs — a phenomenon no less grave for being hidden away. Marginalization of and contempt for the Amerindian and black populations are things we cannot accept, neither as human beings, nor still less as Christians. Today these populations are coming to a more acute awareness of their situation. and consequently are voicing an ever more powerful demand for their most elementary human rights. This raised consciousness is pregnant with implications for the future.

We must also mention the unacceptable, inhumane position of women. One of the most subtle obstacles to its perception is its almost hidden character in habitual, daily life in our cultural tradition — to the point that when we denounce it, we seem a little strange to people, as if we were simply looking for trouble.

This state of affairs among us is a challenge to pastoral work, a challenge to the commitment of the Christian churches. Consequently, it is also a challenge to theological reflection. We still have a long way to go in this area. Matters of culture, race, and gender will be (and have already begun to be) extremely important to liberation theology. Doubtless the most important part of this task will fall to persons who actually belong to these respective human groups, despite the difficulties lying in the way today. No sudden burst of resistance is in the offing, but the voice of these downtrodden has begun to be heard, and this augurs well for the future. Here we surely have one of the richest theological veins for the coming years.

The cargo of inhuman, cruel death with which all of this misery and oppression is laden is contrary to the will of the God of Christian revelation, who is a God of life. But this does not blind us to the positive elements that we have indicated. These things manifest an ever-promising human depth and strength in terms of life. All of this constitutes the complex world of the poor. But our overall judgment remains: real poverty, a lack of the necessities of life (of a life worthy of a human being); social injustice, which plunders the masses and feeds the wealth of the few; the denial of the most elementary of human rights, are evils that believers in the God of Jesus can only reject.

2. *Going to the Causes*

In this complicated, narrow universe of the poor, the predominant notes are, first, its insignificance in the eyes of the great powers that rule the world of today, and second, its enormous human, cultural, and religious wealth, especially in terms of a capacity for the creation of new forms of solidarity in these areas.

This is how the poor are presented to us in scripture. The various books of the Bible paint a powerful picture of the cruel situation of spoliation and abuse in which the poor abide. One of the most energetic denunciations of this state of affairs is in the shatteringly beautiful — despite the painfulness of the topic under consideration — description we find in chapter 24 of the Book of Job. But it is not a matter of a mere neutral presentation of this reality. No, the biblical writers — the prophets, especially — point the finger of blame at those responsible for the situation. The texts are many. These passages denounce the social injustice that creates poverty as contrary to the will of God and to the meaning of the liberative deed of God manifested in the exodus from Egypt.

Medellín, Puebla, and John Paul II have all adopted this outlook in recent times. Today, pointing out causes implies structural analysis. This has always been an important point in the framework of liberation theology. The approach has been a costly one. True, the privileged of this world accept with a certain amount of equanimity the fact of massive world poverty. Such a fact is scarcely to be concealed in our day. But when causes are indicated, problems arise. Pointing out the causes inevitably means speaking of social injustice and socioeconomic structures that oppress the weak. When this happens, there is resistance — especially if the structural analysis reveals the concrete, historical responsibility of specific persons. But the strongest resistance and greatest fear are aroused by the threat of a raised consciousness and resulting organization on the part of the poor.

The tools used in an analysis of social reality vary with time and with the particular effectiveness they have demonstrated when it comes to understanding this reality and proposing approaches to the solution of problems. It is a hallmark of the scientific method to be critical of the researcher's own premises and conclusions. Thereby science constantly advances to new hypotheses of interpretation. For example, the theory of dependency, so frequently employed during the first years of our encounter with Latin American reality, has obviously turned out to be an inadequate tool. It is still an important one; but it has taken insufficient account of the internal dynamics and complexity of each country, and of the sheer magnitude of the world of the poor. Furthermore, Latin American social scientists are becoming more and more attentive to factors, not in evidence until more recent years, that express an evolution in progress in the world economy.

All of this calls for a refinement of our various means of cognition and even for the application of other, new means of the same. The social dimension is very important, but we must go deeper. There has been a great deal of insistence, in recent years, altogether correctly, on the contrast between a developed, wealthy northern world (whether capitalist or socialist), and an underdeveloped, poor, southern one (cf. John Paul II, *Sollicitudo Rei Socialis*). This affords a different view of the world panorama, which cannot be reduced to confrontations of an ideological order or to a limited approach to confrontations between social classes. It also indicates the basic opposition implied in the confrontation between East and West. Indeed, the diversity of the factors that we have cited makes us aware of various types of social oppositions and conflicts prevailing in today's world.

The important transformation surely occurring in the field of social analysis today is needed in the theology of liberation. This circumstance has led liberation theology to incorporate into its examination of the intricate, fluid reality of poverty certain valuable new perspectives being adopted by the human sciences (psychology, ethnology, anthropology). Incorporation does not mean simply adding, without organic splicing. Attention to cultural factors makes it possible for us to penetrate basic mentalities and attitudes that explain important aspects of reality. Economic reality is no longer the same when evaluated from a cultural viewpoint. And surely the reverse is true as well.

It is not a matter of choosing among instruments. As a complex human condition, poverty can only have complex causes. We must not be simplistic. We must doggedly plunge to the root, to the underlying causes of the situation. We must be, in this sense, truly radical. Sensitivity to the new challenges will dictate changes of focus in the process of our selection of the routes to be taken to an authentic victory over the social conflicts that we have cited, and to the construction of a just world, the community of sisters and brothers for which the Christian message calls.

II. The Reason for a Preference

While it is important and urgent to have a scholarly knowledge of the poverty in which the great masses of our peoples live, along with the causes that lie at the origin of this poverty, theological work properly so called begins when we undertake to read this reality in the light of Christian revelation.

The biblical meaning of poverty, then, will be one of the cornerstones of liberation theology. True, this is a classic question of Christian thinking. But the new, active presence of the poor vigorously re-posits that question. A keystone of the understanding of poverty along these theological lines is the distinction among the three notions of poverty, as we have stated. That is the context of a central theme of this theology, one broadly accepted today in the universal church: *the preferential option for the poor*. We are dealing with an outlook whose biblical roots are deep.

1. A Theo-centric Option

Medellín had already encouraged giving "preference to the poorest and neediest, and to those who are segregated for any reason" ("Document on Poverty," no. 9). The very term "preference" obviously precludes any exclusivity; it simply points to who ought to be the first — not the only — objects of our solidarity. From the very first the theology of liberation has insisted on the importance of maintaining both the universality of God's love and the divine predilection for "history's last." To opt for either of these extremes to the exclusion of the other would be to mutilate the Christian message. The great challenge is to maintain a response to both demands, as Archbishop Romero used to say with reference to the church, "From among the poor, the church can be for everyone."

In the harsh, hard years of the late 1960s and early 1970s, this perspective occasioned numerous experiments in the Latin American church, along with a theological reflection bearing on these experiments. Here was a process of the refinement of expressions translating the commitment to the poor and oppressed. This became plain at Puebla, which adopted the formula "the preferential option for the poor" (cf. the chapter of the Puebla Final Document bearing that name). The expression had already begun to be used in the theological reflection of that time in Latin America. Thus, the Puebla Conference bestowed a powerful endorsement. Now the formula and the concept belong to everyone.

The word "option" has not always been well interpreted. Like any slogan, it has its limits. What it seeks to emphasize is the free commitment of a decision. This option for the poor is not optional in the sense that a Christian need not necessarily make it, any more than the love we owe every human being, without exception, is optional. It is a matter of a deep, ongoing solidarity, a voluntary daily involvement with the world of the poor. At the same time, the word "option" does not necessarily mean that those who make it do not already belong to the world of the poor. In many cases they do. But even here it is an option; the poor themselves must make this decision, as well. Some important recent documents issuing from the ecclesiastical magisterium at the universal level, echoing the outlook of the Latin American church, explicitly employ the expression "preferential option for the poor."

Some have claimed that the magisterium would be happy to see the expression "preferential option" replaced with "preferential love" which, we are told, would change the meaning. It seems to us that the matter has been settled by the latest encyclical of John Paul II. Listing certain points and emphases enjoying priority among the considerations of the magisterium today, the pope asserts: "Among these themes, I should like to mention, here, the *preferential option or love* for the poor. This is an option or *special form* of primacy in the exercise of Christian charity" (*Sollicitudo Rei Socialis,* no. 42).

When all is said and done, the option for the poor means an option for the God of the Reign as proclaimed to us by Jesus. The whole Bible, from the story of Cain and Abel onward, is marked by God's love and predilection for the weak and abused of human history. This preference manifests precisely God's gratuitous love. This is what the evangelical Beatitudes reveal to us. The Beatitudes tell us in extremely simple fashion that a predilection for the poor, the hungry, and the suffering has its basis in the Lord's own bounty and liberality.

The ultimate reason for a commitment to the poor and oppressed does not lie in the social analysis that we employ, or in our human compassion, or in the direct experience we may have of poverty. All of these are valid reasons and surely play an important role in our commitment. But as Christians, we base that commitment fundamentally on the God of our faith. It is a theocentric, prophetic option we make, one which strikes its roots deep in the gratuity of God's love and is demanded by that love. Bartolomé de las Casas, immersed in the terrible poverty and destruction of the Indians of this continent, gave this as the reason for his option for them: "Because the least one, the most forgotten one, is altogether fresh and vivid in the memory of God." It is of this "memory" that the Bible speaks to us.

This perception was asserted in the experience of the Latin American Christian communities, and thus it came down to Puebla. Puebla maintains that for the sole reason of the love of God manifested in Christ, "the poor merit preferential attention, whatever may be the moral or personal situation in which they find themselves" (Puebla Final Document, no. 1142). In other words, the poor are preferred not because they are necessarily better than others from a moral or religious standpoint, but because God is God. No one lays conditions on God (cf. Jth. 8:11-18), for whom the last are first. This shocks our ordinary, narrow understanding of justice; it reminds us that God's ways are not our ways (cf. Isa. 55:8).

There has been no shortage of misunderstanding, then, or undue reduction on the part of self-styled champions of this preferential option as well as its overt adversaries. Still, we can safely assert that we are dealing with an indefectible part of the understanding maintained by the church as a whole today of its task in the world. We are dealing with a focus that is fraught with consequences — one which is actually only taking its first steps, and which constitutes the core of a new spirituality.

2. The Last Shall Be First

In a parable that we know from the first gospel alone, Matthew sets in relief — in the contrast between the first and the last — the gratuity of God's love by comparison with a narrow notion of justice (Matt. 20:1-16). "I intend to give this man who was hired last the same pay as you," says the Lord. Then he assails the envious with a pair of incisive questions: "I am free to do as I please with my money, am I not? Or are you envious because I am generous?" Here is the heart of the matter. The literal expression "bad eye" (for "envious") is revealing. In the Semitic mentality it denotes a fierce, jealous look — a look that petrifies reality, that leaves no room for anything new, leaves no room for generosity, and especially, here, undertakes to fix limits to the divine bounty. The parable transmits a clear lesson concerning the core of the biblical message: the gratuity of God's love. Only that gratuity can explain God's preference for the weakest and most oppressed.

"Thus the last shall be first and the first shall be last" (v. 16). Frequently we cite only the first half of the verse: "The last shall be first," forgetting that, by the same token, the first shall be last. But what we have here is an antithesis. The two statements shed light on each other, and therefore should not be separated. The antithesis is a constant in the gospels when the reference is to the addressees of the Reign of God. The gospels tell us of those who shall enter the Reign heralded by Jesus, and at the same time they tell us who shall be unable to do so. This antithetical presentation is highly instructive concerning the God of the Reign. Let us approach this matter by way of certain examples.

1. In Luke (6:20-26), the Beatitudes are followed by the Woes. The Greek word for *poor* here is *ptōchoi.* Its meaning is beyond any doubt: etymologically the word means the "stooped," the "dismayed." It is actually used to speak of the needy, those who must beg in order to live — those whose existence, then, depends on others. In other words, it means the helpless. This connotation of social and economic inferiority was already present in the Hebrew words that *ptōchos* translates in the version known as the Septuagint. Scholars agree that this is the basic meaning of the word *ptōchos* in its thirty-four occurrences in the New Testament (twenty-four of them being in the gospels). Very different is the situation of the rich, who have already received their consolation. Here again the sense is clear: the rich *(plousioi)* are those who possess a great deal of material wealth. Luke frequently contrasts them with the poor: the parable of the rich man and the poor Lazarus, in which, it is worth mentioning, it is not the rich man, but the representative of the anonymous of history, who is designated by a name (16:19-31); the vanity of the highly placed and the oppression of the poor (20:46-47); the widow's mite, accentuating the contrast presented in the parallel text in Mark 12:41-44, its possible source.

We also have a contrast between the hungry and the satiated. The Greek word used by Luke for the hungering, *peinōntes,* like the Hebrew words it translates in the Septuagint, indicates that this is not simple hunger but a deprivation resulting from evil acts of violence perpetrated over an extended period of time. The reference is to an endemic food shortage. "Starving," then, or "famished" would be better words for *peinōntes* than simply "hungry." The satiated, by contrast, are the fully satisfied. Thus, the song placed by Luke on the lips of Mary strikes a definitive contrast between the rich and the hungry (Luke 1:53). Indeed, in Luke we often find poverty and hunger associated, as we find wealth and abundance of nourishment associated.

Those who weep — now we are in the third Beatitude — are those who experience a pain so acute, a sorrow so intense, that they cannot but express it. Weeping is a manifestation of feelings to which Luke is sensitive; he uses the verb *klaiein*, "to weep," eleven times. The pain expressed by this word is not momentary. This suffering is profound and springs from permanent marginalization. Rarely, on the other hand, do the Christian scriptures mention anyone "laughing" *(gela-)*. Laughing can be a legitimate expression of joy (Luke 6:21), but it can also be the manifestation of a merriment that is oblivious of the sufferings of others, one based on privileges (6:25).

These are real situations — even social and economic situations — of poverty and wealth, hunger and satiety, suffering and self-satisfaction. The Reign of God will belong to those who live in conditions of weakness and oppression. For the wealthy to enter the Reign will be more difficult than "for a camel to go through a needle's eye" (Luke 18:25).

2. The gospels let us know, in various ways, that it is the despised, and not persons of importance, who have access to the Reign of God and to knowledge of the word of God. When the Lord cries, "Let the children come to me. Do not hinder them. The kingdom of God belongs to such as these" (Matt. 19:14), we immediately think of childlike docility and trust. We miss the radicality of Jesus' message. In the cultural world of Jesus' time, children were regarded as defectives. Together with the poor, the sick, and women, they were relegated to the status of the inconsequential. This shocks our modern sensitivity. But testimonials to this abound. To be "such as these," therefore, to be as children, means being insignificant, someone of no value in the eyes of society. Children are in the same category as the ignorant, on whom God our Father has willed to bestow a self-revelation (Matt. 11:25), or the "least ones," in whom we encounter Christ himself (Matt. 25:31-46).

Opposite these small, ignorant persons stand "the learned and the clever" (Matt. 11:25), who have seized control of the "key of knowledge" (Luke 11:52), and who despise the lowly, the people — ʿam ha-ʾarets, the people of the earth, of the land — whom they regard as ignorant and immoral ("this lot, that knows nothing about the law" [John 7:49]). The gospel calls them the simple folk, "merest children" (Matt. 11:25) — using the Greek word *nēpioi*, with its strong connotation of ignorance and simplicity.

Here again we find ourselves confronted with concrete, contrasting social situations based on unequal degrees of religious knowledge. Ignorance is not a virtue, nor is wisdom a vice. The biblical preference for simple folk springs not from a regard for their supposed moral and spiritual dispositions, but from their human frailty and from the contempt to which they are subjected.

3. We should actually do better to call the parable of those invited to the wedding banquet, as recorded in Matthew (22:2-10) and Luke (14:16-24), the parable of the *un*invited, since it is really they who constitute the core of its lesson. Exegetes are gradually abandoning the common interpretation of this text as a parable of an Israel called by God, but rejected for its faults, and thereupon a non-Israel called in place of Israel. Today the tendency is rather to understand those who were invited first as the "upper crust" of the time — persons who enjoyed both a high social rank and a knowledge of the Law; and the second group as those to whom Jesus preferentially addressed his message, the poor and the dispossessed — those regarded as sinners by the religious leaders of the people. Matthew goes so far as to say: "The servants then went out into the byroads and rounded up everyone they met, bad as well as good. This filled the wedding hall with banqueters" (Matt. 22:10). "Bad" and "good," we read, in that order. Once more we are dealing not with a question of moral deserts, but with an objective situation of the "poor and the crippled, the blind and the lame" (Luke 14:21).

4. Jesus is emphatic. He has come not for the sake of the righteous, but for sinners; not for the sake of the healthy, but for the sick (cf. Mark 2:17). Once again we have an antithetical presentation of the addressees of Jesus' message. On this occasion the tone is ironic: Are there perhaps righteous, healthy people who have no need of Jesus' salvific love? No, the "righteous," here are the self-righteous, those who pretend to be sinless, while the "healthy" are those who think they do not need God. These, despite the tokens of respect that they receive in society, are the greatest sinners, sick with pride and self-sufficiency. Then who are the sinners and the unhealthy, for whom the Lord has come? In terms of what we have just observed concerning the righteous and the healthy, we must be dealing here with those who are not well regarded by the "upper crust" of the social and religious world.

Those afflicted with serious illnesses or physical handicaps were regarded as sinners (cf. John 9). Hence, for example, lepers were segregated from social life; Jesus returns them to society by restoring them to physical health. Similarly public sinners, like tax collectors and prostitutes, were the dregs of society. It is that condition, and not their moral or religious quality, that makes them first in the love and tenderness of Jesus. Therefore he apostrophizes the great ones of his people: "Tax collectors and prostitutes are entering the kingdom of God before you" (Matt. 21:31). The gratuity of God's love never ceases to amaze us.

III. Church of the Poor

One month before the opening of the Council, John XXIII called into being a church of the poor. His words have become familiar ones: "As for the underdeveloped countries, the church is, and wishes to be, the church of all, and especially the church of the poor" (Discourse of September 11, 1962). This intuition had strong repercussions on Medellín, as well as on the life of the Latin American church, especially by way of the base church communities. An examination of the meaning of the notion of spiritual poverty will help us to understand why the disciple, the person who belongs to the people of God, must express an acceptance of the Reign of God in a commitment of solidarity and loving community with all, especially with the actual poor and dispossessed of this world.

1. Discipleship

The Beatitudes are recorded in two versions in the gospels, one in Luke and the other in Matthew. The contrast between the two versions is frequently attributed to an attempt on the part of Matthew to "spiritualize" the Beatitudes, that is, to convert to a recital of purely interior, disincarnate dispositions what in Luke had been a concrete, historical expression of the coming of the Messiah. We disagree with this interpretation. Among other things, it is scarcely to be denied that Matthew's gospel is particularly insistent on the importance of performing concrete, material deeds in behalf of others, especially the poor (cf. Matt. 25:31-46). What Matthew does is view the Beatitudes through the lens of the central theme of his gospel: discipleship. The spiritual poor are followers of Jesus. The Matthean Beatitudes (Matt. 5:3-12) indicate the basic attitudes of the disciple who receives the Reign of God in solidarity with others. Matthew's text can be divided into two parts.

1. The *first block* of Beatitudes closely resembles Luke's version. Luke, as we hear so frequently, speaks of materially poor persons. To whom is Matthew directing our attention, then, when he says "in spirit" in the first Beati-

tude? In the biblical mentality, spirit connotes dynamism. Spirit is breath, life force — something manifested through cognition, intelligence, virtue, or decision. Thus, "of spirit" transforms a reference to an economic and social situation into a disposition required in order to receive the word of God (cf. Zeph. 2:3). We are confronted with a central theme of the biblical message: the importance of *childlikeness*. We are being exhorted to live in full availability to the will of the Lord — to make that will our sustenance, as Jesus would have us do in the gospel of John. It is the attitude of those who know themselves to be the sons and daughters of God, and the sisters and brothers of the others. To be poor in spirit is to be a *disciple* of Christ.

The *second Beatitude* (the third, in some versions) is sometimes seen as implied in the first. Be this as it may, the fact is that the Hebrew words 'anaw and 'ani ("poor"), too, are translated by the Greek *praeis* (used later in this same block) meaning "lowly," or meek. Thus, we must be dealing with a nuance of the expression "poor in spirit." The meek, the lowly, are the unpretentious. They are open, affable, and hospitable. The quality is specifically a human one. (The Bible never ascribes "lowliness" to God. It does ascribe it to Jesus: cf. Matt. 11:28-29, where Jesus is "gentle and humble of heart.") To be meek is to be as the Teacher. To the meek is promised the earth, the land. The earth, the land, the soil is the first specification of the Reign of God in the Beatitudes, and in the Bible it carries the clear connotation of life.

In the *third Beatitude* Matthew uses a different verb from Luke's, but the meaning is similar: "sorrowing," *penthountes*. The word suggests the sorrow of mourning, catastrophe, or oppression (cf. 1 Macc. 1:25-27). Blessed, then, are those who refuse to resign themselves to injustice and oppression in the world. "They shall be consoled." The verb *parakalein*, "to console, to comfort," is an echo of Second Isaiah: "The Lord comforts his people and shows mercy to the afflicted" (Isa. 49:13). The consolation in question sounds a note of liberation. Luke presents us with a Jesus who fulfills the promise of the consolation of Israel (cf. Luke 2:25). Blessed are those who have known how to share the sorrow of others to the point of tears. For the Lord will console them: he will wipe away their tears, and "the reproach of his people he will remove from the whole earth" (Isa. 25:8; cf. Rev. 21:4).

In the *fourth Beatitude* a central theme for Matthew's gospel appears: the towering importance of *justice*. The use of the verbs "to hunger" and "to thirst" adds a note of special urgency and a religious overtone. The object of this burning desire is justice, or righteousness, as a gift of God and a human task; it determines a manner of conduct on the part of those who wish to be faithful to God. To be righteous or just means to acknowledge the rights of others, especially in the case of the defenseless; thereby it supposes a relationship with God that can appropriately be styled "holiness." The establishment of "justice and right" is the mission entrusted by the God of the Bible to the chosen people; it is the task in which God is revealed as the God of life. To hunger and thirst for justice is to hope for it from God, but it is likewise to will to put it in practice. This desire — similar to the "seeking of holiness" of Matthew 6:33 — will be slaked, and its satisfaction will be an expression of the joy of the coming of the Reign of love and justice.

2. With the *fifth Beatitude,* the second block of Matthew's text begins. This block is constituted for the most part of Beatitudes proper to his gospel. The mercy of God is a favorite theme of Matthew. The parable he recounts in 18:23-35 is an illustration of the fifth Beatitude. The behavior required of the follower of Jesus is characterized by mercy. Matthew dovetails this outlook with that of the Hebrew scriptures when he cites Hosea 6:6: "It is love [i.e., mercy] that I desire, not sacrifice" (cf. Matt. 9:13, 12:7). These are basic attitudes, not formalities. It is practice, and not formality, upon which judgment will be rendered. The text of Matthew 25:31-46 speaks to us precisely of works of mercy. Those who refuse to practice solidarity with others will be rejected. Those who put mercy into practice are declared blessed; they shall receive God's love, which is always a gift. This grace, in turn, demands of them that they be merciful to others.

Who are the "single-hearted"? The common tendency to relegate the religious to the domain of interior attitudes and "recollection" can make the *sixth Beatitude* difficult to understand — or rather, too easy to misunderstand. Single-heartedness implies sincerity, wisdom, and determination. It is not a matter of ritual or appearances. It is a matter of profound personal attitude. This is the reason for Jesus' disputes with the Pharisees, which Matthew presents to us in such energetic terms. Every Christian runs the risk of being a hypocrite: professing one thing and doing another, separating theory from practice. The letter of James — who is like Matthew in so many ways — employs a particularly suggestive term. On two occasions, James rejects "devious" persons — literally, "double-souled" persons, *dipsychoi* (James 1:8, 4:8). The God of the Bible requires a total commitment: "No man can serve two masters. He will either hate one and love the other or be attentive to one and despise the other" (Matt. 6:24). To draw near to God means "cleansing the heart," unifying our lives, having a single soul. Being a disciple of the Lord means having the "same mind" as the Teacher. Thus, a person of pure heart, an integral person, will see God — and "face to face," as Paul says (1 Cor. 13:12). This promise is the cause of the joy of Jesus' followers.

The building of peace is a key task for the Christian. But in order to perceive the scope of this task, we must be rid of a narrow conception of peace as the absence of war or conflict. This is not the peace to which we are invited by the *seventh Beatitude*. The Hebrew word *shalom* is a familiar one and exceedingly rich in connotation. It indicates an overall, integral situation, a condition of life in harmony with God, neighbor, and nature. Shalom is the opposite of everything that runs contrary to the welfare and rights of persons and nations. It is not surprising, then, that there should be an intimate biblical link between justice and peace: "Justice and peace *(shalom)* shall kiss" (Ps. 85:10). The poor are denied both justice and *shalom*. This is why both are promised particularly to those deprived of life and well-being. Peace must be actively sought; the Beatitude is speaking of artisans of peace, not those who are commonly termed pacifists or peaceable individuals. Those who construct this peace, which implies harmony with God and with the divine will in history as well as an integrity of personal life (health) and social life (justice), "shall be called sons of God" — that is, will actually *be* children of God. Acceptance of the gift of filiation implies precisely the forging of community in history.

The *eighth Beatitude* joins two key terms: "reign," and "holiness," or justice. To have life and to establish justice (to hunger and to thirst for justice) is to call down upon one's head the wrath of the mighty. Of this the prophets, and Jesus' own life, are abundant testimonial. Those who have decided to be disciples cannot be above their Teacher (cf. Matt. 10:24). The fourth Lukan Beatitude had already enjoined this outlook on the disciple: "Blessed shall you be when men hate you, when they ostracize you and insult you and proscribe your name as evil because of the Son of Man" (Luke 6:22). A focus on discipleship is not directly present in the first three Lukan Beatitudes; Matthew, however, adopts it in all of his own. Furthermore, Matthew reinforces his statement concerning persecution "for holiness' sake" with a promise, in the following verse, of felicity for those who are abused "because of me." Matthew 5:11, then, comes very close to Luke 6:22, which speaks of persecution "because of the Son of Man," along with establishing an equivalency between justice and Jesus as the occasions of the hostility of which the blessed are the object. In this way, Matthew proclaims the surprising identity, which he will also maintain in chapter 25, between a deed of love in behalf of the poor and a deed done in behalf of the Son of Man come to judge the nations. To give one's life for justice is to give it for Christ himself.

To those who suffer for *justice*, or "holiness' sake," is promised the *Reign of God*. By repeating this term, "Reign of God," which he has already used in the first Beatitude, Matthew closes his text with an impact, through the use of the literary device known as inclusion. The promises of the six Beatitudes enclosed between the first and the last are but specifications of the promise with which the Beatitudes as a unit open and close: the promise of the Reign. The land, consolation, satiety, mercy, the vision of God, the divine filiation are but details of the life, love, and justice of the Reign of God.

These promises are gifts of the Lord. As the fruit of the free divine love, they call for a response in terms of a particular behavior. The Beatitudes of the third evangelist underscore the *gratuity of the love of God,* who "preferentially" loves the concrete poor. Those of Matthew flesh out this picture by indicating the *ethical requirement in order to be a follower of Jesus,* which flows from that loving initiative of God. It is a matter of accent. Both aspects are present in each of our two versions of the Beatitudes. And the focuses are complementary. The followers of Jesus are those who translate the grace received — which invests them as witnesses of the Reign of life — into works in behalf of their neighbor, especially the poor. The disciple is the one who strikes a solidarity — including "material" solidarity — with those for whom the Lord has a preferential love. Behold the sum and substance of the reason why a person is declared blessed and fit to "inherit the kingdom prepared for you from the creation of the world" (Matt. 25:34). Blessed are disciples — those who make the "preferential option for the poor." Gratuity and demand, investiture and dispatch to a mission, constitute the twin poles of the life of discipleship. Only a church in solidarity with the actual poor, a church that denounces poverty as an evil, is in any position to proclaim God's freely bestowed love — the gift that must be received in spiritual poverty (cf. Medellín, "Document on Poverty," no. 4).

2. The Poor Evangelize

The "church of the poor" is a very ancient concept of church. It is as old as Paul, and Paul's description is matchless. To the church living in the splendid, wealthy city of Corinth, the Apostle writes:

> Brothers, you are among those called. Consider your situation. Not many of you are wise, as men account wisdom; not many are influential; and surely not many are well-born: God chose those whom the world considers absurd to shame the wise; he singled out the weak of this world to shame the strong. He chose the world's lowborn and despised, those who

count for nothing, to reduce to nothing those who were something; so that mankind can do no boasting before God. (1 Cor. 1:26-29)

In order to perceive God's predilection for the poor, the Corinthians need only look among themselves in the Christian community. It is a question of historical experience. (2 Corinthians 8:2 will speak of the "deep poverty" of the communities of Macedonia.) But Paul's text does a theological reading of this experience and expresses a comprehension of the church from the true, most demanding focus: the viewpoint of God. The mercy of God and the divine will for life are revealed in this preference for what the world regards as foolish and weak: for the plebeian, for the condemned, for the "nonexistent." The gratuity of God's love is manifested in the confusion and humiliation of the wise, the strong, the "existing."

Thus, the church is a sign of the Reign of God. Luke gives us the content of the proclamation of the Reign in his presentation of the Messiah's program (Luke 4:18-19). The various human situations enunciated in the text (poverty, captivity, blindness, oppression) are set forth as expressions of death. With Jesus' proclamation, death will beat a retreat; Jesus injects into history a principle of life, and a principle that will lead history to its fulfillment. We find ourselves, then, before the disjunction, central to biblical revelation, between death and life. It is a disjunction that calls upon us to make a radical option.

The central fact of the Messiah's proclamation is that the proclamation itself is Good News for the poor. This Good News is then made concrete in the other actions it proclaims: liberating captives, restoring sight to the blind, and bringing freedom to the oppressed. In all of these actions freedom is the dominant notion — even in the case of sight for the blind, if we keep in mind the Hebrew text of Isaiah 61:1-2, which alludes to the deliverance of those chained in the darkness of prisons. Thus, the core of the Good News announced by the Messiah is liberation. The Reign of God, which is a Reign of life, is not only the ultimate meaning of human history. Its presence is already initiated in the attention bestowed by Jesus — and by his followers — on the poor and oppressed.

In response to the cry of the poor for liberation, Medellín proposes a church in solidarity with that aspiration for life, freedom, and grace. A beautiful, synthetic text tells us that the conference seeks to present "the face of an authentically *poor, missionary, and Paschal* church, without ties to any temporal power and boldly committed to the liberation of the whole human being and of all human beings" (Medellín, "Document on Youth," no. 15, emphasis added).

At Medellín, as in the pastoral practice and theological reflection that had preceded that conference, thereupon to be enshrined in its texts, the concept of a church of the poor has a frank Christological focus. That is, there is more at stake here than a sensitivity to the vast majority of the people of our continent, the poor. The basic demand in our pastoral practice, in our theological reflection, and in the Conference of Medellín itself — the element that confers the deepest meaning on the entire matter — comes from faith in Christ. The "Document on Poverty" makes this altogether clear. There are many passages to this effect, of which we shall cite only one: "The poverty of countless people calls for justice, solidarity, witness, commitment, and extra effort to carry out fully the salvific mission entrusted to [the church] by Christ" (Medellín, "Document on Poverty," no. 7). Complete liberation in Christ, of which the church is a sacrament in history, constitutes the ultimate foundation of the church of the poor.

This Christological option is inspired as well in another declaration, this time from Vatican II. In *Lumen Gentium* we read that the church "recognizes in the poor and suffering the image of its poor and patient founder . . . and seeks to serve Christ in them" (*LG*, no. 8). This identification of Christ with the poor (cf. Matt. 25:31-46) is a central theme in our reflection on the church of the poor. Puebla expresses it beautifully in one of its most important texts, speaking of the traits of Christ present in the "very concrete faces" of the poor (Puebla Final Document, nos. 31-39; here, no. 31).

In other words, in addressing the subject of the church of the poor, the Latin American church (in the magisterium, in pastoral practice, and in theology) adopts a "theo-logical" perspective. To speak of such a church is not only to accentuate the social aspects of its mission; it is to refer first and foremost to the very being of that church as a sign of the Reign of God. This is the heart and soul of John XXIII's intuition ("The church is, and wishes to be . . ."), which was developed in depth by Cardinal Lercaro in his interventions at the Council. It is important to underscore this. There is a tendency to view these matters only from the angle of "social problems" and to consider that the church has attended to the question of its poverty by setting up a secretariat for social affairs. The challenge goes deeper than that. What John XXIII had in mind was an in-depth church renewal.

The deep, demanding evangelical theme of the proclamation of the gospel to the poor was broached at Vatican II but did not become its central question, as Cardinal Lercaro had requested at the close of the first session. At Medellín, however, it did become the main question; it was the context of the preferential option for the poor that inspired the major texts of the conference. We have recalled the biblical bases of the proclamation of the gospel to the poor. What we wish to do here is emphasize that this outlook has marked the life of the Latin American church throughout all these years. A great many experiments and commitments have made of this notion — a proclamation of the gospel to the disinherited — their central intuition and have sought to make it a reality. It is by embarking on this course that the church has found its deeper inspiration in its efforts for the liberation of the poor and oppressed of our continent.

All of this has made for a very profound renewal of the activity of the church. The missionary requirement is always to break out of one's own narrow circle and enter a different world. This is what large sectors of the Latin American church have experienced as they have set out along the pathways of an evangelization of the despoiled and insignificant. They have begun to discover the world of the poor, and to encounter the difficulties and misunderstandings that their option provokes on the part of the great ones of this world.

At the same time, years of commitment to a "defense of the rights of the poor, according to the gospel mandate" (cf. Medellín, "Document on Peace," no. 22) and the creation of Christian base communities as the "prime, fundamental, basic nucleus of the church, which should make itself responsible for the wealth and expansion of the faith" (Medellín, "Document on Joint Pastoral Ministry," no. 10) have opened up new perspectives. These experiments with church "have helped the Church to discover the evangelizing potential of the poor" (Medellín, "Document on Poverty," no. 1147). This is one of Puebla's basic declarations. It has its roots in the experience of the church in Latin America. It also demonstrates Puebla's continuity with Medellín.

Not only are the poor the privileged addressees of the message of the Reign of God; they are its vessels as well. One expression of this potential is to be seen in the base ecclesial communities, which are surely among the most promising phenomena of the church of Latin America today. These communities sail in the broad channel opened up by the Council when the latter spoke of the people of God in the world of poverty. They constitute an ecclesial presence of history's insignificant ones — or, to use the words of the Council, of a "Messianic people" (*LG*, no. 9). That is to say, here is a people who walk the roads of history in the hope of the Reign that ever realizes the Messianic paradox: "The last shall be first."

The option for the poor, with all of the pastoral and theological consequences of that option, is one of the most important contributions to the life of the church universal to have emerged from the theology of liberation and the church on our continent. As we have observed, that option has its roots in biblical revelation and the history of the church. Still, today it presents particular, novel characteristics. This is due to our better understanding of the depth and complexity of the poverty and oppression experienced by most of humanity; it is due to our perception of the economic, social, and cultural mechanisms that produce that poverty; and before all else, it is due to the new light which the word of the Lord sheds on that poverty. This outlook thereby becomes the core of the "new evangelization," which got under way in Latin America two decades ago, but which it is so important to keep fresh and up to date. The novelty we cite was acknowledged, in a certain way, by the synod held on the occasion of the twentieth anniversary of the close of Vatican II. Among the synod's conclusions: "Since the Second Vatican Council, the Church has become more aware of its mission to serve the poor, the oppressed, and the outcast."

This service is a perilous one today, in the lands we live in. The vested interests at stake are powerful, and many are the victims of imprisonment, abuse, slander, exile, and death who have met their fate as a result of a wish to enter into solidarity with the poor. This is the reality of martyrdom, a reality at once tragic and fruitful. And it is a fact of life in a church that is learning day by day that it cannot be greater than its Master.

13 The Central Position of the Reign of God in Liberation Theology

Jon Sobrino

I. Liberation Theology as a Theology of the Reign of God

All authentic theological renewal is the fruit of an attempt to answer the question: What is "ultimate" in Christian faith? The question implies that Christian faith is made up of divers elements that can be organized and arranged in a hierarchy. That the truths of faith are hierarchically ordered became obvious at Vatican II, but their actual organization and ordering in respect to an ultimate principle is the task of theology. It is up to theology to seek out that ultimate element that will give the best account of the totality of the faith, and the element selected will determine the character of the theology that selects it.

In our opinion, this is what has been occurring in theology for a century now, with the rediscovery that Jesus' message was eschatological. Those who made the discovery proposed a concrete content for this eschatological message: the Reign of God. But the importance of the discovery went far beyond a determination of content. For theology, it meant the end of a mere theological, dogmatic, or biblical positivism and the inauguration of the eschatological theologies — those theologies that attempted to name the ultimate element in faith and to develop from there.

Translated by Robert R. Barr.

A. Liberation Theology's Answer to the Question of the Eschaton

The theology of liberation is formally and organically integrated into this method and concept of theology. It names an ultimate, which then functions as an organizing and ordering principle for everything else. That to which this theology assigns the primacy is indicated in its very name: liberation, which is understood essentially as liberation of the poor. In this sense, liberation theology is also an eschatological theology, since it assigns liberation more than a mere place (however important a place) in the content of theology; it assigns it an ultimate and ordering content. Thus, it is not a regional theology (a part of theology, or of a particular theology — the part bearing upon liberation). Still less is it a reductionistic theology (a theology whose sole object would be liberation). In assigning a primacy to the liberation of the poor, the theology of liberation is positing the liberation of the poor as that part of the content of theology around which all of theology can be organized — all questions of who God and Christ are, what grace and sin are, what the Church and society are, what love and hope are, and so on.

The analyses conducted in the present chapter constitute an attempt to answer the question, What faith reality, what *eschaton,* most adequately corresponds to a theology that assigns historical primacy to the liberation of the poor? In other words, how might one formulate the ultimate in such a way as to do justice to both the revelation of God and the concrete, historical liberation of the poor?

B. Primacy of the Reign of God

The theology of liberation prefers the Reign of God as the *eschaton.* But it is very important to understand why. There are various reasons. Let us attempt to summarize the most important of them.

1. In its very enterprise, liberation theology has a particular leaning that it cannot deny, whatever the advantages and disadvantages of that leaning or attitude. In this it is not altogether unlike other theologies, but it does emphasize certain dimensions of the theological undertaking that are more specific to itself than to other theologies.

Liberation theology is clearly a *historical* theology. It seeks to locate historically, to verify in history, the entire content of the faith, including strictly transcendent content. Its very name is no more than the historicization of the core of Christian faith: salvation. Liberation theology is the theology of salvation as liberation. Liberation theology is also *a prophetical* theology, which takes account of sin — and historical sin — as central to its concern, something that must be exposed and denounced. It is a *praxic* theology, which understands itself as an ideological moment of an ecclesial, historical praxis. That is, it is interested before all else in transforming reality, although it defends its *theological status* and believes itself to be a theology that can help in the transformation of history. Finally, it is a *popular* theology — although there are various understandings of this concept — a theology that sees in the people, in the twin connotation of "people" as poverty and as collectivity, the addressee, and in some theologians, however analogically, the very subject of theology.

2. Besides corresponding better to liberation theology's posture and scope, the Reign of God evinces a greater potential for systematically organizing the whole of theology, as theology ought to be practiced in a reality like that of the Third World. Ignacio Ellacuría, who places a great deal of emphasis on the Reign of God as the object of theology, exemplifies this. While the passage we are about to cite is a lengthy one, it will spare us an extensive commentary.

> What this conception of faith from a point of departure in the Reign of God does is posit an indissoluble conjunction between God and history.... The Reign of God is immune to a whole series of perilous distortions. It is impervious to a dualism of (earthly) Reign and (heavenly) God, such that those who cultivate the world and history would be doing something merely positivistic, while those who devote themselves to God would be doing something transcendent, spiritual, and supernatural. It rejects an identification of the Reign of God with the church, especially with the institutional church, which would imply both an escape from the world into the church, and an impoverishment of the Christian message and mission that would culminate in a worldly church — a secularization of the church by way of a conformation of its institutional aspect to secularistic values of domination and wealth, and by subordinating to it something greater than it by far, the Reign of God. It rejects a manipulation of God, a taking of the name of God in vain in support of injustice, by insisting that that name and reality are properly invoked in the historical signs of justice, fraternity, freedom, a preferential option for the poor, love, mercy, and so on, and that without these it is vain to speak of a salvific presence of God in history.
>
> The Reign of God in history as a Reign of God among human beings

exposes the historical wickedness of the world, and thereby the reign of sin, that negation of the Reign of God. Over and above a certain natural sin (original sin) and a personal sin (individual sin), the proclamation of the Reign and the difficulty of seeing it implanted evinces the presence of a "sin of the world," which is fundamentally historical and structural, communitarian and objective, at once the fruit and the cause of many other personal and collective sins, and its propagation and consolidation as the ongoing negation of the Reign of God. Not that structures commit sin, as liberation theologians are sometimes accused of saying; but structures manifest and actualize the power of sin, thereby causing sin, by making it exceedingly difficult for men and women to lead the life that is rightfully theirs as the daughters and sons of God.

This sinful power is utterly real. It is intrinsically sin, and the fruit of sin, and here we may recall the traditional explanations of original sin; but further, it causes sin by presenting obstacles to the dynamism of the Reign of God among human beings, to the presence of the life-giving Spirit amidst the principalities and powers of death. Thus, without being deprived of its essential immanence, the evil of the world acquires a transcendent dimension. . . . The destruction of human life, or its impoverishment, is anything but a purely moral problem: it is also, absolutely and unqualifiedly, a theological problem — the problem of sin in action, and the problem of life denied in human existence.[1]

We see very clearly, in this lengthy citation, that the primacy accorded to the Reign of God resides in the capacity of the latter to unify, without either separation or confusion, transcendence and history. It is from this point of departure that essential content such as Christ and the church can and ought to be understood, without hint of idealistic abstractions or spurious substitutions of what the Reign of God is not. Furthermore, although this terminology is not used in our citation, it is the Reign of God that enables us to rediscover the anti-Reign, the world of sin, that is — both historical and transcendent. Reality's ultimate duality, its irreconcilable duality, is properly identified not in the binomial "transcendence and history" — which can and should be reconciled — but in the irreconcilable binomial of Reign and anti-Reign, the history of grace and of sin.

3. One of the reasons for the primacy of the Reign of God in the theol-

---

1. Ellacuría, "Aporte de la teología de la liberación a las religions abrahámicas en la superación del individualism y del positivismo," manuscript of an address to the Congress of Abrahamic Religions held at Córdoba, Spain, in February 1987, pp. 10-12.

ogy of liberation is the thrust and intent of that theology to systematization. But there is an even more basic reason. Theology is always a second act, within and in the presence of a reality, and liberation theology lays explicit emphasis on this point. But it is the reality of Latin America and of the Third World in general that calls for a Reign of God, of whatever conceptual formulation. The major fact in Latin America is the massive, unjust poverty that threatens whole populations with death. At the same time, the most novel fact is the hope of a just life, of liberation. It is this twin reality that calls for reflection and a primary reaction — logically antecedent to any theological reflection and even any specific, determinate faith. It is reality itself that demands to be seen as a reality of life or death, that poses the question of hope or despair, that calls for an option for life or death. A grasp of the primary reality as being unjust poverty and the hope of a just life, requiring one to throw in one's lot with the alternative of life, can then be reformulated in theological reflection as the pre-understanding necessary for an adequate understanding of revelation, and theologized as a sign of the times and a manifestation of the will of God. All of this is true, and liberation theology includes all of it. But in itself this grasp is of something more primordial: it is the grasp of a reality that raises its own, autonomous cry.

After all, when theology sees Latin America's reality in this first, pre-theological moment, it finds, without falling into naiveté or anachronisms, a social situation remarkably akin to that in which the notion of the Reign of God was first formulated, biblically in so many words, or extrabiblically in other terms. It is true today, as well, that entire peoples are unjustly oppressed and that they have a hope of life. It is true today, as well, that this is the most important fact for a grasp of the totality, as well as the various ethical, praxic, and semantic dimensions that emerge from that totality. If this is the case, and if this is historically akin to the reality in which the formulation of utopia in terms of the Reign of God was originally crystallized, then it is fairly obvious why a theologization of third-world reality might be undertaken in terms of the theology of the Reign of God. It is current historical reality that ultimately renders the concept of the Reign of God more useful today than other concepts for a theological elaboration of reality. It is the kinship between both realities, that of the Third World today and that of the peoples who forged the notion of the Reign of God, that makes it possible to have a better understanding of what the Reign of God meant when it was first conceived. The fusion of horizons required by hermeneutics is accomplished first and foremost in reality itself.

What has occurred then in liberation theology is that, in a pre-theological moment, reality has been grasped as an irruption of the poor with a hope of liberation. This grasp comports a prejudgment, if you will, but therein is the origin of the theology of liberation. When that theology is formally constituted a theology in terms of the primacy of the poor, or more precisely, of the liberation of the poor, then a course is set similar to that theologized so many centuries ago in the Hebrew scriptures and with Jesus: the Reign of God. It is the historical situation that ultimately forces this election.

II. Determination of the Reign of God in the Gospel

The fact that the Reign of God is central to the theology of liberation says nothing as yet about the quality and character of that Reign. Such a determination for the present time, which we shall attempt in part III, is no easy matter. But neither is an evangelical determination of the nature of the Reign of God, and this for an obvious reason: while using the expression countless times, and eager as he is to explain it in his parables, Jesus never says exactly *what* this Reign is.

This is not to suggest that nothing can be known of what the Reign of God meant for Jesus. What it does suggest is the need for a method, or to speak more modestly, a way of ascertaining this. To our view, the approaches used by systematic christologies are three. They might be called: (1) the notional way, (2) the way of the practice of Jesus, and (3) the way of the addressee of the Reign. These ways or paths are not mutually exclusive, but complementary. Still, depending on which is used or most emphasized, theologians' conclusions will vary. Liberation theology's contribution to a determination of the Reign of God consists not so much in exegetical discoveries, but in an insistence on the limitations and dangers of taking only the first way, and in its emphasis on the need for the second way, and especially the third. Liberation theology shows this in its own procedure when it analyzes Jesus' proclamation of the Reign of God.

A. *The Notional Way*

The notional way attempts to ascertain what the Reign of God was for Jesus from a starting point in the notion Jesus himself might have had of it. This way analyzes the various notions of the Reign in the Hebrew scriptures and among Jesus' contemporaries (John the Baptist, the Zealots, the Pharisees, the apocalyptic groups, and so on). So, the researcher attempts to ferret out what Jesus thought about the Reign. The substance of these investigations — expressed in formal terms — is usually the following. Jesus proclaimed a utopia, something good and salvific, that was at hand.

All of this is true, of course, and liberation theology embraces it. The problem is how this notion of the Reign of God can become rather more concrete; it is here that we note the importance, or unimportance, attributed to the other two "ways." When the latter are not actively present in the investigation — we say "actively" because they are always present in some way — the notion of the Reign tends to abide in supreme vagueness and abstraction. This does not militate against the fact that what is said of the Reign is something true, good, and holy — something, so to speak, with which Jesus himself would agree. But the vagueness and abstraction are of no help to anyone desirous of learning what, in the concrete, the Reign was for Jesus. Indeed, they can be dangerous if they relegate to a secondary level, or even simply ignore, important things that Jesus meant by the Reign of God.

B. The Way of the Praxis of Jesus

The premise of the way of the praxis of Jesus is that what Jesus did will shed light on what the Reign of God is. This is Schillebeeckx's position. "The concrete content of the Kingdom arises from [Jesus'] ministry and activity considered as a whole."[2] This methodological option is clearly justified in the case of those actions which Jesus himself referred to the Reign of God, whether explicitly (as with the expulsion of demons, or preaching in parables) or implicitly (for example, in his meals). But the option is reasonable for the rest of Jesus' activity as well — certainly for the first great part of his public life, since in that period the proclamation of the Reign was precisely the central element in his work.

In order to clarify the importance of this point, the first thing we must emphasize is the very fact of Jesus' practice, which, in strict logic, needn't have existed at all. Let us ask the following logical, hypothetical questions. If Jesus thought that the Reign of God was imminent and gratuitous, then why might he not have restricted himself to its proclamation? Why not await that

---

2. Edward Schillebeeckx, *Jesus: An Experiment in Christology* (New York: Seabury Press, 1979), p. 143.

coming in passivity and confidence? Why not accept the situation of his world, if it was soon to change? These purely logical questions have only a historical response. Jesus *did* many things. In pure logic, once more, one could ask whether he did them because the Reign was already present, or in order that it might become present. Were Jesus' deeds purely sacramental, the expression of a Reign that drew near in all gratuity, or were they also service to the Reign, deeds performed in order that it might draw near? Whatever the answer to these questions, the important thing is to emphasize that Jesus did many things; he did not passively await the coming of the Reign (or ask this attitude of his hearers). Not even for the short period of hope in the imminence of the end could Jesus tolerate the situation of his world, as Cullmann says.[3]

Jesus' activity in the service of the Reign is understandable, since even in Isaiah (and in Luke's conception) the proclamation of the Good News, the content of the Reign, is essentially accompanied by activity: "This news will only be *good* to the extent that the liberation of the oppressed becomes reality."[4] But such an a priori approach is not the only way to understand Jesus' activity. Besides the programmatic summary of the proclamation of the Reign in Luke, we have other, earlier summaries of Jesus' activity: Jesus "went into their synagogues preaching the Good News and expelling demons throughout the whole of Galilee" (Mark 1:39). Jesus healed many persons, suffering from various illnesses, and drove out many demons (Mark 1:34). In the summary that we find in Acts 10:38, Jesus "went about doing good works and healing all who were in the grip of the devil."

The fact of Jesus' activity is clear. To place it in relationship with the Reign of God is often exegetically justifiable and is systematically reasonable. The important thing, then, is to see what his activity contributes to a determination of the nature of the Reign by making concrete the vagueness of the formulation of the latter. Let us briefly analyze three stages in Jesus' activity, while stating from the outset that it is only for methodological reasons that we separate this second way, the way of Jesus' praxis, from the third, the way of the addressee.

1. Jesus' Miracles   Jesus performed a series of activities that he understood as signs of the Reign. As signs, they are not the totality of the Reign. But if they render it present, then surely they must tell us something about it. Among

---

3. Oscar Cullmann, *Jesus and the Revolutionaries* (New York: Harper & Row, 1970).
4. C. Escudero Freire, *Devolver el evangelio a los pobres* (Salamanca, 1978), p. 270.

the signs of the Reign are Jesus' miracles, his expulsion of demons, and his welcoming of sinners. His meals are signs of the celebration of the Reign. We will concentrate on the miracles.

Taken formally, the miracles are signs that the Reign of God is approaching "with power." They have been called "cries of the Kingdom." Thus, they are not the Reign in its totality, nor do they offer a comprehensive solution for the evils for which the Reign will provide the remedy. As signs of the Reign, the miracles are before all else salvation — beneficent realities, liberative realities in the presence of oppression. Hence, the miracles occasion joy by their beneficent aspect and generate hope by their liberative aspect.

Although they are only signs, the miracles express the character of the Reign of God as salvation from urgent concrete needs. This means liberation, since the needs from which one is saved are those produced by elements of oppression; the reason for the Reign is nothing other than, nothing apart from, these needs themselves.

2. Jesus' Denunciations We have referred to the signs wrought by Jesus as actions in the service of the Reign. But we may ask whether Jesus performed some more comprehensive activity, some activity correlative to the totality of the Reign of God — something from which we might deduce what that Reign meant in its totality. Granted, Jesus formulated no theory of society as such. However, neither can it be said that Jesus has nothing to transmit to us in terms of the Reign's dimension of totality. That dimension appears in his view of the anti-Reign as a totality; from that view we can deduce something of what the Reign itself signified as a totality. After all, the anti-Reign is not only different from the Reign, it is formally its contrary. In this sense, perhaps we might denominate certain activities of Jesus as praxis, since they were intended as a denunciation of society in its totality. The purpose was to expose the causes of the anti-Reign and transform it into the Reign, although on this point Jesus offers no technical means but only calls for conversion.

That Jesus is convinced of the existence of the anti-Reign is clear. The world and the society in which he lived were not totalities in conformity with the will of his Father, God. But more than this, they were strictly the contrary. This is what we are taught by the controversies in which Jesus was caught up. These are never simple exercises in casuistry, or in the resolution of secondary *quaestiones disputatae*. They always deal with the central question of all: who God is. In the religious society of Jesus' time and place, this automatically led to the next question: what would a world according to God be like? In the controversy over the ears of grain plucked on the sabbath day in a stranger's field, for example, what is in question is the priority of life over worship (the religious dimension of the controversy) and over owner-ship (the social dimension). Jesus declares that, for God, life has priority over all else; he holds that, in today's language, God is a God of life, and that therefore society ought to be organized in service of life. What underlies the controversies is the exclusive alternative between the God of life and other gods, between Reign and anti-Reign. What is directly clear in the controver-sies is Jesus' rejection of the anti-Reign. But indirectly they also explain this minimum: in the name of God, there should exist a society organized in ser-vice of life.

Jesus' denunciations demonstrate his forthright condemnation of those responsible for the anti-Reign. Certain anathemas may be directed against individuals, but in general the addressees of the denunciations and anathe-mas are formulated in the plural. Not that Jesus had a theory of social classes, but he does assume the existence of social groups responsible for the anti-Reign. The wealthy, Pharisees, scribes or doctors of the Law, priests, and civil rulers are denounced and anathematized. Various things are thrown up to them: that they are hypocrites, that their existence is vain and empty, that they will have to give an accounting on the Day of Judgment, and so on. But in (almost) all of the denunciations there is a fundamental element: the ad-dressees are the cause of the anti-Reign, they are oppressors, they produce victims. In the abundant denunciations of those responsible we discern a de-nunciation of the society that they mold as an oppressive society, rotten to the core. Here is a society in which power, at its various levels, oppresses the masses. This is the anti-Reign.

In sum, we can say that Jesus rejects these particular social groups and the society that they shape. By way of his denunciations of the groups re-sponsible for it, he denounces the configuration of society that they create. A society that produces this many victims is the anti-Reign; it must change in order to be in conformity with the will of God. From this it is possible to de-duce only a minimum, but it is an important minimum for what the Reign of God is: it will be the contrary of the anti-Reign. There will be no oppres-sion of some by others. In today's language, as in the language of the Hebrew scriptures, the Reign of God will be a reign of justice, a world organized in service of the life of those who had been victims, a world that will tear up death and oppression by the roots. Love as a possible formulation of the sub-stance of the Reign will have to be made concrete in terms of justice. Other-wise Jesus' denunciations and exposés will not make much sense.

3. **Jesus' Lot** Jesus' denunciations and exposés, seen as a whole, function as praxis, independently of his explicit consciousness of it; that is, they are pronounced with the purpose of transforming social reality. This is verified in Jesus' lot, which in turn will explain what the Reign of God is. Almost no one today continues to accept Bultmann's thesis that Jesus' death at the hands of the political authority as a punishment for a political misdemeanor was simply an absurd, tragic mistake. Both trials or processes, the religious more so than the political, make it abundantly clear that Jesus' adversaries knew very well what they were doing and why they were doing it. In the religious process, Jesus stands accused of blasphemy, an accusation whose formulation is religious. But alongside this indictment, which would appear to be redactional, appears the basic accusation: Jesus wants to destroy the temple. In this religious formulation, Jesus is implicitly but unambiguously accused of seeking the radical subversion of society. The temple was the symbol of the totality of society, in the religious, economic, financial, and political areas. In his political trial he is charged with acts of concrete subversion. These charges are dismissed, as they are seen to be unfounded. But he is also accused (and this is the charge on which he is found guilty and sentenced to death) of offering a distinct — and in the formulation of the gospels, exclusive — alternative to the Empire. From a historical viewpoint, the accusation leveled against him in the religious trial is far more solidly founded than his indictment in the political. But the conclusion is the same: Jesus objectively represents a menace to established society, and for that he must die. In situations very much like those in which Jesus lived and acted, Archbishop Romero used to explain, with consummate simplicity and clarity, that anyone who gets in the way is killed. The ultimate agent of Jesus' murder is not to be sought among individuals. The ultimate agent of Jesus' murder is that which Jesus disturbs: his society. In systematic language, the mediator of God is murdered by the mediators of other gods, because God's mediation, the Reign, is an objective threat to the mediations of other gods (the temple theocracy, the Empire). The attempt to do away with Jesus was a historical, structural necessity. Thus, the fact that he was killed is altogether understandable historically. The mystery lies in why God should have permitted it, which is something we cannot investigate here.[5]

But what does Jesus' murder tell us about the Reign of God? Once more,

5. Cf. Sobrino, "Jesús de Nazaret," in *Conceptos fundamentals de pastoral,* ed. C. Floristán and J. J. Tamayo (Madrid, 1983), p. 249; Ignacio Ellacuría, "Por qué muere Jesús y por qué lo matan," *Diakonia* (1978): 65-75.

we learn something minimal, but basic. Persons who preach an exclusively transcendent Reign of God do not get themselves murdered. People who preach a Reign that is only a new relationship with God, or only "love," or only "reconciliation," or only "trust in God," are not murdered. All these things may be legitimately regarded as elements accompanying the message of the Reign of God, but they alone do not explain Jesus' death, and therefore they alone cannot be the central element of the Reign. The Reign of God must have had some bearing on the historico-social, not only on the transcendent. Jesus proclaimed it for religious reasons, surely: because the Reign of God represents the will of God, as does Jesus' proclamation of that Reign. But the content of the Reign was not religious in the sense of being nonhistorical or asocial. To bring out this point, Juan Luis Segundo asserts that the Reign of God proclaimed by Jesus was a political reality — not by contrast with the religious element, but by contrast with the purely transcendent or purely individual.[6] Segundo goes on to say that the purely religious element of the Reign of God only reinforces its political dimension, since concepts like *Reign* (and *poor*) are "all the more crucially political insofar as their underlying motivations are religious."[7] Whether the Reign of God be called a political reality or a historico-social one, the important thing to bring out is the historical, concrete dimension it had in the mind of Jesus. For Jesus, the Reign is the Reign *of God*. It is what happens in history when *God* reigns. But when God reigns, something happens *in history* that transforms that history and shapes it in a particular manner, in contrast with the anti-Reign.

As opposition, it is not an extrapolation from present possibilities; and as opposition to the historical anti-Reign, it is something occurring in history. It is a historico-social reality — a political one, if you will. None of this militates against the character of the Reign as that *of God*. On the contrary, Jesus sees it as such precisely because this is the way he understands *his* God, and he serves that God — to the point of being put to death — because he believes that the Reign is the will of God for this world.

C. The Way of the Addressee of the Reign

The third way, or approach to a determination of what the Reign of God is, is that of the addressee, which we have already sketched out to some extent in

6. Cf. Juan Luis Segundo, *Jesus of Nazareth*, trans. John Drury (Maryknoll, NY: Orbis Books, 1984-88), pp. 87-103.

7. Segundo, *Jesus of Nazareth*, p. 88.

our consideration of the second way. An emphasis on the third way, it seems to us, is liberation theology's most specific contribution to theological methodology. The basic premise of this third approach is that the content and addressees of the Reign are mutually explanatory; all the more so when the addressee is considered not in a vague and undifferentiated manner, but concretely; and especially, when it becomes possible to know the reason why this is the addressee of the Reign. The effect of an analysis of the addressee is a concrete identification of the utopia and salvation of the Reign — and surely a concrete identification of the anti-Reign — such that salvation can no longer be universalized or be found in all manner of interchangeable conceptions, precisely because the addressee is concrete.

The theology of liberation takes this exegetical determination of the addressee very seriously and systematizes the reality of the poor on the basis of the data of the gospel.[8] The poor are an economic and social reality. They are those for whom to live is to bear a heavy burden, by reason of the difficulty of their lives and by reason of their marginalization. The poor are a collective reality; they are poor peoples, or poor as a people. The poor are a historical reality; they are poor not mainly for natural reasons, but historical ones — poor because of injustice. The poor are a dialectical reality; there are poor because there are rich, and vice versa. The poor are a political reality; in their very reality, they have at least a potential for conflict and the transformation of society. This systematization of the reality of the poor is not deduced, especially on the last point, immediately from evangelical data. But it does systematize fundamental traits, and we offer it in order that the reality of the poor not disappear into thin air, as so often happens. In any case, what is of interest to the theology of liberation, and what that theology proposes methodologically, is that it be taken seriously that *these* poor, the poor of the gospel, are the addressees of the Reign of God, and that it is in terms of *these* poor that the nature of the Reign of God can be made concrete. These propositions, which seem so utterly obvious and logical, are nevertheless not usually accepted, or at least not consistently. This is understandable, because they ascribe a "partiality," a partisanship, to God. God is taking sides — being partial to one group rather than to another, and this, today as in Jesus' time, is scandalous. Indeed, the preaching of the Good News to the poor, simply as such, produces scandal (cf. Matt. 11:6, Luke 7:23). After a long analysis in the work previously cited, Segundo emphasizes this partiality:

8. Cf. Ignacio Ellacuría, "Pobres," in *Conceptos fundamentales de pastoral*, ed. C. Floristán and J. J. Tamayo (Madrid, 1983), pp. 786-802.

> The Reign of God is not announced to everyone. It is not "proclaimed" to all. . . . The Reign is destined for certain groups. It is theirs. It belongs to them. Only for them will it be a cause of joy. And, according to Jesus' *mind,* the dividing line between joy and woe produced by the Reign runs between *the poor* and the rich. (p. 90)

He gives the reason for this partiality, which usually causes still greater scandal:

> The Reign comes to change the *situation* of the poor, to put an end to it. As the first Beatitude tells us the poor possess the Reign of God. That is not due to any merit of theirs, much less to any value that poverty might have. On the contrary, the Reign is theirs because of the inhuman nature of their situation as poor people. . . . If the poor were still subject to (moral and religious) conditions in order to enjoy the coming Reign of God, that would mean the collapse of the original Beatitudes and their revelation of God. They could not say of the poor that the Reign is theirs, precisely *because* of what they suffer from their inhuman situation. (pp. 107, 140)

On the basis of the proposition that the poor are the addressees of the Reign of God, and that they are that simply in their quality as poor, two supremely important consequences follow. The first, an obvious one, bears on the content of the Reign. The poor define the Reign of God by what they are. They make concrete a utopia customarily formulated in the abstract — partly out of logical necessity, but for the most part because of a reluctance to make it real — in order that its addressees be not the poor alone, but others as well, and ultimately all. It is not easy to select a single term in which to formulate this reality, since, as we have said, needs — those of the poor, as we can now specify — are plural. But for the purpose of formulating the termination of the misfortunes of the poor, words like *life, justice,* and *liberation* continue to be meaningful. What the best formulation of the Reign of God would be is, at bottom, something only the poor themselves can answer, since theirs is the Reign, and it is they who know that from which the Reign delivers them. But the important thing is that, whatever the formulation, the poor make concrete the content of the Reign as the defeat of poverty. Perhaps we might simply say that the Reign of God is a world, a society, that makes life and dignity possible for the poor.

The second important thing that makes concrete the addressee of the Reign of God is precisely the element denoted by the prepositional phrase "of God" in the name for that Reign; in other words, the transcendent dimension of the Reign. This thesis may sound strange at this point. A determination that the poor, as described, are the addressees of the Reign of God is frequently invoked in support of an indictment of liberation theology for reductionism, economicism, sociologism, or the like. Our proposition may sound strange for another reason, as well. In citing the transcendent, we could seem to be automatically transporting ourselves to some timeless, immaterial world. There is still the tendency, in addressing the question of transcendence and history, not only to distinguish them, but to set them in mutual opposition. Nevertheless, the transcendency of the Reign of God ought to be analyzed, at least in a first moment, in terms of the character of that Reign as being "of God," whatever the manifestation of this being "of God."

To our view, the fact that the Reign is of the poor, that it belongs to the poor, is a very effective way of expressing its being "of God," both with respect to the formality of God as mystery and with respect to the ultimate content of that mystery. As for the former, the poor are addressees of the Reign not in virtue of any moral or religious quality they may happen to possess, not because poverty makes it possible (as it in fact does make it possible) to live in greater openness to God. The reason the Reign is addressed to the poor is simply the way God is. God's being thus, and not otherwise, is neither conceptualized nor conceptualizable (in addition to being, for the adversaries of the poor, neither desired nor desirable). It is a manifestation of the divine reality, which, at least from a historical viewpoint, outstrips, transcends, the expectancies of natural reason, and certainly of sinful reason. Jesus' entire life shows the extent to which "the way God is" transcends conventional notions. The Reign's partiality to the poor occasions scandal and conflict. And having proclaimed to the poor in the Beatitudes that the Reign of God is theirs, in his parables Jesus must constantly defend this partiality of God's, in controversy with his adversaries. It is as if Jesus constantly had to say, "God is *not* the way you think God is, but just the opposite." Jesus cannot actually argue *why* God is this way; he can only assert the fact in the hope that his adversaries will accept a new God, the God who embraces the sinner, who pays the same wage to those who arrive at the eleventh hour as to those who come at the first, who is distraught and anxious over a single sheep that has gone astray.

In terms of Jesus' service to the Reign, as well as in terms of its addressees, then, we think it possible to say what the Reign of God was for Jesus. The Reign of God continues to be utopia, and thereby indefinable. But with what we have seen, we can safely assert that it is the utopia of the poor, the termination of their misfortunes, liberation from their slaveries, and the opportunity to live and to live with dignity. And again, from this point of departure, we can better understand the meaning of the Reign as a Reign "of God": the God of the Reign is a God who desires life for the poor and who delivers them from the anti-Reign.

III. Systematic Concept of the Reign of God

An evangelical determination of the Reign of God is surely of the highest importance for our faith. But in itself it does not furnish a systematic concept of the Reign for today. Liberation theology, which unlike other theologies maintains the central character of the Reign, considers that the systematic concept of the Reign should be based on and should synthesize what is essential to the evangelical concept. But, while necessary, this is insufficient.

> The gospel invites us to creative fantasy, and to the elaboration of ideologies sprung not from some aprioristic quantity, but from an analysis of, and the challenges of, a situation, with a view to a project of liberation. This being the case, the Christian, in faith, should not be afraid to take a concrete decision — with the risks of failure that that decision will involve — a decision that can be the historically mediated coming of the Reign. Therefore he or she can ask, ardently, day after day: "Thy kingdom come to us." Neither faith nor the church knows in advance what the concrete shape of such a decision will be.[9]

This citation from Leonardo Boff forbids an absolute formulation of the Reign. It emphasizes the need (and the risks) of its historicization today. But it demands some notion of what the Reign may mean today — some horizon against which a response to present challenges can be understood as a realization, however provisional, of the Reign.

A. Current Reassertion of the Reign of God

Before all else, it must be observed that the theology of liberation, with all its risks and all its provisional character, reaffirms the need to maintain the

9. Leonardo Boff, *Jesucristo y la liberación del hombre* (Madrid, 1981), p. 388.

Reign of God as a central concept today. We have already seen the specific reasons for this assertion. What remains to be explained is in what sense liberation theology continues to maintain this when other theologies abandon it as their central concept. To make it more understandable, we may recall the celebrated question of *when* the Reign is to come.

What the theology of liberation states is the following. In the first place, this theology insists that the Reign of God has not come at the level of mediation, and that, nevertheless, the will of God continues to come to this world. From the non-arrival of the Reign liberation theology does not adopt the conclusion leapt to by other ideologies, which, being ignorant of mediation, concentrate exclusively on the mediator, who indeed has come. That the mediation has not come raises an intrinsic difficulty for its determination, this is true; but liberation theology asserts that that determination must continue to be sought today. In the second place, liberation theology insists that there is at once a continuity and a discontinuity between the systematic and evangelical concepts of the Reign of God. The discontinuity is obvious, since it is unclear what the will of God is today for the current real world. From this liberation theologians come to their well-known demand for analytical mediations in order to arrive at a determination of the content of the Reign. The continuity is obvious, too — *for faith.* Liberation theology completely agrees that the mediator has indeed come, and that, accordingly, in its view of the Reign, in its activity in behalf of the Reign, there is something essential and permanent. This essential and permanent factor stands in need of becoming concrete but will never have to be canceled. It will always be needed in order to guide any future determination of the Reign of God. Simple as it may appear to say it, liberation theology accepts the fact that, throughout the historical life of Jesus, not only in the Jesus of the resurrection, the will of God for this world has appeared, with ultimacy, and that this has never been revoked in subsequent history.

B. Systematic Concept of the Reign of God

After these reflections we can answer the question of what liberation theology understands systematically by the Reign of God. Formally speaking, by the Reign of God the theology of liberation understands a historical reality that has in itself the potential of openness to and indication of a "more." Materially speaking, it ascribes to the concept of the Reign of God the basic element of the evangelical concept as that concept is historicized in terms of the hermeneutic principles set forth above. Thus, the Reign of God is a reign of life; it is a historical reality (a just life for the poor) and a reality with an intrinsic tendency to be "more" (ultimately, utopia).

It should be clear, in this definition, by virtue of the primacy accorded them in the gospel and in the option, that the poor are the primary addressees of the Reign. A definition of the content of the Reign as *life* must be explained. What is at stake, of course, is not the term in itself; other, equivalent expressions could be found. *Life* is selected, we believe, because it is a better expression of both the historical and the utopian elements of the Reign. *Just* is added to indicate both the route to the attainment of life in the presence of the anti-Reign and to express the condition in which life subsists.

The theology of liberation insists on life as the historical content of the Reign because, in the Third World, poverty means proximity to death. The poor are those "who die before their time" (Gustavo Gutiérrez). *Life* means that, with the advent of the Reign, the poor cease to be poor. Liberation theology insists on the primary sense of life, without being over-hasty to analyze the element of the "more" that is inherent in all life. Paradoxically, it focuses more on (an idealized) protology than on eschatology: more on creation than on fulfillment. Life is not simply a leaven which, kneaded into the dough of reality, gives rise to the truly human, so that at last the Reign of God is here. In the Third World, life is not the premise; it is always the proposition itself. It is a finality in itself. In negative terms, the primary sin of the anti-Reign is not against eschatology, but against creation.

Today it is the concept of a just life that bridges the gap between the systematic and the evangelical concept of the Reign. The words, "a just life," ring as Good News in the ears of millions of human beings. It is they that move people to posit signs whose inner thrust is an overwhelming sense of mercy at the sight of the faces of the poor; and it is they that move people to denounce the pervasive presence of the anti-Reign. Efforts in behalf of life today also constitute a continuing occasion of scandal, conflict, persecution, and death. The upshot of all of this is that the Good News of the Reign can have a meaningful Christian formulation today as the life of the poor.

But life is also a reality which, of its very nature, is always open to the "more." Its concept is dynamic and directional; it points to an unfolding of itself in multilevel realization, a realization charged in turn with new opportunities and exigencies. Life points to the perpetual element of the "more" in the concept of the Reign of God.

In the Reign of God there must be bread — the prime symbol of the Good News today. But this same reality, bread, raises the question of how to obtain it, thereby demanding some kind of activity and toil. Then once there is bread, the question arises how to share it (the ethical element and the communitarian element), the temptation arises not to share it (sin), and the need arises to celebrate it, for the gladness that the bread produces. Bread obtained by some is intrinsically a question of bread for other groups, other communities, for an entire people — and the question of liberation arises. But then the attainment of bread by a whole people means practice, reflection, functional ideologies, risks, perils. And the need can arise to risk one's very life in order that bread be transformed into a symbol not of selfishness but of love.

And now bread is more than bread. It has something of the sacramental about it, and so the festival of maize is celebrated, and those who come together not only eat bread, but sing and recite poems, and bread opens out upon art and culture. And none of this happens mechanically. At each stage of the reality of bread, the need for spirit appears — a spirit of community for sharing and celebrating, a spirit of valor to fight for bread, a spirit of strength to persevere in the struggle, a spirit of love to accept the fact that to toil for the bread of others is the greatest thing a human being can do.

The Good News of bread can lead to an expression of gratitude to God for what God has done, or the question of why God does not see to it that there is plenty of bread for all. It can lead to the question of who that one is who multiplied loaves to satisfy hunger and then was killed for it. It can lead to the question of whether the church takes bread seriously as Good News, and how it relates it to its mission. It can lead to the question of whether there is anything more than bread, whether there is a bread of word needed and Good News, even when there is no material bread; whether, if it is true that at the close of history there will be bread for all, it is worth the trouble to seek and toil in this history for the same thing, though at times darkness is everywhere; whether the hope of bread for all is really wiser than resignation; and so much more. Life is always more, and in bread there is always more than bread. But it must be emphasized that the reality of bread develops in this direction when the bread in question is not just any bread — the bread of luxury, or the bread that produces wealth — but the bread of the poor.

This brief phenomenology of the "more" that is in bread — whatever a description of that "more" may happen to be — is only intended to show how life itself always unfolds into "more." Thus, the theology of liberation emphasizes the historical character of the Reign — life — which intrinsically leads toward the "more." As it places no limits on this "more," the life of the

Reign leads to the utopian. This is the ultimate reason why liberation theology has to speak of an "integral" liberation — not in order to add something that will balance "material" liberation with other, more spiritual, liberations, but because in that primary material that we call the life of the poor is always the germ of a "more" of life. It is in this sense that we can say that the Reign of God is life, abundant life, and a plenitude of life.

Thus, liberation theology emphasizes the historical and utopian aspect of the Reign. This is nothing especially new; what is new is the relationship it posits between the two, by contrast with what other theologies do in this regard.

In the first place, liberation theology insists on and defends the historical element inherent in the Reign of God, both by reason of obvious ethical exigencies, and because it believes that this is the way to come to a better grasp of the utopian element of the Reign without the usual risks of alienation. Its purpose is to prevent the final fulfillment of the Reign from becoming a pretext for ignoring or relegating to a secondary level the realization of the will of God for the poor. As Archbishop Romero said repeatedly: "One must defend the minimum, which is the maximum gift of God: life."

In the second place, the utopian element of the Reign is understood in the theology of liberation as a guide along the pathways to be traversed in history, and not merely as a relativization of the paths already traversed. Unlike other theologies, liberation theology does not emphasize, although of course it accepts, the relativizing character of the utopian Reign where anything historical is concerned. It knows the "eschatological reserve." It would be very surprising if it did not; the reality of the poor makes it abundantly clear that current history is not the Reign of God! A warning of the danger of equating history with the utopia of the Reign would, in Latin America, sound like sarcasm. The theology of liberation does not reject the function of the eschatological reserve, but it interprets it in another way. Eschatology not only posits "reservations" with regard to the historical, but it condemns the historical. In positive terms, eschatology does not relativize historical configurations on an equal basis; it ranks them. A fallacy lurks in an insistence simply that "nothing is the Reign of God" — as if the distance between that Reign and any historical configuration whatsoever is equal to any other because it is infinite. The theology of liberation knows very well that utopia is that which by definition is never realized in history *(ou topos)*. But it also knows that there are *topoi* in history, and that the will of God is better realized in some than in others.

Finally, liberation theology understands the utopian element of the

Reign of God not only as an element of the final event of history, but as a force of attraction that becomes present in history by way of a real anticipation of the end. This force does not reside, as Pannenberg would have it, in the unreality of the utopia, which enables us and requires us to live in a particular way and thus to live as persons saved. With all respect for the provisional nature of all historical achievements, there are formulations of the utopia that draw history onward, that make history to be more than itself: justice, a communion of sisters and brothers, liberation, or, in the great words of Rutilio Grande: "A common board, with a broad tablecloth, and set for everyone, as at this Eucharist. No one left out. Napkins and place settings for everyone." The utopia is like a powerful magnet. It mobilizes. It moves human beings time and again to give their best to make the Reign come true. The theology of liberation believes that the final utopia, while beyond history, moves history here and now.

IV. America and the Church

Introduction

Eric Gregory

Discussions of "America and the Church" often focus on the role of religion in politics, especially in shaping public policy, elections, or cultural divisions. Others track normative debates about the appropriate role of religion in liberal democracies governed by appeals to rights, equality, and freedom. As such, whether in social science or philosophy, religion is evaluated from the perspective of politics. The essays that follow in this section concern the nature and purpose of politics from the perspective of religion. The difference is salient for theological reflection on America.

The essays engage concrete issues and familiar themes about legitimacy, war, political economy, law, nationalism, and pluralism. Many of their questions remain in an era of globalization marked by social and economic inequalities that serve as proxies for political domination. Are there alternatives to capitalism that escape criticisms of socialism and communism? Is the nation-state the only viable political form of democracy? What is the relationship between legality and morality? All three authors have been claimed on different sides of the culture wars, even by those who refuse the term. But their writings resist identification as "liberal" or "conservative."

The calculus of tragic decisions in contemporary American domestic and foreign policy might give each of our authors pause. I suspect they would find aspects of American democracy to embody perversions of justice rather than imperfections. They might criticize varieties of popular and civil religion that claim the mantle of orthodoxy. Yet no one knows what they would think of America as a body politic or the current coalition of democracy and Christianity. This introduction situates these selected essays and focuses briefly on questions they raise about human nature, history, and Christian responsibility in a constitutional democracy.

Reinhold Niebuhr (1892-1971) and John Courtney Murray (1904-1967) were two of the most influential Christian political thinkers in twentieth-century America. They are rivaled only by the quite different character and prophetic legacy of Martin Luther King Jr. H. Richard Niebuhr (1894-1962) towered over Protestant theology and ethics from his scholarly post at Yale Divinity School. Different streams in his writings continue to influence proposals in post-liberal theology, virtue ethics, and the sociological study of American religion.

Reinhold Niebuhr and Murray both defended constitutional arrangements and free democratic institutions against totalitarianism. They endorsed "limited government" that distinguished church, state, and civil society as the fruit of Christian thought. But they were critical of modern ideas and practices that undermine these fragile achievements. For both, secularized religious concepts harbor dangerous temptations in American self-understanding. They were skilled essayists and public intellectuals through periods of national crises, advancing polemical yet ecumenical commentary from their respective theological traditions. Each was featured on covers of *Time* magazine in the decades following World War II, when serious religious ideas garnered national attention beyond the church and academy. Despite dramatic changes in American life, many today invoke them as models of civic engagement in a turbulent world. Still others argue that Niebuhr and Murray perilously put religion in the service of status quo politics. Their moral and theological analyses, it is argued, assume the priority of the nation-state and confuse Christianity with bourgeois "Americanism." They reduce religion to ethics and the task of theology to making Christian ideas safe for the elites of democracy. Christian proclamation becomes a pseudo-religious mood for imperial renewal of Western culture.

Murray, a Jesuit priest, controversially defended religious liberty and the compatibility of Catholicism and democracy grounded in a Thomistic interpretation of natural law. He introduced Catholic social teachings (including just war thinking) to a Protestant establishment that was anti-Catholic or anxious about Catholic participation in politics. His collection of essays, *We Hold These Truths,* was published in the same year as the 1960 election of John F. Kennedy, the country's first Catholic president. At the same time, in the period before Vatican II where he played a key role, Murray sought to transform Catholic hostility or ambivalence regarding the separation of church and state. He did so by distinguishing American liberalism from the ideological atheism of European liberalisms, and by recruiting premodern models of church-state differentiation (i.e., Pope Gelasius I).

Reinhold Niebuhr, son of an immigrant pastor in the German Evangelical Synod, also wrestled with multiple identities in his reading of the American experiment. Under the rubric of "Christian Realism," he is best known for his sober views on the relevance of Christianity between World War I and the Cold War. He was an American Schleiermacher defending biblical religion against cultured despisers for a disappointed modernity. He took delight in puncturing dreams of scientific utopianism as well as the moralistic aspects of the "Social Gospel" and his own liberal Protestantism. This critical edge, which constructed unattractive dogmas, served his purpose of saving the partial truths of Enlightenment optimism and Reformation pessimism in the cause of proximate justice.

"Augustine's Political Realism" demonstrates this dialectical course between idealism and despair. It confirms Niebuhr's reputation for restoring the category of sin as a profound guide to human nature and the limits of politics. For Niebuhr, Augustine's anthropology makes sense of the "social factions, tensions, and competitions" endemic to human communities without abandoning the belief that human creatures bear the image of God. This idea finds political expression in Niebuhr's aphorism: "man's capacity for justice makes democracy possible; but man's inclination to injustice makes democracy necessary." In Augustine's "two cities" theology, he finds a corrective to the pretensions of Aristotelian politics and the excessive realism of Luther and Hobbes. While critical of Murray's ecclesiology and the supposed rationalism of natural law, Niebuhr's Augustinianism also supported a Christian secularity without secularism. But he distances himself from what he takes to be Augustine's account of love's remedy under the aspect of *caritas* and the body of Christ. Niebuhr's stark contrast between sacrificial *agape* and rational justice here parallels his most popular work, *Moral Man and Immoral Society,* which frustrated readers unclear about love's relation to justice within history.

If Niebuhr elevated the political realism of Augustinianism to interpret America, Murray elevated the metaphysical realism of Thomism. Murray's essay displays his characteristic notion that the uniqueness of America poses an intellectual project for a fuller expression of Catholic theology. Turning what many saw as a challenge into an opportunity, Murray tells a providential story about the American founding and its relation to Western thought shaped by presence of the Church and Catholic sensibilities of the common good. Through invitation rather than critique, his essay tries to outnarrate interpretations that accent exclusively Enlightenment or Protestant origins. Murray worries that these stories lend themselves to voluntarism, individualism, and positivism. He reads "the American Proposition," expressed in the Declaration of Independence and the best moments of American public philosophy, as grounded in reason and the sovereignty of God over nations and individuals. As such, "democracy is more than a political experiment; it is a spiritual and moral enterprise." Murray does not rest his claims on the personal piety of the founders. Rather, the framers built "better than they knew" because of the vibrant intellectual presence of natural law and natural rights. Their language betrayed knowledge of realities they did not always adequately profess. Catholics embrace this consensus because republican ordered liberty is responsive to the consent of free persons disciplined by the moral law. For Murray, Catholic civic participation is neither expedient nor concessive. It is a decision of conscience. But it is provisional and open to reevaluation in light of the contingencies of history and dynamism of practical reasoning. Given his specific concerns, he highlights the virtues of America and the irony of Catholic guardianship of its ideals.

The rare public exchange between the Niebuhr brothers also raises issues of conscience, Christian discipleship, and American citizenship. They are profitably read alongside recent debates about the use of torture in a "war on terror." The 1932 essays appeared in *The Christian Century,* a flagship journal of mainline Protestantism. They address the Japanese invasion of Manchuria, which posed a dilemma for emerging international law and Christian pacifists frustrated by alternatives to American intervention. But broader themes parallel what Murray elsewhere characterizes as two approaches to church-society relations in Catholic thought: an "eschatological humanism" that emphasizes the dramatic rupture of cross and resurrection, and an "incarnational humanism" that emphasizes the immanent transformation of human activity in culture.

"The Grace of Doing Nothing" is itself a response to coercive proposals like sanctions that Reinhold entertained in breaking from pacifism. Against pessimism, indignation, or cynicism, H. Richard names the inactivity of depending upon God. But, as he clarifies, this inactivity is the patient yet radical activity of those aware "that something is being done." This something is not sentimental railing against self-interested nations in the name of love. The "something" is the activity of God in judgment and redemption. This primary reality — recognized by a life of repentance and forgiveness in "little cells" of Christian community — is what his brother fails to affirm as historical reality and "emergent" possibility. Reinhold's God, according to his brother, remains a regulative ideal beyond history. His politics accommodates the church to worldly programs of nationalism and capitalism. His religion is tough-minded liberalism dressed up with biblical myths and symbols.

Reinhold's response to this challenge to his self-image is firm. He applauds the diagnosis of naïve idealism and American complicity in teaching the "ways of imperialism." But his confession is not repentant inactivity, even as he allows an eschatological spirit of love to qualify the "judicious uses of the forces of nature." Rather, Reinhold charges his brother with otherworldly perfectionism and apocalyptic waiting. In terms of his later analysis of sin in *The Nature and Destiny of Man,* the sloth that escapes the responsibility of power is a poor antidote to the pride of American self-righteousness. Critique and responsibility — like love and justice — must be held in tension. Relative justice is not the Kingdom of God, but it is a better hope than endless introspection or mysticism. To borrow a metaphor from Murray, Reinhold accused H. Richard of "basketweaving" in the face of social struggle. Christians must be active in politics, not huddle in the catacombs.

H. Richard's response shifts attention from the actual and ideal to divine action. He knew his brother well enough to avoid liberal tropes that he too had rejected since the 1920s. Instead, he turns the table by claiming that it is his brother who adopts an old reform method of "making Christian love an ambulance driver in the wars of interested and clashing parties." This abandons evangelical faith. It separates politics from morality by assuming the power politics of a secular world. Murray also claimed that the *ad hoc* character of Niebuhrian realism is prone to fascination with ambiguity and paradox. Both worried that Reinhold's political vision would lead to troubling forms of consequentialism in the name of responsibility. For them, he carries the doctrine of sin too far. For Reinhold, tragic decisions about lesser evils must be made in a fallen world. Morality does constrain *realpolitik,* even if violated under necessity and reasserted with contrition or lament.

Since 9/11, questions about what it means to be an American and about America's role in the world have returned to prominence. Murray recognized growing fragmentation in public discourse. One remarkable development since his day has been greater Protestant-Catholic theological engagement and understanding. Such dialogue may sponsor a political theology that joins the distinctive Thomism of American Catholicism with the Augustinianism of American Protestantism. Even those committed to reviving natural law on Murray's terms, however, express concerns about an "American consensus." These anxieties solicit renewed efforts to affirm such a consensus even as others question whether a shared *theory* of morality and law is needed for pluralist democracies.

Should Christians contribute to public philosophy? Should their energies attend primarily to the distinctive witness and practices of the Christian community in the service of the world? Different answers to those questions animate much of recent Christian social ethics. Students of political theology, however, might begin by asking, What, if anything, is *theologically* interesting about America? Any answer to that question demands more than empirical analysis or critique of "Christian America." It calls for engaging the fundamental questions these essays raise about God, the Church, and history.

14 Augustine's Political Realism

Reinhold Niebuhr

The terms "idealism" and "realism" are not analogous in political and in metaphysical theory; and they are certainly not as precise in political, as in metaphysical, theory.

In political and moral theory "realism" denotes the disposition to take all factors in a social and political situation, which offer resistance to established norms, into account, particularly the factors of self-interest and power. In the words of a notorious "realist," Machiavelli, the purpose of the realist is "to follow the truth of the matter rather than the imagination of it; for many have pictures of republics and principalities which have never been seen." This definition of realism implies that idealists are subject to illusions about social realities, which indeed they are.

"Idealism" is, in the esteem of its proponents, characterized by loyalty to moral norms and ideals, rather than to self-interest, whether individual or collective. It is, in the opinion of its critics, characterized by a disposition to ignore or be indifferent to the forces in human life which offer resistance to universally valid ideals and norms. This disposition, to which Machiavelli refers, is general whenever men are inclined to take the moral pretensions of themselves or their fellowmen at face value; for the disposition to hide self-interest behind the facade of pretended devotion to values, transcending self-interest, is well-nigh universal. It is, moreover, an interesting human characteristic, proving that the concept of "total depravity," as it is advanced by some Christian realists, is erroneous. Man is a curious creature with so strong a sense of obligation to his fellows that he cannot pursue his own interests without pretending to serve his fellowmen.

The definitions of "realists" and "idealists" emphasize disposition, rather than doctrines; and they are therefore bound to be inexact. It must remain a matter of opinion whether or not a man takes adequate account of all the various factors and forces in a social situation. Was Plato a realist, for instance, because he tried to guard against the self-interest of the "guardians" of his ideal state by divesting them of property and reducing their family responsibilities to a minimum? Does this bit of "realism" cancel out the essential unrealism inherent in ascribing to the "lusts of the body" the force of recalcitrance against the moral norm, or in attributing pure virtue to pure mind?

The Distinctive Nature of Augustine's Realism

Augustine was, by general consent, the first great "realist" in Western history. He deserves this distinction because his picture of social reality in his *Civitas Dei* gives an adequate account of the social factions, tensions, and competitions which we know to be well-nigh universal on every level of community; while the classical age conceived the order and justice of its polis to be a comparatively simple achievement, which would be accomplished when reason had brought all subrational forces under its dominion.

This difference in the viewpoints of Augustine and the classical philosophers lies in Augustine's biblical, rather than rationalistic, conception of human selfhood, with the ancillary conception of the seat of evil being in the self. Augustine broke with classical rationalism in his conception of the human self, according to which the self is composed of mind and body; the mind being the seat of virtue because it has the capacity to bring all impulses into order; and the body, from which come the "lusts and ambitions," being the cause of evil. According to Augustine, the self is an integral unity of mind and body. It is something more than mind and is able to use mind for its purposes. The self has, in fact, a mysterious identity and integrity transcending its functions of mind, memory, and will. "These three things, memory, understanding, and love are mine and not their own," he declares, "for they do what they do not for themselves but for me; or rather I do it by them. For it is I who remember by memory and understand by understanding and love by love."[1] It must be observed that the transcendent freedom of this self, including its capacity to defy any rational or natural system into

1. *De Trin.*, 15.22.

which someone may seek to coordinate it (its capacity for evil), makes it difficult for any philosophy, whether ancient or modern, to comprehend its true dimension. That is why the classical wise men obscured it by fitting its mind into a system of universal mind and the body into the system of nature; and that is also why the modern wise men, for all their rhetoric about the "dignity" of the individual, try to cut down the dimension of human selfhood so that it will seem to fit into a system of nature.

This conception of selfhood is drawn from the Bible, rather than from philosophy, because the transcendent self which is present in, though it transcends, all of the functions and effects of the self, is comprehensible only in the dramatic-historical mode of apprehension which characterizes biblical faith. Augustine draws on the insights of neo-Platonism to illustrate the self's power of self-transcendence; but he rejects Plotinus' mystic doctrine, in which the particular self, both human and divine, is lost in a vast realm of undifferentiated being.

Augustine's conception of the evil which threatens the human community on every level is a corollary of his doctrine of selfhood. "Self-love" is the source of evil rather than some residual natural impulse which mind has not yet completely mastered. This excessive love of self, sometimes also defined as pride or *superbia,* is explained as the consequence of the self's abandonment of God as its true end and of making itself "a kind of end." It is this powerful self-love or, in a modern term, "egocentricity," this tendency of the self to make itself its own end or even to make itself the false center of whatever community it inhabits, which sows confusion into every human community. The power of self-love is more spiritual than the "lusts of the body," of which Plato speaks; and it corrupts the processes of the mind more than Plato or Aristotle knew. That is why Augustine could refute the classical theory with the affirmation that "it is not the bad body which causes the good soul to sin but the bad soul which causes the good body to sin." At other times Augustine defines the evil in man as the "evil will," but with the understanding that it is the self which is evil in the manifestation of its will. "For he who extols the whole nature of the soul as the chief good and condemns the nature of the flesh as if it were evil, assuredly is fleshly both in the love of the soul and in the hatred of the flesh."[2] This concise statement of the Christian position surely refutes the absurd charge of moderns that the Christian faith is "dualistic" and generates contempt for the body. It also establishes the only real basis for a realistic estimate of the forces of recalcitrance which

2. *De Civ. Dei,* 15.5.

we must face on all levels of the human community, particularly for a realistic estimate of the spiritual dimension of these forces and of the comparative impotence of "pure reason" against them.

Compared with a Christian realism, which is based on Augustine's interpretation of biblical faith, a great many modern social and psychological theories, which fancy themselves anti-Platonic or even anti-Aristotelian and which make much of their pretended "realism," are in fact no more realistic than the classical philosophers. Thus modern social and psychological scientists are forever seeking to isolate some natural impulse such as "aggressiveness" and to manage it; with equal vanity they are trying to find a surrogate for Plato's and Aristotle's disinterested "reason" in a so-called "scientific method." Their inability to discover the corruption of self-interest in reason or in man's rational pursuits, and to measure the spiritual dimension of man's inhumanity and cruelty, gives an air of sentimentality to the learning of our whole liberal culture. Thus we have no guidance amid the intricacies of modern power politics, except as the older disciplines, less enamored of the "methods of natural science," and the common sense of the man in the street, supply the necessary insights.

The "City of This World"

Augustine's description of the social effects of human egocentricity or self-love is contained in his definition of the life of the "city of this world," the *civitas terrena*, which he sees as commingled with the *civitas dei*. The "city of this world" is dominated by self-love to the point of contempt of God; and is distinguished from the *civitas dei* which is actuated by the "love of God" to the point of contempt of self. This "city" is not some little city-state, as it is conceived in classical thought. It is the whole human community on its three levels of the family, the commonwealth, and the world.

A potential world community is therefore envisaged in Augustine's thought. But, unlike the Stoic and modern "idealists," he does not believe that a common humanity or a common reason gives promise of an easy actualization of community on the global level. The world community, declares Augustine, is "fuller of dangers as the greater sea is more dangerous."[3] Augustine is a consistent realist in calling attention to the fact that the potential world community may have a common human reason, but it speaks

3. *De Civ. Dei*, 19.7.

in different languages, and "two men, each ignorant of each other's language" will find that "dumb animals, though of a different species, could more easily hold intercourse than they, human beings though they be."[4] This realistic reminder that common linguistic and ethnic cultural forces, which bind the community together on one level, are divisive on the ultimate level, is a lesson which our modern proponents of world government have not yet learned.

Augustine's description of the *civitas terrena* includes an emphasis on the tensions, frictions, competitions of interest, and overt conflicts to which every human community is exposed. Even in the family, one cannot rely on friendship "seeing that secret treachery has often broken it up."[5] This bit of realism will seem excessive until we remember that our own generation has as much difficulty in preserving the peace and integrity in the smallest and most primordial community, the family, as in integrating community on the highest global level.

The *civitas terrena* is described as constantly subject to an uneasy armistice between contending forces, with the danger that factional disputes may result in "bloody insurrection" at any time. Augustine's realism prompts him to challenge Cicero's conception of a commonwealth as rooted in a "compact of justice." Not so, declares Augustine. Commonwealths are bound together by a common love, or collective interest, rather than by a sense of justice; and they could not maintain themselves without the imposition of power. "Without injustice the republic would neither increase nor subsist. The imperial city to which the republic belongs could not rule over provinces without recourse to injustice. For it is unjust for some men to rule over others."[6]

This realism has the merit of describing the power realities which underlie all large-scale social integrations whether in Egypt or Babylon or Rome, where a dominant city-state furnished the organizing power for the Empire. It also describes the power realities of national states, even democratic ones, in which a group, holding the dominant form of social power, achieves oligarchic rule, no matter how much modern democracy may bring such power under social control. This realism in regard to the facts which underlie the organizing or governing power refutes the charge of modern liberals that a realistic analysis of social forces makes for state absolutism; so

---

4. *De Civ. Dei*, 19.7.
5. *De Civ. Dei*, 19.5.
6. *De Civ. Dei*, 19.21.

that a mild illusion in regard to human virtue is necessary to validate democracy. Realistic pessimism did indeed prompt both Hobbes and Luther to an unqualified endorsement of state power; but that is only because they were not realistic enough. They saw the dangers of anarchy in the egotism of the citizens but failed to perceive the dangers of tyranny in the selfishness of the ruler. Therefore they obscured the consequent necessity of placing checks upon the ruler's self-will.

Augustine's realism was indeed excessive. On the basis of his principles he could not distinguish between government and slavery, both of which were supposedly the rule over man by man and were a consequence of, and remedy for, sin; nor could he distinguish between a commonwealth and a robber band, for both were bound together by collective interest; "For even thieves must hold together or they cannot effect what they intend." The realism fails to do justice to the sense of justice in the constitution of the Roman Empire; or, for that matter, to the sense of justice in a robber band. For even thieves will fall out if they cannot trust each other to divide the loot, which is their common aim, equitably. But the excessive emphasis upon the factors of power and interest, a wholesome corrective to Cicero's and modern Ciceronian moralistic illusions, is not fatal to the establishment of justice so long as the dangers of tyranny are weighed as realistically as the dangers of anarchy.

Augustine's realistic attitude toward government rests partly upon the shrewd observation that social peace and order are established by a dominant group within some level of community; and that this group is not exempt from the corruption of self-interest merely because the peace of society has been entrusted to it. (One thinks, incidentally, how accurately the Augustinian analysis fits both the creative and the ambiguous character of the American hegemony in the social cohesion of the free world.)

The realism is partly determined by his conception of a "natural order" which he inherited from the early Christian fathers, who in turn took it from that part of the Stoic theory which emphasized the primordial or primitive as the natural. This Stoic and Christian primitivism has the merit of escaping the errors of those natural law theories which claim to find a normative moral order amid the wide variety of historic forms or even among the most universal of these forms. The freedom of man makes these Stoic conceptions of the "natural" impossible. But it has the weakness which characterizes all primitivism, whether Stoic, Christian, or Romantic, for it makes primitive social forms normative. A primitive norm, whether of communal property relations or unorganized social cohesion, may serve provisionally as an occasion for the criticism of the institutions of an advancing civilization, more particularly the institutions of property and government; but it has the disadvantage of prompting indiscriminate criticism. This lack of discrimination is obvious in primitivistic Stoicism, in early Christianity, in seventeenth-century Cromwellian sectarianism, in Romanticism, and in Marxism and anarchism.

Augustine expressed this idea of a primitive social norm as follows:

> This is the prescribed order of nature. It is thus that God creates man. For "let them," He says, "have dominion over the fish of the sea and the fowl of the air and over every creeping thing, which creepeth on the earth." He did not intend that His rational creature, made in His image, should have dominion over anything but irrational creation — not man over man but man over beasts. And hence the righteous men of primitive times were made shepherds of cattle rather than kings of men.[7]

This primitivism avoids the later error of the absolute sanctification of government. But its indiscriminate character is apparent by his failure to recognize the difference between legitimate and illegitimate, between ordinate and inordinate subordination of man to man. Without some form of such subordination the institutions of civilization could not exist.

The Commingling of the Two Cities

If Augustine's realism is contained in his analysis of the *civitas terrena*, his refutation of the idea that realism must lead to cynicism or relativism is contained in his definition of the *civitas dei*, which he declares to be "commingled" with the "city of this world" and which has the "love of God" rather than the "love of self" as its guiding principle. The tension between the two cities is occasioned by the fact that, while egotism is "natural" in the sense that it is universal, it is not natural in the sense that it does not conform to man's nature as one who transcends himself indeterminately and can only have God rather than self for his end. A realism becomes morally cynical or nihilistic when it assumes that the universal characteristic in human behavior must also be regarded as normative. The biblical account of human behavior, upon which Augustine bases his thought, can escape both illusion and cynicism because it recognizes that the corruption of human freedom

---

7. *De Civ. Dei*, 19.15.

may make a behavior pattern universal without making it normative. Good and evil are not determined by some fixed structure of human existence. Man, according to the biblical view, may use his freedom to make himself falsely the center of existence; but this does not change the fact that love rather than self-love is the law of his existence, in the sense that man can only be healthy, and his communities at peace, if man is drawn out of himself and saved from the self-defeating consequences of self-love.

There are several grave errors in Augustine's account of love and of the relation of love to self-love; but before considering them we might well first pay tribute to his approach to political problems. The virtue of making love, rather than justice, into the norm for the community may seem, at first blush, to be dubious. The idea of justice seems much more relevant than the idea of love, particularly for the collective relationships of men. The medieval tradition, which makes the justice of a rational "natural law" normative even for Christians when they consider the necessities of a sinful world, seems much more realistic than modern forms of sentimental Protestantism, which regards love as a simple alternative to self-love which could be achieved if only we could preach the idea persuasively enough to beguile men from the one to the other.

Augustine's doctrine of love as the final norm must be distinguished from modern sentimental versions of Christianity which regard love as a simple possibility, and which think it significant to assert the obvious proposition that all conflicts in the community would be avoided if only people and nations would love one another. Augustine's approach differs from modern forms of sentimental perfectionism in the fact that he takes account of the power and persistence of egotism, both individual and collective, and seeks to establish the most tolerable form of peace and justice under conditions set by human sin. He inherited the tradition of monastic perfection; and he allows it as a vent for the Christian impulse toward individual perfection, without however changing the emphasis upon the duty of the Christian to perfect the peace of the city of this world. Furthermore, he raises questions about monastic perfection which, when driven home by the Reformation, were to undermine the whole system.

> I venture to say [he writes] that it is good for those who observe continence and are proud of it, to fall that they may be humbled. For what benefit is it to anyone in whom is the virtue of continence, if pride holds sway? He is but despising that by which man is born in striving after that which led to Satan's fall . . . holy virginity is better than conjugal chastity,

but if we add two other things, pride and humility . . . which is better, pride or humility? I have no doubt that a humble married woman is to be preferred to a proud virgin. . . . A mother will hold a lesser place in the Kingdom of Heaven, because she has been married, than the daughter, seeing that she is a virgin. . . . But if thy mother has been humble and thou proud, she will have some sort of place, but thou none.[8]

While Augustine's doctrine of love is thus not to be confused with modern sentimentalities which do not take the power of self-love seriously, one may well wonder whether an approach to politics which does not avail itself of the calculations of justice, may be deemed realistic. We have already noted that Augustine avails himself of the theory of the "natural law," only in the primordial version of the theory. If primordial conditions of a "natural order" are not to be defined as normative, the only alternative is to assume a "rational order" to which the whole of historical life conforms. Aquinas, in fact, constructed his theory of the natural law upon classical, and primarily Aristotelian, foundations. It was the weakness of both classical and medieval theories that they assumed an order in history, conforming to the uniformities of nature. Aristotle was aware of deviations in history, greater than those in nature; but he believed that there was nevertheless one form "which was marked by nature as the best." There is, in other words, no place in this theory of natural law for the endlessly unique social configurations which human beings, in their freedom over natural necessity, construct. The proponents of "natural law" therefore invariably introduce some historically contingent norm or social structure into what they regard as God's inflexible norm. That was the weakness of both classical and medieval social theory; and for that matter of the natural law theories of the bourgeois parties of the eighteenth century, who had found what they regarded as a more empirically perceived "natural law." But the modern empirical intelligence was no more able than the deductive rational processes of classical and medieval times, to construct a social norm not colored by the interests of the constructor, thus introducing the taint of ideology into the supposed sanctities of the law.

We must conclude, therefore, that Augustine was wise in avoiding the alleged solution of a natural law theory, which was the basis of so much lack of realism in both the classical and the medieval period, and which can persist today, long after the Aristotelian idea of fixed form for historical events

8. Sermon cccliv, ix, 9.

has been overcome, as the dogma of a religious system which makes its supposed sanctities into an article of faith. Augustine's conception of the radical freedom of man, derived from the biblical view, made it impossible to accept the idea of fixed forms of human behavior and of social organization, analogous to those of nature, even as he opposed the classical theory of historical cycles. Furthermore, his conception of human selfhood, and of the transcendence of the self over its mind, made it impossible to assume the identity of the individual reason with a universal reason, which lies at the foundation of the classical and medieval natural law theories. It is in fact something of a mystery how the Christian insights into human nature and history, expressed by Augustine, could have been subordinated to classical thought with so little sense of the conflict between them in the formulations of Thomas Aquinas; and how they should have become so authoritative in Roman Catholicism without more debate between Augustinian and Thomistic emphases.

Augustine's formula for leavening the city of this world with the love of the city of God is more adequate than classical and medieval thought, both in doing justice to the endless varieties of historical occasions and configurations and in drawing upon the resources of love rather than law in modifying human behavior.

Every "earthly peace," declares Augustine, is good as far as it goes. "But they will not have it long for they used it not well while they had it." That is, unless some larger love or loyalty qualifies the self-interest of the various groups, this collective self-interest will expose the community to either an overt conflict of competing groups or to the injustice of a dominant group which "when it is victorious . . . will become vice's slave."

Let us use some examples from current national and international problems to illustrate the Augustinian thesis.

There is, or was, a marked social tension between the middle classes of industrial owners and the industrial workers in all modern industrial nations. In some of them, for instance in Germany and France, this tension led to overt forms of the class conflict. In others such as Britain, the smaller European nations, and America, this tension was progressively resolved by various accommodations of interest. Wherein lay the difference? It did not lie in the possession of more adequate formulae of justice in some nations than in others. The difference lay in the fact that in some nations the various interest groups had, in addition to their collective interest, a "sense of justice," a disposition to "give each man his due," and a loyalty to the national community which qualified the interest struggle. Now, that spirit of justice is identical with the spirit of love, except at the highest level of the spirit of love, where it becomes purely sacrificial and engages in no calculation of what the due of each man may be. Two forms of love, the love of the other and the love of the community, were potent, in short, in modifying the acerbities and injustices of the class struggle. The two forms of love availed themselves of various calculations of justice in arriving at and defining their ad hoc agreements. But the factors in each nation and in each particular issue were too variable to allow for the application of any general rules or formulas of justice. Agreements were easier, in fact, if too much was not claimed for these formulas. Certain "principles" of justice, as distinguished from formulas or prescriptions, were indeed operative, such as liberty, equality, and loyalty to covenants; but these principles will be recognized as no more than the law of love in its various facets.

In the same manner, the international community is exposed to exactly the tensions and competitions of interest which Augustine describes. There are no formulas of justice or laws which will prevent these tensions from reaching overt conflict, if the collective interest of each nation is not modified by its loyalty to a higher value, such as the common civilization of the free nations. Where this common loyalty is lacking, as in our relation with Russia, no formula can save us from the uneasy peace in which we live. The character of this peace is just as tentative as Augustine described it. Whenever common loves or loyalties, or even common fears, lay the foundation for community, it must of course be our business to perfect it by calculations of justice which define our mutual responsibilities as exactly as possible.

It must be noted that the Augustinian formula for the leavening influence of a higher upon a lower loyalty or love, is effective in preventing the lower loyalty from involving itself in self-defeat. It corrects the "realism" of those who are myopically realistic by seeing only their own interests and failing thereby to do justice to their interests where they are involved with the interests of others. There are modern realists, for instance, who, in their reaction to abstract and vague forms of international idealism, counsel the nation to consult only its own interests. In a sense, collective self-interest is so consistent that it is superfluous to advise it. But a consistent self-interest on the part of a nation will work against its interests, because it will fail to do justice to the broader and longer interests, which are involved with the interests of other nations. A narrow national loyalty on our part, for instance, will obscure our long-range interests where they are involved with those of a whole alliance of free nations. Thus the loyalty of a leavening portion of a nation's citizens to a value transcending national interest will save a "realistic" nation from defining its interests in such narrow and short-range terms as to defeat the real interests of the nation.

Critique of Augustine's Realism

We have acknowledged some weaknesses in the Augustinian approach to the political order which we must now define and examine more carefully.

(1) Non-Catholics commonly criticize Augustine's alleged identification of the *civitas dei* with the visible Church. But we must absolve him of this charge or insist on a qualification of the criticism. He does indeed accept the Catholic doctrine, which had grown up before his day; and he defines the visible Church as the only perfect society. There are passages in which he seems to assume that it is possible to claim for the members of the Church that they are solely actuated by the *amor dei*. But he introduces so many reservations to this assertion that he may well be defined in this, as in other instances, as the father of both Catholicism and the Reformation. Of the Church, Augustine declared, "by faith she is a virgin. In the flesh she has few holy virgins."[9] Or again: "God will judge the wicked and the good. The evil cannot now be separated from the good but must be suffered for a season. The wicked may be with us on the threshing floor . . . in the barn they cannot be."[10] The reservations which he made upon the identification of the Church and the kingdom laid the foundations for the later Reformation position.

(2) But these reservations about the sinners who might be present in the visible Church cannot obscure a graver error in his thought. This error is probably related to his conception of grace which does not allow for the phenomenon, emphasized by the Reformation, that men may be redeemed in the sense that they consciously turn from self to Christ as their end, and yet they are not redeemed from the corruption of egotism which expresses itself, even in the lives of the saints. This insight is most succinctly expressed in Luther's phrase *"simul justus et peccator"* (both justified and a sinner). When Augustine distinguished between the "two loves" which characterize the "two cities," the love of God and the love of self, and when he pictured the world as a commingling of the two cities, he does not recognize that the commingling is due not to the fact that two types of people dwell together, but because the conflict between love and self-love is in every soul. It is par-

9. Sermon ccxiii, vii, 7.
10. *Comm. on Ps.* cxi, 9.

ticularly important to recognize this fact in political analyses; for nothing is more obvious than that personal dedication is no guarantee against the involvement of the dedicated individual in some form of collective egotism.

(3) We have frequently referred to Augustine's definition of the "two loves" which inform the "two cities" of which "the one is selfish and the other social," the one loving self to the point of contempt of God and the other loving God to the point of contempt of self. The question is whether Anders Nygren is right in *Agape and Eros* in defining the Augustinian conception of *amor dei* as rooted in a classical rather than a biblical concept.

In defense of Augustine it must be said that he is not insensible to the two facets of the love commandment and therefore does not define the *amor dei* in purely mystical terms as a flight from this world. He insists on the contrary that the *amor dei* is "social" and he offers the concord among brethren as a proof of the love of God. But nevertheless Nygren is right in suggesting that the thought of Plotinus has colored Augustine's conceptions sufficiently so that the *agape* of the New Testament is misinterpreted by Augustine's conception of *caritas* and *amor dei*. The *agape* form of love in the New Testament fails to be appreciated particularly in two of its facets:

First, the equality of the "two loves," the love of God and the love of the neighbor (enforced in the Scripture by the words "the second is like unto [the first]"), is violated by Augustine under the influence of Plotinus, even as a later medieval Catholic mystic, St. John of the Cross, violated it when he regarded the love of the creature as a ladder which might lead us to the love of God, but must be subordinated to the latter. Augustine wants us to love the neighbor for the sake of God, which may be a correct formulation; but he wants us to prove the genuineness of our love of God in the love of the neighbor, or by leading him to God. Thus the meeting of the neighbor's need without regard to any ultimate religious intention is emptied of meaning. The love of the neighbor is for him not part of a double love commandment, but merely the instrument of a single love commandment which bids us flee all mortality, including the neighbor, in favor of the immutable good.

The second facet of the *agape* concept of the New Testament which tends to be obscured by Augustine is the notion of sacrificial love, the absurd principle of the cross, the insistence that the self must sacrifice itself for the other. It is not fair to Augustine to say that he neglects this facet of meaning, for he seems to emphasize it so constantly. He comes closest to its meaning when he deals with the relation of humility to love. Yet it seems fair to say that he was sufficiently imbued by classical mystical thought forms so that the emphasis lies always upon the worthiness or unworthiness of the object of our love; the insistence is that only God and not some mutable "good" or person is worthy of our love. This is a safeguard against all forms of idolatry. But it does not answer another important question: when I love a person or a community do I love myself in them or do I truly love them? Is my love a form of alteregoism? The Augustinian *amor dei* assumes that the self in its smallness cannot contain itself within itself, and therefore it is challenged to go out from itself to the most ultimate end. But it hardly reveals the full paradox of self-realization through self-giving, which is a scandal in the field of rational ethics as the cross is a scandal in the field of rational religion. Yet it is the source of ultimate wisdom. For the kind of self-giving which has self-realization as its result must not have self-realization as its conscious end; otherwise the self by calculating its enlargement will not escape from itself completely enough to be enlarged.

The weakness of Augustine in obscuring these facets of the *agape* principle may be illustrated, without unfairness I hope, by referring to his treatment of family love. He questions the love of mate or children as the final form of love, but not for New Testament reasons. He does not say: "When you love your wife and children are you maybe really loving yourself in them and using them as the instruments of your self-aggrandisements?" He declares instead, in effect: "You must not love your family too unreservedly because your wife and children are mortal. They also belong to the rivers of Babylon, and, if you give them absolute devotion, the hour of bereavement will leave you desolate." Of course, Augustine is too much the Christian to engage in a consistent mystic depreciation of the responsibilities and joys of this earthly life. After all, his whole strategy for the "commingling" of the two cities revolves around the acceptance of the ordinary responsibilities of home and state, but in performing these tasks for the ultimate, rather than the immediate end. He asks:

> What then? Shall all perish who marry and are given in marriage, who till the fields and build houses? No, but those who put their trust in these things, who prefer them to God, who for the sake of these things are quick to offend God, these will perish. But those who either do not use these things or who use them as though they used them not, trusting more in Him who gave them than in the things given, understanding in them His consolation and mercy, and who are not absorbed in these gifts lest they fall away from the giver, these are they whom the day will not overtake as a thief unprepared.[11]

11. *Comm. on Ps.* cxx, 3.

Modern Illusions and "The River of Babylon"

We must not, in criticizing Augustine for neo-Platonic elements in his thought, obscure the Christian elements which will be equally an offense to modern men who regard the world as self-sufficing and self-explanatory, who reject as absurd the Christian faith that there is not only a mystery behind and above the world of observed phenomena and intelligible meanings, but that it is a mystery whose meaning has been disclosed as a love which elicits our answering love. This modern generation, with its confidence in a world without mystery, and without meaning beyond simple intelligibility, will not be beguiled from its unbelief by a reminder that its emancipation from God has betrayed it into precisely those idolatries — the worship of false gods, the dedication to finite values as if they were ultimate — of which Augustine spoke. But it must be recorded nevertheless as a significant fact of modern history. While it is an offense to regard communism as the inevitable end-product of secularism, as some Christians would have us believe, it is only fair to point out that the vast evils of modern communism come ironically to a generation which thought it would be easy to invest all the spiritual capital of men, who mysteriously transcend the historical process, in some value or end within that process; and communism is merely the most pathetic and cruel of the idolatrous illusions of this generation.

We must be clear about the fact that all the illusions about man's character and history, which made it so difficult for either the classical or the modern age to come to terms with the vexing problems of our togetherness, seem to stem from efforts to understand man in both his grandeur and his misery by "integrating" him into some natural or rational system of coherence. Thereby they denied the mystery of his transcendence over every process which points to another mystery beyond himself, without which man is not only a mystery to himself but a misunderstood being.

We cannot deny that from a Christian standpoint the world is like a "river of Babylon," to use Augustine's symbol; and that Augustine is right in suggesting that ultimately we cannot find peace if we are merely tossed down the river of time. We must find security in that which is not carried down the river. "Observe, however," declares Augustine (in a simile which will seem strange to generations which have made the "rivers of Babylon," the stream of temporal events, into forces of redemption, but which will not seem so strange as the modern experience proves history as such to be less redemptive than we had believed):

The rivers of Babylon are all things which are here loved, and pass away.

For example, one man loves to practice husbandry, to grow rich by it, to employ his mind on it, to get his pleasure from it. Let him observe the issue and see that what he has loved is not a foundation of Jerusalem, but a river of Babylon.

Another says, it is a grand thing to be a soldier; all farmers fear those who are soldiers, are subservient to them, tremble at them. If I am a farmer, I shall fear soldiers; if a soldier, farmers will fear me. Madman! thou hast cast thyself headlong into another river of Babylon, and that still more turbulent and sweeping. Thou wishest to be feared by thy inferior; fear Him Who is greater than thou. He who fears thee may on a sudden become greater than thou, but He Whom thou oughtest to fear will never become less.

To be an advocate, says another, is a grand thing; eloquence is most powerful; always to have clients hanging on the lips of their eloquent advocate, and from his words looking for loss or gain, death or life, ruin or security. Thou knowest not whither thou hast cast thyself. This too is another river of Babylon, and its roaring sound is the din of the waters dashing against the rocks. Mark that it flows, that it glides on; beware, for it carries things away with it.

To sail the seas, says another, and to trade is a grand thing — to know many lands, to make gains from every quarter, never to be answerable to any powerful man in thy country, to be always travelling and to feed thy mind with the diversity of the nations and the business met with, and to return enriched by the increase of thy gains. This too is a river of Babylon. When will the gains stop? When wilt thou have confidence and be secure in the gains thou makest? The richer thou art, the more fearful wilt thou be. Once shipwrecked, thou wilt come forth stripped of all, and rightly wilt bewail thy fate *in* the rivers of Babylon, because thou wouldest not sit down and weep *upon* the rivers of Babylon.

But there are other citizens of the holy Jerusalem, understanding their captivity, who mark how human wishes and the diverse lusts of men, hurry and drag them hither and thither, and drive them into the sea. They see this, and do not throw themselves into the rivers of Babylon, but sit down upon the rivers of Babylon and upon the rivers of Babylon weep, either for those who are being carried away by them, or for themselves whose deserts have placed them in Babylon.[12]

---

12. *Comm. on Ps.* cxxxvi, 3, 4.

Whatever the defects of the Augustine approach may be, we must acknowledge his immense superiority both over those who preceded him and who came after him. A part of that superiority was due to his reliance upon biblical rather than idealistic or naturalistic conceptions of selfhood. But that could not have been the only cause, else Christian systems before and after him would not have been so inferior. Or were they inferior either because they subordinated the biblical-dramatic conception of human selfhood too much to the rationalistic scheme, as was the case with medieval Christianity culminating in the thought of Thomas Aquinas, or because they did not understand that the corruption of human freedom could not destroy the original dignity of man, as was the case with the Reformation with its doctrines of sin, bordering on total depravity and resulting in Luther's too pessimistic approach to political problems?

As for secular thought, it has difficulty in approaching Augustine's realism without falling into cynicism, or in avoiding nihilism without falling into sentimentality. Hobbes' realism was based on an insight which he shared with Augustine, namely, that in all historical encounters, the mind is the servant and not the master of the self. But he failed to recognize that the self which thus made the mind its instrument was a corrupted and not a "normal" self. Modern "realists" know the power of collective self-interest as Augustine did; but they do not understand its blindness. Modern pragmatists understand the irrelevance of fixed and detailed norms; but they do not understand that love must take the place as the final norm for these inadequate norms. Modern liberal Christians know that love is the final norm for man; but they fall into sentimentality because they fail to measure the power and persistence of self-love.

Thus Augustine, whatever may be the defects of his approach to political reality, and whatever may be the dangers of a too slavish devotion to his insights, nevertheless proves himself a more reliable guide than any known thinker. A generation which finds its communities imperiled and in decay from the smallest and most primordial community, the family, to the largest and most recent, the potential world community, might well take counsel of Augustine in solving its perplexities.

15 *E Pluribus Unum:* The American Consensus

John Courtney Murray

As it arose in America, the problem of pluralism was unique in the modern world, chiefly because pluralism was the native condition of American society. It was not, as in Europe and in England, the result of a disruption or decay of a previously existent religious unity. This fact created the possibility of a new solution; indeed, it created a demand for a new solution. The possibility was exploited and the demand was met by the American Constitution.

The question here concerns the position of the Catholic conscience in the face of the new American solution to a problem that for centuries has troubled, and still continues to trouble, various nations and societies. A new problem has been put to the universal Church by the fact of America — by the uniqueness of our social situation, by the genius of our newly conceived constitutional system, by the lessons of our singular national history, which has molded in a special way the consciousness and temper of the American people, within whose midst the Catholic stands, sharing with his fellow citizens the same national heritage. The Catholic community faces the task of making itself intellectually aware of the conditions of its own coexistence within the American pluralistic scene. We have behind us a lengthy historical tradition of acceptance of the special situation of the Church in America, in all its differences from the situations in which the Church elsewhere finds herself. But it is a question here of pursuing the subject, not in the horizontal dimension of history but in the vertical dimension of theory.

The argument readily falls into two parts. The first part is an analysis of the American Proposition with regard to political unity. The effort is to make a statement, later to be somewhat enlarged, of the essential contents of the American consensus, whereby we are made "e pluribus unum," one society subsisting amid multiple pluralisms. Simply to make this statement is to show why American Catholics participate with ready conviction in the American consensus. The second part of the argument, to be pursued in the next chapter [of Murray's book], is an analysis of the American Proposition with regard to religious pluralism, especially as this proposition is embodied in our fundamental law. Again, simply to make this analysis is to lay bare the reasons why American Catholics accept on principle the unique American solution to the age-old problem.

The Nation Under God

The first truth to which the American Proposition makes appeal is stated in that landmark of Western political theory, the Declaration of Independence. It is a truth that lies beyond politics; it imparts to politics a fundamental human meaning. I mean the sovereignty of God over nations as well as over individual men. This is the principle that radically distinguishes the conservative Christian tradition of America from the Jacobin laicist tradition of Continental Europe. The Jacobin tradition proclaimed the autonomous reason of man to be the first and the sole principle of political organization. In contrast, the first article of the American political faith is that the political community, as a form of free and ordered human life, looks to the sovereignty of God as to the first principle of its organization. In the Jacobin tradition religion is at best a purely private concern, a matter of personal devotion, quite irrelevant to public affairs. Society as such, and the state which gives it legal form, and the government which is its organ of action are by definition agnostic or atheist. The statesman as such cannot be a believer, and his actions as a statesman are immune from any imperative or judgment higher than the will of the people, in whom resides ultimate and total sovereignty (one must remember that in the Jacobin tradition "the people" means "the party"). This whole manner of thought is altogether alien to the authentic American tradition.

From the point of view of the problem of pluralism this radical distinction between the American and the Jacobin traditions is of cardinal importance. The United States has had, and still has, its share of agnostics and unbelievers. But it has never known organized militant atheism on the Jacobin, doctrinaire Socialist, or Communist model; it has rejected parties and theories which erect atheism into a political principle. In 1799, the year of the Napoleonic *coup d'état* which overthrew the Directory and established a dictatorship in France, President John Adams stated the first of all American first principles in his remarkable proclamation of March 6:

> . . . it is also most reasonable in itself that men who are capable of social arts and relations, who owe their improvements to the social state, and who derive their enjoyments from it, should, as a society, make acknowledgements of dependence and obligation to Him who hath endowed them with these capacities and elevated them in the scale of existence by these distinctions. . . .

President Lincoln on May 30, 1863, echoed the tradition in another proclamation:

> Whereas the Senate of the United States, devoutly recognizing the supreme authority and just government of Almighty God in all the affairs of men and nations, has by a resolution requested the President to designate and set apart a day for national prayer and humiliation; And whereas it is the duty of nations as well as of men to own their dependence upon the overruling power of God, to confess their sins and trespasses in humble sorrow, yet with the assured hope that genuine repentance will lead to mercy and pardon. . . .

The authentic voice of America speaks in these words. And it is a testimony to the enduring vitality of this first principle — the sovereignty of God over society as well as over individual men — that President Eisenhower in June, 1952, quoted these words of Lincoln in a proclamation of similar intent. There is, of course, dissent from this principle, uttered by American secularism (which, at that, is a force far different in content and purpose from Continental laicism). But the secularist dissent is clearly a dissent; it illustrates the existence of the American affirmation. And it is continually challenged. For instance, as late as 1952 an opinion of the United States Supreme Court challenged it by asserting: "We are a religious people whose institutions presuppose a Supreme Being." Three times before in its history — in 1815, 1892, and 1931 — the Court had formally espoused this same principle.

The Tradition of Natural Law

The affirmation in Lincoln's famous phrase, "this nation under God," sets the American proposition in fundamental continuity with the central political tradition of the West. But this continuity is more broadly and importantly visible in another, and related, respect. In 1884 the Third Plenary Council of Baltimore made this statement: "We consider the establishment of our country's independence, the shaping of its liberties and laws, as a work of special Providence, its framers 'building better than they knew,' the Almighty's hand guiding them." The providential aspect of the matter, and the reason for the better building, can be found in the fact that the American political community was organized in an era when the tradition of natural law and natural rights was still vigorous. Claiming no sanction other than its appeal to free minds, it still commanded universal acceptance. And it furnished the basic materials for the American consensus.

The evidence for this fact has been convincingly presented by Clinton Rossiter in his book, *Seedtime of the Republic*,[1] a scholarly account of the "noble aggregate of 'self-evident truths' that vindicated the campaign of resistance (1765-1775), the resolution for independence (1776), and the establishment of the new state governments (1776-1780)." These truths, he adds, "had been no less self-evident to the preachers, merchants, planters, and lawyers who were the mind of colonial America." It might be further added that these truths firmly presided over the great time of study, discussion, and decision which produced the Federal Constitution. "The great political philosophy of the Western world," Rossiter says, "enjoyed one of its proudest seasons in this time of resistance and revolution." By reason of this fact the American Revolution, quite unlike its French counterpart, was less a revolution than a conservation. It conserved, by giving newly vital form to, the liberal tradition of politics, whose ruin in Continental Europe was about to be consummated by the first great modern essay in totalitarianism.

The force for unity inherent in this tradition was of decisive importance in what concerns the problem of pluralism. Because it was conceived in the tradition of natural law the American Republic was rescued from the fate, still not overcome, that fell upon the European nations in which Continental Liberalism, a deformation of the liberal tradition, lodged itself, not least by the aid of the Lodges. There have never been "two Americas," in the sense in which there have been, and still are, "two Frances," "two Italys," "two Spains." Politically speaking, America has always been one. The reason is that a consensus was once established, and it still substantially endures, even in the quarters where its origins have been forgotten.

Formally and in the first instance this consensus was political, that is, it

1. New York: Harcourt, Brace and Co., 1953.

embraced a whole constellation of principles bearing upon the origin and nature of society, the function of the state as the legal order of society, and the scope and limitations of government. "Free government" — perhaps this typically American shorthand phrase sums up the consensus. "A free people under a limited government" puts the matter more exactly. It is a phrase that would have satisfied the first Whig, St. Thomas Aquinas.

To the early Americans government was not a phenomenon of force, as the later legal positivists would have it. Nor was it a "historical category," as Marx and his followers were to assert. Government did not mean simply the power to coerce, though this power was taken as integral to government. Government, properly speaking, was the right to command. It was authority. And its authority derived from law. By the same token its authority was limited by law. In his own way Tom Paine put the matter when he said, "In America Law is the King." But the matter had been better put by Henry of Bracton (d. 1268) when he said, "The king ought not to be under a man, but under God and under the law, because the law makes the king." This was the message of Magna Charta; this became the first structural rib of American constitutionalism.

Constitutionalism, the rule of law, the notion of sovereignty as purely political and therefore limited by law, the concept of government as an empire of laws and not of men — these were ancient ideas, deeply implanted in the British tradition at its origin in medieval times. The major American contribution to the tradition — a contribution that imposed itself on all subsequent political history in the Western world — was the written constitution. However, the American document was not the *constitution octroyée* of the nineteenth-century Restorations — a constitution graciously granted by the King or Prince-President. Through the American techniques of the constitutional convention and of popular ratification, the American Constitution is explicitly the act of the people. It embodies their consensus as to the purposes of government, its structure, the extent of its powers and the limitations on them, etc. By the Constitution the people define the areas where authority is legitimate and the areas where liberty is lawful. The Constitution is therefore at once a charter of freedom and a plan for political order.

The Principle of Consent

Here is the second aspect of the continuity between the American consensus and the ancient liberal tradition; I mean the affirmation of the principle of the consent of the governed. Sir John Fortescue (d. 1476), Chief Justice of the Court of King's Bench under Henry VI, had thus stated the tradition, in distinguishing between the absolute and the constitutional monarch: "The secounde king [the constitutional monarch] may not rule his people by other laws than such as thai assenten to. And therefore he may set uppon thaim non imposicions without their consent." The principle of consent was inherent in the medieval idea of kingship; the king was bound to seek the consent of his people to his legislation. The American consensus reaffirmed this principle, at the same time that it carried the principle to newly logical lengths. Americans agreed that they would consent to none other than their own legislation, as framed by their representatives, who would be responsible to them. In other words, the principle of consent was wed to the equally ancient principle of popular participation in rule. But, since this latter principle was given an amplitude of meaning never before known in history, the result was a new synthesis, whose formula is the phrase of Lincoln, "government by the people."

Americans agreed to make government constitutional and therefore limited in a new sense, because it is representative, republican, responsible government. It is limited not only by law but by the will of the people it represents. Not only do the people adopt the Constitution; through the techniques of representation, free elections, and frequent rotation of administrations they also have a share in the enactment of all subsequent statutory legislation. The people are really governed; American political theorists did not pursue the Rousseauist will-o'-the-wisp: how shall the individual in society come to obey only himself? Nevertheless, the people are governed because they consent to be governed; and they consent to be governed because in a true sense they govern themselves.

The American consensus therefore includes a great act of faith in the capacity of the people to govern themselves. The faith was not unrealistic. It was not supposed that everybody could master the technical aspects of government, even in a day when these aspects were far less complex than they now are. The supposition was that the people could understand the general objectives of governmental policy, the broad issues put to the decision of government, especially as these issues raised moral problems. The American consensus accepted the premise of medieval society, that there is a sense of justice inherent in the people, in virtue of which they are empowered, as the medieval phrase had it, to "judge, direct, and correct" the processes of government.

It was this political faith that compelled early American agreement to the institutions of a free speech and a free press. In the American concept of them, these institutions do not rest on the thin theory proper to eighteenth-century individualistic rationalism, that a man has a right to say what he thinks merely because he thinks it. The American agreement was to reject political censorship of opinion as unrightful, because unwise, imprudent, not to say impossible. However, the proper premise of these freedoms lay in the fact that they were social necessities. "Colonial thinking about each of these rights had a strong social rather than individualistic bias," Rossiter says. They were regarded as conditions essential to the conduct of free, representative, and responsible government. People who are called upon to obey have the right first to be heard. People who are to bear burdens and make sacrifices have the right first to pronounce on the purposes which their sacrifices serve. People who are summoned to contribute to the common good have the right first to pass their own judgment on the question, whether the good proposed be truly a good, the people's good, the common good. Through the technique of majority opinion this popular judgment becomes binding on government.

A second principle underlay these free institutions — the principle that the state is distinct from society and limited in its offices toward society. This principle too was inherent in the Great Tradition. Before it was cancelled out by the rise of the modern omnicompetent society-state, it had found expression in the distinction between the order of politics and the order of culture, or, in the language of the time, the distinction between *studium* and *imperium*. The whole order of ideas in general was autonomous in the face of government; it was immune from political discipline, which could only fall upon actions, not ideas. Even the medieval Inquisition respected this distinction of orders; it never recognized a crime of opinion, *crimen opinionis;* its competence extended only to the repression of organized conspiracy against public order and the common good. It was, if you will, a Committee on un-Christian Activities; it regarded activities, not ideas, as justiciable.

The American Proposition, in reviving the distinction between society and state, which had perished under the advance of absolutism, likewise renewed the principle of the incompetence of government in the field of opinion. Government submits itself to judgment by the truth of society; it is not itself a judge of the truth in society. Freedom of the means of communication whereby ideas are circulated and criticized, and the freedom of the academy (understanding by the term the range of institutions organized for the pursuit of truth and the perpetuation of the intellectual heritage of society) are immune from legal inhibition or government control. This immunity is a civil right of the first order, essential to the American concept of a free people under a limited government.

A Virtuous People

"A free people": this term too has a special sense in the American Proposition. America has passionately pursued the ideal of freedom, expressed in a whole system of political and civil rights, to new lengths; but it has not pursued this ideal so madly as to rush over the edge of the abyss, into sheer libertarianism, into the chaos created by the nineteenth-century theory of the "outlaw conscience," *conscientia exlex,* the conscience that knows no law higher than its own subjective imperatives. Part of the inner architecture of the American ideal of freedom has been the profound conviction that only a virtuous people can be free. It is not an American belief that free government is inevitable, only that it is possible, and that its possibility can be realized only when the people as a whole are inwardly governed by the recognized imperatives of the universal moral law.

The American experiment reposes on Acton's postulate, that freedom is the highest phase of civil society. But it also reposes on Acton's further postulate, that the elevation of a people to this highest phase of social life supposes, as its condition, that they understand the ethical nature of political freedom. They must understand, in Acton's phrase, that freedom is "not the power of doing what we like, but the right of being able to do what we ought." The people claim this right, in all its articulated forms, in the face of government; in the name of this right, multiple limitations are put upon the power of government. But the claim can be made with the full resonance of moral authority only to the extent that it issues from an inner sense of responsibility to a higher law. In any phase civil society demands order. In its highest phase of freedom it demands that order should not be imposed from the top down, as it were, but should spontaneously flower outward from the free obedience to the restraints and imperatives that stem from inwardly possessed moral principle. In this sense democracy is more than a political experiment; it is a spiritual and moral enterprise. And its success depends upon the virtue of the people who undertake it. Men who would be politically free must discipline themselves. Likewise institutions which would pretend to be free with a human freedom must in their workings be governed from within and made to serve the ends of virtue. Political freedom is endangered in its foundations as soon as the universal moral values, upon whose shared possession the self-discipline of a free society depends, are no longer vigorous enough to restrain the passions and shatter the selfish inertia of men. The American ideal of freedom as ordered freedom, and therefore an ethical ideal, has traditionally reckoned with these truths, these truisms.

Human and Historical Rights

This brings us to the threshold of religion, and therefore to the other aspect of the problem of pluralism, the plurality of religions in America. However, before crossing this threshold one more characteristic of the American Proposition, as implying a consensus, needs mention, namely, the Bill of Rights. The philosophy of the Bill of Rights was also tributary to the tradition of natural law, to the idea that man has certain original responsibilities precisely as man, antecedent to his status as citizen. These responsibilities are creative of rights which inhere in man antecedent to any act of government; therefore they are not granted by government and they cannot be surrendered to government. They are as inalienable as they are inherent. Their proximate source is in nature, and in history insofar as history bears witness to the nature of man; their ultimate source, as the Declaration of Independence states, is in God, the Creator of nature and the Master of history. The power of this doctrine, as it inspired both the Revolution and the form of the Republic, lay in the fact that it drew an effective line of demarcation around the exercise of political or social authority. When government ventures over this line, it collides with the duty and right of resistance. Its authority becomes arbitrary and therefore nil; its act incurs the ultimate anathema, "unconstitutional."

One characteristic of the American Bill of Rights is important for the subject here, namely, the differences that separate it from the Declaration of the Rights of Man in the France of '89. In considerable part the latter was a parchment-child of the Enlightenment, a top-of-the-brain concoction of a set of men who did not understand that a political community, like man himself, has roots in history and in nature. They believed that a state could be simply a work of art, a sort of absolute beginning, an artifact of which abstract human reason could be the sole artisan. Moreover, their exaggerated individualism had shut them off from a view of the organic nature of the human community; their social atomism would permit no institutions or associations intermediate between the individual and the state.

In contrast, the men who framed the American Bill of Rights understood history and tradition, and they understood nature in the light of both. They too were individualists, but not to the point of ignoring the social nature of man. They did their thinking within the tradition of freedom that was their heritage from England. Its roots were not in the top of anyone's brain but in history. Importantly, its roots were in the medieval notion of the *homo liber et legalis*, the man whose freedom rests on law, whose law was the age-old custom in which the nature of man expressed itself, and whose lawful freedoms were possessed in association with his fellows. The rights for which the colonists contended against the English Crown were basically the rights of Englishmen. And these were substantially the rights written into the Bill of Rights.

Of freedom of religion there will be question later. For the rest, freedom of speech, assembly, association, and petition for the redress of grievances, security of person, home, and property — these were great historical as well as civil and natural rights. So too was the right to trial by jury, and all the procedural rights implied in the Fifth- and later in the Fourteenth-Amendment provision for "due process of law." The guarantee of these and other rights was new in that it was written, in that it envisioned these rights with an amplitude, and gave them a priority, that had not been known before in history. But the Bill of Rights was an effective instrument for the delimitation of government authority and social power, not because it was written on paper in 1789 or 1791, but because the rights it proclaims had already been engraved by history on the conscience of a people. The American Bill of Rights is not a piece of eighteenth-century rationalist theory; it is far more the product of Christian history. Behind it one can see, not the philosophy of the Enlightenment but the older philosophy that had been the matrix of the common law. The "man" whose rights are guaranteed in the face of law and government is, whether he knows it or not, the Christian man, who had learned to know his own personal dignity in the school of Christian faith.

The American Consensus Today

Americans have been traditionally proud of the earlier phases of their history — colonial and Revolutionary, constitutional and Federalist. This pride persists today. The question is, whether the American consensus still endures — the consensus whose essential contents have been sketched in the foregoing. A twofold answer may be given. The first answer is given by Professor Rossiter:

> Perhaps Americans could achieve a larger measure of liberty and prosperity and build a more successful government if they were to abandon the language and assumptions of men who lived almost two centuries ago. Yet the feeling cannot be downed that rude rejection of the past, rather than levelheaded respect for it, would be the huge mistake. Americans may eventually take the advice of their advanced philosophers and adopt a political theory that pays more attention to groups, classes, public opinion, power-élites, positive law, public administration, and other realities of twentieth-century America. Yet it seems safe to predict that the people, who occasionally prove themselves wiser than their philosophers, will go on thinking about the political community in terms of unalienable rights, popular sovereignty, consent, constitutionalism, separation of powers, morality, and limited government. The political theory of the American Revolution — a theory of ethical, ordered liberty — remains the political tradition of the American people.

This is a cheerful answer. I am not at all sure that it is correct, if it be taken to imply that the tradition of natural law, as the foundation of law and politics, has the same hold upon the mind of America today that it had upon the "preachers, merchants, planters, and lawyers who were the mind of colonial America." There is indeed talk today about a certain revival of this great tradition, notably among more thoughtful men in the legal profession. But the talk itself is significant. One would not talk of reviving the tradition, if it were in fact vigorously alive. Perhaps the American people have not taken the advice of their advanced philosophers. Perhaps they are wiser than their philosophers. Perhaps they still refuse to think of politics and law as their philosophers think — in purely positivist and pragmatist terms. The fact remains that this is the way the philosophers think. Not that they have made a "rude rejection of the past." They are never rude. And they can hardly be said to have rejected what they never knew or understood, because it was never taught to them and they never learned it. The tradition of natural law is not taught or learned in the American university. It has not been rejected, much less refuted. We do not refute our adversaries, said Santayana; we quietly bid them goodbye. I think, as I shall later say, that the American university long since bade a quiet goodbye to the whole notion of an American consensus, as implying that there are truths that we hold in common, and a natural law that makes known to all of us the structure of the moral universe in such wise that all of us are bound by it in a common obedience.

There is, however, a second answer to the question, whether the original American consensus still endures. It is certainly valid of a not inconsiderable portion of the American people, the Catholic community. The men of learning in it acknowledge certain real contributions made by positive sociological analysis of the political community. But both they and their less learned fellows still adhere, with all the conviction of intelligence, to the tradition of natural law as the basis of free and ordered political life. Historically, this tradition has found, and still finds, its intellectual home within the Catholic Church. It is indeed one of the ironies of history that the tradition should have so largely languished in the so-called Catholic nations of Europe at the same time that its enduring vigor was launching a new Republic across the broad ocean. There is also some paradox in the fact that a nation which has (rightly or wrongly) thought of its own genius in Protestant terms should have owed its origins and the stability of its political structure to a tradition whose genius is alien to current intellectualized versions of the Protestant religion, and even to certain individualistic exigencies of Protestant religiosity. These are special questions, not to be pursued here. The point here is that Catholic participation in the American consensus has been full and free, unreserved and unembarrassed, because the contents of this consensus — the ethical and political principles drawn from the tradition of natural law — approve themselves to the Catholic intelligence and conscience. Where this kind of language is talked, the Catholic joins the conversation with complete ease. It is his language. The ideas expressed are native to his own universe of discourse. Even the accent, being American, suits his tongue.

Another idiom now prevails. The possibility was inherent from the beginning. To the early American theorists and politicians the tradition of natural law was an inheritance. This was its strength; this was at the same time its weakness, especially since a subtle alteration of the tradition had already commenced. For a variety of reasons the intellectualist idea of law as reason had begun to cede to the voluntarist idea of law as will. One can note the change in Blackstone, for instance, even though he still stood within the tradition, and indeed drew whole generations of early American lawyers into it with him. (Part of American folklore is Sandburg's portrait of Abraham Lincoln, sitting barefoot on his woodpile, reading Blackstone.) Protestant Christianity, especially in its left wing (and its left wing has always been dominant in America), inevitably evolved away from the old English and American tradition. Grotius and the philosophers of the Enlightenment had cast up their secularized versions of the tradition. Their disciples were to better their instruction, as the impact of the methods of empirical science made itself felt even in those areas of human thought in which knowledge is noncumulative and to that extent recalcitrant to the methods of science. Seeds of dissolution were already present in the ancient heritage as it reached the shores of America.

Perhaps the dissolution, long since begun, may one day be consummated. Perhaps one day the noble many-storeyed mansion of democracy will be dismantled, leveled to the dimensions of a flat majoritarianism, which is no mansion but a barn, perhaps even a tool shed in which the weapons of tyranny may be forged. Perhaps there will one day be wide dissent even from the political principles which emerge from natural law, as well as dissent from the constellation of ideas that have historically undergirded these principles — the idea that government has a moral basis; that the universal moral law is the foundation of society; that the legal order of society — that is, the state — is subject to judgment by a law that is not statistical but inherent in the nature of man; that the eternal reason of God is the ultimate origin of all law; that this nation in all its aspects — as a society, a state, an ordered and free relationship between governors and governed — is under God. The possibility that widespread dissent from these principles should develop is not foreclosed. If that evil day should come, the results would introduce one more paradox into history. The Catholic community would still be speaking in the ethical and political idiom familiar to them as it was familiar to their fathers, both the Fathers of the Church and the Fathers of the American Republic. The guardianship of the original American consensus, based on the Western heritage, would have passed to the Catholic community, within which the heritage was elaborated long before America was. And it would be for others, not Catholics, to ask themselves whether they still shared the consensus which first fashioned the American people into a body politic and determined the structure of its fundamental law.

What has been said may suffice to show the grounds on which Catholics participate in the American consensus. These grounds are drawn from the materials of the consensus itself. It has been a greatly providential blessing that the American Republic never put to the Catholic conscience the questions raised, for instance, by the Third Republic. There has never been a schism within the American Catholic community, as there was among French Catholics, over the right attitude to adopt toward the established polity. There has never been the necessity for nice distinctions between the regime and the legislation; nor has there ever been the need to proclaim a policy of *ralliement*. In America the *ralliement* has been original, spontaneous, universal. It has been a matter of conscience and conviction, because its motive was not expediency in the narrow sense — the need to accept what one is powerless to change. Its motive was the evident coincidence of the principles which inspired the American Republic with the principles that are structural to the Western Christian political tradition.

16 The Grace of Doing Nothing

H. Richard Niebuhr

MARCH 23, 1932

It may be that the greatest moral problems of the individual or of a society arise when there is nothing to be done. When we have begun a certain line of action or engaged in a conflict we cannot pause too long to decide which of various possible courses we ought to choose for the sake of the worthier result. Time rushes on and we must choose as best we can, entrusting the issue to the future. It is when we stand aside from the conflict, before we know what our relations to it really are, when we seem to be condemned to doing nothing, that our moral problems become greatest. How shall we do nothing?

The issue is brought home to us by the fighting in the East. We are chafing at the bit, we are eager to do something constructive; but there is nothing constructive, it seems, that we can do. We pass resolutions, aware that we are doing nothing; we summon up righteous indignation and still do nothing; we write letters to congressmen and secretaries, asking others to act while we do nothing. Yet is it really true that we are doing nothing? There are, after all, various ways of being inactive, and some kinds of inactivity, if not all, may be highly productive. It is not really possible to stand aside, to sit by the fire, in this world of moving times; even Peter was doing something in the court-yard of the high-priest's house — if it was only something he was doing to himself. When we do nothing we are also affecting the course of history. The problem we face is often that of choice between various kinds of inactivity rather than of choice between action and inaction.

Our inactivity may be that of the pessimist who watches a world go to pieces. It is a meaningful inactivity for himself and for the world. His world, at all events, will go to pieces the more rapidly because of the inactivity. Or it may be the inactivity of the conservative believer in things as they are. He does nothing in the international crisis because he believes that the way of Japan is the way of all nations, that self-interest is the first and only law of life, and that out of the clash of national, out of that of individual, self-interests the greater good will result. His inactivity is one of watchful waiting for the opportunity when, in precisely similar manner, though with less loss of life and fortune, if possible, he may rush to the protection of his own interests or promote them by taking advantage of the situation created by the strife of his competitors. This way of doing nothing is not unproductive. It encourages the self-assertive and it fills them with fear of the moment when the new competition will begin. It may be that they have been driven into their present conflict by the knowledge or suspicion that the watchful waiter is looking for his opportunity, perhaps unconsciously, and that they must be prepared for him.

The inactivity of frustration and moral indignation is of another order. It is the way of those who have renounced all violent methods of settling conflicts and have no other means at hand by which to deal with the situation. It is an angry inactivity like that of a man who is watching a neighborhood fight and is waiting for the police to arrive — for police who never come. He has renounced for himself the method of forcible interference, which would only increase the flow of blood and the hatred, but he knows of nothing else that he can do. He is forced to remain content on the sidelines, but with mounting anger he regards the bully who is beating the neighbor, and his wrath issues in words of exasperation and condemnation. Having tied his own hands he fights with his tongue and believes that he is fighting because he inflicts only mental wounds. The bully is for him an outlaw, a person not to be trusted, unfair, selfish, one who cannot be redeemed save by restraint. The righteous indignation mounts and mounts, and must issue at last — as the police fail to arrive — either in his own forcible entry into the conflict, despite his scruples, or in apoplexy.

The diatribes against Japan which are appearing in the secular and religious press today have a distressing similarity to the righteously indignant utterances which preceded our conflicts with Spain and with Germany. China is Cuba and Belgium over again; it is the Negro race beaten by Simon Legree. And the pacifists who have no other program than that of abstention from the unrighteousness of war are likely to be placed in the same quandary in which their fellows were placed in 1860, 1898, and 1915, and — unless human attitudes have been regenerated in the interim — they are likely to share the same fate, which was not usually incarceration. Here is a situation which they did not foresee when they made their vow; may it not be necessary to have one more war to end all war? Righteous indignation not allowed to issue in action is a dangerous thing — as dangerous as any great emotion nurtured and repressed at the same time. It is the source of sudden explosions or the ground of long, bitter, and ugly hatreds.

If this way of doing nothing must be rejected, the Communists' way offers more hope. Theirs is the inactivity of those who see that there is indeed nothing constructive to be done in the present situation, but that, rightly understood, this situation is after all preliminary to a radical change which will eliminate the conditions of which the conflict is a product. It is the activity of a cynicism which expects no good from the present, evil world of capitalism, but also the inactivity of a boundless faith in the future. The Communists know that war and revolution are closely akin, that war breeds discontent and misery, and that out of misery and discontent new worlds may be born. This is an opportunity, then, not for direct entrance into conflict, not for the watchful waiting of those who seek their self-interest, but for the slow laborious process of building-up within the fighting groups those cells of communism which will be ready to inherit the new world and be able to build a classless international commonwealth on the ruins of capitalism and nationalism. Here is inactivity with a long vision, a steadfast hope, and a realistic program of non-interfering action.

But there is yet another way of doing nothing. It appears to be highly impracticable because it rests on the well-nigh-obsolete faith that there is a God — a real God. Those who follow this way share with communism the belief that the fact that men can do nothing constructive is no indication of the fact that nothing constructive is being done. Like the Communists they are assured that the actual processes of history will inevitably and really bring a different kind of world with lasting peace. They do not rely on human aspirations after ideals to accomplish this end, but on forces which eliminated slavery in spite of abolitionists. The forces may be as impersonal and as actual as matching production, rapid transportation, the physical mixtures of races, and so on, but as parts of the real world they are as much a part of the total divine process as are human thoughts and prayers.

From this point of view, naively affirming the meaningfulness of reality, the history of the world is the judgment of the world and also its redemption, and a conflict like the present one is — again as in communism — only the prelude both to greater judgment and to a new era. The world being what it is, these results are brought forth when the seeds of national or individual self-interest are planted; the actual structure of things is such that our wishes for a different result do not in the least affect the outcome. "As a man soweth so shall he reap."

This God of things as they are is inevitable and quite merciless. His mercy lies beyond, not this side of, judgment. This inactive Christianity shares with communism also the belief in the inevitably good outcome of the mundane process and the realistic insight that good cannot be achieved by the slow accretion of better habits alone but more in consequence of revolutionary change which will involve considerable destruction. While it does nothing it knows that something is being done, something which is divine both in its threat and in its promise.

This inactivity is like that of the early Christians whose millenarian mythology it replaces with the contemporary mythology of social forces. (Mythology is after all not fiction but a deep philosophy.) Like early Christianity and like communism today radical Christianity knows that nothing constructive can be done by interference, but that something very constructive can be done in preparation for the future. It also can build cells of those within each nation who, divorcing themselves from the program of nationalism and of capitalism, unite in a higher loyalty which transcends national and class lines of division and prepare for the future.

There is no such Christian international today because radical Christianity has not arrived as yet at a program and a philosophy of history, but such little cells are forming. The First Christian International of Rome has had its day; the Second Christian International of Stockholm is likely to go the way of the Second Socialist International. There are need and opportunity for a Third Christian International.

While the similarities of a radically Christian program with the Communist program are striking, there are also great dissimilarities. There is a new element in the inactivity of radical Christianity which is lacking in communism. The Christian reflects upon the fact that his inability do anything constructive in the crisis is the inability of one whose own faults are so apparent and so similar to those of the offender that any action on his part is not only likely to be misinterpreted but is also likely — in the nature of the case — to be really less than disinterested. He is like a father who, feeling a righteous indignation against a misbehaving child, remembers that this misbehavior is his fault as much as the child's and that indignation is the least helpful, the most dangerous of attitudes to take; it will solve nothing, though it may repress.

So the American Christian realizes that Japan is following the example of his own country and that it has little real ground for believing America to be a disinterested nation. He may see that his country, for which he bears his own responsibility as a citizen, is really not disinterested and that its righteous indignation is not wholly righteous. An inactivity then is demanded which will be profoundly active in rigid self-analysis. Such analysis is likely to reveal that there is an approach to the situation, indirect but far more effective than direct interference, for it is able to create the conditions under which a real reconstruction of habits is possible. It is the opposite approach from that of the irate father who believes that every false reaction on the part of his child may be cured by a verbal, physical, or economic spanking.

This way of doing nothing the old Christians call repentance, but the word has become so reminiscent of emotional debauches in the feeling of guilt that it may be better to abandon it for a while. What is suggested is that the only effective approach to the problem of China and Japan lies in the sphere of an American self-analysis which is likely to result in some surprising discoveries as to the amount of renunciation of self-interest necessary on the part of this country and of individual Christians before anything effective can be done in the East.

The inactivity of radical Christianity is not the inactivity of those who call evil good: it is the inaction of those who do not judge their neighbors because they cannot fool themselves into a sense of superior righteousness. It is not the inactivity of a resigned patience, but of a patience that is full of hope and is based on faith. It is not the inactivity of the non-combatant, for it knows that there are no non-combatants, that everyone is involved, that China is being crucified (though the term is very inaccurate) by our sins and those of the whole world. It is not the inactivity of the merciless, for works of mercy must be performed though they are only palliates to ease present pain while the process of healing depends on deeper, more actual and urgent forces.

But if there is no God, or if God is up in heaven and not in time itself, it is a very foolish inactivity.

17 Must We Do Nothing?

Reinhold Niebuhr

MARCH 30, 1932

There is much in my brother's article, "The Grace of Doing Nothing," with which I agree. Except for the invitation of the editors of *The Christian Century* I would have preferred to defer voicing any disagreement with some of his final conclusions to some future occasion; for a casual article on a specific problem created by the contemporary international situation hardly does justice to his general position. I believe the problem upon which he is working — the problem of disassociating a rigorous gospel ethic of disinterestedness and love from the sentimental dilutions of that ethic which are current in liberal Christianity — is a tremendously important one. I owe so much to the penetrating thought which he has been giving this subject that I may be able to do some justice to his general position even though I do not share his conviction that a pure love ethic can ever be made the basis of a civilization.

He could not have done better than to choose the Sino-Japanese conflict, and the reactions of the world to it, in order to prove the difficulty, if not the futility, of dealing redemptively with a sinful nation or individual if we cannot exorcise the same sin from our own hearts. It is true that pacifists are in danger of stirring up hatred against Japan in their effort to stem the tide of Japanese imperialism. It is true that the very impotence of an individual who deals with a social situation which goes beyond his own powers tempts him to hide his sense of futility behind his display of violent emotion. It is true that we have helped to create the Japan which expresses itself in terms of materialistic imperialism. The insult we offered her in our immigration laws was a sin of spiritual aggression. The white world has notoriously taught her the ways of imperialism, but has pre-empted enough of the yellow man's side of the world to justify Japan's imperialism as a vent for pent-up national energies.

It is also true that American concern over Japanese aggression is not wholly disinterested. It is national interest which prompts us to desire stronger action against Japan than France and England are willing to take. It is true, in other words, that every social sin is, at least partially, the fruit and consequence of the sins of those who judge and condemn it, and that the effort to eliminate it involves the critics and judges in new social sin, the assertion of self-interest and the expression of moral conceit and hypocrisy. If anyone would raise the objection to such an analysis that it finds every social action falling short only because it measures the action against an impossible ideal of disinterestedness, my brother could answer that while the ideal may seem to be impossible the actual social situation proves it to be necessary. It is literally true that every recalcitrant nation, like every antisocial individual, is created by the society which condemns it, and that redemptive efforts which betray strong ulterior motives are always bound to be less than fully redemptive.

My brother draws the conclusion from this logic that it is better not to act at all than to act from motives which are less than pure, and with the use of methods which are less than critical (coercion). He believes in taking literally the words of Jesus, "Let him who is without sin cast the first stone." He believes, of course, that this kind of inaction would not really be inaction; it would be, rather, the action of repentance. It would give every one involved in social sin the chance to recognize how much he is involved in it and how necessary it is to restrain his own greed, pride, hatred, and lust for power before the social sin is eliminated.

This is an important emphasis particularly for modern Christianity with its lack of appreciation of the tragic character of life and with its easy assumption that the world will be saved by a little more adequate educational technique. Hypocrisy is an inevitable by-product of moral aspiration, and it is the business of true religion to destroy man's moral conceit, a task which modern religion has not been performing in any large degree. Its sentimentalities have tended to increase rather than to diminish moral conceit. A truly religious man ought to distinguish himself from the moral man by recognizing the fact that he is not moral, that he remains a sinner to the end. The sense of sin is more central to religion than is any other attitude.

All this does not prove, however, that we ought to apply the words of Jesus, "Let him who is without sin cast the first stone," literally. If we do we will never be able to act. There will never be a wholly disinterested nation. Pure disinterestedness is an ideal which even individuals cannot fully achieve, and human groups are bound always to express themselves in lower ethical forms than individuals. It follows that no nation can ever be good enough to save another nation purely by the power of love. The relation of nations and of economic groups can never be brought into terms of pure love. Justice is probably the highest ideal toward which human groups can aspire. And justice, with its goal of adjustment of right to right, inevitably involves the assertion of right against right and interest against interest until some kind of harmony is achieved. If a measure of humility and of love does not enter this conflict of interest it will of course degenerate into violence. A rational society will be able to develop a measure of the kind of imagination which knows how to appreciate the virtues of an opponent's position and the weakness in one's own. But the ethical and spiritual note of love and repentance can do no more than qualify the social struggle in history. It will never abolish it.

The hope of attaining an ethical goal for society by purely ethical means, that is, without coercion, and without the assertion of the interests of the underprivileged against the interests of the privileged, is an illusion which was spread chiefly among the comfortable classes of the past century. My brother does not make the mistake of assuming that this is possible in social terms. He is acutely aware of the fact that it is not possible to get a sufficient degree of pure disinterestedness and love among privileged classes and powerful nations to resolve the conflicts of history in that way. He understands the stubborn inertia which the ethical ideal meets in history. At this point his realistic interpretation of the facts of history comes in full conflict with his insistence upon a pure gospel ethic, upon a religiously inspired moral perfectionism, and he resolves the conflict by leaving the field of social theory entirely and resorting to eschatology. The Christian will try to achieve humility and disinterestedness not because enough Christians will be able to do so to change the course of history, but because this kind of spiritual attitude is a prayer to God for the coming of his kingdom.

I will not quarrel with this apocalyptic note, as such, though I suspect many *Christian Century* readers will. I believe that a proper eschatology is necessary to a vigorous ethic, that the simple idea of progress is inimical to the highest ethic. The compound of pessimism and optimism which a vigorous ethical attitude requires can be expressed only in terms of religious eschatology. What makes my brother's eschatology impossible for me is that he identifies everything that is occurring in history (the drift toward disaster, another world war, and possibly a revolution) with the counsels of God, and then suddenly, by a leap of faith, comes to the conclusion that the same God who uses brutalities and forces, against which man must maintain conscientious scruples, will finally establish an ideal society in which pure love will reign.

I have more than one difficulty with such a faith. I do not see how a revolution in which the disinterested express their anger and resentment, and assert their interests, can be an instrument of God, and yet at the same time an instrument which religious scruples forbid a man to use. I should think that it would be better to come to ethical terms with the forces of nature in history, and try to use ethically directed coercion in order that violence may be avoided. The hope that a kingdom of pure love will emerge out of the catastrophes of history is even less plausible than the Communist faith that an equalitarian society will eventually emerge from them. There is some warrant in history for the latter assumption, but very little for the former.

I find it impossible to envisage a society of pure love as long as man remains man. His natural limitations of reason and imagination will prevent him, even should he achieve a purely disinterested motive, from fully envisaging the needs of his fellow men or from determining his actions upon the basis of their interests. Inevitably these limitations of individuals will achieve cumulative effect in the life and actions of national, racial, and economic groups. It is possible to envisage a more ethical society than we now have. It is possible to believe that such a society will be achieved partly by evolutionary process and partly by catastrophe in which an old order, which offers a too stubborn resistance to new forces, is finally destroyed.

It is plausible also to interpret both the evolutionary and the catastrophic elements in history in religious terms and to see the counsels of God in them. But it is hardly plausible to expect divine intervention to introduce something into history which is irrelevant to anything we find in history now. We may envisage a society in which human cooperation is possible with a minimum amount of coercion at all — unless, of course, human beings become quite different from what they now are. We may hope for a society in which self-interest is qualified by rigorous self-analysis and a stronger social impulse, but we cannot imagine a society totally without the assertion of self-interest and therefore without the conflict of opposing interests.

I realize quite well that my brother's position both in its ethical perfectionism and in its apocalyptic note is closer to the gospel than mine. In confessing that, I am forced to admit that I am unable to construct an adequate social ethic out of a pure love ethic. I cannot abandon the pure love ideal because anything which falls short of it is less than the ideal. But I cannot use it fully if I want to assume a responsible attitude towards the problems of society. Religious perfectionism drives either to asceticism or apocalypticism. In the one case the problem of society is given up entirely; in the other individual perfection is regarded as the force which will release the redemptive powers of God for society. I think the second alternative is better than the first, and that both have elements which must be retained for any adequate social ethic, lest it become lost in the relativities of expediency. But as long as the world of man remains a place where nature and God, the real and the ideal, meet, human progress will depend upon the judicious use of the forces of nature in the service of the ideal.

In practical, specific, and contemporary terms, this means that we must try to dissuade Japan from her military venture, but must use coercion to frustrate her designs if necessary, must reduce coercion to a minimum and prevent it from issuing in violence, must engage in constant self-analysis in order to reduce the moral conceit of Japan's critics and judges to a minimum, and must try in every social situation to maximize the ethical forces and yet not sacrifice the possibility of achieving an ethical goal because we are afraid to use any but purely ethical means.

To say all this is really to confess that the history of mankind is a perennial tragedy; for the highest ideals which the individual may project are ideals which he can never realize in social and collective terms. If there is a law in our members which wars against the law that is in our minds as individuals, this is even more true when we think of society. Individuals set the goal for society but society itself must achieve the goals, and society is and will always remain sub-human. The goal which a sensitive individual sets for society must therefore always be something which is a little outside and beyond history. Love may qualify the social struggle of history but it will never abolish it, and those who make the attempt to bring society under the dominion of perfect love will die on the cross. And those who behold the cross are quite right in seeing it as a revelation of the divine, of what man ought to be and cannot be, at least not so long as he is enmeshed in the processes of history.

Perhaps that is why it is inevitable that religious imagination should set goals beyond history. "Man's reach is beyond his grasp, or what's a heaven for." My brother does not like these goals above and beyond history. He wants religion and social idealism to deal with history. In that case he must not state his goal in absolute terms. There can be nothing absolute in history, no matter how frequently God may intervene in it. Man cannot live without a sense of the absolute, but neither can he achieve the absolute. He may resolve the tragic character of that fact by religious faith, by the experience of grace in which the unattainable is experienced in anticipatory terms, but he can never resolve in purely ethical terms the conflict between what is and what ought to be.

18 The Only Way into the Kingdom of God

H. Richard Niebuhr

APRIL 6, 1932

Sir: Since you have given me leave to fire one more shot in the fraternal war between my brother and me over the question of pacifism, I shall attempt to place it as well as I can, not for the purpose of demolishing my opponent's position — which our thirty years' war has shown me to be impossible — but for the sake of pointing as accurately as I can to the exact locus of the issue between us. It does not lie in the question of activity or inactivity, to which my too journalistic approach to the problem directed attention; we are speaking after all of two kinds of activity. The fundamental question seems to me to be whether "the history of mankind is a perennial tragedy" which can derive meaning only from a goal which lies beyond history, as my brother maintains, or whether the "eschatological" faith, to which I seek to adhere, is justifiable. In that faith tragedy is only the prelude to fulfillment, and a prelude which is necessary because of human nature; the kingdom of God comes inevitably, though whether we shall see it or not depends on our recognition of its presence and our acceptance of the only kind of life which will enable us to enter it, the life of repentance and forgiveness.

For my brother, God is outside the historical processes, so much so that he charges me with faith in a miracle-working deity which interferes occasionally, sometimes brutally, sometimes redemptively in this history. But God, I believe, is always in history; he is the structure in things, the source of all meaning, the "I am that I am," that which is that it is. He is the rock against which we beat in vain, that which bruises and overwhelms us when we seek to impose our wishes, contrary to his, upon him. That structure of the universe, that creative will, can no more be said to interfere brutally in

265

history than the violated laws of my organism can be said to interfere brutally with my life if they make me pay the cost of my violation. That structure of the universe, that will of God, does bring war and depression upon us when we bring it upon ourselves, for we live in the kind of world which visits our iniquities upon us and our children, no matter how much we pray and desire that it be otherwise.

Self-interest acts destructively in this world; it calls forth counter-assistance; nationalism breeds nationalism, class assertion summons up counter-assertion on the part of exploited classes. The result is war, economic, military, verbal; and it is judgment. But this same structure in things which is our enemy is our redeemer; "it means intensely and it means good" — not the good which we desire, but the good which we would desire if we were good and really wise. History is not a perennial tragedy but a road to fulfillment and that fulfillment requires the tragic outcome of every self-assertion, for it is fulfillment which can only be designated as "love." It has created fellowship in atoms and organisms, at bitter cost to electrons and cells; and it is creating something better than human selfhood but at bitter cost to that selfhood. This is not a faith in progress, for evil grows as well as good, and every self-assertion must be eliminated somewhere and somehow — by innocence suffering for guilt, it seems.

If, however, history is no more than tragedy, if there is no fulfillment in it, then my brother is right. Then we must rest content with the clash of self-interested individuals, personal or social. But in that case, I see no reason why we should qualify the clash of competition with a homeopathic dose of Christian "love."

The only harmony which can possibly result from the clash of interests is the harmony imposed by the rule of the strong or a parallelogram of social forces, whether we think of the interclass structure or the international world. To import any pacifism into this struggle is only to weaken the weaker self-assertions (India, China, or the proletariat) or to provide the strong with a facade of "service" behind which they can operate with a salved conscience. (Pacifism, on the other hand, as a method of self-assertion is not pacifism at all but a different kind of war.)

The method which my brother recommends, that of qualifying the social struggle by means of some Christian love, seems to me to be only the old method of making Christian love an ambulance driver in the wars of interested and clashing parties. If it is more than that, it is a weakening of the forces whose success we think necessary for a juster social order. For me the question is one of "either-or"; either the Christian method, which is not the method of love but of repentance and forgiveness, or the method of self-assertion; either nationalism or Christianity, either capitalism-communism or Christianity. The attempt to qualify the one method by the other is hopeless compromise.

I think that to apply the terms "Christian perfectionism" or "Christian ideal" to my approach is rather misleading. I rather think that Dewey is quite right in his war on ideals; they always seem irrelevant to our situation and betray us into a dualistic morality. The society of love is an impossible human ideal, as the fellowship of the organism is an impossible ideal for the cell. It is not an ideal toward which we can strive, but an "emergent," a potentiality in our situation which remains unrealized so long as we try to impose our pattern, our wishes upon the divine creative process.

Man's task is not that of building utopias, but that of eliminating weeds and tilling the soil so that the kingdom of God can grow. His method is not one of striving for perfection or of acting perfectly, but of clearing the road by repentance and forgiveness. That this approach is valid for societies as well as for individuals and that the opposite approach will always involve us in the same one ceaseless cycle of assertion and counter-assertion is what I am concerned to emphasize.

V. In the Shadow of Auschwitz

Introduction

George Hunsinger

Political theology falls into two general categories, namely, the descriptive and the normative. They need not be mutually exclusive. Descriptive accounts may have a normative agenda, while normative accounts usually incorporate elements of political description. Descriptive accounts look at how theology functions in political contexts; normative accounts, at how it ought to function.

Normative accounts usually assume that the right sort of theology correlates with the right sort of political function (+/+), and the wrong sort of theology with the wrong sort of function (-/-). The mixed possibilities, however, are rarely entertained. In actuality, however, as a sign of human imperfection or inconsistency, the right sort of theology may correlate with the wrong sort of function (+/-), and the wrong sort of theology with the right sort of function (-/+). In the readings in this section, these general possibilities are illustrated in various ways.

Carl Schmitt seems to set forth a descriptive account with a normative agenda. He purports to describe the political function of theology in modern social thought and under modern social circumstances. He is especially interested in how modern political theory is covertly a form of secularized theology. Schmitt's descriptive terminology, which does not always conform to current usage (e.g., "sociology"), is fuzzy at best, and the writers he discusses have sometimes lapsed into total obscurity. Despite appearing to be a mile wide and an inch deep — here he attempts to cover more than two centuries of material in very short compass — his freewheeling remarks are not without insight, especially when discussing figures still of interest, like Rousseau, Mill, and Hegel. Under Hitler, Schmitt was a professed Nazi in political affiliation and an authoritarian Catholic in religion. Notoriously, he justified Nazi anti-Semitism and various atrocities. Descriptively, however, he developed an interesting theory of dictatorship as well as an analysis of how a "state of exception" can be used to justify it. For Schmitt the right sort of theology (arbitrary divine sovereignty as seen in "miracles") correlated with the right sort of political theory (dictatorship, anti-Semitism, and brutal repression as necessary exceptions to the rule of law). Normatively, many would see him today as a double negative, that is, both theologically and politically.

A Christ-centered interpretation of political reality is offered by Dietrich Bonhoeffer. More considered and less dilettantish than Schmitt, Bonhoeffer sketches an interesting typology of ecclesiastical social thought that is itself highly normative or theory-laden. He argues for the advantages of interpreting political reality from a center "in Christ" as opposed to one "in human nature" or "in sin." If Jesus Christ is the origin and the goal of all things, as well as the medium though whom they are governed by God, then he is also the origin, goal, and medium of divine governance in the political realm — whether through the church or apart from it or even against it. The legitimacy of secular government is seen as both grounded in Christ and delimited by him, and especially by his cross, through which, paradoxically, he reigns in power as the Lord. Bonhoeffer's political interpretation of the cross potentially created an opening for nonviolent forms of direct action and political witness, an opening he only partially glimpsed and never developed. Contemporary political scientists such as Gene Sharp and others have argued that in the latter half of the twentieth century nonviolent direct action, when organized on a massive scale, often turned out to be a force more powerful than violence in effecting progressive social change. If so, then by resorting to tyrannicide, not to mention by aligning himself with certain less than democratic social forces, Bonhoeffer may have partially obscured his best insights. From this point of view, his achievement would be mixed.

Although Karl Barth is more detailed on church and state than Bonhoeffer, Bonhoeffer, in a sense, is more Barthian than Barth. He takes a more Christ-centered approach than Barth does in the excerpt reproduced here, which was written prior not only to the German church struggle under Hitler but also to *Church Dogmatics.* Although in principle Barth, like Bonhoeffer, sees both church and state as participating in the order of redemption, he does not seem to break as clearly as Bonhoeffer does from older ideas inherited from the Reformation. In particular, unlike Bonhoeffer, Barth gives little or no attention to the cross of Christ when thinking about politics and political authority in the secular realm. On the basis of these selections, it would be easier to integrate Barth's best insights into the framework that Bonhoeffer sets forth than the reverse. More attention to the theme of the cross might have enabled Barth to ground his concern for the exploited and oppressed (the working class) more clearly than he does. His concern for the neighbor's welfare, for the rule of law, and for democratic accountability might also have benefited from a more explicitly Christ-centered approach. His later anti-imperialistic and anti-militaristic emphases are in little evidence. Noteworthy is his allowance for armed struggle against a grievously unjust state, a view that would later be tempered by his advocacy of a practical pacifism. Furthermore, why the church should be seen as more of a human work than as the work of Christ is never made entirely clear. Barth's idea of the church as something that will wither away in the eschaton, his relatively non-sacramental understanding of worship, and his anti-episcopal sentiments are all dated views that would need to be carefully reconsidered in light of the ecumenical movement and its progress after Vatican II. In the end, Barth's social and political views seem more commendable in this excerpt than the normative grounding he provides for them, and his best theological insights did not develop on these matters until later.

Johann Baptist Metz, in the selection reproduced here, proposes to discuss political theology without once mentioning the name of Jesus Christ. In Metz's other writings Christ is very often presented as the object of ethical imitation. To that extent he would seem to be presenting his readers with a merely exemplarist Christology. However, as a Roman Catholic theologian, Metz is surely presupposing more about Christ than he manages in these cases to make clear. Nevertheless, the apparent eclipse of Christ, if not his drastic reduction to being little more than a moral symbol or a "dangerous memory" (is not the Risen Christ, even for Metz, the living Lord?), would seem, from an ecclesial standpoint, to impose severe limits on the adequacy of Metz's proposals about political theology insofar as he wishes them to be taken seriously in the church. How social and historical circumstances can impose a "paradigm shift" in theology — the question Metz proposes to explore — cannot be convincingly answered if it fails to be convincingly formulated. Sweeping cultural and historical claims, which take the form of pronouncements from on high, do not make matters any easier. Placing these defects to one side, however, Metz is undoubtedly correct that Christian theology can no longer afford to ignore social problems like anti-Semitism, racism, and, in general, the sufferings of victims of deep-seated social injustice.

Political theology needs to explore how these sufferings can be, and too often are, obscured and exacerbated by religion. It also needs to develop theological remedies to religion in its socially dysfunctional forms. Serious remedies, however, will require not only more careful social and cultural analysis but also more perceptive retrievals from the theological tradition.

According to Dorothee Sölle, the history of the word *father* to name God has been nothing less than a history of barbarism. Masculine divine symbols like "Father" have served to legitimize male supremacy, and male supremacy, especially when institutionalized as patriarchy, has been coterminous with subjugating women through outright violence and abuse. Under these cultural and historical circumstances, God the Father cannot possibly be God the Liberator, and if God is indeed Liberator, God the Father, as traditionally understood, will have to go. Obedience as a theological concept will also have to go, since liberation means solidarity, equality, and freedom, not servile compliance to authority, not to mention illegitimate authority. The hermeneutic represented by Sölle is almost entirely a hermeneutic of suspicion, rejection, and finally perhaps schism. Little place is left for an alternative hermeneutic of reconsideration, repentance, and retrieval. Women and others who do not wish to follow Sölle down the path of blanket rejection are, presumably, in danger of becoming benighted collaborators in their own oppression. Most women in Christian communities, however, even when they are not unsympathetic to Sölle's forceful critique, are not prepared to jettison traditional Christian language for God, including its familiar trinitarian meanings. Apart from a relatively small enclave in academic and ecclesial circles, they are more inclined to take the path of reinterpretation and retrieval. They don't want subjugation and abuse any more than Sölle does, but they take a more moderate view. They are not content with simply defecting in place. They believe that abuse of theological language does not bar use, and they sense that the needed antidote to abuse is not disuse but proper use. Beyond what Sölle seems to envision, they seek renewal and retrieval in the church along these lines.

19 Political Theology

Carl Schmitt

state → sovereign

All significant concepts of the modern theory of the state are secularized theological concepts not only because of their historical development — in which they were transferred from theology to the theory of the state, whereby, for example, the omnipotent God became the omnipotent lawgiver — but also because of their systematic structure, the recognition of which is necessary for a sociological consideration of these concepts. The exception in jurisprudence is analogous to the miracle in theology. Only by being aware of this analogy can we appreciate the manner in which the philosophical ideas of the state developed in the last centuries.

The idea of the modern constitutional state triumphed together with deism, a theology and metaphysics that banished the miracle from the world. This theology and metaphysics rejected not only the transgression of the laws of nature through an exception brought about by direct intervention, as is found in the idea of a miracle, but also the sovereign's direct intervention in a valid legal order. The rationalism of the Enlightenment rejected the exception in every form. Conservative authors of the counterrevolution who were theists could thus attempt to support the personal sovereignty of the monarch ideologically, with the aid of analogies from a theistic theology.

I have for a long time referred to the significance of such fundamentally systematic and methodical analogies.[1] A detailed presentation of the mean-

---

1. *Der Wert des Staates* (Tübingen, 1914); *Politische Romantik* (Munich and Leipzig, 1919); *Die Diktatur: Von den Anfängen des modernen Souveränitätsgedankens bis zum proletarischen Klassenkampf* (Munich and Leipzig, 1921).

ing of the concept of the miracle in this context will have to be left to another time. What is relevant here is only the extent to which this connection is appropriate for a sociology of juristic concepts. The most interesting political application of such analogies is found in the Catholic philosophers of the counterrevolution, in Bonald, de Maistre, and Donoso Cortes. What we immediately recognize in them is a conceptually clear and systematic analogy, and not merely that kind of playing with ideas, whether mystical, natural-philosophical, or even romantic, which, as with everything else, so also with state and society, yields colorful symbols and pictures.

The clearest philosophical expression of that analogy is found in Leibniz.[2] Emphasizing the systematic relationship between jurisprudence and theology, he rejected a comparison of jurisprudence with medicine and mathematics: "We have deservedly transferred the model of our division from theology to jurisprudence because the similarity of these two disciplines is astonishing." Both have a double principle, reason (hence there is a natural theology and a natural jurisprudence) and scripture, which means a book with positive revelations and directives.

Adolf Menzel noted in an essay[3] that today sociology has assumed functions that were exercised in the seventeenth and eighteenth centuries by natural law, namely, to utter demands for justice and to enunciate philosophical-historical constructions or ideals. He seems to believe that sociology is inferior to jurisprudence, which is supposed to have become positive. He attempts to show that all heretofore sociological systems end up by making "political tendencies appear scientific." But whoever takes the trouble of examining the public law literature of positive jurisprudence for its basic concepts and arguments will see that the state intervenes everywhere. At times it does so as a *deus ex machina,* to decide according to positive statute a controversy that the independent act of juristic perception failed to bring to a generally plausible solution; at other times it does so as the graceful and merciful lord who proves by pardons and amnesties his supremacy over his own laws. There always exists the same inexplicable identity: lawgiver, executive power, police, pardoner, welfare institution. Thus to an observer who takes the trouble to look at the total picture of contemporary jurisprudence, there appears a huge cloak-and-dagger drama, in which the state acts in many disguises but always as the same invisible person. The "omnipotence" of the modern law-

2. *Nova Methodus,* paras. 4, 5.
3. *Naturrecht and Soziologie* (Vienna and Leipzig, 1912).

giver, of which one reads in every textbook on public law, is not only linguistically derived from theology.

Many reminiscences of theology also appear in the details of the argumentation, most of course with polemical intent. In a positivistic age it is easy to reproach an intellectual opponent with the charge of indulging in theology or metaphysics. If the reproach were intended as more than mere insult, at least the following question could suggest itself: What is the source of this inclination for such theological and metaphysical derailments? One would have had to investigate whether they may be explained historically, perhaps as an aftereffect of monarchical public law, which identified the theistic God with the king, or whether they are underpinned by systematic or methodical necessities. I readily admit that because of an inability to master intellectually contradictory arguments or objections, some jurists introduce the state in their works by a mental short circuit, just as certain metaphysicians misuse the name of God. But this does not yet resolve the substantive problem.

Until now one was generally satisfied with casual intimations only. In his publication on the law in the formal and material sense, Albert Hanel[4] raised the old objection that it is "metaphysics" to demand, for the sake of the uniformity and reliability of the state's will (both of which he thus does not deny), the concentration of all functions of the state in one organ. Hugo Preuss[5] too attempted to defend his association concept of the state by relegating his opponents to theology and metaphysics. The concept of sovereignty in the theory of the state by Laband and Jellinek and the theory of the "sole supremacy of the state" make the state an abstract person so to speak, a *unicum sui generis,* with a monopoly of power "mystically produced." To Preuss this was a legal disguise of the theory of the divine right of kings, a repetition of the teachings of Maurenbrecher with the modification that the religious fiction is replaced by the juristic fiction. Thus Preuss, a representative of the organic theory of the state, reproached his opponent for theologizing. In his critical studies of the concept of the juristic person, Bernatzik[6] maintained, on the other hand, that it is precisely the organic doctrine of the state that is theology. Bernatzik attempted to destroy the organic ideas of Stein, Schulze, Gierke, and Preuss with the sneering remark

---

4. *Das Gesetz im Formellen and Materiellen Sinne* (Leipzig, 1888), p. 150. [2d printing (Darmstadt, 1968) — tr.]

5. *Festgabe fur Laband,* vol. 2 (1908), p. 236. [I was unable to verify this citation — tr.]

6. "Kritische Studien über den Begriff der juristischen Person und über die juristische Personlichkeit der Behörden insbesondere," *Archiv des offentlichen Rechts* 5 (1890): 210, 225, 244.

that if the organs of the collective legal person should once again be persons, then every administrative authority, every court, and so on, would be a juristic person and the state in its entirety would also once again be such a sole juristic person. "The attempt to comprehend the dogma of the Trinity would, by comparison, be an easy matter." He also dismissed Stobbes's opinion that the entire collective personality is a legal person with the sentence that he does not understand "twists like this one that are reminiscent of the dogma of the Trinity." Yet he himself said, "It already resides in the concept of legal competence that its source, the state's legal order, must posit itself as the subject of all law, consequently as a juristic person." This process of positing itself was apparently so simple and plausible to Bernatzik that he mentioned a deviating opinion as representing "only a curiosity." Nevertheless, he did not ask himself why there is a greater logical necessity for the source of legal competence, namely, the legal order, that is, the state's legal order, to posit itself as a product than there is for Stahl's dictum that only a person can be the basis for another person.

Kelsen has the merit of having stressed since 1920 the methodical relationship of theology and jurisprudence. In his last work on the sociological and the juristic concepts of the state[7] he introduced many analogies. Although diffuse, these analogies make it possible for those with a deeper understanding of the history of ideas to discern the inner heterogeneity between his neo-Kantian epistemological point of departure and his ideological and democratic results. At the foundation of his identification of state and legal order rests a metaphysics that identifies the lawfulness of nature and normative lawfulness. This pattern of thinking is characteristic of the natural sciences. It is based on the rejection of all "arbitrariness," and attempts to banish from the realm of the human mind every exception. In the history of the parallel of theology and jurisprudence, such a conviction finds its place most appropriately probably in J. S. Mill. In the interest of objectivity and because of his fear of arbitrariness, he too emphasized the validity without exception of every kind of law. But he probably did not assume, as did Kelsen, that the free deed of legal perception could shape just any mass of positive laws into the cosmos of its system, because this would nullify the objectivity already achieved. For a metaphysics that suddenly falls into the pathos of objectivity, it should make no difference whether an unconditional positivism directly adheres to the law that presents itself, or whether it bothers to first establish a system.

---

7. [Tr.] *Der Soziologische und der juristische Staatsbegriff* (Tübingen, 1922).

Kelsen, as soon as he goes one step beyond his methodological criticism, operates with a concept of causation that is entirely natural-scientific. This is most clearly demonstrated by his belief that Hume's and Kant's critique of the concept of substance can be transferred to the theory of the state.[8] But he fails thereby to see that the concept of substance in Scholastic thought is entirely different from that in mathematical and natural-scientific thinking. The distinction between the substance and the practice of law, which is of fundamental significance in the history of the concept of sovereignty,[9] cannot be grasped with concepts rooted in the natural sciences and yet is an essential element of legal argumentation. When Kelsen gives the reasons for opting for democracy, he openly reveals the mathematical and natural-scientific character of his thinking:[10] Democracy is the expression of a political relativism and a scientific orientation that are liberated from miracles and dogmas and based on human understanding and critical doubt.

For the sociology of the concept of sovereignty it is altogether vital to be clear about the sociology of legal concepts as such. The aforementioned systematic analogy between theological and juristic concepts is stressed here precisely because a sociology of legal concepts presupposes a consistent and radical ideology.[11] Yet it would be erroneous to believe that therein resides a spiritualist philosophy of history as opposed to a materialist one.

The political theology of the Restoration offers an exemplary illustration of the sentence Max Weber articulated in his critique of Rudolf Stammler's philosophy of right, namely, that it is possible to confront irrefutably a radical materialist philosophy of history with a similarly radical spiritualist philosophy of history. The authors of the counterrevolution explained political change as a result of change in outlook and traced the French Revolution to the philosophy of the Enlightenment. It was nothing more than a clear antithesis when radical revolutionaries conversely attributed a change in thought to a change in the political and social conditions. That religious, philosophical, artistic, and literary changes are closely linked with political and social conditions was already a widespread dogma in western Europe, especially in France, in the 1820s.

In the Marxist philosophy of history this interdependence is radicalized to an economic dependence; it is given a systematic basis by seeking a point of

8. *Der Soziologische und der juristische Staatsbegriff*, p. 208.

9. *Die Diktatur*, pp. 44, 105, 194.

10. "Vom Wesen and Wert der Demokratie," *Archiv für Sozialwissenschaft und Sozialpolitik* 47 (1920-21): 84.

11. [Tr.] Schmitt uses the word *radical* here in the sense of "thought out to the end."

ascription also for political and social changes and by finding it in the economic sphere. This materialist explanation makes a separate consideration of ideology impossible, because everywhere it sees only "reflexes," "reflections," and "disguises" of economic relations. Consequently, it looks with suspicion at psychological explanations and interpretations, at least in their vulgar form. Precisely because of its massive rationalism, this philosophy can easily turn into an irrationalist conception of history, since it conceives all thought as being a function and an emanation of vital processes. The anarchic-syndicalist socialism of Georges Sorel thus linked in this fashion Henri Bergson's philosophy of life with Marx's economic conception of history.

Both the spiritualist explanation of material processes and the materialist explanation of spiritual phenomena seek causal relations. At first they construct a contrast between two spheres, and then they dissolve this contrast into nothing by reducing one to the other. This method must necessarily culminate in a caricature. Just as Engels saw the Calvinist dogma of predestination as a reflection of capitalist competition in terms of its senselessness and incalculability, it would be just as easy to reduce the modern theory of relativity and its success to currency relations in today's world market, and thus to find the economic basis of that theory. Some would call such a procedure the sociology of a concept or a theory. This, however, is of no concern to us.

It is otherwise with the sociological method, which, with a view to certain ideas and intellectual constructions, seeks the typical group of persons who arrive at certain ideological results from the peculiarity of their sociological situations. In this sense one can speak of a sociology of juristic concepts, in the case of Max Weber, who traced the differentiation of the various legal fields to the development of trained jurists, civil servants who administer justice, or legal dignitaries.[12] The sociological "peculiarity of the group of persons who professionally concern themselves with forming law" necessitates definite methods and views of juristic thinking. But this is still not a sociology of a legal concept.

To trace a conceptual result back to a sociological carrier is psychology; it involves the determination of a certain kind of motivation of human action. This is a sociological problem, but not a problem of the sociology of a concept. If this method is applied to intellectual accomplishments, it leads to explanations in terms of the milieu, or even to the ingenious "psychology" that is known as the sociology of specific types, that is, of the bureaucrat, the attorney, or the professor who is employed by the state. The Hegelian system,

---

12. *Rechtssoziologie*, II, 1.

for example, if investigated by applying this method, would have to be characterized as the philosophy of the professional lecturer, who by his economic and social situation is enabled to become, with contemplative superiority, aware of absolute consciousness, which means to practice his profession as a lecturer of philosophy; or it would be possible to view Kelsen's jurisprudence as the ideology of the lawyer-bureaucrat practicing in changing political circumstances, who, under the most diverse forms of authority and with a relativistic superiority over the momentary political authority, seeks to order systematically the positive decrees and regulations that are handed down to him. In its consequent manner this type of sociology is best assigned to belles-lettres; it provides a socio-psychological "portrait" produced by a method that cannot be distinguished from the brilliant literary criticism of a Sainte-Beuve, for example.

Altogether different is the sociology of concepts, which is advanced here and alone has the possibility of achieving a scientific result for a concept such as sovereignty. This sociology of concepts transcends juridical conceptualization oriented to immediate practical interest. It aims to discover the basic, radically systematic structure and to compare this conceptual structure with the conceptually represented social structure of a certain epoch. There is no question here of whether the idealities produced by radical conceptualization are a reflex of sociological reality, or whether social reality is conceived of as the result of a particular kind of thinking and therefore also of acting. Rather this sociology of concepts is concerned with establishing proof of two spiritual but at the same time substantial identities. It is thus not a sociology of the concept of sovereignty when, for example, the monarchy of the seventeenth century is characterized as the real that is "mirrored" in the Cartesian concept of God. But it is a sociology of the concept of sovereignty when the historical-political status of the monarchy of that epoch is shown to correspond to the general state of consciousness that was characteristic of western Europeans at that time, and when the juristic construction of the historical-political reality can find a concept whose structure is in accord with the structure of metaphysical concepts. Monarchy thus becomes as self-evident in the consciousness of that period as democracy does in a later epoch.

The presupposition of this kind of sociology of juristic concepts is thus a radical conceptualization, a consistent thinking that is pushed into metaphysics and theology. The metaphysical image that a definite epoch forges of the world has the same structure as what the world immediately understands to be appropriate as a form of its political organization. The determination of such an identity is the sociology of the concept of sovereignty. It proves that in fact, as Edward Caird said in his book on Auguste Comte, metaphysics is the most intensive and the clearest expression of an epoch.

"Imitate the immutable decrees of the divinity." This was the ideal of the legal life of the state that was immediately evident to the rationalism of the eighteenth century. This utterance is found in Rousseau's essay *Political Economy*. The politicization of theological concepts, especially with respect to the concept of sovereignty, is so striking that it has not escaped any true expert on his writings. Said Emile Boutmy, "Rousseau applies to the sovereign the idea that the philosophes hold of God: He may do anything that he wills but he may not will evil."[13] In the theory of the state of the seventeenth century, the monarch is identified with God and has in the state a position exactly analogous to that attributed to God in the Cartesian system of the world. According to Atger, "The prince develops all the inherent characteristics of the state by a sort of continual creation. The prince is the Cartesian god transposed to the political world."[14]

There is psychologically (and, from the point of view of a phenomenologist, phenomenologically as well) a complete identity. A continuous thread runs through the metaphysical, political, and sociological conceptions that postulate the sovereign as a personal unit and primeval creator. The fine tale of the *Discours de la méthode* provides an extraordinarily instructive example. It is a document of the new rationalist spirit. In the depth of doubt, it finds consolation by using reason unswervingly: "*J'étais assuré d'user en tout de ma raison.*" But what is it that becomes clear in the first place to the mind suddenly forced to reason? That the works created by several masters are not as perfect as those created by one. "One sole architect" must construct a house and a town; the best constitutions are those that are the work of a sole wise legislator, they are "devised by only one"; and finally, a sole God governs the world. As Descartes once wrote to Mersenne, "It is God who established these laws in nature just as a king establishes laws in his kingdom."

The seventeenth and eighteenth centuries were dominated by this idea of the sole sovereign, which is one of the reasons why, in addition to the decisionist cast of his thinking, Hobbes remained personalistic and postulated an ultimate concrete deciding instance, and why he also heightened his

13. "La declaration des droits de l'homme et du citoyen et M. Jellinek," *Annales des sciences politiques* 4 (1902): 418.

14. *Essai sur l'histoire des doctrines du contrat social* (1906), p. 136.

state, the Leviathan, into an immense person and thus point-blank straight into mythology. This he did despite his nominalism and natural-scientific approach and his reduction of the individual to the atom. For him this was no anthropomorphism — from which he was truly free — but a methodical and systematic postulate of his juristic thinking. But the image of the architect and master builder of the world reflects a confusion that is characteristic of the concept of causality. The world architect is simultaneously the creator and the legislator, which means the legitimizing authority. Throughout the Enlightenment period until the French Revolution, such an architect of world and state was called the legislator.

Since then the consistency of exclusively scientific thinking has also permeated political ideas, repressing the essentially juristic-ethical thinking that had predominated in the age of the Enlightenment. The general validity of a legal prescription has become identified with the lawfulness of nature, which applies without exception. The sovereign, who in the deistic view of the world, even if conceived as residing outside the world, had remained the engineer of the great machine, has been radically pushed aside. The machine now runs by itself. The metaphysical proposition that God enunciates only general and not particular declarations of will governed the metaphysics of Leibniz and Nicolas Malebranche. The general will of Rousseau became identical with the will of the sovereign; but simultaneously the concept of the general also contained a quantitative determination with regard to its subject, which means that the people became the sovereign. The decisionistic and personalistic element in the concept of sovereignty was thus lost. The will of the people is always good: "The people are always virtuous." Said Emmanuel Sieyes, "In whatever manner a nation expresses its wishes, it is enough that it wishes; all forms are good but its will is always the supreme law."

But the necessity by which the people always will what is right is not identical with the rightness that emanated from the commands of the personal sovereign. In the struggle of opposing interests and coalitions, absolute monarchy made the decision and thereby created the unity of the state. The unity that a people represents does not possess this decisionist character; it is an organic unity, and with national consciousness the ideas of the state originated as an organic whole. The theistic as well as the deistic concepts of God become thus unintelligible for political metaphysics.

It is true, nevertheless, that for some time the aftereffects of the idea of God remained recognizable. In America this manifested itself in the reasonable and pragmatic belief that the voice of the people is the voice of God — a belief that is at the foundation of Jefferson's victory of 1801. Tocqueville in his account of American democracy observed that in democratic thought the people hover above the entire political life of the state, just as God does above the world, as the cause and the end of all things, as the point from which everything emanates and to which everything returns. Today, on the contrary, such a well-known legal and political philosopher of the state as Kelsen can conceive of democracy as the expression of a relativistic and impersonal scientism. This notion is in accord with the development of political theology and metaphysics in the nineteenth century.

To the conception of God in the seventeenth and eighteenth centuries belongs the idea of his transcendence vis-à-vis the world, just as to that period's philosophy of state belongs the notion of the transcendence of the sovereign vis-à-vis the state. Everything in the nineteenth century was increasingly governed by conceptions of immanence. All the identities that recur in the political ideas and in the state doctrines of the nineteenth century rest on such conceptions of immanence: the democratic thesis of the identity of the ruler and the ruled, the organic theory of the state with the identity of the state and sovereignty, the constitutional theory of Krabbe with the identity of sovereignty and the legal order, and finally Kelsen's theory of the identity of the state and the legal order.

After the writers of the Restoration developed a political theology, the radicals who opposed all existing order directed, with heightened awareness, their ideological efforts against the belief in God altogether, fighting that belief as if it were the most fundamental expression of the belief in any authority and unity. The battle against God was taken up by Proudhon under the clear influence of Auguste Comte. Bakunin continued it with Scythian fury. The battle against traditional religiosity can be traced naturally to many different political and sociological motives: the conservative posture of ecclesiastical Christianity, the alliance of throne and altar, the number of prominent authors who were "déclassé," the appearance of an art and literature in the nineteenth century whose genial representatives, at least in the decisive periods of their lives, had been spat out by the bourgeois order — all this is still largely unrecognized and unappreciated in its sociological detail.

The main line of development will undoubtedly unfold as follows: Conceptions of transcendence will no longer be credible to most educated people, who will settle for either a more or less clear immanence-pantheism or a positivist indifference toward any metaphysics. Insofar as it retains the concept of God, the immanence philosophy, which found its greatest systematic architect in Hegel, draws God into the world and permits law and the state to emanate from the immanence of the objective. But among the most extreme radicals, a consequent atheism began to prevail. The German left-Hegelians were most conscious of this tendency. They were no less vehement than Proudhon in proclaiming that mankind had to be substituted for God. Marx and Engels never failed to recognize that this ideal of an unfolding self-conscious mankind must end in anarchic freedom. Precisely because of his youthful intuition, the utterance of the young Engels in the years 1842-1844 is of the greatest significance: "The essence of the state, as that of religion, is mankind's fear of itself."[15]

If viewed from this perspective of the history of ideas, the development of the nineteenth-century theory of the state displays two characteristic moments: the elimination of all theistic and transcendental conceptions and the formation of a new concept of legitimacy. The traditional principle of legitimacy obviously lost all validity. Neither the version of the Restoration based on private law and patrimony nor the one founded on a sentimental and reverent attachment was able to resist this development. Since 1848 the theory of public law has become "positive," and behind this word is usually hidden its dilemma; or the theory has propounded in different paraphrases the idea that all power resides in the *pouvoir constituant* of the people, which means that the democratic notion of legitimacy has replaced the monarchical. It was therefore an occurrence of utmost significance that Donoso Cortes, one of the foremost representatives of decisionist thinking and a Catholic philosopher of the state, one who was intensely conscious of the metaphysical kernel of all politics, concluded in reference to the revolution of 1848, that the epoch of royalism was at an end. Royalism is no longer because there are no kings. Therefore legitimacy no longer exists in the traditional sense. For him there was thus only one solution: dictatorship. It is the solution that Hobbes also reached by the same kind of decisionist thinking, though mixed with mathematical relativism. *Autoritas, non veritas facit legem.*

A detailed presentation of this kind of decisionism and a thorough appreciation of Donoso Cortes are not yet available. Here it can only be pointed out that the theological mode of thought of the Spaniard was in complete accord with the thought of the Middle Ages, whose construction was juristic. All his perceptions, all his arguments, down to the last atom, were juristic; his lack of understanding of the mathematical natural-scientific thinking of the nineteenth century mirrored the outlook of natural-scientific thinking toward decisionism and the specific logic of the juristic thinking that culminates in a personal decision.

15. Friedrich Engels, *Schriften aus der Frühzeit,* ed. G. Mayer (Berlin, 1920), p. 281.

20 State and Church

Dietrich Bonhoeffer

1. The Concepts Involved

The concept of the state is foreign to the New Testament. It has its origin in pagan antiquity. Its place is taken in the New Testament by the concept of government ("power"). The term "state" means an ordered community; government is the power which creates and maintains order. The term "state" embraces both the rulers and the ruled; the term "government" refers only to the rulers. The concept of the *polis,* which is a constituent of the concept of the state, is not necessarily connected with the concept of *exousia.* For the New Testament the *polis* is an eschatological concept; it is the future city of God, the new Jerusalem, the heavenly society under the rule of God. The term "government" does not essentially refer to the earthly *polis;* it may go beyond it; it is, for example, applicable even in the smallest form of community, in the relation of father and child or of master and servant. The term "government" does not, therefore, imply any particular form of society or any particular form of state. Government is divinely ordained authority to exercise worldly dominion by divine right. Government is deputyship for God on earth. It can be understood only from above. (Government does not proceed from society, but it orders society from above.) If it is exegetically correct to regard it as an angelic power, this would still serve only to define its position between God and the world. Only the concept of government, and not the concept of the state, can have a theological application. Nevertheless, in a concrete study the concept of state naturally cannot be avoided.

In using the term "church," and especially in clarifying its relation to the terms "government" and "state," we have to distinguish between the spiritual office or ministry and the congregation or the Christians. The spiritual office is the divinely ordained authority to exercise spiritual dominion by divine right. It does not proceed from the congregation, but from God. A clear distinction must be drawn between the secular and the spiritual authority, but the Christians are, nevertheless, at the same time citizens, and the citizens, whether they be believers or not, are at the same time subject to the claim of Jesus Christ. Consequently the relationship of the spiritual office to the government differs from that of the Christians. In order to avoid constant misunderstandings this difference should be kept clearly in view.

2. The Basis of Government

A. In the Nature of Man

The ancients, especially Aristotle, base the state on the character of man. The state is the supreme consummation of the rational character of men, and to serve it is the supreme purpose of human life. All ethics is political ethics. Virtues are political virtues. This theory of the state was taken over in principle by Catholic theology. The state is a product of human nature. Man's ability to live in society derives from the Creation, as does also the relation of rulers and ruled. The state fulfills the assigned purpose of the human character within the sphere of the natural and creaturely. The state is the "highest development of the natural society" (Schilling, *Moraltheologie*, II, p. 609). This Aristotelian and Thomist doctrine is found in a somewhat modified form in Anglican theology. And indeed it has also penetrated into modern Lutheranism. With the Anglicans the connection between natural theology and incarnational theology opens up the possibility of a peculiar natural-cum-Christian theory of the state. (Incidentally, the questionableness of this combination of natural and incarnational theology is now clearly perceived by the young Anglo-Catholics, who provide the corrective of a *theologia crucis*.) Modern Lutheranism acquired the notion of the natural state through Hegel and romanticism. In this case the state is the fulfillment not of the universally human and rational character of man, but of the creative will of God in the people. The state is essentially a nation-state. The people fulfill its divinely willed destiny in such a state. The detailed contents are of no significance here. The Ancient Greek concept of the state persists in the forms of the rational state, the nation-state, the culture-state, the social state, and finally, as the decisive factor, the Christian state. The state is the executor of certain given contents, and indeed, when this theory is carried to its ultimate conclusion, the state becomes the actual subject or originator of these contents, i.e., of the people, the culture, the economy or the religion. It is "the real god" (Hegel). All these theories alike regard the state as a community, so that it is only with difficulty and by indirect means that they admit of the idea of government. Fundamentally it is necessary in these cases to derive government, too, from the natural character of man. It consequently becomes difficult to understand it at the same time as the coercive power which directs itself against man, for it is precisely this coercive power which essentially distinguishes the government of the state from that voluntary priority and subordination which is to be found in every community. Whenever the basis of the state is sought in the created nature of man, the concept of government is broken up and is then reconstructed from below, even when this is not at all intended. Whenever the state becomes the executor of all the vital and cultural activities of man, it forfeits its own proper dignity, its specific authority as government.

B. In Sin

The Reformation, by taking up ideas of St. Augustine, broke away from the ancient Greek concept of the state. The Reformation does not represent the state as a community arising from the created nature of man, although traces of this idea, too, can be found in the writings of some of the Reformers; it places the origin of the state, as government, in the Fall. It was sin that made necessary the divine institution of government. The sword which God has given to government is to be used by it in order to protect men against the chaos which is caused by sin. Government is to punish the criminal and to safeguard life. Thus a reason is provided for the existence of government both as a coercive power and as the protector of an outward justice. The Reformation attached equal importance to both of these aspects, but its thinking subsequently developed along two divergent lines. Some thinkers subordinated the concept of justice to the concept of coercive force, and were thus led on to the concept of the state which is founded on power; others subordinated power to justice, and so attained to the concept of the state which is founded on law and order. The former believed that there was *exousia* only where there was power, the latter only where there was justice. In this way both parties failed to give its full meaning to the Reformation concept of *exousia*. Both parties perceived that the state is not a consummation of creaturely characteristics but an institution of God which is ordained from above. They did not understand the state "from below," on the basis of the people, the culture, etc., but from above, that is to say, in the true sense, as government. In this way the original idea of the Reformation and of the Bible was faithfully followed out. Thus the state is not essentially a culture-state, etc. These are only possible, divinely permitted forms of political society, and there may well be an abundance of other such forms which have hitherto remained unknown to us. Unlike these forms of society, which are merely permitted by God, government is actually established and ordained by God Himself. People, culture, social organization, etc., are of the world. Government is order in the world, an order which bears the authority of God. Government is not itself of the world, but of God. On this basis the notion of the Christian state is also untenable; for the state possesses its character as government independently of the Christian character of the persons who govern. There is government also among the heathen.

C. In Christ

It becomes clear from these last remarks, and indeed from everything that we have said so far on this subject, that the basing of the state on sin or on the nature of man leads to a conception of the state as a self-contained entity, a conception which fails to take account of the relation of the state to Jesus Christ. Whether it be as an institution of creation or as an institution of preservation, the state exists here by itself, more or less independently of the revelation of God in Jesus Christ. This conclusion cannot be avoided even in the case of the second theory, which is in many ways superior to the first. But now the question arises, what basis can there be for a theologically tenable assertion (as distinct from a philosophy, in general Christian terms) with regard to Paradise and the Fall — what basis can there be other than Jesus Christ? It is through Jesus Christ and for Jesus Christ that all things are created (John 1:3; I Cor. 8:6; Heb. 1:2), and in particular "thrones, dominions, principalities and powers" (Col. 1:16). It is only in Jesus Christ that all these things "consist" (Col. 1:17). And it is He who is "the head of the church" (Col. 1:1). A theological proposition with regard to government, with regard, that is to say, to the government which is instituted by God and not to some general philosophical idea of government, is therefore in no circumstances possible, without reference to Jesus Christ, and to Jesus Christ as the head of His Church; no such proposition is possible without reference to the Church of Jesus Christ. The true basis of government is therefore Jesus Christ Himself. The relation of Jesus Christ to government can be expressed under seven headings.

- a. As the Mediator of Creation, "through whom" government, too, is created, Jesus Christ is the sole and necessary medium between government and the Creator. There is no immediate relation between government and God. Christ is its Mediator.
- b. Government, like all created things, "consists only in Jesus Christ"; in other words, it is only in Him that it has its essence and being. If Jesus Christ did not exist there would be no created things; all created things would be annihilated in the wrath of God.
- c. Government, like all created things, is designed and directed "towards Jesus Christ." Its goal is Jesus Christ Himself. Its purpose is to serve Him.
- d. Jesus Christ possesses all power in heaven and on earth (Matt. 28:18), and He is, therefore, also the Lord of government.
- e. Through the atonement on the cross Jesus Christ has restored the relation between government and God (Col. 1:20 — τὰ πάντα).
- f. In addition to these relations to Jesus Christ which government shares with all created things, there is also a special relation in which government stands with respect to Jesus Christ.
    - I. Jesus Christ was crucified with the permission of government.
    - II. By acknowledging and openly declaring the innocence of Jesus (John 18:38; cf. also the part played by Lysias, Felix, Festus and Agrippa in the trial of St. Paul), government gave evidence of its proper character.
    - III. When government did not dare to exercise its governmental power in maintaining its own knowledge and judgment, it abandoned its office under pressure from the people. This does not constitute a condemnation of the office, but only of the faulty discharge of this office.
    - IV. Jesus submitted to government; but He reminded government that its power is not human arbitrary will, but a "gift from above" (John 19:11).
    - V. With this Jesus showed that government can only serve Him, precisely because it is a power which comes down from above, no matter whether it discharges its office well or badly. Both in acquitting Him of guilt and in delivering Him up to be crucified, government was obliged to show that it stands in the service of Je-

sus Christ. Thus it was precisely through the cross that Jesus won back His dominion over government (Col. 2.15), and, at the end of all things, "all dominion and government and power" will be both abolished and preserved through Him.

g. So long as the earth continues, Jesus will always be at the same time Lord of all government and Head of the Church, without government and Church ever becoming one and the same. But at the end there will be a holy city *(polis)* without temples, for God and the Lamb will Themselves be the Temple (Rev. 21), and the citizens of this city will be the faithful of the congregation of Jesus throughout all the world, and dominion in this city will be exercised by God and the Lamb. In the heavenly *polis* state and Church will be one.

Only the derivation of government from Jesus Christ can supersede the derivations in terms of natural law which are the ultimate consequences of the derivations from the nature and the sin of man. The derivation from the nature of man regards the actual conditions of peoples, etc., as providing the basis for the state in terms of natural law. This argument affords a justification for imperialism and for revolution (for both inward and outward revolution). The derivation from sin has to devise natural-law standards in order to restrict the concept of power by means of the concept of justice; these standards will imbue it with a more strongly conservative tendency. But both the concept and the contents of natural law are equivocal (depending on whether this natural law is derived from certain particular data or from certain particular standards); and it therefore fails to provide an adequate basis for the state. Natural law can furnish equally cogent arguments in favor of the state which is founded on force and the state which is founded on justice, for the nation-state and for imperialism, for democracy and for dictatorship. A solid basis is afforded only by the biblical derivation of government from Jesus Christ. Whether and to what extent a new natural law can be established on this foundation is a theological question which still remains open.

3. The Divine Character of Government

A. In Its Being

Government is given to us not as an idea or a task to be fulfilled but as a reality and as something which "is" (αἱ δὲ οὖσαι, Rom. 13:1c). It is in its being that it is a divine office. The persons who exercise government are God's "ministers," servants and representatives (Rom. 13:4). The being of government is independent of the manner of its coming into being. No matter if man's path to governmental office repeatedly passes through guilt, no matter if almost every crown is stained with guilt (cf. Shakespeare's histories), the being of government lies beyond its earthly coming into being; for government is an institution of God, not in its coming into being but in its being. Like all existing things, government, too, stands in a certain sense beyond good and evil; that is to say, it possesses not only an office but also a historical existence. An ethical failure does not *eo ipso* deprive it of its divine dignity. This situation is clearly expressed in the saying "my country, right or wrong." This is that historical relationship of one actual entity to another which is found again in the relationship between father and child, between brother and brother, and between master and servant, and which is immediately obvious in these cases. There can be no ethical isolation of the son from his father, and indeed, on the basis of actual being, there is a necessity of sharing in the assuming and carrying of the guilt of a father or a brother. There is no glory in standing amid the ruins of one's native town in the consciousness that at least one has not oneself incurred any guilt. That is rather the self-glorification of the moral legalist in the face of history. The clearest expression of this dignity of government, one source of which is its historical existence, is its power, the sword which it wields. Even when the government incurs guilt and is open to ethical attack, its power is from God. It has its existence solely in Jesus Christ, and through the cross of Christ it is reconciled with God *(vide supra).*

B. In Its Task

The being of government is linked with a divine commission. Its being is fulfilled only in the fulfillment of the commission. A total apostasy from its commission would jeopardize its being. But by God's providence this total apostasy is possible only as an eschatological event, and as such it leads amidst grievous torments to a total separation of the congregation from the government as the embodiment of Antichrist. The mission of government consists in serving the dominion of Christ on earth by the exercise of the worldly power of the sword and of justice. Government serves Christ by establishing and maintaining an outward justice by means of the sword which is given to it, and to it alone, in deputyship for God. And it has not only the negative task of punishing the wicked, but also the positive task of praising the good or "them that do well" (I Pet. 2:14). It is therefore endowed, on the one hand, with a judicial authority, and on the other hand, with a right to educate for goodness, i.e., for outward justice or righteousness. The way in which it exercises this right of education is, of course, a question which can be considered only in the context of the relation of government to the other divine mandates. The much-discussed question of what constitutes this goodness or outward justice which government is charged with promoting is easily resolved if one keeps in view the derivation of government from Jesus Christ. This good cannot in any case be in conflict with Jesus Christ. Good consists in allowance being made in every action of government for the ultimate purpose, namely, the service of Jesus Christ. What is intended here is not a Christian action, but an action which does not exclude Christ. Government achieves such an action if it takes the contents of the second table as its criterion in its various particular historical situations and decisions. But whence does government derive its knowledge of these contents? Primarily from the preaching of the Church. But for pagan government the answer is that there is a providential congruity between the contents of the second table and the inherent law of historical life itself. Failure to observe the second table destroys the very life which government is charged with preserving. Thus, if it is properly understood, the task of protecting life will itself lead to observance of the second table. Does this mean that the state is after all based on natural law? No; for in fact it is a matter here only of the government which does not understand itself but which now is, nevertheless, providentially enabled to acquire the same knowledge, of crucial significance for its task, as is disclosed to the government which does understand itself in the true sense in Jesus Christ. One might, therefore, say that in this case natural law has its foundation in Jesus Christ.

Consequently, whether or not government is aware of its own true basis, its task consists in maintaining by the power of the sword an outward justice in which life is preserved and is thus held open for Christ.

Does the task of government also include observance of the first table, that is to say, the decision for the God and Father of Jesus Christ? We intend to consider this question in the section on government and Church, and at this point we will say only that the knowledge of Jesus Christ is part of the assignment of all men, including, therefore, those persons who exercise government. But the praise and the protection of the righteous (I Pet. 2:14) is an integral part of the mission of government, independently of the decision of faith of the persons who exercise government. Indeed it is only in protecting the righteous that government fulfills its true mission of serving Christ.

The mission of government to serve Christ is at the same time its inescapable destiny. Government serves Christ no matter whether it is conscious or unconscious of this mission or even whether it is true or untrue to it. If it is unwilling to fulfill this mission, then, through the suffering of the congregation, it renders service to the witness of the name of Christ. Such is the close and indissoluble relation of government to Christ. It cannot in either case evade its task of serving Christ. It serves Him by its very existence.

C. In Its Claim

The claim of government, which is based on its power and its mission, is the claim of God and is binding upon conscience. Government demands obedience "for conscience' sake" (Rom. 13:5), which may also be interpreted as "for the Lord's sake" (I Pet. 2:13). This obedience is combined with deference (Rom. 13:7; I Pet. 2:17). In the exercise of the mission of government the demand for obedience is unconditional and qualitatively total; it extends both to conscience and to bodily life. Belief, conscience and bodily life are subject to an obligation of obedience with respect to the divine commission of government. A doubt can arise only when the contents and the extent of the commission of government become questionable. The Christian is neither obliged nor able to examine the rightfulness of the demand of government in each particular case. His duty of obedience is binding on him until government directly compels him to offend against the divine commandment, that is to say, until government openly denies its divine commission and thereby forfeits its claim. In cases of doubt obedience is required; for the Christian does not bear the responsibility of government. But if government violates or exceeds its commission at any point, for example by making itself master over the belief of the congregation, then at this point, indeed, obedience is to be refused, for conscience' sake, for the Lord's sake. It is not, however, permissible to generalize from this offence and to conclude that this government now possesses no claim to obedience in some of its other demands, or even in all its demands. Disobedience can never be anything but a concrete decision in a single particular case. Generalizations lead to an apocalyptic diabolization of government. Even an anti-Christian government is still in a certain sense government. It would, therefore, not be permissible to refuse to pay taxes to a government which persecuted the Church. Conversely, the fact of obedience to government in its political functions, payment of taxes, acceptance of loyalty oaths and military service, is always a proof that this government is not yet understood in the sense of the apocalypse. An apocalyptic view of a particular concrete government would necessarily have total disobedience as its consequence; for in that case every single act of obedience obviously involves a denial of Christ (Rom. 13:7). In all political decisions the historical entanglement in the guilt of the past is too great to be assessed, and it is therefore generally impossible to pass judgment on the justice of a single particular decision. It is here that the venture of responsibility must be undertaken, but the responsibility for such a venture on the part of the government can be borne *in concreto* (i.e., apart from the general share in responsibility for political action which is borne by individuals) only by the government. Even in cases where the guilt of the government is extremely obvious, due consideration must still be given to the guilt which has given rise to this guilt. The refusal of obedience in the case of a particular historical and political decision of government must therefore, like this decision itself, be a venture undertaken on one's own responsibility. A historical decision cannot be entirely resolved into ethical terms; there remains a residuum, the venture of action. That is true both of the government and of its subjects.

4. Government and the Divine Institutions in the World

Government has the divine task of preserving the world, with its institutions which are given by God, for the purpose of Christ. For this purpose government alone bears the sword. Everyone is subject to an obligation of obedience towards government. But, both with its task and with its claim, government always presupposes the created world. Government maintains created things in their proper order, but it cannot itself engender life; it is not creative. However, it finds already in the world which it governs two institutions through which God the Creator exercises His creative power, and upon which it must therefore, in the nature of things, rely; these are marriage and labor. The Bible discloses both of these to us already in Paradise, and thereby shows that they are part of God's creation, which is through and for Jesus Christ. Even after the Fall, i.e., in the only form in which we know them, both are still divine institutions of discipline and grace, because God desires to show Himself even to the fallen world as the Creator, and because He causes the world to consist in Christ and makes it Christ's own. Marriage and labor are from the beginning subject to a definite divine mandate which must be executed in faith and obedience towards God. Marriage and labor, therefore, possess their own origin in God, an origin which is not established by government, but which requires to be acknowledged by government. Through marriage bodily life is propagated and men are brought into being for the glorification and service of Jesus Christ. But this implies also that marriage is there not only for begetting children but also for educating them in obedience to Jesus Christ. The parents are for the child the deputies of God, both as its begetters and as its educators. Through labor a world of values is created for the glorification and service of Jesus Christ. Here, too, as in the case of marriage, there is not a divine creation out of nothing, but on the basis of the first creation there is a creation of new things, in marriage of new life and in labor of new values: Labor embraces here the whole range of work which extends from agriculture by way of industry and commerce to science and art (cf. Gen. 4.17ff.). Thus, for the sake of Jesus Christ, a right of their own is conferred both upon marriage, together with the family, and upon labor, together with economic life, culture, science and art. This means that for these fields the significance of government is regulative and not constitutive. Marriage is performed not by government but in the presence of government. Industry and commerce, science and art, are not cultivated by government itself, but they are subject to its supervision, and within certain limits (which cannot be discussed in detail here) to its direction. But government never becomes the subject or originator of these fields of labor. If it asserts its authority beyond the limits of its assigned task it will in the long run forfeit its genuine authority over these fields.

Distinct from the order or institution of marriage and that of labor is the order or institution of the people. According to Scripture, its origin lies neither in Paradise nor in an explicit divine mandate. The people is, on the one hand (according to Gen. 10), a natural consequence of the spreading of the succeeding generations; on the other hand (Gen. 11), it is a divine institution which causes mankind to live in dissension and mutual incomprehension, and which thereby reminds men that their unity does not lie in their own achievements of complete power but solely in God, the Creator and Redeemer. Yet in Scripture there is no special commission of God for the people. Marriage and labor are divine offices, but the people is a historical reality, which in a special sense has reference to the divine reality of the one people of God, the Church. Scripture offers no indication with regard to the relation between people and government; it does not demand the nation-state; it recognizes the possibility that several peoples may be united under one government. It knows that the people grows from below, but that government is instituted from above.

5. Government and Church

Government is instituted for the sake of Christ; it serves Christ, and consequently it also serves the Church. Yet the dominion of Christ over all government does not by any means imply the dominion of the Church over government. But the same Lord, whom government serves, is the Head of the congregation, the Lord of the Church. The service of government to Christ consists in the exercise of its commission to secure an outward justice by the power of the sword. This service is thus an indirect service to the congregation, which only by this is enabled to "lead a quiet and peaceable life" (I Tim. 2:2). Through its service towards Christ, government is ultimately linked with the Church. If it fulfills its mission as it should, the congregation can live in peace, for government and congregation serve the same Master.

A. Government's Claim on the Church

The claim of government to obedience and deference extends also to the Church. With respect to the spiritual office, government can indeed only demand that this office shall not interfere in the secular office, but that it shall fulfill its own mission, which does, in fact, include the admonition to obey government. Government possesses no authority over this mission itself, as it is exercised in the pastoral office and in the office of Church management. So far as the spiritual office is an office which is exercised publicly, government has a claim to supervise it, to see that everything is done in an orderly manner, that is to say, in accordance with outward justice. It is only in this connection that it has a claim to intervene in the question of appointments and organization within the office. The spiritual office itself is not subject to government. Yet government possesses a full claim to obedience with regard to the Christian members of the congregation. In this it does not appear as a second authority side by side with the authority of Christ, but its own authority is only a form of the authority of Christ. In his obedience to government the Christian is obedient to Christ. As a citizen the Christian does not cease to be a Christian, but he serves Christ in a different way. This in itself also provides an adequate definition of the contents of the authentic claim of government. It can never lead the Christian against Christ; on the contrary, it helps him to serve Christ in the world. The person who exercises government thus becomes for the Christian a servant of God.

B. The Church's Claim on Government

The Church has the task of summoning the whole world to submit to the dominion of Jesus Christ. She testifies before government to their common Master. She calls upon the persons who exercise government to believe in Christ for the sake of their own salvation. She knows that it is in obedience to Jesus Christ that the commission of government is properly executed. Her aim is not that government should pursue a Christian policy, enact Christian laws, etc., but that it should be true government in accordance with its own special task. Only the Church brings government to an understanding of itself. For the sake of their common Master, the Church claims to be listened to by government; she claims protection for the public Christian proclamation against violence and blasphemy; she claims protection for the institution of the Church against arbitrary interference, and she claims protection for Christian life in obedience to Jesus Christ. The Church can never abandon these claims; and she must make them heard publicly so long as government itself maintains its claim to acknowledge the Church. Of course, if government opposes the Church, explicitly or in fact, there may come a time when the Church no longer wastes her words, even though she still does not give up her claim; for the Church knows that, whether government performs its mission well or badly, it must always serve only its Master, and therefore also the Church. The government which denies protection to the Church thereby places the Church all the more patently under the protection of her Master. The government which blasphemes its Master testifies thereby all the more evidently to the power of this Master who is praised and glorified in the torments and martyrdoms of the congregation.

C. The Ecclesiastical Responsibility of Government

To the claim of the Church there corresponds the responsibility of government. Here it becomes necessary to answer the question of the attitude of government to the first commandment. Must government make a religious decision, or does its task lie in religious neutrality? Is government responsible for maintaining the true Christian service of God, and has it the right to prohibit other kinds of divine service? Certainly the persons who exercise government ought also to accept belief in Jesus Christ, but the office of government remains independent of the religious decision. Yet it pertains to the responsibility of the office of government that it should protect the righteous, and indeed praise them, in other words that it should support the practice of religion: A government which fails to recognize this undermines the root of the true obedience and, therefore, also its own authority (e.g., France in 1905). At the same time the office of government as such remains religiously neutral and attends only to its own task. And it can, therefore, never become the originator in the foundation of a new religion; for if it does so it disrupts itself. It affords protection to every form of service of God which does not undermine the office of government. It takes care that the differences between the various forms of service of God do not give rise to a conflict which endangers the order of the country. But it achieves this purpose not by suppressing one form of service of God, but by a clear adherence to its own governmental commission. It will thereby become evident that the true Christian service of God does not endanger this commission, but, on the contrary, continually establishes it anew. If the persons who exercise government are Christian they must know that the Christian proclamation is delivered not by means of the sword but by means of the word. The idea of *cuius regio eius religio* was possible only in certain quite definite political circumstances; namely, the agreement of the princes to admit each other's exiles; as a general principle it is incompatible with the office of government. In the case of some special situation of ecclesiastical emergency it would be the responsibility of the Christians who exercise government to make their power available, if the Church requests it, in order to remove the source of the disorder. This does not mean, however, that in such circumstances government as such would take over the functions of ecclesiastical control. It is here exclusively a matter of restoring the rightful order within which the spiritual office can be rightfully discharged and both government and Church can perform their own several tasks. Government will fulfill its obligation under the first commandment by being government in the rightful manner and by discharging its governmental responsibility also with respect to the Church. But it does not possess the office of confessing and preaching faith in Jesus Christ.

D. The Political Responsibility of the Church

If political responsibility is understood exclusively in the sense of governmental responsibility, then it is clearly only upon government that this responsibility devolves. But if the term is taken to refer quite generally to life in the *polis,* then there are a number of senses in which it is necessary to speak of political responsibility of the Church in answer to the claim of government upon the Church. Here again we distinguish between the responsibility of the spiritual office and the responsibility of the Christians. It is part of the Church's office of guardianship that she shall call sin by its name and that she shall warn men against sin; for "righteousness exalteth a nation," both in time and in eternity, "but sin is perdition for the people," both temporal and eternal perdition (Prov. 14:34). If the Church did not do this, she would be incurring part of the guilt for the blood of the wicked (Ezek. 3:17ff.). This warning against sin is delivered to the congregation openly and publicly, and whoever will not hear it passes judgment upon himself. The intention of the preacher here is not to improve the world, but to summon it to belief in Jesus Christ and to bear witness to the reconciliation which has been accomplished through Him and to His dominion. The theme of the proclamation is not the wickedness of the world but the grace of Jesus Christ. It is part of the responsibility of the spiritual office that it shall devote earnest attention to the proclamation of the reign of Christ as King, and that it shall with all due deference address government directly in order to draw its attention to shortcomings and errors which must otherwise imperil its governmental office. If the word of the Church is, on principle, not received, then the only political responsibility which remains to her is in establishing and maintaining, at least among her own members, the order of outward justice which is no longer to be found in the *polis,* for by so doing she serves government in her own way.

Is there a political responsibility on the part of individual Christians? Certainly the individual Christian cannot be made responsible for the action of government, and he must not make himself responsible for it; but because of his faith and his charity he is responsible for his own calling and for the sphere of his own personal life, however large or however small it may be. If this responsibility is fulfilled in faith, it is effectual for the whole of the *polis.* According to Holy Scripture, there is no right to revolution; but there is a responsibility of every individual for preserving the purity of his office and mission in the *polis.* In this way, in the true sense, every individual serves government with his responsibility. No one, not even government itself, can deprive him of this responsibility or forbid him to discharge it, for it is an integral part of his life in sanctification, and it arises from obedience to the Lord of both Church and government.

E. Conclusions

Government and Church are connected in such various ways that their relationship cannot be regulated in accordance with any single general principle. Neither the separation of state and Church, nor the form of the state church can in itself constitute a solution of the problem. Nothing is more dangerous than to draw theoretical conclusions by generalizing from single particular experiences. The recommendation for a withdrawal of the Church from the world and from the relations which she still maintains with the state under the impact of an apocalyptic age is, in this general aspect, nothing but a somewhat melancholy interpretation of the times in terms of the philosophy of history. If it were really acted upon in earnest, it would necessarily lead to the most drastic consequences, which are described in Rev. 13. But, conversely, a philosophy of history may equally easily be the source for a scheme for a state church or a national church. No constitutional form can as such exactly represent the actual relative closeness and remoteness of government and Church. Government and Church are bound by the same Lord and are bound together. In their task government and Church are separate, but government and Church have the same field of action, man. No single one of these relationships must be isolated so as to provide the basis for a particular constitutional form (for example in the sequence state church, free church, national church); the true aim is to provide room within every given form for the relationship which is, in fact, instituted by God and to entrust the further development to the Lord of both government and Church.

6. The Church and the Form of the State

In both Protestant and Catholic political theory the question of the form of the state is always treated as a secondary problem. Certainly, so long as government fulfills its assigned mission, the form in which it does so is of no great importance for the Church. Still, there is justification for asking which form of the state offers the best guarantee for the fulfillment of the mission of government and should, therefore, be promoted by the Church. No form of the state is in itself an absolute guarantee for the proper discharge of the office of government. Only concrete obedience to the divine commission justifies a form of the state. It is, nevertheless, possible to formulate a few general propositions in order to discern those forms of the state which provide a relatively favorable basis for rightful governmental action and, therefore, also for a rightful relationship between church and state; precisely these relative differences may be of great practical consequence.

a. That form of the state will be relatively the best in which it becomes most evident that government is from above, from God, and in which the divine origin of government is most clearly apparent. A properly understood divine right of government, in its splendor and in its responsibility, is an essential constituent of the relatively best form of the state. (Unlike other western royalty, the kings of the Belgians called themselves kings "by the grace of the people.")

b. That form of the state will be relatively the best which sees that its power is not endangered but is sustained and secured
   I. by the strict maintenance of an outward justice,
   II. by the right of the family and of labor, a right which has its foundation in God, and
   III. by the proclamation of the gospel of Jesus Christ.

c. That form of state will be relatively the best which does not express its attachment to its subjects by restricting the divine authority which has been conferred upon it, but which attaches itself to its subjects in mutual confidence by just action and truthful speech. It will be found here that what is best for government is also best for the relationship between government and church.

21 Church and State

Karl Barth

Humility is the disposition of the creature that says Yes to the fact that its existence is spoiled by its guilt and lives by the divine patience, that confesses the mercy of God which meets it in its lostness, that understands and wants fellowship with God as a fellowship which is mediated by the divine incarnation. This creature is sinful man to whom God has been gracious in Christ. In being what he is called to be in the new covenant between God and man, in believing therefore, man obeys the commandment of humility. He obeys in mediated fellowship with God. He obeys the incarnate God. He obeys the order set up by the incarnate God. We have understood this obedience as sacrifice, as the vicarious achievement, corresponding to our guiltiness before God, of a life that signifies and represents our forfeiture to God as our Judge. We have tried to understand the two fundamental determinations of this life: toward God, repentance, and toward men, service. If our reconciliation is to be understood as reconciliation by the God-man, our life in reconciliation, insofar as it is obedience and therefore humility and therefore sacrifice, is obviously to be understood as repentance and service. This is what God wants of us in Christ. The concrete and visible divine order in which man is obedi-

---

This section of §13 is not found in the 1929 text. Except in subsection III it follows the new version prepared for the repetition of the lectures in 1930/31. Up to the end of II, then, it is all Text B and the additions denoted by [ ] do not here (as elsewhere) indicate materials found in B as against A but marginal insertions by Barth with hints perhaps of the 1933 revision. The 1928/29 original is preserved in a copy by an unknown hand and is reproduced in the Appendix [of the *Ethics*].

ent in this new covenant, and thus brings sacrifice and repents and serves, is, however, the double order of church and state. That Christian service is linked here to this concrete and visible order rests on the fact that the fellowship with God is a mediated fellowship, mediated through the incarnation of God. The concrete and visible orders as such are a sign of Christ's humanity, and in their claim for acknowledgment and acceptance they are a sign of his deity. They are thus to be recognized in faith and affirmed in obedience. That Christian obedience is referred to those two orders of church and state rests again on the fact that it is obedience to the God-man Christ, first to the fact that the obedience of faith calls man on the one side to repentance before God and on the other to service to the neighbor, and second to the fact that it is one thing to be obedient as a sinner to the *grace of God* and another to be obedient to the grace of God as a *sinner.* As repentance before God includes service to the neighbor, but as the acknowledgment of the grace of God is also more than this, there is as a comprehensive outer circle the order of the church and obedience as action within it. As service to the neighbor is included in repentance before God and acknowledgment of the grace of God, but as the acknowledgment of human sin is less than this, there is as a narrower inner circle the order of the state and Christian obedience as action within it. The relation of the one divine order of life in the kingdom of grace is as follows: The church always has the state in it but it is not the state. Alongside the state, which it has in it, it is in a distinctive way *only* the church. The state is wholly church, too, but it is so in *its own* way and it is not the whole church. The relative dualism of the two orders expresses the provisional character of the kingdom of grace as the kingdom of faith and antithesis, of decision and hope in relation to the kingdom of God in which the relative distinction of the functions of church and state is removed.

I. The Church

1. The church is the sign, set up by God's revelation, of the concrete and visible order of life by and in which people are summoned to repentance before God on the basis of accomplished reconciliation. This calling takes place, the order of the church is effective, and the sign comes into force "where and when it pleases God" (CA V),[1] i.e., in the promised free act of grace in which

---

1. [CA denotes Confession of Augsburg (1530), T. G. Tappert, *The Book of Concord* (Philadelphia, 1959), pp. 23ff.]

God makes his revelation and saving action present. On the presupposition of this divine action, the church is both the divine institution and establishment of a constantly new affirmation of the reconciliation that God has accomplished in Christ, and at the same time human fellowship in this constantly affirmed reconciliation. In accordance with the character of the church as a divine institution those united in it achieve repentance before God by the proclamation and hearing of the Word of God in preaching and sacrament. In accordance with its character as a gathering of sinners saved by grace, it achieves repentance by common worship. As those who are called by this institution and in this fellowship to render service to the neighbor along with repentance before God, its members finally give the witness of free acts of love in the church. In relation to the decisive presupposition they know that this can be done in a right and holy way only by faith and therefore only to the honor of God who has accomplished reconciliation, who has willed this sign, and who has promised its fulfillment, i.e., the confirmation of accomplished reconciliation.

2. The church is not the kingdom of God. This means (a) that the church is not an order of creation. According to Luther a "most bare and pure and simple" nonchurchly religion accords with creaturely life in obedience (EA 1, 133).[2] (b) The church, however, is also not an order of eternal life. In the heavenly Jerusalem there will be no more temple according to Revelation 21:22. The contrast between promise and fulfillment, as between proclamation and worship or repentance and service, but also the "where and when it pleases God" as these are essential characteristics of the church, presuppose the antithesis between sin and grace which is not yet present in creation and will no longer be so in the redemption. At the beginning and the end there is no church. As a sign of the mediated fellowship between God and man the church belongs to the middle, to the time between the times, to history.

3. As an order of reconciliation the church, affirmed and willed in faith and to the honor of God, is one, legitimate, free from error, and binding on everyone. The norm by which it is measured and must direct itself is [the promise that is given to it, i.e.,] the prophetic-apostolic witness to the completed atonement whose recipient and bearer it will be continually. The confessions of the church document its earlier recognition of the necessity and nature of this continuity. But for all its concern to be right and holy in obe-

2. [EA denotes M. Luther, *Werke* (Erlangen Edition), 1826ff., rev. E. L. Enders, 1862ff., (opera) exegetica Latina.] WA [M. Luther, *Werke. Kritische Gesamtausgabe* (Weimar Edition), 1883ff.] 42, 80, 41-81, 1 (LW, 1, 106).

dience to scripture and respect for its own confessions, the church can understand the divine verdict, in virtue of which it really is this, only as grace, and therefore it can count upon the validity of this verdict only in faith, i.e., only in the fulfillment of repentance.

4. The humility of the sinner saved by grace, which is required of the individual, implies concretely, therefore, that his acts be done in this order of reconciliation and be a confirmation of this order. Reconciliation rests upon the enacted incarnation of God. Participation in it is conditioned by its promised constant confirmation, i.e., by faith in this promise, and therefore by the divine institution and human fellowship in which this faith is exercised. Here in the elements of proclamation, worship, and loving action the sign is set up which humility can never in any circumstances ignore. To take human reality seriously as a state of sin *and* grace is to accept and want the church; [fundamental] denial of the church, on the other hand, presupposes a Romantic or sectarian view of humanity which no longer corresponds to the reality, or does not yet do so. The possibility of a practical break with the existing concrete form of the church, as at the Reformation, is a special case for which those who venture it must not only claim but also prove an insight resting on extraordinary divine authority and commission.

5. As a human work, the church's activity shares in the folly and wickedness of those whose sin is forgiven, yet has not for this reason ceased to be sin, but rather demonstrated itself therein. The church will not let itself be diverted from its promise or its task [by its loneliness and impotence,] by the indifference and opposition that is shown it by the rest of the world. All this will constantly remind it of its own worldliness, but also of its call to continual return to its starting point in the free grace of God. The same humility in which it constitutes itself will prevent it both from flight into inwardness or invisibility, i.e., from abandoning itself as a concrete and visible order, and equally from claiming or seeking any abstract fullness of the truth and power of the community or its offices, i.e., from abandoning its foundation in the free divine act of grace. As the bride of Christ it is also his handmaiden, and therefore it must do its work aright, yet it must do it within its limits as service, not with any confusion or presumption. As the earthly body of its heavenly Lord, it will take its *earthly* existence quite seriously, fully affirming, willing, and practicing it as such.

6. The human work of the church is divine service as the setting up of the sign of proclamation, worship, and acts of love. Generally understood, it is fundamentally the work of the whole life of all its members done with regard to all human reality. To this extent, repentance before God embraces

service to the neighbor and the church embraces the state. But as, in fact, not all the life of those gathered in the church is identical with the doing of this work, so our fellowship with God does not coincide in fact with our fellowship with our neighbor, the sinfulness of both being manifested in this. [Similarly the church is not visible as Christ's church in the state, but concealed,] and the church needs a special and distinctive function, a specific existence as the church, in distinction from that of the state. In this distinctive existence, it is uniquely [visible as] a sign of God's free grace that establishes fellowship between God and man, forgiving all sin and covering it. This distinctive function and existence consists of divine service in the narrower and proper sense of the term, i.e., of worship.

7. The decisive elements in the divine service of the church in the narrower sense are (a) preaching as the personal [repetition and] transmission of the biblical testimony to Christ, and the administration of the sacraments as a necessary confirmation of the existence of this testimony prior to all human speech; (b) congregational prayer and praise as the church's attestation of its responsibility to this testimony; and (c) the voluntary work of aid to all kinds of threatened and disadvantaged people as a witness to the unity of repentance and service and also to the hope of the kingdom of God by which the church lives.

8. A series of subsidiary tasks flows from this task of divine service: (a) the Christian education of young people as a mediation of the [intelligible re]cognition of the elements in the divine service of the church in the narrower and broader sense; (b) individual pastoral care, both physical and spiritual, understood as concrete personal proclamation supplementing public proclamation, as a demonstration of the directness of the divine address which proclamation must serve; (c) evangelization and overseas mission as a necessary expression of the life of the church and its responsible communication to the rest of the world for which Christ also died and which, even though it may seem strange to it at first, it must humbly reckon to be God's; and (d) theology, i.e., the never- and nowhere-superfluous reflection of the church on its divine origin, on the consolations and warnings of its human history, and on its task, which is the same in every age but which must be taken up afresh in every age.

9. The promise and task of divine service in the narrower sense is given fundamentally to the church as such, i.e., to all its members. The special offices of pastor, deacon, superintendent, and theological teacher are [certainly gifts of the Holy Spirit but also] commissions of the community in its discharge of the office of Christ entrusted to it, although the office of a bishop

construed as a pastor set over other officers in the church, when seen in the light of Christ's position as alone the chief shepherd, is not a possibility in the church but mistakenly copies the monarchical form of state government. In the community of Christ all can serve only the sovereign Lord and therefore each must render equal service to the other.

II. The State

1. The state, too, is an "external means of grace" (Calvin, *Inst.* IV).[3] It is the sign, set up by God's revelation, of the concrete and visible order of life by which and in which, on the basis of accomplished reconciliation, we are summoned to serve our neighbor. This order, too, is effective in the free act of God's grace and, under the presupposition of this act, but *only* under it, is both a divine institution and a divinely willed human society. The state fulfills its aim and purpose by making all responsible for each and each for all through the establishment and maintaining of public law and the control and support of public education. Because truly mutual service in this sphere is conditioned by the existence of repentance before God, the true and ultimate aim and goal of the order of the state has to coincide with that of the church; people should be not only with others but for them in the state, too, on the basis of mutual forgiveness. Each specific state has to ask therefore, whether, in order to be a real state, it not only has law and culture but is also a Christian state in the church's sense.

2. The state, then, is not the city of the devil deriving from the fall of the wicked angels, resting on human self-love, and standing over against the church as Cain stood over against Abel (Augustine, *De civitate Dei* XI, 34; XIV, 28; XV, 1.17; XXI, 1). Yet it is no more identical than the church is with the incarnation (Hegel)[4] or the kingdom of God (Rothe).[5] It is not an order

---

3. [*Inst.* denotes J. Calvin, *Christianae Religionis Institutio* 1559.] Book IV, in which the discussion of the state forms chap. 20, bears the general heading "The External Means or Aims by Which God Invites Us into the Society of Christ and Holds Us Therein," or, in brief, "Means of Grace."

4. G. W. F. Hegel, *Sämtliche Werke*, Jubilee ed., in 20 vols., ed. H. Glockner, vol. 11 (Stuttgart, 1949), pp. 85f. Hegel refers here to the principles of the state as determinations of the divine nature.

5. Cf. R. Rothe, *Theologische Ethik*, 3 vols. (Wittenberg, 1845-1848); 5 vols. (Wittenberg, 1867-1871²), vol. 2, §§449-458. Rothe refers here to the general organism of the state as essentially the absolutely completed kingdom of God, absolute theocracy (quoting J. G. Fichte, *Politische Fragmente* (*Werke* VIII), p. 613.

of creation, for it did not exist before the fall and is a necessary remedy against corrupt nature (Luther, EA 1, 130).[6] Nor is it an order of eternal life. It is an order of the sustaining patience of God which is necessary and good because even those who have been blessed in Christ are wholly and utterly sinners. It, too, presupposes that repentance before God and service to the neighbor are in an antithesis that has not yet been overcome. It, too, rests on the "where and when it pleases God." It, too, is a sign of the mediated fellowship between God and man. It, too, once was not and one day will not be, so that it belongs with the church to the time between the times, to the kingdom of grace.

3. As an order of reconciliation the state in all possible forms can serve in God's stead (Rom. 13; the authorities, according to Calvin, are God's "vicars" [Op. 20, 320][7] or "lieutenants" [Op. 49, 637f.]).[8] To the extent that it is the free act of divine grace which alone can make, but can really make, Nero's Rome or Calvin's Geneva into what the state ought to be as an order of reconciliation, its divine dignity and its character as a divine institution and a divinely willed human society are, as in the case of the church, a subject of revelation and faith, so that in the historical situation of the Reformation period the recognition rather than the contesting of temporal authority is rightly made a subject of the church's confession.[9] This means that God acknowledges the requirement of obedience to specific forms of state although he is not bound to any one in particular and may at any time call any of them in question, either in part or as a whole.

4. Concretely, then, the humility demanded of the sinner saved by grace consists in detail of action within this order and of a confirmation of it. Here again we must think indeed of the incarnation of God, in which we have a share only within the divine institution and divinely willed human society, in which faith in the promise is confirmed. The state is an institution and society of this kind, and a given state can be so. True humility, truly taking seriously the reality of the human condition as one of both grace and sin, can-

6. Cf. WA 42, 79, 7ff.

7. This reference is wrong, but cf. *Inst.* IV, 20, 4, 6: "acting as his viceregents"; "if they remember that they are vicars of God."

8. Cf. CR [Corpus Reformatorum] LXXVII, 637f. "God ordains that there should be justice and those who are elected and authorized to govern are like his lieutenants."

9. Cf. CA XVI, 1 (Apol. XVI, 53); XXVIII, 18; Small Catechism; Large Catechism; Geneva Catechism, 1542, 194f.: Ecclesiastical Discipline, 1559, 39; Confession, 1560, chap. 24; Belgic Confession, 1561, art. XXXVI; Heidelberg Catechism, 1563; Second Helvetic Confession, 1566, art. XXX (cf. P. Schaff, *Creeds of Christendom, Evangelical Creeds*).

not ignore this sign, in contrast to all romanticism and sectarianism. It is Christian obedience, then, to give the state what belongs to it [cf. Mark 12:17 par.], i.e., to affirm and desire it as a sign of obligatory service to the neighbor and to be a sincere and consistent citizen of it. Concrete affirmation of the state in a specific form is limited, of course, by God's freedom over against any form. We must obey man, i.e., the existing form, for God's sake. But we must obey God rather than man [cf. Acts 5:29]. We can obey man only in obedience to God. We cannot obey man in disobedience to God. It may be, then, that in obedience to God we cannot obey. Concrete affirmation of the state must sometimes take the form, then, of working with a party which seeks to improve or alter the form of the state. A revolutionary alteration of the form of the state, because of the use of force that seems to be unavoidable in such a case, and especially because of the temporary overthrow of the state in general which it undoubtedly entails, because of the danger of its total jeopardizing, is a last resort to which (as to the reformation of the church) one may have recourse only in extreme and very rare circumstances. As Christian obedience, the desire for this or that form of the state is not inviolable, but in contrast to anarchy, which forgets the reality of man, the desire for the state may be described as such. This desire for the state in general is the decisive and by no means time-bound content of the Reformation confession of the state.

5. As a human work, the state shares in the corruption with which man, far from forgiving sin, pursues his own ends with cunning and force in the struggle for existence, something which is no different or better because it is here done collectively. The existence of a specific state is questionable at every point as service to the neighbor. For (a) each state [even a liberal one,] will finally be self-willing and self-seeking in its sponsoring of education and culture, not teaching each to serve the other but all to serve itself. (b) Each state [even the conservative one] will order the common life on the untenable presuppositions that the right of the individual to order his own life, apart from the state's own claim upon him, is an ultimately inviolable good which must be protected by every available means, and conversely that each must be brought to account for his own offenses. (c) The final weapon whereby each state defends itself against its members is the coercion with which it dares to forestall God's own claim to men. (d) Each state is simply one among many others over against which it relies upon the usurped right of force, and appeals to it, to maintain its own existence. [(e) Almost every state is a nation-state, i.e., the state of a particular people that rules in it but is confronted by national minorities whose nationhood is more or less suppressed in this

state.] Thus each state contradicts its very nature as an order of service to the neighbor. This participation of the individual state in sin can sometimes mean that as it is before God it will not be tolerated but rejected, that it will thus have to be altered or renewed by its members, although we have to realize that even a new and better form will in its own way still participate in sin. Yet the participation of an individual state in sin can also take place under the divine patience and forgiveness as a necessary fulfillment of the divine will of the Creator, although we have to realize that it is not thereby justified. Hence the dignity of any given state can be regarded only as inauthentic, and the respect that must be shown it only as provisional. The individual state can be willed and affirmed as service to the neighbor only in repentance before God, i.e., under the proviso of God's grace and in faith that God will make good what we cannot help but do badly.

6. The human work of the state is generally understood as the building up of society among men by establishing the sign of [commonly discovered and accepted] right or law, [protected if necessary by force,] and [commonly sought] education. This is fundamentally the work of the total life of all its members and it relates fundamentally to this total reality of human life. It thus embraces the work of the church as well, inasmuch as this, too, is service to the neighbor. The distinctive function of the state in comparison with that of the church may be seen first in the concrete state, which is primarily oriented to sin and not to grace, and which on the one side, as a nation-state, desires and seeks to build up society only within geographical and ethnographical boundaries, and on the other side, as a mere state of law and culture, does not press on to the perfecting of human society by mutual forgiveness, needing in both areas to be supplemented by the church, which is different from it.

7. The decisive elements in the upbuilding of society by the nation-state with its law and culture are (a) the constitution, i.e., the basic regulation of the relation among the legislative, executive, and judicial powers which needs, if not the express will and cooperation of the citizens, at least (even in the case of the dictatorship of a minority or majority) their freely given confidence; (b) legislation, i.e., the regulation of common life for the ends of state, the best possible safeguarding of its unity, law, and freedom;[10] (c) proper government, i.e., concern for the full, equal, and appropriate execution of the exist-

---

10. Cf. the beginning of the last strophe of A. H. Hoffman von Fallersleben's (1798-1874) "Song of Germany" (1841), the later national anthem: "Unity and law and freedom, for the German fatherland . . ."

ing laws; (d) the administration of justice to give definitive and independent rulings (independent even of the 'current' government) in cases of dispute.

8. [Concrete] tasks of the legislative and executive branches of a nation-state, with its law and culture, include at all events (a) the [making possible] supervision, consolidation, and protection of national labor; (b) the counteracting of the temporary or permanent favoring of individual groups of citizens which might arise through faults in economic organizations when this is left in private hands; this might take the form of the partial or total taking over the economy by the state itself; (c) the [external] protection both of the social structures of marriage, family, and people, which rest on the order of creation, and of the formation of freer societies of particular interests or concerns insofar as these new groups can be understood as an affirmation of the state, i.e., of the common social structure which is superior to all of them; (d) the [external] protection of the existence of free scientific research and the supervision and appropriate organization of education and culture for its members; (e) the external protection of the free activity of the church as the specific society in which there is recollection of the ultimate and sustaining purpose of the state outside its own sphere.

9. The task and promise of the work of the state derive from God. It is correct, then, that the validity and goodness of this work depend on God's grace. But because its task and promise are from God, it demands fundamentally, if in different ways, the will and deed of all. Not just the male sex, or one of the constituent peoples, or a single family or group of families to the exclusion of all others, is called by God's grace to do the work of the state. [In this sense all the power of the state comes from the people.] To lead the work one individual may be called in a smaller or larger circle, who in virtue of the confidence reposed in him does in fact more or less lead the many. The question of leadership is thus one of an event which is the mutual venture of the leader and the led. [The leader may also be a usurper with a great power of suggestion, and confidence in his leadership may be a matter of hypnosis.] A specific decision about the sacred place from which the leadership comes cannot precede this venture. [Before, as, and after it is ventured it stands under the question whether it is to be regarded as obedience to God or service to the neighbor.]

III. Church and State

1. As Boniface VIII rightly presupposed (Bull *Unam Sanctam*, 1302), church and state, expressing one and the same temporally, though not eternally,

valid divine order, are two swords of the one power of Jesus Christ.[11] The dualism of the orders is conditioned and demanded by the dualism of man as the saved sinner who is reconciled to God. Christian humility will acknowledge equally the *relativity* of their distinctness and the *necessity* of their relative distinctness. It can thus accept neither an absolutizing (metaphysical separation of religious and secular spheres) nor a one-sided eliminating (caesaropapism or theocracy) of this distinctness.

2. Between church and state there is no equality, but superiority in the church's favor. The temporal authority must be subject to the spiritual, as Boniface says.[12] The temple comes before the home (Luther, EA 1, 130).[13] State and church coinhere. Yet the church is not first in the state but the state in the church, just as repentance before God establishes but does not presuppose service to the neighbor, and conversely service to the neighbor presupposes but does not establish repentance before God. The Christian is always a member of the church first, and only then, and as such, a citizen.

3. The church, if its responsible representatives are not to cease to be humble, can assert its basic superiority over the state only to God's glory as Lord of both church and state and not to its own glory, and only with its given weapons of proclamation of the Word and repentance, and not, like Boniface, with the direct or indirect uniting of both swords in its hand, with the exercise of a quasi-temporal authority in competition with that of the state.[14]

4. Insofar as the church acts as such, it will renounce not only any appeal to the individual instinct of self-preservation or any assertion of the distinction between good and evil, not only the use of external compulsion within and force without, but fundamentally, too, the establishment and enforcement of any fixed law [corresponding to the laws of the state]. Canon and dogma are not legal but spiritual norms and may be used only as such. Church law in the strict sense can only be the church-recognized law of the state itself existing in the church. The formation of a special church law, as an unavoidable change into another genus, can be regarded only as an inci-

---

11. Nov. 18, 1302. The bull argues that the two swords produced at the last supper are both in the hands of the disciples and represent the spiritual and temporal powers, both in the hands of the church, the former to be used by it, the latter for it, and the former superior to the latter; Denz. [H. Denzinger, *Enchiridion Symbolorum*, 30th ed. (Freiburg, 1955)] no. 468, 469.

12. See above, n. 11.

13. WA 42, 79, 7 (LW, 1, 104).

14. See above, n. 11.

dental and doubly inauthentic function of the church. It comes under the rule: The less, the better.

5. The church will in practice be subject to the state, the guardian of law, as one society among others. Things being as they are, it will have to accept the concrete national individuality of the state and its own necessary national separation and distinction from other parts of the church.[15] The freedom and superiority which it reserves for itself precisely in this way are not linked to the measure of independence of its leadership and organization in relation to those of the state, nor to the presence of a visible international unity of the church, but to the measure of confidence with which it maintains itself as a fellowship of proclamation of the Word and repentance over against the justified and unjustified claims of the state, with a much larger task which is in fact a uniform one and therefore international. A state church which knows and is loyal to its own cause, and to the unity of this cause, is to be preferred to even the most vital of free churches as a symbol of the final unity of church and state.

6. The church recognizes and helps the state inasmuch as service to the neighbor, which is the purpose of the state, is necessarily included in its own message of reconciliation and is thus its own concern. It will take up a reserved attitude toward the state to the extent that this diverges from its purpose, being unable as the church to accept co-responsibility in this regard. Finally, with its own given weapons, it will move on to protest against the state if the latter's actions mean a denial of its purpose, if it is no longer manifest and credible as the order of God. In one way or the other, it will positively confess the purpose of the state and the individual state with it.

7. The state, if its responsible representatives do not cease to be humble, can assert its practical superiority over the church only to the glory of God as Lord of both church and state and not to its own glory — and only in its own field as the guardian of law, not as the preacher of a world-view that fits in with the state's own *raison d'être*, nor with the desire to set up a special civil Christianity. It gives freedom to the church to set up its own worship, dogma, [and constitution,] and to promote its own preaching and theology.

8. The state for its part cannot in principle be tied to a specific form of the church. It recognizes and supports the church insofar as its own purpose is grounded and included in that of the church. To that extent it is neither

---

15. An allusion to the lively debate in Germany after 1918 as to whether state boundaries should also be church boundaries; cf. O. Dibelius, *Das Jahrhundert der Kirche* (Berlin, 1926, 1927²), pp. 98f.

nonreligious nor non-confessional. But it is supra-confessional to the extent that it is tolerant in face of the confessional division of the church, i.e., to the extent that within the limits of the law it fundamentally assures all church fellowships of the same freedom.

9. Yet in practice, without intolerance to other churches, and as an expression of the distinctness with which it is aware of its own purpose, it can claim that one form of the church is in a particular way the form of the church and treat it as such, just as the church does not shrink from recognizing the concrete nation-state. A qualified recognition and support of the church as a symbol of the unity of church and state is, even from the state's own standpoint, more appropriate than the system of a real [organizational] separation of church and state.

22 Theology in the New Paradigm: Political Theology

Johann Baptist Metz

1. Paradigm Change in Theology?

1. Let me (incautiously) assume for the moment that there is something like "progress" in theology. How can this progress be assessed? Perhaps on the basis of paradigm change, in analogy to Kuhn's suggestion? I would hesitate here, and should like to put a number of questions, without aiming at completeness, and without claiming any competence in scientific theory.

What Kuhn understands by progress derives explicitly from an etiological evolution logic,[1] and is therefore also formulated in neo-Darwinian terms.[2] But is the *logos* of Christian theology, with its underlying apocalyptic-eschatological structure, not molded by a different logic of time, history and development (if indeed we can speak of development here at all)?[3] At all events, for the *logos* of this theology, "tradition" and "remembrance," for example, cannot simply be replaced by "historical reconstruction" on an evolutionistic basis. It is not evident how the evolutionary model could permit a normative use of history, let alone a "canonical" one.[4]

---

1. In which — to take up a saying of the "Darwinian" Nietzsche — evolution aims at nothing except — evolution.

2. Cf. Thomas S. Kuhn, *The Structure of Scientific Revolutions* (Chicago & London, 1962), ch. 13. But see also Toulmin's criticism of Lakatos (Popper) taken up by Lamb in his paper in *Paradigm Change in Theology*, ed. Hans Küng and David Tracy, trans. Margaret Kohl (New York: Crossroad, 1989). Here the question about time and history could be reconsidered.

3. On the question about the relation between history and evolution, cf. J. B. Metz, *Faith in History and Society*, trans. D. Smith (London & New York, 1980), ch. 10.

4. Cf. here Metz, *Faith in History and Society*, chs. 11 & 12.

Is there such a thing as a "pure" history of theology at all, analogous to the "pure" history of science and to Kuhn's hermetic scientific community — a history of theology separate from church history, for example, or from political history? Is a new paradigm ever produced internally by theology at all? Is there any such thing as a theological paradigm change independent of reformative processes in the context of the church? Is the history of theological thought not always shaped by the social history of religion and the church?

Who is the conscious subject of theology? What is the place where theology is done? Is this as unequivocally clear for theology as it is when we apply the paradigm theory to scientific history? Does not a change in the subjects of theology and the places where theology is practiced perhaps actually belong to the specific theological paradigm change?[5] Finally, are there not always several competing paradigms in theology — constitutionally, and not merely temporarily?[6]

2. I shall therefore use "paradigm" and "paradigm change" in theology in a rather broad sense.[7] As *criteria* for a "new paradigm in theology" I should like tentatively to propose the following:

(a) the awareness of crisis and the capacity for dealing with it;
(b) the capacity for reduction.

I mean this in two ways: first, as a non-regressive reduction of over-complexity and wordiness — language-run-riot (in which the crises of theology are pushed below the surface and covered up);[8] and second, as the non-trivial reduction of doctrine to life, of doxography to biography, because the *logos* of theology always aims at a form of knowledge that is *a form of living*.[9] For the idea of God to which Christian theology is bound is in it-

5. Cf. J. B. Metz, *A New Paradigm of Doing Theology?* (Lima, 1983). Cf. also *Concilium* (May, 1978): *Doing Theology in New Places*.

6. In the light of its content (cf. n. 9) and in the light of its subjects and the places where it is pursued (the theology of the religious orders, university theology, basis theology, and so on).

7. Modifications can also be found in contributions by Küng, Tracy, and Lamb to *Paradigm Change in Theology* (cf. n. 2).

8. "Reduction" as the criterion of a theological paradigm change must not be confused semantically with the same term as it is employed in system theory.

9. Cf. here my attempt to interpret Karl Rahner's theology as a kind of new paradigm: "Karl Rahner — ein theologisches Leben," in J. B. Metz, *Unterbrechungen* (Gütersloh, 1981). I should also like in this connection to point to a paradigm discussion in modern Protestant theology which has meanwhile become a classic: the correspondence between Karl Barth

self a practical idea. It continually cuts across the concerns of people who try "merely to think" it. The histories of new beginnings, conversion, resistance, and suffering belong to the very definition of this idea of God. The pure concept "God" is the contraction, the shorthand, so to speak, of histories, in response to which theology must repeatedly decode its terms.[10]

I should like therefore to name the crises which provide the impulse for a paradigm change in theology (section 2); and shall then try to show why, and in what sense, the "new" theology which is able to absorb these crises productively and tries to achieve the reductions I have described, is a political theology, or has a political dimension (section 3).

2. The Crises

Let me mention three crises which have sparked off new ways of doing theology.[11] They are incidentally so constituted that their productive theological absorption is necessarily ecumenical in its very approach, not merely in its result.

1. *Theology in the face of the modern era:* that is, theology after the end of the religious and metaphysical views of the worldviews which still provided the context for Reformation theology.

---

and Adolf von Harnack, which was published sixty years ago. Barth stresses over against Harnack the apocalyptically tense crisis structure of faith, and the proclamation character of theology:

10. In this approach the difference between *logos* and myth, history and histories remains *within* theology.

11. On the following signs of crisis or of the End-time cf. among others J. Habermas, *Legitimation Crisis,* trans. T. McCarthy (London, 1976); R. Spaemann, "Die christliche Religion und das Ende des modernen Bewusstseins," *Communio* 8 (1979): 251-70; J. B. Metz, *The Emergent Church,* trans. P. Mann (New York & London, 1981); L. Gilkey, "The New Watershed in Theology," *Soundings* (1981): 118-31; also Gilkey's paper in *Paradigm Change in Theology* (cf. n. 2).

2. *Theology in the face of Auschwitz:* that is, theology after the end of idealism, or all systems of meaning without conscious subjects.
3. *Theology in the face of a socially divided and culturally polycentric worldwide church:* that is, theology at the end of its cultural monocentricism. In my view this "end" shelters within itself promising signs of a change.

3. The Political Dimension of Theology in the New Paradigm

The "new" theology which perceives these crises as fundamental crises of theology and which tries to overcome them in productive reduction is a "political" theology.

1. Theology After the End of the Religious and Metaphysical Views of the World

The theological discernment and absorption of this end — that is, the productive grappling with the processes of the Enlightenment — bring to the fore the political dimension of theology under two aspects. Both these aspects have given rise to misunderstanding and semantic confusion in the past, and still do so today. This is because, on the one hand, people have tried to fit this political theology into the already existing divisions of theological labor. This has led to a misreading of its character as *fundamental theology* (see section (a) below). On the other hand, another misunderstanding was due to the fact that, after the Enlightenment, this political theology was identified with the legitimizing political theology of the pre-Enlightenment era. Its *critical* character was therefore overlooked (see section (b) below).

(a) With regard to the first point: the very project of a fundamental theology after the Enlightenment may be termed political theology. The disintegration of the religious and metaphysical world pictures has put an end to the era of theology's cognitive innocence. Theology must now come to terms with the denials of historical innocence through historicism, and with the denials of its social innocence through ideological criticism in both its bourgeois and its Marxist versions. Theology can no longer push the questions invoked here away from its center into the fringe zones of apologetics. Its very *logos* is affected.

As fundamental theology, it can therefore no longer be content with the usual assignment of historical and social themes in theology to different divisions of labor. As fundamental theology it must be hermeneutics, and its hermeneutics must be political hermeneutics.[12] For it cannot simply leave "history" to a separate historical theology, as if theology had any foundation without history and without a thinking subject.[13] Nor can it view "society" as the exclusive domain of social ethics, or the social teachings of the church,[14] as if theology's search for truth and witness to that truth had any foundation completely removed from social concerns and conflicts. Moreover, since the Enlightenment a fundamental theology can no longer simply assume that the relation between theory and practice is, as far as it is concerned, sufficiently settled by way of the customary division of labor between systematic and practical theology. For to assume this would be to conceal from itself the practical foundation of all theological wisdom and the specific form, or *Gestalt*, its theory takes. Fundamental theology, that is to say, must be practical, political hermeneutics.[15] In my view, a fundamental theology of this kind must ultimately again take up the question about the cognitive subjects of theology, and the places where theology is to be done — a question which was supposed to have been dealt with by way of the division of labor in the church.[16]

(b) Now of course the disintegration of religious and metaphysical world pictures in the Enlightenment must not be interpreted as if the result were an utterly demythologized and secularized world, with a total divorce between religion and politics.[17] Religion was not completely privatized, and

12. Cf. here the project of a practical fundamental theology as practical theology: J. B. Metz, *Faith in History and Society*, chs. 1-4.

13. Cf. here Tracy's paper on hermeneutics in *Paradigm Change in Theology* (cf. n. 2). Recent discussions about the narrative structure of theology also belong here.

14. For criticism of this division of labor see now above all W. Kroh, *Kirche im gesellschaftlichen Widerspruch* (Munich, 1982). Here Kroh carries on the first detailed discussion between the new political theology and the traditions of Catholic social teaching.

15. H. Peukert, *Science, Action, and Fundamental Theology* (ET Cambridge, MA, 1984), has developed this approach and carried it further in discussion with contemporary theories of science and action. Cf. also Lamb's paper and the work of his own he cites there. From the point of view of liberation theology, of particular importance is the epistemological work by C. Boff and F. Castillo, *Theologie aus der Praxis des Volkes* (Munich & Mainz, 1978). Boff includes criticism of J. B. Metz, J. Moltmann, and D. Sölle.

16. Cf. the work cited in n. 5.

17. "The dialectic of Enlightenment" has already taught us how much the notion of the total demythologization or secularization of the world, and the concept of progress molded by this idea, became the real myth of early modern times.

politics was not entirely secularized.[18] Even politically "enlightened" societies have their political religions, with the help of which they seek to legitimize and stabilize themselves. We are familiar with this political religion in the "civil religion" of the United States, for example, as well as in what we in Germany call *bürgerliche Religion*. Although linguistically the two phrases "mean" the same thing (for example, *bürgerliches Recht* = civil law), civil religion and *bürgerliche Religion* can by no means simply be equated, for they derive from very different political cultures.[19] So when in Germany neo-conservatism also recommends the introduction of a "civil religion,"[20] this amounts ultimately to a reproduction of the traditional patterns in which politics is legitimized by religion — in the guise of political theology in its classic form.[21] Of course both political religions, American and German, serve to politicize religion — a politicization which means that religion is assigned a strict social purpose: it is functionalized.

But it is just this politicization of religion which political theology criticizes, and for two reasons. On the one hand, it criticizes it as religion, since political theology contests a religion which acts as legitimation myth and which purchases its discharge from society's criticism of religion through the suspension of its claim to truth. On the other hand, it criticizes the politicization of religion on theological grounds, contesting all theologies which, appealing to their non-political character, become pre-eminently theologies of just this political religion. If we do not want to establish the essence of religion in politics, not even an enlightened politics, we must not suppress theology's political dimension.

Of course this interpretation also provokes questions, and above all this one: if neither civil religion nor its German equivalent is available as the place where, since the Enlightenment, religion and politics can legitimately be reconciled theologically, what then? How then can the universalistic norms of Christianity be brought into harmony with political life at all, since that political life certainly cannot and must not revert to the time be-

18. For important observations here and on the definition of the tasks of a new political theology see F. Fiorenza, "Religion und Politik," in *Christlicher Glaube in moderner Gesellschaft* 27 (Freiburg, 1982).

19. Cf. J. Habermas, "Neokonservative Kulturkritik in den USA and in der Bundes-republik," *Merkur* (November, 1982).

20. Recently, above all, H. Lubbe, following N. Luhmann.

21. Cf. here the critical comments by J. Moltmann, "Das Gespenst einer Zivilreligion," *Evangelische Kommentare* (March, 1983). I should like to associate myself specifically with his criticism.

fore the achievements of the political Enlightenment — the separation of powers, the right to opposition, liberty of opinion, and so forth? Do these universalistic norms make themselves felt when questions about ultimate goals crop up in political life, not merely questions about methods and their application? That is to say, do these norms make their impact when prevailing conditions themselves come under pressure and require legitimation — when a political ethic is required, not merely as an ethic for order but as an ethic for change?[22]

2. Auschwitz — or Theology After the End of Idealism

Here Auschwitz stands for the end of the modern era. In this context we have to notice first of all that the catastrophe of Auschwitz takes on paradigmatic character through its very incomparability. It points theology's historical and political conscience away from the singular "history" to the plural "histories of suffering," which cannot be idealistically explained, but can only be recollected in the context of a practical intent.[23] But which theology does not live from a catastrophic background, either by turning its back on it — that is, idealistically — or by being profoundly chafed and disturbed by it?

There is no meaning which one could salvage by turning one's back on Auschwitz, and no truth which one could thereby defend. Theology therefore has to make an about-turn, a turn which will bring us face-to-face with the suffering and the victims. And this theology is political theology. Its hermeneutics is a political hermeneutics, a hermeneutics in the awareness of danger.[24] It criticizes the high degree of apathy in theological idealism, and its defective sensibility for the interruptive character of historical and political catastrophes.

This political theology after Auschwitz is not a theology in terms of a system. It is theology in terms of human subjects, with a practical foundation. It continually introduces into public awareness "the struggle for recol-

22. See here as long ago as 1969 J. B. Metz in H. Peukert, ed., *Diskussion zur "politischen Theologie"* (Munich & Mainz, 1969). At present this question, for example, is discussed under the heading of "monotheism and politics."

23. Cf. J. B. Metz, *Faith in History and Society*, ch. 9.

24. Important elements for a "hermeneutics in the face of danger" may be found in W. Benjamin's work; cf. O. John's pertinent dissertation, ". . . *und dieser Feind hat zu siegen nicht aufgehört." Die Bedeutung Walter Benjamins für eine Theologie nach Auschwitz* (Münster, 1983).

lection," for the recollecting knowledge which is related to the human subjects concerned. For this theology, the "system" can no longer be the place of theological truth — not, at least, since the catastrophe of Auschwitz, which no one can ignore without cynicism or can allow to evanesce into an "objective" system of meaning.

This theology formulates the question about God in its oldest and most controversial form, as the theodicy question, though not in an existentialistic version but in a political one. It begins with the question about the deliverance of those who have suffered unjustly, the victims of our history and the defeated. It continually brings this question anew into the political awareness as indictment, and expounds the concept of a strict universal solidarity, which also includes the dead, as a practical and political idea, on which the fate of human beings as clear and evident subjects depends.

For without this solidarity the life of human beings as subjects tends more and more towards anthropomorphism. The public invitation to apply for the post as successor to the human being as subject has already gone out. The applicant is to have no recollection of past suffering and is to be tormented by no catastrophes. *Time* magazine has already portrayed the successful candidate on its front cover, as the man of the year for 1983: the robot, an intelligence without memory, without feeling and without morals.[25]

3. Theology at the End of Its Cultural Monocentricism

Is our paradigm discussion not too Eurocentrically aligned from the outset? I must ask this, because it is only in the light of this question that I can discuss the political dimension of the "new" theology adequately. It is a fact that the church no longer merely *has* a third world church but *is* a third world church with, historically, West European origins. What does this fact mean for Catholic theology, for example?

On the one hand it means that the social antagonism in the world is moving to the center of attention in the church and in theology. Conditions which are directly inconsistent with the gospel, such as exploitation and oppression or racism, are becoming challenges to theology. They demand that

---

25. Cf. here — in connection with the work of Metz and Peukert — M. Lamb, *Solidarity with Victims* (New York, 1982).

faith be formulated in categories of resistance and change. Thus theology is impelled to become political by its own *logos*.

On the other hand, in this new situation in which the church finds itself, a process of theological significance is emerging which we should not fail to take into account in our discussion about a paradigm change. The church is on the move from a culturally more or less monocentric European and North American church to one that is world-wide and culturally polycentric. In order at least to indicate the theological import of this transition, I should like[26] hypothetically to divide the history of theology and the church, up to the present day, into three eras: a first relatively brief founding era of Jewish Christianity; a second, very long era, in a more or less homogeneous cultural area — the age of the Gentile Christianity that grew up on hellenistic soil, the West European culture and civilization that was bound up with that and which lasted down to our own day; and a third era, the era of a world-wide cultural polycentricism in the church and theology, which is emerging at the present time. In this era the modern division between the churches, for example, appears mainly as an internal fate affecting European Christendom.[27]

Of course the end of cultural monocentricism does not mean disintegration into an arbitrary or random contextual pluralism. Nor does it mean the enthronement of a new, non-European monocentricism in the church and in theology. The church's original western history, which in concrete terms was always also a history of guilt where non-European cultures were concerned, will remain an immanent part of the cultural polycentricism of church and theology. But what is at stake now is mutual inspiration and mutual productive assimilation. This seems to me to be important for our European outlook on the churches and theology of the third world. For I see a reforming impulse coming upon western Christianity from there and, linked with that, the offer of a "paradigm change" in theology as well. I can

---

26. Following a suggestion of Karl Rahner's about the beginnings of a genuinely worldwide church in Vatican II; cf. his *Theological Investigations,* vol. 20 (London, 1981): "Concern for the Church."

27. Of course, in this hypothesis I have to assume much which I cannot discuss and substantiate here; for example, that there really is such a thing as this cultural polycentricism, and that it has not already been corrupted in germ by the profane Europeanization of the world which we call technology or technological civilization — that is, through the world-wide rule of western rationality, in which far more of the politics, history, and anthropology of Europe is concealed than the technocrats of all political colors would have us believe.

do no more than indicate that here, in the context of the political dimension of theology which I have been asked to talk about.[28]

With us this new beginning is associated rather abstractly with concepts such as basis church, liberation theology, and so forth. But here the gospel is related in a highly direct and immediate way to the specific political conditions in which people live. This "application" generally seems to us too naive, too pre-modern, too simplistic, in view of our own over-complex situation, which has been heightened into extreme abstraction, particularly in the context of all the problems of interpretation in Scripture and tradition which have accumulated in our theology ever since the Enlightenment, and which may be summed up under the catchword of "hermeneutics." But if we examine the matter more closely, it becomes evident that in this "application" we see a new form of theological hermeneutics, which I should like to call a political hermeneutics of danger. The awareness of danger as a basic category of a theological hermeneutics has a sound biblical foundation. The flash of danger lights up the whole biblical landscape; danger, present and impending, runs through all the biblical utterances, especially in the New Testament. As we know, the discipleship narratives in the synoptic Gospels are not simply entertaining stories. They are not really even didactic stories. They are stories told in the face of danger: they are dangerous stories. And we have only to read John (15:18f., for instance) or Paul (for example II Cor. 4:8f.): what do we understand about texts like these and their *logos* if, and as long as, the awareness of danger is systematically screened out in our hermeneutics?

Now, this political hermeneutics of danger is certainly reductive — to some degree oversimplifying — and that in the sense of the reductions I named at the beginning as criteria for a paradigm change: practice returns home to pure theory, logic is joined again by mysticism, resistance and suffering once more find their proper place in the theological definition of grace and Spirit. If then there really is "progress" in theology, and anything like a paradigm change, should we not have to pay particular attention to new impulses like these in the culturally polycentric space for learning offered by the world church and the worldwide Christian faith?[29] Are these

28. More detail may be found in my essay "Aufbruch zur Reformation," *Süddeutsche Zeitung* (April 9-10, 1983). Cf. also Metz, "Toward the Second Reformation," in *The Emergent Church* (cf. n. 11).

29. Of course, this raises the question how Christian universalism can be so understood in the encounter with other religions and cultures that it does not simply, without more ado,

things not always bound up with the reformative situations in which Christianity "returns to its roots"?[30]

"imperialistically" integrate and subordinate them, but discerns them in their authentic message. I have tried to offer a solution in my reflections on the narrative-practical understanding of Christianity (as distinct from a transcendental-idealistic one) in *Faith in History and Society*, ch. 9 (cf. n. 3). It seems to me that this approach also offers an indication of how the deadlocks (formulated by L. Gilkey in his paper in *Paradigm Change in Theology* [cf. n. 2]) of a Christian absolutism in the encounter with other religions and cultures could be solved.

30. Could we not, therefore, after all tentatively include the new paradigm of theology under the heading of "liberation"? If, for the moment, we start from the assumption that the paradigm that has hitherto molded modern theology was "liberty," then the paradigm change in theology would be the change from liberty to liberation. Cf. here my reflections in "Toward the Second Reformation" in *The Emergent Church* (see n. 11), and the references in n. 28. In *The Emergent Church,* in the same chapter, I also discuss the dilemma of Catholic theology in the face of the "liberty" paradigm.

23 Fatherhood, Power, and Barbarism: Feminist Challenges to Authoritarian Religion

Dorothee Sölle

One of the names of God in the Jewish-Christian tradition is Father. What are the practical implications of this symbolic name at the present time? I want to consider, not the history of the origins of the symbol, but the history of its effects; not the question "What was its original intent?" but rather "What happened to it?" And so I come to two theological realities: the Father-God and the culture of obedience. Both expressions cause me major difficulties, which I will formulate in three questions:

1. Has obedience produced and helped to shape a culture or a barbarism?
2. Can the word *father* still stand for God when we have learned to think of God and liberation as inseparable?
3. What elements of the father-symbol are indispensable?

These questions should not be dehistoricized or desubjectivized. I am posing them as a German, as a woman, and as someone who is trying to be a Christian at the end of the twentieth century, and I do not wish to deny my national, my sexual, or my socioeconomic identity. That makes it difficult, because the rules of theological language, while they know how to differentiate between the God of the philosophers and the God of Abraham, Isaac, and Jacob, are still ignorant of the God of Sarah, Rebecca, and Rachel. The fathers in faith are reduplicated in the father in heaven; the mothers of faith are still in the dark: prehistorical, unremembered, forgotten, and suppressed.

I. The Culture of Obedience and Barbarism

My oldest difficulty with a culture of obedience stems from my national identity. The history of my people is colored by a central event in this century that changed its language, ideas, conceptions, and images. Words and concepts have ineluctably acquired a different quality because of that event; they have lost their innocence. Precisely as someone who lives after that event and who deals with language, I cannot and I will not forget. In a particular text — a poem, for example — certain words carry their historical fate with them. Star, smoke, hair all still had in 1942 a different meaning in German from the one they have now, after the greatest crime and misery in the history of my people.

My first question to a "Christian culture of obedience" is whether obedience is not one of those ideas that can no longer remain intact after the Holocaust.[1] It is for historians to decide how much weight is to be given to Christian training in obedience in Germany as a preparation for fascism. For theologians, repeated references to obedience by Adolf Eichmann, whose parents had registered him in the YMCA, or by Rudolf Hess, whose father had marked him for a priest, are enough to rob the concept of its theological innocence. Nor does it help much to seek the most obvious way out by trying to distinguish between "genuine" or "proper" obedience to God and that owed to human beings. Can one ask for an attitude toward God and train people in that attitude while at the same time criticizing the same behavior toward people and institutions?

Must obedience lead to barbarism? This question should not be limited to historical fascism. Obedience today defines itself independently of charismatic leaders in terms of the so-called givens of economics, the consumption of energy and expanding militarism. The technocrats have long since inherited the mantle of the priests. But the structural elements of authoritarian religion remain, even in the new relations of obedience, although these prefer to disguise themselves as merely the "rules of the game," and the relics of religious training prepare increasingly religion-less people for an obedience from which all personal traits and any relationship to trust and self-surrender have vanished. The new, computerized obedience has three structural elements in common with the older religious type:

---

1. On what follows, see also my 1968 critique of the Christian ideology of obedience: D. Sölle, *Beyond Mere Obedience*, trans. L. W. Denef (New York: Pilgrim, 1982).

1. Recognition of a higher power that has our fate in its hands and excludes any self-determination.
2. Submission to the rule of this power, which needs no moral legitimation such as love or justice.
3. A deep pessimism about the human person: she/he is not capable of love or truth, but is a powerless and meaningless being whose obedience feeds on the very denial of her or his own strength.

The cardinal virtue of authoritarian religion is obedience; the cardinal sin is resistance — in contrast to a humanitarian religion, where the corresponding virtue and vice are, respectively, self-realization and misspent life.[2] In terms of social history, this kind of authoritarian religiosity functions to affirm the society and stabilize its dominant tendencies. Within authoritarian religion, emancipatory willingness to change and critical transcendence of what is are rejected, even and especially when they are religiously founded: God's justice and love are less important than God's power. Authoritarian religion reveals an infantile need for consolation that expresses itself aesthetically and in the history of piety as sentimentality; it is matched, however, by a compulsive need for order, fear of confusion and chaos, and a desire for comprehensibility and dominance. It is precisely its rigidity that outlasts the other moments of a dying religion; the authoritarian ties remain as part of the technocratic interpretation of life. The Milgram experiment, in which an overwhelming majority of ordinary people were prepared to torture innocent people with electric shocks at the direction of scientists, fits very well in the context of a culture of obedience. Obedience functions well within fascist or technocratic barbarism.

II. God and Liberation

Erich Fromm distinguished between humanitarian and authoritarian forms of religion. The historical Jesus, early Buddhism, and the mystics in most religions are examples of a nonrepressive religion that does not rest on one-sided, asymmetrical dependence or realize itself by means of internalized compulsion. It is precisely at this point that the sociopsychological questions about the father-symbol begin.

2. Cf. Erich Fromm's fundamental distinction between humanitarian and authoritarian religion in his *Psychoanalysis and Religion* (New Haven, CT: Yale University Press, 1950).

Why do people revere a God whose most important quality is power, whose interest is in subduing, who fears equality, a being who is addressed as Lord, for whom mere power is not enough, so that his theologians have to credit him with omnipotence? The most important question posed by a developing feminist theology to those in authority is directed against phallocratic fantasies, against the adoration of power. Why should we honor and love a being that does not transcend the moral level of a culture currently shaped by men, but instead serves to stabilize it?

To put it in terms of my own theological autobiography: My difficulties with the great and powerful arise out of the experience of Auschwitz. In 1965 I published my first book, *Stellvertretung. Ein Kapitel Theologie nach dem Tode Gottes.*[3] The position I defended there is radically Christocentric, in the tradition of Bonhoeffer. Godself, God as acting and speaking, cannot be experienced. We can relate to the powerless Christ who was independent of authority, who has nothing but his love with which to win and save us. His powerlessness is an inner authority; we are not his because he has begotten, created, or made us, but because his weaponless power is love, which is stronger than death.

My difficulties with the father, begetter, possessor of power, and determiner of history were deepened as I began to understand more clearly what it means to be born a woman — that is, "mutilated" — and to live in a patriarchal society. How could I wish to make power the central category in my life; how could I revere a God who is not more than a man? With male power I associate things like the ability to roar, giving orders, learning to shoot. I do not think that I in particular have been damaged by patriarchal culture more than other women. It has simply become more and more obvious to me that any identification with the aggressor, with the powerful, with the rapist, is the most terrible fate that can overtake any woman.

Nor does the father-symbol have the same fascination for those who can never be fathers. Even power combined with mercy, even the kind father, is not a solution for this problem. A good slaveowner may be loved and honored by his slaves; female piety is frequently a kind of Uncle Tom devotion. But submission to the roles defined as "feminine" and obedience to God, who has supposedly established these rules in our nature, destroy our chance to be full human beings. A father cannot free us from the history of

---

3. English trans.: *Christ the Representative: An Essay in Theology after the Death of God*, trans. David Lewis (Philadelphia: Fortress, 1967).

my people or from the sexism of the ruling culture. Can the father-symbol still represent what we mean by the word *God?*

If we understand that we can only speak symbolically about God, every symbol that sets itself up as absolute must be relativized. God really transcends our talk about God, but only when we no longer lock God up in symbolic prisons. I can admit that "father" is one way of talking about God, but when it is made compulsory as the only way, the symbol becomes a prison for God. All the other symbolic expressions that people have used to describe their experience of God are repressed by the obligatory language or are demoted to a lower level in the hierarchy.

Pope John Paul I said, in a remark that has drawn a lot of attention, that God is at least as much mother as father. But in practical religious life we are still far behind this relativizing of the symbolic language. After a worship service in St. Catharine's Church in Hamburg that began "In the Name of the Father and the Mother, the Son and the Spirit," there was an excited discussion about whether one may speak that way. Changing sanctified liturgical language is one step outside the prison and therefore is felt as threatening. Four women gave the blessing together: "May God bless and protect you. May she let her face shine upon you and give you peace."

These are examples of tentative efforts that are being made everywhere today where women have become aware of their situation. The desire for another image of God, for new symbols and different hopes, is important for those who need a different God because they are insulted, humiliated, and disgusted by the culture in which we live. After all, it is not primarily men who suffer from the sexism of theological language.

The relativizing of a God-symbol, like "father," that has been used absolutely, is a minimal demand in this context. There are other symbols for God: we can say "mother" or "sister" to her, if we want to remain within the framework of family. However, I find that symbols drawn from nature are clearer, because of their nonauthoritarian quality. A theological language free of dominance can draw on the mystical tradition: "fountain of all goodness," "living wind," "water of life," "light" are all God-symbols without authority or power, without any chauvinist flavor. The recognition of the "higher power," the adoration of dominance, the denial of our own strength, have no place in mystical piety.

The master-slave relationship has often been expressly criticized, but it is especially the use of creative language that has made it outdated. Religion here is the experience of oneness with the whole, of belonging, not of submission. People do not worship God because of God's power and domination; they "sink" into God's love, which is "ground," "depth," "ocean." Mother- and nature-symbols are preferred where the relationship to God does not demand obedience but unity, where God is not a distant Other who demands sacrifice and self-denial, but where, instead, agreement and one-ness with the Living One are the theme of religion. Solidarity will then re-place obedience as the most important virtue.

III. The Father-Symbol

Are there elements in the symbol of God as father that are indispensable for a liberating theology? Does a personal language about God have precedence over other possible symbols? Do we need a "thou" interpreted as "father" to be partner to the human "I"?

In patriarchal culture, the father represents the dependence of the indi-vidual. It is biologically given in the fact of being begotten and in the long dependency of the human young, who must be cared for and protected. But does our long childhood justify a religious language essentially oriented to a parent-child relationship? And does not the exclusion of the mother from this relationship, as if it were the father alone who is responsible for concep-tion and survival, emphasize the authoritarian element still more?

The image of the father in Judaism is oriented to the function of the head of the household, who represents a particular legal, religious, pedagog-ical, and economic authority. He is judge, priest, teacher, and he controls the means of production. Those within this culture who address God as father have experienced these concrete forms of dependence in their own lives, with double intensity if they are women. Only mercy, as the other element in the father-symbol, can make this dependency bearable; the joining of abso-lute authority with compassion is the mark of the Father-God. Closeness and distance, fatherly kindness and juridical dominion are the poles that de-termine the image of the father. The history of the Father-God in our culture can be described in terms of the tension between these two poles. But when the concentration of biological and social power roles falls apart and in-creasingly becomes a thing of the past, is not their religious superelevation also without foundation? What is there in the image of the father that is in-dispensable?

I think that the central question in every feminist philosophical and theological discussion is about the relationship between dependence and in-dependence. Is independence a liberating word, a central value that women are discovering for themselves, or are there dependencies that cannot be denied? Is it good to make oneself emotionally independent, or does that only get us to where the men are, with their superficial ties that dare not limit the ideologized independence of the male hero? What does it mean anthropologically to be dependent? And what does it mean in society? The field of this internal feminist discussion is also the field of theological decision. Is dependence nothing but a repressive inheritance, or does it belong to our createdness?

We have not made, invented, or located ourselves historically or geographically. The context of our life has a before and after to which we are related and from which we cannot divorce ourselves without injury. We are not alone ontologically. There is — this we must believe — a unity of the world, a wholeness, a goal.

Does not the language about God, the father of the living, express precisely this dependence as solidarity? The text of one of Johann Sebastian Bach's religious songs, taken from Simon Dach (1605-1659), says:

> I am, O Lord, within thy might,
> 'tis thou hast brought me to the light,
> and you preserve for me my life,
> you know the number of my moons,
> and when I to this vale of gloom
> again must say my last good night.
> Where, how and when I am to die,
> you know, O Father, more than I.

The "power" of the Lord, who at the end is called "Father," is described here with exactitude: it is begetting, life-creating, life-preserving, and life-ending power. Our being born and our dying are not in our hands. Saying "father" to God means that we do not surrender life and death to vitalistic chance. Seeing the world as creation means to see it as willed, as planned, as good. If speaking of God as father helps us not just to accept our dependence as an earthly lot to be overcome, but to welcome it, accepting our finiteness and creaturehood, then there can be no objection to it. Familial symbols can be liberating if they interpret our dependence theologically, as trust in the father and mother.

Familial symbols for God, speaking of God our Father and God our Mother, can have a liberating character, not because they soften the antihumanist, repressive features of patriarchy, but because they anchor us in nature and in the human family. Then talk of God the Father will no longer be sociologically exploited to strengthen the determination of roles and false dependency; it will not be employed to make us eternal children. Instead, it makes us able to trust in the life that goes beyond our own. It endows us also with confidence in Brother Death.

VI. Confronting the Powers

Introduction

Ched Myers

To argue that theology should be fundamentally politically grounded in context, content, and method begs the question of what *kind* of concrete political practices are being assumed or advocated. About this there has been considerable vagueness or equivocation, perhaps because of the academic social location from which most North Atlantic political theology, Third-World liberation theology, and post-colonial theology has been generated. This section addresses the issue head on: Christian political engagement should be *militant* but *nonviolent* in its efforts to resist structural injustice and to build a more humane world.

It is hardly accidental that our three selections come from the margins of, or outside altogether, the theological academy. Dorothy Day (1897-1980) located her life and witness among the urban poor in New York's Bowery neighborhood, founding the influential Catholic Worker movement during the Great Depression. René Girard is a French social philosopher and literary critic whose formidable work has been widely influential, yet has earned only a relatively small (though loyal) following among theologians. New Testament scholar Walter Wink did much of his work from the non-degree-granting "seminary without borders" at Auburn in New York, and in recent years has concentrated his efforts on popular education in churches and social change organizations in the U.S. and South Africa. Each of the three has made a significant contribution to the development of the theory and practice of Christian active nonviolence, and thus to political theology.

Dorothy Day's work spanned a half-century of American religious activism. As a young journalist Day was deeply influenced by the resurgence of radical social thought in the wake of World War I, particularly socialism and anarchism. Living in New York, she was active in radical politics, but struggled with failed relationships. Converting to Catholicism in the late 1920s, she founded the Catholic Worker movement with French anarchist Peter Maurin in 1933, in the depths of the Depression. Based on a philosophy of serving Christ by offering hospitality to the poor, resisting state violence, and nurturing "clarification of thought," the Catholic Worker movement has (without central decision-making or institutionalization) grown to some 185 communities around North America and abroad (see www.catholicworker.org). Just as importantly, Catholic Worker thought and practice have disproportionately influenced several generations of Christian activists, from antiwar actions in the 1960s to Central American solidarity and Sanctuary organizing in the 1980s to young anarcho-primitivist communities today.

Day was the author of several books, most notably her autobiography, *The Long Loneliness* (1952), and her story of the Catholic Worker movement, *Loaves and Fishes* (1963). But her main expression was in the pages of *The Catholic Worker* monthly paper, and the selection below from a 1948 edition is vintage. As was typical of her style, Day railed against both U.S. militarism and American Catholic conformity to Cold War anti-communist culture. Her polemics were backed up by street-level activism, in this case, leafleting against universal conscription at local colleges.

Their pacifist stance brought Catholic Workers notoriety in the late 1950s, when they publicly refused to cooperate with air raid drills in New York City that were "preparing" the citizenry for nuclear war. Similarly, Workers were among the first to burn draft cards in the Vietnam era — the embodiment of Day's call for "wholesale disloyalty to Americanism, wholesale refusal to fight." Such radical, gospel-rooted nonviolence cut sharply against the grain of mid-century Catholicism, yet helped to birth the creative experiments in symbolic nonviolent direct action of the Berrigan brothers and the subsequent Plowshares disarmament movement. Dorothy Day's legacy has measurably pushed American Catholics on questions of war and poverty, while her witness as a lay woman continues to inspire faith-based activists of all stripes.

René Girard's interdisciplinary thought ranges wide and deep, with a particular focus on the origins of violence in human culture. Girard (b. 1923 in France) studied history in Paris before doing his doctoral work in the U.S. He taught literature and criticism at several American universities before coming to Stanford in 1981, from where he retired in 1995. His most theologically important works are *Violence and the Sacred* (1972), *Things Hidden since the Foundation of the World* (1987), and *I See Satan Fall like Lightning* (2001). Girard formulated an anthropological theory of "mimetic desire" to explain how human individuals and groups build solidarity through scapegoating a common enemy (explained simply by Brian McDonald in the introduction to his interview with Girard, below).

A Roman Catholic, Girard argued that all violence has its roots in rituals or myths of scapegoating, but that the biblical narrative in general and Christ's death in particular exposed this lie and overturned the sovereignty of sacrificial religion. As McDonald points out below, "Girard's belief about the death of Christ may be no less controversial among Christians than his allegiance to Christ is scandalous to the secular world." Girard's work has stimulated fresh theological thinking around nonviolence;[1] non-propitiatory understandings of the Cross;[2] and has even inspired two websites that offer Girardian resources to those preaching the Lectionary (http://girardianlectionary.net and www.preachingpeace.org).

Walter Wink's little book *The Bible in Human Transformation* (1973) challenged the gulf between academic inquiry and personal spirituality in biblical studies, and launched his quest to understand the relevance of Scripture to the work of personal and political change. His best-known work is the "Powers" trilogy:

- *Naming the Powers: The Language of Power in the New Testament* (1984) summarized and extended the efforts of, for example, G. B. Caird, H. Berkhof, John Howard Yoder, and William Stringfellow to rehabilitate the importance of principalities and powers language in the New Testament.
- *Unmasking the Powers: The Invisible Forces That Determine Human Existence* (1986) attempted to decode the New Testament cosmology (or worldview) using the insights of depth psychology and what one reviewer called a "phenomenology of oppression," showing its relevance for contemporary religion and politics; his thesis is neatly summarized and popularized in the selection below.
- *Engaging the Powers: Discernment and Resistance in a World of Domination* (1992) articulated three of Wink's most important contributions: the "myth of redemptive violence" that legitimates conventional think-

---

1. See, e.g., W. Swartley, ed., *Violence Renounced: René Girard, Biblical Studies and Peacemaking* (Telford, PA: Pandora Press, 2000).

2. E.g., J. Weaver, *The Nonviolent Atonement* (Grand Rapids: Eerdmans, 2001).

ing concerning retributive justice and just war; the "Domination system" as shorthand for the whole complex of personal and political delusion and oppression (also summarized in the selection below); and the gospel centrality of nonviolence. This volume was influenced by Wink's hands-on experiences in a context of revolutionary struggle (articulated in his *Violence and Nonviolence in South Africa: Jesus' Third Way* [1987]).

Wink's work has helped to animate a renaissance in Christian nonviolent activism, at least in the First World. While he occasionally suffers from "new paradigm" optimism, Wink's "translation" of New Testament semantics, which have so long been captive to modern spiritualism, represents an enormous contribution to political theology. I share his deep conviction that central to the church's vocation in the world is the militantly evangelical and political task of "making known the wisdom of God to the rulers and authorities in the highest places" (Eph. 3:10).

Twenty years ago I argued that the nonviolent cross of Jesus, who lived and died resisting empire and renewing Israel's alternative social vision, represented a "stumbling block" for political theologies.[3] Indeed, the theory and practices of revolutionary nonviolence have too often been overlooked or marginalized by those seeking a politically engaged faith, including most of the voices represented in this volume. The logic of what Wink calls "redemptive violence" dies hard, not least in contexts of oppression. On the other hand, too often theological advocates of nonviolence have done so from a safe academic distance, failing to embody Gandhi's dictum that the truth is revealed only in the *midst* of actual conflicts.

Wink, Girard, and Day (along with a few others in this volume such as Yoder, Tutu, and Hauerwas), in contrast, understand the cross, not as a blood sacrifice to propitiate an angry deity, but as the ultimate form of resistance to the logic of retributive "justice" — to lie at the center of both Christian theology *and* politics. For Girard, Christ's death spells the cosmic demise of scapegoating politics and religion. For Wink, Jesus' way of nonviolence subverts the Powers by refusing to recognize their sovereignty over life and death. And for Day, pacifism rooted in solidarity with the least is constitutive of Christian discipleship.

Wink and Girard provide theological and anthropological grounding for nonviolence as a way of life that political theology needs to take more se-

---

3. Ched Myers, *Binding the Strong Man: A Political Reading of Mark's Story of Jesus* (Maryknoll, NY: Orbis, 1988/2008), pp. 469ff.

riously. Their approach accords well with recent studies analyzing the socio-political context of the Bible and its testimony of resistance to empire.[4] Elaine Enns and I have tried to integrate these trajectories to extend the case for a biblical theology of nonviolence in *Ambassadors of Reconciliation,* vol. 1: *New Testament Reflections on Restorative Justice and Peacemaking.*[5]

The witness of Dorothy Day, meanwhile, challenges political theology to translate its insights concretely into daily practice. While the issue of "social location" has only recently been embraced by theologians, its importance has long been understood by the Catholic Worker movement. One can only truly assess the truth of what Day famously called the "filthy rotten system" from the perspective of the poorest — yet our seminaries are well insulated from such contexts. Political theology must be about *where, how,* and *with whom* we do our reflection. Dorothy Day practiced what we might call "somatic politics": on the one hand tending to the bodies of the broken as a way of communing with the Body of Christ; on the other hand placing her own body in public space in a way that nonviolently "confronted the Powers." This dialectic between the works of mercy and prophetic dissent has its roots, of course, in the Jesus story itself. But it also illustrates a first principle of Gandhian nonviolence: our mobilized, empowered, but disarmed bodies are our most powerful political tool.

For theology to be political, the following selections agree, it must engage the Powers; but for politics to be theological, it must aspire to nonviolence.

4. E.g., R. Horsley, ed., *In the Shadow of Empire: Reclaiming the Bible as a History of Faithful Resistance* (Louisville: Westminster/John Knox, 2008).
5. Maryknoll, NY: Orbis, 2009.

24 We Are Un-American: We Are Catholics

Dorothy Day

Is it Soviet Russia who is the threat to the world? Is it indeed? Then may we quote from Scott Nearing's *The Way of the Transgressor?*

> What nation today has a navy bigger than all other navies combined? The USA. What nation today is steadily adding to the only known stockpile of atom bombs? The USA. What nation today is tops in the development of buzz bombs, jet planes, bacterial poisons and death rays? The USA. What nation today is spending the largest sums on military preparations? The USA. What nation today is permitting representatives of the armed forces to take over the direction of domestic and foreign policy? The USA. What nation today is arming its neighbors (in Latin America), intervening in the internal affairs of Europe and Asia, threatening the world peace and security and rapidly surrounding itself with a black curtain of anxiety, suspicion and hatred? The USA.

If we are to accept the materialistic and atheistic philosophy of the capitalist state which holds sway in the United States, then there can be but little objection to this state of affairs. If our values are derived from the stock exchange, if we are to join in the psychopathic mania that has made war an end in itself, which has made it the norm of the American economy, if we are to be united against an ideology rather than for an ideology — then we are on the right track.

Some of us at *The Catholic Worker* have been going to the colleges and distributing a leaflet against UMT [Universal Military Training]. And most everyone to whom we gave the leaflet has expressed acceptance of UMT, has thought it a good thing. There are no antiwar organizations in the colleges these days, at least not in the Catholic colleges. There is a sense of the inevitable, that war is to come, that morality has nothing to do with it, that it is a question of licking Russia before she gets too strong, before she gets the atomic bomb. Around the local churches they are distributing leaflets and cards asking the Italians here to write to their relatives in Italy not to vote Communist. It would be interesting to know who is financing this campaign. It would be interesting to know why Communism has become such a threat in Italy. Is it perhaps that we have failed? And that, to cover that failure, we attribute the influence of Communists to trickery? Have Catholics in Italy been radicals, have they worked for freedom, those who control official policy? Has there been as much concern for worker ownership of the means of production and distribution, for decentralization, for a peaceful liquidation of acquisitive classes, as there has been in establishing a *modus vivendi* with fascism, as there has been in cooperating with elements of the Right? Have not we Catholics, by and large, gone down the road of compromise so far that we can awaken no enthusiasm among the people? That the only thing we can whip up enthusiasm for, in conjunction with the Hearst press, is an anti-Communist crusade? A crusade that utilizes the anti-Christian and Mohammedan concept of a "holy war." A defense of Jesus Christ by bombs, a blood-soaked earth, quick death, hate. A hate that always exists in war despite the unreal and pedantic distinctions of theologians whose love of refinements is equaled only by their ignorance of psychology, of what happens to a man to get him prepared to murder. To get the poor in a state of mind where they will attribute every decent sentiment, every cry for justice, all love of man for his neighbor, to "Communists." Because to go to war means to go against every decent sentiment and against all cries for justice and against all love of man for his neighbor. The policy of the United States is anti-Catholic because it is atheistic. God does not enter into it for in place of Him there is *expediency*. It has become expedient that we murder, it has become expedient that we ignore the precepts of Jesus Christ laid down in the Sermon on the Mount and applicable to *all men,* not just to a chosen few who are to be perfect. It has become expedient that we preach hatred of Communists to the people, that we fasten signs of hate on Church doors and sell comic strip hate books in the Church vestibule. Christianity has been reduced by the theologians to a rule of expediency, Christianity has been made to identify itself with Americanism, with the scum of the Right!

Why is *The Catholic Worker* opposed to UMT and to war? Because we are Communists? No! For we were opposed to World War II when the Communists were for it. Because we are indifferent to the fate of the Church? No! For she is our Mother, the Bridegroom of Jesus Christ. But she is more than real estate, she is more than temporal power, her spirit is not the spirit of the world and she has no need to be defended by the arms of the world. No more than her Divine Master who refused such defense.

We are against war because it is contrary to the spirit of Jesus Christ, and the only important thing is that we abide in His spirit. It is more important than being American, more important than being respectable, more important than obedience to the State. It is the only thing that matters. We are against Universal Military Training because it is preparation for sin, for the sin that is war. It is better that the United States be liquidated than that she survive by war.

What would we advocate? Wholesale disloyalty to Americanism. Wholesale refusal to fight. Wholesale withdrawal of labor (a general strike) from all industries that further the war effort. We would urge a mighty band of Catholic Conscientious Objectors who will refuse induction, who will follow Jesus of Nazareth, Prince of Peace, in the way of non-violence, in love for all mankind!

25 Violence and the Lamb Slain:
An Interview with René Girard

Brian McDonald

René Girard is both one of the twentieth century's most prominent theorists of culture and a devout Roman Catholic. Born and raised in France, Girard received his Ph.D. in history from Indiana University and has lived and taught for most of his life in America.

He combines a "deconstructionist" and "debunking" analysis of the origins and bases of human culture with an essentially traditionalist affirmation of Christianity. His cultural analysis has been praised by secular critics, even as his insistence that this very analysis should lead to Christian affirmation has shocked them. Christians are pleased that a giant of modernist and postmodernist thought is a solid Christian, but some are disturbed that he seems to "debunk" the propitiatory view of Christ's death on the Cross. A brief outline of his thought and its development may therefore be useful before presenting the interview.

Girard's Thought

Picture two young children playing happily on their porch, a pile of toys beside them. The older child pulls a G.I. Joe from the pile and immediately his younger brother cries out, "No, my toy!" pushes him out of the way, and grabs it. The older child, who was not very interested in the toy when he picked it up, now conceives a passionate need for it and attempts to wrest it back. Soon a full fight ensues, with the toy forgotten and the two boys busy pummeling each other.

As the fight intensifies, the overweight child next door wanders into their yard and comes up to them, looking for someone to play with. At that point, one of the two rivals looks up and says, "Oh, there's old fat butt!" "Yeah," says his brother. "Big fat butt!" The two, having forgotten the toy, now forget their fight and run the child back home. Harmony has been restored between the two brothers, though the neighbor is now indoors crying.

It would not be much of an exaggeration to say that Girard builds his whole theory of human nature and human culture through a close analysis of the dynamics operating in this story. Most human desires are not "original" or spontaneous, he argues, but are created by imitating another whom he calls the "model." When the model claims an object, that tells another that it is desirable — and that he must have it instead of him. Girard calls this "mimetic" (or imitative) desire. In the subsequent rivalry, the two parties will come to forget the object and will come to desire the conflict for itself. Harmony will only be restored if the conflicting parties can vent their anger on a common enemy or "scapegoat."

With the lucidity characteristic of French thought before the "deconstructionist" writers, and a consistency reminiscent of Calvin, Girard shows, throughout the body of his work, how his theory of "mimetic" desire can illuminate and unify an extraordinarily disparate set of human phenomena. It can explain everything from sacrifice to conflict, from mythology to Christianity.

Mimetic desire accounts for the nature of human culture. Early human cultures, thinks Girard, must have been marked by violence as mimetic desire drew human beings into unceasing conflict. Ultimately, the object would disappear from view and be replaced by the conflict itself. Thus, most conflicts, either ancient or modern, are almost literally over "nothing," with essentially identical rivals seeking only the prestige that comes from achieving victory over each other. (St. Augustine noted this in his *Confessions*, when he analyzed sports and games and marveled that the only object won in these contests was prestige gained through victory over a rival.)

Primitive societies would have few mechanisms for containing the spreading contagion of mimetic violence, so Girard concludes that such societies would have inevitably decimated themselves had they not found a mechanism for containing the conflict.

This mechanism he locates in another fundamental human characteristic: our propensity for "scapegoating." At some stage in a cycle of mimetic violence, the community spontaneously turns on one of its members as the one who is to blame for it all. (Remember that point in innumerable movie

Westerns where, in the midst of some scene of agitation and confusion, a finger gets pointed at someone and immediately a thicket of fingers is pointing at him and a lynch mob is instantly created?)

While mimetic violence divides each against each, *scapegoating* violence unites all against one. Thus the destruction of the scapegoat produces a genuinely unifying experience, the peace and relief of which makes such a profound impact that, over time, the hated scapegoat is turned into a god, and the community tries to perpetuate the peace-bringing effect of this original lynching by commemorating it ritually and sacrificially. Ultimately this ritualized violence becomes the basis for religion, mythology, kingship, and the establishment of those differences in role and status that are so essential to bring about internal peace. (Differentiation cuts down on mimetic rivalry since only "equals" can compete for the same object.)

Desire and Repentance

Girard's key idea (if not the term) made its first appearance in *Deceit, Desire, and the Novel* (1959), the work that first brought him to prominence. In this analysis of great writers from Cervantes to Proust, Girard found that all the great novels dealt with the theme of what he then called "triangular desire" and ended with a kind of repentance: a protagonist awakening into a recognition of the wrong-headedness of a life built on the illusion of imitated desire and rivalry with others.

In *Violence and the Sacred* (1972), he moved from the realm of literature to that of culture itself, and added to his concept of mimetic desire that of scapegoating. This analysis of the way religion, mythology, and culture are built upon an unrecognized foundation of mimetically caused violence and scapegoating brought him considerable acclaim when it was published.

However, *Things Hidden Since the Foundation of the World* (1979), though a best-seller in France, lost him much of that acclaim, for in this latter work Girard dared to assert that the shackles of sacrificial religion were broken for a large portion of mankind by the force of the biblical story in which a number of narratives reversed the classical mythological pattern by *exonerating* the scapegoat and showing the *community* to be guilty of gratuitous murder.

What most offended his secular audience was that he saw in the culmination of the biblical witness, the passion of Christ, a permanent exposé of "the things hidden from the foundation of the world" — that both the order and disorder of human life are founded on the clashes of mimetic desire relieved by the lie of the scapegoat mechanism.

Hence, Girard identifies the foundational principle of culture as "Satan," since it mirrors perfectly Christ's description of "the Prince of this world," who was moved by envy and was "a liar and a murderer from the first." By laying down his life to expose and overthrow this kingdom built on violence and untruth, Christ also introduced the world to another kingdom, one "not of this world," whose fundamental principles are repentance for sins instead of the catharsis of scapegoating and love of God and neighbor rather than the warfare of mimetic desire.

The death of Christ and its effects move Girard's theory from "naturalism" to Christian affirmation, since he is convinced that the mindset of natural humanity is so wholly immersed in the "intervidual" psychology of sacrificial religion that only a divine revelation could break us free of it — or even make us *recognize* the suppressed lie at the basis of our existence. Hence, the very appearance of the Christ, and his successful exposure of the lies at the base of human life and culture, is a proof of his divinity, since "no human is able to reveal the scapegoat mechanism."

Girard's belief about the death of Christ may be no less controversial among Christians than his allegiance to Christ is scandalous to the secular world. Against the view of Christ's death that would see him as a propitiatory sacrifice offered to the Father, Girard would argue that Christ's death was intended to overthrow in its entirety the religion of propitiatory sacrifice, since he sees that religion as of the very essence of fallen man.

The Interview

The following interview was conducted by telephone and has been edited for clarity.

BRIAN MCDONALD: *You were led to Christianity through a process that many people would find unusual: that of studying the structure of some of our great Western novels. Could you explain how the "shape" of novelistic works became a factor in your embracing of Christianity?*

RENE GIRARD (RG): Yes. A great novel involves an experience that is spiritual; the novelist engages in reflection and comes to sense that his whole life has been based upon illusion. The character in a novel then experiences a conversion that involves a recognition that he is like those he despises. But this experience of the character is in reality a reflection of what has happened to the novelist. It is what makes him able to write the novel.

In language you use elsewhere, the novelist ceases to "scapegoat" his characters and identifies with them.

RG: Yes, yes. Now this experience of conversion is not necessarily the Christian experience of conversion, but it has that pattern. It has the Christian form in *Crime and Punishment,* but the same form, though not overtly Christian, takes place in Marcel Proust's *The Past Recaptured.*

And you yourself?

RG: I would say that it is my own life I am describing when I discuss these matters.

I believe you have stated somewhere that this novelistic pattern originated in Augustine's Confessions.

RG: Yes, this I think is true. Though the *Confessions* is different in that the conversion happened before the book was written. You see, I always think of it as something happening at the end. In my view the novelist writes the novel twice. The first time, he finishes it, but unlike God after creating the world, he looks at his work and says, "It is bad!" What is missing is something that must happen to the novelist himself. And when it happens, the novel is really viewed from a different perspective. But the pattern of conversion changing the way everything former is seen is established in the *Confessions.*

Reading Christ's Death

You have advocated what is seen as a "non-sacrificial" reading of the death of Christ that is significantly at odds with the usual understanding of that death as a "hilasterion" that satisfies the wrath and justice of God. Could you describe that view and how your study of the formation and maintenance of human cultures has led you to it?

RG: Oh, this is a question that will require a long answer! It is not quite true that I take what you have called a "non-sacrificial reading of the death of Christ." We must establish first of all that there are two kinds of sacrifice.

Both forms are shown together (and I am not sure anywhere else) in the story of Solomon's judgment in the third chapter of 1 Kings. Two prostitutes bring a baby. They are doubles engaging in a rivalry over what is apparently a surviving child. When Solomon offers to split the child, the one woman says "yes," because she wishes to triumph over her rival. The other woman then says, "No, she may have the child," because she seeks only its life. On the basis of this love, the king declares that "she is the mother."

Note that it does not matter who is the biological mother. The one who was willing to sacrifice herself for the child's life is in fact the mother. The first woman is willing to sacrifice a child to the needs of rivalry. Sacrifice is the solution to mimetic rivalry and the foundation of it. The second woman is willing to sacrifice everything she wants for the sake of the child's life. This is sacrifice in the sense of the gospel. It is in this sense that Christ is a sacrifice since he gave himself "for the life of the world."

What I have called "bad sacrifice" is the kind of sacrificial religion that prevailed before Christ. It originates because mimetic rivalry threatens the very survival of a community. But through a spontaneous process that also involves mimesis, the community unites against a victim in an act of spontaneous killing. This act unites rivals and restores peace and leaves a powerful impression that results in the establishment of sacrificial religion.

But in this kind of religion, the community is regarded as innocent and the victim is guilty. Even after the victim has been "deified," he is still a criminal in the eyes of the community (note the criminal nature of the gods in pagan mythology).

But something happens that begins in the Old Testament. There are many stories that reverse this scapegoat process. In the story of Cain and Abel, the story of Joseph, the book of Job, and many of the psalms, the persecuting community is pictured as guilty and the victim is innocent. But Christ, the son of God, is the ultimate "scapegoat" — precisely because he is the son of God, and since he is innocent, he exposes all the myths of scapegoating and shows that the victims were innocent and the communities guilty.

You use the word "Satan" to describe the structural principle of human existence in which both disorder and order are built upon untruth and violence: disorder created by mimetic conflict and order restored and established by per-

secution and destruction of scapegoats. In the purely "anthropological" portions of your work, you seem to view this structure as a kind of necessity for early human beings. In the more "theological" portions of your work, you seem to treat it very much as what has traditionally been called Original Sin. Do you view the satanic structure as a kind of historical necessity — given the conditions of early human existence — or do you view it as a "fall" that could have been avoided? (Or is this a false either/or?)

RG: Well, I must stay within the scientific use. This is the language people speak and understand in this time. I am an anthropologist. As I view the process of hominization, it is a kind of historical inevitability. We don't know of any other creature that practices sacrifice, and there seem to be neurological features that required this, based upon the fact that we are the most mimetic of all animals.

On the other hand, even if this had a kind of historical necessity, it is also a form of a lie. The scapegoat mechanism is something men "do but know not what they do." It is indeed from that Original Sin and something from which redemption is required.

As a cultural theorist sticking within the limits of your discipline, you must bracket the question of Satan as a "personal" being. I am interested, however, in whether as a Christian you see Satan as a kind of "being" as well as a structure.

RG: (Laughs.) Well, I don't know. Does it really matter? Whether Satan is a personal being or not, he is still the "prince of this world." Existence is satanically structured whether or not he is a personal being. He is a liar and a murderer from the first, and the religion of murder and lie has founded our existence from the first. Perhaps we shouldn't become too preoccupied with him, should we?

Besieged Christians

Most Christians have a siege mentality when confronted with modern and postmodern thought, finding the "unmaskings" of Freud, Nietzsche, Marx, or Derrida purely and simply as nihilistic threats to the gospel. However, you seem to have an essentially positive (if critical) reading of the trends of contemporary thought, believing that if its practitioners fully understood their own insights, they would find them leading toward the Christian revelation instead of away from it. If this is a correct assessment of what you are saying, what in contemporary thought seems most "retrievable" to you?

RG: Well, they are nihilistic. Nietzsche actually describes the full reality of Dionysian religion as sacrificial — and endorses it! But *without* the endorsement his thought is precisely what I am saying!

You have described yourself as a deconstructionist.

RG: Yes, but then one must have something to deconstruct *to*. Deconstructing when you are looking for the foundation underneath is a good thing.

In a striking phrase, you say that "Everything which happened to Jesus is now happening to the gospel texts." Could you explain what you mean by this?

RG: The texts are scapegoated. They are blamed for what is wrong. And yet it is precisely these texts that have brought the scapegoating mechanism to light!

You assert that the Gospels appear to be myth but in reality are "poles apart" from myth. Why do they appear to be myth and why are they in reality "poles apart"?

RG: They appear to be myth because the death of Christ is presented as a sacrifice, and sacrifice of the scapegoat is the origin and theme of all mythology. But it is a sacrifice that refutes the whole principle of violence and sacrifice. God is revealed as the "arch-scapegoat," the completely innocent one who dies in order to give life. And his way of giving life is to overthrow the religion of scapegoating and sacrifice — which is the essence of myth.

The heart of Christ's sacrifice is shown in his prayer, "Not my will, but thine be done." It was inevitable that if someone lived this life, he would suffer the death of a scapegoat, so the sacrifice was inevitable from the moment he began his ministry. But the end of that death would not be to make men feel confirmed in their lives, but to call men into question. Unlike the myths, we have a choice. Christ's kingdom or the kingdom of Satan. When one does not accept Christ's offer, he is of course a member of that kingdom.

Your thought at one end is extremely naturalistic and "unspiritual" (for instance, there is no inborn sense of the transcendent: the sacred is quite literally a "by-product" of our misunderstanding of the scapegoat mechanism). According to your theory, human culture seems to be explained without "remainder" as a product of wholly naturalistic combinations of biological and social forces. I do not fully understand the leap that allows you to affirm God, Christ, eternal life, and so forth, not as a revelation that simply "trumps" your naturalism (as Barth might do), but as a kind of end result of that process of thought when carried out to its logical conclusion.

RG: Well, we must speak the language of the times — which is naturalistic. My thought is no more reductionist than Paul's when he says: "I determined to know nothing among you but Christ and him crucified." Paul did not mean to say that there was nothing besides the death of Christ, but that all knowledge took place in understanding the crucifixion of Christ. It is from that death and the place of that death that all understanding comes. I believe that it is in that sense that my hypothesis, though I keep repeating it over and over again, is not reductionist.

26 Identifying the Powers

Walter Wink

This book is unashamedly about things spiritual. It assumes that spiritual reality is at the heart of everything, from photons to supernovas, from a Little League baseball team to Boeing Aircraft. It sees spirit — the capacity to be aware of and responsive to God — at the core of every institution, every city, every nation, every corporation, every place of worship. It issues from a world unlike that inhabited by skeptics and unbelievers, on the one hand, and the credulous and "overbelievers" on the other. What I have written celebrates a divine reality that pervades every aspect of our existence, where the harmony intended for the universe can already begin to be experienced. And it invites those who are suffering from spiritual malnutrition to a heavenly feast like nothing this society can offer.

In our godless, soulless world, however, it is not easy to speak of spiritual things. Materialism outlaws the divine, while organized religion has all too often neglected the soul in its preoccupation with institutional maintenance.

The world is, to a degree at least, the way we imagine it. When we think it to be godless and soulless, it becomes for us precisely that. And we ourselves are then made over into the image of godless and soulless selves. If we want to be made over into the image of God — to become what God created us to be — then we need to purge our souls of materialism and of other worldviews that block us from realizing the life God so eagerly wants us to have.

Understanding worldviews is key to breaking free from the ways the Powers control people's minds. Yet there is remarkably little discussion of worldviews. Spirituality writer Morton Kelsey first woke me to their importance. Even the term "worldview" is fairly recent. The Germans had the word *Weltanschauung* ("view of the world"), but that referred more to one's personal philosophy of life. A worldview, by contrast, dictates the way whole societies see the world. A worldview provides a picture of the nature of things: where is heaven, where is earth, what is visible and invisible, what is real and unreal. As I am using the term, worldviews are not philosophies, theologies, or even myths or tales about the origin of things. They are the bare-bones structures with which we think. They are the foundation of the house of our minds on which we erect symbols, myths, and systems of thought. Through the lens of our worldview we make sense of our experiences. In the very act of opposing another person's thought, we often share the same worldview.

There have been only a handful of worldviews in all of Western history. Normally, a worldview functions on an unconscious level. People are unaware of its existence. It is just the way things are. It is just now becoming possible to bring these worldviews to awareness. Here is a simple typology of the worldviews that have shaped human existence over much of Western history.

1. The Ancient Worldview

This is the worldview reflected in the Bible. In this conception, everything earthly has its heavenly counterpart, and everything heavenly has its earthly counterpart. Every event is thus a combination of both dimensions of reality. If war begins on earth, then there must be, at the same time, war in heaven between the angels of the nations in the heavenly council. Likewise, events initiated in heaven are mirrored on earth. This is a symbolic way of saying that every material reality has a spiritual dimension, and every spiritual reality has physical consequences. There can be no event or entity that does not consist, simultaneously, of the visible and the invisible.

The Jewish rabbis had a whimsical way of reflecting this worldview. Once, according to Rabbi Hoshaiah (c. 250 C.E.), when the angels who serve God in heaven asked God when the New Year was going to be, God answered them, "You ask me? You and I, we will ask the law court below!" According to the Talmud, after the temple of Jerusalem had been destroyed, the ministering angels, thinking of the correspondence of the earthly with the heavenly, begged God not to destroy the heavenly dwelling place also.

Not only the writers of the Bible, but also the Greeks, Romans, Egyptians, Babylonians, Indians, and Chinese — indeed, most people in the ancient world — shared this worldview, and it is still held by large numbers of people today. There is thus nothing uniquely biblical about this worldview. It just happened to be the view current at the time the Bible was written. That means that there is no reason that the Bible cannot be interpreted within the framework of other worldviews as well.

2. The Spiritualist Worldview

In the second century C.E., a new worldview emerged, one that radically challenged the Judeo-Christian notion that the creation is basically good. In this worldview, creation was the fall. Spirit is good, matter is evil. The world is a prison into which spirits have fallen from the good heaven. Having become trapped in bodies, these spirits became subject to the deformed and ignorant Powers that rule the world of matter. Consequently, sex, the body, and earthly life in general were considered evil. The religious task was to rescue one's spirit from the flesh and these Powers and regain that spiritual realm from which one has fallen.

This worldview is historically associated with religions such as Gnosticism and Manichaeism, philosophies such as Neo-platonism, and the sexual attitudes we associate, however unfairly, with Puritanism. It continues to be a powerful factor today in spiritualism, sexual hang-ups, eating disorders, negative self-images, and the rejection of one's body. The UFO phenomenon may reflect this longing to escape our planet for a better world, as in the case of the "Heaven's Gate" cult. But the spiritualist worldview is also reflected in those forms of Christian faith that place all the emphasis on getting to heaven when one leaves this "vale of tears."

3. The Materialist Worldview

This view became prominent during the Enlightenment but is as old as Democritus (who died about 370 B.C.E.). In many ways it is the antithesis of the world-rejection of spiritualism. The materialist view claims that there is no heaven, no spiritual world, no God, no soul; nothing but what can be known through the five senses and reason. The spiritual world is an illusion. There is no higher self; we are mere complexes of matter, and when we die we cease to exist except as the chemicals and atoms that once constituted us. Matter is ultimate. There is a "hard" of philosophical materialism that sees the universe as devoid of spirit, and a "soft" materialism associated with consumerism, self-gratification, and an absence of spiritual values. It is also the dominant ethos of most universities, the media, and culture as a whole. Since there can be no intrinsic meaning to the universe, people have to create values, purposes, and meanings for themselves. There is no right and wrong except what society agrees upon for purposes of survival or tranquility.

This materialistic worldview has penetrated deeply even into many religious persons, causing them to ignore the spiritual dimensions of systems or the spiritual resources of faith. I myself received a deep dose of materialism in college (even though it was a Methodist school!) that I have been struggling to free myself from ever since. Materialism has in fact become so pervasive in modern society that it is virtually identified with the scientific point of view, even though the new physics has moved beyond materialism into a re-enchanted universe.

4. The Theological Worldview

In reaction to materialism, theologians created or postulated a supernatural realm. Acknowledging that this higher realm could not be known by the senses, they conceded earthly reality to science and preserved a privileged "spiritual" realm immune to confirmation or refutation. The materialists were only too glad to concede to the theologians the "heavenly" realm, since they did not believe it existed anyway. The slogan that many clergy were taught in seminaries was "Science tells us *how* the world was created, religion tells us *why*." This means splitting reality in two and hermetically sealing off theology from the discoveries of science and science from the wisdom of theology. An extreme example of this split was a friend who was a doctoral student in geology at Columbia University. As a religious fundamentalist, he believed on Sundays that the universe was created in 4004 B.C., but during the rest of the week he accepted the theory that it was created around fifteen billion years ago. But that is only a flagrant form of the split accepted by virtually all the great theologians of the twentieth century. In a world inundated with scientific data and discoveries, they simply have not been interested in science. The price paid for this schizoid view of reality was the loss of a sense of the whole and the unity of heavenly and earthly aspects of existence. The earth reveals the glory of God, and scientists uncover God's majesty. Science and religion cannot be separated.

5. An Integral Worldview

This new worldview is emerging from a number of streams of thought: the new physics; liberation theology; feminist theology; the reflections of psychologist Carl Jung and paleontologist Teilhard de Chardin; process philosophers such as Alfred North Whitehead, Charles Hartshorne, John Cobb, and David Ray Griffin; theologians such as Morton Kelsey, Thomas Berry, Matthew Fox; the Buddhists Thich Nhat Hanh and Joanna Macy; and many Native American religions. This integral view of reality sees everything as having an outer and an inner aspect.

Heaven and earth are seen here as the inner and outer aspects of a single reality. This integral worldview affirms spirit at the core of every created thing. But this inner spiritual reality is inextricably related to an outer form or physical manifestation. This new worldview takes seriously all the aspects of the ancient worldview, but combines them in a different way. Both worldviews use spatial imagery. The idea of heaven as "up" is a natural, almost unavoidable way of indicating transcendence. But if the world turns, there is no longer an "up" anywhere in the universe, just as north is no more "up" than south is "down." Few of us in the West who have been deeply touched by modern science can actually think that God, the angels, and departed spirits are somewhere in the sky, as most ancients literally did. (And as some people today who disbelieve still do — including atheists. Remember the glee of the Soviet cosmonauts in announcing to the world that they had encountered no supernatural beings in space?) The integral worldview reconceives that spatial metaphor not as "up" but "within."

In this worldview, soul permeates the universe. God is not just within me, but within everything. The universe is suffused with the divine. This is not pantheism, where everything is God, but panentheism (*pan*, everything; *en*, in; *theos*, God), where everything is in God and God in everything. Spirit is at the heart of everything, and all creatures are potential revealers of God. This integral worldview is no more essentially "religious" than the ancient worldview, but I believe it makes the biblical data more intelligible for people today than any other available worldview, the ancient one included.

The Reverend James Forbes, pastor of the Riverside Church in New York City, commented regarding the issue of worldviews:

> Black people in my community talk about God and sometimes talk to God. It's always interesting when some of them have been in mental hospitals and they're getting ready to meet staff and get a chance to come out if

they prove to be well from their neurosis or their psychosis. And we have to counsel them: Now, when they ask you, do you hear voices, don't you tell them, "Yes, I heard God tell me this morning that everything was gonna be all right." I mean, it is so real that someone who did not understand the worldview would think that here's somebody hallucinating. For us God talks and walks with us. So I think we have a kind of integral worldview.[1]

This integral worldview is also evident in the Native American representation of Sky Father and Earth Mother, and in the Chinese yin/yang figure. It is given modern representation by the Moebius strip, which can be demonstrated by taking a long strip of paper, forming a loop, and then rotating one end of the strip 180 degrees, or onto its back side. If you follow the loop with your finger, it will be now on the inside, now on the outside, and within again, and so on, illustrating the constant oscillation between the inner and the outer.

Worldviews determine what we are allowed to believe about the world. Most of us have chunks of each of these worldviews in our psyches. We may have been sexually repressed or sexually abused as children; for us the spiritualist worldview may still be operative, leading us to deny our relationship to our bodies and locate our true essence in a transcendent, nonphysical world. Or we may have taken deeply to heart the materialistic ethos of university life, or we may have been bombarded by materialist consumerism our whole life long through the media and the malls. Or we may cling to the theological worldview as a way of fending off the materialism of modern science. Or we may embrace the integral worldview as a way of reuniting science and religion, spirit and matter, inner and outer. The important point here is that *we may be the first generation in the history of the world that can make a conscious choice between these worldviews.* We can decide which worldview best describes the world as we encounter it, and whether we still want to be controlled by the others.

Opening to Spiritual Reality

The writers of the Bible had names that helped them identify the spiritual realities that they encountered. They spoke of angels, demons, principalities

1. James Forbes, *The System Belongs to God*, a six-part video from EcuFilm, 810 Twelfth Ave. South, Nashville, TN 37203.

and powers, Satan, gods, and the elements of the universe. Materialism had no use for such things and so dismissed them. The theological worldview could hardly make room in the universe for God; these spiritual powers were an extravagance that worldview could scarcely afford. And "modern" people were supposed to gag on the idea of angels and demons. The world had been mercifully swept clean of these "superstitions," and people could sleep better at night knowing that they were safe from spirits.

Recently, however, there has been a spate of books on angels (and several movies, including the highly acclaimed *Wings of Desire*), and a whole battery of movies and novels on satanism and exorcism, going back to *Rosemary's Baby* and *The Exorcist*. It is as if modern people, stripped of life's spiritual depths by a shallow materialist culture, are crying out for transcendence. People want to believe that the world is more than a consumer's paradise and that they themselves are more than food for worms.

Much of this interest in angels is as shallow as the materialism it opposes. It is comforting to believe that we are all protected by guardian angels, for example. But these guardian angels seem to work best in middle-class neighborhoods where there are plenty of resources; they don't do so well protecting children in ghettos from drive-by shootings. If we want to take the notion of angels, demons, and the principalities and powers seriously, we will have to go back to the biblical understanding of spirits in all its profundity and apply it freshly to our situation today.

Latin American liberation theology made one of the first efforts to reinterpret the "principalities and powers," not as disembodied spirits inhabiting the air, but as institutions, structures, and systems. But the Powers, as we have seen, are not just physical. The Bible insists that they are *more* than that (Eph. 3:10; 6:12); this "more" holds the clue to their profundity. In the biblical view the Powers are at one and the same time visible *and* invisible, earthly *and* heavenly, spiritual *and* institutional (Col. 1:15-20). Powers such as a lumberyard or a city government possess an outer, physical manifestation (buildings, personnel, trucks, fax machines) and an inner spirituality, corporate culture, or collective personality. The Powers are simultaneously an outer, visible structure and an inner, spiritual reality. Perhaps we are not accustomed to thinking of the Pentagon, or the Chrysler Corporation, or the Mafia as having a spirituality, but they do. The New Testament uses the language of power to refer at one point to the outer aspect, at another to the inner aspect, and yet again to both together. What people in the world of the Bible experienced as and called "principalities and powers" was in fact the actual spirituality at the center of the political, economic, and cultural institutions of their day.

When people tell of their experiences of evil in the world, they often lapse into the language of the ancient worldview. Demons and angels are depicted as separate beings soaring about in the sky rather than as the spirituality of institutions and systems. When I suggest restating the same thought using an integral worldview, they often respond, "Oh, yes, that's what I meant." But it is not at all what they have said; in fact, they have just said something utterly different. This contradictory behavior is not sloppy thinking (these are generally very perceptive people, or they would not have discerned these spiritual realities). Rather, it shows how ready people are to shift from the ancient worldview to a more integral one. People use the old way of putting it merely because they lack a better way to say it. When they are provided a more adequate language, they instantly recognize that these new words fit their experience; they say what they wanted to say all along yet were not equipped to verbalize. People are groping for a more adequate language to talk about spiritual realities than the tradition provides. A rapid and fundamental sea change has been taking place in the contemporary worldview. It has gone largely unnoticed, but more and more people are beginning to become aware of it. A new conceptual worldview is *already* in place, like the wiring in the hard drive of a computer, and can be activated by its mere articulation.

The lesser-known aspect of the Powers is the *spiritual,* or *invisible,* dimension. We generally perceive it only indirectly, by means of projection. In New Testament times, people did not read the spirituality of an institution directly from its outer manifestations. Instead, they projected its felt or intuited spiritual qualities onto the screen of the universe and perceived them as cosmic forces reigning from the sky.

Some first-century Jews and Christians perceived in the Roman Empire a demonic spirituality which they called Satan (the "Dragon" of Revelation 12). But they encountered this spirit in the actual institutional forms of Roman life: legions, governors, crucifixions, payment of tribute, Roman sacred emblems and standards, and so forth (the "beast" of Revelation 13). The spirit that they perceived existed right at the heart of the empire, but their worldview equipped them to discern that spirit only by intuiting it and then projecting it out, in visionary form, as a spiritual *being* residing in heaven and representing Rome in the heavenly council.

In the ancient worldview, where earthly and heavenly reality were inextricably united, this view of the Powers worked effectively. But for many modern Westerners it is impossible to maintain that worldview. Instead, fundamentalists treat the Powers as actual demonic beings in the air, largely divorced from their manifestations in the physical or political world (the theological worldview), and secularists deny that this spiritual dimension even exists (the materialistic worldview).

To complete the projection process, we must *withdraw* the projections and recognize that the real spiritual force that we are experiencing emanates from actual institutions. Our task, working within the emerging unitary worldview, is to withdraw those projections from on high and relocate them in the institutions where they actually reside.

Projection does not falsify reality. Sometimes it is the only way we can know the inner spirit of things. The demons projected onto the screen of the cosmos really are demonic, and play havoc with humanity. Only they are not *up there* but *over there*, in the socio-spiritual structures that make up the one and only real world. They exist in factories, medical centers, airlines, and agribusiness, to be sure, but also in smaller systems such as families, churches, the Boy Scouts, and programs for senior citizens. The New Testament insists that demons can have no impact on us unless they are able to embody themselves in people (Mark 1:21-28; Matt. 12:43-45; Luke 11:24-26), or pigs (Mark 5:1-20), or political systems (Rev. 12–13).

It is merely a habit of thought that makes people think of the Powers as personal beings. In fact, many of the spiritual powers and gods of the ancient world were not conceived of as personal at all. I prefer to think of the Powers as impersonal entities, though I know of no sure way to settle the question. Humans naturally tend to personalize anything that seems to act intentionally. But we are now "discovering" from computer viruses that certain systemic processes are self-replicating and "contagious," behaving almost willfully even though they are quite impersonal. Anyone who has lost computer files to a virus knows how personal this feels. For the present, I have set aside the question of the actual status of these Powers, and instead have attempted to describe what it was that people in ancient times were *experiencing* when they spoke of "Satan," "demons," "powers," "angels," and the like.

For instance, we might think of "demons" as the actual spirituality of systems and structures that have betrayed their divine vocations. When an entire network of Powers becomes integrated around idolatrous values, we get what can be called *the Domination System*. From this perspective, "Satan" is the world-encompassing spirit of the Domination System. Do these entities possess actual metaphysical *being*, or are they the "corporate personality" or ethos of an institution or epoch, having no independent existence apart from their incarnation in a system? That is for the reader to decide. My main objection to personalizing demons is that by doing so, we give them a "body" or form separate from the physical and historical institutions through which we experience them. I prefer, therefore, to regard them as the impersonal spiritual realities at the center of institutional life.

Think, for example, of a riot at a championship soccer game. For a few frenzied minutes, people who in their ordinary lives behave on the whole quite decently suddenly find themselves bludgeoning and even killing opponents whose only sin was rooting for the other team. Afterward people often act bewildered and wonder what could have possessed them. Was it a "riot demon" that leapt upon them from the sky, or was it something intrinsic to the social situation: a "spirituality" that crystallized suddenly, caused by the conjunction of an outer permissiveness, heavy drinking, a violent ethos, a triggering incident, and the inner violence of the fans? And when the riot subsides, does the "riot demon" rocket back to heaven, or does the spirituality of the rioters simply dissipate as they are scattered, subdued, or arrested?

Or take a high school football team. Its team spirit is high during the season, then cools at the season's close, although it does persist to a degree in history (memories) and hope (the coming season). Similarly, the spirit of a nation endures beyond its actual rule in the lasting effects of its policies, its contributions to culture, and its additions to the sheer weight of human suffering.

None of these "spiritual" realities has an existence independent of its material counterpart. None persists through time without embodiment in a people or a culture or a regime or a corporation or a dictator. An ideology, for example, is invisible, but it does not just float in the air; it is always the justification for some actual group, be it the AFL-CIO or General Motors, Greenpeace, or the oil industry. As the soul of systems, the Powers in their spiritual aspect are everywhere around us. Their presence is inescapable. The issue is not whether we "believe" in them but whether we can learn to identify them in our actual, everyday encounters. The apostle Paul called this the gift of discerning spirits. When a particular Power becomes idolatrous — that is, when it pursues a vocation other than the one for which God created it and makes its own interests the highest good — then that Power becomes demonic. The spiritual task is to unmask this idolatry and recall the Powers to their created purposes in the world. But this can scarcely be accomplished by individuals. A group is needed — what the New Testament calls an *ekklesia* (assembly) — one that exists specifically for the task of recalling these Powers to their divine vocation. That was to be the task of the church, "so that through the church *(ekklesia)* the wisdom of God in its rich variety might now be made known to the rulers and authorities ['principalities and powers'] in the heavenly places" (Eph. 3:10). And the church must perform this task despite its being as fallen and idolatrous as any other institution in society.

There is a growing recognition, even among secular thinkers, of the spiritual dimension of corporate entities. Terence Deal, for example, has written a text for businesses entitled *Corporate Cultures,* and other analysts have discerned the importance of a business's symbolic system and mission as clues to enhancing its efficiency. The corporate spirits of IBM and General Electric are palpably real and strikingly different, as are the national spirits of the United States and Canada. What distinguishes the notion of the angel of an institution is the Bible's emphasis on vocation. The angel of a corporate entity is not simply the sum total of all it is, but also bears the message of what it ought to be.

It has recently become stylish to develop mission statements for institutions. But a sense of mission implies a sender, just as a vocation ("calling") implies one who calls. The biblical understanding is that no institution exists as an end in itself, but only to serve the common good. The principalities and powers themselves are created in and through and for Christ, according to Colossians 1:16, which means that they exist only on behalf of the humanizing purposes of God revealed by Jesus — and by all others who were in touch with that divine reality as well.

Many business and corporation executives ignore God's humanizing purposes, and speak rather of profit as the "bottom line." But this is a capitalist heresy. According to the eighteenth-century philosopher of capitalism Adam Smith, businesses exist to serve the general welfare. Profit is the means, not the end. It is the reward a business receives for serving the general welfare. When a business fails to serve the general welfare, Smith insisted, it forfeits its right to exist. It is part of the church's task to remind corporations and businesses that profit is *not* the "bottom line," that as creatures of God they have as their divine vocation the achievement of human well-being (Eph. 3:10). They do not exist for themselves. They were bought with a price (Col. 1:20). They belong to the God who ordains sufficiency for all.

The relevance of the Powers for an understanding of evil should by now be clear. Evil is not just personal but structural and spiritual. It is not simply the result of human actions, but the consequence of huge systems over which no individual has full control. Only by confronting the spirituality of an institution *and* its physical manifestations can the total structure be transformed. Any attempt to transform a social system without addressing both its spirituality and its outer forms is doomed to failure. Materialism knows nothing of an inner dimension, and so is blind to its effects.

Transforming the Powers

It is hard not to wonder if such massive institutions can really be transformed. If evil is so profoundly systemic, what chance do we have of bringing them into line with God's purposes for them? The answer to that question hinges on how we conceive of institutional evil. Are the Powers intrinsically evil? Or are some good? Or are they scattered all along the spectrum from good to evil? The answer seems to be: none of the above. Rather, they are at once good and evil, though to varying degrees, and they are capable of improvement. Put in stark simplicity:

> The Powers are good.
>
> The Powers are fallen.
>
> The Powers must be redeemed.

These three statements must be held together, for each by itself is not only untrue but downright mischievous. We cannot affirm governments or universities or businesses as good unless at the same time we recognize that they are fallen. We cannot face their oppressiveness unless we remember that they are also a part of God's good creation. And reflection on their creation and fall will seem to legitimate these Powers and blast any hope for change unless we assert, at the same time, that these Powers can and must be redeemed. But focus on their redemption will lead to utopian disillusionment unless we recognize that their transformation takes place within the limits of the fall.

This theological framework is of utmost importance for understanding the nature of the Powers. They are good by virtue of their creation to serve the humanizing purposes of God. They are all fallen, without exception, because they put their own interests above the interests of the whole. And they can be redeemed, because what fell in time can be redeemed in time. We must view this schema as both temporal and simultaneous, in sequence and all at once. Temporally: the Powers *were* created, they *are* fallen, and they *shall be* redeemed. This can be asserted as belief in the final triumph of God over the forces of evil. But this schema is also simultaneous: God at one and the same time *upholds* a given political or economic system, since some such system is required to support human life; *condemns* that system insofar as it is destructive of fully human life; and *presses for its transformation* into a more humane order. Conservatives stress the first, revolutionaries the second, reformers the third. The Christian is expected to hold together all three.

An institution may place its own good above the general welfare. A corporation may cut corners on costs by producing highly inflammable infant sleepwear that endangers children's lives. Union leadership may become more preoccupied with expanding its own powers and prerogatives than fighting for better working conditions for the rank and file. The point is not that anything goes, but that no matter how greedy or idolatrous an institution becomes, it cannot escape the encompassing care and judgment of the One in and through and for whom it was created (Col. 1:16). In that One "all things hold together" (Col. 1:17 — literally, "receive their systemic place"; *synistēmi* is the Greek source of our word *system*). The Powers are inextricably locked into God's system, whose human face is revealed by Jesus. They are answerable to God. And that means that every subsystem in the world is, in principle, redeemable. Nothing is outside the redemptive care and transforming love of God. The Powers are not intrinsically evil; they are only fallen. Fallen does not mean depraved, as some Calvinists alleged. It simply refers to the fact that our existence is not our essence: we are, none of us, what we are meant to be. We are alienated from God, each other, nature, and our own souls, and cannot find the way back by ourselves. But the situation is not without hope, for what sinks can be made to rise again.

We may pollute our water supply and the air we breathe with no concern for the future. But we are systemically inseparable from the ecosystem, and there comes a point of irreversibility when the toxic wastes we dump become our own drink, and we come under the "judgment" of the ecosystem. No subsystem that attempts to rival the status of God's system itself can last very long. The story of Satan's rebellion and expulsion from heaven symbolically depicts the fate of any creature that lusts after ultimate power and authority.

By acknowledging that the Powers are good, bad, and salvageable — all at once — we are freed from the temptation to demonize those who do evil. We can love our enemies or nation or church or school, not blindly, but critically, calling them back time and again to their own highest self-professed ideals and identities. We can challenge institutions to live up to the vocation that is theirs from the moment they were created. We can oppose their actions while honoring their necessity.

We must be careful here. To assert with Colossians 1:15-20 that God created the Powers does not imply that God endorses any particular Power at any given time. God did not create capitalism or socialism, but human life requires some kind of economic system. Some institutions and ideologies such as Nazism or sexism can be transformed only by being abandoned or destroyed and replaced by forms of governance or gender relations that are more true to God's intent. But the necessary social function they have idolatrously perverted will abide. Germany still needed a government; men and women still need ways to relate.

To say that the Powers are created in, through, and for the humanizing purposes of God, then, does not imply divine endorsement of systems that have been overcome by evil (such as the American prison system). It is God's plan for human beings to cooperate in fulfilling basic needs. To this end God wills that there be subsystems whose sole purpose is to serve human need (we need *some* way of protecting society from sociopathic criminals).

Naming the Powers identifies our experiences of these pervasive forces that dominate our lives. Unmasking the Powers takes away their invisibility, and thus their capacity to coerce us unconsciously into doing their bidding. Engaging the Powers involves joining in God's endeavor to bend them back to their divine purposes.

The good news is that God not only liberates us from the Powers, but liberates the Powers from their destructive behavior as well. Their evil is not intrinsic but the result of idolatry. Therefore they can be redeemed. Even when they veer off course from their created vocations, the Powers are incapable of separating themselves from the divine order. Subsystems may violate the harmony of the whole system by elevating their own purposes above all others, but they cannot separate themselves from the larger order of things — any more than cancer can live apart from its host. And like a cancer, the Powers are able to do evil only by means of processes embedded in them as a result of their good creation. Even gangs manifest the human need for security, support, and love.

The task of redemption is not restricted to changing individuals, then, but also to changing their fallen institutions. That redemption will culminate in the salvation, not just of people, but of their nations as well. Thus, according to the vision of the New Jerusalem in Revelation 21:24-26, the nations come marching into the holy city, bearing their gifts to humankind. Awaiting them there is the Tree of Life, whose leaves are "for the healing of the nations" (Rev. 22:2). Personal redemption cannot take place apart from the redemption of our social structures.

Redemption means actually being liberated from the oppression of the Powers, being forgiven for both one's own sin and for complicity with the Powers, and setting about liberating the Powers themselves from their bondage to idolatry. The good news is nothing less than a cosmic salvation, a restitution of all things (Acts 3:21), when God will "gather up all things in [Christ], things in heaven and things on earth" (Eph. 1:10). This universal rectification will entail both a healing and subordination of rebellious structures, systems, and institutions to their rightful places, in service to the One in and through and for whom they exist. The gospel, then, is not a message about the salvation of individuals *from* the world, but news about a world transfigured, right down to its basic structures.

The Powers That Be are good creations of God (as we are), are fallen (as we are), and can be redeemed (as we can be). They are creatures like us — at once magnificent and abysmal, beneficial and harmful, indispensable and unendurable. If they were each isolated from the other, we might approach their transformation piecemeal, one at a time. Unfortunately, they are linked together in a bewilderingly complex network, in what we can call the Domination System. In that system, even Powers that directly compete with each other for territory or markets preserve the system by the very interactions by which they try to destroy each other. Like a massive family system, no institution or organization is allowed to "get better" without repercussions from other, more pathological Powers. The Domination System does not permit deviations from its values. If we are to take seriously the redemption of the Powers, we must follow their track into the labyrinth of the Domination System.

VII. Gender and Race

Introduction

Emilie M. Townes

The readings for this section provide a window into contemporary black theology and feminist theologies. Feminist theologies encompass a wide arena: white feminist, womanist, *mujerista,* lesbian, Asian and Asian American, Two-Thirds world, and more. The four readings in feminist theologies display the common themes of patriarchy, ecclesiology, worship, and the importance of women's experience and context in theological discourse and imagination. Isasi-Díaz and Williams note the inadequacies of white Western middle-class-based feminism in addressing the diversity of women's experiences based on race and class. Williams develops a new term, "demonarchy," to highlight the distinct history and experiences of black women in a patriarchal society. Isasi-Díaz focuses on *lo cotidiano* to do the same for Latinas.

These essays are representative of a large body of work produced by feminist theologians and bookmark the conversation among feminists in the 1980s and 1990s. Ruether's work spans her contemporaries (e.g., Letty Russell and Elisabeth Schüssler-Fiorenza), second-generation theologians (e.g., Susan Brooks Thistlethwaite and Mary McClintock Fulkerson), and third-generation feminist theologians (e.g., Laurel Schneider and Jennifer Harvey). Williams joins Katie Geneva Cannon and Jacqueline Grant as foundational figures in womanist thought. Second-generation womanist theologians include M. Shawn Copeland and Kelly Brown Douglas. Third-generation womanist theologians include Monica Coleman and Dianne Stewart. The Asian women's conference statement is representative of such key figures as Chung Hyun Kyung and Nam-Soon Kang (South Korea),

Aruna Gnanadason (India), and Kwok Pui-lan (Hong Kong). It presages the emergence of Asian American feminist theologians such as Rita Nakashima Brock and Nami Kim. Isasi-Díaz's work is in conversation with Latina feminist theologians such as María Pilar Aquino (Roman Catholic) and Daisy Machado (Protestant) as well as the *mujerista* theologian Yolanda Tarango.

Cone's and Carter's contributions to this section form a call and response as Carter's essay responds to Cone's call for contemporary black theologians to develop a more rigorous and integrative racial analysis in their work as a theological project. Their contributions are joined by Victor Anderson, Dwight Hopkins, Peter Paris, Anthony Pinn, and Cornel West. Jonathan Walton and Sylvester Johnson represent the younger generation of black theologians. Each thinker recognizes the deeply theological character of race and racism and the social impact that the failure to recognize this wreaks historically and in the contemporary theological imagination.

Rosemary Radford Ruether is a leading Roman Catholic feminist theologian. The excerpt from her classic text in feminist theology, *Sexism and God-Talk* (1984), was the first systematic treatment of Christian symbols and doctrines. Ruether employs a dialectical approach to expose repressed elements of the Christian tradition and moves beyond these to form a new synthesis that is the core of an alternative worldview of a new society. The critical norm of this dialectical approach is the prophetic strand of biblical faith (Hebrew prophets) and Jesus' critique of dominant power systems that ultimately promotes women's full humanity.

The selection from Ruether's book focuses on her affirmation of the "equality of woman in the image of God and restoration of her full personhood in Christ" and her insistence that redemption in Christ has a social dimension that warns against individualizing and spiritualizing salvation and sin. Her working assumption is that feminist theology is the "dynamic unity of creation and redemption." She explores three forms of feminism — liberal, socialist, and radical — to answer the question, "Can we begin to envision a more comprehensive vision that encompasses all three traditions rather than sets them up as competitors of each other?" Not surprisingly, her answer is yes, and she argues for an integrated vision that includes liberal, socialist, and radical feminist traditions to help build a new society. However, she ends with a caution and a possibility: the caution is that this alternative vision eludes on a global scale because of the insufficient collective power of those already converted to an alternative vision; the possibility is that "The nucleus of the alternative world remains, like the Church (theologically, *as* the Church), harbingers and experimenters with new human possibilities within the womb of the old."

The 1987 Conference Statement excerpt is part of a 360-page report. The conference emerged from discussions in the Christian Conference of Asia (CCA) and the Ecumenical Association of Third World Theologians. Several women theologians, including the late Korean theologian Sun Ai Lee Park, played a key role. The report documents one of the early ecumenical gatherings of Asian Protestant and Catholic women. The conference design encouraged theologizing from one's own context in order to discover the liberating message of the Bible and Jesus' life and ministry. All participants were encouraged to analyze their own national situation, to examine the social, political, religious, cultural, and psychological aspects from a woman's perspective. The participants began by examining their contexts in South Asia, South East Asia, East Asia, and the Pacific (New Zealand, Australia, Indonesia, and Singapore). They then developed composite papers on theological topics that were presented to the plenary.

National reports comprise the first part of the document. The excerpt in this section is part of the second part of the document and addresses the theological topics of Asian women's spirituality, the Holy Spirit, Christ, Mary, and ecclesiology. These topics are taken up after an analysis of the impact of a culture of militarism, classism, racism, and castism that has spawned undemocratic governments in the region. Additionally, the attendees note the presence of international Western capitalism, the nuclear arms race, and war. These contextual realities are foundational for the institutionalized patriarchy that "underlie[s] even the apparently most democratic nations."

Delores S. Williams critiques black theology and feminist theology for ignoring the specific concerns of black women who must address the devastating impact of the interlocking oppressions of classism, racism, and sexism in their daily lives. Womanist thought introduces the importance of the influence and contributions of black women to black culture, black and feminist theologies, the black church, and society at large. Williams begins by exploring what is necessary for feminism to be "colorized" so that it speaks to black women's experiences in the U.S. She develops the term "demonarchy" to describe the overarching oppression in black women's lives. The roots of demonarchy are found in U.S. slavery, and it continues today in white-controlled U.S. institutions where racial and gender oppression affect black women and the economic well-being of black families. Williams's critique does not exempt white women. To the degree to which they are the beneficiaries of the privileges of whiteness, white women participate in the creation and maintenance of demonarchy.

Her understanding of ecclesiology is found in the ways in which she addresses black worship and biblical foundations for the church's mission. Williams argues that the black church must cast out social, political, economic, and spiritual demonic rule within the church in the lives of its members. For her, the demonic is socio-political-spiritual, and its "social organization based upon racist-gender oppression, economic oppression, and the oppression of the human spirit does not intend merely to maim. It intends to destroy the very lives of black women and black peoplehood." The black church must recognize that it is in an encounter with radical evil and discard black male imitations of white manhood and patriarchy and embrace the equality of men and women inclusively.

The excerpt from Ada María Isasi-Díaz is the first comprehensive statement of *mujerista* theology's method. Like Williams, she addresses feminist theology's inability to deal with difference, to share power equally, or to understand the intersection of racism/ethnic prejudice, classism, and sexism, and its apparent rejection of liberation as its goal, replacing it instead "with limited benefits for some women within present structures, benefits that necessitate some groups of women and men to be oppressed in order for some others to flourish."

Isasi-Díaz, a Cuban-born Roman Catholic theologian, notes that *mujerista* theology emerges from a liberative praxis that enables Latinas to understand the daily oppressive structures they must contend with, the centrality of eschatology in the life of every Christian, and how they have internalized their own oppression. This leads to three distinctive characteristics: the "locus theologicus" of *mujerista* theology as *mestizaje* and *mulatez* (the racial and culture mixture of U.S. Latino/as or Latinoas), *lo cotidiano* (the "stuff," the everyday of Latinas' lives) as its theological source, and *mujerista* theology as a particular kind of liberation theology with its focus on praxis and popular religion. She concludes with the various challenges *mujerista* theology poses to traditional theologies in terms of epistemological vigilance, theology as communal task, and the importance of differences.

The essay by James Cone begins with a brief intellectual autobiography that contextualizes his work and explains how the civil rights and black power movements woke him from his "theological slumber." Long critical of white supremacy and the ways in which white politicians and ministers colluded to suppress black folk, of the anti-intellectualism of many black churches, and of the uncritical faith they espouse, Cone believes that the black experience is a valid starting point for theology. His work is distinguished for its passionate and precise anger at the silence of white theologians regarding racism and their failure to recognize that critiquing racism is "just as crucial for the integrity of Christian theology as any critique in the modern world," and he finds it amazing that, given the prevalence and violence of racism in the U.S., this theme remains absent from white theological discourse.

He is also critical of the failure of black theologians to develop a thorough racial critique of the sort of Christian theology that makes it impossible to do theology without engaging in white supremacy. Although he is appreciative of the recent work of womanists, second-generation black male theologians, biblical scholars, and historians, his concern remains. Ending the silence of white and black theologians regarding racism is crucial for Cone, and in particular, the challenge of black theology for the twenty-first century is to develop an integrated, comprehensive, and enduring theological critique that makes it impossible to forget the "horrible crimes of white supremacy in the modern world."

J. Kameron Carter's excerpt takes up Cone's challenge to contemporary black theologians. Carter explores how race, religion, and the modern state form civil society and public culture. He does so by showing the connection between race and the Jewish question in modernity to reveal how race is a religious problem and therefore theopolitical because it is tied to modern politics and to what is religious in modernity. In exploring how theology has influenced and continues to influence how humanity becomes racialized and a part of empire-building (his discussion of sovereignty in the excerpt), Carter takes up Cone's challenge by arguing that theology reconstituted itself to establish race as the defining characteristic of modernity. Contemporary racial reasoning has emerged as a result of severing Christianity's Jewish roots such that the modern West began to see Jews as an alien and inferior race that is the adversary of Christianity.

Carter turns to Michel Foucault to reveal the deep structure of modern racial reasoning "by raising the question of race, religion, and the mythical, even as he reinscribed the structural logic of the problem at the point where these lines intersect on the theological meaning of Jewish existence in the modern world." Appealing to Foucault's understanding of biopower (how a state can exert total control over its constituents), biohistory (the pressures through which the movements of life and the processes of history interfere with one another), and counterhistory (history that follows the usual progressive, linear, memory model), Cameron underscores the mythology that upholds modernity. However, he notes that Foucault's genealogy joins Cornel West's genealogy in *Prophesy Deliverance* (1982) in not going far enough because both do not fully engage the theological in their genealogies of modernity and racial discourse.

The thinkers in this section offer a challenging set of questions for the contemporary reader.

- Why should colonialism, racism, sexism, and other forms of oppression and empire building be considered theological problems? Traditional forms of theology separate theological categories and social categories. Black and feminist theologies systematically challenge this false dualism and suggest that there is little in a creation shaped by God that falls outside of a robust and inclusive theological imagination.
- How do we sort out the moral ambiguities of contemporary life? Clearcut decisions fade before a world of multiple options that are both viable and just. The theologies in this section stress this in varying ways and suggest that personhood is a vital starting point for us to face our moral options today.
- Is difference a problem or a gift? In a theological and moral universe that is often built on an either/or dichotomy, the theologies represented in this section suggest that we will be better served to think in terms of both/and. These theologies suggest the need to develop a usable theology that can respond to the daily challenges we face as not only sociopolitical but deeply theoethical.
- Is the search for questions to help us create a more just world as important as finding the answers to our questions? Rather than posing the answer to this question as either/or, it may be that we need to recognize that it is just as important to be able to formulate and ask the questions about the nature of injustices and various forms of oppression in our world as it is to find the answers to them and implement the answers to these questions.

27 The New Earth: Socioeconomic Redemption from Sexism

Rosemary Radford Ruether

Christianity has, in its New Testament foundations, traditions that would affirm the equality of woman in the image of God and the restoration of her full personhood in Christ. But even the primarily marginalized traditions that have affirmed this view through the centuries have not challenged the socioeconomic and legal subordination of women. Equality in Christ has been understood to apply to a new redeemed order beyond creation, to be realized in Heaven. Even when anticipated on earth, equality in Christ is confined to the monastery or the Church, the eschatological community. Patriarchy as order of nature or creation remains the underlying assumption of mainstream and radical Christianity alike. If woman becomes equal as virgin, prophetess, martyr, mystic, or even preacher, it is because these roles are seen as gifts of the Spirit and harbingers of a transcendent order. Only with the Enlightenment is there a shift to an egalitarian concept of "original nature" that challenges the "naturalness" of hierarchical social structures.

The claim that redemption in Christ has a social dimension has come about in modern Christianity only by an identification of its inherited messianic symbols with their secular interpretation in liberalism and socialism. But this new consciousness is still under continuous challenge by conservative Christians who seek to invalidate any theology, whether from a feminist, class, or racial minority perspective, that would make socioeconomic liberation an intrinsic part of the meaning of redemption. Such Christians would claim that redemption is a purely spiritual matter and has nothing to do with socioeconomic changes.

This individualizing and spiritualizing of salvation is the reverse side of the individualizing of sin. Sin is recognized only in individual acts, not structural systems. One is called to examine one's sinfulness in terms of abuses of oneself and personal unkindness to one's neighbor, but not in terms of the vast collective structures of war, racism, poverty, and, least of all, the oppression of women. In more sophisticated circles, Reinhold Niebuhr's division between "moral man" and "immoral society" is used to declare that altruism and love is possible, if at all, only on the interpersonal level. Collective groups, especially large ones, like nation-states, can only pursue an ethic of self-interest.

This "realism" is distorted by neoconservatives into an attack on any effort to create a more just society as fanatical and utopian. Liberation theology is condemned as a "heretical" effort to transcend the limits of historical existence, as though the present Western capitalist society represented the "limits" of historical existence and the "best of all possible worlds."[1] Such thinking neglects the early Niebuhr for whom such reflections on human limits are also an effort to find a solid basis for building a more just society. Niebuhr's working model of a more just society was democratic socialism. And he did not hesitate to think that even violent revolution might be ethically justified, at times, to break chains of colonial oppression and bring about the basis for such a new possibility.[2]

The working assumption of this feminist theology has been the dynamic unity of creation and redemption. The God/ess who underlies creation and redemption is One. We cannot split a spiritual, antisocial redemption from the human self as a social being, embedded in sociopolitical and ecological systems. We must recognize sin precisely in this splitting and deformation of our true relationships to creation and to our neighbor and find liberation in an authentic harmony with all that is incarnate in our social, historical being. Socioeconomic humanization is indeed the outward manifestation of redemption.

The search for the good self and the good society exists in an unbreakable dialectic. One cannot neglect either side. One cannot assume, with Marxism, that new, just social institutions automatically will produce the "new humanity." But one also cannot suppose that simply building up an aggregate of converted individuals will cause those individuals to act differ-

---

1. Peter L. Berger, *Pyramids of Sacrifice: Political Ethics and Social Change* (New York: Basic Books, 1974). See also Dennis P. McCann, *Christian Realism and Liberation Theology* (Maryknoll, NY: Orbis, 1981).

2. Reinhold Niebuhr, *Moral Man and Immoral Society: A Study in Ethics and Politics* (New York: Scribner's, 1932).

ently, changing society without any attention to its structures. The sensitized consciousness causes individuals to band together to seek a transformed society, and new and more just social relations cause many people to act and become different.

In this chapter I examine different traditions of feminist liberation, specifically liberal, socialist, and radical feminism. I summarize the main aspects of each perspective and also the limits that seem to appear in each. We will ask on the socioeconomic level the question that we have asked on anthropology: Can we begin to envision a more comprehensive vision that encompasses all three traditions rather than sets them up as competitors of each other?

Liberal Feminism

Liberal feminism has its roots in a feminist appropriation of the liberal traditions of equal rights, rooted in the doctrine of a common human nature of all persons. The liberal feminist agenda has been focused on the historic exclusion of women from access to and equal rights in the traditional male public sphere. It has sought to dismantle the historic structure of patriarchal law that denied women civil rights as autonomous adults. It has sought the full equality of women before the law, as citizens. This has entailed the repeal of discriminatory laws that denied property rights to married women especially, under the common-law rubric that the married woman was "civilly dead" and that her husband was her legal representative.

The apex of the campaign for autonomous civil status was suffrage, the granting of the vote to women, which also opened up all other political rights under the Constitution, such as the holding of political office. Another major emphasis of liberal feminism has been in the educational and professional spheres. Women sought full access to higher education, which historically had been denied to them. Education was seen both as an expression of women's human right to develop their intellectual potential and also as the key to all those professions of power and profit that men monopolized by denying women educational credentials and licenses, particularly law, medicine, and the ministry. Liberal feminists also sought to change marriage laws: Loss of property rights in marriage and inequitable divorce and child custody laws were areas of early and continuing concern.[3]

3. Eleanor Flexner, *Century of Struggle: The Woman's Rights Movement in the United States* (New York: Atheneum, 1972).

Twentieth-century liberal feminism has taken this quest for equal rights further: equal pay for equal work, equal access to all levels of a profession once women are admitted to it, the breaking down of formal and informal structures of power by which women in professions are excluded from top leadership roles. Caucuses within every profession spring up to examine these structures and act as advocates and networks of power and communication.

Liberal feminism has also turned to the whole underside of male control over women's bodies which nineteenth-century feminists only began to question: women's right to reproductive self-determination, sex education, birth control, and abortion. It has focused on women's right to dignity and control over their sexual persons, against sexual harassment on the job, wife battering in the home, rape in the streets (or home), and pornography, which dehumanizes the cultural imagination about women. Lesbianism also has achieved its place in the liberal feminist agenda, although not without considerable stress. Liberalism defines the lesbian as a "minority" person who should not be denied human and civil rights because of sexual preference.

The consistent pursuit of the liberal feminist agenda of equal rights continually pushes the limits of liberalism itself. Zillah Eisenstein, in *The Radical Future of Liberal Feminism*,[4] shows how the pursuit of the egalitarian claims by women continually transcends and challenges the limits of the patriarchal-capitalist system. The search for equality for women cannot be accommodated within this system, and consistent liberal feminists come increasingly to recognize the need to transform fundamentally the larger system.

In the socioeconomic sphere, liberal feminism begins to analyze the basic inequality of women in the economic hierarchy of paid labor and also the interconnections between women's work role in the home and the treatment of women on the job. Corporate capitalism treats women as a marginal labor force to be hired when needed and fired at will. In times of expanding industrialization, women were needed to work in factories and they were exploited with low pay and miserable working conditions. But more advanced industrialism, with a shrinking need for labor-intensive production, allies with "reform" measures that aim at removing women from the labor force and returning them to the home as their "true sphere."[5]

4. Zillah R. Eisenstein, *The Radical Future of Liberal Feminism* (New York: Longman, 1981).

5. Walter Rauschenbusch, *Christianizing the Social Order* (New York: Macmillan, 1912), pp. 413-14.

Likewise, in wartime all the ideological media of communication of society reverse their usual messages and call women to become truck drivers and workers in heavy industry, to fill the empty seats in the universities, and even the pulpits, as their "patriotic duty." But when the war is over the old messages return. Women are told to go home, to make room for the returning males who have prior rights to the jobs, and to produce babies to replace the slaughtered population.

Women in the work force are confined primarily to a female job ghetto. The kinds of work women do at home condition fundamentally the work to which they are directed in the paid labor force. Child care, nursery school and primary school teaching, food service, office maintenance — all this is women's work, although men may act as managers in more sophisticated and prestigious versions of such work. Above all, women have become the clerical workers of advanced industrialism, coping with the vast piles of paperwork and communication systems that hold this global apparatus together. They do the rote labor of the paper and electronic empire but have almost no input or control over its content. The male executive elite stands on a vast pyramid of female labor: file clerks, "charwomen," and, finally, their own wives, who free them for exclusive attention to decision making. The richer and more powerful the executive, the higher and more intricate the pyramid of class-, race-, and gender-based division of labor that supports his power and profits.

Female work in this system is typically poorly paid and has little job security. It is the least likely to be protected by unions or secure contracts. Perhaps no more than ten percent of women work in what are considered professional occupations, but even these are often segregated as female professions. Nurses, teachers, medical technicians, and librarians receive much lower remuneration than men in comparable positions demanding a similar level of specialization and education. A tiny number, about three percent, of women work in the prestigious male professions: university professor, lawyer, doctor, minister. Here, too, women are generally found to have lower rank and poorer pay.[6]

Women in the United States achieved their largest percentages in the male professions between 1900 and 1920, and their numbers declined thereafter. Only with the spectacular efforts of the feminist revival in the late 1960s to the present have their proportional numbers in these professions

---

6. Eleanor Leacock, "History, Development and the Division of Labor by Sex: Implications for Organization," *Signs* 7, no. 2 (Winter 1981): 474-91.

begun to equal what they were in 1920! Thus, despite all appearances of women crowding into law, medical, and theological schools, graduate departments of science, and so on, the economic structure of industrial capitalism is one of pervasive, structural discrimination against women.

Women's work role in the home both doubles the burden and reinforces the stereotype of women's low status on the job. Despite recent adjustments in dual-career marriages, in which men seek to share housekeeping and childraising, the structure and culture of corporate industrialism are deeply set against allowing them to do so. Despite all goodwill, men seldom have any real understanding of the extent and complexity of the work that goes into homemaking. Women are so socialized to feel they have to do this work (and men to think they don't have to do it) that they generally find it easier to do most of it themselves rather than expend the emotional energy trying to get men (or children) to do their share. Males tend to assume that if they have picked up a child from nursery school once a week, wiped the dishes, and helped with the shopping, they have "shared" housework.

Statistical studies of women's domestic work continue to show that when women work, they still do almost all the housework. The housework is simply squeezed into the after-hours and less is done.[7] This adds to a woman's sense of harassment since she feels constantly responsible for a sector of work that she cannot accomplish adequately. This is not simply a matter of her own psychology, because the culture constantly scapegoats married working women as the cause of a variety of social problems, from homosexuality to juvenile delinquency, because they are not full-time mothers and homemakers.

This "second shift" of domestic work also fundamentally mitigates women's equality in the paid work force, in three ways. First, the psychological and cultural model of women's work in the home creates a model of women's work on the job that makes men hostile to women's equality with them in the same type of work. Second, women's time commitments to domestic work prevent them from putting in extra time after hours for travel, education, and committee work, which advance people in the meritocracy. Third, the first two factors shut women out of the networks of communication that are used to compete on the job.

The ideology of equal rights obscures as much as it aids women's real equality. Official liberalism may have won all the laws on the books that ap-

7. Heidi Hartmann, "The Family as the Locus of Gender, Class and Political Struggle: The Example of Housework," *Signs* 6, no. 3 (Spring 1981): 366-94.

pear to grant women full equality. It is very hard to uncover the actual structures that prevent this in practice and that relegate women to low-paid and low-status sectors of the work force. Appearances justify the impression that women simply don't have the "drive" to achieve equality with men. The hidden work role of women masks the fact that women have to work at least half again as hard as men in order to be "equal" in this system.

Zillah Eisenstein argues that these contradictions between the liberal ideology of equality and the structures of job hierarchy and the double work shift that prevent equality give rise to the radicalization of liberal feminism. The more women analyze these contradictions, the more they realize their inability to achieve this equality within the structures of capitalism. A fundamental transformation of the work structures both in the home and in the paid labor force is necessary. Only socialist feminism provides tools for analyzing these contradictions and envisions a new system that might solve them. Liberal feminism and socialist feminism are not in irreconcilable conflict, however. The logical and social contradictions of liberal feminism lead to its transformation into socialist feminism.

One should not assume that those operating within a liberal feminist perspective will automatically be led in this direction. The traditional complaint of socialist feminists against liberal feminism was that its ideology and practice are encapsulated within the class interests of the bourgeois. Liberal feminists sought political rights and educational and professional roles within the same framework as male roles of their own class. But they seldom realized the very different concerns of working-class women, racial minority women, and poor women, who were shut out of exercising class-based "rights." This bias came out clearly in the later phases of the suffrage struggle in the late nineteenth century when a sizable part of the movement switched from arguing for the vote on the basis of equal rights to arguing for it on the basis of "expediency." It was said that middle-class Anglo-Saxon women had the education and culture to exercise the vote "properly." To give it to them would double the vote of the "responsible citizens" (WASP middle class). This drift took place at a time when blacks and immigrants were being disenfranchised by Jim Crow and literacy laws.[8]

Women always occupy two interlocking kinds of social status. As a gender, all women are marginalized and subjugated relative to males. But as members of class and race hierarchies, women occupy class levels compara-

8. Eileen Kraditor, *The Ideas of the Woman's Suffrage Movement, 1880-1920* (New York: Norton, 1980).

ble to, although as secondary members of, their class and race. Any strategy of women's liberation must recognize the interface and contradictions between these two ways of determining women's social status. Marginalization as women can lead to a sense of cross-class and cross-race solidarity of women along lines of common gender discrimination. But women's membership in class and race hierarchies can draw women into a primary identification with the males of their class and race, against women and men of other classes and races.

White middle-class women are tempted to compensate for gender discrimination by using women of the lower class to do their "women's" work, thereby freeing themselves to compete as equals with men of their group. The dual-career family at upper executive levels is made possible by the affluence that can hire the housekeeper and the private secretary. This is then touted as the fulfillment of the promise of liberal feminism, although actually the economic position of the white upper middle class is being reinforced against women and men of lower classes and races. Such equality at affluent levels remains token. Its visibility and acclaim only serve to disaffect poor women, working-class women, minority women, and women as housewives from feminism. The glitter of feminist "equality," as displayed in *Cosmopolitan* and *Ms.*, both eludes and insults the majority of women who recognize that its "promise" is not for them.

Socialist Feminism

Is socialist feminism, then, the answer to the insufficiencies and limits of liberal feminism? Does one not have to lead liberal feminism explicitly to an analysis of the class contradictions of women under capitalism, rather than waiting for liberal feminism to "automatically" produce this radicalization? I believe this is the case. Yet socialist feminism also produces its own contradictions, some of them analogous to those of liberal feminism.

The tradition of socialist feminism goes back to the classic study by Friedrich Engels, *The Origin and History of the Family, Private Property and the State* (1884). Engels recognized that the ideology of woman as weak, timid, and incompetent was fundamentally a class myth of bourgeois society shaped to sanctify the family patterns of middle-class men who did not need their wives' labor in the work force. But working-class women had to go into the factories to provide income for the survival of their families, in a system of exploitative wages for working-class men and women. The woman who dragged coal carts in the mines or labored for ten hours a day at machines could not cultivate the pretenses of "feminine" delicacy, nor was she given the deference and protection of the "lady." This same woman returned from long hours at work only to take on a second work role in the family. In so doing, she exposed and contradicted the class-based myths of female weakness by her very ability to cope with these exhausting conditions.

The key to Marxist feminism, as developed by Engels and his successors, was the restoration of women to economic autonomy, under socialist conditions in which the exploitation of the proletariat had been abolished. Modern industrialization was in fact beginning this liberation of women by forcing working-class women into wage labor. But it was doing so under oppressive capitalist conditions. Under socialism, the means of production would be owned and managed by the workers themselves. Then women, along with men, as workers, would have an equal share in the fruits of their productive labor. Under these conditions, women as independent wage earners would be able to relate to men as equal partners, both on the job and within marriage. Economic independence, not simply civil rights, was seen as the key to women's liberation. Without economic independence under equal working conditions, the civil rights that liberal feminism would win — the rights to vote, to be educated, and to own property — remained class privileges.

Socialist and Communist governments, in practice, have carried through the basic outlines of this tradition of socialist feminism. On gaining power, such governments have legislated civil equality for women. They have dismantled the patriarchal laws that discriminated against women in marriage and divorce and that denied women political rights and access to education and employment. They have done this with the assumption that these rights are effective only within a socialist society in which women have full and equal employment with men. So the main socialist agenda has been to integrate women into the work force.[9]

Moreover, socialist societies have recognized that women cannot compete with men as equals as long as they are handicapped by the second shift of domestic work. They have tried to alleviate this handicap by socializing certain aspects of women's work. Most typically, this means state-supported daycare centers and nursery schools, which allow mothers to return to work within a year of childbearing. Maternity leave and guaranteed reentry to jobs

9. Sheila Rowbotham, *Women, Resistance and Revolution: A History of Women and Revolution in the Modern World* (New York: Random House, 1974), pp. 140-41, 185-86.

further compensate for women's work in reproduction. Some socialist societies have also experimented with collective laundries and kitchens. Low-cost or free contraceptives and abortions encourage planned childbearing.

All this represents a significant advantage for women in socialist societies in contrast to capitalist societies, which have resisted such efforts to alleviate women's domestic role by various appeals to the sanctity of the (patriarchal) family. The result is that the contradictions between women's work and domestic role are exacerbated and rendered chaotic, with a worsening of the very conditions of stress on the family that bourgeois patriarchy claims to deplore by blaming them on "working mothers."

Although socialism has ameliorated the handicap of women in industrial society, it has not fundamentally altered it. An analysis of women's work in socialist or communist societies shows that the same contradictions between unpaid domestic and low-paid wage labor continue. Despite the efforts of government to integrate women equally into the work force, women are still found at the lower levels of every job hierarchy, from politics to business to factory work. They receive lower pay and fewer benefits than men at the same level. The stereotype of women's inferiority persists, and men object to having a woman in a superior position.

Why is this? It has been concluded in various studies that the primary cause of this continuing inequality of women in communist societies is the double work burden of unpaid domestic labor. Women work approximately four hours a day more than men in order to provide domestic services. This second job sends women scurrying to shops (to stand in long lines), to nurseries, and to kitchens after work. By contrast, their male "peers" use this time to volunteer for political offices, to sit on factory committees, to take refresher courses, or to go to the gyms or bars where they win points in the meritocracy and forge the vital links with their male colleagues that advance them up the job ladder.

Women's second job has the same effects in socialist societies as in capitalist countries: preserving the stereotype of women as low-level workers under men, leaving women exhausted and unable to compete with men, and eliminating women from the after-hours roles by which men advance in the meritocracy. It would seem that patriarchy plus industrialism is the cause of this pattern. Socialism rationalizes, but does not fundamentally solve these contradictions.[10]

10. Hilda Scott, *Does Socialism Liberate Women? Experiences from Eastern Europe* (Boston: Beacon Press, 1974), pp. 191-208.

The answer of socialist feminism has been to analyze women's domestic work role as a major source of gender-based "class structure." As long as women continue to carry a double work role, they cannot compete as equal with men in the paid labor force. But it is not clear that socialist feminism has an answer to this, except to extend further the socialization of women's domestic role. This means collective kitchens, collective laundries, collective housecleaning — indeed, the collectivization of housing altogether in dormitories that would abolish the home as a private space. Perhaps some socialists would even go further and imagine some technology that would alleviate women's role as childbearers with test-tube fertilizations and mechanical wombs.[11] Presumably, such technology would provide jobs well paid and shared by men and women alike.

But one must ask whether such a vision is the ultimate liberation or the ultimate enslavement. If collectivism means state control, then an abolition of the home would be the total alienation of one's life to institutions external to one's own control and governed by a managerial elite. In the name of the liberation of women, we would hand over the remnants of that self-employed and autonomous sphere of life where we own and control our own means of production — our reproductive organs, our kitchens, and so on.

Socialism, like liberalism, operates under an unstated androcentric bias. It assumes that the male work role is the normative human activity. Women are to be liberated by being incorporated into the male realm. Liberalism would extend to women the legal right to do so, while socialism would provide women with the economic capacity to take advantage of such rights. Both assume that women are liberated insofar as they are enabled to function like men in the public realm.

One must ask whether the dominant socialist traditions (democratic socialism and Marxism-Leninism) have not fundamentally misconstrued the socialist agenda of restoring ownership of the means of production to the people. In terms of factories and workplaces, this should mean giving ownership and management into the hands of local committees of workers, rather than making the workers employees of a state bureaucracy. Socialist ideology seems to contain a fundamental contradiction: It has seen itself as restoring ownership of the means of production to the people, while at the same time it continues the process of industrialization, that is, collectivization of work outside the home. It has identified ownership by the people with ownership by the state and management by the party bureaucracy. The

11. Shulamith Firestone, *Dialectic of Sex* (New York: Bantam, 1971), p. 11.

result has been a deepening of the alienation of people from their labor and the creation of a new ruling class, the party bureaucracy.

When the question of collectivization of work is applied to the remaining roles of women in the home, this issue becomes radicalized. Do we want to continue this process of further alienation of our life processes? Is it not necessary to imagine an entirely different model for socialization — namely, taking back to communalized households work functions that have been taken over by capitalist or state party managers? In this light, the work functions of women in the home appear as the remnants of a preindustrial world of home-based economy. In contrast to state socialism, communitarian or utopian socialism has understood socialism as the communalization of work on the base of a communal family. The split between home and work, women's work and men's work, is overcome by reintegrating them in a community that both raises its children collectively and owns and manages its own means of production. It is not accidental that feminists who have tried to imagine a reconstructed, nonsexist society have instinctively gravitated toward some form of the utopian socialist model rather than to state socialism.

Thus the feminist issue, when pursued within socialism, also seems to explode the limits of the dominant socialist traditions and to suggest that the feminist question cannot be solved within the limits of its system. Instead, we are forced to ask, in a much more fundamental way, the difference between women's role as childbearer and nurturer and the male economic and political role that has been defined over against it. Feminism needs to ask whether, instead of making the male sphere the human norm and attempting to assimilate women into it, it is not necessary to move in the opposite direction. Should we not take the creation and sustaining of human life as the center and reintegrate alienated maleness into it? This leads to the third tradition of feminism — radical feminism — which takes the gender division as primary and insists that women's liberation is first and foremost liberation from male domination.

Radical Feminism

For radical feminism the core issue is women's control over their own persons, their own bodies as vehicles of autonomous sexual experience, and their own reproduction. Patriarchy means, above all, the subordination of women's bodies, sexuality, and reproduction to male ownership and control. Rape, wife beating, sexual harassment, pornography, the ideologies, culture, and fashions that socialize women to becoming objects of male sexual control, the denial of birth control and abortion, and, ultimately, the denial of female initiation and control over sexual relations — all are ramifications of the fundamental nature of patriarchy, the expropriation of woman as body by man. Any theory of women's liberation that stops short of liberating women from male control over their bodies has not reached the root of patriarchy.

For many, the logic of this position leads to lesbian separatism. Women can't be liberated from patriarchy until they are liberated from men. Women need to see the community of women as their primary base. Women bonding together both in love relationships and for primary support, together with their (female?) children, is women's base and identity. It is on this base that feminism needs to build an alternative women's world. Women must question not only the ideologies of sexism but of heterosexism, that is, the basic assumption that men and women are naturally attracted to each other sexually and that male-female couples are necessary for human families.

In feminist utopian novels, ranging from Charlotte Perkins Gilman's *Herland* (1915)[12] to Sally Gearhart's *Wanderground,*[13] we have visions of a world of women liberated from men. Men are seen in these novels as alien to women, as creatures in some fundamental way inhuman. They are characterized by aggressive sexuality and domineering attitudes toward women and nature. Theirs is literally a "rape culture." In the feminist utopia, a select community of women have escaped from male control. Key to this is a recovery of love between women and, with it, the ability to reproduce independent of men. (This, in fact, is not biologically implausible. The male sperm acts to stimulate the female egg to start to divide and grow. It has been postulated that this could be done by another agent, such as another female egg, in which case all the offspring would be female.)[14]

The female utopia cultivates a women's culture. High values are placed on intuitive and poetic forms of communication and on mutuality and care

12. Charlotte Perkins Gilman, *Herland: A Lost Feminist Utopian Novel* (New York: Pantheon, 1979).

13. Sally Gearhart, *Wanderground: Stories of the Hill Women* (Watertown, MA: Persephone, 1979).

14. For discussion of uniparental female reproduction see D. G. Whittingham, "Parthenogenesis in Mammals," in *Oxford Review of Reproductive Biology,* ed. C. A. Finn (Oxford: Oxford University Press, 1980), pp. 205-31. Also see P. C. Hoppe and K. Illmensee, "Microsurgically Produced Homozygons — Diploid, Uniparental Mice," *Proceedings of the National Academy of Science, U.S.A.* 74, no. 12 (December 1977): 5657-61.

for the earth. Eden is restored. One might say that, with the ejection of men, evil is eliminated from human (female) relationships. But men still roam like beasts of prey outside the magic circle of women's world. Women must be constantly on guard against letting men into their good land of peace and plenty.

Various radical feminist writers have developed aspects of this separatist vision. Mary Daly concentrates on a passionate exposé of the inhumanity of males and their culture of rape, genocide, and war. The history of women becomes a trail of crucifixions, with males as the evil archons of an anticosmos where women are entrapped. For Daly, liberation for women is primarily spiritual. They discover an alternative land within their inner selves, then learn to communicate with a new language that breaks apart and transforms the dominant language. They escape together through the holes rent in the fabric of patriarchal ideology into a separate and higher realm of female interiority.[15] Daly's vision moves to a remarkable duplication of ancient Gnostic patterns, but now built on the dualism of a transcendent spirit world of femaleness over against the deceitful anticosmos of masculinity.[16]

Goddess religion represents a somewhat different movement, which may or may not be lesbian separatist. But in either case the dominant divine symbol is the Great Mother, linking Womanhood and Nature. Authentic humanity and the good earth reign under the sign of the Mother. Eden can be restored only by subordinating the male to the female. The horned God or male consort of the Goddess is not her equal, much less her "father," but her son-lover. Men, if they are accepted, must recognize their subordinate place in the female-centered world.[17] The male characteristics of linear thinking and objectification can be deprived of their evil-making tendencies only when assimilated into and under the female properties of love,

15. Mary Daly, *Beyond God the Father: Toward a Philosophy of Women's Liberation* (Boston: Beacon Press, 1973).

16. The pattern of Daly's thought moves increasingly toward a concept of the male as generically evil and thus necessarily generating evil structures. The atmosphere of Daly's thought is a kind of other-worldly incantation by which one demystifies and escapes out of the existing demonic male world. See *Gyn/Ecology: The Metaethics of Radical Feminism* (Boston: Beacon Press, 1979). This is strikingly similar to the mood and worldview of ancient Gnosticism. See Hans Jonas, *The Gnostic Religion: The Message of the Alien God and the Beginnings of Christianity* (Boston: Beacon Press, 1958), pp. 48-96.

17. Z. Budapest, *The Holy Book of Women's Mysteries,* parts 1 and 2 (Los Angeles: Susan B. Anthony Coven, No. 1, 1979, 1980). Naomi Goldenberg, *Changing of the Gods* (Boston: Beacon Press, 1979). Starhawk, *The Spiral Dance: The Rebirth of the Ancient Religion of the Goddess* (New York: Harper & Row, 1979).

mutual service, and intuitive knowledge. The suppressed powers of the human self are released to become the basis of a new culture and mode of relating and communicating.[18]

Other radical feminists concentrate more on the alternative social base for a women's world. They seek to build women's work collectives in which women are no longer dependent on male ownership and male hierarchical methods of organization of work. Such work collectives can be developed in urban settings in a variety of professions: women's health centers, law collectives, media collectives, and the like. The ultimate separatist vision moves toward the country collective, where women create an alternative, communitarian society. Here the women's community — as female bonding, family, culture, spirituality, and participatory, nonhierarchical ways of organizing — can flourish in an organic community.

Is this direction of radical feminism the ultimate vision of feminism? Do feminists who wish to be radical (to get to the root of patriarchy) and consistent necessarily have to break their ties with men and move into this separatist perspective? I believe that this stance, although attractive in many ways, is delusive. Women's affirmation of their own humanity as more fundamental than their sexist conditioning demands a like affirmation of the humanity of males. Separatism reverses male hierarchicalism, making women normative humanity and males "defective" members of the human species. This enemy-making of males projects onto males all the human capacities for competitive relations and ego-power drives and hence denies that women too possess these capacities as part of their humanity.

Such enemy-making of men would ultimately subvert the whole dream of a women's culture based on mutuality and altruism. The very process of projecting the negative part of their own psychic potential onto males, and failing to own these themselves, would tend to make such women's groups fanatical caricatures of that which they hate. The dehumanization of the other ultimately dehumanizes oneself. One duplicates evil-making in the very effort to escape from it once and for all, by projecting it on the "alien" group.

This does not mean that women's communes and collectives and lesbian families cannot exist as good human relationships, as well as experimental bases for an alternative humanity. One could indeed look to such communities as harbingers of an alternative culture of nonhierarchical relationships. But they can function in this way only when they do not wall

18. Starhawk, *The Spiral Dance*, pp. 21-22, 129-37.

themselves into a separatist ideology that identifies femaleness with goodness and maleness with evil and when they take responsibility for the ambiguity of their own humanity. On that basis we can then see the development
of women's culture and modes of organization as experiments on behalf of
humanity, male and female. We draw on capacities for mutuality that men
possess as well as women. We criticize tendencies toward egoism that women
possess as well as men. It is true that women, because of their relative powerlessness within history, have cultivated values and modes of relationships
that are less dehumanized than male culture. But the effort to imagine symbols and systems of life that draw on these must do so for the sake of liberating these capacities in men as well, on behalf of the whole of humanity.

Is There an Integrative Feminist Vision of Society?

The search for an integrative vision starts with the assumption that feminism must include the liberal, socialist, and radical traditions. Each of these
traditions shows its limitations precisely at the point where it tries to become final and to encapsulate itself within its own system. It remains insightful and authentic to the extent that it also remains open-ended. We have
seen how the insufficiencies of each perspective suggest the need for the others. Liberal feminism opens into the questions of the economic hierarchies
of work explored by socialist feminism. Radical feminism moves into an increasingly isolated, separatist utopianism that largely fails to address the real
possibilities of most women and men, and so calls for its reintegration back
into questions of social reorganization of mainstream society. Each of these
perspectives can provide a part of a larger whole to the extent that we refuse
the temptation to set up any one in a mutually exclusive relationship to the
others.

What is the society we seek? We seek a society that affirms the values of
democratic participation, of the equal value of all persons as the basis for
their civil equality and their equal access to the educational and work opportunities of the society. But more, we seek a democratic socialist society that
dismantles sexist and class hierarchies, that restores ownership and management of work to the base communities of workers themselves, who then create networks of economic and political relationships. Still more, we seek a
society built on organic community, in which the processes of childraising,
of education, of work, of culture have been integrated to allow both men
and women to share child nurturing and homemaking and also creative ac-

tivity and decision making in the larger society. Still more, we seek an ecological society in which human and nonhuman ecological systems have been
integrated into harmonious and mutually supportive, rather than antagonistic, relations.

There are two ways to imagine going about building this new society.
One is to build an alternative, communitarian system by a small voluntary
group with a high intentionality and consciousness. Such a group would
seek to put together all aspects of this feminist, socialist, communitarian,
and ecological vision in a small experiment conducted on a separate social
and economic base from the larger society. Such communal experiments
have been carried out within history. They can be reasonably successful in
fusing all aspects of the vision. Their limitation lies precisely in their inability to move beyond the small voluntary group and create a base for the larger
society.

A second method is to work on pieces of the vision separately: a communal child-care unit within an educational institution or workplace; an alternative energy system for an apartment building; solar greenhouses for a
neighborhood; a women's collective that produces alternative culture for the
society. We might develop within a self-managed institution less hierarchical
forms of organization, more equal remuneration for all workers, men and
women, regardless of their jobs. We might plan communities that allow
more humanized relationships between the various aspects of people's lives.
We might encourage a plurality of household patterns, homosexual as well
as heterosexual, voluntary as well as blood- and marriage-related, where
groups can share income and homemaking. We can think of these separate
pieces of a mosaic that we are putting in place, gradually replacing the present picture with a new vision.

But the alternative nonsexist, nonclassist and nonexploitative world
eludes us as a global system. This is not so much because of our inability to
imagine it correctly as because of the insufficient collective power of those
already converted to an alternative vision. The powers and principalities are
still very much in control of most of the world. The nucleus of the alternative world remains, like the Church (theologically, as the Church), harbingers and experimenters with new human possibilities within the womb of
the old.

28 Conference Statement from the 1987 Asian Women's Theology Consultation

We, 32 delegates from 16 countries in Asia, met in Singapore, November 20-29, 1987, and reflected prayerfully on theology in the light of our national and regional situations, especially the situation of women.

The Situation of Women in the Region

Many governments of the region claim to be democratic but are not authentically so. There is large-scale misuse of power at various levels, affecting the lives of the majority. Extremes of poverty and wealth, corruption, widespread unemployment, and oppression of minorities exist alongside one another. In many countries this has provoked organized revolt and confrontation from different sections of society. In some situations the government has assumed an increasingly repressive and authoritarian character by their use of law and courts or by their expansion of police and paramilitary apparatus. There is a culture of militarism alongside classism, racism, and castism.

The international operations of western capitalism intrude into our countries, as do the arms race and the threat of nuclear war.

All of these situations are the outcome of institutionalized patriarchy, and they underlie even the apparently most democratic nations.

Within this general situation, it is the women who suffer the most because of their sex and the restrictions culture places on women. They are oppressed in the church as well as in society. Often sexism is sanctioned by religion.

The exact form of sexism varies from country to country but within each culture women are marginalized in a number of ways. Sexism erupts into overt violence, e.g. in rape, domestic violence, sexual harassment, incest, prostitution, pornography, female feticide, infanticide, and sati. Customs like dowry can also lead to violence. Even in countries where discrimination against women is outlawed, customary attitudes to women mean that, as in other countries, women are less well educated than men in general, are given jobs of lower status, and receive lower income than men. Women often work in bad conditions. They often live in poverty. Higher education often does not lead to good jobs or higher income, and can lead to more demanding work and social expectations. The education of women is wasted instead of being used for development of society and church. Within both church and society, women are excluded from decision-making bodies, even when the matters they are considering affect women's lives directly.

Few churches actively encourage women to study theology. Women hold up the church and are most of the congregations, but the number of women in decision-making bodies and in theological colleges does not reflect the number of women in the church. Very few churches ordain women and the number of ordained women is still very small. Ordination of women has not led to structural change which is liberating to women. Until now, the church's theology has been done by men, and women's experience and spirituality have had no place in their work. The same is true of indigenous people who suffer colonization and invasion.

Emerging Asian Women's Spirituality

Asian women identify and define spirituality as faith experiences which motivate our thought processes and behavior patterns in relation to God and neighbor. Spirituality is awakened souls urging dignified humanhood.

Traditional spirituality was understood to be individualistic and inward looking. It is passive and distinguishes holy from the non-holy. In contrast, contemporary spirituality is integral, outgoing, community-oriented, active, holistic, and all-embracing.

The challenges of the new spirituality are manifested in our dying to ourselves in order to live for others. Feminist spirituality is prophetic and has a mission with commitment. It is born of a new vision. It challenges the technical, scientific, and capitalistic world. The new spirituality involves a change in this world so that Jesus Christ is incarnated in our lives enabling us to discover our own identity and strength. This strength enables women to struggle for their well-being and survival, for human rights, social justice, and peace; to participate in socio-political, economic, culture life, and decision-making processes; to struggle against the caste system and for equality of tribal and all oppressed people and structures. Feminist spirituality empowers us against sexism.

The Holy Spirit

The Trinitarian image of God gives us a great insight into the whole process of creation of the world with human beings made in God's image. The spirit is understood as the all-pervading presence and the moving force of God. The Holy Spirit in relation to women is a life-giving, comforting, liberating, and creative Spirit. It is a powerful Spirit who empowers women as individuals and also as community.

The Holy Spirit enables us to have a unitive vision of reality. From an inherited, male-dominant theology, we move to a theology of partnership in Asia, which in the true sense can be called an Asian Human Theology.

Women's Understanding of Christ

The Asian women's understanding of Jesus is that of one who transcends the evil order of patriarchy. Jesus is the prophetic Messiah, whose role is that of the suffering servant, who offers himself as a ransom for many. Through his suffering Messiahship, he creates a new humanity. In contrast is the classical view of God as male and of the Christ as the male image of God. In this traditional view, Jesus is a triumphal king and an authoritarian High Priest. This view has served to support a patriarchal religious consciousness in the church and theology. It has justified male dominance and perpetuated the subordinate status of women. The evil patriarchal order which subjugates and oppresses women in society is seen to operate also in the church. But women participate in the messianic prophetic role of Jesus through the suffering of oppressed women and through the solidarity and struggle of women who seek freedom from patriarchal structures.

Who Is Mary?

It is the task of all women to reclaim Mary and redefine her as liberator of oppressed people, especially women of all ages and cultures. We reject the distortion of Mary's identity which comes from male interpretation. We claim the right to liberate the church's teaching about Mary. The doctrine of the Virgin Birth has been used to oppress women. We understand that the real meaning of the Virgin Birth is the end of the patriarchal order. We reject this order in ourselves, our families, and church and society.

The Magnificat is a rallying point for women and for all denominations to work together with the poor and oppressed to overcome injustice. We believe in a new creation in which we all claim our full humanness. We must therefore overcome economic and political oppression in our own contexts as well as in First/Third World relationships.

In response to Mary, we commit ourselves to the work of creating new partnerships.

The Church

The church and its institutions have been heretical in discriminating against women, in being hierarchical in structure, and in not using the gifts which the Holy Spirit gives to all the members of the church. We challenge the church to show in its life that it believes the Gospel — that women as well as men are created in the image of God, that women as well as men are saved and set free by Jesus the Christ, and that because women and men are baptized into one Lord Jesus Christ, distinctions between men and women disappear and should not affect the life of the church. God calls the church to share in the struggle for liberation of all people, especially women. The church can only do so when it ceases to oppress its own members, and lets those of its members who suffer oppression in society direct its mission.

As Asian women our theological image of the church is a circle of God's people in which Jesus the Christ is the center. There are various inequalities in Asian society, based on sex, class, race, and the north-south divide. But in this circle, all the people are the same distance from Jesus Christ, guaranteeing full equality and human dignity. Jesus Christ being the Alpha and the Omega, this community, this ecclesia, this circle, aims for the final completion which is the Christian hope.

29 The Color of Feminism:
Or Speaking the Black Woman's Tongue

Delores S. Williams

The title of my address issues from two sources. The first part of the topic —
"The Color of Feminism" — came from the editors of *Christianity and Crisis*
who used these words to title my response to an article written by feminist
theologian, Rosemary Ruether.[1] The second part of the title — "Speaking
the Black Woman's Tongue" — came from my experience with two groups
of black Christian women who asked me to speak to them about feminism
and feminist theology. When I finished discussing feminism (its source and
contemporary character) and describing the positions of representative
feminist theologians, one woman in each group gave a response that has
plagued me from that day until this. For the purposes of this address, I will
refer to these women as group "A" and group "B." The black woman in group
"A" said:

> "Honey [addressing me], I want to say something about this feminism if
> you can bear with me. [I nodded my head indicating I could.] This all re-
> minds me of the day I went into a fancy dress shop downtown and saw a
> real pretty dress. The colors in the dress blended right. The design was
> modern and fashionable. The buttons in front looked real pretty with the
> material. Everything about that dress looked just right. There was only
> one problem when it came right down to me. The dress was size five, and I
> wear size twenty. The saleslady told me that shop didn't carry no dresses
> over size thirteen. I can sew real good, but I knew there was no way for me

1. Delores S. Williams, "The Color of Feminism," *Christianity and Crisis* 45, no. 7 (April
29, 1985): 164-65.

398

to alter that dress and still have the same thing. There just wasn't enough material in that dress to make it fit me. Now that's my point, honey. This feminism looks real pretty, but there just ain't enough in it to fit me. And what I'm wondering is: if you black feminists try to make feminism fit me, will you have the same thing?"

The woman in group "B" asked questions that were even more probing. In this group, I had used the work of bell hooks *(Ain't I a Woman?)* and Angela Davis *(Women, Race and Class)* to present some black female scholars' views of the politics of some of the leading nineteenth- and twentieth-century feminists. Instantly, the women in the group became interested in Davis' and hooks' descriptions of the racist ideas and actions of some of the white feminists. Then a small black woman in the group walked up to the front. She faced me and asked the following questions:

"If the work of women's liberation in this country has always accomplished white supremacy and the work of the Ku Klux Klan is for white supremacy, is the label 'feminist' comparable to the label 'Klansman'? Do the words 'black feminist' equal the same kind of terrible contradiction as the words 'black Klansman'? Since you are a feminist, ma'am, are you advancing the cause of white supremacy? Are you extending white woman's privilege rather than fighting for the liberation of black women and all other black people? What are your feminist politics about?"

I could discern that my responses to these women left them uneasy, unsatisfied. While I could make some correlations between white and black women's oppression and could point to the work of individual white feminists who also struggled for all women's liberation, I could not deliver on the "biggies" that bell hooks pointed out in *Ain't I a Woman?* For instance, I could not convince them that the contemporary feminist movement was any more *seriously concerned* about black women's liberation than the early white suffragettes were *seriously concerned* about black women getting the vote. Like many poor, oppressed people who cannot afford to live above the level of practical reality, these Afro-American Christian women apparently believed the truth of feminism lay in the incongruity between feminist rhetoric and feminist action.

These experiences (i.e., having *Christianity and Crisis* editors title my article "The Color of Feminism," and hearing the response of black Christian women to feminism) have caused me to shape some questions which are now at the center of my work. As I teach religious studies; as I participate in the life of the church; as I struggle with groups of women caught up in the problems generated by racist social structures, low self-esteem, and abusive men, I ask myself: "Is it only the racism of a few white feminists that causes most black women not to become involved in the feminist movement in church and society? How (or can) feminism be 'colorized' so that it also speaks the black woman's tongue, so that it tells the very truth of the black woman's historical existence in North America? What are the materials that have to be put into feminism to make it fit black women? If feminism is 'colorized' so that it also speaks the black woman's tongue, so that it (feminism) does not reinforce white supremacy, will feminism still be feminism?"

Here, I will share with you my reflections upon these questions. Though my observations and analysis are far from conclusive, they do represent my first public attempt to respond to the call for accountability that undergirded the questions of the black Christian women in groups "A" and "B."

Is It Only Racism?

Within the last five years, black female scholars have documented the biases toward black women that have existed in the women's liberation movements in America since their beginning in the nineteenth century. Angela Davis describes the first women's rights convention held in America at Seneca Falls in 1848. She comments on the white women's lack of concern for the slave women:

> While at least one Black man was present among the Seneca Falls conferees, there was not a single Black woman in attendance. Nor did the convention's documents make even a passing reference to Black women. In light of the organizers' abolitionist involvement it would seem puzzling that slave women were entirely disregarded.[2]

At the 1851 Women's Convention held in Akron, Ohio (when Sojourner Truth delivered her famous "Ain't I a Woman?" speech), "some of the white women . . . had been initially opposed to a Black Woman having a voice in their convention." Davis claims, however, that by 1869 when the Equal Rights Association was ending its life, Sojourner Truth had begun to recognize

> . . . the dangerous racism underlying the feminists' opposition to Black male suffrage. . . . When Sojourner Truth insisted that "if you bait the

2. Angela Davis, *Women, Race and Class* (New York: Vintage Books, 1983), p. 57.

suffrage-hook with a woman, you will certainly catch a black man," she issued yet another profound warning about the menacing influence of racist ideology.[3]

Another black female scholar, bell hooks, declares that "every women's movement in America from its earliest origin to the present day has been built on a racist foundation. . . ."[4] hooks claims "the first white women's rights advocates were never seeking social equality for all women; they were seeking social equality for white women."[5] Refuting the contemporary white poet, Adrienne Rich, who said that white women's activity in the Abolitionist movement provides a "strong anti-racist female tradition" for the contemporary feminist movement, hooks says:

> They [the nineteenth-century white women's rights' advocates] attacked slavery, not racism. The basis of their attack was moral reform. . . . While they strongly advocated an end to slavery, they never advocated a change in the racial hierarchy that allowed their caste status to be higher than that of black women or men. In fact, they wanted that hierarchy to be maintained. Consequently, the white women's rights movements, which had a lukewarm beginning in earlier reform activities, emerged in full force in the wake of efforts to gain rights for black people precisely because white women wanted to see no change in the social status of blacks until they [white women] were assured that their demands for more rights were met.[6]

Even more devastating for black women and black men in the nineteenth century were the racist strategies individual white feminists employed to gain white women's rights. Paula Giddings describes some of the debased activities of women's suffrage leaders Susan Anthony and Elizabeth Cady Stanton. Giddings says:

> More revealing — and disturbing — was the vicious campaign launched by Anthony and Stanton. Black women like [Francis] Harper may have had their complaints against Black men, but they must have looked down on White women using them as fodder to further their own selfish ends.

3. Davis, *Women, Race and Class,* p. 83.

4. bell hooks, *Ain't I a Woman? Black Women and Feminism* (Boston: South End Press, 1981), p. 124.

5. hooks, *Ain't I a Woman?* p. 124.

6. hooks, *Ain't I a Woman?* pp. 125-26.

That this was Anthony and Stanton's strategy became clear when they allied with a millionaire Democrat, George Train, who financed their feminist newspaper, *The Revolution*. Within its pages was venom of the worst kind.[7]

The Revolution carried Susan Anthony's observation that the Republican Party had elevated two million black men and given them the dignity of citizenship by giving them the vote. "With the other hand," Anthony claimed, "they [the Republicans] dethroned FIFTEEN MILLION WHITE WOMEN — their own mothers and sisters, their own wives and daughters — and cast them under the heel of the lowest orders of manhood."[8] Elizabeth Cady Stanton was more vicious. She wrote about a black man lynched in Tennessee. "The point of the story," says Giddings, "wasn't the awful injustice of lynching, but that giving black men the vote was virtually a license to rape."[9] Stanton also attempted to use class as a weapon in her battle to secure voting rights for white, upper-class women. When she announced she would run for the New York Legislature in 1866, Stanton had this to say:

> In view of the fact that the freed men of the South and the millions of foreigners now crowding our shores, most of whom represent neither property, education nor civilization, are all in the progress of events to be enfranchised, the best interests of the nation demand that we outweigh this incoming pauperism, ignorance and degradation, with the wealth, education, and refinement of the women of the republic.[10]

When Stanton was pressured to clarify this position, she condescendingly responded: "We prefer Bridget and Dinah at the ballot box to Patrick and Sambo."[11]

It is no wonder that subsequent feminists made racist statements equal to those of Anthony and Stanton. In 1903, a leading southern feminist, Belle Kearney, proclaimed:

> Just as surely as the North will be forced to turn to the South for the nation's salvation, just so surely will the South be compelled to look to its

---

7. Paula Giddings, *Where and When I Enter: The Impact of Black Women on Race and Sex in America* (New York: William Morrow & Company, 1984), p. 66.

8. Giddings, *Where and When I Enter*, p. 66.

9. Giddings, *Where and When I Enter*, p. 66.

10. Giddings, *Where and When I Enter*, p. 67.

11. Giddings, *Where and When I Enter*, p. 67.

Anglo-Saxon women as the medium through which to retain the supremacy of the white race over the Africans.[12]

Apparently the contemporary feminist movement — in both its secular and religious manifestations — is no less infested with racism than its predecessor, the women's suffrage movement. Feminists of color are protesting. In the book *This Bridge Called My Back,* a Chicana woman declares that ". . . women of color are veterans of a class and color war that is still escalating in the feminist movement." Black feminist poet Audre Lorde chides Mary Daly, a white feminist scholar in religious studies, about using her words (Lorde's) to corroborate her (Daly's) analysis of what she sees as sexist practices in black cultures. In "An Open Letter to Mary Daly" about Daly's book *Gyn/Ecology,* Lorde says, "For my part, I felt . . . you . . . misused my words, utilized them only to testify against myself as a woman of color. . . . For my words you used were no more, or less, illustrative of this chapter than . . . any number of my other poems might have been." Lorde asks Daly, "So the question arises in my mind, Mary, do you ever really read work of black women?"[13] In a recent issue of *Christianity and Crisis,* a black female minister, the Reverend Angelique Walker-Smith, directed some questions to white feminist theologian Rosemary Ruether about an article she (Ruether) wrote. Walker-Smith expressed serious concern over what she saw as Ruether's use of the term "Christian feminism" to signify only white feminism. Walker-Smith says:

> I am very disturbed about Ruether's labeling of "Christian Feminism" in her article [Ruether's "Feminist Theology and the Academy" appearing in *Christianity and Crisis,* March 4, 1985]. Why does she use the term "Christian Feminism" to label what really is "Christian feminism for white women"? Is she trying to suggest that Asian Christian feminism and black Christian feminism or any other minority Christian feminism is somehow subject to "white woman Christian feminism"? The insinuation that "white woman feminism" is somehow the true Christian feminism is clearly made when it is made to look synonymous with "Christian feminism. . . ."[14]

12. Quoted by Elizabeth Hood, "Black Woman, White Woman: Separate Paths to Liberation," *The Black Scholar* 4, no. 7 (April 1978): 49.

13. Audre Lorde, "Open Letter to Mary Daly," in *This Bridge Called My Back,* ed. Cherrie Moraga and Gloria Anzaldua (Watertown, MA: Persephone Press, 1981).

14. Angelique Walker-Smith, "Exclusive Language Reflects Inner Beliefs," *Christianity and Crisis* 45, no. 7 (April 29, 1985): 146.

On the basis of the preceding evidence, one can conclude that the racist activity of white feminists has been prevalent enough to discourage many Afro-American women from participating in the feminist movement. However, I want to suggest an additional problem that might account for black women's absence from the feminist movement. This problem centers upon an idea that is significant for feminist thought and action. My discussion here will also touch on the second and third questions I am considering here — i.e., "How can (if it can) feminism be 'colorized' so that it also speaks the tongue of black women . . . ?" and, "if feminism can so speak, what additional materials have to be added to make it fit black women's experience?"

Speaking Black Women's Tongue?

For feminist thinking, an important idea is that patriarchy is the major source of all women's oppression. However, this idea becomes limited and problematic when one attempts to use it to understand the Afro-American woman's total experience of oppression in North America.

In feminist literature, patriarchy is the power relation between men and women and between women and society's institutions controlled by men. White-American feminist Adrienne Rich describes it as

> . . . the power of the fathers: a familial-social, ideological, political system in which men — by force, direct pressure, or through ritual, tradition, law, and language, customs, etiquette, education, and division of labor — determine what part women shall or shall not play, and in which the female is everywhere subsumed under the male.[15]

While Mary Daly, in *Beyond God the Father*, reveals how the patriarchal religions (e.g., Judaism and Christianity) reinforce women's oppression and validate male supremacy, her understanding of patriarchy apparently concurs with Rich's definition. It is not reductionist, I think, to suggest that most feminist writing on the subject does support Rich's understanding of the meaning of patriarchy.[16]

15. Adrienne Rich, *Of Woman Born: Motherhood as Experience and Institution* (New York: W. W. Norton & Company, 1976), p. 40.

16. For a discussion of patriarchy in several contexts see Kate Millett, *Sexual Politics* (Garden City, NY: Doubleday, 1970); see also bell hooks' discussion in *Ain't I a Woman?*; Elizabeth Dodson Gray, *Patriarchy as a Conceptual Trap* (Wellesley, MA: Roundtable Press, 1982).

However, a simple interpolation of Rich's definition reveals its limitation as far as black women are concerned. To be congruent with the Afro-American woman's experience of oppression in this country, patriarchy would have to be defined as

> . . . the power of . . . [white men and white women]: a familial-social, ideological, political system in which [white men and white women] — by force, direct pressure, or through ritual, tradition, law and language, customs, etiquette, education, and division of labor — determine what part [black] women shall or shall not play, and in which the [black] female is everywhere subsumed under the [white female and white] male.[17]

Thus defined, patriarchy loses its identity. It is no longer just the power of fathers, or men, to oppress women. It is also the power of a certain group of females to oppress other groups of females. This inclusion of a group of women as oppressors — an assessment that speaks the truth of the Afro-American woman's history in North America — renders the feminist patriarchal critique of society less valid as a tool for assessing black women's oppression *resulting from their relation to white-controlled American institutions.* Therefore, one cannot claim that patriarchy, as it is understood by feminists, is the major source of all women's oppression.

Another limitation of the feminist understanding of patriarchy is that it fails to place emphasis upon what appears to be a positive side of patriarchy with regard to the development of white-American women. It is also the operation of this positive side that indicates a clear distinction between white women's and black women's oppression.

White American patriarchy, in its institutional manifestations, affords many white female children and white female adults (as groups) the care, protection, and resources necessary for intellectual development and physical well-being.[18] White American patriarchy has thus provided white women with the education, skills, and support (and often financial resources) they need to get first chance at the jobs and opportunities for women resulting from the pressures exerted by the civil rights movements in America. White American patriarchy, in its private and institutional manifestations, also intends to support the life, physical growth, intellectual de-

---

17. Rich, *Of Woman Born,* author's interpolations.

18. While many feminists are to be admired for refusing to take the white woman's traditional place upon the pedestal, few have turned down the privileges bestowed upon them by fathers, brothers, and sons.

velopment, and economic well-being of the female and male fruit of the white woman's womb — *when that fruit issues from her sexual union with white males.* From a black female perspective, then, it is possible to speak of *the productive patriarchal intent of white patriarchy* for the female and male fruit of the white woman's womb. And this productive patriarchal intent permeates the relation between white women (as a group) and the white-controlled institutions of American society.

However, the same institutions have no such productive intent for black women or for the fruit of black women's wombs (even if that fruit derived from sexual union between a black female and a white male).[19] Rather, these institutions intend the retardation of the intellectual, emotional, spiritual, economic, and physical growth of black women and the fruit of their wombs, male and female. This is partly demonstrated in the current operation of the white-controlled public school system in America. The black struggle for equality through integration into that system has exposed black children to a host of white male and white female teachers who daily undermine (often through ignorance of their own racism) the confidence, the intellectual stamina, the spirit, and the leadership development of black children. Convinced that black people are intellectually inferior to whites, many of these white teachers and school administrators "do not encourage black children to excel like they do white children," a black female student in my freshman English class once told me. "If you keep quiet, act nicely, and do a little work they will pass you," she said. "It doesn't matter that nobody taught you to read or write a theme."

In my own dealings with the white-controlled public school system, I have often come face-to-face with the "exclusion tactics" some white female and white male teachers use to retard black children's interest in the school's talent-shaping activities. I am reminded of the time my daughter wanted to try out for a role in a school play. The assistant drama coach, a white female, told her there was no need for her to try out because there were no black parts in the play. To this day, I have trouble understanding the term "black parts" in relation to Shakespeare's "A Midsummer Night's Dream." In my encounter with this school's drama department, I discovered any white child, male or female, could try out for roles in plays. Black children were discouraged from trying out for all plays except those designating that a black character was needed — usually a nurse for white children, or a maid, janitor, or

---

19. Afro-American slave narratives contain many accounts about slave owners who fathered children by slave women and then sold these children as slaves.

jester.[20] The drama coach (white) tried to console the aspiring young black actresses and actors by telling them the drama department would put on a black play at the end of the year. Later, the same teacher told the black children that her department had decided not to put on a black play because nobody would come to see it; the school population was mostly white. In this school, white children interested in acting did not experience this kind of humiliation. The white drama coaches were not retarding the development of white female and male children. Some of the black children became discouraged and gave up their interest in acting.

With regard to black women's oppression and the feminist idea that patriarchy is the primary source of women's oppression, two points should be reiterated. The first is that the feminist understanding of the patriarchal relation between women and society's institutions does not include black women's oppression resulting from *their relation to the white-controlled American institutions governing their lives.* As far as black women's experience is concerned, it is a misnomer to name oppressive-rule with words that only identify men as oppressors of women. Since white women join white men in oppressing black women (and in maintaining white supremacy), black women need nomenclature and language which reflect this reality. One cannot accept the argument that white women, in their affiliation with American institutions, are forced by patriarchal structures (or by patriarchal conditioning) to oppress black women, and therefore, patriarchy — or male rule — really is responsible for the oppression of all women relating to society's institutions. Davis, hooks, and Giddings have shown how independent white feminists (at odds with and supposedly rejecting patriarchal rule) did, of their own volition and for their own political benefit, oppress black women and other black people. White American women cannot be relieved of the responsibility for choices they made/make in their roles as oppressors.

The second point to be reiterated here is that while white patriarchy may ultimately cause the oppression of white women, it constantly provides resources for the development of white women. Many black women who work in white settings have seen white feminist groups use the positive side of white patriarchy to gain political, economic, and educational advantages that mostly benefit white women. The positive side of patriarchy provides

20. In the October 27, 1985, issue of *The New York Times Magazine* a black middle-class mother expressed her anger about a play performed by students at a predominantly white school her child attended. In the play, all the black children were cast as monkeys and wore no masks. A little white boy was cast as a gorilla and he wore a mask.

the media and means for keeping white women's issues at the forefront of the liberation movement and at the forefront of American conscience.[21]

The failure of white feminists to emphasize the *substantial difference* between their patriarchally-derived-privileged-oppression and black women's demonically-derived-annihilistic-oppression renders black women invisible in feminist thought and action. It is no wonder that in most feminist literature written by white-American women, the words "woman" and "women" signify only the white woman's experience. By failing to insert the word "white" before "woman" and "women," some feminists imperialistically take over the identity of those rendered invisible. Therefore, one can encounter instances in white feminist literature when feminists make appropriations from Afro-American culture without identifying the source of the appropriation and without admitting that American feminism has roots deep in black culture. This is glaringly obvious in the following claim made by white feminist scholar Jo Freeman:

> The most prevalent innovation developed by the younger branch [of feminism] has been the "rap group." Essentially an education technique, it has spread far beyond its origins and become a major organizational unit of the whole movement, most frequently used by suburban housewives. From a sociological perspective, the rap group is probably the most valuable contribution by the women's liberation movement to the tools for social change.[22]

Even the most casual student of black culture knows that the "rap" and the "rap group" have been alive in the oral tradition of the Afro-American Community (nation-wide) for more than fifty years. During the civil rights movements in the late 1950s and early 1960s, rap groups performed in black homes and in black churches. These groups had several purposes. One major purpose was to educate black people about the various strategies to be used in demonstrations. Another purpose was to allow black people to share

21. For some time now, black women have been complaining about the nature of the women's studies programs planned by feminists but financed by white male money. Black women say these programs are primarily about white women. See *All the Women Are White, All the Blacks Are Men, but Some of Us Are Brave: Black Women's Studies,* ed. Gloria T. Hull, Barbara Snaith, and Patricia Bell Scott (Old Westbury, NY: Feminist Press, 1982). Pay special attention to the article written by Barbara Smith.

22. Jo Freeman, "The Women's Liberation Movement: Its Origins, Structures, Import and Ideas," in *Women: A Feminist Perspective,* ed. Jo Freeman (New York: Mayfield Publishing Company, 1975), p. 451.

their experiences so that the black community could see how racism had affected every area of black life. Before the 1950s and 1960s, individual blacks used the rap to expound on social and moral issues. Today, in Afro-American and some Hispanic communities, the "rap" provides the rhythmic accompaniment for the famous "break dancing" which originated among northern Hispanic and black youth forming the street cultures of both communities. The "rap" and the "rap group" certainly did not originate among white feminists. If anything, the rap was *borrowed* from black people by white women who touched black culture, perhaps through the civil rights movements or through one-on-one involvements with black men and women.

The implication of all the preceding discussion is that black women, *in their relation to white-controlled American institutions,* do not experience patriarchy.[23] It is necessary, then, for black women — when describing their own oppressed relation to white-controlled American institutions — to use new words, new language, and new ideas that fit their experience. These new words, language, and ideas will help black women develop an appropriate theoretical foundation for the ideology and political action needed to obtain the liberation of black women and the black family.[24]

Therefore, as a beginning, I suggest that there are at least two ways of institutional white-rule effecting the oppression of many American women. Certainly one of these is patriarchy as described by Adrienne Rich earlier in this paper. There is also the demonic way of institutional white-rule which controls black women's lives. This way can be named demonarchy.[25] Patriarchy, *in its white institutional form,* can also be understood as the systemic governance of white women's lives by white women's fathers, brothers, and sons using care, protection, and privilege as instruments of social control. Demonarchy can be understood as the demonic governance of black

23. Black women should, as they name their experience, consider the following: "White males experience the world from the top side of history. White females experience the world from the underside of history. Black men experience the world from the underside of the underside of history. Black women experience the world from rock-bottom." Such a position for black women logically suggests a different naming of reality and certainly a different view of history.

24. For some years now, I have heard many black women say that they could not conceive of their own liberation apart from the liberation of the black family because black children, female and male, are as oppressed by white-controlled American institutions as they (black women) are.

25. Democracy has no relation to demonarchy, which posits beings intermediate between humans and the divine.

women's lives by white male and white female ruled systems using racism, violence, violation, retardation, and death as instruments of social control. Distinguished from individual violent acts stemming from psychological abnormalities on the part of the perpetrator, demonarchy is a traditional and collective expression of white government in relation to black women. It belongs to the realm of normalcy. It is informed by a state of consciousness that believes white women are superior to and more valuable than any woman of color and that white men are the most valuable and superior forms of life on earth. While sexism is a kind of women's oppression issuing from patriarchy, racist-gender oppression of black women issues from demonarchy. Black women cannot disjoin race and gender as they describe their oppression resulting from their relation to white-controlled American institutions.

Demonarchy has its roots in American slavery in the governance that allowed black women to be used as breeder women, that allowed black women to be indiscriminately raped by white men of every class, that allowed black women to be used as work-horses for white females controlling the domestic/private sphere of the slavocracy.[26] Note the following example of the demonic governance (demonarchy) of the Afro-American slave woman's life:

> Women [on the slave ships] were lashed severely for crying. They were stripped of their clothing and beaten on all parts of their body. Ruth and Jacob Weldon, an African couple who experienced the horrors of the slave passage, saw "mothers with babes at their breast basely branded and scarred, till it would seem as if the very heavens might smite the infernal tormentors with the doom they so richly merited." After the branding all slaves were stripped of any clothing. . . . Rape was a common method of torture slavers used to subdue recalcitrant black women. The threat of rape or other physical brutalization inspired terror in the psyches of displaced African females. Robert Shufeldt, an observer of the slave trade, documented the prevalence of rape on slave ships. He asserts, "In those days many a negress was landed upon our shores [sic] already impregnated by some one of the demonic crew that brought her over."[27]

Demonarchy prevailed beyond slavery as white men continued to rape black women and as both white males and white females put the blame for

---

26. Much literature about black women describes the inhumane treatment that black women received as they worked for white women as domestics and as housekeepers.

27. hooks, *Ain't I a Woman?* p. 18.

this rape on the alleged ". . . immorality of black women."[28] Demonarchy prevailed in World War II America as white women severely exploited the labor of black female domestic workers. In *Women, Race and Class,* Angela Davis reports that

> . . . in the 1940's, there were street-corner markets in New York and other large cities — modern versions of slavery's auction block — inviting white women to take their pick from the crowds of Black women seeking work.

Quoting from Louise Mitchell's account, Davis describes the actual situation:

> Every morning, rain or shine, groups of [black] women with brown paper bags or cheap suitcases stand on street corners in the Bronx and Brooklyn waiting for a chance to get some work. . . . Once hired on the "slave market," the women often find after a day's backbreaking toil, that they worked longer than was arranged, got less than was promised, were forced to accept clothing instead of cash, and were exploited beyond human endurance. Only the urgent need for money makes them [black women] submit to this routine daily.[29]

During the Second World War, northern white women were not alone in their desire to exploit black women's labor so that the domestic/private sphere of white American life could offer comfort and well-being for white families. Discussing black female employment in the defense industries in America during the 1940s Paula Giddings reports that

> . . . a Black newspaper, "The Baltimore Afro-American," ran a story in 1945 about Black women struggling to be hired by the Naval Ordnance Plant in Macon, Georgia: "The chief opposition to employment of colored women did not come from management or the employees . . . but from white local housewives, who feared lowering the barriers would rob them of maids, cooks and nurses."[30]

As a way of controlling black women's lives, demonarchy thrives today in white-controlled American institutions where *racist-gender* oppression

28. See bell hooks' discussion of this in *Ain't I a Woman?* pp. 36-37.
29. Davis, *Women, Race and Class,* p. 95.
30. Giddings, *Where and When I Enter,* p. 237.

not only affects black women. It also affects the economic well-being of the black family. As Paula Giddings reminds us:

> Both the past and the present tell us it is not a question of race *versus* sex, but race *and* sex. In a time when so many Black women and children need sufficient income, the concerns about sex are necessary for the progress — indeed, the economic survival — of Afro-Americans as a group.[31]

As the source of the *racist-gender* oppression black women experience in their relation to white-controlled American institutions, demonarchy causes a qualitative difference between the oppression of black women and white women. Therefore, black women, understanding the demonic character of their oppression, are apt to emphasize issues different from those empha-sized by white feminists informed by the patriarchal critique of women's op-pression. White feminists struggle for women's liberation *from male domina-tion* with regard for such *priority* issues as rape, domestic violence, women's work, female bonding, inclusive language, the gender of God, economic au-tonomy for women, and heterosexism. Black women liberators would per-haps consider *women's liberation and family liberation from white-male–white-female domination* with regard for such priority issues as physical sur-vival and spiritual salvation of the family (with equality between males and females); the re-distribution of goods and services in the society (so that white families no longer get the lion's share of the economic, educational, political, and vocational resources available in every social class); encounter-ing God as family (masculine and feminine, father, mother, and child); end-ing white supremacy, male supremacy (or any gender supremacy), and upper-class supremacy in all American institutions.

This does not mean that black women are not concerned about such is-sues as rape, domestic violence, and women's work. Neither does this mean that white feminists should refrain from indicating these issues as priorities for *white* women. Nor does this mean that black women liberators should refrain from supporting white feminist action to alleviate domestic violence, rape, and exclusion of women. All black women should support the aboli-tion of these atrocities. However, these issues are not priorities for Afro-American liberators who understand the demonic nature of their oppres-sion resulting from their relation to white-controlled American institutions.

Inasmuch as Afro-American women's history shows that black women

---

31. Giddings, *Where and When I Enter*, p. 237.

have struggled *simultaneously* for their own liberation and that of other black people (males, females, and children), it is appropriate to suggest that a women's movement, informed by an understanding of demonarchy, would have at least three primary goals. These would be (1) liberation of women and the family simultaneously; (2) establishing a positive quality of life for women and the family simultaneously; (3) forming political alliances with other marginal groups struggling to be free of the oppression imposed by white-controlled American institutions. Hence, the black women's issues cited above emerge from these goals. Liberation of black women and black families involves survival, salvation of black people's spirits, and equality between males and females. A positive quality of life is achieved through the redistribution of goods and services and new encounters with God. As they form the appropriate political alliances, black women liberators raise the issue of ending white supremacy, gender supremacy, and class bias. (It must be emphasized that a positive quality of life for black women and the family should be based upon *both* a reinforcement of Afro-American cultural and religious heritage *and* a realistic/scientific analysis of black people's relation to the means of production in the societies in which Afro-Americans live.)

Hence, if black women's tongue is to be spoken within feminism, i.e., if feminism is also to be "colorized," feminist consciousness must be raised to:

1) understand the limitation of the feminist patriarchal critique for assessing the nature of black women's oppression derived from black women's *relation to white-male–white-female-dominated social systems;*

2) recognize the need to assess the ethical significance of white feminists using "white patriarchal power" to gain privileges that benefit mostly white women;

3) realize that black American women and white American women are apt to use different linguistic configurations to express the terms of their oppression. For instance, white women may claim that women's primary oppression issues from male subjugation of females; therefore, women must struggle for their liberation which, when achieved, also liberates oppressor-men. Afro-American females may say that white American families (fathers, mothers, children) in every social class have the power to oppress the black family (mothers, fathers, and children). Black women must struggle for the liberation of women within the context of the broader struggle for the liberation of the black family where equality must exist between females and males. Therefore, feminist consciousness must also be raised to:

4) consider women's liberation and family liberation as *inseparable* goals;

5) realize that the family (whether nuclear or extended) can be an effective unit for consciousness-raising with regard to gender, racial, and class oppression.

The multi-racial feminist collective called Mud Flower has already begun to suggest what it means to color feminism so that black women and other women of color are seriously included. They say, "An analysis of sexism that is not also an assessment of racism, ethnic prejudice, and economic injustice is not . . . a feminist analysis."[32] In accord with this Mud Flower statement, black female liberators might want to make an additional affirmation — i.e., that an analysis of racial oppression which is not also an assessment of women's oppression, of the black family's oppression, and of the economic injustices in society is not a valid assessment of black oppression in North America. Mud Flower reminds us that "We do not have to be economists, anthropologists, or sociologists to know that race, class and gender are critical, even determinative, forces in the ordering of human life and religion."[33] We merely have to be determined to confront the forces in our society that create and perpetuate oppression based on race, gender, and class.

Materials to Be Added?

While the preceding discussion suggests that additional "materials" must be added to feminism to make it also fit black women's experience, there are parts of feminism that "sound pretty," as the black Christian woman observed in group "A" above. Hence, some aspects of feminism are already attractive to some Afro-American women. Certainly, the feminist emphasis upon equal pay for equal work done by men and women in the work place is appealing — as is also the feminist claim that women should have control of their own bodies and that nurturing responsibilities within the family should be shared equally by males and females.

Even though there is a split between rhetoric and action in some feminist approaches to the Afro-American woman's rights and liberation, the feminist movement in America has provided some useful tools for black

32. Katie G. Cannon, Beverly W. Harrison, Carter Heyward, et al., *God's Fierce Whimsy* (New York: The Pilgrim Press, 1985), p. 34.

33. Cannon, Harrison, Heyward, et al., *God's Fierce Whimsy*, p. 34.

women to begin to evaluate their relationship to black men, to the black family, and to the institutions in the Afro-American community where black males have the authority (e.g., the black church). Some Afro-American female thinkers have shown that the feminist understanding of sexism — oppression of a person because of gender — aptly describes the oppression black women receive in their relationships with some black men and with black-male-dominated Afro-American institutions, e.g., the black church. This means, then, that even though the feminist understanding of patriarchy (from which sexism derives) is limited when one attempts to use it to describe black women's oppression *resulting from their relation to white-male–white-female-dominated social systems,* it is useful for assessing black women's relation to black males and to those institutions where black males have the authority. This state of affairs exists because black males, since slavery, have tended to re-create their manhood to conform to the model of manhood sanctioned in American society. Of course, this sanctioned manhood was white and was understood by white people to be patriarchal. So, while we add the demonarchal critique to feminism, we must maintain relevant aspects of the patriarchal critique feminists have provided. But some caution must be exercised. We must insist that our feminist definitions of patriarchy be adjusted so that they show clearly (and not by inference) that white people have the power and authority to oppress black men, and they exercise this authority in every area of American life.

The question of whether these new additions will distort feminism is an open one. Feminists, themselves, will have to deal with the questions. But we can say that feminism as a language of women's experience will become stagnant unless new concepts are added to its linguistic store of word and wisdom.

Ecclesiological Import

In conclusion, some brief consideration must be given to the significance of the demonarchal critique for the life and mission of the black church. The naming of demonic rule (i.e., demonarchy) suggests new ways to talk about black worship and new biblical foundations for the mission of the church. Informed by the demonarchal critique of black women's relation to white-controlled American institutions, one can now understand the black church's shouts, rhythms, and music not as uncontrolled frenzy, but as its way of casting out the intolerable pain demonic rule *instills* in its victims.

This process of casting out pain in the worship space of the black church happens in a transactional relation between the rhythm of song, the rhythm of words, the black preacher's charisma, and the black woman. Time, in its ordinary sense, is suspended as black women give up their pain in the rhythm of the flow of music, of word, and of charisma. The joyful noise that results — e.g., shouts, moans, claps, etc. — represents the black woman's thanks to God for the revitalization of her spirit which demonarchy has tried to destroy. The deep spirituality that often characterizes the black church results from this process of casting out pain and women giving thanks to God for the spirit.

In terms of its mission to the black community and to the world, the black church (informed by the demonarchal critique) will be about the business of casting out the demonic — the socially, politically, economically, and spiritually demonic rule that threatens the life of black people and the life of the human spirit. This casting out of demonic rule can be named "the church's liberation activity" which finds its biblical validation in such texts as: Mark 3:14-15 ("Jesus . . . appointed twelve — designating them apostles — that they might be with him and that he might send them out to preach and to have authority to drive out demons. . . ."); Matthew 10:1 ("He called his twelve apostles to him and gave them authority to drive out evil spirits. . . ."); Matthew 10:7-8 ("As you [the disciples] go, preach this message: 'The kingdom of heaven is near.' Heal the sick, raise the dead, cleanse those who have leprosy, drive out demons. . . ."); Luke 9:1 ("When Jesus had called the twelve together, he gave them power and authority to drive out all demons. . . .").[34] The importance of this emphasis upon casting out the work of the demonic is that it allows the black church to understand its liberation action in terms of the connection between the spiritual and political dimensions of its life and history.

Apart from modern psychological theory which understands the demonic as a constitutive element of human personality, the black church (if informed by the demonarchal critique) will see the demonic in socio-political-spiritual terms. The church will understand that social organization based upon racist-gender oppression, economic oppression, and oppression of the human spirit does not intend merely to maim. It intends to destroy the very lives of black women and black peoplehood. For this reason, the church cannot be naive, nor can it underestimate the *power* of the demonic governance it challenges. The black church's mission of casting out

34. From the *New International Version of the Bible.*

the demonic in the social world can only be successful if the church realizes that its liberation encounter is with *nothing less* than radical evil.

Finally, if the black church is to understand its mission to itself, it must see that part of its mission is to enlighten its congregations so that the oppression of women in the church is alleviated — so that black male imitations of white manhood and white male patriarchy are discarded. Due to the split in the black church between power and authority, this oppression is reinforced. Black women are the economic, spiritual, numerical powers in the churches while black males have the authority. When black women *take* the lead and heal the split by giving authority to black women (especially black women ministers), the black church will indeed become a more representative model of the kingdom in our midst. But in order to do this, the black church — like feminism — must add materials to its life and thought which speak the black woman's tongue — materials that show women and men to be equal in both power and authority — materials that speak in new, meaningful, and inclusive theological categories.

30 *Mujerista* Theology:
A Challenge to Traditional Theology

Ada María Isasi-Díaz

One of the reviewers of my book *En la Lucha* pointed out that I have spent the last ten years of my life working at elaborating a *mujerista* theology. When I read this, I realized the reviewer was right: the elaboration of *mujerista* theology has been and will continue to be one of my life-projects. Since I know myself to be first and foremost an activist, an activist-theologian, the reason why *mujerista* theology is so important to me is that to do *mujerista* theology is a significant and important way for me to participate in the struggle for liberation, to make a contribution to the struggle of Latinas in the USA.

What is *mujerista* theology? In the first part of this chapter, after a general description of *mujerista* theology, I will explain some of the key characteristics and elements of *mujerista* theology. In the second part I will deal with the challenges that *mujerista* theology presents to traditional theology. So, what is *mujerista* theology?

Mujerista Theology

General Description

To name oneself is one of the most powerful acts a person can do. A name is not just a word by which one is identified. A name also provides the conceptual framework, the point of reference, the mental constructs that are used in thinking, understanding, and relating to a person, an idea, a movement. It is with this in mind that a group of us Latinas[1] who live in the United States and who are keenly aware of how sexism,[2] ethnic prejudice, and economic oppression subjugate Latinas, started to use the term *mujerista* to refer to ourselves and to use *mujerista* theology to refer to the explanations of our faith and its role in our struggle for liberation.[3]

The need for having a name of our own, for inventing the term *mujerista* and investing it with a particular meaning became more and more obvious over the years as Hispanic women attempted to participate in the feminist Anglo-European movement in the United States. Latinas have become suspicious of this movement because of its inability to deal with differences, to share power equally among all those committed to it, to make it possible for Latinas to contribute to the core meanings and understandings of the movement, to pay attention to the intersection of racism/ethnic prejudice, classism, and sexism, and because of the seeming rejection of liberation as its goal, having replaced it with limited benefits for some women within present structures, benefits that necessitate some groups of women and men to be oppressed in order for some others to flourish. These serious flaws in the Euro-American feminist movement have led grassroots Latinas to understand "feminism" as having to do with the rights of Euro-American middle-class women, rights many times attained at the expense of Hispanic and other minority women. As the early 1992 national survey conducted by the Ms Foundation in New York City and the Center for Policy Alternatives in Washington, D.C., called the "Women's Voices Project" showed:

> the term feminism proved unattractive . . . women of color saying it applied only to white women. The survey shows that, while 32 percent of all women reported they would be likely to join a woman's group devoted to job and educational opportunities, or supporting equal pay, and equal rights for women, substantially fewer reported they would join a "feminist" group devoted to these tasks. Thus we must demonstrate to women

1. There is no agreement among Latinas whether to refer to ourselves as "Hispanic women" or as "Latina women." My choosing to use "Latina" is done indiscriminately.

2. In *mujerista* theology heterosexism is understood to be a distinct element of sexism.

3. It is important to notice that we do not use the term *mujerismo* since it can be understood to indicate that Latinas' natural entity is based on being women when in fact our natural entity as women is based on being human. See Raquel Rodríguez, "La marcha de las mujeres . . . ," *Pasos* 344 (March-April 1991): 11, n. 6.

that "feminism" means devotion to the concerns women report, or we must find another term for women's activism.[4]

Mujerista is the word we have chosen to name devotion to Latinas' liberation.

A *mujerista* is someone who makes a preferential option for Latina women, for our struggle for liberation.[5] Because the term *mujerista* was developed by a group of us who are theologians and pastoral agents, the initial understandings of the term came from a religious perspective. At present the term is beginning to be used in other fields such as literature and history. It is also beginning to be used by community organizers working with grassroots Hispanic women. Its meaning, therefore, is being amplified without losing as its core the struggle for the liberation of Latina women.

*Mujerista*s struggle to liberate ourselves not as individuals but as members of a Hispanic community. We work to build bridges among Latinas/os while denouncing sectarianism and divisive tactics. *Mujeristas* understand that our task is to gather our people's hopes and expectations about justice and peace. Because Christianity, in particular the Latin American inculturation of Roman Catholicism, is an intrinsic part of Hispanic culture, *mujeristas* believe that in Latinas, though not exclusively so, God chooses once again to lay claim to the divine image and likeness made visible from the very beginning in women. *Mujeristas* are called to bring to birth new women and new men — Hispanics willing to work for the good of our people (the "common good") knowing that such work requires the denunciation of all destructive sense of self-abnegation.[6]

Turning to theology specifically, *mujerista* theology, which includes both ethics and systematic theology, is a liberative praxis: reflective action that has as its goal liberation. As a liberative praxis *mujerista* theology is a process of enablement for Latina women which insists on the development

4. Linda Williams, "Ending the Silences: The Voices of Women of Color," *Equal Means* 1, no. 4 (Winter 1993): 13.

5. Though the rest of this chapter refers more directly to *mujerista* Latinas, we intend here to make explicit that Latino men as well as men and women from other racial/ethnic groups can also opt to be *mujeristas*.

6. Rosa Marta Zárate Macías, "Canto de mujer," in *Concierto a mi pueblo*, tape produced by Rosa Marta Zárate Macías, P.O. Box 7366, San Bernardino, CA 92411. Much of this description is based on this song composed and interpreted by Rosa Marta in response to several Latinas' insistence on the need for a song that would help to express who they are and that would inspire them in the struggle. For the full text of her song in English and Spanish see Ada María Isasi-Díaz, "*Mujeristas:* A Name of Our Own," *Christian Century* (May 24-31, 1989): 560-62.

of a strong sense of moral agency and clarifies the importance and value of who we are, what we think, and what we do. Second, as a liberative praxis, *mujerista* theology seeks to impact mainline theologies, those theologies which support what is normative in church and, to a large degree, in society — what is normative having been set by non-Hispanics and, to the exclusion of Latinas and Latinos, particularly Latinas.

Mujerista theology engages in this two-pronged liberative praxis, first by working to enable Latinas to understand the many oppressive structures that almost completely determine our daily lives. It enables Hispanic women to understand that the goal of our struggle should be not to partici-pate in and to benefit from these structures but to change them radically. In theological and religious language this means that *mujerista* theology helps Latinas discover and affirm the presence of God in the midst of our com-munities and the revelation of God in our daily lives. Hispanic women must come to understand the reality of structural sin and find ways of com-bating it because it effectively hides God's ongoing revelation from us and from society at large.

Second, *mujerista* theology insists on and aids Latinas in defining our preferred future: What will a radically different society look like? What will be its values and norms? In theological and religious language this means that *mujerista* theology enables Hispanic women to understand the central-ity of eschatology in the life of every Christian. Latinas' preferred future breaks into our present oppression in many different ways. Hispanic women must recognize those eschatological glimpses, rejoice in them, and struggle to make those glimpses become our whole horizon.

Third, *mujerista* theology enables Latinas to understand how much we have already bought into the prevailing systems in society — including the religious systems — and have thus internalized our own oppression. *Mujerista* theology helps Hispanic women to see that radical structural change cannot happen unless radical change takes place in each and every one of us. In theological and religious language this means that *mujerista* theology assists Latinas in the process of conversion, helping us see the real-ity of sin in our lives. Further, it enables us to understand that to resign our-selves to what others tell us is our lot and to accept suffering and self-effacement is not a virtue.

Main Characteristics

Following are descriptions of three main elements or key characteristics of *mujerista* theology that are closely interconnected. I develop the role of *lo cotidiano* at greater length since I have not done so before.

Locus Theologicus The locus theologicus, the place from which we do *mujerista* theology, is our *mestizaje* and *mulatez,* our condition as racially and culturally mixed people; our condition of people from other cultures living within the USA; our condition of people living between different worlds, a reality applicable to the Mexican Americans living in the Southwest, but also to the Cubans living in Miami and the Puerto Ricans living in the Northeast of the USA.

Mestizaje refers to the mixture of white people and native people living in what is now Latin America and the Caribbean. *Mulatez* refers to the mixture of black people and white people. We proudly use both words to refer both to the mixture of cultures and to the mixture of races that we Latinas and Latinos in the USA embody. Using these words is important for several reasons.[7] First of all, it proclaims a reality. Even before the new *mestizaje* and *mulatez* that are happening here in the USA, we all have come from *mestiza* and *mulata* cultures, from cultures where the white, red, and black races have been intermingled, from cultures where Spanish, Amerindian, and African cultural elements have come together and new cultures have emerged.[8] *Mestizaje* and *mulatez* are important to us because they vindicate "precisely that which the dominant culture, with its pervading racism [and ethnic prejudice], condemns and deprecates: our racial and cultural mixture."[9] *Mestizaje* and *mulatez* also point to the fact that "if any would understand us, they must come to us, and not only to our historical and cultural.] ancestors."[10] *Mes-*

---

7. Our usage of these words goes beyond their original meaning to include the mixing of Hispanics/Latinos in the USA with those of other races-cultures who live in this country, and the mixing among ourselves, Hispanics/Latinos coming from different countries of Latin America and the Caribbean.

8. I use *mulato* and *mulata* in Spanish to indicate that the social connotation that we give to this word is not as derogatory as the one given to it in the USA. By using the Spanish spelling I also seek not to offend African Americans in this country who find the use of the word "mulatto" offensive.

9. Justo L. González, "Hispanics in the United States," *Listening Journal of Religion and Culture* 27, no. 1 (Winter 1992): 14.

10. González, "Hispanics in the United States," p. 15.

tizaje and *mulatez* are what make "it possible for our cultures to survive. 'Culture' is a total way of responding to the total world and its ever changing challenges."[11] Culture has to do with a living reality, and as such it must grow, change, adapt. And our "new" *mestizaje* and *mulatez* here in the USA are just that, our actual ongoing growing, based on our past but firmly grounded in the present and living into our future.

Finally, *mestizaje* and *mulatez* are our contribution to a new understanding of pluralism, a new way of valuing and embracing diversity and difference. Later, we will discuss the issue of differences in greater detail. Suffice it to say here that the kind of pluralism that does embrace differences is about distributing opportunities, resources, and benefits in an inclusive way. To embrace differences at the structural level goes well beyond recognizing the multiplicity of interests and identities that exist in this society and their multiple claims on the institutions of the USA. Embracing differences, real pluralism, is first and foremost about making sure that

> institutional and economic elites are subjected to effective controls by the constituencies whose welfare they affect, that neither the enjoyment of dominance nor the suffering of deprivation is the constant condition of any group, and that political and administrative officers operate as guardians of popular needs rather than as servants of wealthy interests.[12]

Theologically, how do *mestizaje* and *mulatez* function? *Mestizaje* and *mulatez* are what "socially situates" us Hispanics in the USA. This means that *mestizaje* and *mulatez* as the theological locus of Hispanics delineate the finite alternatives we have for thinking, conceiving, expressing our theology.[13] For example, because *mestizaje* and *mulatez* socially situate our theology, our theology cannot but understand all racism and ethnic prejudice as sin and the embracing of diversity as virtue. This means that the coming of the kin-dom[14] of God has to do with a coming together of peoples, with no one being excluded and at the expense of no one. Furthermore, *mestizaje* and *mulatez* mean that the unfolding of the kingdom of God happens when

11. González, "Hispanics in the United States," p. 15.

12. Michael Parenti, *Power and the Powerless* (New York: St. Martin's Press, 1978), p. 28.

13. Otto Maduro, *Religion and Social Conflict* (Maryknoll, NY: Orbis Books, 1982), pp. 42-43.

14. I use "kin-dom" to avoid using the sexist and elitist word "kingdom." Also, the sense of family of God that "kin-dom" represents is much in line with the centrality of family in our Latina culture. I am grateful to Georgene Wilson, O.S.F., from whom I learned this word.

instead of working to become part of structures of exclusion we struggle to do away with such structures. Because of the way mainline society thinks about mestizas and mulatas, we cannot but think about the divine in non-elitist, non-hierarchical ways.

Mestizaje and *mulatez* for us Latinas and Latinos is not a given. In many ways it is something we have to choose repeatedly, it is something we have to embrace in order to preserve our cultures, in order to be faithful to our people, and from a theological-religious perspective, in order to remain faithful to the struggle for peace and justice, the cornerstone of the gospel message. Because we choose *mestizaje* and *mulatez* as our theological locus, we are saying that this is the structure in which we operate, from which we reach out to explain who we are and to contribute to how theology and religion are understood in this society in which we live. *Mestizaje* and *mulatez* and the contributions they make to society's understanding of pluralism, therefore, are one of the building blocks of a *mujerista* account of justice.

Latinas' *Cotidiano* as Theological Source From the very beginning of *mujerista* theology, we have insisted that the source of our theological enterprise is the lived experience of Hispanic women. We have insisted on the capacity of Latinas to reflect on their everyday life and the struggle to survive against very difficult obstacles. When in *mujerista* theology we talk about liberative daily experience, about Hispanic women's experience of struggling every day, we are referring to *lo cotidiano*. *Lo cotidiano* has to do with particular forms of speech, the experience of class and gender distinctions, the impact of work and poverty on routines and expectations, relations within families and among friends and neighbors in a community, the experience of authority, and central expressions of faith such as prayer, religious celebrations, and conceptions of key religious figures.[15]

These key religious figures are not only those of Christianity, Jesus and Mary his mother, but also those more exclusively Catholic like the saints, and those of popular religion, such as the *orishas* of different African religions and the deities of different Amerindian religions. However, in *mujerista* theology, *lo cotidiano* is more than a descriptive category. *Lo cotidiano* also includes the way we Latinas consider actions, discourse, norms, established social roles, and our own selves.[16] Recognizing that it is

15. Daniel H. Levine, *Popular Voices in Latin American Catholicism* (Princeton, NJ: Princeton University Press, 1992), p. 317.

16. Levine, *Popular Voices in Latin American Catholicism*, p. 317.

inscribed with subjectivity, that we look at and understand what happens to us from a given perspective, *lo cotidiano* has hermeneutical importance. This means that *lo cotidiano* has to do with the daily lived experiences that provide the "stuff" of our reality. *Lo cotidiano* points to "shared experiences," which I differentiate from "common experience." "Shared experiences" is a phrase that indicates the importance differences play in *lo cotidiano*. On the other hand, "common experience" seems to mask differences, to pretend that there is but one experience, one way of knowing for all Hispanic women.[17] And *lo cotidiano* points precisely to the opposite of that: it points to transitoriness and incompleteness.

Lo cotidiano is not a metaphysical category, it is not an attempt to see Latinas' daily lived experience as fixed and universal. Rather it is a way of referring to the "stuff" and the processes of Hispanic women's lives.[18] *Lo cotidiano* is not something that exists a priori, into which we fit the daily lived experience of Hispanic women. *Lo cotidiano* of Latinas is a matter of life and death, it is a matter of who we are, of who we become, and, therefore, it is far from being something objective, something we observe, relate to, and talk about in a disinterested way. Finding ways to earn money to feed and clothe their children and to keep a roof over their heads is part of *lo cotidiano* for Latinas. Finding ways to survive corporal abuse is part of *lo cotidiano*. Finding ways to effectively struggle against oppression is part of *lo cotidiano*.[19]

Besides its descriptive and hermeneutical task, *mujerista* theology appropriates *lo cotidiano* as the epistemological framework of our theological enterprise. Therefore, *lo cotidiano,* the daily experience of Hispanic women, not only points to their capacity to know but also highlights the features of their knowing. *Lo cotidiano* is a way of referring to Latinas' efforts to understand and express how and why their lives are the way they are, how and why they function as they do.[20] Of course there are other ways of coming to know

17. This has very serious methodological implications for *mujerista* theology. See Ada María Isasi-Díaz, *En la Lucha: Elaborating a Mujerista Theology* (Minneapolis: Fortress Press, 1993), chapter 3.

18. Sharon Welch, "Sporting Power — American Feminists, French Feminists and an Ethic of Conflict," in C. W. Maggie Kim, Susan M. St. Ville, and Susan M. Simonaitis, eds., *Transfigurations: Theology and the French Feminists* (Minneapolis: Fortress Press, 1993), p. 174.

19. I want to make absolutely clear that *lo cotidiano* is not to be understood as housekeeping chores in the sense that women's daily work is usually conceptualized: cleaning, doing laundry, driving the children to extracurricular activities. However, neither do I wish to diminish the importance of those kinds of tasks.

20. Otto Maduro, *Mapas para la fiesta* (Buenos Aires: Centro Nueva Tierra para la Promoción Social y Pastoral, 1992), p. 17.

what is real; there are many forms and types of knowledge. Our emphasis on *lo cotidiano* as an epistemological category, as a way of knowing, has to do, in part, with the need to rescue Hispanic women's daily experience from the category of the unimportant. *Lo cotidiano* has been belittled and scorned precisely because it is often related to the private sphere, to that sphere of life assigned to women precisely because it is considered unimportant. Or is it the other way around?

In *mujerista* theology, then, *lo cotidiano* has descriptive, hermeneutical, and epistemological importance. The valuing of *lo cotidiano* means that we appreciate the fact that Latinas see reality in a different way from the way it is seen by non-Latinas. And it means that we privilege Hispanic women's way of seeing reality insofar as the goal of their daily struggle is liberation. This is very important for *mujerista* theology for, though for us *lo cotidiano* carries so much weight, it is not the criterion used for judging right and wrong, good and bad. It is only insofar as *lo cotidiano* is a liberative praxis, a daily living that contributes to liberation, that *lo cotidiano* is considered good, valuable, right, salvific.[21] Were we to claim *lo cotidiano* as an ethical/theological criterion, norm, or principle we would be romanticizing *lo cotidiano*. Yes, there is much that is good and life-giving in *lo cotidiano* but there also is much that "obstructs understanding and tenderness, allowing to appear an abundance of postures of self-defense that are full of falsehoods, of lies, that turn *lo cotidiano* into a behavior that is not open to life."[22]

The importance we give to *lo cotidiano* steers *mujerista* theology away from any essentialism that would obscure precisely what is at the core of *lo cotidiano*: difference. At the same time *lo cotidiano* moves us from the "add and stir" version of feminist theology. As an epistemological category *lo cotidiano* goes well beyond adding another perspective and points to the need to change the social order by taking into consideration the way Latinas see and understand reality. *Lo cotidiano* points to the fact that how we Hispanic women, women who struggle from the underside of history, constitute ourselves and our world is an ongoing process. It takes into consideration

---

21. In *mujerista* theology salvation and liberation are intrinsically united. There can be no salvation without liberation. The realization of the kin-dom of God, which is what salvation refers to, begins to be a reality in history, and that is what liberation is. Liberation has to do with fullness of life, a prerequisite of the full realization of the kin-dom of God. For a fuller explanation see *En la Lucha*, pp. 34-45.

22. Ivone Gebara, *Conócete a ti misma* (São Paulo: Ediciones Paulinas, 1991), p. 24.

many different elements that we use to define ourselves as Latinas within the USA in the last years of the twentieth century.[23]

This does not mean, however, that *lo cotidiano* leads us to total relativism.[24] The fact that *lo cotidiano* is not the criterion, norm, or principle we use in *mujerista* theology does not mean that we use no criterion to judge right and wrong. As we have already said, we do recognize and hold liberation to be the criterion or principle by which we judge what is right or wrong, what is good or bad, what is salvific or condemnatory. By insisting as we have done on the "shared experiences" that constitute *lo cotidiano* we are trying to counter the isolationism inherent in individualism, the superiority inherent in claims of uniqueness, the hegemonic effect of false universalisms, all of which are intrinsic elements of absolute relativism. By saying that liberation is the criterion we use in *mujerista* theology, we are insisting on making it the core element, yes, the essential element of Hispanic women's morality and of all morality. In making liberation our central criterion *mujerista* theology attempts to contribute to an elaboration of morality that revolves around solidarity with the oppressed and the search for ways of an ever more inclusive social justice.[25]

In no way is the specificity of *lo cotidiano* to be taken as an "anything goes" moral attitude. That attitude is possible only in those who have power, in those whose social-political reality is entrenched and, therefore, do not feel threatened by the rest of humanity. That attitude is possible only in those who feel their world is completely stable, that nothing needs to change and that nothing will change. That is why *lo cotidiano* of Latinas is totally unimaginable for the dominant group; that is why they are totally disengaged from *lo cotidiano* of two-thirds of the world; that is why they are incapable of conceiving new ideas, of creating new ways of organizing society, even ways that would help them to perpetuate the status quo.[26]

---

23. For an explanation of the elements that are key to the self-understanding of Latinas see *En la Lucha*.

24. My main dialogue partners for these following paragraphs have been Margaret Farley and Leonardo Boff, whom I cite below. See Margaret Farley, "Feminism and Universal Morality," in Gene Outka and John P. Reeder, eds., *Prospect for a Common Morality* (Princeton, NJ: Princeton University Press, 1993), pp. 170-90.

25. Leonardo Boff, "La postmodernidad y la miseria de la razón liberadora," *Pasos* 54 (July-August 1994): 13.

26. Boff, "La postmodernidad y la miseria de la razón liberadora," p. 13. I am reminded here of one of the reasons Míguez Bonino gives for the preferential option for the poor and oppressed. According to him, since they have nothing to gain from the present structures,

Our insistence on *lo cotidiano* indeed should be seen as a denunciation of inadequate and false universalisms that ignore Latinas' daily lived experience. It also is a denunciation of the oppression Hispanic women suffer. Our insistence on *lo cotidiano* is an attempt to make our Latinas' experience count, to question the "truth" spoken by those who have the power to impose their views as normative. But our insistence on *lo cotidiano* must not be read as denying the viability and need for shared agendas and strategies. On the contrary, *mujerista* theology is anxious to participate in developing those strategies for liberation, which we know can grow only out of real solidarity, and this, in turn, depends on a real engagement of differences rather than a superficial acknowledgment of them.

In *mujerista* theology *lo cotidiano* has made it possible to appeal to the daily lived experience of Hispanic women as an authentic source without ignoring social location. On the contrary, *lo cotidiano* makes social location explicit for it is the context of the person in relation to physical space, ethnic space, social space. Furthermore, *lo cotidiano* for Latinas points both to the struggle *(la lucha)* against the present social order and to the liberating alternative which constitutes the core of our historical project: community *(la comunidad)*. This means that *lo cotidiano* constitutes the arena where Hispanic women are confronted by the groups of which they are members. This makes it possible for them to judge their own personal understandings, aspirations, ambitions, projects, and goals in their lives. So *lo cotidiano* is where morality begins to play a role for Latinas.[27] *Lo cotidiano* becomes the lived-text in which and through which Hispanic women understand and decide what is right and good, what is wrong and evil.[28] As such *lo cotidiano* is not a private, individual category, but rather a social category. *Lo cotidiano* refers to the way Latinas know and what we know to be the "stuff" *(la tela,* literally, the cloth) out of which our lives as a struggling community within the USA is fabricated.[29]

Lo cotidiano for us is also a way of understanding theology, our attempt

---

the poor and the oppressed are capable of imagining a different future, something those who are set in protecting the present are not capable of doing. See José Míguez Bonino, "Nuevas tendendas en teologia," *Pasos* 9 (January 1987): 22.

27. Cecilia Mino G., "Algunas refleciones sobre pedagogia de género y cotidianidad," *Tejiendo Nuestra Red* 1, no. 1 (October 1988): 11-12.

28. To claim *lo cotidiano* as lived-text is in no way to say that it is a moral criterion.

29. Though I do not agree with all of Mary McClintock Fulkerson's ideas, her book gives much to think about in our own *mujerista* theological enterprise. See her book *Changing the Subject: Women's Discourses and Feminist Theology* (Minneapolis: Fortress Press, 1994).

to explain how we understand the divine, what we know about the divine. I contrast this to the academic and churchly attempts to see theology as being about God instead of about what we humans know about God. *Lo cotidiano* makes it possible for us to see our theological knowledge as well as all our knowledge as fragmentary, partisan, conjectural, and provisional.[30] It is fragmentary because we know that what we will know tomorrow is not the same as what we know today but will stand in relation to what we know today. What we know is what we have found through our experiences, through the experiences of our communities of struggle. What we know is always partisan, it is always influenced by our own values, prejudices, loyalties, emotions, traditions, dreams, and future projects.[31] Our knowing is conjectural because to know is not to copy or reflect reality but rather to interpret in a creative way those relations, structures, and processes that are elements of what is called reality. And, finally, *lo cotidiano* makes it clear that, for *mujerista* theology, knowledge is provisional for it indicates in and of itself how transitory our world and we ourselves are.[32]

The insistence on *lo cotidiano* brings up the issue of how *mujerista* theology deals with the past. Does *mujerista* theology pay any attention to what Scriptures tell us about God, what the doctrines and dogmas of our churches tell us about the divine, what theologians throughout the centuries have said about God? We certainly reject any and all regurgitation of the past. Reflexive use of the past is no good. But reflective use of the past is an important method in *mujerista* theology. Our communities have their own living religious traditions. The religious beliefs and practices of grassroots Latinas are not ex nihilo, but rather are rooted in traditions passed on from our ancestors and certainly rooted in Catholic and, more recently, in Protestant religious teachings.

Using *lo cotidiano* of Hispanic women as the source of *mujerista* theology is an act of subversion. Our theology challenges the absolutizing of mainline theology as normative, as exhaustively explaining the gospels or Christian beliefs. Using *lo cotidiano* as the source of our theology means that Latinas are not the object of *mujerista* theology. Hispanic women are the subjects, the agents of *mujerista* theology.

30. Maduro, *Mapas para la fiesta*, p. 137.

31. And in *mujerista* theology we are very clear about our partisan perspective. We make a clear option for the perspective of Latinas based on the fact that we believe the Christian message of justice and peace is based on an option for the oppressed.

32. I have here adapted Maduro's synthesis about knowledge. See *Mapas para la fiesta*, pp. 136-38.

A Specific Kind of Liberation Theology The third characteristic of *mujerista* theology is that it is a liberation theology, a specific kind with its own characteristics. As in other liberation theologies for us the unfolding of the kin-dom of God does not happen apart from history. We talk about "salvation-liberation," believing that both are interconnected and that to work for liberation for us Christians, which has to do with establishing justice in concrete ways in our world, is not necessarily different from being good Christians. For Latinas our religious practices and beliefs contribute significantly to the struggle for liberation, the struggle for survival.

Part of this understanding is the fact that for us theology is a praxis. By praxis I mean reflective, liberative action. To understand theology as praxis means that we accept the fact that we cannot separate thinking from acting. *Mujerista* theology is not reflection upon action but a liberative action in and of itself. The daily actions of our communities as they struggle to survive need intentional thinking, and religion plays a role in the thinking and the motivation for action, as well as in the kind of action done and the reason for doing it. Furthermore, the insistence that grassroots Latinas do *mujerista* theology and that so doing is a liberative praxis indicates that they too are intellectuals. The regular understanding of "intellectual" connotes a social function, a professional category. Unfortunately, however, this meaning is usually extended to mean that intellectuals, in contrast to nonintellectuals, are the ones who are capable of intellectual activity. In reality, however,

> although one can speak of intellectuals, one cannot speak of non-intellectuals, because non-intellectuals do not exist. . . . Each [one] participates in a particular conception of the world, has a conscious line of moral conduct, and therefore contributes to sustain a conception of the world or to modify it, that is, to bring into being new modes of thought.[33]

Women in general (but in particular poor women with little formal education, and even more so women whose first language is not English — as is the case with many Hispanic women) are commonly not considered quite capable of articulating what they think. Yes, many consider that Latinas' ability to think is at best limited. It is clear to see, then, why *mujerista* theology's claim that grassroots Hispanic women are "organic intellectuals," that their articulation of their religious understandings is an element of this theology, is in itself a liberative praxis.

33. Antonio Gramsci, *Prison Notebook,* ed. and trans. Quintin Hoare and Geoffrey Norwell Smith (New York: International Publishers, 1975), p. 9.

Another important element of *mujerista* theology as a liberation theology is the part popular religion plays in it.[34] It is precisely this aspect of the religion of Latinas that provides the greatest impetus for our struggle for liberation. There is no way you can deal with Hispanics, study our culture, or read our literature without encountering popular religion. After the Spanish language, popular religion is the most important identifying characteristic of Latinas, the main carrier of our culture. Hispanic women's Christianity is of a very specific variety. Its main vehicle, the signs and symbols that it uses, and a significant part of its theology are based on medieval Christianity, the pre-Reformation, sixteenth-century Christianity of southern Spain. But this sixteenth-century Spanish Christianity is mingled with the religious beliefs and rituals of African and Amerindian cultures as well.[35]

Now "dominant North Atlantic theology has generally regarded popular religion as a primitive force of religious expression needing to be evangelized."[36] *Mujerista* theology, as most of Hispanic/Latino theology, on the other hand, "recognizes popular religion as a credible experience of the . . . [divine]; and as a positive reservoir of values for self-determination."[37] In other words, in *mujerista* theology we insist on "the normative, graced, and even universal dimensions of the 'salvific' manifestations of non-Christian religions."[38]

Popular religion plays a significant role in our struggles for survival and liberation. Many of us know from experience that it is mainly due to popular religion that Christianity is alive and flourishing among Latinas in spite of the lack of care and attention we have experienced from the churches. In popular religion we find a sense of embracing diversity that makes it possible for very different elements to influence each other to the point where each element is reformulated, maintaining its own specificity but not without taking into consideration the specificity of the other elements.

34. Generally popular religion is understood along the lines of less sophisticated, nonsystematic, almost dealing with magic. Here it means nothing of that but simply refers to "the religion of the people."

35. At present certain Pentecostal elements are beginning to be integrated into Latino popular religion.

36. Arturo Bañuelas, "U.S. Hispanic Theology," *Missiology* 20, no. 2 (April 1992): 290-91.

37. Bañuelas, "U.S. Hispanic Theology," pp. 290-91.

38. This quotation is taken from unpublished notes of Orlando Espín and Sixto Garcia for a presentation they made at the Catholic Theological Society of America. An edited version of their presentation/workshop can be found in the Catholic Theological Society of America *Proceedings* 42 (1987): 114-19.

Challenges to Traditional Theologies

In pointing out the ways in which *mujerista* theology challenges traditional theologies I do not want to suggest that there is nothing good about traditional theology. But I do want to make it very clear that its relevance to what is going on in our world today is waning mainly because of the way in which it insists on dealing with tradition, because it does not take seriously the religion of the people but seems to prefer the doctrines and dogmas of the church, and because traditional theologies seem to be content with seeing themselves as accountable only, or at least mainly, to the institutional churches.

"Epistemological Vigilance"

The first challenge is born of a need we *mujerista* theologians recognize as primary: we must have "epistemological vigilance."[39] We need to be epistemologically vigilant as indeed traditional theology should also be. But, while we recognize this need and embrace it, traditional theology rejects it or simply ignores it. Now, what understandings are encompassed within this term "epistemological vigilance"?

First, we *mujerista* theologians make a very serious and ongoing effort to be aware of our subjectivity. We need to have a "critical consciousness of the limits of our capacity to know reality, and of the 'concealing and distorting' tendencies of this same capacity."[40] We work hard at being aware of our ideological biases and, though it is not easy, we work hard at revealing such biases. This means that we have to be aware of how our own social situation colors our analysis of the religion of our communities and colors the way we say what we say in our theological writings.

Second, epistemological vigilance here refers to the constant need to evaluate how our theological enterprise contributes to the liberation of our people. And here I am referring not only to the results of our theology, our writings, but also to the way in which we conduct our research. The question "Who benefits from this?" should never be far away from our minds. We need to apply a hermeneutics of suspicion to our constructive proposals, to our narratives, to our whole theological enterprise.

39. This term is used by Maduro. In his work it refers mainly to the meaning I notice in the next paragraph. See Maduro, *Religion and Social Conflict*, pp. 27-29.

40. Maduro, *Religion and Social Conflict*, p. 27.

Third, epistemological vigilance refers to the need to avoid avoidance. *Mujerista* theologians need to be able to grapple with differences, with contradictions. We need to engage each other, to press each other for greater clarity, to question each other. In order to do this we need to work very hard at maintaining our sense of community, at not giving in to destructive competition or, what is worse, ignoring each other.

Now, all of this is a challenge to traditional theology because one of the key elements of traditional theology is its so-called objectivity, its so-called immutability, its sense of being "official" and, precisely because it is official, of being the only perspective that is correct.

Mujerista theology denounces any and all so-called objectivity. What passes as objectivity in reality merely names the subjectivity of those who have the authority and/or power to impose their point of view. So instead of objectivity what we should be claiming is responsibility for our subjectivity. All theology has to start with self-disclosure. Self-disclosure as part of theology should give all those who in one way or another come into contact with our theological work our "actional route."[41] As a theologian I am obliged to reveal my concrete story within the framework of the social forces I have lived in. I am called to reveal the pivotal forces and issues that have formed me and that serve as my main points of reference. The idea in this kind of self-disclosure is to situate the subject, in this case myself, so that my discourse is understandable to others not only out of their own experience but insofar as they have the ability to go beyond the limits of their experience and see how my experience, because it is part of the processes of living, relates to and intersects with their experience, no matter how different both experiences are. In other words, the particulars of my life might not be something others can relate to easily, but, by knowing a little about them, others will be able to find some point of contact, at least because of similarities in the processes of our lives. Thanks to those points of contact, others will be able to understand me and assess what I say without necessarily agreeing with me or limiting me to the scope of their experience.

Because subjectivity embraces the question "Who benefits from this?" *mujerista* theology challenges the so-called objectivity of traditional theology that refuses to recognize that it often tends to benefit the status quo at the expense of those who are marginal in church and society. The status quo is not a natural arrangement but rather a social construct originating with

41. Mark Kline Taylor, *Remembering Esperanza* (Maryknoll, NY: Orbis Books, 1990), pp. 1-18.

and maintained mainly by white, Euro-American males. Traditional theology offers intellectual backing for religious understandings and practices at the core of our churches, and it is easy to see who are those in charge of our churches.

Finally, *mujerista* theology's insistence on recognizing and disclosing subjectivity challenges the official "status of traditional theology that results in avoidance of engagement. Traditional theology has clothed itself with the immutability that it claims is God's. Or does perhaps not that traditional theology make God immutable because it makes God in its own image and likeness?

Theology as a Communal Task

Our second challenge to traditional theology has to do with the centrality which community has in our Latino culture and in our theology. This means that we will continue to use the lived-experience of our grassroots communities as the source of our theology. So the themes of our theology are those that are suggested to us by the religious understandings and practices of our communities and not by the doctrines and dogmas of our churches. The goal of *mujerista* theology is not to come up with a Summa, or with three volumes entitled Systematic Theology #1, #2, and #3. The themes *mujerista* theology deals with are those that are required by Latinas' struggle for liberation. Thus, in our first book we dealt with what grounds the struggle for many of us, our understanding of God.[42] The second book dealt with issues of self-identity — of ethnicity and of moral agency.[43] And now we are working on issues of embodiment, for what is most commonly used against us, to oppress us, is our bodies.[44]

Yes, we need to continue to approach theology from the perspective of the religious understandings and practices of our communities. This means that we must resist the temptation to do theology as usual, not only by using different methods but also by resisting the temptation to follow the "regular" themes and divisions of traditional theology. In no way does this mean that our theology is not, should not be rigorous. We owe to ourselves and our

42. Ada María Isasi-Díaz and Yolanda Tarango, *Hispanic Women: Prophetic Voice in the Church* (San Francisco: Harper & Row, 1988; reprint, Minneapolis: Fortress Press, 1992).

43. *En la Lucha.*

44. We are in the process of doing reflection weekends with Latinas all around the country to collect material on how Latinas understand and relate to our bodies.

communities the very best theology that we can do. But good theology for us *mujerista* theologians is a theology that helps our people in their struggle for survival, not a theology that receives the blessing of the status quo because it follows traditional patterns.

In a way traditional theology, even the best of traditional theology, by insisting on following the patterns established long ago, in my opinion closes itself to the ongoing revelation of the divine in our midst. Those who do traditional theology call their way of proceeding "faithfulness to the past." I call it "blindness to the present" and "ignoring the God-in-our-midst today."

The Importance of Differences

A third challenge *mujerista* theology presents to traditional theology has to do with *mestizaje* and *mulatez,* with how we understand and deal with diversity, with differences. For us differences are not something to be done away with but rather something to be embraced. In our theology we do not aim at assimilation, at making all that is different fit into some preconceived norm or center. That is not how we deal with diversity. Both our understanding of *mestizaje* and *mulatez* as well as our understanding of popular religion and how it functions in *mujerista* theology make explicit what we mean when we talk about embracing diversity.

Let me explain this further here. Usually in mainline discourse, in traditional theological discourse, difference is defined as absolute otherness, mutual exclusion, categorical opposition.[45] This is an essentialist meaning of difference in which one group serves as the norm against which all others are to be measured. Those of us who do not measure up are considered to be deviant, and our ideas are heretical. Difference of opinion, difference of perspective, arising most of the time from different life-experiences, any and all differences are defined as exclusion and opposition.

This way of defining difference expresses a fear of specificity and a fear of making permeable the boundaries between oneself and the others, between one's ideas and those of others. Specificity tends to be understood as unique — lending it a certain air of "the unknown" of which one is afraid or which is romanticized as exotic.

45. I am indebted to the work of Iris Marion Young on the issue of diversity. See Iris Marion Young, *Justice and the Politics of Difference* (Princeton, NJ: Princeton University Press, 1990), particularly chapter 6.

In *mujerista* theology we posit embracing differences as a moral option. We work at seeing those who are different from us as mirrors of ourselves and what we think. Ideas that are different from ours are mirrors — not the only ones — we have for our ideas (ideas similar to ours, of course, also are mirrors of our ideas) for they do make us see our ideas in a new light, maybe even make it possible for us to better understand our own ideas, to clarify them for ourselves and for others, a result that might not be achieved if we were to ignore ideas different from ours.

To embrace differences we have to stop being lazy and have to know what others really think. But that requires self-conscious interaction, and we are afraid of interacting with those with whom we disagree. Also, to be able to interact with others we have to affirm difference as something positive, we have to affirm plurality, to make permeable the boundaries of our categories. All of this requires embracing ambiguity, something those of us who live at the margins know much about. But traditional theology is not willing to do that because instead of risking ambiguity it rests secure in its impermeable and immutable center.

In *mujerista* theology difference, then, means not otherness or exclusive opposition but specificity and heterogeneity. Difference is understood as relational rather than as a matter of substantive categories and attributes. Difference is not then a description of categories, descriptions set one against the other across a barbed wire fence. Rather difference points to the specificity of each description and seeks ways to relate those different descriptions, different because they come from people with dissimilar life-experiences.

Embracing difference, welcoming ambiguity, is not in any way to be conceived as wishy-washiness! We are not advocating total relativity. As a matter of fact because *mujerista* theology is a strategy for liberation, there is a certain discipline of action that we demand of each other. Also, in Latino culture tradition is something very important: So tradition is taken into consideration. But the role of tradition is not to impose itself perennially without any changes. The role of tradition is to make present the wisdom of generations past which we are then called to evaluate and apply to the present in view of our need for survival, our need for liberation. And, unfortunately, that is an understanding of tradition that traditional theology is not willing to consider.

Conclusion

In many ways what has guided *mujerista* theology from the beginning are those wonderful words of Miriam in the book of Numbers, "Has Yahweh indeed spoken only through Moses?" (Num. 12:2). Well aware of the fact that she suffered severe penalties for daring to scold Moses, for daring to claim that Yahweh also spoke to her and through her, our sister Miriam invites *mujerista* theologians to throw our lot with the people of God and to hope that, just as in her case, the authorities will catch up with us, that they will eventually also see that we have no leprosy, that we are clean. But their declaration of cleanliness is not what makes us clean; their saying is not what makes *mujerista* theology a worthwhile and important task for us. It is rather the fact that *mujerista* theology is part of the struggle for survival, the struggle for liberation — that is what makes it right and just for us to pursue it. Doing *mujerista* theology is an intrinsic element of our struggle, of our lives, because indeed, for Latinas in the USA to struggle is to live, *la vida es la lucha.*

31 Looking Back, Going Forward: Black Theology as Public Theology

James H. Cone

This Black Theology Conference provides an opportunity for me to reflect on the origin and development of my theological perspective. When I think about my vocation, I go back to my childhood years in Bearden, Arkansas — a rural community of approximately 1,200 people. I do not remember Bearden for nostalgic reasons. In fact, I seldom return there in person, because of persistent racial tensions in my relations with the whites and lingering ambivalence in my feelings toward the blacks. I am not and do not wish to be Bearden's favorite son. My brother, Cecil, also a theologian and a preacher, has been bestowed that honor by the African American community, a distinction he gladly accepts and a role he fulfills quite well.

I remember Bearden because it is the place where I first discovered myself as black and Christian. There, the meaning of black was defined primarily by the menacing presence of whites, which no African American could escape. I grew up during the age of Jim Crow (1940s and early 1950s). I attended segregated schools, drank water from colored fountains, went to movies in balconies, and — when absolutely necessary — greeted white adults at the back doors of their homes. I also observed the contempt and brutality that white law meted out to the blacks who transgressed their racial mores or who dared to question their authority. Bearden white people, like most southerners of that time, could be mean and vicious, and I, along with other blacks, avoided them whenever possible, as if they were poisonous snakes.

The Christian part of my identity was shaped primarily at Macedonia A.M.E. Church. Every Sunday and sometimes on weeknights, I encoun-

438

tered Jesus through rousing sermons, fervent prayers, spirited gospel songs, and the passionate testimonies of the people. Jesus was the dominant reality at Macedonia and in black life in Bearden. The people walked with him and told him about their troubles as if he were a trusted friend who understood their trials and tribulations in this unfriendly world. They called Jesus "the lily of the valley and the bright and morning star," the "Rose of Sharon and the Lord of life," a "very present help in time of trouble." The people often shouted and danced, clapped their hands and stamped their feet as they bore witness to the power of Jesus' Spirit in their midst — "building them up where they are torn down and propping them up on every leaning side."

As he did for the people of Macedonia, Jesus became a significant presence in my life, too. I do not remember the exact date or time I "turned to Jesus," as the conversion experience was called. At home, church, and school, at play and at work, Jesus was always there, as the anchor of life, giving it meaning and purpose and bestowing hope and faith in the ultimate justice of things. Jesus was that reality who empowered black people to know that they were not the worthless human beings that white people said they were.

There were no atheists in the "Cotton Belt," as the "colored" section of Bearden was called — no proclaimers of Nietzsche's "God is dead" philosophy and none of the "cultured despisers" of religion that Friedrich Schleiermacher wrote to in 1799. The closest to Nietzsche's atheists and Schleiermacher's cultured despisers were the bluespeople who drank corn whiskey and boogied slowly and sensually to the deep guttural sound of the raunchy music at the juke joints every Friday and Saturday night. The sounds of Bessie Smith, Muddy Waters, and Howlin' Wolf took center stage as they belted out "I Used to Be Your Sweet Mama," "Hoochie Coochie Man," and "Somebody in My Home." Such music was called the "lowdown dirty blues."

Unlike the church people, the bluespeople found the Sunday religion of Jesus inadequate for coping with their personal problems and the social contradictions they experienced during the week. As church people soothed their souls with the song, "Lord, I want to be a Christian in my heart," the people at the honky-tonk transcended their agony by facing it with stoic defiance or, as James Baldwin called it, "ironic tenacity."[1] "I got the blues, but I'm too damned mean to cry."

1. James Baldwin, *The Fire Next Time* (New York: Dell, 1964), p. 61.

Sometimes sharp tensions emerged between the celebrants of Saturday night and those of Sunday morning. But each group respected the other, because both knew that they were seeking, in their own way, to cope with the same troubles of life. Some people moved between the two groups during different periods of their lives, as my father did. But it was not possible to be a member in good standing in both groups at the same time, because the church demanded that an individual make a choice between the blues and the spirituals, between the "devil's music" and the "sweet melodies of Jesus." Baptist and Methodist churches, the only black denominations in Bearden, regularly accepted backsliders back into the fold, provided they repented of their wrongdoing and declared their intentions to lead a good and righteous life in service to the Lord. My father had a few lapses in faith, because he found it hard to cope with life's adversities without taking a nip of gin and hanging out with the bluespeople in order to add a little spice to life not found at the church. But my mother monitored him closely, and Macedonia readily received him back into the community of the faithful as often as he publicly repented.

During my childhood what puzzled me most about the religion of Jesus was not the tension between Saturday night and Sunday morning in black life but rather the conspicuous presence of the color bar in white churches. In Bearden, like the rest of America, Sunday was the most segregated day of the week, and 11 A.M., the most segregated hour. Black and white Christians had virtually no social or religious dealings with each other, even though both were Baptists and Methodists — reading the same Bible, worshiping the same God, and reciting the same confessions of faith in their congregations.

Although whites posted "Welcome" signs outside their churches, ostensibly beckoning all visitors to join them in worship, blacks knew that the invitation did not include them. "What kind of Christianity is it that preaches love and practices segregation?" my brother Cecil and I, budding young theologians, often asked each other. "How could whites exclude black people from their churches and still claim Jesus as their Savior and the Bible as their holy book?" We talked about testing the theological integrity of white faith by seeking to integrate one of their churches but felt that the risks of bodily harm were too great.

Despite the ever-present reality of white supremacy, I do not ever remember experiencing a feeling of inferiority because of what whites said about me or about other black people. One reason was the stellar example my father and mother set before me. They were part of that cloud of black witnesses that James Baldwin wrote about who "in the teeth of the most terrible odds, achieved an unassailable and monumental dignity."[2] They taught me what Baldwin told his nephew: "You can only be destroyed by believing that you really are what the white world calls a nigger."[3]

My parents were strong and self-confident, exhibiting a determined opposition to white supremacy and creative leadership and great courage when they and the black community faced adversity. Charlie and Lucy, as the people in Bearden called them, were immensely intelligent, even though they had little opportunity for formal education, having completed only the sixth and ninth grades respectively. (With the support and encouragement of my father, my mother went back and completed high school where her sons had graduated earlier and also went on to finish her college degree four years later. She then returned to teach in Bearden. I was struck by her determination.) Their education, they often told their sons, came from the "school of hard knocks," the experience of surviving with dignity in a society that did not recognize black humanity.

The faith of Macedonia, which my parents imbibed deeply, was a powerful antidote against the belief that blacks were less than whites. According to this faith, God created all people equal — as brothers and sisters in the church and in society. No person or group is better than any other. As evidence for that claim, preachers and teachers often cited the text from the prophet Malachi: "Have we not all one father? Hath not one God created us?" (2:10 KJV). They also quoted Paul, selectively — carefully avoiding the ambiguous and problematic texts, especially in Philemon where Paul returned the slave Onesimus to his master and in Ephesians where servants were told to "be obedient to them who are your masters . . . as unto Christ" (Eph. 6:5 KJV).

Preachers and Sunday school teachers at Macedonia were quite skilled in picking biblical texts that affirmed their humanity. They especially liked Luke's account of Paul's sermon on Mars Hill where he said God made of one blood all nations of men [and women] to dwell on the face of the earth (Acts 17:26 KJV). They also quoted Paul's letter to the Galatians: "There is neither Jew nor Greek . . . neither slave nor free, . . . neither male nor female." We are "all one in Christ Jesus" (3:28 KJV) — blacks and whites, as well as other human colors and orientations. When one truly believes that gospel and internalizes it in one's way of life, as I and many black Christians in

2. Baldwin, *The Fire Next Time*, p. 21.
3. Baldwin, *The Fire Next Time*, p. 14.

Bearden did, it is possible to know that you are somebody even though the world treats you like nobody.

From the time I was conscious of being black and Christian, I recognized that was a problem for America's white politicians and invisible to most of its practitioners of religion. I did not quite understand what made me problematic or invisible since skin color appeared to be a minor difference between human beings. Yet politicians found it difficult to pass laws to protect black humanity. Even those that were passed were rarely enforced. White ministers seemed not to notice the daily white assault on black humanity. They preached sermons about loving God and the neighbor as if the violence that whites committed against blacks did not invalidate their Christian identity.

While struggling to understand how whites reconciled racism with their Christian identity, I also encountered an uncritical faith in many black churches. They not only seemed to tolerate anti-intellectualism as whites tolerated racism; but they, like most whites in relation to racism, often promoted it. It was as if the less one knew and the louder one shouted Jesus' name, the closer one was to God.

I found it hard to believe that the God of Jesus condoned ignorance as if it was a virtue. It contradicted what my parents and teachers taught me about the value of education and a disciplined mind. It also contradicted what I read in history books about black slaves who risked life and limb in order to learn to read and write so they could understand more clearly the meaning of the freedom to which God had called them. I was, therefore, deeply troubled by the anti-intellectualism that permeated many aspects of the ministry in the black church.

How could ministers preach the gospel in a world they did not understand? How could they understand the gospel without disciplined reflection and critical debate? "A religion that won't stand the application of reason and common sense," wrote W. E. B. Du Bois, "is not fit for an intelligent dog."[4]

The search for a reasoned faith in a complex and ever-changing world was the chief motivation that led me to study at Garrett Theological Seminary (now Garrett-Evangelical). It seemed that the more I learned about the gospel through a critical study of the Bible, history, theology, and the practice of ministry the more I needed and wanted to know about it. I wanted to

---

4. In Manning Marable, "The Black Faith of W. E. B. Du Bois: Sociocultural and Political Dimensions of Black Religion," *The Southern Quarterly* 23, no. 3 (Spring 1985): 21.

explore its meanings for different social, political, and cultural contexts, past and present.

Theology quickly became my favorite subject in seminary because it opened the door to explore faith's meaning for the current time and situation in which I was living. I loved the give-and-take of theological debate and eagerly waited for the opportunity during and after classes to engage my professors and fellow students on the burning theological issues of the day. That was why I remained at Garrett and Northwestern University for the Ph.D. in systematic theology. After I completed the doctorate in spring 1965, writing a dissertation on Karl Barth's anthropology, I thought I had enough knowledge of the Christian faith to communicate it to persons anywhere in the world. Who would not feel adequately endowed after reading twelve volumes of Barth's *Church Dogmatics*?

But the Civil Rights and Black Power movements of the 1960s awakened me from my theological slumber. As I became actively involved in the black freedom movement that was exploding in the streets all over America, I soon discovered how limited my seminary education had been. The curriculum at Garrett and Northwestern had not dealt with questions that black people were asking as they searched for the theological meaning of their fight for justice in a white racist society. And as individuals and isolated students within a demanding educational system, neither I nor the token number of black students had the intellectual resources to articulate those questions. I found myself grossly ill-prepared, because I knew deep down that I could not repeat to a struggling black community the doctrines of the faith as they had been reinterpreted by Barth, Bultmann, Niebuhr, and Tillich for European colonizers and white racists in the United States. I knew that before I could say anything worthwhile about God and the black situation of oppression in the United States, I had to discover a theological identity that was accountable to the life, history, and culture of African American people.

In a way, my education had pulled me away from my people. The educational quest had been to master the theological systems of the well-known European theologians of the past and present. As students, we obediently spent most of our time reading books, listening to lectures, and writing papers about their views of God, Jesus, the Holy Spirit, and the church. But recognizing the community to whom I was accountable, I wanted to know more than just what Europeans and white Americans who emulated them thought about sacred reality. I was searching for a way to create a Christian theology out of the black experience of slavery, segregation, and the struggle for a just society. When I asked my professors what theology had to do with the black struggle for racial justice, they seemed surprised and uncomfortable with the question, not knowing what to say, and anxious to move on with the subject matter as they understood it. I was often told that theology and the struggle for racial justice were separate subjects, with the latter belonging properly in the disciplines of sociology and political science. Although I felt a disquieting unease with that response, I did not say much about it to my professors as they skirted around talking about what the gospel had to say to black people in a white society that had defined them as nonpersons.

While reading Martin Luther King, Jr., and Malcolm X, the blackness in my theological consciousness exploded like a volcano after many dormant years. I found my theological voice. Using the cultural and political insights of Malcolm and Martin, I discovered a way of articulating what I wanted to say about theology and race: it not only rejected the need for my professors' approval, but challenged them to exorcise the racism in their theologies. Malcolm taught me how to make theology black and never again to despise my African origin. Martin showed me how to make and keep theology Christian and never allow it to be used to support injustice. I was transformed from a Negro theologian to a Black theologian, from an understanding of theology as an analysis of God ideas in books to an understanding of it as a disciplined reflection about God arising out of a commitment to the practice of justice for the poor.

The turn to blackness was an even deeper metanoia-experience than the turn to Jesus. It was spiritual, radically transforming my way of seeing the world and theology. Before I was born again into thinking black, I thought of theology as something remote from my history and culture, something that was primarily defined by Europeans whom I, at best, could only imitate. Blackness gave me new theological spectacles, which enabled me to move beyond the limits of white theology and empowered my mind to think wild, heretical thoughts when evaluated by white academic values. Blackness opened my eyes to see African American history and culture as one of the most insightful sources for knowing about God since the Bible was declared a canon. Blackness whetted my appetite for learning how to do theology with a black signature on it and thereby make it accountable to poor black people and not to the privileged white theological establishment. The revolution that Malcolm X created in my theological consciousness meant that I could no longer make peace with the intellectual mediocrity in which I had been trained. The more I trusted my experience the more new thoughts about God and theology whirled around in my head — so fast I could hardly contain my excitement.

Using the black experience as the starting point of theology raised the theodicy question in a profound and challenging way that was never mentioned in graduate school. It was James Baldwin's *The Fire Next Time* which poignantly defined the problem for me: "If [God's] love was so great, and if He loved all His children, why were we, the blacks, cast down so far?"[5] This was an existential, heart-wrenching question, which challenged the academic way in which the problem of evil was dealt with in graduate school. It forced me to search deep into a wellspring of blackness, not for a theoretical answer that would satisfy the dominant intellectual culture of Europe and the United States, but rather for a new way of doing theology that would empower the suffering black poor to fight for a more liberated existence.

In writing *Black Theology and Black Power* (1969), I suddenly understood what Karl Barth must have felt when he first rejected the liberal theology of his professors in Germany. It was a liberating experience to be free of my liberal and neo-orthodox professors, to be liberated from defining theology using abstract theological jargon that was unrelated to the life-and-death issues of black people. Although separated by nearly fifty years and dealing with completely different theological situations and issues, I felt a spiritual kinship with Barth, especially his writing of *The Epistle to the Romans* (1921) and in his public debate with Adolf Harnack, his former teacher.

As I think back to that time in the late 1960s, when white American theologians were writing and talking about the "death of God theology" as black people were fighting and dying in the streets, the energy swells once again. I was angry and could not keep it to myself. Like Malcolm X, I felt I was the angriest black theologian in America.[6] I had to speak out, as forcefully as I knew how, against the racism I witnessed in theology, the churches, and the broader society. And that was why I began to write.

The anger I felt while writing *Black Theology and Black Power* was fueled by the assassination of Martin Luther King, Jr. Thirty years later as I prepared the "Aims of Religion" address on the anniversary date of King's death, I am still just as angry, because America, when viewed from the perspective of the black poor, is no closer to King's dream of a just society than

5. Baldwin, *The Fire Next Time*, p. 46.

6. Many people called Malcolm X "the angriest Negro in America." See his *Autobiography* (New York: Ballentine Books, 1965), p. 366.

when he was killed. While the black middle class has made considerable economic progress, the underclass, despite America's robust economy, is worse off in 1998 than in 1968. While the statistics are well known, they still fail to shock or outrage most Americans. One-third of young black males are involved in the criminal justice system. One-half of black babies are born in poverty, and their life expectancy in the urban ghetto is lower than that of Bangladesh.

America is still two societies: one rich and middle class, the other poor and working class. One-third of the African American population is poor. Predominantly women and children, they are, in the words of William J. Wilson, the truly disadvantaged,[7] with few skills that enable them to compete in this technological, informational age. To recognize the plight of the poor does not require academic dissection. It requires only a drive into the central cities of the nation to see people living in places not fit for human habitation.

What deepens my anger today is the appalling silence of white theologians on racism in the United States and the modern world. Whereas this silence has been partly broken in several secular disciplines, theology remains virtually mute. From Jonathan Edwards to Walter Rauschenbusch and Reinhold Niebuhr and up to the present moment, progressive white theologians, with few exceptions, write and teach as if they do not need to address the radical contradiction that racism creates for Christian theology. They do not write about slavery, colonialism, segregation, and the profound cultural link these horrible crimes created between white supremacy and Christianity. The cultural bond between European values and Christian beliefs is so deeply enmeshed in the American psyche and thought process that their identification is assumed. White images and ideas dominate the religious life of Christians and the intellectual life of theologians, reinforcing the "moral" right of white people to dominate people of color economically and politically. White supremacy is so widespread that it becomes a "natural" way of viewing the world. We must ask therefore: Is racism so deeply embedded in Euro-American history and culture that it is impossible to do theology without being anti-black?

There is historical precedent for such ideological questioning. After the Jewish Holocaust, Christian theologians were forced to ask whether anti-Judaism was so deeply woven into the core of the gospel and Western history that theology was no longer possible without being anti-Semitic. Recently

---

7. See William Julius Wilson, *The Truly Disadvantaged: The Inner City, the Underclass and Public Policy* (Chicago: University of Chicago Press, 1987).

feminists asked an equally radical question regarding whether patriarchy was so deeply rooted in biblical faith and its male theological tradition that one could not do Christian theology without justifying the oppression of women. Gay and lesbian theologians are following the feminist lead and are asking whether homophobia is an inherent part of biblical faith. And finally, Third World theologians, particularly in Latin America, forced many progressive First World theologians to revisit Marx's class critique of religion or run the risk of making Christianity a tool for exploiting the poor.

Critiquing racism is just as crucial for the integrity of Christian theology as any critique in the modern world. Christianity was blatantly used to justify slavery, colonialism, and segregation for nearly five hundred years. Yet this great contradiction is consistently neglected by the same white male theologians who would never ignore the problem that critical reason poses for faith in a secular world. They still do theology as if white supremacy creates no serious problem for Christian belief. Their silence on race is so conspicuous that I sometimes wonder why they are not greatly embarrassed by it.

How do we account for such a long history of white theological blindness to racism and its brutal impact on the lives of African people? Is it because white theologians do not know about the tortured history of the Atlantic slave trade, which according to British historian Basil Davidson "cost Africa at least fifty million souls"?[8] Have they forgotten about the unspeakable crimes of colonialism? In the Congo alone, "Reputable estimates suggest that between five and eight million [people] were killed in the course of twenty-three years."[9]

Two hundred forty-four years of slavery and one hundred years of legal segregation, augmented by a reign of white terror that lynched more than five thousand blacks, defined the meaning of America as "white over black."[10] White supremacy shaped the social, political, economic, cultural, and religious ethos in the churches, the academy, and the broader society. Seminary and divinity school professors contributed to America's white nationalist perspective by openly advocating the superiority of the white race over all others. The highly regarded church historian, Philip Schaff of Union Seminary in New York (1870-1893), spoke for most white theologians in the

---

8. Basil Davidson, *The African Slave Trade: Precolonial History 1450-1850* (Boston: Little, Brown, 1961), p. 80.

9. Louis Turner, *Multinational Companies and the Third World* (New York: Hill and Wang, 1973), p. 27.

10. See especially Winthrop D. Jordan, *White Over Black: American Attitudes toward the Negro 1550-1812* (Baltimore: Penguin Books, 1969).

nineteenth century when he said: "The Anglo-Saxon and Anglo-American, of all modern races, possess the strongest national character and the one best fitted for universal dominion."[11]

Present-day white theologians do not express their racist views as blatantly as Philip Schaff. They do not even speak of the "Negro's cultural backwardness," as America's best-known social ethicist Reinhold Niebuhr did as late as 1965.[12] To speak as Schaff and Niebuhr spoke would be politically incorrect in this era of multiculturalism and color blindness. But that does not mean that today's white theologians are less racist. It only means that their racism is concealed or unconscious. As long as religion scholars do not engage racism in their intellectual work, we can be sure that they are as racist as their grandparents, whether they acknowledge it or not. By not engaging America's crimes against black people, white theologians are treating the nation's violent racist past as if it were dead. But as William Faulkner said, "The past is never dead; it is not even past." Racism is so deeply embedded in American history and culture that we cannot get rid of this cancer by simply ignoring it.

There can be no justice without memory — without remembering the horrible crimes committed against humanity and the great human struggles for justice. But oppressors always try to erase the history of their crimes and often portray themselves as the innocent ones. Through their control of the media and religious, political, and academic discourse, "They're able," as Malcolm put it, "to make the victim look like the criminal and the criminal look like the victim."[13]

Even when white theologians reflect on God and suffering, the problem of theodicy, they almost never make racism a central issue in their analysis of the challenge that evil poses for the Christian faith. If they should happen to mention racism, it is usually just a footnote or only a marginal comment. They almost never make racism the subject of a sustained analysis. It is amazing that racism could be so prevalent and violent in American life and yet so absent in white theological discourse.

President Clinton's call for a national dialogue on race has created a

11. Cited in Martin E. Marty, *Righteous Empire: The Protestant Experience in America* (New York: Dial Press, 1970), p. 17.

12. See Reinhold Niebuhr, "Man's Tribalism as One Source of His Inhumanity," in *Man's Nature and His Communities* (New York: Charles Scribner's Sons, 1965), pp. 84-95; and his "Justice to the American Negro from State, Community and Church," in *Pious and Secular America* (New York: Charles Scribner's Sons, 1958), pp. 78-85.

13. *Malcolm X Speaks* (New York: Grove Press, 1965), p. 165.

context for public debate in the churches, the academy, and the broader society. Where are the white theologians? What guidance are they providing for this debate? Are they creating a theological understanding of racism that enables whites to have a meaningful conversation with blacks and other people of color? Unfortunately, instead of searching for an understanding of the great racial divide, white religion scholars are doing their searching in the form of a third quest for the historical Jesus. I am not opposed to this academic quest. But if we could get a significant number of white theologians to study racism as seriously as they investigate the historical Jesus and other academic topics, they might discover how deep the cancer of racism is embedded not only in the society but also in the narrow way in which the discipline of theology is understood.

Although black liberation theology emerged out of the Civil Rights and Black Power movements of the 1960s, white theologians ignored it as if it was not worthy to be regarded as an academic discipline. It was not until Orbis Books published the translated works of Latin American liberation theologians that white North American male theologians cautiously began to talk and write about liberation theology and God's solidarity with the poor. But they still ignored the black poor in the United States, Africa, and Latin America. Our struggle to make sense out of the fight for racial justice was dismissed as too narrow and divisive. White U.S. theologians used the Latin American focus on class to minimize and even dismiss the black focus on race. African Americans wondered how U.S. whites could take sides with the poor out there in Latin America without first siding with the poor here in North America. It was as if they had forgotten about their own complicity in the suffering of the black poor who were often only a stone's throw from the seminaries and universities where they taught theology.

White theology's amnesia about racism is partly due to the failure of black theologians to mount a persistently radical race critique of Christian theology, one so incisive and enduring that no one could do theology without engaging white supremacy in the modern world. American and European theologians became concerned about anti-Semitism only because Jews did not let them forget the Christian complicity in the Holocaust. Feminists transformed the consciousness of American theologians through persistent, hard-hitting analysis of the evils of patriarchy, refusing to let any man anywhere in the world forget the past and present male assault against women. It is always the organic intellectuals of an exploited group who must take the lead in exposing the hidden crimes of criminals.

While black theologians' initial attack on white religion shocked white theologians, we did not shake the racist foundation of modern white theology.[14] With the assistance of James Forman's "Black Manifesto"[15] and the black caucuses in Protestant denominations, black theological critiques of racism were successful in shaking up the white churches. But white theologians in the seminaries, university departments of religion, divinity schools, and professional societies refused to acknowledge racism as a theological problem and continued their business as usual, as if the lived experience of blacks was theologically vacuous.

One reason why black theologians have not developed an enduring radical race critique stems from our uncritical identification with the dominant Christian and integrationist tradition in African American history. We are the children of the black church and the Civil Rights movement. The spirituals have informed our theology more than the blues, Howard Thurman more than W. E. B. Du Bois, Martin Luther King, Jr., more than Malcolm X, and male preachers more than women writers. We failed to sustain the critical side of the black theological dialectic and opted for acceptance into white Christian America. When whites opened the door to receive a token number of us into the academy, church, and society, the radical edge of our race critique was quickly dropped as we enjoyed our new-found privileges.

Womanist and second-generation black male theologians, biblical scholars, and historians are moving in the right directions. The strength of these new intellectual developments lies in their refusal to simply repeat the ideas of the original advocates of black theology. They are breaking new theological ground, building on, challenging, and moving beyond the founders of black theology. Using the writings of Zora Neale Hurston, Alice

14. In addition to *Black Theology and Black Power* (Maryknoll, NY: Orbis Books, 1997; originally 1969), my contribution to black theology's race critique included *A Black Theology of Liberation* (Maryknoll, NY: Orbis Books, 1985; originally 1970) and *God of the Oppressed* (Maryknoll, NY: Orbis Books, 1998; originally 1975). Other critiques were Albert B. Cleage, *The Black Messiah* (New York: Sheed & Ward, 1968); J. Deotis Roberts, *Liberation and Reconciliation: A Black Theology* (Maryknoll, NY: Orbis Books, 1994; originally 1971); *A Black Political Theology* (Philadelphia: Westminster, 1974); and Gayraud S. Wilmore's *Black Religion and Black Radicalism* (Maryknoll, NY: Orbis Books, 1998; originally 1972). Significant essays included Vincent Harding, "Black Power and the American Christ," *Christian Century,* January 4, 1967; "The Religion of Black Power," in *Religious Situation 1968,* ed. D. R. Cutler (Boston: Beacon, 1968); and Herbert O. Edwards, "Racism and Christian Ethics in America," *Katallagete* (Winter 1971).

15. See "The Black Manifesto," in James H. Cone and Gayraud S. Wilmore, eds., *Black Theology: A Documentary History,* vol. 1, *1966-1979* (Maryknoll, NY: Orbis Books, 1993), pp. 27-36.

Walker, Toni Morrison, and a host of other women writers past and present, womanist theologians broke the monopoly of black male theological discourse. They challenged the male advocates of black theology to broaden their narrow focus on race and liberation and to incorporate gender, class, and sexuality critiques and the themes of survival and quality of life in our theological discourse.[16] Some younger black male critics locate the limits of black theology in its focus on blackness,[17] and others urge a deeper commitment to it, focusing especially on the slave narratives.[18] Still others suggest that the Christian identity of black theology contributes to black passivity in the face of suffering.[19] Biblical scholars and historians are laying exegetical and historical foundations for a critical re-reading of the Bible in the light of the history and culture of black people.[20] All these critiques and proposals make important contributions to the future development of black theology. But what troubles me about all these new theological constructs is the absence of a truly radical race critique.

Malcolm X was the most formidable race critic in the United States during the twentieth century. He was the great master of suspicion in regard to

16. See "Womanist Theology," in James H. Cone and Gayraud S. Wilmore, eds., *Black Theology: A Documentary History*, vol. 2, *1980-1992* (Maryknoll, NY: Orbis Books, 1993), pp. 257-351.

17. See Victor Anderson, *Beyond Ontological Blackness: An Essay on African American Religious and Cultural Criticism* (New York: Continuum, 1995).

18. See "The Second Generation," in James H. Cone and Gayraud S. Wilmore, eds., *Black Theology: A Documentary History*, vol. 2, pp. 15-75; see also Josiah U. Young, *A Pan-African Theology: Providence and the Legacies of the Ancestors* (Trenton, NJ: Africa World Press, 1992); Dwight N. Hopkins and George Cummings, eds., *Cut Loose Your Stammering Tongue: Black Theology in the Slave Narratives* (Maryknoll, NY: Orbis Books, 1991); Dwight N. Hopkins, *Shoes That Fit Our Feet: Sources for a Constructive Black Theology* (Maryknoll, NY: Orbis Books, 1993); Garth Kasimu Baker-Fletcher, *Xodus: An African American Male Journey* (Minneapolis: Fortress, 1996); Riggins R. Earl, *Dark Symbols, Obscure Signs: God, Self, and Community in the Slave Mind* (Maryknoll, NY: Orbis Books, 1993).

19. See Anthony B. Pinn, *Why, Lord? Suffering and Evil in Black Theology* (New York: Continuum, 1995). Pinn is building on an earlier critique of black theology by William R. Jones, *Is God a White Racist? A Preamble to Black Theology* (Boston: Beacon, 1998; originally 1973).

20. See "New Directions in Black Biblical Interpretation," in James H. Cone and Gayraud S. Wilmore, eds., *Black Theology: A Documentary History*, vol. 2, pp. 177-254; Cain H. Felder, *Troubling Biblical Waters: Race, Class, and Family* (Maryknoll, NY: Orbis Books, 1989); Cain H. Felder, ed., *Stony the Road We Trod: African American Biblical Interpretation* (Minneapolis: Fortress, 1991); Brian K. Blount, *Go Preach! Mark's Kingdom Message and the Black Church Today* (Maryknoll, NY: Orbis Books, 1998); Theophus H. Smith, *Conjuring Culture: Biblical Formations of Black America* (New York: Oxford University Press, 1994).

American democracy and the Christian faith. His critique of racism in Christianity and American culture was so forceful that even black Christians were greatly disturbed when they heard his analysis. His contention that "Christianity was a white man's religion" was so persuasive that many black Christians left churches to join the Nation of Islam. The rapid growth of the religion of Islam in the African American community is largely due to the effectiveness of Malcolm's portrayal of Christianity as white nationalism. It was Malcolm via the Black Power movement who forced black theologians to take a critical look at white religion and to develop a hermeneutic of suspicion regarding black Christianity. How can African Americans merge the "double self" — the black and the Christian — "into a better and truer self,"[21] especially since Africa is the object of ridicule in the modern world and Christianity is hardly distinguishable from European culture?

While we black theologians appropriated Malcolm in our initial critique of white religion, we did not wrestle with Malcolm long enough. We quickly turned to Martin King. The mistake was not in moving toward King but rather in leaving Malcolm behind. We need them both as a double-edged sword to slay the dragon of theological racism. Martin and Malcolm represent the yin and yang in the black attack on racism. One without the other misses the target — the affirmation of blackness in the beloved community of humankind.

Malcolm X teaches us that African Americans cannot be free without accepting their blackness, without loving Africa as the place of our origin and meaning. Martin King teaches us that no people can be free except in the beloved community of humankind — not just blacks with blacks or whites with whites but all of us together (including Indians, Asians, Hispanics, gays, lesbians, and bisexuals) in a truly multicultural community. Malcolm alone makes it too easy for blacks to go it alone and for whites to say "Begone!" Martin alone makes it easy for whites to ask for reconciliation without justice and for middle-class blacks to grant it, as long as they are treated specially. Putting Martin and Malcolm together enables us to overcome the limitations of each and to build on the strengths of both and thereby to move blacks, whites, and other Americans toward racial healing and understanding.

There can be no racial healing without dialogue, without ending the white silence on racism. There can be no reconciliation without honest and

21. W. E. B. Du Bois, *The Souls of Black Folk* (Greenwich, CT: Fawcett Publications, 1961), p. 23.

frank conversation. Racism is still with us in the academy, in the churches, and in every segment of the society because we would rather push this problem under the rug than find a way to deal with its past and present manifestations.

Most whites do not like to talk about racism because it makes them feel guilty, a truly uncomfortable feeling. They would rather forget about the past and think only about the present and future. I understand that. But I only ask whites to consider how uncomfortable the victims of racism must feel, as they try to cope with the attitudes of whites who act as if racism ceased with the passage of the 1964 Civil Rights Bill. At least when people express their racism overtly, there is some public recognition of its existence and a possibility of racial healing. Silence is racism's best friend.

"A time comes when silence is betrayal,"[22] Martin King said. That time has come for white theologians. Racism is one of the great contradictions of the gospel in modern times. White theologians who do not oppose racism publicly nor rigorously engage it in their writings are part of the problem and must be exposed as the enemies of justice. No one, therefore, can be neutral or silent in the face of this great evil. We are either for it or against it.

Black theologians must end their silence too. We have opposed racism much too gently. We have permitted white theological silence in exchange for the rewards of being accepted by the white theological establishment. This is a terrible price to pay for the few crumbs that drop from the white master's table. We must replace theological deference with courage, and thereby confront openly and lovingly silent white racists or be condemned as participants in the betrayal of our own people.

In 1903, W. E. B. Du Bois prophesied, "The problem of the twentieth century is the problem of the color-line — the relation of the darker to the lighter races of [people] in Asia and Africa, in America and the islands of the sea."[23] As we stand at the threshold of the next century, that remarkable prophecy is as relevant today as it was when Du Bois uttered it. The challenge for black theology in the twenty-first century is to develop an enduring race critique that is so comprehensively woven into Christian understanding that no one will be able to forget the horrible crimes of white supremacy in the modern world.

22. Martin Luther King, Jr., "Beyond Vietnam," a pamphlet of the Clergy and Laymen Concerned about Vietnam, April 4, 1967.
23. W. E. B. Du Bois, *The Souls of Black Folk*, p. 23.

32 The Prospects of Foucault's Analysis: Linking Race, Religion, and Modern Sovereignty

J. Kameron Carter

If Foucault's genealogy of sexuality as laid out in *History of Sexuality* seeks to answer the question of when people began to think of themselves as sexual beings and what instigated this new mode of human self-knowledge, his genealogy of modern racism seeks to answer a similar, interrelated set of questions: When did people begin thinking of themselves as principally racial beings, and what factors instigated such thinking? Answering these questions is part of Foucault's project of describing how the body is disciplined and controlled, how it is governed, in modern and late-modern society. Foucault makes clear in the concluding chapter of volume I of *History of Sexuality* ("Right of Death and Power over Life," a chapter that he took to be "the fundamental part of the book"[1]) that the questions of sexuality and race are not parallel. Rather, they are intersecting inquiries. What links them, he tells us, is the advent in late modernity, particularly beginning in the nineteenth century, of power's new modus operandi, its "new procedures."[2] The new procedures of power are the procedures of "biopower"; its new historical analytic is that of "biohistory."[3] The problem of modern racism — along with the problem of sexuality, Foucault believes — is to be located here.

. . .

Foucault is interested in the continuity-in-discontinuity, in the con-

---

1. Michel Foucault, *Power/Knowledge: Selected Interviews and Other Writings, 1972-1977* (New York: Pantheon, 1981), p. 222.

2. Michel Foucault, *The History of Sexuality* (New York: Vintage, 1980), p. 148.

3. Foucault, *History of Sexuality*, p. 143.

stants, so to speak, that hold together how "the people" are constituted within the latest two moments in the unfolding of the modern world. The first is the moment in which "the people," or the modern subject as a sociopolitical unit, is constituted through individuals' handing themselves over to the sovereignty of states. This is the basic logic by which "the nation" as a territorialized people comes to be. The second moment is biopolitical and concerns how peoplehood comes to exceed any particular national territory. In becoming transnational, the territory of the power becomes omniversal. Fulfilling the Enlightenment's quest for cosmopolitan universality, the territory of power becomes *bios* or life itself and in its totality. . . . [T]his is not to say that the nation vanishes. Rather, it is to say that the horizon within which it operates has shifted. It has become borderless.

Now, while sensitive to the differences between these moments in the constitution of modern peoplehood and subjectivity, Foucault, as already mentioned, is more interested, I think, in what holds them together. Sexuality, insofar as it is an important index of biology, of borderless and unmediated *bios*, is a vector from which to probe this bond. But there is a deeper dimension to the problem of sexuality in the constitution of territorialized and deterritorialized, modern and postmodern (or hypermodern), subjectivity. The deep structure of the problem of sexuality as a vector onto life itself in the production of modern subjects, of modern man, is race, and it is race that links the different forms of peoplehood in early and late modernity, respectively. Foucault begins to spell this out in the concluding section of *History of Sexuality*. There one of his chief concerns is to assert that racial thinking does new work in the nineteenth century and into the twentieth century even as it remains in some sense continuous with the work it once did in prior phases of modernity's unfolding; biopower is the term under which he names this new work. That is, race comes to work in a decentralized and deterritorialized way. It begins to work biopolitically, and it begins to articulate itself within the global flows, communications, and currencies of power-flows and currencies that exceed any one nation's borders. . . . [I]n the course of delimiting this new, biopolitical work that race does, Foucault also gives insight into what is continuous in how the discourse of race functions across the transition from early modernity's territorialized constitution of subjectivity and peoplehood to late modernity's deterritorialized constitution of them.

. . .

[T]he lecture series is important, given my purposes, because even as the lectures chart these lines of inquiry, they also indicate, if in the end inadequately, the theological and religious nature of the problem of race and thus the quasi-theological and religious nature of the constitution of the modern state and presumably its ongoing pseudotheological constitution across the field of biopower. Foucault, in short, points to . . . the convergence of the plotlines of race, religion, and the modern state. Shortly I show how Foucault conceives of this convergence as taking place around the meaning of the life of ancient, biblical Israel and what that life signifies for the modern world. Yet I argue that despite this insight, he does not probe it deeply enough. This is because the method of genealogy blinds him precisely at this juncture from seeing how modernity's anxiety has to do with its obfuscation of the *theological* meaning of Israel's understanding of themselves as a people. Rather than reckoning with this and its rippling effects throughout modernity, Foucault reenacts a nontheological, racialized interpretation of this people. In so doing, he repeats modernity's supersessionism. This problem reached its first crystalline expression in the thought of Immanuel Kant. Allow me to trace the route to this conclusion by looking more closely at Foucault's 1975-1976 lecture series, especially the third and fourth lectures.

Foucault begins his third lecture by briefly summarizing the accomplishment of the previous two. In those lectures, he says, "We said a sort of farewell to the theory of sovereignty . . . as a method for analyzing power relations."[4] Such a theory and method are inadequate chiefly because they presuppose something like the statist unity of sovereignty; that is, they reduce power to the unity of a sovereign, be it the sovereignty "of one individual over others, of one group over others, of one class over others."[5] In this conception of power, sovereignty never has to account for itself, though it accounts for and grounds all else. It is that "from which powers spring."[6] Foucault's problem with this conception is that it does not take account of the fact that "power . . . circulates" as a "chain," a "network," or a web.[7] As discussed, Foucault in *History of Sexuality* asserts that the concentration of power in the unity of the sovereign is but the terminal form that power takes; power itself

must be understood . . . as the multiplicity of force relations . . . ; as the process which, through ceaseless struggles and confrontations, trans-

4. Foucault, *"Society Must Be Defended": Lectures at the Collège de France, 1975-1976,* trans. David Macey (New York: Picador, 2003), p. 43.

5. Foucault, *"Society Must Be Defended,"* p. 29.

6. Foucault, *"Society Must Be Defended,"* p. 45.

7. Foucault, *"Society Must Be Defended,"* p. 29.

forms, strengthens, or reverses [those relations]; as the support which these force relations find in one another; . . . and lastly . . . the strategies in which they take effect . . . embodied in the state apparatuses, in the formulation of the law, in the various social hegemonies.[8]

In addition and most important, an understanding of power in terms of the unity of a sovereign remains oblivious to power's modern modes of operation. With the advent of modernity, power functions no longer in feudal fashion, in which a potentate rules "over the land and over the produce of the land," and in which the political collective, the people, is constituted as the corporal body of the king.[9] Rather, in the modern modes of power, "bodies and what they do"[10] are the field over which power operates. Power in its new modes constitutes the political collective, not as the corporal body of the king, but as the social body of the nation — that is, as the people itself, without the mediation of a sovereign. This constitution of the people as the social body of the nation occurs through what Foucault calls the "normalization" of bodies. Insofar as power's constitution of the modern political collective eschews sovereignty, it presents an antihegemonic aspect.

Foucault uses the problem of war to analyze this antihegemonic aspect and thus to account for the power relations at work in the constitution of the people in modernity. He observes that over the course of time from the Middle Ages to the dawning of the modern era, the nature of warfare was transformed: war ceased being a private affair.[11] The state thus came to have the sole prerogative of waging war, and with this distinguishing prerogative in hand, the state banished warfare to the margins of society. The business of warfare became the responsibility of a carefully "defined and controlled military apparatus," left to a class of "technical and professional" practitioners, namely, soldiers.[12] This is the story of the birth of the army as a modern institution.

But there is another side to the story. Might it be the case, Foucault asks, that "if we look beneath peace, order, wealth, and authority, beneath the calm order of subordinations, beneath the State and State apparatuses, be-

---

8. Foucault, *History of Sexuality*, pp. 92-93.

9. The classic text that explores the corporal nature of the king in medieval thought and life is Ernst H. Kantorowicz, *The King's Two Bodies: A Study in Mediaeval Political Theology* (Princeton: Princeton University Press, 1985).

10. Foucault, *"Society Must Be Defended,"* p. 35.

11. Foucault, *"Society Must Be Defended,"* p. 48.

12. Foucault, *"Society Must Be Defended,"* pp. 48-49.

neath the laws, and so on, [that we will] hear and discover a sort of primitive and permanent war," that we will discover that war is being waged "just beneath the surface of peace," and that it will prove true that bellicosity is "the principle that allows us to understand order, the State, its institutions, and its history"?[13] Foucault's rhetorical answer to this battery of questions is "Yes"; but in so answering, he recognizes that he must explore the principle that lies behind his affirmation. The principle he isolates is this: "Politics is the continuation of war by other means."[14]

. . . Thus, with his inversion of [Karl von] Clausewitz's axiom[,] Foucault . . . [is] implicitly claiming that . . . modernity functions under a perpetual state of exception or emergency, the uninterrupted condition of the crisis of politics. Indeed, the state of exception or emergency — namely, the condition of war — is modernity's inner analytic, its syntax and grammar.[15]

Foucault unpacks this principle by analyzing the emergence in modernity of a "new . . . strange discourse," "a historico-politico" one about how society came to be the way it is.[16] This new historical discourse, the discourse of "counterhistory,"[17] was committed to disclosing how "war" in fact "is the uninterrupted frame of history."[18] While in one respect war in modernity is relegated to the periphery of the social body, the discourse of counterhistory gives rise to the view that war in a different form occupies the center of the social body and, in fact, constitutes the social body.[19] Hence, this new discourse of and about history stands against the way in which history as a discourse had functioned to this point. Foucault tells us in the fourth lecture that through the late Middle Ages, history functioned on the model of the Roman annalists,[20] who, like Livy for example, were bent on providing a "politico-legendary history of the Romans" or, more specifically, a "Jupiterian" history of the sovereignty of the Caesars.[21] A central objective of this form of historical discourse was implicitly to "[identify] . . . people

13. Foucault, *"Society Must Be Defended,"* pp. 46-47.

14. Foucault, *"Society Must Be Defended,"* p. 15.

15. For an interesting recent engagement with modernity read under the aspect of the state of exception, see Giorgio Agamben, *State of Exception,* trans. Kevin Attell (Chicago: University of Chicago Press, 2005). The chief foil for Agamben's argument is early-twentieth-century German political theorist Carl Schmitt.

16. Foucault, *"Society Must Be Defended,"* p. 49.

17. Foucault, *"Society Must Be Defended,"* p. 70.

18. Foucault, *"Society Must Be Defended,"* p. 59.

19. Foucault, *"Society Must Be Defended,"* p. 49.

20. Foucault, *"Society Must Be Defended,"* pp. 66, 71.

21. Foucault, *"Society Must Be Defended,"* pp. 71, 68.

with monarch, and nation with sovereign."[22] Its goal was to subsume "the entire social body" under the dazzling light, glory, and power effects of sovereignty,[23] which was bent on "[binding] everything together into a unity — which is of course the unity of the city, the nation, or the State" as that unity was embodied in the sovereign.[24]

What distinguishes the new history from the old is that it is anti-Roman and thus historical precisely by being counterhistorical. It does not proceed on the model of the Roman annalists. Instead, . . . the new (counter)historical discourse reveals history as the story of the struggle between races, between those held up in the light by sovereign power and those left in the darkness by it. It is the story of taking sides, and as such a story, counterhistory discloses what side sovereignty is finally on. It no longer occludes the fact that there are winners and losers. That is, historical discourse is no longer the discourse that explains how the Romans became Romans, or the Gauls Gauls, or the French French, or what have you. It is discovered that "[the] history of some is not the history of others" and that "the history of the Saxons," for example, "after their defeat at the Battle of Hastings is not the same as the history of the Normans who were the victors in that same battle. It will be learned that one man's victory is another man's defeat."[25]

What Foucault points out here is how modern historical discourse shows that war is the analytic of the identity of people groups or nations, and no longer simply that by which glory accrues to potentates — how war is an analytic of the identity not just of the victors as a people group, and not just of the vanquished as a people group, but of victors and vanquished in their *continued* group opposition to one another even under the conditions of so-called peace, and how this peaceful opposition comes to be expressed in politics and codified in law and finally enforced by government, by the state, as the means through which to produce itself as a people. It is in this way that the nation — the "We" in "We the People," so to speak — is forged[26] and legally and politically organized as "the State" in order to secure itself as "the People." Counterhistory, therefore, is an act of memory — to speak theologically, of anamnesis — of remembering in a certain way: counterhistory remembers how the unifying light of the present order of things presupposes and is sustained by group opposition. What all of this means is that a funda-

22. Foucault, *"Society Must Be Defended,"* p. 69.
23. Foucault, *"Society Must Be Defended,"* p. 70.
24. Foucault, *"Society Must Be Defended,"* p. 69.
25. Foucault, *"Society Must Be Defended,"* p. 69.
26. Foucault, *"Society Must Be Defended,"* p. 142.

mental and ineradicable rift runs through the fabric of society, and this rift produces and founds the state. It means that "[we] are . . . at war with one another; [and that] a battlefront runs through the whole of society, continuously and permanently. . . . [It] is this battlefront that puts us all on one side or the other. There is no such thing as a neutral subject. We are all inevitably someone's adversary. A binary structure runs through society."[27]

But it means something else as well. Foucault spends the better part of the lectures telling us that the continued bellicosity simmering just beneath the surface of peace, law, and government, a bellicosity that both produces and reproduces subjects and peoples in binary opposition to one another, is, in fact, racial. Bellicosity produces the people, the nations, and the state by producing and reproducing the social body along the axis of race. Indeed, war produces and reproduces racial subjects even as it produces and reproduces "the racial state."[28] "The war that is going on beneath order and peace, the war," Foucault says, "that undermines our society and divides it in a binary mode is, basically, a race war . . . [one in which the] social body is articulated around two races."[29]

Now, it is important that Foucault not be read as conflating race war with racism, for he, in fact, carefully distinguishes the two. He praises race war for its emancipatory possibilities, for the fact that, as he sees it, it inaugurates a history that counters the history of sovereignty. . . . [In contrast, r]acism reflects how the otherwise praiseworthy "race-ing" of the social body bears within itself the seeds of its own destruction — indeed, the destruction of the very social body that it constitutes; for in late modernity the principle of race struggle is employed in the reinvention of the logic of sovereignty.

The return of sovereignty into the constitution of the modern political collective does not imply a return of the feudal, sovereign-to-subject model of power; rather, the social body itself becomes the locus of sovereignty. It is important to note that Foucault in no way suggests that one theoretically begins with an already constituted modern collective social entity and that power ripples out from there. This would simply reinvent the model of feudal sovereignty that sees power as unified in a potentate and then moving outward from that center. Instead, Foucault says that it is in the very manner by which power produces and reproduces the social body that sovereignty

---

27. Foucault, *"Society Must Be Defended,"* p. 51.

28. Cf. David Theo Goldberg, *The Racial State* (Malden, MA: Blackwell Publishers, 2002).

29. Foucault, *"Society Must Be Defended,"* pp. 59-60.

makes its return. The struggle *between* the races that counterhistorical discourse brings to the fore as the primary constituting force of the modern state begins in the nineteenth century to transmute into a struggle *within* "the race." It becomes an internal matter of the people against the people, and so a matter of the people, of bios, against itself. When this happens, the in-itself emancipatory notion of races gets redeployed biologically to secure the collective, the race. Security takes the form of protecting the collective, the race, from contamination and degeneracy. It takes the form of defending society from itself. Race struggle as a struggle against sovereignty thus devolves, as Foucault tells the story, into statist, biological racism as the means of unifying and defending the sovereign social body.

The various disciplines of modern scientific knowledge act both as medium and justification of this form of racial sovereignty. It is the "tight grid of disciplinary coercions that actually guarantees the cohesion of [the] social body," the cohesion, that is, of the sovereign collective.[30] These disciplines, which "create apparatuses of knowledge . . . and multiple fields of expertise" and which "refer to [the] theoretical horizon . . . [of] the field of the human sciences . . . , constitute the silent basement of the great mechanics of power" in its quest for norms or rules through which to secure the social body.[31] Stated differently, fields of knowledge such as the disciplinary practices of medicine, the biological sciences, the social sciences, and especially the discourse of history emerge to greatly expand knowledge, but with a view to assist in protecting "the integrity, the superiority, and the purity of the race": that is, of the collective conceived racially.[32]

The task of Foucault's lectures, then, was to persuade his auditors — and now his readers — of the veracity of his social theory, and in the course of doing this to simultaneously praise the shift in how power now operates in modernity to resist sovereignty, while also taking seriously its limits, limits that account for the eventual rise of modern racism in the nineteenth century. It can be said that, for Foucault, modernity is a pharmakon — both a medicinal potion and a poison. Foucault points out the limits of the modern social order in the interests of overcoming them, and thus, one might say, in the interests of salvaging the best of modernity and its counterhistorical, counterhegemonic possibilities. Thus in properly reckoning with the limits inherent in how modernity is constituted, one is better positioned

30. Foucault, *"Society Must Be Defended,"* p. 37.
31. Foucault, *"Society Must Be Defended,"* p. 38.
32. Foucault, *"Society Must Be Defended,"* p. 81.

to "[look] for a new right," a right that is neither of the old feudal, pre-modern sort nor of the modern variety rooted as it is in collective biopower and thus in a recuperated notion of sovereignty. This new right — the right of justice — must be one "that is both antidisciplinary and emancipated from [the disciplinary] principle" altogether.[33]

. . . [I]n the constitution of modernity, for Foucault, . . . the discourse of race or, more specifically, of race struggle, functions mythically, religiously, and in the end quasi-theologically. Indeed, it is a mythical discourse according to which the social order that is modernity moves in a cyclical logic of fall and redemption. The people that paradigmatically express this logic of race struggle and counterhistory, and hence the logic of modernity at its best in resisting sovereignty, is the Jewish people, the people of ancient, biblical Israel. A careful reading of Foucault's fourth lecture justifies this claim insofar as it points to how both the real (or lived) and the mythological (or "imagined") dimensions of race in the modern world converge on the religious and theological significations of Jewish existence.

Here is where I want to begin finalizing the justification of my claim that Foucault taps into the deep structure of the problem of modern racial reasoning by raising the question of race, religion, and the mythical, even as he reinscribes the structural logic of the problem at the point where these lines intersect on the theological meaning of Jewish existence for the modern world.

The Problems with Foucault's Analysis: Reinscribing Christian Supersessionism

That modernity is born of counterhistory; that at its best, it is counter-history (and at its worst, it reiterates sovereignty); and that it has inaugurated a mode of historical consciousness by which identity is seen as liberated through the struggle of races: these are all themes mentioned above as central to the argument of Foucault's 1975-1976 lectures. What is yet to be more fully expounded is the mythical, religious, and even quasi-theological nature of Foucault's narrative. He mentions both in the lectures and in the last chapter of *History of Sexuality* that myth, particularly myths about blood purity, was a crucial component of nineteenth-century and twentieth-century racism, especially the racism of Nazi Germany. More than just an ad

---

33. Foucault, *"Society Must Be Defended,"* p. 40.

hominem remark, Foucault's comments about myth open an important perspective on his argument. In *History of Sexuality* he observes that what came to mediate the shift from the administration of power through "a symbolics of blood" to its administration through "an analytics of sexuality" was race.[34]

In the former state of affairs, "blood was a reality with a symbolic function" that worked in the interests of upholding that zone of power that was imagined as above the social field of everyday life. Functioning symbolically, "power spoke *through* blood" and thus was a sign of such so-called superior realities as "the honor of war, the fear of famine, the triumph of death, the sovereign with his sword, executioners, and tortures."[35] So understood, blood spoke beyond itself, beyond its reference to bodies as such. One could very well say . . . that blood functioned symbolically to uphold power's centralizing capacities — its capacity, that is, to draw everything together around the territorialized state and within the limits of society, insofar as those limits follow the territorial limits of the state.

Things change with the transition from a "symbolics of blood" to "an analytics of sexuality." "In a society of 'sex,'" Foucault tells us, "the mechanisms of power are addressed to the body, to life, to what causes it to proliferate, to what reinforces the species, its stamina, its ability to dominate, or its capacity for being used."[36] Functioning now in a decentralized way, power came to work in the interests of "the blood of the caste . . . [indeed, in the interests of] the blood of the people" so as to bring about a perfect, "eugenic ordering of society."[37] This was the new way in which nation and peoplehood were conceived. Besides making use of a number of new modes of knowledge (such as statistics, census studies, and medicine, to name a few) to justify itself, and besides making use of themes such as "health, progeny, race, the future of the species, [and] the vitality of the social body,"[38] late-modern sovereignty also drew on myth to justify itself.[39] This general logic is at work in the following passage from *History of Sexuality*:

Beginning in the second half of the nineteenth century, the thematics of blood was sometimes called on to lend its entire historical weight toward

34. Foucault, *History of Sexuality*, p. 148.
35. Foucault, *History of Sexuality*, p. 147.
36. Foucault, *History of Sexuality*, p. 147.
37. Foucault, *History of Sexuality*, pp. 148-49.
38. Foucault, *History of Sexuality*, p. 147.
39. Foucault, *History of Sexuality*, p. 149.

revitalizing the type of political power that was exercised through the devices of sexuality. Racism took shape at this point (racism in its modern, "biologizing," statist form): it was then that a whole politics of settlement *(peuplement)*, family, marriage, education, social hierarchization, and property, accompanied by a long series of permanent interventions at the level of the body, conduct, health, and everyday life, received their color and their justification from the mythical concern with protecting the purity of the blood and ensuring the triumph of the race. Nazism was doubtless the most cunning and the most naïve (and the former because of the latter) combination of the fantasies of blood and the paroxysms of a disciplinary power. A eugenic ordering of society with all that implied in the way of extension and intensification of micro-powers, in the guise of an unrestricted state control *(étatisation)*, was accompanied by the oneiric exaltation of a superior blood; the latter implied both the systematic genocide of others and the risk of exposing oneself to a total sacrifice. It is an irony of history that the Hitlerite politics of sex remained an insignificant practice while the blood myth was transformed into the greatest blood bath in recent memory.[40]

In this passage we can read Foucault as offering a condensed answer to an implied question: How could a symbolics of blood continue to have cachet under conditions of an "analytics," or a science, of sexuality? His answer is that it could because the critical issue is neither primarily the symbolics of blood nor the analytics, or the science, of sexuality in their own right; rather, the crucial issue is the mythology underlying both. This mythology is two-edged: on the one hand, it inspires liberation from or resistance to Roman-style history and sovereignty; on the other hand, it can be made to invest the logic of sovereignty with new energy and in the process, as mentioned above, convert the discourse of the struggle of *races* against sovereignty and tyranny into a discourse of *race* and thereby give birth to racism.[41]

The question, then, is, How is this transformation possible? What is it about the mythology undergirding modernity that enables this possibility? It can be said that in seeking an answer to this question, Foucault is in fact seeking a genealogical explanation of the phenomenon, an account of how the discourse of *races* could metastasize into a discourse of *race*, and in this sense he is seeking a genealogy of modern racism(s). For racism represents a falling back into sovereignty, albeit the tyrannical sovereignty of the collec-

40. Foucault, *History of Sexuality*, pp. 149-50.
41. Cf. Stoler, *Race and the Education of Desire*, p. 81.

tive, of the group, now figured racially. The fourth lecture suggests that religious myth provides Foucault with his genealogical explanation of how this fall could occur; for within the religious myth that Foucault sees as upholding modernity, he sees as well the mechanism by which the collective itself can become the new site of sovereignty. That is, he sees how the mythology that upholds modernity in its rise from sovereignty simultaneously entails the possibility of its fall — its religious and mythological fall — back into sovereignty. Thus in some sense, religious myth — at least as presently configured and functioning to ground modernity — never fully overcomes sovereignty but is part of its dialectic. Indeed, it can be said that in a fundamental but unspoken way the mythological orientation of modernity harbors the attitude of sovereignty, allowing it to endlessly ramify or reproduce itself in ever-new permutations.

Another way to express this is to say, employing language from Foucault's essay "What Is Enlightenment?" that the mythical orientation that both is modernity and grounds modernity is at once "modern" (in its sense of undermining sovereignty) and antimodern or "countermodern." The ultimate implication of this assertion is that the religious myth underwriting modernity harbors both its redemption and its fall; indeed, it is always already a fallen or compromised redemption. Enlightenment will always be in need of enlightenment. What emerges, then, between the lines and in the interstices between "the said and the unsaid"[42] of Foucault's explanation of the place of religious myth in modernity's apparatuses of power is that modernity is a religious performance of mythic proportions, one that is ever poised, with respect to sovereignty, between redemptive liberation and a sinful fall back into the oppression of sovereignty, now at the site of the collective. We learn from other places in Foucault's oeuvre and also from James Miller, Foucault's biographer, that as Foucault saw it, the answer to this problem is to be liberated — or, perhaps better, to be disentangled — from the collective. This entails seeing neither the sovereign nor the collective as life's precondition but, rather, seeing the body as such — albeit, as subject to a different "ascetic" script, a different way of caring or being "[concerned] for the self as the practice of freedom" — as life's ultimate precondition and as the place where the ultimate agon against sovereignty is to be waged.

What is worth paying particular attention to for my purposes is how Foucault positions Jewish faith in his narrative, how it becomes the means

---

42. Foucault, *Power/Knowledge,* p. 194.

through which to reflect the modern world at its "counterhistorical" best — and also at its "historical" worst — back to itself. I am interested, in other words, in how Foucault's reading of the myth that founds and that *is* modernity positions the Jew — more specifically, the people of ancient, biblical Israel — in relationship to his genealogy of race. I am also interested in how as a result of his mythical reading of modernity, Jews provide modernity with a hermeneutic of itself: that is, they provide modernity with an interpretive grid of "the said and the unsaid" that constitutes its apparatuses of power and the systems of relation linking those apparatuses together. And last, I am interested in how it is that Foucault's way of imagining all of this unwittingly reenacts modernity's anxiety-filled relationship to the theopolitical significance of Jewish existence.

Allow me now to textually substantiate my worry over how Foucault seems unwittingly to harbor modernity's anti-Jewish anxiety. Having given an account of what he means by counterhistory, Foucault then elaborates on it by imputing religious qualities to counterhistory. In so doing he can be read as also expounding on claims made in *History of Sexuality* to link myth to the rise of the state racism of Nazi Germany. Understood against the backdrop of the lectures, Foucault's claim is that in the case of Nazi Germany, myth was deployed in a religiously problematic way. Through the lectures, Foucault also lets us know that there can nevertheless be a positive use of religious myth, and this is evident from his claim that the counterhistory of the struggle of races "prophetic[ally] rupture[s]" the static, unifying aura of sovereignty. This rupturing should be understood in the Old Testament scriptural sense. Hence "[the] new discourse," he informs us, "is similar to a certain number of epic, religious, or mythical forms which, rather than telling of the untarnished and uneclipsed glory of the sovereign, endeavor to formulate the misfortune of ancestors, exiles, and servitude . . . [while waiting] for the promised land and the fulfillment of the old promises." Moreover,

> [with] this new discourse of race struggle, we see the emergence of something that, basically, is much closer to the mythico-religious discourse of the Jews than to the politico-legendary history of the Romans. We are much closer to the Bible than to Livy, in a Hebraic-biblical form much more than in the form of the annalist who records, day by day, the history of the uninterrupted glory of power. . . . At least from the second half of the Middle Ages onward, the Bible was the great form for the articulation of religious, moral, and political protests against the power of kings and the despotism of the church. Like the references to biblical texts itself, this

form functioned, in most cases, as a protest, a critique, and an oppositional discourse. . . . To that extent, it is not surprising that we see, at the
end of the Middle Ages, in the sixteenth century, in the period of the Reformation, and at the time of the English Revolution, the appearance of a
form of history that is a direct challenge to the history of sovereignty and
kings — to Roman history — and that we see a new history that is articulated around the great biblical form of prophecy and promise.[43]

I quote this passage at length because in it — and throughout the rest of the
fourth lecture — Foucault exposes the mythico-religious and even quasi-
theological undercurrent of his account of modernity, an account that views
modernity as an agon of history and counterhistory and the notion of race
as that which fuels the antagonism.

One discovers that the story being told in the lectures about the confrontation of counterhistory and history is actually another way of genea-
logically peering behind the Protestant Reformation and the principle of
revolution it inaugurates so as to view the Reformation not simply as a discrete historical event but, instead, as a religious disposition, a mythical posture, or (as he says in the essay "What Is Enlightenment?") an "attitude," the
"attitude of modernity [itself] . . . [in its struggle] with attitudes of
'countermodernity.'"[44] It is important to observe that for Foucault, the Protestant Reformation, both as historical event and as exemplifying the principle of modernity, operates in this schema according to the analytic of the
war of races in its resistance to "the power of kings and the despotism of the
church [read: Roman Catholic Church]."[45] The Reformation, in short, displays the attitude of modernity; the attitude of *dandysme,* of experimenta-
tion for the sake of self-realization and artistic self-elaboration; and lastly of
"heroic," rather than merely tragic, existence on the boundary of death so as
to finally plunge the stake into the heart of sovereignty.[46]

But modernity, exemplified at its counterhistorical best in this way under the aspect of the Protestant Reformation, plays the role of type to another, one might say "proto-counterhistorical" race: namely, the Jews. The
fourth lecture seems to imply an analogy between the principle or attitude
of modernity as exemplified in the Protestant Reformation in its challenge

43. Foucault, *"Society Must Be Defended,"* p. 71.
44. Foucault, "What Is Enlightenment?" in Paul Rabinow, ed., *The Foucault Reader*
(New York: Pantheon, 1984), p. 39.
45. Foucault, *"Society Must Be Defended,"* p. 71.
46. Foucault, "What Is Enlightenment?" pp. 40-42.

to the despotism of the church and the tyranny of kings on the one hand and "the mythico-religious discourse of the Jews" on the other. Jews, in the guise of ancient, biblical Israel, are either the prototype or the antitype of modernity. As a people of prophetic resistance to the tyranny and oppression meted out to them at the hands of sovereigns such as the ancient Egyptian pharaohs and Babylonian rulers, ancient Israel is the sociocollective embodiment of the principle or attitude of counterhistory. They embody it not through recourse to the logic of sovereignty; rather, it could be said that in the history of Western political thought and practice, ancient Israel is the fountainhead of a different political ordo, a counterhistorical one in which Israel's existence as a people is founded on seeing the struggle of races as the inner, redemptive mechanism of history. Israel, in its ancient and in its modern embodiment, does this by defining itself as a collective, a distinct people — that is, as Jews — in contrast to its oppressors, who down through history have defined themselves through the unifying glory of the sovereign, be he the Egyptian pharaoh, the Babylonian king, the German Führer, or any other tyrannical figure.

Thus to sum up this particular point: counterhistory or the inner attitude of modernity has a twofold mythological and religious signification. First, there is the implication that the principle of counterhistory, which functions according to a logic of race struggle, in fact enacts the Protestant principle of reformation, which for Foucault is about revolution, the principle of counterhegemonic resistance to sovereignty. Second, there is the further implication from this that the inner basis of the principle of Protestantism, and thus the inner basis of the principle of race (struggle), lies in the mythological and religious discourse of the Jews. This means that Foucault, at least on this score, reads Jewish existence in positive terms, as that which must be embraced. Jews are the vantage from which to understand the counterhegemonic. This is because they deliver to Western civilization and political thought a mode of life figured through a discourse of the races that tends toward freedom (at least an Enlightenment notion of freedom). In so doing, they provide a mythological and religious basis for the counterhistorical "attitude of modernity," rooted as it is in a discourse of *races,* of race struggle. . . . Foucault has tapped into the fact that the question of race arises inside the question of Israel, inside the question of the theopolitical meaning of Jewish existence.

And yet there is a troubling downside to reading the life of Israel in this way — as the index or interpretive grid or religious symbol of the modern world. Such a reading also makes Israel the index of modernity's discontents insofar as those discontents cluster around the way (racial) collectivity can also spawn a new form of hegemonic sovereignty, the sovereignty of the collective conceived of as the *race*. It is the sovereignty of the collective, particularly when its meanings are interpolated through the knowledges that the biological and health sciences yield, that generates a discourse of *race* and so of racism. All of this means that Israel occupies an odd mythopoetic position in the Foucauldian scheme of things. On the one hand, Israel must be embraced to the extent that it is the fountainhead of the attitude of counterhistory and thus prototypically of the attitude that is modernity. Simultaneously, Jewish existence must be overcome to the extent that its racializing of existence (through the war of races figured through the Jew-Gentile distinction) can lead to racism, to a notion of blood purity or racial group superiority, and thus to preventing modernity from fully elaborating itself and living into its *dandysme* or counterhistorical attitude. In other words, Israel's prototypical racializing of existence can lead to a problematic performance of the nation and constitution of the state.

Foucault's tenth lecture can be read as addressing just this problem in nineteenth-century historical discourse. That is, Foucault is trying to account for the shift in how counterhistory itself came to no longer be so much a (counter)narrative that exposes sovereignty's source in past acts of invasion and thus leads to the struggle *between races* but, rather, came to be internalized as a struggle *within* the present state, a struggle over the defense of society and so of "the *race*." He wants to account for how it transpired that "the fundamental moment is no longer the origin, and intelligibility's starting point is no longer the archaic element; it is, on the contrary, the present."[47]

Foucault calls attention here to a shift in late modernity in how historical discourse conceived the nation and its future. This shift manifested itself in the fact that counterhistory ceased to speak of a current coded race struggle arising out of past events and started to cast it in terms of an ongoing war with occupying forces. In his account of the way in which historical discourse functioned among the English Levellers and Diggers in their explanation of who the Normans and William the Conqueror really were, Foucault intends to show how this shift began.[48] Historical discourse functioned less and less to suggest that the current state of things reflects the effects of an invasion and occupation; instead, the purveyors of history began to view the present as being in a sense ahistorical and replete in itself. Thus "the present

47. Foucault, *"Society Must Be Defended,"* p. 227.
48. Foucault, *"Society Must Be Defended,"* pp. 87-111.

becomes the fullest moment, the moment of greatest intensity," despite the many (racial) rifts and cleavages that mark it. Indeed, it is from these aberrant rifts that the present must be saved for the sake of its future; the present must be purged so that the "virtual" and "functional totality of the nation" can become the "actual" and "real universality of the state."[49]

The critical implication that Foucault calls attention to is the way in which the privileged moment for historical discourse shifts from a supposedly pristine past in need of counterhistorical resistance to the nation's present endeavor to produce and reproduce and realize itself as the perfect state. Under these circumstances, historical discourse comes to function under a "principle of national universality."[50] To be sure, this universality is not a sanguine state of affairs, for in every productive and reproductive effort the social rift, the binary opposition, continues to be produced and reproduced. But it is produced and reproduced now *within* the race, not *between* the races. The task of society, which has become a civilian rather than a militaristic one, is the still bellicose task of achieving victory, but now by eliminating its internal rifts. Its task, in short, is to defend itself against itself. It is now a war for purity within the race, a war for racial purity, one might say. According to Foucault, this shift in social dynamics, which follows the shift in the nature of historical discourse, lays the groundwork for racism, particularly statist, biological racism. Such racism is actualized when the effort to produce and reproduce the nation is coupled with the biological and medical sciences.

None of what has been said commits us to a reading of Foucault that suggests that he somehow intends to implicate Jews as complicit in the nineteenth- and twentieth-century racism meted out against them. Indeed, he unequivocally opposes racism (and especially anti-Semitism) and understood his work as an intellectual labor to expose its causes and to change its reality. My point, however, is that consideration of Foucault's claims regarding the mythical basis of race, religion, and the modern state suggests an unwitting reenactment of modernity's anxiety about the theopolitical meaning of Jewish existence. That anxiety shows itself here around this question of the meaning of the people, of the collective, of the nation, of the state. It centers on an insufficient theological grasp of the covenantal status of this people and its election.

Hence, what the lectures have no way of interrogating are the ways in

49. Foucault, *"Society Must Be Defended,"* p. 227.
50. Foucault, *"Society Must Be Defended,"* p. 239.

which Israel embodies and is called to a performance of what it means to be a people, more specifically, YHWH's people, beyond the modern nation-state as an "imagined community," even if in late modernity the nation-state is in many ways borderless.[51] That is to say, Foucault's lectures cannot imagine Israel as a covenantal people and therefore as a people constituted (however, imperfectly) beyond modernity's hegemonic and counterhegemonic alternatives. He fails to query how modernity represents a deformation of Israel's covenantal status into a racial status. Indeed, by not acknowledging the *theological* significance of Israel's existence or interrogating how modernity represents an attempt to triumph over what Israel theologically signifies, Foucault's discourse remains trapped within the story of the modern racializing — we can even say, orientalizing — of the Jew. My claim, stated differently then, is this: Foucault's genealogical inquiry did not — and perhaps, due to its presuppositions, could not — go far enough. In the end, he, as Cornel West did, brackets the theological from his genealogy of modernity and thus from his analysis of modern racial discourse. Foucault, in fact, admits as much in the introductory remarks to the fifth of his 1975-1976 Collège de France lectures:

> The divide, the perception of the war between races predates the notions of social struggle or class struggle, but it certainly cannot be identified with a racism of, if you like, the religious type. It is true that I haven't talked [so far in these lectures] about anti-Semitism. I intended to say a bit about it last time, . . . but I did not have time. What I think we can say . . . is this: Insofar as it is a religious and racial attitude, anti-Semitism had so little influence on the history I was trying to trace for you that it does not have to be taken into account until we reach the nineteenth century.[52]

He continues by claiming that anti-Semitism as a distinctively religious or theological problem is of recent vintage:

> The old religious-type anti-Semitism was reutilized by State racism only in the nineteenth century, or at the point when the State had to look like, function, and present itself as the guarantor of the integrity and purity of the race, and had to defend itself against the race or races that were infiltrating it, introducing harmful elements into its body, and which there-

51. Benedict Anderson, *Imagined Communities: Reflections on the Origin and Spread of Nationalism,* revised ed. (London: Verso, 1991).
52. Foucault, *"Society Must Be Defended,"* p. 88.

fore had to be driven out for both political and biological reasons. It is at this point that anti-Semitism develops, picking up, using, and taking from the old form of anti-Semitism all the energy — and a whole mythology — which had until then been devoted solely to the political analysis of the internal war, or the social war. At this point the Jews came to be seen as — and were described as — a race that was present within all races, and whose biologically dangerous character necessitated a certain number of mechanisms of rejection and exclusion on the part of the State. It is therefore, I think, the reutilization within State racism of an anti-Semitism which had developed for other reasons that generated the nineteenth-century phenomena of superimposing the old mechanisms of anti-Semitism on this critical and political analysis of the struggle between races within a single society.[53]

[It is necessary to] challenge Foucault's claim that "[insofar] as [the Jewish question] is a religious and racial attitude, [it] had so little influence on the [story of modernity or more specifically on the story of the rise of the modern State and of the political in the modern world] . . . that it does not have to be taken into account until we reach the nineteenth century." . . . [C]ontra Foucault, . . . the story of the modern invention of race had every-thing to do with the story of the modern invention of religion; . . . both of these stories were of a piece with the story of the rise of the modern nation-state as a new form of political economy or sociopolitical governance; and . . . the so-called Jewish problem was a key subtext in all of this.

This new form of governance was soteriological in character but was able to be so only by absorbing key features of Christian thought, with the result that the modern state, through its pretensions toward (especially European) nationalism, gets figured as the new agent of redemption. In this sense, modernity from the first harbors quasi-theological or pseudotheological pretensions, pretensions that were at work in the formation of modern racial discourse as one of its supporting discourses for the "total revolution" of society.[54] It is worth stating again that a key subtext of this revolutionary saga is the *Judenfrage*. The negotiation of this question in the struggle to constitute the modern (nation) state, to use Immanuel Kant's language, was nothing short of a grand religious drama.

---

53. Foucault, *"Society Must Be Defended,"* pp. 88-89.

54. I take this phrase from Bernard Yack, *The Longing for Total Revolution: Philosophic Sources of Social Discontent from Rousseau to Marx and Nietzsche* (Berkeley: University of California Press, 1992).

VIII. Postcolonial Challenges

Introduction

Joerg Rieger

While definitions of the postcolonial are multiple, two are especially relevant for us. According to one of the meanings of the term, the postcolonial emerges in the midst of the struggle with the colonial, early on.[1] This serves as an important reminder that there is never a pure colonial situation, devoid of resistance and lacking alternatives. Christianity itself might serve as an example for this definition, as it has been shaped under the influence of various empires and colonialisms, without ever having been assimilated altogether by these contexts.[2] Another definition understands the postcolonial as that which comes after the official end of mostly European colonialism, which happened at various times during the past two centuries around the globe. What both of these definitions share in common, nevertheless, is a sense of the ongoing need for resistance.

While resistance is a way of life for the colonized in a colonial situation, most postcolonial theorists understand that even in postcolonial situations, after the end of colonialism, the struggle against oppression continues. While the times of colonialism, with viceroys, governors, standing armies of soldiers and clerks, and established government apparatuses on foreign terrain are by and large in the past, we are now dealing with what elsewhere I have called the postcolonial empire. Here power is located increasingly in

1. This is the approach taken in *The Postcolonial Studies Reader,* ed. Bill Ashcroft, Gareth Griffiths, and Helen Tiffin (London: Routledge, 1995).

2. I show this for several theological turning points from the first to the twenty-first century in my book *Christ and Empire: From Paul to Postcolonial Times* (Minneapolis: Fortress Press, 2007).

economic and cultural processes of globalization, many of them related to the U.S.[3]

Theological Challenges

It is often overlooked that the close relation of Christianity with various empires and colonialisms has produced what should be classified as colonial theology. For the most part, such colonial theology is not self-identified. It is produced less by intention than by default, due to the fact that empire and colonialism affect not only the realms of politics and economics but also the realms of the cultural, the intellectual, and the religious. It is this situation that creates the postcolonial challenge for theology: at stake is the question whether theology supports empire and the colonial, implicitly or explicitly, or whether theology resists these structures and provides alternatives. *Tertium non datur:* a third option does not exist in a world that is permeated by the vast power differentials that go with empire and the colonial.

While issues of postcolonial theory have been addressed in biblical studies for some time, in theology the methodological challenges of postcolonial theory have been addressed only in more recent years. In this anthology, the work of Kwok Pui-lan and Mark Lewis Taylor represent these more recent developments. Nevertheless, postcolonial challenges as such have been addressed for some time by theologians who have taken seriously the fact that Christianity can never be assimilated to empire and colonialism altogether, and who thus have kept providing alternatives to the status quo. Such alternatives, to be sure, are usually not discovered at the desks of mainline theology but emerge in relation to the real-life struggles of the colonized and the victims of empire. This is the common thread that ties together the chapters in this section.

Desmond Tutu, the former Anglican Archbishop of Cape Town, has achieved international acclaim for his resistance to South African apartheid. Experiencing oppression firsthand sharpened his theological astuteness to matters of empire and colonialism. It is no surprise, therefore, that in his reflections on Rwanda he notes not only the much-publicized conflict between Hutus and Tutsis but also the role that the "colonial overlords" played in laying the groundwork for this situation. In situations like that, true reconciliation cannot be cheap; it requires an "acknowledgement by the cul-

---

3. See Rieger, *Christ and Empire,* chapter 7.

476

prit," and it requires also that the disparities will be rectified. Still, the meaning of forgiveness in such situations remains hotly contested. Tutu reports that his public acceptance of a plea for forgiveness by theologian Willie Jonker for his Afrikaner community was disputed, because it could seem that this would let the white church "get away with murder."

Emmanuel Katongole, writing from the perspective of Uganda, notes the shallowness of a postmodern situation where otherness and difference have become valued terms. He finds "something sinister about the postmodern celebration of difference" because, while creating fresh interest in Africa, it also defuses the challenges that difference can pose. Worse yet, such celebration of difference tends to go hand in hand with economic globalization. While Katongole does not address the theological underpinnings of the current situation, he searches for an alternative theological perspective. African religious developments, he finds, might fit the bill if seen not as a "strategy" but as a "tactic," understanding a "tactic" as the "art of the weak" (Michel De Certeau), who may not have what it takes to take on the enemy as a whole.

Kim Yong-Bock, one of the fathers of Korean minjung theology, and Arvind Nirmal, a Dalit theologian from India, both focus on the reality of the colonized and oppressed, and on the challenges that they pose to theological reflection. These approaches came into their own in the 1970s and 1980s and have been with us ever since. Kim notes the fact that the minjung — composed of all people who experience oppression — are not just suffering but, to a certain extent, are also active subjects who are making a difference in the world. The power of the minjung resembles the power of Jesus, in that it resists the dominant powers and seeks to establish "messianic servanthood," modeled according to the biblical notion of the Suffering Servant. Nirmal notes the difference between elite Indian Christian theology, which has been the norm, and a people's theology that originates with the Dalit community, the diverse communities of untouchables or outcastes in Indian society. The theological liberation motif that emerges here is profoundly Indian in that it confronts the particular forms of oppression in that context. Rather than seeking premature reconciliation, Nirmal insists that the protest of the Dalits "should be so loud that the walls of Brahmanism . . . come tumbling down." In the process the "dalitness" of Jesus of Nazareth and of God becomes clear: the divine is taking sides once again, as in the biblical stories of old.

Kosuke Koyama and Rafiq Khoury speak from situations of destruction, one from the defeated Japan of 1945 and the other from the Palestinian perspective since the founding of the modern State of Israel. Koyama, a Japanese Christian theologian who taught in the U.S. for many years, deals with the experience of destruction during World War II, as well as the need for repentance for Japanese imperial aggression against other Asian countries. In this context, the religion of empire is exposed for what it is — idolatry — and it is out of the destruction of idolatry that new religious sensitivities can develop. From the perspective of Palestinian Christianity, Khoury examines the complex religious character of the situation in Israel. In this context, colonial theology endorsing "classic colonialist methods" is still alive and well, and it finds expression in literalist interpretations of the Bible and of theological notions such as election and promise, boosted by "a guilt-complex regarding the Jewish people." In a context of destruction and death supported by theology, the Palestinian people pose a profound theological challenge to the identity of the Holy Land, which now needs to be reconsidered from the perspective of the least of these.

Some Conceptual Challenges

While the texts of Musa Dube, Kwok Pui-lan, and Mark Lewis Taylor are no less rooted in struggles against colonialism and empire, they add some explicit reflections on the conceptual challenges of postcolonial theory to religion and the study of theology. All three authors are in agreement that the failure to address the history of empire and colonialism in our own contexts is the biggest problem, as it helps to maintain the structures of empire in our own time, particularly in the United States.

Dube's text, written from Botswana, Africa, constitutes a systematic exploration of a feminist postcolonial method for the study of the Bible. Her concern is not with "historical accusations" but with a "committed search and struggle for decolonization and liberation of the oppressed." While postcolonial theory at times plays down dualisms and binaries, Dube emphasizes the sharp contrast between the colonized and the colonizers in a colonial setting: one group is depicted as helpless, undeveloped, and evil, the other group as authoritative, developed, and good. In such a context of grave power differentials, common modern sensitivities about inclusion and exclusion in the biblical traditions are reversed: an inclusive approach might support common cause with the colonizers and collaboration with the empire, while an exclusive approach might support resistance.

Kwok, a theologian from Hong Kong teaching in the United States, notes the limitations of the modern notion of religion, and she concludes that theology never emerges in a vacuum but in an ongoing process of negotiation with economic, political, and ecclesial power structures. Once this is clear, we need to deal with the challenges of colonialism and empire at a deeper level, which considers its impacts on religion and theology itself. Theology and politics are not separate spheres, as is commonly assumed, but interact with each other. Hybridity, the fusion of elements that the dominant approach would like to keep separate, is one of the consequences of this situation. It is manifest especially as theologians from marginalized communities fuse elements from dominant and indigenous traditions, including the perspectives of those marginalized by ethnicity and gender, thereby shifting the basis of authority.

Taylor admits that it is not easy for postcolonial theology in the United States to find religious or ecclesial groups as "social mediator(s)," but he nevertheless notes the existence of movements of "people with spirit from diverse religious, moral, and political orientation" with whom this approach finds its home. The resources for a new movement in the U.S. are not as insignificant as is often assumed, beginning with the Jesus movement itself; the Latin American, African American, and women's communities that generated liberation theologies, which are alive and well; hidden religious revolutionary traditions in the North Atlantic; and loose-knit interreligious coalitions that focus on justice. Taylor notes the specific challenge of relating the postcolonial notion of hybridity to resistance, which includes the effort to balance "discourses of difference" with "discourses of liberation."

Achieving this balance, I would argue, may well be the primary task of postcolonial theology, as the notions of hybridity as well as difference are often taken to mean the demise of the antithesis of colonizers and the colonized in a postcolonial setting. While hybridity reminds us that pure categories of colonizers and colonized, oppressors and oppressed, do not exist, since these groups constantly reshape each other in complex mutual interactions, we must not overlook the power differentials that remain in place even in a postcolonial context. Hybridity, it must be remembered, works only on the basis of power differentials, and it is in a special way the reality of those who find themselves located on the underside of the colonial or postcolonial world, because they cannot escape the impact of those in power; those in power, on the other hand, usually have more flexibility. For the colonized, this often means that they are shaped by the colonial world to such a degree that, to the casual observer, it can appear as if they are becoming more and more like the colonizers.

479

One of the most important insights of postcolonial theory, however, is that the colonized never become exactly identical to the colonizers. Here is where the hope for an alternative theology lies. When the colonized mimic the colonizers, an important difference remains — a difference that can also be observed in their theologizing and that might ultimately point us to the different reality of God. The postcolonial term "mimicry," informed by poststructuralist philosophical observations, emphasizes the difference between the original and that which is imitated. In this difference lies the potential for subversion and ultimately for resistance.[4] As a result, hybridity and mimicry point not to the celebration of difference, multiculturalism, and plurality, but to the ultimate liberation from suffering and oppression.

Conclusion

In an age in which hard power is becoming less fashionable and when difference and multiculturalism are widely affirmed, we need to recall that grave power differentials continue to exist. Our problem resembles, to some degree, what happens in the transition from physical abuse of others (spouses, children, and other dependents) to other more hidden forms of abuse on the basis of deep-seated economic, cultural, religious, and psychological dependencies. The reason why postcolonial notions like hybridity and mimicry are important today is not because dualisms of power and binaries would have finally disappeared, but because of the persistence of grave power differentials, shifting from the more visible realm of politics to the less visible realm of the economy.

The ethnocentrisms that have often been challenged by postcolonial critics may serve as a case in point. Without the backing of the power differentials of a capitalist economy, even Eurocentrism would be merely another ethnocentrism,[5] and Anglo culture in the U.S. might have to wait for the latest polls in order to find out whether it was still in charge. This insight also serves as a reminder why so many Europeans and so many Anglos in the U.S. reap only limited benefits from buying into ethnocentric positions: capitalism does not provide the same amount of support to Europeans and Anglos

---

4. For the terms "hybridity" and "mimicry" see Homi Bhabha, *The Location of Culture* (London: Routledge, 1994).

5. This is an observation by Arif Dirlik, referenced in Rebecca Todd Peters, *In Search of the Good Life: The Ethics of Globalization* (New York: Continuum, 2004), p. 141.

who do not belong to the ruling classes. Nevertheless, the good news is that these power differentials are being challenged and that alternatives are emerging even in theology. As postcolonial theologians might add: Thanks be to God.

33 Without Forgiveness There Really Is No Future

Desmond Tutu

A year after the genocide of 1994 in Rwanda, when at least half a million people were massacred, I visited that blighted land. I went as the president of the
continental ecumenical body, the All Africa Conference of Churches. In my
ten-year, two-term presidency I had tried to take the AACC to its member
churches through pastoral visits, especially to those countries that were experiencing crises of one sort or another. So I and other AACC officers had
visited Nigeria; Liberia during its civil war; Angola and others. We also went
to celebrate successes when, for instance, democracy replaced repression and
injustice in Ethiopia. But usually we wanted to demonstrate solidarity with
our fellow Christians in lands that were experiencing some trial or another.
So the AACC leadership had gone to Rwanda.

We visited Ntarama, a village near the capital, Kigali, where Tutsi had
been mown down in a church. The new government had not removed the
corpses, so that the church was like a mortuary, with the bodies lying as they
had fallen the year before during the massacre. The stench was overpower-
ing. Outside the church building was a collection of skulls of some of those
who had been brutally done to death — some of the skulls still had *pangas*
(machetes) and daggers embedded in them. I tried to pray. Instead I broke
down and wept.

The scene was a deeply disturbing and moving monument to the vi-
ciousness that as human beings we are capable of unleashing against fellow
human beings. Those who had turned against one another in this gory fashion had often lived amicably in the same villages and spoken the same language. They had frequently intermarried and most of them had espoused

482

the same faith — most were Christians. The colonial overlords had sought to maintain their European hegemony by favoring the main ethnic group, the Tutsi, over the other, the Hutu, thus planting the seeds of what would in the end be one of the bloodiest episodes in modern African history. (The third group was the Twa, much fewer in numbers.) That genocide made one think anew about blaming racism for every conceivable ill that has befallen humankind, because, while whites had a hand in fomenting the ethnic internecine strife, the actual perpetrators were black against fellow black.

A few kilometers from this church, some women had begun to build a settlement which they named the Nelson Mandela Village. It was to be a home for some of the many widows and orphans created by the genocide. I spoke to the leaders of this women's movement. They said, "We must mourn and weep for the dead. But life must also go on, we can't go on weeping." How wonderfully impressive, how indomitable. Over at Ntarama, we might say, there was Calvary, death and crucifixion. Here in the Nelson Mandela Village was Resurrection, new life, new beginning, new hope. Once more it was noteworthy to see how women have this remarkable resilience and an instinct for nurturing life.

I also visited the overcrowded Kigali Prison, packed to the rafters with those suspected of being involved in genocide. Almost all were Hutus. There were women, men, and even young children, people of every age and from every social group — including priests and nuns, teachers and lawyers. Some people had died from suffocation. I told President Pasteur Bizimungu that that prison was a disaster waiting to happen and that it would add to the bitter memories and exacerbate the resentment of Hutu toward Tutsi.

I also attended a rally in the main stadium of Kigali. It was amazing that people who had so recently experienced such a devastating trauma could sing and laugh and dance as they did at that rally. Most of the leading politicians were present, from the President on down. I had been asked to preach. I began by expressing the deepest condolences of all their sisters and brothers in other parts of Africa, for people elsewhere had been profoundly shocked at the carnage and destruction. (It turns out now that, had the international community heeded the many warnings that were being given at the time, perhaps the United Nations might have had the resources to intervene and the genocide might very well not have happened. The Rwandese felt a deep anger against the UN. The victims and survivors felt they had been let down very badly, with disastrous consequences.) I said that the history of Rwanda was typical of a history of "top dog" and "underdog." The top dog wanted to cling to its privileged position and the underdog strove to topple the top dog. When that happened, the new top dog engaged in an orgy of retribution to pay back the new underdog for all the pain and suffering it had inflicted when it was top dog. The new underdog fought like an enraged bull to topple the new top dog, storing in its memory all the pain and suffering it was enduring, forgetting that the new top dog was in its view only retaliating for all that it remembered it had suffered when the underdog had been its master. It was a sad history of reprisal provoking counter-reprisal. I reminded the Tutsi that they had waited for thirty years to get their own back for what they perceived to be the injustices that had been heaped on them. I said that extremists among the Hutu were also quite capable of waiting thirty years or more for one day when they could topple the new government, in which the Tutsi played a prominent role, and in their turn unleash the devastation of revenge and resentment.

I said there was talk about tribunals because people did not want to tolerate allowing the criminals to escape punishment. But what I feared was that, if retributive justice was the last word in their situation, then Rwanda had had it. Most Hutu would feel that they had been found guilty not because they were guilty but because they were Hutu, and they would wait for the day when they would be able to take revenge. Then they would pay back the Tutsi for the horrendous prison conditions in which they had been held.

I told them that the cycle of reprisal and counterreprisal that had characterized their national history had to be broken and that the only way to do this was to go beyond retributive justice to restorative justice, to move on to forgiveness, because without it there was no future.

The President of Rwanda responded to my sermon with considerable magnanimity. They were ready to forgive, he said, but even Jesus had declared that the devil could not be forgiven. I do not know where he found the basis for what he said, but he was expressing a view that found some resonance, that there were atrocities that were unforgivable. My own view was different, but I had been given a fair and indeed friendly hearing. Later I addressed the parliamentary and political leadership of that country and I was not shouted down as I repeated my appeal for them to consider choosing forgiveness and reconciliation rather than their opposites.

Why was I not rebuffed? Why did these traumatized people, who had undergone such a terrible experience, listen to an unpopular point of view? They listened to me particularly because something had happened in South Africa that gave them reason to pause and wonder. Was this not a viable way of dealing with conflict? Might those who had been at one another's throats try to live amicably together? The world had expected that the most ghastly blood bath would overwhelm South Africa. It had not happened. Then the world thought that, after a democratically elected government was in place, those who for so long had been denied their rights, whose dignity had been trodden underfoot, callously and without compunction, would go on the rampage, unleashing an orgy of revenge and retribution that would devastate their common motherland. Instead there was this remarkable Truth and Reconciliation Commission to which people told their heartrending stories, victims expressing their willingness to forgive and perpetrators telling their stories of sordid atrocities while also asking for forgiveness from those they had wronged so grievously.

The world could not quite believe what it was seeing. "[Y]ou get new hope for the future," the former President of the Federal Republic of Germany, Richard von Weizsacker, told a symposium in Berlin in April 1999 after hearing our country's story. South Africans managed an extraordinary, reasonably peaceful transition from the awfulness of repression to the relative stability of democracy. They confounded everyone by their novel manner of dealing with a horrendous past. They had perhaps surprised even themselves at first by how much equanimity they had shown as some of the gory details of that past were rehearsed. It was a phenomenon that the world could not dismiss as insignificant. It was what enabled me to address my sisters and brothers in Rwanda in a manner that under other circumstances could have been seen as insensitive and presumptuous.

I have had the same experience when visiting other parts of the world where people are seeking to come to terms with their history of conflict and disagreement. In 1998, I went to Dublin and to Belfast. In both these cities audiences warmed to the message that our South African experience showed that almost no situation could be said to be devoid of hope. Our problem had been one which most had abandoned as ultimately intractable. I said, "Yes, we have lived through a ghastly nightmare, but it has ended." The Irish were on the way to an end to their nightmare, for had there not already been the Good Friday Agreement? I said they ought not to grow despondent over the obstacles preventing the implementation of that crucial agreement; our experience had been that quite frequently the enemies of peace would respond to breakthroughs by redoubling their efforts to derail the process. I said the Irish should redouble their own determination and vigilance to ensure that such a priceless gift as the end of their "troubles" should not elude them just when it was within their grasp.

I told them that in South Africa it had often felt as if we were on a roller-coaster ride. At one moment we would experience the most wonderful joy, euphoria even, at some new and crucial initiative. We would see the promised land of peace and justice around the corner. Then, just when we thought we had entered the last lap, something ghastly would happen — a massacre, a deadlock, brinkmanship of some kind, a walkout by one delegation or another — and we would be scraping the bottom of despair and despondency. I told them this was normal. The prize at the end is so wonderful that they should not let go of their dream of a new Ireland; of a time when they would be amazed that they had been blind for so long; of a time when they would realize that they had wasted many years and many lives when in fact goodness and peace and tolerance were wonderful and ultimately uncomplicated. I reminded them of how it had seemed so unlikely for us to have got where we now were in South Africa. Just as our nightmare had ended, so too would theirs end, as sure as day follows night.

They heard this message as if in a sense it had been uttered by an oracle. What gave a heightened credibility to what I said was the fact that we had had a relatively peaceful transition and had found this novel way of dealing with the legacy of our past. I want to believe that it helped them a little when I exhorted them not to despair because of a deadlock over the decommissioning of weapons. In Belfast, I was deeply impressed by the many dedicated individuals working away in strife-torn communities, building bridges between alienated and traumatized people, being extraordinary agents of peace and reconciliation. I said to them that nothing is ever lost; that their work did not evaporate into the ether and disappear into oblivion, even if it appeared a failure. No, in a way that we could not fathom, their work went to impregnate the atmosphere. We know that happens. We can sense that a home is happy even before anyone tells us because we are able to catch the "vibes" — it is in the very stones. We know when a church is redolent of sanctity, of holiness; when it has been prayed in. We can almost catch the odor of holiness and sense the energy and reverence of those many who have gone before. It is there in the atmosphere, in the very fabric. A prayed-in church is qualitatively different from one that has the atmosphere of a concert hall. So I told those dedicated workers for peace and reconciliation that they should not be tempted to give up on their crucial work because of the frustrations of seemingly not making any significant progress; that in our experience nothing was wasted, for in the fullness of time, when the time was right, it would all come together and those looking back would realize what a critical contribution they had made. They were part of the cosmic movement toward unity, toward reconciliation, that has existed from the beginning of time.

It is and has always been God's intention that we should live in friendship and harmony. That was the point of the story of the Garden of Eden, where there was no bloodshed, not even for religious sacrifice. The lion and the lamb gamboled together and all were vegetarian. Then the primordial harmony that was God's intention for all God's creation was shattered and a fundamental brokenness infected the entire creation. Human beings came to be at loggerheads, blaming one another and being at one another's throats. They were alienated from their Maker. Now they sought to hide from the God who used to stroll with them in the garden. Creation, was now "red in tooth and claw." Where there had been friendship, now we experienced enmity. Humans would crush the serpent's head before it bruised their heels. This story is the Bible's way of telling a profound existential truth in the form of highly imaginative poetry.

Prosaic, literal-minded spirits who cannot soar in the realms of the muse will be dismissive of this highly imaginative storytelling. And yet even if we doubt that there has ever been such harmony in a mythical Garden of Eden, none but the most obtuse can doubt that we are experiencing a radical brokenness in all of existence. Times are out of joint. Alienation and disharmony, conflict and turmoil, enmity and hatred characterize so much of life. Ours has been the bloodiest century known to human history. There would be no call for ecological campaigning had nature not been exploited and abused. We experience the ground now bringing forth thistles as soil erosion devastates formerly arable land and deserts overtake fertile farms. Rivers and the atmosphere are polluted thoughtlessly and we are fearful of the consequences of a depleted ozone layer and the devastation of the greenhouse effect. We are not quite at home in our world, and somewhere in each of us there is a nostalgia for a paradise that has been lost.

Believers say that we might describe most of human history as a quest for that harmony, friendship, and peace for which we appear to have been created. The Bible depicts it all as a God-directed campaign to recover that primordial harmony when the lion will again lie with the lamb and they will learn war no more because swords will have been beaten into plowshares and spears into pruning hooks. Somewhere deep inside us we seem to know that we are destined for something better. Now and again we catch a glimpse of the better thing for which we are meant — for example, when we work together to counter the effects of natural disasters and the world is galvanized by a spirit of compassion and an amazing outpouring of generosity; when for a little while we are bound together by bonds of a caring humanity, a universal sense of *ubuntu*, when victorious powers set up a Marshall Plan to help in the reconstruction of their devastated former adversaries; when we establish a United Nations Organization where the peoples of the earth can parley as they endeavor to avoid war; when we sign charters on the rights of children and of women; when we seek to ban the use of antipersonnel land mines; when we agree as one to outlaw torture and racism. Then we experience fleetingly that we are made for togetherness, for friendship, for community, for family, that we are created to live in a delicate network of interdependence.

There is a movement, not easily discernible, at the heart of things to reverse the awful centrifugal force of alienation, brokenness, division, hostility, and disharmony. God has set in motion a centripetal process, a moving toward the center, toward unity, harmony, goodness, peace, and justice, a process that removes barriers. Jesus says, "And when I am lifted up from the earth I shall draw everyone to myself"[1] as he hangs from His cross with outflung arms, thrown out to clasp all, everyone and everything, in a cosmic embrace, so that all, everyone, everything, belongs. None is an outsider, all are insiders, all belong. There are no aliens, all belong in the one family, God's family, the human family. There is no longer Jew or Greek, male or female, slave or free — instead of separation and division, all distinctions make for a rich diversity to be celebrated for the sake of the unity that underlies them. We are different so that we can know our need of one another, for no one is ultimately self-sufficient. The completely self-sufficient person would be subhuman.

It was God's intention to bring all things in heaven and on earth to a unity in Christ, and each of us participates in this grand movement. Thus Teilhard de Chardin, the paleontologist, in a passage from *Le Milieu divin* declares:

> We are sometimes inclined to think that the same things are monotonously repeated over and over again in the history of creation. That is because the season is too long by comparison with the brevity of our individual lives, and the transformation too vast and too inward by comparison with our superficial and restricted outlook, for us to see the progress of what is tirelessly taking place in and through all matter and spirit. Let us believe in revelation, once again our faithful support in our most human forebodings. Under the commonplace envelope of things and of all our purified and salvaged efforts, a new earth is being slowly engendered.
>
> One day, the Gospel tells us, the tension gradually accumulating be-

---

1. John 12:32.

tween humanity and God will touch the limits prescribed by the possibilities of the world. And then will come the end. The presence of Christ, which has been silently accruing in things, will suddenly be revealed — like a flash of light from pole to pole. Breaking through all the barriers within which the veil of matter and the watertightness of souls have seemingly kept it confined, it will invade the face of the earth. . . . Like lightning, like a conflagration, like a flood, the attraction exerted by the Son of Man will lay hold of all the whirling elements in the universe so as to reunite them or subject them to his body. . . . As the Gospel warns us, it would be in vain to speculate as to the hour and the modalities of this formidable event. But we have to expect it . . . that is perhaps the supreme Christian function and the most distinctive characteristic of our religion. . . . The Lord Jesus will only come soon if we ardently expect him. . . . Successors to Israel, we Christians have been charged with keeping the flame of desire ever alive in the world. Only twenty centuries have passed since the Ascension. What have we made of our expectancy?

A rather childish haste, combined with the error in perspective which led the first generation of Christians to believe in the immediate return of Christ, has unfortunately left us disillusioned and suspicious. Our faith in the Kingdom of God has been disconcerted by the resistance of the world to good. A certain pessimism has encouraged us . . . to regard the world as decidedly and incorrigibly wicked. And so we have allowed the flame to die down in our sleeping hearts . . . in reality we should have to admit, if we were sincere that we no longer expect anything.[2]

And so I was able to say to those remarkable people in Belfast that nothing is lost. What they were doing advanced the course of reconciliation. What each of us does can retard or promote, can hinder or advance the process at the heart of the universe. Christians would say the outcome is not in question. The death and resurrection of Jesus Christ puts the issue beyond doubt: ultimately goodness and laughter and peace and compassion and gentleness and forgiveness and reconciliation will have the last word and prevail over their ghastly counterparts. The victory over apartheid was proof positive of the truth of this seemingly utopian dream.

May the time come when men (and women) having been awakened to the close bond linking all the movements of this world in the single all-

2. Quoted by Mary McAleese in *Reconciled Being: Love in Chaos* (New York: Continuum Publishing Group, 1999).

embracing work of the Incarnation, shall be unable to give themselves to any one of their tasks without illuminating it with the clear vision that their work, however elementary it may be, is received and put to good use by a Centre of the Universe.[3]

I had visited the Holy Land over Christmas 1989 and had the privilege during that visit of going to Yad Vashem, the Holocaust museum in Jerusalem. When the media asked me for my impressions, I told them it was a shattering experience. I added that the Lord whom I served, who was himself a Jew, would have asked, "But what about forgiveness?" That remark set the cat among the pigeons. I was roundly condemned. I had also expressed my dismay at the treatment meted out to the Palestinians, which was in my view quite at variance with what the Jewish prophets taught and what the Jewish rabbi that we Christians followed demanded from his followers. I was charged with being anti-Semitic and graffiti appeared on the walls of St. George's Anglican Cathedral in Jerusalem in whose close I was staying. It read, "Tutu is a black Nazi pig."

I was thus somewhat apprehensive about going there again in January 1999, when I was to preach at an Anglican church on the West Bank, speak to a group in Jerusalem, and attend a meeting in Tel Aviv of the Peres Peace Center, on whose board of directors I serve. But I need not have worried. Our hosts at the meeting in Jerusalem had to turn people away. It was clear everywhere we went that what had occurred in South Africa fascinated people greatly. Shimon Peres, the former Prime Minister, Foreign Minister, and Nobel Peace laureate, hailed our reconciliation process as something unique in history.

In the Jerusalem meeting, which was packed, there really was a deep interest among Israelis in the process of the commission and in the concept of forgiveness and reconciliation. I was able to point out that we had learned in South Africa that true security would never be won through the barrel of a gun. True security would come when all the inhabitants of the Middle East, that region so revered by so many, believed that their human rights and dignity were respected and upheld, when true justice prevailed. I had not changed my own points of view: I still felt there was a need for forgiveness and that there ought to be both security for the state of Israel and justice and equity for the Palestinians. But somehow in Israel I was seen in a new light.

It was clear in all of these countries — Rwanda, Ireland, Israel, and Pal-

---

3. Teilhard de Chardin, again quoted by Mary McAleese.

estine — that the process in which South Africa had been engaged lent a credibility to whatever I might say. People could listen to perhaps difficult things without accusing me of being presumptuous and insensitive. More than anything else, it did seem as if many who listened to me were people who derived hope from what we had attempted to do in South Africa. We happened to have been blessed with leaders who were ready to take risks — when you embark on the business of asking for and granting forgiveness, you are taking a risk.

In relations between individuals, if you ask another person for forgiveness you may be spurned; the one you have injured may refuse to forgive you. The risk is even greater if you are the injured party, wanting to offer forgiveness. The culprit may be arrogant, obdurate, or blind, not ready or willing to apologize or to ask for forgiveness. He or she thus cannot appropriate the forgiveness that is offered. Such rejection can jeopardize the whole enterprise. Our leaders were ready in South Africa to say they were willing to walk the path of confession, forgiveness, and reconciliation with all the hazards that lay along the way. And it seems their gamble might be paying off, since our land has not been overwhelmed by the catastrophe that had seemed so inevitable.

It is crucial, when a relationship has been damaged or when a potential relationship has been made impossible, that the perpetrator should acknowledge the truth and be ready and willing to apologize. It helps the process of forgiveness and reconciliation immensely. It is never easy. We all know just how difficult it is for most of us to admit that we have been wrong. It is perhaps the most difficult thing in the world — in almost every language the most difficult words are, "I am sorry." Thus it is not at all surprising that those accused of horrendous deeds and the communities they come from, for whom they believed they were committing these atrocities, almost always try to find ways out of even admitting that they were indeed capable of such deeds. They adopt the denial mode, asserting that such-and-such has not happened. When the evidence is incontrovertible they take refuge in feigned ignorance. The Germans claimed they had not known what the Nazis were up to. White South Africans have also tried to find refuge in claims of ignorance. The former apartheid cabinet member Leon Wessels was closer to the mark when he said that they had not wanted to know, for there were those who tried to alert them. For those with eyes to see there were accounts of people dying mysteriously in detention. For those with ears to hear there was much that was disquieting and even chilling. But, like the three monkeys, they chose neither to hear, nor see, nor speak of evil. When some did own up, they passed the blame to others, "We were carrying out orders," refusing to acknowledge that as morally responsible individuals each person has to take responsibility for carrying out unconscionable orders.

We do not usually rush to expose our vulnerability and our sinfulness. But if the process of forgiveness and healing is to succeed, ultimately acknowledgment by the culprit is indispensable — not completely so but nearly so. Acknowledgment of the truth and of having wronged someone is important in getting to the root of the breach. If a husband and wife have quarreled without the wrongdoer acknowledging his or her fault by confessing, so exposing the cause of the rift, if a husband in this situation comes home with a bunch of flowers and the couple pretend all is in order, then they will be in for a rude shock. They have not dealt with their immediate past adequately. They have glossed over their differences, for they have failed to stare truth in the face for fear of a possible bruising confrontation. They will have done what the prophet calls healing the hurt lightly by crying, "Peace, peace where there is no, peace."[4] They will have only papered over the cracks and not worked out why they fell out in the first place. All that will happen is that, despite the beautiful flowers, the hurt will fester. One day there will be an awful eruption and they will realize that they had tried to obtain reconciliation on the cheap. True reconciliation is not cheap. It cost God the death of His only begotten Son.

Forgiving and being reconciled are not about pretending that things are other than they are. It is not patting one another on the back and turning a blind eye to the wrong. True reconciliation exposes the awfulness, the abuse, the pain, the degradation, the truth. It could even sometimes make things worse. It is a risky undertaking but in the end it is worthwhile, because in the end dealing with the real situation helps to bring real healing. Spurious reconciliation can bring only spurious healing.

If the wrongdoer has come to the point of realizing his wrong, then one hopes there will be remorse, or at least some contrition or sorrow. This should lead him to confess the wrong he has done and ask for forgiveness. It obviously requires a fair measure of humility, especially when the victim is someone in a group that one's community had despised, as was often the case in South Africa when the perpetrators were government agents.

The victim, we hope, would be moved to respond to an apology by forgiving the culprit. As I have already tried to show, we were constantly amazed in the commission at the extraordinary magnanimity that so many

4. Jeremiah 6:14 and 8:11.

of the victims exhibited. Of course there were those who said they would not forgive. That demonstrated for me the important point that forgiveness could not be taken for granted; it was neither cheap nor easy. As it happens, these were the exceptions. Far more frequently what we encountered was deeply moving and humbling.

In forgiving, people are not being asked to forget. On the contrary, it is important to remember, so that we should not let such atrocities happen again. Forgiveness does not mean condoning what has been done. It means taking what happened seriously and not minimizing it; drawing out the sting in the memory that threatens to poison our entire existence. It involves trying to understand the perpetrators and so have empathy, to try to stand in their shoes and appreciate the sort of pressures and influences that might have conditioned them.

Forgiveness is not being sentimental. The study of forgiveness has become a growth industry. Whereas previously it was something often dismissed pejoratively as spiritual and religious, now because of developments such as the Truth and Reconciliation Commission in South Africa it is gaining attention as an academic discipline studied by psychologists, philosophers, physicians, and theologians. In the United States there is an International Forgiveness Institute attached to the University of Wisconsin, and the John Templeton Foundation, with others, has started a multimillion-dollar Campaign for Forgiveness Research. Forgiving has even been found to be good for your health.

Forgiving means abandoning your right to pay back the perpetrator in his own coin, but it is a loss that liberates the victim. In the commission we heard people speak of a sense of relief after forgiving. A recent issue of the journal *Spirituality and Health* had on its front cover a picture of three U.S. ex-servicemen standing in front of the Vietnam Memorial in Washington, D.C. One asks, "Have you forgiven those who held you prisoner of war?" "I will never forgive them," replies the other. His mate says: "Then it seems they still have you in prison, don't they?"[5]

Does the victim depend on the culprit's contrition and confession as the precondition for being able to forgive? There is no question that, of course, such a confession is a very great help to the one who wants to forgive, but it is not absolutely indispensable. Jesus did not wait until those who were nailing him to the cross had asked for forgiveness. He was ready, as they drove in

---

5. *Spirituality and Health* 2, no. 1 (New York, Trinity Church: Spirituality & Health Publishing).

the nails, to pray to his Father to forgive them and he even provided an excuse for what they were doing. If the victim could forgive only when the culprit confessed, then the victim would be locked into the culprit's whim, locked into victimhood, whatever her own attitude or intention. That would be palpably unjust.

I have used the following analogy to try to explain the need for a perpetrator to confess. Imagine you are sitting in a dank, stuffy, dark room. This is because the curtains are drawn and the windows have been shut. Outside the light is shining and a fresh breeze is blowing. If you want the light to stream into that room and the fresh air to flow in, you will have to open the window and draw the curtains apart; then that light which has always been available will come in and air will enter the room to freshen it up. So it is with forgiveness. The victim may be ready to forgive and make the gift of her forgiveness available, but it is up to the wrongdoer to appropriate the gift to open the window and draw the curtains aside. He does this by acknowledging the wrong he has done, so letting the light and fresh air of forgiveness enter his being.

In the act of forgiveness we are declaring our faith in the future of a relationship and in the capacity of the wrongdoer to make a new beginning on a course that will be different from the one that caused us the wrong. We are saying here is a chance to make a new beginning. It is an act of faith that the wrongdoer can change. According to Jesus,[6] we should be ready to do this not just once, not just seven times, but seventy times seven, without limit — provided, it seems Jesus says, your brother or sister who has wronged you is ready to come and confess the wrong they have committed yet again.

That is difficult, but because we are not infallible, because we will hurt especially the ones we love by some wrong, we will always need a process of forgiveness and reconciliation to deal with those unfortunate yet all too human breaches in relationships. They are an inescapable characteristic of the human condition.

Once the wrongdoer has confessed and the victim has forgiven, it does not mean that is the end of the process. Most frequently, the wrong has affected the victim in tangible, material ways. Apartheid provided the whites with enormous benefits and privileges, leaving its victims deprived and exploited. If someone steals my pen and then asks me to forgive him, unless he returns my pen the sincerity of his contrition and confession will be considered to be nil. Confession, forgiveness, and reparation, wherever feasible, form part of a continuum.

6. Matthew 18:22.

In South Africa the whole process of reconciliation has been placed in very considerable jeopardy by the enormous disparities between the rich, mainly the whites, and the poor, mainly the blacks. The huge gap between the haves and the have-nots, which was largely created and maintained by racism and apartheid, poses the greatest threat to reconciliation and stability in our country. The rich provided the class from which the perpetrators and the beneficiaries of apartheid came and the poor produced the bulk of the victims. That is why I have exhorted whites to support transformation taking place in the lot of blacks.

For unless houses replace the hovels and shacks in which most blacks live, unless blacks gain access to clean water, electricity, affordable health care, decent education, good jobs, and a safe environment — things which the vast majority of whites have taken for granted for so long — we can just as well kiss reconciliation goodbye.

Reconciliation is liable to be a long-drawn-out process with ups and downs, not something accomplished overnight and certainly not by a commission, however effective. The Truth and Reconciliation Commission has only been able to make a contribution. Reconciliation is going to have to be the concern of every South African. It has to be a national project to which all earnestly strive to make their particular contribution — by learning the language and culture of others; by being willing to make amends; by refusing to deal in stereotypes by making racial or other jokes that ridicule a particular group; by contributing to a culture of respect for human rights, and seeking to enhance tolerance — with zero tolerance for intolerance; by working for a more inclusive society where most, if not all, can feel they belong — that they are insiders and not aliens and strangers on the outside, relegated to the edges of society.

To work for reconciliation is to want to realize God's dream for humanity — when we will know that we are indeed members of one family, bound together in a delicate network of interdependence.

Simon Wiesenthal in the anthology, *The Sunflower: On the Possibilities and Limits of Forgiveness,* tells the story of how he was unable to forgive a Nazi soldier who asked to be forgiven. The soldier had been part of a group that rounded up a number of Jews, locked them up in a building, and proceeded to set it alight, burning those inside to death. The soldier was now on his deathbed. His troubled conscience sought the relief that might come through unburdening himself, confessing his complicity and getting absolution from a Jew. Simon listened to his terrible story in silence. When the soldier had ended his narration, Simon left without uttering a word, certainly

495

not one of forgiveness. He asks at the end of his account, "What would you have done?"

The Sunflower is a collection of the responses of various people to Simon Wiesenthal's question. An updated version[7] contains a contribution from me. The dilemma Wiesenthal faced was very real. His own view, which seems to be that of many Jews, is that the living have no right to forgive on behalf of those who were killed, those who suffered in the past and are no longer alive to make the decision for themselves. One can understand their reluctance, since if they were to forgive it might appear they were trivializing the awful experience of the victims; it also might seem the height of presumption to speak on behalf of people who suffered so grievously, especially perhaps if one had not oneself suffered to the same extent. I understand the nature of their dilemma and would not want to seem to minimize it, but I hold a slightly different view.

At the end of 1990 the various South African churches gathered in Rustenburg to the west of Pretoria in one of the most fully ecumenical and representative church meetings to have taken place in our country. This meeting was called the Rustenburg Conference. Present were those churches that had been very vocal in opposing apartheid through their membership in the South African Council of Churches, as well as the major white Dutch Reformed Church (Nederduitse Gereformeerde Kerk, or DRC), which had supported apartheid by providing its theological rationale (but which had already retreated significantly from that posture). Then there were the many so-called charismatic or pentecostal churches that had tried to be apolitical, though they must have been aware that their imagined neutrality in reality supported the unjust status quo. There were representatives, too, from overseas partner churches and from the so-called African independent churches, which had taken varying political stances.

Quite early in the proceedings a leading DRC theologian, Professor Willie Jonker, made an eloquent plea for forgiveness to his black fellow Christians on behalf of Afrikaners, specifically those in the Dutch Reformed Church. It was not clear whether he had a mandate to be a spokesperson for his church, but as its official delegation subsequently endorsed his statement we can say he was representing that denomination. One could well have asked whether he could claim to speak for past generations of its members, though it would be an oddly atomistic view of the nature of a community

---

7. Harry James Carps and Bonny V. Fetterman, eds. (New York: Schocken Books, 1998), p. 275.

not to accept that there is a very real continuity between the past and the present and that the former members would share in the guilt and the shame as in the absolution and the glory of the present. A church is a living organization, otherwise history is of no significance and we should concentrate only on those who are our contemporaries. But clearly this is not how human beings normally operate. We boast about the past achievements of those who are no longer with us and point to them with pride even when they are in the dim and distant past. Their influence is as real as when the achievements were first attained, if not more so. It is the same with failures and disgraces: they too are part of who we are, whether we like it or not. When we speak, we speak as those who are aware of the cloud of witnesses surrounding us. No one would doubt that ultimately a confession such as that made by Dr. Jonker, if it was not repudiated by those on whose behalf it was purportedly being made, would be accepted as speaking for the living and the dead, for those present and those no longer with us.

I consulted with Frank Chikane, who was at the time general secretary of the South African Council of Churches, and we agreed that such an impassioned plea, such a heartfelt confession, could not be treated as just another example of rhetoric. Theologically, we knew that the gospel of our Lord and Savior constrained us to be ready to forgive when someone asked for forgiveness. This was also happening at an important time in the history of our land. Nelson Mandela had been released earlier that year and there was a genuine striving for a negotiated settlement to help the delicate transition from repression to democracy. If the churches, with their immense potential as agents of reconciliation, could not reconcile with each other it could very well send the wrong message to the politicians and to the people of God. If the churches, despite their distressing baggage, could find one another in a public act of forgiveness and reconciliation that would be a massive shot in the arm for a peaceful transition. And so I got up to say that we accepted the deeply moving and sincere plea for forgiveness.

This could, of course, have been interpreted as a monstrous act of presumption on my part. Who had given me the right to claim to speak on behalf of the millions of contemporary victims of apartheid and, even more seriously, for those many millions who were no longer alive? The DRC had introduced apartheid into church structures, establishing separate churches for members classified under apartheid as black, Indian, and "Coloured." Some of the black delegates at the conference, particularly those from these segregated churches — first called the "daughter" and later the "sister" churches of the DRC — were quite incensed with me because they felt the white church was being allowed to get away with murder, literally and figu-ratively. They questioned the seriousness of the confession since they were upset that the DRC was dragging its feet on the question of uniting with the black churches. They were also distressed because the white denomination was balking at the prospect of accepting the "Belhar Confession," which the other churches in the DRC family had endorsed. This confession, among other things, condemned apartheid as a heresy. However, while I was chal-lenged to justify my position, which I did try to do, happily I was not repudi-ated, and what happened at Rustenburg perhaps did advance the cause of a peaceful transition.

It is a little difficult for me to understand how it is that Jews should be willing to accept the substantial compensation being paid out as reparation by European governments and institutions for complicity in the Holocaust. For if we accept the argument that they cannot forgive on behalf of those who suffered and died in the past, logic would seem to dictate that those who did not suffer directly as a result of the action for which the reparation is being paid should also be incapable of receiving compensation on behalf of others. Their stance also means that there is still a massive obstacle to the resumption of more normal and amicable relationships between the com-munity of the perpetrators and the community of those who were wronged. There will always be this albatross hanging around the neck of the erstwhile perpetrators, whatever they might want to do about acts of reparation and whatever new and better attitudes they may want to bring to the situation. It is a time bomb that could explode at any time, rendering the new relation-ship vulnerable and unstable.

I hope that philosophers, theologians, and thinkers within the Jewish community will reopen this issue and consider whether it is possible to come to a different conclusion for the sake of the world. Their influence on world morality is far too precious to be jeopardized by their current stance. I can just imagine what would happen if Africans were to say that there is nothing that Europeans could do to make amends for the sordid-ness of the slave trade; that Africans alive today can never have the temer-ity to forgive Europeans for the outrage that was slavery, in which at a con-servative estimate some forty million people died, apart from all its other pernicious consequences — the families which were destroyed, the women who were abused, and the toll that this scourge took on so many of God's children.

If we are going to move on and build a new kind of world community there must be a way in which we can deal with a sordid past. The most effective way would be for the perpetrators or their descendants to acknowledge the awfulness of what happened and the descendants of the victims to respond by granting forgiveness, providing something can be done, even symbolically, to compensate for the anguish experienced, whose consequences are still being lived through today. It may be, for instance, that race relations in the United States will not improve significantly until Native Americans and African Americans get the opportunity to tell their stories and reveal the pain that sits in the pit of their stomachs as a baneful legacy of dispossession and slavery. We saw in the Truth and Reconciliation Commission how the act of telling one's story has a cathartic, healing effect.

If the present generation could not legitimately speak on behalf of those who are no more, then we could not offer forgiveness for the sins of South Africa's racist past, which predates the advent of apartheid in 1948. The process of healing our land would be subverted because there would always be the risk that some awful atrocity of the past would come to light that would undermine what had been accomplished thus far, or that people would say: "It is all right so far as it goes in dealing with the contemporary situation, but it is all utterly ineffectual because it has failed to deal with the burden of the past."

True forgiveness deals with the past, all of the past, to make the future possible. We cannot go on nursing grudges even vicariously for those who cannot speak for themselves any longer. We have to accept that what we do we do for generations past, present, and yet to come. That is what makes a community a community or a people a people — for better or for worse.

I have wished desperately that those involved in seeking solutions for what have seemed intractable problems in places such as Northern Ireland and the Middle East would not despise the value of seemingly small symbolic acts that have a potency and significance beyond what is apparent. I have been distressed to learn that some of those most intimately connected to the peace process in Northern Ireland have not been seen shaking hands in public, that some have gone to odd lengths not to be photographed together with those on the other side, their current adversaries. It was wonderful that, at the funeral of King Hussein of Jordan, President Ezer Weizman of Israel had the courage to shake hands with the leader of a radical Palestinian group. It was a gesture that helped to humanize his adversary where before much had conspired to demonize him. A small handshake can make the unthinkable, the improbable — peace, friendship, harmony, and tolerance — not quite so remote.

I also hope that those who are at this moment enemies around the world might consider using more temperate language when describing those with whom they disagree. Today's "terrorist" could very well be tomorrow's president. That has happened in South Africa. Most of those who were vilified as terrorists are today our cabinet ministers and others sitting in the government benches of our National Assembly. If those we disagree with today are possibly going to be our colleagues tomorrow, we might begin by trying to describe them in language that won't be an embarrassment when that time of change does come.

It is crucial too that we keep remembering that negotiations, peace talks, forgiveness, and reconciliation happen most frequently not between friends, not between those who like one another. They happen precisely because people are at loggerheads and detest one another as only enemies can. But enemies are potential allies, friends, colleagues, and collaborators. This is not just utopian idealism. The first democratically-elected government of South Africa was a government of National Unity made up of members of political parties that were engaged in a life-and-death struggle. The man who headed it had been incarcerated for twenty-seven years as a dangerous terrorist. If it could happen there, surely it can happen in other places. Perhaps God chose such an unlikely place deliberately to show the world that it can be done anywhere.

If the protagonists in the world's conflicts began to make symbolic gestures for peace, changed the way they described their enemies, and began talking to them, their actions might change too. For instance, what is it doing for future relations in the Middle East to go on constructing Jewish settlements in what is accepted to be Palestinian territory when this causes so much bitterness and resentment among the Palestinians, who feel belittled and abused? What legacy does it leave for the children of those who are destined to be neighbors? I have asked similar questions when Arab nations have seemed so completely unrealistic in thinking they could destroy Israel. What a wonderful gift to the world, especially as we enter a new millennium, if true peace would come in the land of those who say salama, or shalom, in the land of the Prince of Peace.

Peace is possible, especially if today's adversaries were to imagine themselves becoming friends and begin acting in ways that would promote such a friendship developing in reality. It would be wonderful if, as they negotiated, they tried to find ways of accommodating each other's needs. A readiness to make concessions is a sign of strength, not weakness. And it can be worthwhile sometimes to lose a battle in order in the end to win the war. Those who are engaged in negotiations for peace and prosperity are striving after such a splendid, such a priceless goal that it should be easier to find ways for all to be winners than to fight, for negotiators to make it a point that no one loses face, that no one emerges empty-handed, with nothing to place before his or her constituency. How one wishes that negotiators would avoid having bottom lines and too many preconditions. In negotiations we are, as in the process of forgiveness, seeking to give all the chance to begin again. The rigid will have a tough time. The flexible, those who are ready to make principled compromises, end up being the victors.

I have said ours was a flawed commission. Despite that, I do want to assert as eloquently and as passionately as I can that it was, in an imperfect world, the best possible instrument so far devised to deal with the kind of situation that confronted us after democracy was established in our motherland. With all its imperfections, what we have tried to do in South Africa has attracted the attention of the world. This tired, disillusioned, cynical world, hurting so frequently and so grievously, has marveled at a process that holds out considerable hope in the midst of much that negates hope. People in the different places that I have visited and where I have spoken about the Truth and Reconciliation process see in this flawed attempt a beacon of hope, a possible paradigm for dealing with situations where violence, conflict, turmoil, and sectional strife have seemed endemic, conflicts that mostly take place not between warring nations but within the same nation. At the end of their conflicts, the warring groups in Northern Ireland, the Balkans, the Middle East, Sri Lanka, Burma, Afghanistan, Angola, the Sudan, the two Congos, and elsewhere are going to have to sit down together to determine just how they will be able to live together amicably, how they might have a shared future devoid of strife, given the bloody past that they have recently lived through. They see more than just a glimmer of hope in what we have attempted in South Africa.

God does have a sense of humor. Who in their right minds could ever have imagined South Africa to be an example of anything but the most ghastly awfulness, of how not to order a nation's race relations and its governance? We South Africans were the unlikeliest lot and that is precisely why God has chosen us. We cannot really claim much credit ourselves for what we have achieved. We were destined for perdition and were plucked out of total annihilation. We were a hopeless case if ever there was one. God intends that others might look at us and take courage. God wants to point to us as a possible beacon of hope, a possible paradigm, and to say, "Look at South Africa. They had a nightmare called apartheid. It has ended. Northern Ireland (or wherever), your nightmare will end too. They had a problem regarded as intractable. They are resolving it. No problem anywhere can ever again be considered to be intractable. There is hope for you too."

Our experiment is going to succeed because God wants us to succeed, not for our glory and aggrandizement but for the sake of God's world. God wants to show that there is life after conflict and repression — that because of forgiveness there is a future.

34 Postmodern Illusions and the Challenges of African Theology: The Ecclesial Tactics of Resistance

Emmanuel M. Katongole

As Marlow travels into the heart of what was the Belgian Congo, he begins to search for Mr. Kurtz, who was sent by the "gang of virtue," the Europeans who saw themselves as bringing Enlightenment and progress or Civilization to the Africans. Marlow believes that Kurtz will restore his faith in the vision of enlightened imperialism that is at odds with the pervasive evidence of corruption, lethargy, violence, and disease. As he reaches the interior, Marlow learns that Kurtz is dying. And meeting the dying Mr. Kurtz, he discovers the ultimate corruption. At the bottom of the report which Kurtz has prepared to send back to the company in Belgium along with his shipment of ivory, he has scrawled the words which were to be enacted repeatedly in the twentieth century: the final solution to the problem of difference — "exterminate all the brutes."

Carol Gilligan, *In a Different Voice*
(Cambridge, MA: Harvard University Press, 1982), pp. xxiv-xxv,
in reference to Joseph Conrad's *The Heart of Darkness*

I make reference to Conrad's 1902 classic novella in the epigram above in order to make clear from the very start the main argument of this essay. Present-day discourse on Africa is often premised on a certain postmodern optimism and spurious reference to the "New World Order," the "Global Village," a "World Economy," an "African Renaissance," etc. In spite of these various and honorific titles, there will be nothing radically new or liberating for many Africans in this "New Deal." Instead, many will find themselves still

503

caught as the innocent and unsuspecting victims of Kurtz's chilling prescription, namely, "exterminate all the brutes." It is difficult to understand what might have motivated Kurtz to come to such an extreme "solution" except to see it within the context of his modernist revulsion to what he saw as the "barbaric" and "primitive" customs of the Congolese people.

In spite of its declared sensitivity to difference and otherness, postmodernism is still so much caught up in this modern predicament and failure by Western culture to accept and respect tastes and habits, in general, ways of life or rationalities which are different from her own way of life. In other words, just like Kurtz's enlightened modernism, whose history we are sadly aware of in Africa, postmodernism involves the same determination to destroy whatever is local or different. However, while Marlow seems to have come to the realization of (and be haunted by) "The horror! The horror" which lay at the heart of such human depravity undertaken in the name of progress and virtue,[1] we in Africa may easily fail to notice the despair and even the terror that is part and parcel of our postmodern condition. Instead, we may find ourselves as the all too willing victims of its enchanting machinations. In other words, it looks like a postmodernism culture easily invents subtle ways to "exterminate the brutes," even as the latter continue to "celebrate" their inception within the new world order.

In this essay, by focusing on three aspects, (1) the postmodern celebration of difference, (2) the global economy, and (3) "condomization," I will show how there is something like a postmodern "re-invention"[2] of Africa al-

---

1. I use "seems," for it appears that even though Marlow himself was shocked by Kurtz's extremism, he adored the man and shared his mission. Accordingly, Marlow saw himself as "an emissary of light, something like a lower apostle" whose job included "weaning those ignorant millions from their horrid ways" as his aunt had insisted (Joseph Conrad, *Heart of Darkness* [New York: Dover Publications, 1990], p. 10). Nevertheless, I am grateful to Keith Maiden, my co-guest professor at Molloy College, New York (Spring 1999), for the many interesting discussions we had on Conrad's *Heart of Darkness*. Maiden tended to regard Marlow in a far less harsh manner by pointing out how, on returning to England (leaving the dead Kurtz buried in the Congo), Marlow was haunted by his ultimate realization of the depravity and despair ("The horror! The horror!") at the heart of the colonial project. It could just be that our differences reflect nothing but our biographical and literary differences. Maiden is English, and a professor of English literature at Lancaster, while I am Ugandan, and a professor of African Studies. However, even such biographical differences are crucial to the way in which one approaches such a compact and powerful book as Conrad's *Heart of Darkness*. For a more detailed discussion of this novel in a way that I find particularly instructive, see Edward Said, *Culture and Imperialism* (New York: Alfred Knopf, 1993), especially pp. 19-31.

2. I mean this in the sense in which Mudimbe talks about the "invention" of Africa. By using the work of Michel Foucault, Mudimbe shows how European conceptions of "Reason"

ready underway. Even more significantly, I hope to show that there is nothing radically new or liberating within this postmodern re-invention. Rather, it represents a heightened (modernist) determination in the destruction of whatever is local, particular, or different. The effect of this re-invention is nothing less than the creation of superficial characters and societies, people, in other words, who have lost not just hope for a meaningful existence but even the power to locate their lives and activities within any historically meaningful narrative. Accordingly, I see the greatest challenge facing the Christian churches in Africa in the twenty-first century in terms of whether they will be able to generate enough critical skills and resources to enable Christians to survive postmodernism, as well as allow African Christians to recapture a sense of hope and dignity. Such a task forms the wide context for African biblical hermeneutics in the twenty-first century.

I must confess, though, that it took me a long time to realize that African Christian theology might have a negative stake within postmodernism. In fact, on one occasion I had even suggested[3] that postmodernism offered a unique possibility for us in Africa to develop local theologies — narrative theologies away from the totalizing master narratives against which we had up till now defined ourselves. Both Foucault's genealogical exposition of the power relations which lie behind the standard regimes of "knowledge," "truth," and "objectivity"[4] and Lyotard's announcement of the end of master narratives[5] — two authors I mostly associated with a postmodern trend — seemed to confirm these advantages. In fact, I saw the new directions being charted by hitherto excluded voices like African women theologians and African Independent Church theologies as con-

---

and "Civilizations" were in need of, and succeeded in "constructing," an alter-ego of a "savage" and "primitive" Africa. See V. Y. Mudimbe, *The Invention of Africa: Gnosis, Philosophy and the Order of Knowledge* (Bloomington, IN: Indiana University Press, 1988). Here I argue that postmodern realities (especially the media and the market) are engaged in a similar "construction" of a new postmodern Africa. However, with the "age of Europe" giving way to "the age of America," a postmodern Africa will increasingly bear the stamp of an "Africa made in America."

3. Emmanuel Katongole, "African Christian Theology Today: On Being a Pre-modern Postmodernist." Unpublished paper read at the Graduate School of Theology, University of Natal, Pietermaritzburg, June 1998.

4. See particularly Michel Foucault, *The Archeology of Knowledge,* trans. A. M. Sheridan Smith (London: Tavistock Press, 1972), and *Power/Knowledge: Selected Interviews and Other Writings 1972-1977,* ed. C. Gordon (Brighton: Harvest Press, 1980).

5. J.-F. Lyotard, *The Postmodern Condition: A Report on Knowledge,* trans. G. Bennington and B. Massurni (Minneapolis: University of Minnesota Press, 1984).

firming this optimism.[6] With a postmodern mood in place, I had thought that it was time to use the favored expression, "to drink from our own wells."[7] What better possibility to do so than in the space opened by the postmodern death of grand narratives, and rehabilitation of difference?

Looking back, I realize that my naive enthusiasm was greatly due to the fact that I associated postmodernism almost exclusively with an intellectual style — one that casts suspicion on "classical notions of truth, reason, identity and objectivity, of the idea of universal progress or emancipation, of single frameworks, grand narratives or ultimate grounds of explanation."[8] Even though I still think there are decisive advantages in postmodernism as an intellectual style or set of moods, I have come to see that its cultural expressions are by far more determinative than its intellectual roots. I do not claim that one can neatly separate the two, but it is true that while very few of us would have heard of the name of Foucault, and even fewer of Lyotard, the most unlettered peasant in the Transkei or Amuria has to confront, and negotiate her life around, the media and market forces of late capitalism.[9]

6. See T. Maluleke, "Recent Developments in the Christian Theologies of Africa: Towards the Twenty-First Century," *Journal of Constructive Theology* 2, no. 2 (1996): 33-60.

7. Not unlike Mugambi and Bediako, I was anxious to get away from the theologies of inculturation and liberation which had dominated the African theological scene. For as Mugambi notes, even though the latter have been useful foundations within African theology, they have become inadequate to the requirements of the new world order. One reason why Mugambi feels these theologies are inadequate is that they have tended to be merely "reactive" to the physical and ideological misrepresentations of the old world order. Now that the old world order is gone, Mugambi proposes a theology of "Reconstruction" which, he hopes, will relate more fully to the actual and ongoing Christian responses to the life-experiences of Africans. See J. N. K. Mugambi, *From Liberation to Reconstruction: African Christian Theology After the Cold War* (Nairobi: East African Educational Publishers, 1995). For Kwame Bediako, too, "the era of African theological literature as reaction to Western representation is past. What lies ahead is a critical theological construction which will relate more fully to the widespread confidence in the Christian faith [and] to actual and ongoing Christian responses to the life-experiences of Africans." Kwame Bediako, "Understanding African Theology in the 20th Century," *Bulletin for Contextual Theology in Southern Africa and Africa* 3, no. 2 (1996): 6. Maluleke rightly notes the uncritical optimism that marks these suggestions, as well as the failure to question this so-called "new world order" (Maluleke, "Recent Developments in the Christian Theologies of Africa," p. 167). I am in fact arguing that the new (postmodern) world order presents forces that call for resistance and an even far more "reactive" stance than what was adopted in the older world order.

8. Terry Eagleton, *The Illusions of Postmodernism* (Oxford: Basil Blackwell, 1996), p. viii.

9. For the media and market as key postmodern institutions, see Fredric Jameson, *Postmodernism, or, The Cultural Logic of Late Capitalism* (Durham, NC: Duke University Press, 1991).

Thus, by focusing on three cultural expressions of postmodernism within Africa, I will show why and in what way a postmodern culture provides one of the greatest challenges for African Christian theology in general, African biblical hermeneutics in particular.

1. Africa Under "the Global Gaze": The Postmodern Celebration of Difference

It may not be immediately clear that postmodernism involves a determination to destroy whatever is particular and local. In fact, such a claim may sound surprising, since we are more used to associating postmodernism with a renewed interest in, and appreciation of, difference. This interest goes beyond the epistemological shift which, associated with such names as MacIntyre, Rorty, and Kuhn, has drawn attention to the historical nature of truth — and thus to the possibility of different and tradition-dependent rationalities and claims to truth. One also notices, from a Western cultural perspective, a renewed interest in African culture. This interest ranges from a tourist fascination with Africa's unique wildlife, and "tribal" customs, to an academic interest, which makes African Studies one of the favorite and competitive courses within the curriculum of a number of universities, particularly in the United States. Similarly, there is a growing number of cultural environmentalists fighting for the preservation of the unique cultural heritage of non-Western civilizations. Shouldn't we in Africa see this as a great opportunity for African culture and history, indeed for Africa's voice to be recognized and accepted?

We must be careful not to come to this conclusion too easily. For there is something sinister about the postmodern celebration of difference, which at the same time renders differences ineffectual or inconsequential. In other words, the ability to recognize otherness and difference everywhere might just as well amount to an ironic shielding of oneself from listening or attending to the particular and historical claims of the "other." Looked at in this way, there is nothing radically new or liberating about this postmodern celebration of difference. Instead, the fascination seems to mask a heightened crisis in respect to the same old problem of difference. The point here can well be amplified by drawing attention to the particularly interesting work of Bernard McGrane.

In *Beyond Anthropology*, McGrane provides a history of different conceptions of "alien cultures" from roughly the sixteenth to the early twentieth century.[10] McGrane argues that four "general paradigms" have been used by Europeans and Westerners to interpret and "explain" non-European cultures and peoples: a theological, an Enlightenment, a sociological, and a cultural paradigm respectively.

(i) Up to and including the sixteenth century, the dominant cosmography represented the non-European "other" in terms of a theological horizon.

> . . . the alienness of the non-European other was experienced and interpreted on the horizon of Christianity. It was Christianity which fundamentally came between the European and non-European other. Anthropology did not exist; there was, rather, demonology. It was in relation to the Fall and to the influence of Sin and Satan that the other took on his historically specific meaning.[11]

As a manifestation of the "Prince of Darkness," the other "could never be anything but a 'pagan', and hence (s)he inhabited a 'space' that was necessarily the inversion of the only real 'space' — the Christian 'space', the 'space' of divine salvation. Christianity is the only religion, and those who did not profess it simply had no religion."[12] They dwelled entirely in the "hollow of absence," or as Mudimbe would say, in a *terra nullius,* whose only hope lay in being "discovered," "named," and "converted" by the organizing presence of Christians/Europeans.[13]

(ii) In the Enlightenment, McGrane argues, this Christian paradigm was largely supplanted by an epistemological one. Such categories as "ignorance," "error," "untruth," and "superstition" were used to articulate the differences between the European and non-European "other." "For, it was in *man's relation to truth* (light) at the same time as it was in the obscuring of that relation to truth . . . that the Enlightenment *located and accounted for*

---

10. Bernard McGrane, *Beyond Anthropology: Society and the Other* (New York: Columbia University Press, 1989). I am grateful to Kenneth Surin's article, "A Certain 'Politics of Speech': 'Religious Pluralism' in the Age of the McDonald's Hamburger," *Modern Theology* 7, no. 1 (1990): 68-100, which drew my attention to the work of McGrane in the first place.

11. McGrane, *Beyond Anthropology,* p. ix.

12. Surin, "A Certain 'Politics of Speech,'" p. 73.

13. Non-Christians, Mudimbe notes, "have no rights to possess or negotiate any dominion in the then-existing international context, and thus their land is objectively a *terra nullius* (no-man's land) that may be occupied and seized by Christians in order to exploit the richness meant by God to be shared by all humankind. Thus, these colonizing Christians will be helping the inferior "brethren" to insert themselves in the real and true history of salvation." See Mudimbe, *The Invention of Africa,* p. 30.

Difference."[14] The "other" was thus precisely because (s)he belonged to a society that was "unenlightened." In an interesting manner, McGrane devotes a number of pages to the description of the trajectory that resulted in the radical transformation of the West's self-understanding: from regarding themselves primarily as "European-Christians" to the conception of themselves as "*civilized-Europeans*." What the trajectory amounts to, however, is that it is within the Enlightenment, "at this epistemological moment, that the European *becomes civilized*," while the "other" typically comes to be regarded as "primitive." It is also within this Enlightenment space that "anthropology" emerges (and replaces "demonology") as the discursive practice whose systematic and administrative function is to maintain belief in and confirm the existence of exotic and alien worlds, and to explain the "primitive mentality" of the aliens who dwell in these worlds.[15]

(iii) In the nineteenth century, McGrane argues, there was another paradigm shift as the preceding Enlightenment paradigm gave way to an evolutionary paradigm, in which *time* constitutes the difference between European and the non-European "other."

> ". . . there was a vast hemorrhage in time: geological time, developmental time lodged itself between the European and the non-European other." Anthropology, as practiced by, for example, E. B. Taylor, became the discipline which organized and administered the comparison between past and present, between different "stages of development," between the prehistorically fossilized "primitive" and evolutionary advancement of modern western science and civilization.[16]

Compared to its Enlightenment predecessor, nineteenth-century anthropology comes therefore to be grounded in what McGrane calls a double transformation: "first, it transformed difference into *historical* difference, and

14. McGrane, *Beyond Anthropology*, p. 56.

15. In this respect, McGrane rightly notes that there is great similarity between what we term modern "anthropological discourse" and "science fiction": for with the non-European Other as with the aliens-from-other-planets, "what is significant is not whether such beings exist or not, but, rather, *the fact that they are conceivable*." Thus, anthropology turns out to be, in this respect, "terrestrial science fiction, dealing with terrestrial aliens, as indeed, science fiction soon becomes extraterrestrial anthropology dealing with extraterrestrial aliens" (McGrane, *Beyond Anthropology*, p. 3). The possible beings that could be encountered on earth and in the heavens were the same — the terrestrial "other" and the celestial "other" were, of necessity, of the same order.

16. McGrane, *Beyond Anthropology*, p. 73.

then it transformed history into evolution (progressive evolution)."[17] As a result, the world, "which hitherto had been everywhere contemporary with itself, became partitioned off into different times, different time epochs."[18] It is here, on the horizon of historical evolutionary development opened up by nineteenth-century anthropology, that the notion of a "Third World" becomes meaningful, as also the different "theories of development" meant to expedite the former's "inevitable" evolution to the Positive, Modern, Developed, "First World" status.

(iv) Finally, McGrane argues that in the early twentieth century, the dominant paradigm for representing the difference between the European and non-European changed again. Now it was "culture" which accounted for this difference.

> We think under the hegemony of the ethnological response to the alienness of the Other; we are today contained within an anthropological concept of the Other. Anthropology has become our modern way of seeing the Other as, fundamentally and merely, culturally different.[19]

McGrane's work is helpful for a number of reasons. First, as an attempt at an "archeology of anthropology" it is able to uncover the crisis, "the perpetually present identity crisis" which underpins the successive characterization of "alien cultures." For the key to understanding the various conceptions of alienness is to see that they are "constructed by a systematic thought-process of inversion." The alien "other" is everyone else except the European, but who, in his or her abnormal difference, specifies the European identity. This is the reason, McGrane concludes, that "the European's images of non-European man are not primarily, if at all, descriptions of real people, but rather projections of his own nostalgia and feeling of inadequacy." Consequently, the history of anthropology turns out to be little more than the "history of an identity crisis, and the history of the different identities we have existed."[20]

Secondly, and more significantly for our argument here, McGrane makes clear how the postmodern celebration of difference is but an aspect

---

17. McGrane, *Beyond Anthropology*, p. 93.
18. McGrane, *Beyond Anthropology*, p. 94.
19. McGrane, *Beyond Anthropology*, p. x.
20. For the direct quotations in this paragraph see McGrane, *Beyond Anthropology*, pp. 1-6. The similarity and complementarity between McGrane and Mudimbe's work should be immediately obvious.

of the twentieth-century paradigm of looking at the "other" as merely culturally different. This means that with culture as the only, all-defining lens, "difference" now becomes "democratized," such that the non-European "other" is no longer immured in the depths of some petrified "past," but is reasserted into the present, "our" present, and is now "our" contemporary: *"the Other is not — inferior — but different,"*[21] merely and only culturally different.

This of course may give the misleading impression that within the global project the West has become more sensitive to the historical and moral claims of other cultures. Not quite. For along with the "democratization" of difference (one's culture is just one-among-many), there is here what McGrane calls a "paradoxical domestication and annihilation of difference."[22] If all cultures are relative, then in this respect, in this deep respect, none are different. They are only culturally, i.e., superficially different, *merely* different.

Moreover, with the advantages of travel, and with the simultaneous transposition of different cultures and cultural artifacts that the post-liberal media puts before us for our "info-tainment," differences are easily stripped of their moral and historical claims, and become merely "aesthetic" — another aspect (commodity) for the post-liberal individual to enjoy, especially if he lives in the rich countries of the North.[23] Economic globalization thus becomes an intricate and structural aspect of postmodernism whose ideological effect is to obscure the deep social, historical, and economic inequalities between post-liberal consumers of the rich North and the peasants in the South.[24] As a result, what is promoted is a very superficial celebration of particularity, what

21. McGrane, *Beyond Anthropology*, p. 129.

22. McGrane, *Beyond Anthropology*, p. 117.

23. As Bill Cavanaugh notes, "Global mapping produces the illusion of diversity by the juxtaposition of all the varied products of the world's traditions and cultures in one space and time in the marketplace. Mexican food and tuna hotdish, mangoes and mayonnaise all meet the gaze of the consumer. For the consumer with money, the illusion is created that all the world's peoples are contemporaries occupying the same space-time." William T. Cavanaugh, "The World in a Wafer: A Geography of the Eucharist as Resistance to Globalization," *Modern Theology* 15, no. 2 (April 1999): 187.

24. "So the conceit is advanced that my consumption contributes to your well-being through mutually beneficial global trade. The consumption of others' particularity absorbs them into a simulated catholicity while it simultaneously hides the way that space remains rigidly segmented between the [rich] Minnesotans who enjoy mangoes in the dead of winter and the [poor] Brazilian Indians who earn forty cents an hour picking them." Cavanaugh, "The World in a Wafer," pp. 187-188.

one might call a frivolous fascination with difference.[25] Seen from this perspective, the postmodern celebration of difference, just like its previous characterizations of difference, turns into nothing but a monologue about difference. As McGrane notes, "anthropology never listened to the voices of 'alien cultures', it never *learned* from them, rather it studied them; in fact studying them, making sense out of them, making a 'science' about them, has been the modern *method* of *not* listening, of avoiding listening, to them."[26] With the postmodern celebration of difference we seem to be faced with the same monologue, where the postmodern liberal or cosmopolitan can always see the "other" (from the comfort of his living room); he can even "speak well *of* the other, but never to the other, and indeed cannot do otherwise because there really is no intractable other," since the "other" is just or *merely* different.[27] Where Kurtz's enlightened imperialism announced its "superiority" openly, and thus justified the conquest and elimination of the "brutes," the postmodern monologue about difference sedately but ruthlessly domesticates and assimilates the "other" — any other — in the name of difference.

This discussion, albeit long and involved, at least helps show why a postmodern interest in African culture is not necessarily liberating. In fact, I think that one of the greatest challenges facing us will be whether we can mobilize enough intellectual and moral skills to resist the postmodern celebration of Africa's cultural difference and uniqueness. African theology can unwittingly play up to this spectacularization (say, by a superficial "inculturation," which may just promote the picture of a playing, singing, and dancing Africa). What is needed, instead, is a more deeply entrenched theological practice which can challenge the different histories and politics which tend to obscure the actual historical struggles, conflicts and aspirations of the African peoples. An even more serious challenge facing us is how theology and biblical scholarship in Africa can help Africa's voice — its distinctive history and unique challenges — to be heard, instead of being reduced to just another merely different, "neat," or "beautiful" chorus in the endless cacophony of inconsequential differences.

25. McGrane calls it a "trivialization of the encounter with the Other" (*Beyond Anthropology*, p. 129), and Said warns against the "fetishization and relentless celebration of difference and otherness, which takes no account of the politics and particular histories which produce and reproduce the other." Edward Said, "Representing the Colonized: Anthropology's Interlocutors," *Critical Inquiry* 15 (1989): 205-25. See also Jonathan Friedman, "Beyond Otherness," *Telos* 71 (1987): 161-70.

26. McGrane, *Beyond Anthropology*, p. 127, emphasis his.

27. Surin, "A Certain 'Politics of Speech,'" p. 77.

2. Africa Under the Global Economy:
The Endless Futility of "Leap-Frogging"

The global market will perhaps remain one of the greatest cultural expressions of a postmodern era. But as a few voices from the so-called Third World have begun to point out, far from ushering an "African renaissance" and the expected eradication of poverty, this institution is negatively affecting — indeed bringing impoverishment to — the lives of millions of people in the so-called Third World.[28] This is not just because of "unfair" trade balances between the rich North and the poor South. Nor is it just because of the heavy debt owed to the rich countries and international monetary institutions, which stifle or cripple any chances for sustainable development. Even if the debt of the poor nations would completely be written off — as I think it should — with the global economy in place, the poor nations would still be caught in a system that involves a systematic destruction of whatever is *locally* significant. In other words, what we are looking at here is a terribly sick system with the poor nations trapped at the bottom in an endless and futile exercise of "leap-frogging."

This metaphor of "leap-frogging" comes from an undergraduate student — an economics major at the Washington and Lee University in Virginia. In a seminar organized by Prof. Harlan Beckley of the Shepherd Poverty Program, I had pointed out how the market in many parts of Africa is at the service of highly superficial needs. I used the example of Microsoft Windows 98, and how the inauguration of this by the then "latest" software program had been all over the news in Kampala. Both Radio Uganda and Uganda Television had hailed the "advantages" of Windows 98, especially the fact that it made "surfing the net so much easier." One would completely miss the irony if one did not realize that this occurred in a country where only a tiny fraction of the population (about 2%) have ever seen, let alone used, a computer. Whereas Windows 98 might be a great event for some of us who fall within that select minority, I pointed out, what the greatest majority of people in many parts of Africa needed was perhaps not even a typewriter, but pens and paper, not to mention basic

28. For my own previous discussion of the global market, see "Globalization and Economic Fundamentalism in Africa" [in *The Cries of the Poor in Africa: Questions and Responses for African Christianity*, ed Peter Kanyandago (Kisubi, Uganda: Marianum Publishing Press, 2002), pp. 57-78]; "African Renaissance and Narrative Theology in Africa," *Journal of Theology for Southern Africa* 102 (1998): 29-40; and "Modernization or Token Development: Africa and the New Deal" (unpublished).

writing skills. How can you "celebrate" Windows 98 when over 60% of the population does not even have access to clean and regular drinking water, I remarked. It was then that the economics student pointed out that "Africa had no choice." She must leap-frog to "where we are," if she is not to be left behind.

It strikes me that this perceptive economics student's description of Africa's situation is indeed true, but that is precisely the problem, and not the solution. In fact, is this not what Africa has been doing all along: leap-frogging (tied up with the notion of "development" as catching up with the fashions and achievements of the West)? But whereas within the nineteenth-century evolutionary paradigm this "development" was mapped on a lineal evolutionary trajectory — and thus took a more predictable progression — the postmodern "where we are" paradigm has become de-centered, highly unstable, an endless stream of "signifiers without a signified." Postmodern reality is thus based not on any lasting, stable, or predictable pattern, but is increasingly determined by what is "fashionable," the novel, the "in-thing." This really is what is going to make Africa's leap-frogging in the twenty-first century not just more erratic, but also tragically comic. One gets a sense of this comic leap-frogging when one notices how many leaders in Africa feel increasingly compelled to address themselves to the same "global" problems. Recently, the Prime Minister of one of the poorest African countries appeared on television advising the West to come up with a quick solution to the Y2K! I suspect that such a leader feels constrained to leap-frog to the same "global" problems every respectable leader must address. I am sure we are going to see even more tragic cases of leap-frogging on the part of African leaders. What many may perhaps not realize is that thanks to the destabilizing of time and space within the postmodern crave for novelty, the Western "where we are" is becoming increasingly a "virtual" reality of Windows 98 (or is that now 2000?!), the cellular phone, the Yahoo search engine, the Internet, etc.

Given the frantic and desperate leap-frogging that is required if one is to catch up with the operations of such "virtual" realities, it seems impossible, perhaps even out of step, to think about focusing on such "local" issues as cassava, millet, or goats — the lifeline of the man and woman in Malube or Umutata (their "actual," not their "virtual" reality). This is one reason, I suspect, that the language of globalization easily masks the true identity of that reality: a tantalizing form of tragic leap-frogging which effectively obscures from vision and attention issues that are *just* local and particular. As with the earlier language of "conversion," "civilization," and "development," "leap-frogging" bears the same assumption that the only real space to be is where the West is.[29]

What about the millions excluded from this space by the very nature of its internal logic? They are easily condemned to a "local" existence of precipitous and marginal survival, which easily degenerates into a form of what Jack Morris has called "rebel madness,"[30] i.e., the perpetuation of war and violence for its own sake. Is it not surprising, for instance, that in spite of Uganda's internationally acclaimed "economic miracle of recovery" it hosts one of the biggest concentrations of rebel groups on the African continent? All these rebel groups do not pose any serious threat to the government, and in any case none of them has any serious political agenda. On the contrary, the rank and file of these groups is made up of mostly kids and young adults, who either have nowhere else to be or nothing meaningful to do. Participation in such rebel activities at least gives them a sense of purpose or goal in life, but also a voice which would otherwise never have received any attention from the leaders, whose focus and energy seem to be spent in an endless but futile exercise of leapfrogging. I suspect that with the global economy and the logic of leap-frogging at its center, we will see more of this sort of rebel madness. To be sure, this rebel madness might as well be an indication (an extreme indication) that the playful nihilism of postmodernism is already upon us ("killing as a game"). And so, perhaps, we need to focus on another postmodern practice which encourages precisely this sort of posture within Africa.

3. "Condomization" as Playful Nihilism

In an interesting work, George Ritzer describes modern capitalist society as a "McDonaldized" society.[31] The image is not only powerful; it rightly depicts the global spread of modern culture, which is characterized by the logic of standardization, efficiency, calculability, predictability, and control, for

---

29. This is what might be misleading about McGrane's *history* of the various conceptions of "otherness." It might give the impression that the different paradigms are neatly successive. This certainly is not the case, so that conceptualization of difference in the twentieth century involves fragments of the previous conceptions of "otherness."

30. Jack Morris, "A Lesson from the Massacre of Foreign Tourists in Uganda," *America* 180, no. 19 (May 1999): 12-14.

31. George Ritzer, *The McDonaldization of Society: An Investigation in the Changing Character of Contemporary Social Life,* revised edition (Thousand Oaks, CA: Pine Forge Press, 1996).

which the McDonald's hamburger is both a metaphor and the most popular symbol. Ritzer does not make a sharp distinction between modern and post-modern culture, and, in fact, understands (rightly in my opinion) the latter as but a heightened form of McDonaldization.[32] The fact that a great major-ity of Africans do not even know what a McDonald's hamburger is, does not mean that they are strangers to the modern and postmodern culture. It just means that the latter culture has come to Africa through a different (back?) door. For example, the current process of *condomization* underway in many African countries seems to depict well the face postmodernism is taking in many African countries. In other words, not the McDonald's hamburger, but the condom is the symbol of postmodern culture in Africa.

If you ask any eleven-year-old child in Uganda, for instance, she will be able to tell you the names of at least five different brands of condoms. She may never have used one, but she certainly would have heard about their wonderful benefits on one of the many FM radio stations. A visitor immedi-ately notices the clear signs of "condomization" in place: the endless com-mercials about condoms on radio and TV, and on billboards everywhere in towns and along highways in the countryside. Condoms are readily available everywhere. They are sold in supermarkets, by hawkers on the street, on makeshift candle-light stalls in the suburbs where they are placed next to ready-to-go meals; in the countryside, the single-shelf kiosks may run out of sugar and paraffin, but not of their supply of condoms, clearly displayed.

The issue here is not whether condoms do or do not protect against the spread of AIDS, even though one may question the validity of some of the statistics that are often cited as a confirmation of the success of this anti-AIDS drive. The issue is not even the narrow ethical concern of whether it is right or wrong to use a condom; and certainly not whether condom use is sanctioned by God, or a clear violation of God's will. The issue is to see that

---

32. One reason I find Ritzer's small book so interesting is that he clearly points out that this heightened state of McDonaldization shows how modern society has already been thrust far into what Max Weber named "the iron cage of rationality," or what Ritzer calls the "irrationality of rationality." He argues for the need to resist or subvert the McDonaldization process through the cultivation of personal alternatives and/or individual patterns and atti-tudes of resistance. I find both Ritzer's analysis and argument interesting, even though I doubt whether such *individual* or *personal* nonrational niches of resistance is all that we need. In fact, the latter seem to be alternatives open only to "those who can afford it" — i.e., a leisured class of economic elite, the result of the same process of McDonaldization from which they are supposed to flee. I suggest that more than personal or individual niches of re-sistance we need ecclesial communities of resistance and hope.

"condomization" is about the promotion of a certain culture[33] — a postmodern culture.

(i) *Disposability*. One reason why the use of condoms is so popular, I suspect, is their disposability. Of course, one could see this as just an aspect of the same consumer culture of Coca-cola cans, disposable diapers, and throwaway shaving sticks. Such disposability, however, fits quite well with the postmodern announcement of reality as an endless play of signifiers without any stable or permanent base, fueled by global capitalism's ever accelerating need for growth. Disposability, not simply of goods, but of relationships and particular attachments of any kind, is the hallmark of consumption in the new economy.[34] Thus, "condomization" is not just about the convenience of disposable condoms, but more importantly it is about the popularization of a certain form of sexual activity, i.e., one detached from any serious attachment or stable commitment, but which serves to promote a certain nihilistic playfulness of the unstable, de-centered, and post-liberal self.

There is a certain ideological inversion of goals at play here. For "condomization" in Africa is often based on the assumption that Africans are naturally sexually promiscuous, and so the only way to curtail the spread of AIDS is through the promotion of condom use. But as Kanyandago rightly notes, such an assumption is just a myth.[35] What the assumption in fact does is to set up certain expectations, which ends up producing those very expectations (in this case, sexually promiscuous individuals or people incapable of any deep attachments). Such lack of attachment or stable rela-

---

33. The Catholic association Human Life International had at least this right: that condom use promotes a certain culture. However, by identifying all artificial methods of contraceptives alongside abortion and euthanasia, and rejecting everything under the rubric of "culture of death" (as opposed to the Gospel "culture of life"), they do not allow a more critical analysis of the historical and moral complexities involved in each of the practices.

34. Cavanaugh, "The World in a Wafer," p. 188.

35. The way facts about AIDS in Africa are presented, Kanyandago notes, "is inspired by the belief of the WHO and the Western medical establishment that Africans are sexually promiscuous. 'But apart from the fact that the first European Christian missionaries in Africa held this belief, there is absolutely no scientific evidence for this view. On the contrary, Americans lead the world as far as changing sexual partners is concerned. They are followed by France, Australia, and Germany. South Africa, like Thailand, is well back in the middle of the sex league. . . . But there is of course a long Christian tradition of fantasizing about the supposedly licentious life of Africans.'" P. Kanyandago, "The Role of Culture in Poverty Eradication," in Deirdre Carabine and Martin O'Reilly, eds., *The Challenge of Eradicating Poverty in the World: An African Response* (Uganda: Martyrs University Press, 1998), p. 138. Citing C. Fiala, "Dirty Tricks: How the WHO Gets Its AIDS Figures," *New African* (April 1998): 36-38.

tionships and commitments is often paraded within postmodernism as a high mark of flexibility and freedom.

(ii) *Freedom.* "Condomization" concerns itself with, and thus promotes a certain view of, *freedom.* This is the freedom of what the political theorist, Michael Sandel, portrayed as the "unencumbered self."[36] By this he meant the modern individual who assumes that one's commitments and responsibilities are not determined by any tradition, be it church or society, but by one's own *choices.* The *Straight Talk* programs, which currently are in vogue in many African countries, bombard their young audiences with exactly the same message; namely, that nobody has any right to tell them what to do or not do with their bodies. They have a right to decide if and when (or not) they have sex. The major, and perhaps the only consideration in this choice is to make sure it is "safe" or protected. Behind such recommendations is the assumption that young people are naturally capable of making the right choices as long as they have the relevant facts (which *Straight Talk* is meant to provide). Of course, the real target of these recommendations are those familial, tribal, or church traditions which insist that freedom does not come naturally, but is a result of *training* into the relevant practices and habits or virtues. For it is not of course that these traditions discourage people from making choices. It is only that these traditions realize that whatever choices an individual makes are but means of realizing one's potentialities as a member of the family, clan, church, or tribe. But now, by summarily dismissing their requirement for training as both archaic and authoritarian, *Straight Talk* encourages young people to believe that one can be free even without training in a particular tradition as long as one is able to make the right (informed) choices. This not only helps to undermine the authority of the traditional institutions of the family, tribe, or church, but also creates free-floating individuals who easily become prey to their own whimsical needs and choices.

(iii) *Feels Good.* A lot can also be said about the playfulness that "condomization" promotes. One clear observation has to do with the way the playfulness is constructed over and beyond everyday expectations and forms of life, the way it is detached from any meaningful form of material production. That is one reason why the most popular images associated with condom commercials are: baggy jeans, Coca-cola, rap music, and pale skin — not the images of an "ordinary" African life — but a certain "it feels good" culture more typical of American MTV. One wonders, however, whether we

36. Michael Sandel, "The Procedural Republic and the Unencumbered Self," *Political Theory* 12, no. 1 (1984): 81-96.

in Africa can afford the playfulness of such an "it feels good" culture, which in the West is not only made possible by the economic infrastructure of advanced capitalism, but also masks the deep frustration and nihilism within postmodernism.[37]

This, then, is what makes "condomization" an appropriate metaphor for the set of practices (call it a certain politics) whose goal is to transform Africans into postmodern individuals: free-floating *individuals,* incapable of any deep attachments, but who are characterized by a certain superficial feeling and playfulness. To the extent that they become such individuals, they not only lose the possibility of locating themselves within any meaningful history, but more crucially they become increasingly prey to the manipulations and misrepresentations of the media and market forces. And, as I noted earlier, it is not such a big step to move from this nihilistic playfulness to the violence of rebel madness. Accordingly, one of the greatest challenges for African Christian theology and biblical scholarship for the twenty-first century will be to confront realistically, and even to survive, such postmodern illusions.

I suggest that for African Christians the best hope for survival lies in the opposite direction of "condomization," i.e., in the ability to find appropriate re-location within some forms of community which are able to offer not only resistance, but an alternative, to the nihilistic playfulness of postmodern culture. Since nihilism cannot be overcome merely by theory, the crucial issue is the possibility of communities whose way of life and practices embody a "prophetic vision of resistance and hope."[38] In this essay's fi-

---

37. This frustration is certainly apparent in Rorty, one of the key voices who have helped to deconstruct modernity's quest for an independently given notion of Truth and Objectivity. In the absence of any such foundation, Rorty suggests that an individual adopt, on the one hand, a certain attitude of suspicion (irony) to one's commitments and a pragmatic playfulness (light-minded pragmatism) on the other. It is as if Rorty is suggesting that with the postmodern condition we must learn not to take ourselves and our commitments too seriously. See Richard Rorty, *Irony, Contingency and Solidarity* (Cambridge: Cambridge University Press, 1989), pp. xv and *passim.*

38. Gerald O. West, *Biblical Hermeneutics of Liberation: Modes of Reading the Bible in the South African Context* (Pietermaritzburg: Cluster Publications, 1991), p. 45. Theology, African theology in particular, Gerald West remarks, must necessarily be prophetic if it is to be meaningful. Citing from the famous 1985 *Kairos Document,* West surmises, "To be truly prophetic, our response would have to be, in the first place, solidly grounded in the Bible. Our KAIROS impels us to *return to the Bible* and to search the word of God for a message that is relevant to what we are experiencing. This will be no mere academic exercise. Prophetic theology differs from academic theology because, whereas academic theology deals with all biblical themes in a systematic manner and formulates general Christian principles and doctrines, prophetic theology concentrates on those aspects of the Word of God that have

nal section, I will broadly portray the sort of self-understanding which makes it possible for the Christian churches in Africa to exist as such communities of resistance and hope.

4. The Church as a Community of Resistance and Hope

(i) Resistance communities and new forms of fundamentalism

We have recently witnessed unprecedented growth in religious fundamentalism in Africa, giving rise to a number of new sects within both Islam and Christianity. While there might be many reasons to explain this fundamentalist religious outburst, I suspect that an implicit motive of resistance inspires many of these Christian and Islamic sects. The latter call their adherents to a strict observance of the "revealed morality" (contained either in the Bible or the Koran) whose prescriptions are clearly at odds with forms of postmodern playfulness. They similarly encourage strong fellowship and solidarity among the "brothers and sisters" — a call for a "return" to some traditional form of community as a way to resist the "acids" of a postmodern culture. The one thing I find striking about these groups, then, is their sense of resistance as rooted in community. In other words, they bear witness to the fact that resistance is not just an individual thing, because individually it cannot be sustained. If it is to be sustained, such resistance must be grounded within and sustained by the life and practices of a given community. Without such a community, resistance may become just another heroic but narcissistic attempt by the post-liberal individual to make it into the headlines.

While these fundamentalist groups may be communities of resistance, they are insufficiently tactical inasmuch as they are characterized by a total rejection of the postmodern "culture of death." Such wholesale rejection fails to take seriously the ubiquitous nature of postmodern reality. For being postmodern is not a choice we have to make. Postmodernism and its cultural expressions are already upon us. The challenge for us is not to withdraw into some kind of "brethren" enclave, but to deal, critically and selectively, with postmodern culture. In other words, it is not enough for the church to be a community of resistance; it must be a *tactical* community of resistance.

---

an immediate bearing upon the critical situation in which we find ourselves. The theology of the prophets does not pretend to be comprehensive and complete, it speaks to the particular circumstances of a particular time and place — the KAIROS" (p. 58).

(ii) Tactical Communities: The Survival of the Weak

Those familiar with Stanley Hauerwas' work will immediately recognize that I am drawing heavily on his understanding of the church as a community, particularly his reference to the church as a tactical community.[39] Against constant and misplaced charges of "sectarianism" directed at his work by critics, Hauerwas shows that with the collapse of the Christian empire (Christendom), the church always finds herself on alien ground, totally surrounded by (post)modern culture, with no place that she could properly call her own — which means that there can be no enclave to which she can "withdraw." This not only makes any sectarian position unsustainable; it means also that the church must give up any pretensions of being a strategy, but must concern herself by being a tactic. Here Hauerwas draws upon Michel de Certeau's distinction between strategies and tactics.[40] By strategy De Certeau means any

> calculation (or manipulation) of power relationships that becomes possible as a subject that will empower (a business, an army, a city, a scientific institution) can be isolated. It postulates a *place* that can be delimited as its *own* and serve as the base from which relations with an *exteriority* composed of targets or threats (customers or competitors, enemies, the country surrounding the city, objectives and objects of research, etc.) can be managed. As in management, every "strategic" rationalization seeks first of all to distinguish its "own" place, that is, the place of its own power and will, from an "environment." A Cartesian attitude, if you wish: it is an effort to delimit one's own place in a world bewitched by the invisible

---

39. Stanley Hauerwas, *Against the Nations: War and Survival in a Liberal Society* (Nashville: Abingdon Press, 1991), pp. 16-22. Hauerwas' influence in the position I develop in this essay, as well as in the overall evolution of my thinking, is far beyond any explicit acknowledgment. The immediate motivation behind this article, for example, owes a great deal to Hauerwas' "The Christian Difference: Surviving Postmodernism," *Cultural Values* 3, no. 2 (April 1999): 164-81.

40. Michel de Certeau, *The Practice of Everyday Life* (Berkeley: University of California Press, 1988), pp. 35-36. The chapter in question (III) is significantly entitled "'Making Do': Uses and Tactics." In this chapter, de Certeau is concerned with the everyday relations or transactions between the strong and weak, and especially with the "actions" which remain possible for the latter. De Certeau argues that in spite of the disciplines, order, and constraints which dominating systems impose, by an art of "being in between" an individual can find "ways of using" and/or composing "new stories" within those constraining orders.

powers of the Other. It is also the typical attitude of modern science, politics, and military strategy.[41]

In sharp contrast to a strategy, a tactic, according to de Certeau, is

> a calculated action determined by the absence of a proper locus. No delineation of exteriority, then, provides it with the condition necessary for autonomy. The space of a tactic is the space of the other. Thus it must play on and with the terrain imposed on it and organized by the law of a foreign power.[42]

Tactic, in other words, does not have power to plan a general strategy or to view the adversary as a whole. It must operate in isolated actions taking advantage of opportunities without a base where it can build up stockpiles for the next battle. It has mobility, but it gains mobility only by being willing to take advantage of the possibilities that offer themselves at given moments. As de Certeau notes, the tactic is the art of the weak.[43]

For Hauerwas this concretely means that, as a tactic, the church's primary preoccupation is not her own institutional existence, but that of providing her members with skills which will enable them to engage critically and selectively with the (post)modern culture in which they find themselves, and in which they live as "Resident Aliens." Such a posture is only possible to the extent that Christians find themselves members of a community whose story is powerful enough to sustain their tactical existence with hope.

(iii) Biblical Communities: The Bible as a Story of Hope

It is in the above context that Hauerwas underscores the moral authority of the Bible as a "story" — the story of a particular community who, given their

41. Hauerwas, *Against the Nations,* pp. 16-17.

42. De Certeau, *The Practice of Everyday Life,* p. 37.

43. Hauerwas, *Against the Nations,* pp. 17-18, reference to de Certeau, *The Practice of Everyday Life,* pp. 36-37. Tactic is particularly the art of a guerrilla warfare, for, as de Certeau notes, "it operates in isolated actions, blow by blow. It takes advantage of 'opportunities' and depends on them, being without any base where it could stockpile its winnings, build up its position, and then plan raids. What it wins it cannot keep. . . . It must vigilantly make use of the cracks that particular conjunctions open in the surveillance of the proprietary [sic strategic] powers. It poaches in them. It creates surprises in them, it can be where it is least expected. It is a guileful ruse" (p. 37).

unique experience of and with God, move on through history, through different challenges and trials, as a community of resistance and hope.[44] This narrative character of scripture, however, is often obscured in an attempt to objectify scripture as "Word of God" which then can be mined for individual tips for salvation or for some kind of "revealed morality." Whereas scripture no doubt offers such possibilities, Hauerwas' claim is to the effect that there is no way one can understand the full import of scripture if it is abstracted from the history of the community which produced it, and whose experience of and with God it reflects, and in turn shapes. That is to say, scripture is not only an account of a community's journey with God; it in turn creates a "community of memory" — people capable of reading and re-living the same story by placing themselves in the biblical tradition. This overall *political* context not only endows scripture with moral authority; it allows us to see that the reading of scripture is not just some pious exercise, but a political exercise, and even a subversive form of politics.

I have drawn attention to Hauerwas' understanding of church and scripture, for it is precisely such an understanding we need to recover if Christian churches in Africa are to help Christians survive postmodernism, but also meet with hope and dignity the challenges of the twenty-first century. I am certainly aware that historically Christianity and the Bible have played an ambivalent role in Africa.[45] The argument I am making, however, presupposes that Christianity will be able to exploit the theme of resistance which has somehow always been implicit within African Christianity,[46] and thus turn the Bible into a formidable weapon of struggle. What such a recovery requires, however, is the ability to free the Bible from the liberal and individualistic notions of salvation so that we allow its full potential as the story of a pilgrim community to inspire new forms of community which embody the same prophetic vision of resistance and hope. Such communities will not only critically challenge, but also embody much needed alternatives to,

44. See particularly Hauerwas, *A Community of Character: Toward a Constructive Christian Social Ethics* (Notre Dame: University of Notre Dame Press, 1981), pp. 53-71.

45. The movement of Black theology in South Africa, for example, is a response to this "historical dilemma," i.e., the fact that the Bible has been used as an instrument of social control and discrimination. See Takatso Mofokeng, "Black Christians, the Bible and Liberation," *Journal of Black Theology in Southern Africa* 2, no. 1 (1988): 34-42.

46. The recent work by the Comaroffs is perhaps the most comprehensive study to date of the relations between Christianity, power, and resistance within colonial Africa. See particularly John L. and Jean Comaroff, *Of Revelation and Revolution: Christianity, Colonialism and Consciousness in South Africa*, vol. 1 (Chicago: University of Chicago Press, 1991).

the playful nihilism of a postmodern culture. In any case, given the sort of postmodernism illusions which are already upon us, the formation of such churched-communities who read and take the Bible seriously is not only a challenge; it is an urgent necessity for Africa in the twenty-first century.

35 Messiah and Minjung: Discerning Messianic Politics over against Political Messianism

Kim Yong-Bock

In this essay we intend to use the category of messianism as a conceptual tool to determine the relation between minjung and power. We shall first define the term "minjung" as the subject of history and clarify an approach to historical reality. In the context of such an understanding of history, the relationship between the people and power will be clarified. To do this we will do three things. First, we will trace messianic traditions in Korea. Second, we will use messianic categories to analyze Japanese colonial power in Korea, the Korean Communist regime, and the present government of Korea. Finally, we will seek to shed light on the messianic politics of the minjung in terms of the liberation of the minjung.

The minjung are the permanent reality of history. Kingdoms, dynasties, and states rise and fall; but the minjung remain as a concrete reality in history, experiencing the comings and goings of political powers. Although the minjung understand themselves in relation to the power which is in command, they are not confined by that power. The minjung transcend the power structures which attempt to confine them through the unfolding of their stories. Power has its basis in the minjung. But power as it expresses itself in political powers does not belong to the minjung. These powers seek to maintain themselves; and they rule the minjung.

When we view minjung in relation to power, we define the minjung in political terms. The political definition of minjung also includes their socio-economic determination. The political and socio-economic conditions of the minjung are not just objective realities for socio-economic analysis. Rather, we have in mind the total subjective experiences of the minjung —

their aspirations and sufferings, their struggles and defeats which form their social biography. Therefore, our reflection on the minjung involves not only objective socio-economic analysis, but also an empathy for their expressive language and culture.

The identity and reality of the minjung are known not by a philosophical or scientific definition of their essence or nature, but rather through their own stories — their social biographies which the minjung themselves create and therefore can tell best. This story of the minjung or their social biography is told vis-à-vis the power structure that rules the people; and therefore power is the antagonist in the story, while the people are the subjects. The minjung themselves are the protagonists. Thus the story of the minjung entails a historical understanding which regards them as subjects — not as objects — of their own story and destiny.

In discussions of the minjung as the subjects of history there have arisen several questions. The first is about the unclearness of the concept of the minjung. The second is about the social determination or definition of the minjung; the third is whether or not the minjung have been "glorified" into an ideal notion.

We have an obligation to clarify these questions, but before we do so we should indicate our basic position. "Minjung" is not a concept or object which can be easily explained or defined. "Minjung" signifies a living reality which is dynamic, changing, and complex. This living reality defines its own existence and generates new acts and dramas in history; and it refuses in principle to be defined conceptually.

One of the issues involved in the above questions is the difference between the minjung and the Marxist proletariat. The proletariat is defined socio-economically, while the minjung is known politically. Politics as power relations is understood comprehensively and thus includes socio-economic relations. Philosophically speaking, the proletariat is "confined" to socioeconomic (materialistic) determination, so that it is bound to historical possibilities and the internal logic of history. The minjung suffers these limitations in reality; yet the minjung as historical subject transcends the socioeconomic determination of history, and unfolds its stories beyond mere historical possibilities to historical novelty — a new drama beyond the present history to a new and transformed history.

This difference between the minjung and the proletariat entails different views of history. Minjung history has a strong transcendental or transcending dimension — a beyond history — which is often expressed in religious form. There is a close relationship between religion and the minjung's perception of history. Even if minjung history does not involve religious elements in an explicit manner, its folklore or cultural elements play a transcending function similar to religion in the perception of history.

In scope too there is a difference between the minjung and the proletariat. The former is a dynamic, changing concept. Woman belongs to minjung when she is politically dominated by man. An ethnic group is a minjung group when it is politically dominated by another group. A race is minjung when it is dominated by another powerful ruling race. When intellectuals are suppressed by the military power elite, they belong to minjung. Of course, the same applies to the workers and farmers. However, the proletariat is rigidly defined in socio-economic terms in all political circumstances. It is even a name through which a totalitarian political dictatorship is justified.

Historically, the minjung is always in the condition of being ruled, a situation which they seek to overcome. Therefore, minjung history will never permit the glorification of the minjung so that its name may be used to justify any kind of political dictatorship, especially the totalitarian kind. In many ways, the minjung view of history has an affinity with the cultural values of Western democracy; but the constituency of the minjung is the poor and the suppressed who are alienated in their political and socio-economic condition.

Often we are asked about the difference between the idea of minjung and the Maoist notion of *"inmin."* Here, we should recognize the fact that the Maoist notion upholds the supremacy of the proletariat, and that total dictatorship — which is antagonistic to the minjung and therefore contrary to minjung politics — is an integral part of Maoism.

The minjung is not a self-contained or completely defined concept, but a living entity, which has an ever-unfolding drama and story. The minjung has a social and political biography. The minjung reality is known only through its biography, its story, its hope, and sufferings. The socio-political biography of the minjung is the key historical point of reference for minjung theology in addition to references of biblical stories. The problem with philosophical and ideological views of history is that they reduce the total sociopolitical biography (the record of socio-political experiences) of the minjung to an appendix to their systems or concepts. Rather than co-opt the story of the minjung into their systems, philosophy and ideology should serve to clarify the story of the minjung, in which the pain and suffering of the people as well as their hopes and aspirations are expressed.

The next question we need to clarify concerns the historical subjecthood or subjectivity of the minjung. The minjung is the protagonist in the historical drama. It is the subject and its socio-political biography is the predicate. In the Korean context, one may suspect that the notion of the subjecthood from North Korean Communism has sneaked into minjung theology. Once again, we should not mistake the fact that in North Korea the notion of *"juche"* refers to the autonomy of the national totalitarian dictatorship which uses the name of the proletariat. It is a sort of "realized" subjecthood in the form of a dictatorial state. But in minjung theology, the subjecthood of the minjung is in between the times of the "not yet" and the "already."

The minjung are not yet fully the subjects of history. However, their subjectivity is being realized through their struggles against oppressive powers and repressive social structures. In so doing, the minjung have risen up to be subjects of their own destiny, refusing to be condemned to the fate of being objects of manipulation and suppression. The minjung have their own stories to tell over against the stories or the dominant ideologies of the rulers. When we say that the minjung are the subjects of history, we are not exalting them in political terms but are affirming as authentic their identification of themselves as the masters of their own history which is told in their socio-political biography. We should neither glorify nor absolutize the minjung, for they suffer under their historical predicament. In traditional theological terms we may say that they are under and in a state of sin.

Up to now, historical writings have usually centered on the ruling power. A typical example of this is Confucian historiography. It is the chronicle of the king as the ruler. Here the people do not appear as actors in history.[1] Our proposal is that we read history from below, from the point of view of the minjung, rather than from the point of the view of the ruling power. History is the process in which the minjung realize their own destiny to be the free subjects of history and to participate in the Messianic Kingdom. This theological notion of Messianic Kingdom has been chosen to develop a minjung perspective on history.

The messianic aspirations of the people arise out of the historical confrontation between the people and the powers. The Messianic Kingdom is not an illusory or utopian dream, but is the core of the history for which the suffering people, the poor and oppressed, struggle. It is therefore concrete. Herein lie the origin and the basis of messianic language. It does not come from a dreamlike world. When we talk about messianism, we are implying a

---

1. The traditional Korean historical books, *Samguksagi* (Historical Records of Three Kingdoms) and Royal Chronicles of Yi Korea Dynasty, are typical examples of this.

messiah who is of the people and whom the people feel to be theirs. Both terms, "messianism" and "messiah," are often used to indicate a certain "fanaticism" or to describe a hero or elitist cult. Although these negative qualities exist in the history of messiahs and messianisms, they are external to the essence of true messianism. Here, the Messiah emerges from the suffering people and identifies with the suffering people.

Theologically, the messianic expectation of the people is based upon theodicy, which is the victory of the justice of God over evil in history. The Messiah and the people actualize the justice of God in history. This historical process is a radical transformation, in which the new one arrives as the old one departs. Messianism is an eschatological phenomenon closely linked to an apocalyptic perception of history.

From our point of view, the focal point of messianism is the general resurrection of all the people (the minjung), for historical judgment against Evil and its followers. The general resurrection of all the people is a concrete vision of history in which the people realize their corporate subjectivity in participating in the Messianic Kingdom. The content of the Messianic Kingdom may be viewed as *justice, koinonia,* and *shalom* (peace or becoming whole). *Justice* is a faithful relation or a faithful interweaving of the stories of the people and power so that there is no contradiction between them; *koinonia* is the content of the creative interaction that will take place among the people; and *shalom* is the wholesome development of humanity and its well-being. These messianic categories which we have described briefly can be developed into a social philosophy which takes into account the story of the minjung and operates with a messianic view of history.

In a brief paper, it is not possible to enter into a discussion of all aspects of the large and complex issue of messianism. In this paper, we will concentrate on the conceptual difference between power-messianism and Jesus-messianism, or ruler-messianism and minjung-messianism, or political messianism and messianic servanthood. Jesus-messianism or messianic servanthood is a radical challenge to all forms of political, royal, and power messianisms. It is concerned with saving and transforming the minjung so that its subjecthood may be realized. Hence, all powers must be under the rule of Jesus the Messiah, who came to be the Servant of the minjung, who died for them, and who rose from the dead so that the minjung may rise from the power of death historically and not just at the end of time.

With this conceptual background we will turn very briefly to an examination of Korean messianic movements. The oldest significant instance of messianism in Korea came with the introduction of Buddhism, particularly the Maitreya Buddhist tradition. The Maitreya Buddha is known as the Messianic Buddha who comes from the West Paradise to rescue the people from suffering. As yet there has been no substantial study of the Maitreya Messianic Buddha movement although there are several indications of its influence in Korean history. The first such indication is the commentary of Won Hyo, a Silla scholar-monk, on the scriptures concerning the Maitreya Buddha. Won Hyo's famous doctrine that "the ordinary person is Buddha" indicates a strong influence of the popular egalitarian ethics of messianism. Recent archaeological discoveries suggest that the Maitreya formed a decisive ideological backbone for the Unified Silla dynasty of the Three Kingdoms Period. Toward the end of that dynasty, Maitreya Messianic Buddhism influenced the popular resistance movements against dynastic regimes. One may conclude that the people in Korea have been under the strong influence of the messianic movement and ideology of Maitreya Buddhism throughout history.[2] Even during the Yi dynasty, which was dominated by neo-Confucian orthodox ideology, the idea of the Maitreya Buddha was *alive* among the people.

Recently the question has come up about the role Buddhism, especially Maitreya Buddhism, played in undergirding the ideology of the state. It is a question in the area of political messianism which attributes to the state a redemptive messianic role. The historical facts which will answer this question have yet to be determined; but Maitreya Buddhism seems to have played two rather contradictory roles during the time of the Silla dynasty.

The second messianic tradition in Korea is the tale of Hon Kil-dong.[3] Ho Kyun, a Chungin (member of the social class between the ruling *yangban* class and the commoners), wrote this popular novel in the vernacular language of Korea so that the common people could read it easily. The story was told and retold and was most popular during the Yi dynasty, when the ruling power was making the people suffer most.

The scenario is as follows: The alienated social hero Hong Kil-dong, like the author a Chungin, leaves home and joins a group of bandits, because he cannot fulfill his life's ambitions and goals in the existing society. Collecting a gang around him he calls it *"hwalbindang"* (party to rescue the poor). The

2. The Korean Buddhist scholar Ko Eun recently developed this theme under Minjung Buddhism. Maitreya Buddhism had two moments, one being the royal messianic leader and the other being the leader of the suffering people (minjung).

3. "The Tale of Hong Kil-dong" is a paradigm of the social biography of the minjung. It contains popular Buddhist and Taoist elements and is full of social imagination, humor, and satire.

hero of the story attacks the rich and distributes wealth to the poor. This creates great social disturbances. Finally, the hero is persuaded by his father to leave the country, and he goes off to an island called Yuldo — his paradise, which is characterized by the absence of social division and contradiction between the yangban class and the common people. With its picture of a messianic kingdom, the novel prompted much social imagination among the people. This novel seems to have been heavily influenced by Maitreya Messianic Buddhist ideas.

The third is the famous Donghak messianic movement. This movement emerged in the middle of the nineteenth century, when the Yi dynasty was progressively becoming decadent and the suffering of the people reached extreme proportions. During this time the ruling yangban population increased but agricultural production decreased at an alarming rate. The Japanese invasion under Hideyoshi caused many disruptions and not much land was put under cultivation. There was also a decrease in the number of common people, the productive base of society. Therefore the exploitation of the poor peasants by the yangban was extremely severe.

In this historical context, the Donghak religious movement manifested itself as a messianic religion among the common people. This may be called a truly indigenous minjung messianic religion. It played a powerful role in the Donghak Peasant Rebellion of 1895, and in the March First Independence movement of 1919.

In 1860, Choe Je-u (Choe Messiah or Choe Jesus) founded the Donghak religious movement. Although he was disillusioned and alienated from society, he was a religiously sensitive person. His basic teaching or doctrine was that humanity is heaven. On this basis he advocated egalitarian ethical practice. He believed that there will be a second apocalypse when the whole world will be destroyed and a new era will emerge. This hope led his believers to revolutionary actions. This movement may owe something to Catholic literature which was appearing in the early nineteenth century when Catholics were being severely persecuted. However, there is no doubt that the messianism in Donghak is unmistakably indigenous. It played a powerful role in people's movements in the late nineteenth and early twentieth centuries.

The fourth is the Christian movement in Korea. Although to start with it was a Western missionary movement, it soon became a Korean Christian movement among the suffering people of Korea.

The messianic impact of Christianity upon the Korean people took place during the Great Revival of 1907. Here the messianic dynamic of this Korean Christianity unfolded itself in the successive actions of the National

Liberation movement against Japanese colonial rule. Korean Christians were agents of messianism in the people's movement. Christians struggled against the Japanese Imperial Education Rescript; and they participated in the March First Independence movement of 1919. The next historical expression of the Korean Christian messianic movement was when it confronted the Japanese Imperial Authority and Japan's ultranationalism over the issue of Jinja worship. The story of martyrdom of Pastor Chu Ki-chol, a devout Christian nationalist, reveals the nature of this struggle.

The most dramatic manifestation of minjung messianism in Korea was the March First Independence movement of 1919. Korean historians have carefully documented this movement and show the minjung to be its motive power.[4] They also show that the messianic traditions of Buddhism, Donghak religion, and Christianity joined together to form a minjung messianic religious foundation which became the backbone and the dynamic of the March First movement. This movement produced an axial transformation in the history of modern Korean people; and it has become the paradigmatic or root experience of the Korean people. It supplies the motivation, scope, and direction for the minjung to create their own new future.[5]

The Christian messianic movement of the people can be understood more clearly when we see it against the background of *political messianism* in Korea during the last fifty years or so.

Basically, there are five types of political messianism in Korea. Two are traditional, namely, Buddhist political messianism, an example being the Unified Silla dynasty, and Confucian orthodox political ideology, which found expression in the Yi dynasty. One may dispute the messianic character of Confucianism; but the ideology itself contains definite messianic characteristics.

The next three experiences of political messianism by the Korean people were: Japanese ultranationalism in its colonial form; the North Korean Communist movement; and the emerging modern technocracy in Korea.[6] One might argue that modern technocracy may not be classified as messianic, but as we will show, it has strong messianic tendencies.

---

4. Prof. Ahn Pyong-Jik of Seoul National University has, through socio-economic analysis, determined the constituency of the March First Independence movement to be a minjung movement.

5. For a detailed analysis, see Kim Yong-Bock, "Historical Transformation, People's Movement and Messianic Koinonia" (Ph.D. diss., Princeton Theological Seminary, 1976), especially chapter 5.

6. The first draft of this paper was written in 1979. The reference is to the so-called Yushin system.

For the sake of brevity, we will deal with these three cases of political messianism in a schematic manner.

These three political regimes are totalitarian in different ways and to different degrees on the political level; and at the same time on the religious level each claims absolute authority in different ways by assuming divine and messianic roles for the people.

According to the polity of Japanese ultranationalism all values and institutions come under the Imperial Authority of the Emperor. Hence, the government, the military, business, all truth, beauty, and morality belong to the institution of Emperor. The infamous Education Rescript was an open declaration of the fact that the Japanese state, being a religious, spiritual, and moral entity, claimed the right to determine all values. This was the spirit of Japanese national polity which was combined with the doctrine of the divinity of the Emperor. This messianic motive, championed by the Japanese military as the holy army of the Emperor, launched the mission to bring the "Light of the Emperor" to the eight corners of the world.

With regard to the Communist political messianism in North Korea, we do not have all the information we need to deal with it fully. However, it seems clear that the personal messianic or cultic role of Kim Il-sung is very much emphasized. Communism is a secularized form of messianism. Its messianic role, understood in terms of the dictatorship of the proletariat, is in fact assumed by the political leader, and finds expression in a totalitarian political structure.

Finally, modern technocracy, in its Korean form, is being experienced as another form of national messianism. There seems to be a conviction that technology and science, organized into the capitalist system, can solve all the human problems of the Korean people; and the political regime integrates and controls all the economic, military, and cultural institutions. While doing this, the regime places itself and its authority above the law and criticism and claims the loyalty of the people by emphasizing filial piety, which was formerly a cardinal virtue of Japanese ultranationalism. It is not yet totalitarian and absolutist in the classical sense, but such tendencies are unmistakably present.

These three manifestations of political messianism have common characteristics, not only in their totalitarian and absolutist character, but also in sharing a common theory of contradiction. Their view of history is that there are two powers which are struggling against each other, and that one must destroy the other. One is absolutely good and the other is absolutely evil. The justice of God (theodicy) is alleged to be immanent in the established political regime, be it that of the Emperor, a Communist leader, or the military technocracy.

The theodicy immanent in Japanese ultranationalism was seldom obvious or well-defined and thus had an air of mystery about it. It showed itself, however, in opposing its internal enemies, which included liberal, political, and intellectual movements. It also waged a holy war on the so-called Western barbarians and attempted to expand the realm of the Emperor. Communism believes that its manifest destiny is to bring about the victory of the international proletariat, with imperialism (the United States) as its chief enemy. The military technocracy sees irrationality, traditionality, and chaos (instability) as characteristics of its internal enemies, who oppose its messianic claims, and suppresses them. It has Communist North Korea as its external enemy.

In claiming absolute authority, these three kinds of political messianism advocate radical reforms in society. However, these are to be carried out from the top working toward the bottom. For instance, the North Korean regime was not established by the process of a popular revolution, but rather was imposed from the outside by the Soviet Union, against the popular will of the Korean people.

These so-called radical reforms — all in the name of an earthly millennium — are undertaken with a great deal of social and political cost which has to be borne by the minjung. Indeed, the sufferings of the Korean people under these three political messianisms were and are extreme. The free subjectivity of the people is reduced to nothing in history. Socio-economic and cultural analyses of the Korean people's sufferings under these conditions bear witness to the fact that political messianism is antagonistic to the people (the minjung). They experience it as a contradiction.

Therefore, besides making and maintaining false claims to messianism, political messianism sets itself up against the minjung, who face it as a contradiction.

As we have already shown, messianism is a political process or a history in which the minjung join with the Messiah in realizing his messianic role. While political messianism attempts to make the minjung a historical nothing or an object of its messianic claims, the messianic politics of Jesus are the politics that will realize for the minjung their historical subjectivity, thus making them masters of their own historical destiny. Fundamentally, messianic politics must be understood as that of the minjung, not that of the leader, especially not that of the ruling power. The relationship between the minjung and the Messiah should be understood as a relation between the minjung as the subject and the Messiah as their function. However, the messianic function of the people should not be understood in terms of an elite who are at the top of a political hierarchy but in terms of the Suffering Servant.

To be sure, there are many images or models in the Bible which will help to illuminate this notion of messianic politics. For instance, there is the model of King David; there is the figure of the Son of Man in apocalyptic literature; and other kingly ("the anointed") images of the Messiah. However, these have a corrupting influence, for we see the Messiah as a power personality (political messianism) who embodies self-righteousness and triumphalism. However, the most appropriate and convincing of all messianic images is that of Jesus as the Suffering Servant, in the light of which we must examine and reshape other images like that of David, Son of Man, etc. What is noteworthy about the figure of the Suffering Servant is that it provides the two messianic qualities of identification with the suffering people and functioning as servant to the aspiration of the people for liberation.

Such an understanding of messianic politics will provide the means for purging Christian confessions and theologies of elements of political messianism which have come from the ideology of Christendom. The claims of Christendom did not serve the messianic politics of the people to be subjects of history; and this was deliberate. It may be one of the critical tasks especially of Third World theologians to purge elements of political messianism from our Christian confessions, proclamations, and theologies.

Furthermore, to expose the reality of political messianism in the modern state, no matter however secular they claim to be, is one of the fundamental political hermeneutics of the Christian community today.

This task needs to be performed when the Christian community seeks to serve the suffering people as Jesus the Messiah did, and when we seek to realize the hope expressed through his resurrection and his promise of the general resurrection of all the minjung. This task needs to be done in this context because the struggle to realize the messianic aspirations of the minjung is not just a religious or spiritual matter isolated from the political arena. In fact, the political field is the center stage on which the messianic struggle is carried out. Therefore, the confession that Jesus is the Messiah of the people entails political service to the people.

On the basis of the analyses given above, several tasks emerge in the Korean situation.

The first is to expose the long history of political messianism which has enslaved us and to struggle against it. This involves critical evaluations of political values, political structures, and political leadership.

The second is to rediscover the popular messianic traditions inherent in

Maitreya Messianic Buddhism and Donghak religion, both through a research of extant literature and through dialogue with Buddhist and Donghak leaders who have concerns similar to ours. In undertaking this task we must remember that messianic traditions are not immune to influences from political messianism once they are linked to the ruling power. We know of this process in the history of Christianity which has justified absolute power like that of the Divine Right of the King.

The third is to evolve in a concrete way a Christian political perspective based on the following ideas: (1) The general resurrection of the people (bodily as well as spiritual) understood in terms of the messianic subjectivity of the people. (2) *Shalom* in relation to the unification of Korea. (3) *Koinonia* (participation) and justice in relation to the social and political development of the Korean people. In order to do all this we need a general understanding of Korean history and we should dialogue with secular intellectuals who seek to serve the people.

The fourth is to tackle the issue of the use of power in a political struggle. It is not simply a question of the use of violence. The issue concerns the nature and use of power in politics. Although there can be no general rule on the use of power, including force and violence, in the process of realizing the messianic hope of the people, a few general things can be said.

1. Ultimately, power, as we know it, has no ontological status in the framework of the Messianic Kingdom. Jesus not only did not use power as we know it, but he could not use power, since he himself was the embodiment and reality of the Messianic Kingdom which is the powerless status of Jesus the Messiah and the people.

2. However, as we have indicated, history shows the continuous contradiction between political messianism and messianic politics, the power and the people. Therefore, some tamed measure of political realism should be allowed, although an absolute political cynicism or "realpolitik" should never be permitted.

In considering a realistic posture on the part of Christians, the notion of people's power should be taken into account. It is infinitely creative; and various forms of it are evident especially at the grassroots level, where identification and participation with people are easiest.

The people will be the subjects of their own historical destiny. Jesus the Messiah died to expose Roman political messianism and its historical antecedents and descendants; and Jesus the Messiah was resurrected as a foretaste and affirmation of the raising of all the dead minjung to inaugurate the messianic rule of *justice, koinonia* (participation), and *shalom*.

36 Towards a Christian Dalit Theology

Arvind P. Nirmal

Introduction

Let us first of all recognize the fact that this is a historic moment for Indian Christian theology. At this moment Indian Christian theology has ceased to be an enterprise of the elite and on behalf of the elite and allowed itself to be an enterprise of peoples. These peoples are the Dalits: (1) the broken, the torn, the rent, the burst, the split, (2) the opened, the expanded, (3) the bisected, (4) the driven asunder, the dispelled, the scattered, (5) the downtrodden, the crushed, the destroyed, (6) the manifested, the displayed.

If we want to grasp the full significance of this historic movement, we must look back at the tradition of Indian Christian theology. In the seventies, I had made the following observation in one of my articles:

> Broadly speaking, Indian Christian theology in the past has tried to work out its theological systems in terms of either *Advaita Vedanta* or *Vaishisahtha Advaita*. Most of the contributions of Indian Christian theology in the past came from caste converts to Christianity. The result has been that Indian Christian theology has perpetuated within itself what I prefer to call the "Brahminic" tradition. This tradition has further perpetuated an institutional interiority oriented approach to the theological task in India. One wonders whether this kind of Indian Christian theology will ever have a mass appeal.

This brief observation can be spelt out a little more fully. To speak in terms of the traditional Indian categories, Indian Christian theology, following the Brahminic tradition, has trodden the *jnana marga*, the *bhakti marga*, and the *karma marga*. In Brahma Bandhav Upaddhyaya, we have a brilliant theologian who attempted a synthesis of Sankara's *Advaita Vedanta* and Christian theology. In Bishop A. J. Appasamy, we had a *bhakti margi* theologian who tried to synthesize Ramanuja's *Vashishtha Advaita* with Christian theology. In M. M. Thomas we have a theologian who has contributed to theological anthropology at the international level and who laid the foundations for a more active theological involvement in India — the *karma marga*. In Chenchiah we find an attempt to synthesize Christian theology with Sri Aurobindo's "Integral Yoga."

If we look at India's involvement in the ecumenical movement, we recapture the following story:

> The International Missionary Conference held at Edinburgh in 1910, set an official seal on the "fulfillment theory" expounded by J. N. Faruhar. The second International Missionary Conference held in Jerusalem in 1928 encouraged the efforts of the supporters of the fulfillment theory, but warned against the danger of "syncretism." It is also said that different world religions should co-operate with one another against the common enemy of "secularism." Between the Jerusalem Conference and the Madras meeting of the same body in 1938, Barth's neo-orthodoxy became the dominant theology of at least continental Europe. Hendrik Kraemer, the Dutch theologian, applied the Barthian insights to the "problem" of non-Christian faiths. He worked out what might be called the "gospel-judging religion" model. Kraemer argued that there was a basic difference between the gospel of revelation on the one hand and religion on the other.

All religions were human attempts at salvation and as such they had to be judged by the gospel. Christianity, on the other hand, was not a religion, but a gospel — rather the gospel of Jesus Christ. It was a revelation from above. The gospel was not addressed to a Hindu, a Muslim, or a Buddhist, but to a sinful and fallen man. Kraemer's thesis was published under the title *The Christian Message in a Non-Christian World*, on the eve of the Third International Missionary Conference in 1938. Thus, from the early days of India's ecumenical involvement, it had concerned itself with the "problem" of other faiths. Out of this ecumenical involvement emerged the concern for dialogues with other faiths and this concern continues to be taken seriously. But this concern again has contributed to Indian Christian theology's obsession with the Brahminic tradition. As a matter of fact, in connection with the International Missionary Conference at Tambaram several research studies in the economic and social environment of the Indian Church were conducted by various Christian colleges.

They gave a very sober picture of particularly the economic condition of rural Christians. It also became clear that Depressed class converts continued to complain of indifference and neglect. All this, however, did not make any change to Indian Christian theology's obsession with the Brahminic tradition. It had no time or inclination to reflect theologically on the Dalit converts who formed the majority of the Indian Church.

The situation did not change till the seventies. It was in the seventies that Indian theologians began to take the questions of socio-economic justice more seriously. The Indian theological scene thus changed considerably and there emerged what is known as "Third World theology." The advocates of the Third World theology were held together by their allegiance to "liberation theology." It was yet another imported theology. Its chief attraction was the liberation motif which seemed entirely relevant in the Indian situation where the majority of the Indian people face the problem of poverty.

But somehow, I felt that liberation *motifs* in India were of a different nature, the Indian situation was different and that we had to search for liberation *motifs* that were authentically Indian. The Latin American liberation theology in its early stages at least used the Marxist analysis of socio-economic realities, the haves and the have-nots. The socio-economic realities in India, however, are of a different nature and the traditional doctrinaire Marxist analysis of these realities is inadequate in India. It neglects the caste factor which adds to the complexity of Indian socio-economic realities. A journalist-scholar like V. T. Rajashekar Shetty tells us *How Marx Failed in Hindu India.*

The Indian advocates of the Third World theology also ignored the incidents of violence against Dalits in the seventies. The seventies saw several caste wars. Belchi in Bihar in 1977, the urban areas of the North and the South (Agra and Velluparam), both in May, 1978, and Kanjhwala, near the heart of the country's capital are a few of the places which witnessed organized violence against Dalits by caste-Hindus in the seventies. This real life context was overlooked by our Indian third world theologians and they continued to engage in the Latin American liberation rhetoric. The sixties and the seventies were also the decades when the Dalit *Sahitya* (literature) movement and the Dalit Panther movement were making headway in Maharashtra.

Somehow our theologians failed to see in these Dalit movements and struggles a potential for theological reflection. To sum up then, whether it is the traditional Indian Christian theology or the more recent Third World theology, they failed to see in the struggle of Indian Dalits for liberation a subject matter appropriate for doing theology in India. What is amazing is the fact that Indian theologians ignored the reality of the Indian Church. While estimates vary, between 50% and 80% of all the Christians in India today are of Scheduled Caste origin. This is the most important commonality cutting across the various diversities of the Indian Church which would have provided an authentic liberation *motif* for Indian Christian theology. If our theologians failed to see this in the past, there is all the more reason for our waking up to this reality today and for applying ourselves seriously to the task of doing Dalit theology.

My friend Prof. John Webster, in his article "From Indian Church to Indian Theology: An Attempt at Theological Construction," has seen three stages in the history of the Depressed Class Movement in India. The three stages are somewhat overlapping chronologically, but they all have their own distinctive characteristics. The first stage is dated from the 1860s or the 1870s, through the 1930s. The chief characteristic of this first phase is the phenomenon of mass conversion, especially to Christianity. The second stage of this movement begins around 1900 and goes up to 1955. The chief characteristic of the second stage is the caste Hindu efforts to improve the conditions of the Depressed classes.

Initially, such voluntary organizations as the Depressed Classes Mission (1906) and the All Indian Shuddhi Sabha (1909) were involved in these efforts; later, Mahatma Gandhi and the Harijan Sevak Sangh (1932) expanded the work.

After 1937 the government agencies were used to pass laws and to finance and to administer programs for the welfare of the Depressed classes.

The third and the last stage is dated from the 1920s to the present day. This stage is characterized by self-assertion on the part of the Depressed classes themselves. Webster's study is important because it underlines the point I have made earlier, the fact that so much was happening on the Dalit front but Indian Christian theology failed to take note of it.

It is the contention of this paper that the struggle of Indian Dalits is a story that provides us with a liberation *motif* that is authentically Indian. This story needs to be analyzed and interpreted theologically. The struggle is far from over. All the argumentations on the situation of the Dalits are clear indications of the fact that the liberation story of Indian Dalits is incomplete as yet. Theirs (or rather ours) is an ongoing struggle. This liberation struggle needs to be undergirded theologically.

Having looked at the background of and the need for a Christian Dalit theology or Dalit theologies, we should now attempt to answer the question: What is Dalit theology? It is rather difficult to answer this question in simple and straightforward language. For one thing, Dalit theology is still in the process of emergence. We are still trying to construct a Dalit theology or theologies. This is why I have titled this paper "Towards a Christian Dalit Theology." What I am trying to do in this paper is to indicate the possible shape or form that Indian Christian Dalit theology may take. The task that I have set before myself is to anticipate the possible shape of Dalit theology in terms of our understanding of the Holy Trinity.

What Is Dalit Theology?

This question, according to Webster, may be answered in at least three different ways:

The first answer may be that it is a theology *about* the Dalits or theological reflection upon the Christian responsibility to the Depressed classes.

Secondly, the answer may be that it is the theology *for* the Depressed classes, or the theology of the message addressed to the Depressed classes and to which they seem to be responding.

Thirdly, the answer may be that it is the theology *from* the Depressed classes, that is the theology which they themselves would like to expound.

This paper will expound the third answer as I happen to be a Dalit Christian myself. There is a parallel for my stand in the Dalit literature of Maharashtra. In 1970, Bagul published his long story entitled "Sood" (Revenge) with the foreword by the late M. N. Wankhade, the former Principal of Milind Maha Vidhyalaya. Wankhade defined Dalit literature as "*Sahitya* produced by Dalits giving expression to their anger against those who have made them *Dalits*."

Wankhade's definition of Dalit literature was followed by a stormy discussion in the traditional circles of literary criticism. Along with Wankhade, I would say that a Christian Dalit theology will be produced by Dalits. It will be based on their own Dalit experiences, their own sufferings, their own aspirations, and their own hopes. It will narrate the story of their *pathos* and their protest against the socio-economic injustices they have been subjected to throughout history. It will anticipate liberation which is meaningful to them. It will represent a radical discontinuity with the classical Indian Christian theology of the Brahminic tradition.

This Brahminic tradition in the classical Indian Christian theology needs to be challenged by the emerging Dalit theology. This also means that a Christian Dalit theology will be a counter-theology. I submit that people's theologies are essentially counter-theologies; it is necessary that they are also exclusive in character. This will be a methodological exclusivism. This exclusivism is necessary because the tendency of all dominant traditions — cultural or theological — is to accommodate, include, and assimilate; therefore, we need to be on our guard and to shut off the influences of the dominant theological tradition.

In such a theological venture the primacy of the term "dalit" will have to be conceded as against the primacy of the term "Christian" in the dominant theological tradition. This again will be a question of methodological primacy. What this means is that the non-Dalit world will ask us, "What is Christian about Dalit theology?" Our reply will have to be: It is the *dalitness* which is "Christian" about Dalit theology. That is what I mean by the primacy of the term "Dalit." The "Christian" for this theology is *exclusively* the "Dalit." What this exclusivism implies is the affirmation that the Triune God — the Father, the Son, and the Holy Spirit — is on the side of the Dalits and not of the non-Dalits who are the oppressors. It is the common Dalit experience of Christian Dalits along with the other Dalits that will shape a Christian Dalit theology.

Historical Dalit Consciousness

The historical Dalit consciousness is the primary datum of a Christian Dalit theology. The question of Dalit consciousness is really the question of Dalit identity, the question of our roots. If we leave aside the so-called Apostles' Creed and the so-called Nicene Creed and examine some of the Biblical creeds and confessions we will see that the question of identity is an integral part of any faith-affirmation. Take for instance the Deuteronomic creed found in Deuteronomy 26:5-9.

> And you shall make response before the Lord your God. A wandering Aramean was my father; and he went down into Egypt and sojourned there, few in number, and there he became a nation, great, mighty, and populous. And the Egyptians treated us harshly and afflicted us and laid upon us harsh bondage. Then we cried to the Lord, the God of our Fathers, and the Lord heard our voice, and saw our affliction, our toil, and

our oppression, and the Lord brought us out of Egypt with a mighty hand and an outstretched arm, with great terror, with signs and wonders; and he brought us into this place and gave us this land, a land flowing with milk and honey.

I would like to expound this passage in full because it has tremendous implications for a Dalit theology. For the Latin American liberation theologians it is the Exodus experience which is important. It opens with the calling to memory the roots of the people who experienced the Exodus liberation. A creed, a confession, a faith affirmation, therefore, must first exercise in laying bare the roots of the believing community; "A wandering Aramean was my father" recalls the nomadic consciousness. To confess that "once we were no people" is also an integral part of a confession, before we come to the claim "now we are God's people." It is only when we recognize our roots, our identity that we become truly confessional. A truly confessional theology, therefore, has to do with the question of the roots, identity, and consciousness.

Secondly, we notice that this wandering Aramean is also described as "few in number." The Aramean ancestor, therefore, stands for the entire community. The question of identity and roots is inseparably bound with the sense of belonging to a community. In our search for a Dalit theology it is well worth remembering that what we are looking for is community consciousness. The vision of a Dalit theology, therefore, ought to be a *unitive* vision — or rather a "communitive" vision.

Thirdly comes the recalling of their affliction, the harsh treatment meted out by the Egyptians and their bondage. Then comes their cry to the Lord. A theology, a Christian Dalit theology, therefore, is a story of the afflictions, the bondage, the harsh treatment, the toil, and the tears of the Dalits. A genuinely Dalit theology will be characterized by pathos, by suffering.

Fourthly, the Exodus liberation is symbolized by "a mighty hand," "an outstretched arm," and by "terror." "Signs" and "wonders" are low in the order. Liberation does not come only through "signs" and "wonders." A certain measure of "terror" is necessary to achieve it. In terms of Dalit theology, this would mean that the Dalits cannot afford to have a fatalistic attitude to life. They must protest and agitate and change their lot. The late Dr. B. R. Ambedkar's *mantra* for the Dalits was: "unite, educate, and agitate"; and finally, we should also notice that the "land flowing with milk and honey" comes last. It is an outcome of the liberation already achieved. Liberation is its own reward. The "land flowing with milk and honey" is not the chief goal of the Exodus. Rather it is the release from the captivity and slavery, and the liberation struggle we are involved in is primarily a struggle for our human dignity and for our right to live as a free people — people created in the "image of God."

This historic Deuteronomic creed has paradigmatic value for our Dalit theological construct.

The historical Dalit consciousness in India depicts even greater and deeper *pathos* than is found in the Deuteronomic creed. My Dalit ancestor did not enjoy the nomadic freedom of the wandering Aramean. As an outcaste, he was also cast out of his village. The Dalit *bastis* (localities) were always and are always on the outskirts of the Indian village. When my Dalit ancestor walked the dusty roads of his village, the *Sa Varnas* tied a tree-branch around his waist so that he would not leave any unclean foot-prints and pollute the roads. The *Sa Varnas* also tied an earthen pot around my Dalit ancestor's neck to serve as a spittoon. If ever my Dalit ancestor tried to learn Sanskrit or some other sophisticated language, the oppressors gagged him permanently by pouring molten lead down his throat.

My Dalit mother and sisters were forbidden to wear any blouses and the *Sa Varnas* feasted their eyes on their bare bosoms. The *Sa Varnas* denied my Dalit ancestor any access to public wells and reservoirs. They denied him entry to their temples and places of worship. That, my friends, was my ancestor — many in Maharashtra. My Dalit consciousness, therefore, has an unparalleled depth of *pathos* and misery, and it is this historical Dalit consciousness, this Dalit identity, that should inform my attempt at a Christian Dalit theology.

Our paradigmatic creed tells us that "signs and wonders" are not enough for the liberation we are seeking. We need a "mighty hand" and an "outstretched arm" and a certain measure of "terror" — in short, we need an activist struggle for liberation, a movement informed by its action towards its theological reflection. Our *pathos* should give birth to our protest — a very loud protest. Our protest should be so loud that the walls of Brahminism should come tumbling down. A Christian Dalit theology will be a theology full of *pathos*, but not a passive theology.

The Gentile-consciousness of the New Testament can confess that "once we were no people but now we are God's people." The Dalit consciousness in India cannot say even that much. We were not only "no people" but we were also "no humans." For the *Sa Varnas*, humans were divided into the four castes — the *Brahmins*, the *Kshatriyas*, the *Vaishyas*, and the *Shudras*. But we were the outcastes, the *Avarnas*, no humans, below even the *Shudras* in the social ladder. We were the *Panchamas*, the *Chandalas*, and the *Mlecchhas*.

544

This "no-humanness" also should become a part of our theological affirmation or confession.

The Dalit consciousness should realize that the ultimate goal of its liberation movement cannot be the "land flowing with milk and honey." For a Christian Dalit theology it cannot be simply the gaining of the rights, the reservations, and the privileges. The goal is the realization of our full humanness, or conversely, our full divinity, the ideal of the *Imago Dei*, the Image of God in us. To use another biblical metaphor, our goal is the "glorious liberty of the children of God."

Our Exodus Experience

The ideal of *Imago Dei* in us leads us to the question of God. What kind of God are we talking about? What kind of divinity does Dalit theology envision? But before that question is answered, I must make one final comment about the Deuteronomic creed under study. The creed speaks not only about the roots and the historical nomadic consciousness of the people of Israel, but also about their changed status and their thanksgiving. The nomadic experience is brought to memory, but also is the Exodus experience. "Few in number" are now a "nation," great, mighty and "populous." "No people" are now "God's people."

But Christian Dalits in India also affirm their own Exodus experience. What I mean is that, as we should be aware of our historical consciousness, our roots, and our identity, we should also be aware of our present Christian consciousness. We are not just Dalits. We are Christian Dalits. Something has happened to us. Our status has changed. Our Exodus from Hinduism — which was imposed upon us — to Christianity or rather to Jesus Christ is a valuable experience — a liberating experience. The non-Dalits of this country have teased us as "rich Christians" or "bulgar Christians." But we know that this is not true.

Both the 1935 Constitution under the British and the Constitution of the Indian Republic deprived us of our economic rights, political rights, privileges, and reservations. We have been discriminated against in the past and we continue to be discriminated against in the present. Notwithstanding all this, we have followed Jesus Christ. Our exodus to him has enabled us to recognize our own Dalitness, the Dalitness of Jesus of Nazareth, and also the Dalitness of his Father and our Father — our God. In our Exodus to Jesus Christ, we have had a liberating experience. Although we have not reached our ultimate goal, we are confident that the Jesus of Palestine or, the more immediately, the Jesus of India is in the midst of the liberation struggle of the Dalits of India. A Christian Dalit theology, therefore, should also be doxological in character. Our struggle is not over as yet, but we ought to be thankful that it is undergirded by our own Exodus experience and our own Exodus hope.

The Question of God

Now I return to the question of God. I have already said that our Exodus experience has enabled us to recognize the Dalitness of Jesus and his Father. It is in this recognition that the mystery of our Exodus lies. This recognition means that we have rejected non-Dalit deities. A non-Dalit deity cannot be the God of Dalits. This is why our other Dalit friends have rejected Rama — the deity whom millions of Hindus worship and pray to. The story goes that Rama killed Shambuka-Dalit, because Shambuka had undertaken *tapas-charya,* a life of prayer and asceticism.

The dominant religious tradition denied the right to pray to the Dalit. Rama, therefore, simply killed Shambuka and performed *dharma,* religious act. This is why Dalits have rejected Rama. For Dalits, Rama is a killer God — killer and murderer of the Dalits.

But the God whom Jesus Christ revealed and about whom the prophets of the Old Testament spoke is a Dalit God. He is a servant God — a God who serves. Service to others has always been the privilege of Dalit communities in India. The passages from *Manu Dharma Sastra* say that the *Shudra* was created by the self-existent (Svayambhu) to do servile work and that servitude is innate in him. Service is the *Svadhartna* of the *Shudra.* Let us remember the fact that in Dalits we have people who are *avarnas* — those below the *Shudras.* Their servitude is even more pathetic than that of the *Shudras.* Against this background the amazing claim of a Christian Dalit theology will be that the God of the Dalits, the self-existent, the *Svayambhu* does not create others to do servile work, but does servile work Himself. Servitude is innate in the God of the Dalits. Servitude is the *sva-dharma* of our God; and since we the Indian Dalits are this God's people, service has been our lot and our privilege.

Unfortunately, this word "service," ministry or *diakonia,* has lost its cutting edge. A shop tells you, "Service is our motto." Is it? Isn't profit the real motto? A dentist pulls your tooth out and sends you a bill saying, "for the professional services rendered." A member of the State Cabinet or of the Central Cabinet calls himself or herself a "minister" — a servant — whereas what he or she really enjoys is power, *satta,* and not *seva* (service). The word has become an "in thing." Originally, the word *diakonia* was associated with waiting at the dining table. The "servant," therefore, means a waiter. Our house-maid and the sweeper who cleans commodes and latrines are, truly speaking, our servants. Do we realize that? Let us be prepared for a further shock.

Are we prepared to say that my house-maid, my sweeper, my *bhangi* is my God? It is precisely in this sense that our God is a servant God. He is a waiter, a *dhobi,* a *bhangi;* traditionally, all such services have been the lot of Dalits. This means we have participated in this servant God's ministries. To speak of a servant God, therefore, is to recognize and identify Him as a truly Dalit Deity. The Gospel writers identified Jesus with the Servant of God of Isaiah. In his service, he was utterly faithful to God. But what kind of language is used to describe this servant?

> He had no form or comeliness that we should look at him,
> and no beauty that we should desire him.
> He was rejected by men,
> a man of sorrows, and acquainted with grief,
> and as one from whom men hide their faces;
> he was despised, and we esteemed him not.
> Surely he has borne our griefs
> and carried our sorrows;
> yet we esteemed him stricken,
> smitten and afflicted.
> He was oppressed, and he was afflicted,
> yet he opened not his mouth;
> like a lamb that is led to the slaughter,
> and like a sheep that before its
> shearers is dumb,
> so he opened not his mouth.
> By oppression and judgement he was taken away;
> and as for his generation, who considered
> that he was cut off out of the land of the living,
> stricken for the transgression of my people?

That is the language used to describe the servant-language full of pathos. That is the language used for God — the God of the Dalits. But that is also the language which mirrors our own *pathos* as the Dalits. The language that mirrors the God of Dalits and Dalits themselves. Incredible, isn't it? Isaiah also thought so. Therefore, he asks a question right at the beginning of this passage, the Servant song: "Who has believed what we have heard? And to whom has the arm of the Lord been revealed?" We the Christian Dalits in India can answer that question. We should, with full confidence, tell Isaiah, "We have believed what you have heard. And to us has the arm of the Lord been revealed. That is why, Isaiah, we are Christian Dalits and not just Dalits."

Dalit Christology

But what does it mean when we say that we are Christian Dalits and not just Dalits? This statement has Christological implications which must be faced boldly. It means first of all that we proclaim and affirm that Jesus Christ whose followers we are was himself a Dalit — despite his being a Jew. It further means that both his humanity and his divinity are to be understood in terms of his Dalitness. His Dalitness is the key to the mystery of his divine-human unity.

Let us note some of the features of his Dalitness. Let us forget for a moment the wonderful story of his birth colored by the angelic choir, the bright Star, and the Wise Men. Let us have a close look at his genealogy as given in the Gospel according to Matthew (Matthew 1:1-17). We seldom read this genealogy carefully. Among Jesus' ancestors there are a few names which should startle and shock us.

The first name is that of Tamar, the daughter-in-law of Judah. She outwitted her father-in-law by sleeping with him and conceiving from him (Genesis 38:1-30).

Secondly, there is Rahab — the harlot who helped the Israelite spies (Joshua 2:1-21).

Thirdly, there is King Solomon. We should not forget that Solomon was an illegitimate child of David. These small details of Jesus' ancestry should not be forgotten as they are suggestive of his Dalit conditions. He is also referred to as a "carpenter's son." That sounds like looking down upon his father's profession.

The title that Jesus preferred to use for himself is "The Son of Man." The title is used in three different ways, so say the New Testament scholars. Firstly, it simply means man in an ordinary way. For instance, in one place when a scribe wanted to follow him, Jesus said, "Foxes have holes, and birds of the air have nests; but the Son of Man has nowhere to lay his head" (Matt. 8:20).

The second group of the Son of Man sayings is indicative of Jesus' present sufferings and imminent death.

The third group of the Son of Man sayings is called the eschatological Son of Man sayings.

There is some debate about the order of the second and the third groups, but we have no time to go into that. The second group of the Son of Man sayings is significant for developing a Dalit Christology. These sayings speak of the Son of Man as encountering rejection, mockery, contempt, suffering, and finally death. Let us look at a few of these sayings:

And he began to teach them that the Son of Man must suffer many things, and be rejected by the elders and the chief priests and the scribes, and be killed, and after three days rise again. (Mark 8:31)

And he said to them. "Elijah does come first to restore all things; and how it is written of the Son of Man, that he should suffer many things and be treated with contempt." (Mark 9:12)

For the Son of Man also came not to be served but to serve and to give his life as a ransom for many. (Mark 10:45)

These sayings indicate that Jesus as the Son of Man had to encounter rejection, mockery, contempt, suffering, and finally death. All this was from the dominant religious tradition and the established religion. He underwent these Dalit experiences as the prototype of all Dalits. The last saying quoted above also connects the theme of service with the Son of Man.

Another noteworthy feature of Jesus' life is his total identification with the Dalits of his day. Again and again Jesus is accused of eating and drinking with publicans, tax-collectors, and "sinners" of his day (Mark 2:15-16).

In his study entitled "Jesus' Attitude to Caste: A Bible Study" (*Madras Diocesan News and Notes,* January 1982), M. Azariah has drawn our attention to Jesus' approach and attitude towards Samaritans, the Dalits of his day, and has demonstrated that Jesus loved and cared for the Dalits.

The Nazareth manifesto in the Gospel according to Luke has often been commented upon in recent times — especially during the emergency of the seventies. Some of our church leaders even compared it with the twenty-point program of the Indira Congress. What is generally overlooked is its significance for a Christian Dalit theology. "Today this scripture has been fulfilled in your hearing"; we read that "all spoke well of him and wondered at the gracious words which proceeded out of his mouth." But then Jesus goes on to tell his audience for whom his liberation is meant.

His two illustrations indicate that the liberation he is talking about is meant for the Dalits and not for non-Dalits. In his first illustration he speaks about Zarephath, the widow in Sidon to whom Elijah was sent. But he also makes the point that there were many widows in Israel, but Elijah went to none of them. Similarly, it was only Naaman the Syrian, the leper, whom Elisha cleansed. Of course, there were many lepers in Israel, but they were not cleansed. The "Dalits" were set over against "Israel." The gospel that Jesus brought was the gospel for Dalits and not for non-Dalits — not for Israel. The whole situation changes at Jesus' explosive words, and we read, "When they heard this, all in the synagogue were filled with wrath. And they rose up and put him out of the city, and led him to the brow of the hill on which their city was built, that they might throw him down headlong" (Luke 4:16-29). The Nazareth manifesto then is really the manifesto for Dalits.

Another episode from Jesus' ministry, full of significance for a Christian Dalit theology, is that of the cleansing of the temple. The account is as follows:

> And they came to Jerusalem. And he entered the temple and began to drive out those who sold and those who bought in the temple, and he overturned the tables of the money-changers and the seats of those who sold pigeons; and he would not allow any one to carry anything through the temple. And he taught, and said to them, "Is it not written: My House shall be called a House of Prayer *for all the nations?* But you have made it a den of robbers." And the chief priests heard it and sought a way to destroy him, for they feared him; because all the multitude was astonished at his teachings. And when the evening came they went out of the city. (Mark 11:15-19)

This incident is interpreted in various ways by the New Testament scholars. The evangelists other than St. Mark tell us that Jesus was angry on this occasion. On the other hand they omit the words *"for all the nations"* in their account and leave the quotation from Isaiah incomplete. It has been suggested that the evangelists see in this passage a fulfillment of Malachi 3:1, Zechariah 14:21, and Hosea 9:15. All these passages refer to God's *final* intervention in history. Jesus' action then would seem to be that of the Messianic king on his final visit to his Father's house and people and embodying God's ultimate judgment upon the life and religion of Israel.

The second suggestion is that Jesus' cleansing of the temple was in line with the prophetic antithesis between prayer and sacrifice, and he, like the prophets before him, upheld the first and condemned the second.

The third suggestion is that Jesus' anger was directed against the greed and dishonesty of the dealers and the way they were fleecing the poor, but we must note that Mark omits any reference to Jesus' anger.

The fourth and final suggestion comes from Lightfoot, who maintains that the incident must be understood in terms of its implications for the Gentiles. All the buying and selling and money exchanging took place in the part of the temple precincts which were reserved for Gentile worship. It was the Gentile court. The Gentiles had no access to the inner precincts where the Jewish worship proper was conducted. The *bazaar* that was held in the Gentile court thus effectively prevented them from conducting their worship in a peaceful and quiet manner. Jesus the Messianic King thus restores to the Gentiles their religious rights.

Lightfoot's interpretation makes sense to the Indian Dalits who had to struggle for their temple entry rights, and we know about temple entry legislation in the various states of India. We, the Indian Dalits, know what it means to be denied entry to the temple and to be denied the right to pray and worship. Ambedkar and his followers had to agitate for entry to the Kala Rama temple in Nasik. We know about many such temple entry agitations. In his act of restoration of the Gentile rights to worship, we see a prefiguration of the vindication of the Indian Dalits' struggle for their prayer and worship rights.

There are many other examples of Jesus' sympathy for the Dalits of his day. But his Dalitness is best symbolized by the Cross. On the Cross, he was the broken, the crushed, the split, the torn, the driven asunder man — the Dalit in the fullest possible meaning of that term. "My God, my God, why hast thou forsaken me?" he cries aloud from the cross. The Son of God feels that he is God-forsaken. That feeling of being God-forsaken is at the heart of our Dalit experiences and Dalit consciousness in India. It is the Dalitness of the divinity and humanity that the Cross of Jesus symbolizes.

The Holy Spirit

My treatment of a Dalit *pneumatology* will be necessarily brief and sketchy as I did not have enough time to work it out. In our understanding of the beneficial activity of the Holy Spirit, we will have to make use of the metaphors and images of the Holy Spirit. Read for example the story of the valley of the dry bones in Ezekiel 37. "Can these bones live?" is the most important question. I am aware of the fact that the bones in Ezekiel represent Israel. But Israel here is under Dalit conditions. The bones are dead, dry, and lifeless. The Holy Spirit revives these dry bones, gives them life, unifies them, and makes an army out of them. For us Dalits, then, the Spirit is the life-giver, unifier, and empowerer for the liberation struggle of the Indian Dalits. But in our Dalit experiences, He is our *comforter.* He "groans" along with us in our sufferings.

In the story of Cornelius, Peter speaks of "how God anointed Jesus of Nazareth with the Holy Spirit and with power; how he went about doing good and healing all that were oppressed . . ." (Acts 10:38). The Holy Spirit, the Spirit of Jesus, heals all that are oppressed. While Peter was preaching, the Holy Spirit descended on the Gentiles. The baptism was to come later. The Holy Spirit did not wait for the baptism of the Gentiles — the Dalits — to descend upon them. The Holy Spirit is the Spirit on the side of the Dalits.

This is a very brief statement of the triune nature of a Christian Dalit theology.

In a quotation from John 9:3, we read, "It was not that this man sinned, or his parents, but that the works of God might be made manifest in him." This is also true of ourselves as Dalits. We have suffered in the past and we continue to suffer in the present. This is not because of our own sins or the sins of our ancestors — we need not and should not subscribe to any doctrine of *karma samsara.* Our sufferings and our Dalitness have their place in the economy of salvation foreordained by God. It is in and through us that God will manifest and display His glorious salvation.

The sixth group of meanings associated with the term "Dalit" is "manifested" or "displayed." It is through us that God will manifest and display His salvation. It is precisely in and through the weaker, the downtrodden, the crushed, the oppressed, and the marginalized that God's saving glory is manifested or displayed. This is because brokenness belongs to the very being of God. God's divinity and His humanity are both characterized by His Dalitness. He is one with the broken. He suffers when His people suffer. He weeps when His people weep. He laughs when His people laugh. He dies in His people's death and He rises again in His people's resurrection.

This is one possible version of a people's theology. Shall I perhaps say "no people's theology"? But there again, it is always the "no people," the "Dalits," who are the real people, God's very own people.

552

37 Wilderness Tokyo

Kosuke Koyama

The waste arid void confronted me. Even the sun
momentarily became a stranger to me.

15 August 1945: a cloudless, blue summer day. Even now I remember the strangeness of it. Exactly at noon we heard the Diamond Voice of the Emperor, the *akitsu mikami,* the god manifested in human form, through a radio broadcast. This voice for some fifty years had been thought too sacred for any mortal to hear. Now it spoke in a special imperial language, far removed from the Japanese one hears in everyday life. It said:

> To our good and loyal subjects:
> After pondering deeply the general trends of the world and the actual conditions obtaining in our Empire today, we have decided to effect a settlement of the present situation by resorting to an extraordinary measure.
> We have ordered our Government to communicate to the Governments of the United States, Great Britain, China and the Soviet Union that our Empire accepts the provisions of their joint declaration.
> To strive for the common prosperity and happiness of all nations as well as the security and well-being of our subjects is the solemn obligation which had been handed down by Our Imperial Ancestors and we lay it close to the heart. . . .[1]

1. David J. Lu, ed., *Sources of Japanese History* (New York: McGraw-Hill, 1974), vol. II, p. 176.

The war was over. With five hundred other high school students who had been mobilized to work in a military factory, I listened to the broadcast, standing at attention in a badly bombed compound. I went home . . . to a small hovel in which our family had taken shelter after our house had been destroyed. Physically and mentally exhausted from the lack of food and sleep and from the fear of death by the constant air raids, I stood like a ghost and once again saw Tokyo. As far as my eyes could survey Tokyo had become a wilderness. Familiar landmarks were gone: rice shops, temples and shrines at which the people had prayed for victory . . . even railway stations had disappeared. The inhabited world had become a desolate world. A threatening silence enveloped the place which had been called Tokyo, City of the East. The land, it seemed, "had vomited out its inhabitants" (Lev. 18:25). I was dwelling in wilderness Tokyo. I slept, and in the morning I watched the sun rise over a horizon of utter destruction. The sun itself, I felt at that moment, had become a part of the cosmic "waste and void" (Gen. 1:2). Several years later the scene was brought back vividly when I heard these words of Jeremiah which touched me deeply:

> I looked on the earth, and lo, it was waste and void; and to the heavens, and they had no light. I looked on the mountains, and lo, they were quaking, and all the hills moved to and fro. I looked, and lo, there was no man, and all the birds of the air had fled. I looked, and lo, the fruitful land was a desert, and all its cities were laid in ruins before the Lord, before his fierce anger. (Jer. 4:23-26)

What I have felt is that the mythological "waste and void" of which Genesis speaks became concrete in human experience when thousands of B29s, made in Wichita, Kansas, rained down fire on Tokyo until it was completely devastated. In 1945 the mythological became historical for me fused by the American fire-bombing of Tokyo. I was struck by the truth that is contained in the myth, and later was able to appreciate the view of Mircea Eliade and others that myth does not mean "false story" but it contains a "true story" when it describes the crisis moments of human existence.

By their own standards the Japanese had created chaos in Asia. The ancient Japanese definition of sin *(tsumi)* is said to be breaking down the ridges (between rice paddies), covering the irrigation ditches, opening the sluices (causing flood), double planting (sowing other seeds between the rows of rice), setting up stakes (denoting false ownership), skinning alive, flaying (an animal) backwards, and defecation in the wrong place.[2] *Tsumi* disturbs social organization in an agricultural community. It brings chaos into ordered society. Japan broke down the ridges between the Southeast Asian nations for her own advantage, opened the sluices and damaged the welfare of other peoples, setting up stakes and occupying the territories of other nations, murdering Koreans and Chinese by skinning alive, defecating in the sacred places of other peoples. We did not know that what we were doing to other peoples would come home to us. Chaos did come to us, extensively and profoundly. I have become aware of the boomerang effect in history. I have seen "waste and void" concretely and personally in history. It descended upon Tokyo.

On the same day that General MacArthur, the conqueror of Japan, arrived in Tokyo, 30 August 1945, the Prime Minister, Prince Higashikuni, gave his first press conference after the war. "All one hundred million Japanese must repent" *(ichioku so zange),* he said, in order to start a new national life. In the confusion and emptiness of wilderness Tokyo, I welcomed gladly the suggestion of national repentance. My Christian sentiment told me that the suggestion was right and timely. We had committed a crime against humanity, as the Americans had put it.

To my surprise I began to hear from my friends and others strong objections to the *ichioku so zange.* They argued that the Japanese people were victims, not perpetrators, of the crimes committed by their military and fascist rulers. Our leaders must repent, but we were innocent. The brutal truth about human community, I learned, was that the majority of the people can be hostaged by a tiny section of the community. "Japan did not go to war," I repeated to myself. "Some Japanese leaders took the Japanese nation to war." This was my first experience with the complexity of history. There is no destruction without manipulation. Historical "waste and void" comes to us when one section of humanity manipulates others. The manipulators must indeed repent of their crime against humanity. Yet, I felt that the manipulated are not completely innocent. The leaders of Japan were able to act violently against her neighbors because the majority of the people allowed themselves to be manipulated by the few.

"Repent!" the Prince Prime Minister Higashikuni had shouted in wilderness Tokyo. News reporters asked him whether the government would immediately and clearly tell the entire nation the reasons why Japan lost the war. He answered:

2. From the *Engi* Period Law *(Engi-Shiki)* of AD 907.

We were defeated because of the rapid destruction of our military power. . . . In addition to this, the appearance of the nuclear bomb of incredible annihilating capacity and the military advance by the Soviet Union caused the defeat. So many rules and laws had been issued almost indiscriminately during the war years, and they had incapacitated national life. This may be one of the major reasons for the defeat we suffered. Then I am afraid that the government itself, government bureaucrats and military persons led our nation unconsciously and unknowingly in this context. I mean that they thought they were struggling for the country while in truth during that time our country had fallen into the illness of arteriosclerosis, and the result was that the nation suffered a sudden death by stroke. I must also mention the miserably low quality of national morality to be one of the reasons for the defeat. That is to say, the military and government people openly and the people at large secretly had engaged in activities of black market. I of course understand that the bad policies of the government had driven people to black market, but I still maintain that the general low standard of national morality was one of the reasons for the defeat. Now I make a call to all Japanese people, including those in the military and government, that we must examine what we had done and repent. The first step for the reconstruction of our nation begins with the repentance by the hundred million Japanese people. This is, I believe, the first step to unite the nation.[3]

The Prime Minister reviews the war years and enumerates possible reasons for the defeat of the war. Japan was defeated primarily because of the inadequacy in military might. Then comes this mysterious yet very useful Japanese expression: "unconsciously and unknowingly," which implies that the leaders were not really responsible for the war and its tragic end. They were sincere and dedicated to the war aims, but somewhere, where their knowledge could not reach, "arteriosclerosis" was taking place. They were not directly responsible for this illness. One day, suddenly, came a stroke and the nation died. We encounter this "sudden stroke" view of history in the Rescript of Ending War.

But now the war has lasted for nearly four years. Despite the best that has been done by everyone — the gallant fighting of the military and naval forces, the diligence and assiduity of our servants of the State and the de-

---

3. *Hidaka Rokuro*, ed., *Sengo Shiso no Shuppatsu* (Beginning of the Post War Thought) (Chikuma Shobo, 1976), p. 54.

voted service of our one hundred million people — the war situation has developed not necessarily to Japan's advantage, while the general trends of the world have all turned against her interest.

In this paragraph and in the rest of the Rescript there was not one word or one line that calls for a critical examination of Japanese ideology and behavior up to the end of the war. The Rescript says that all Japanese worked diligently to achieve the war aim, but "the war situation has developed not necessarily to Japan's advantage." Japan is, somehow, from the emperor to everyone on the streets, not really responsible for what had happened to her and to her neighbors. She was diligent. She suffered a stroke and died.

"Repent!" But to whom? To ourselves? To the emperor? To the Americans? To the Buddha? To the principle of humanity? The emperor "repented" "before the hallowed spirits of the imperial ancestors" as he indicated in the Rescript of Ending War. What did it mean to repent before the "hallowed spirits of the imperial ancestors" under whose protection we began the war? They had not saved the nation. When fanatical state shintoists and military leaders committed suicide by *harakiri* to atone for their sin before the emperor I felt their act, though intensely patriotic, to be futile. There is something common between suffering a stroke and committing *harakiri* in the context of a historical crisis which poses questions regarding human responsibility. In both cases the persons involved escape, ultimately escape, the question of responsibility. And what does it mean to feel responsible to the departed spirits, even the spirits of the imperial ancestors? Should we not acknowledge our guilt to living persons? To the Koreans, Indonesians, Singaporeans, and Burmese?

Would it be appropriate to repent before the spirits of the war dead, military and civilian, of our own people and of other nations, who lost their lives in a war which we started? When thought goes to the dead, the Japanese culture places more emphasis upon the "pacification of departed spirits" (*irei*) than upon the repentance of the living. The tradition of *irei* is a deep stream in Japanese religiosity. Unpacified spirits (*onryo*) are greatly feared by the people for the havoc they can cause among the living. Yet I have never heard, at least from the official quarters, the suggestion that the defeat in 1945 was caused by the countless *onryo* the recent violent history of Japan had produced. Should we be consistent to our own ancient tradition about the vengeful acts of the *onryo*, then, we must honestly say that the defeat came because of the retaliation by the unpacified spirits.

In the ancient tradition no distinction had been made between the dead as to whether they had fought for the emperor or not. All spirits must be equally pacified. But this tradition has been changed since 1869 when the Japanese government established the Shrine of Pacification of the War Dead, inviting 3,588 spirits that had been loyal to the emperor only to be enshrined. This partial arrangement, I would suppose, must have produced many *onryo*. This point, however, has been conveniently ignored since such discussion will effect anti-patriotic feeling about the state. The important point is that it is thought to be possible to engage in the efficacious act of the pacification of the spirits without going through spiritual repentance on the part of the living. That the living must receive decisive importance over the pacification of the dead, and that it is by not repeating war we may in truth pacify the spirits of the war dead, goes against the "sudden death by stroke" type of view of history. It asks with all seriousness the location of responsibility for the war. We are responsible to history. We must not becloud this clear sense of historical responsibility by rhetoric of "the spirits of imperial ancestors."

Should we repent before the victorious Americans? This was a good possibility. Many people apologized to the Americans for what we had done. But then we remembered the saturation bombings of population centers and the nuclear attack upon two cities which had taken place only a month earlier. If we had destroyed others, they had destroyed us. Was it necessary for American bombers to draw a circle of fire with the fire-bombs and then to crisscross within the circle so that no one could escape the fire? The important difference between Japan and the United States at that moment seemed to be that Japan was defeated and the United States was victorious. Somehow, we sensed, in history to be victorious is not necessarily to be righteous. When we thought of repenting to the Americans we were faced with the disturbing image of saturation bombing. In spite of the atrocities we ourselves had committed during war, how could we repent of our sin to a nation that had dropped nuclear bombs upon two fully inhabited cities? In the concrete historical situation of 1945 the question to whom should they repent was not an easy one for the Japanese.

It seemed to me that we should repent before the defenseless peoples upon whom we had inflicted injury: the Chinese, Filipinos, Koreans, Malaysians, Burmese, Indonesians, and others. We had scarcely known these people. Japanese education had mentioned them only as "inferior" and "subordinate" peoples. We had not studied their cultures and languages. They were just people "over there" without any human reality. How could we repent before people of whom we had no knowledge? In the frantic history of our self-righteousness we had ignored the peoples. Self-righteousness had destroyed our education and finally it deprived us of our mental ability to repent meaningfully.

Japan had perpetrated a great injury outside herself. Yet when the moment of repentance came she retreated into her own parochial mythology, to the "hallowed spirits of the imperial ancestors." We were not happy with this parochial retreat, but what could we do, finding ourselves so ill-equipped to repent? There was no way to communicate our sense of repentance to the neighboring peoples through such "hallowed spirits." The call to repentance made by the first prime minister in the post-war period, which seemed so noble, was miscarried. I envied the simple straightforwardness of the son in the parable of Jesus who was able to say, "Father, I have sinned against heaven and before you . . ." (Luke 15:18); I was particularly impressed by the words "against heaven and before you." They indicate both universal and particular contexts in which his repentance took place. What he did was wrong in the eyes of universal humanity, or simply before "God," and in particular it injured the person to whom he was in the most fundamental sense related. I know that no nation, as nation, would engage in an act of repentance, even though some of its members may do so. It is perhaps the lack of a sense of responsibility for historical events that made even personal repentance difficult for the Japanese people. How one understands history has a determinative effect upon the spiritual capacity for repentance.

Yet, by the grace of God, the moment of defeat was a time of purification. The demonically inflated ideology of the state was eliminated — it came violently and it went away violently — and we began to search after a universal perspective of human value from which we could look at ourselves. The historical experience of "nearing to zero" was a strangely creative moment. I cannot read the story of the prodigal son without thinking of that time in 1945.

> So he went and joined himself to one of the citizens of that country, who sent him into his fields to feed swine. And he would gladly have fed on the pods that the swine ate; and no one gave him anything. But when he came to himself . . . (Luke 15:15-17)

He became a spiritually awakened person when he was forced to feed the swine!

In wilderness Tokyo we were hungry. We were confused. The wilderness outside invaded our souls. There was, however, one attractive aspect of the desolation as I know it now. Desolation is uncluttered. It has a stark simplicity. The wilderness threatens but it also issues an invitation to meditate upon the essentials. Desolation had purified our souls. With a certain sense of surprise I was able to appreciate a bit from Jeremiah: "I remember the devotion of your youth, your love as a bride, how you followed me in the wilderness, in a land not sown" (2:2). In my Christian experience the image of baptism and that of wilderness became inexpressibly united. Baptism, the renewal of life, has meant to me, all these years, an experience of spiritual purification "in the wilderness, in a land not sown." In my mind an outer event, the destruction of proud, violent Japan, and an inner event, my baptismal death in the hope of new life in the risen Christ, coincided. What happened in 1945 to Japan has become a part of my Christian identity.

I understand that in the wilderness we also show our worst stubbornness and destructiveness. The uncluttered space contains the intersection of schemings and mutual oppressions and of spiritual purification. Yet, basically my experience of wilderness Tokyo was expressed in the words of Jeremiah quoted above. It is a strange feeling to see the wilderness Tokyo in the light of the prophet who lived in such a distant time and place. I was looking at the Japan of 1945 not in the light of the "hallowed spirits of the imperial ancestors" but in the words of the sixth century BC prophet, Jeremiah. This experience, which, with all its implications, was not clear to me then, has stayed with me ever since. In the post-war years I became the Jeremiah-theologian.

On 11 September 1945, from the Headquarters of General MacArthur, Supreme Commander of the Allied Powers, came the directive for the arrest of the wartime leaders. As the International Military Tribunal for the Far East progressed, the Japanese people came to know how irresponsible their wartime leaders had been. They had enjoyed a "sacred" system of irresponsibility built upon the divinity of the emperor.

On 27 September the emperor paid a visit to Douglas MacArthur. A photograph taken at the time of their meeting was published by the Japanese press. Here we saw a small man, whom we had thought to be divine, standing with a tall Westerner. Whatever the intention of MacArthur may have been, the impact of that photograph upon the Japanese people was shocking. It was driven home to us that the Japanese people are not a special people, but a very ordinary people — even an inferior people — among other peoples of the world.

A few days later, on 4 October, the Supreme Command of Allied Powers issued the Directive on the Removal of Restrictions on Political and Other

Liberties which since then has been called "The Japanese Bill of Rights." It began in the following manner:

> In order to remove restrictions on political, civil and religious liberties and discriminations on grounds of race, nationality, creed or political opinion, the Imperial Japanese Government will: (a) Abrogate and immediately suspend the operation of all provisions of all laws, decrees, orders, ordinances and regulations which; (1) Establish or maintain restrictions on freedom of thought, of religion, of assembly and of speech, including the unrestricted discussion of the Emperor, the Imperial Institution and the imperial Japanese Government.[4]

"Unrestricted discussion of the Emperor"! This had been unthinkable for about eighty years. An invitation to free exercise of reason has been issued to the Japanese people. Article 97 of the post-war Constitution of Japan (1947) reads:

> The fundamental human rights by this Constitution guaranteed to the people of Japan are fruits of the age-old struggle of man to be free; they have survived the many exacting tests for durability and are conferred upon this and future generations in trust, to be held for all time inviolate.[5]

During the years when the discussion of the Emperor was strictly forbidden, deemed as treason, there was a small number of people who fought for fundamental human rights. They were brutally suppressed by the government. We must remember their costly sacrifices for their vision of human rights as we think of the great history of struggle unfolded in the nations of the West over many centuries. The fruits of that age-old struggle reached Japan in 1947. In the language of the fundamental law of the land, now Japan has been grafted to the sacred heritage of Western humanity.

The victor treated us more generously than we deserved. In 1948 on the day when seven A-Class War Criminals were hanged in Tokyo, the president of Tokyo Union Theological Seminary read II Kings 25:6, 7 in the morning worship service:

---

4. Arnold J. Toynbee, ed., *Survey of International Affairs* (published under the auspices of the British Institute of International Affairs, Oxford University Press), p. 507.

5. Fujii Shinichi, *The Constitution of Japan: A Historical Survey* (Kokushikan University, 1965), p. 322. The English text of the constitutions, both of 1889 and 1947, is taken from this book.

Then they captured the king, and brought him up to the king of Babylon at Riblah, who passed sentence upon him. They slew the sons of Zedekiah before his eyes, and put out the eyes of Zedekiah, and bound him in fetters and took him to Babylon.[6]

The members of the imperial family were not put to death in front of the emperor. The emperor did not lose his eyes. We were not taken into exile to slavery. Japan was not divided into West Japan and East Japan, or North Japan and South Japan. We were well treated by the Americans even to the degree that our Asian neighbors, the people who had suffered much under Japan during the war, felt that justice had not been done.

What had happened in 1945?

Tokyo, like many other Japanese cities, had become a wilderness. "How lonely sits the city that was full of people! How like a widow has she become, she that was great among the nations!" (Lam. 1:1). The glory of Tokyo was broken, discontinued. So complete a destruction of the great cities of the nation gave the people the despairing impression that the life of the nation was discontinued. But this is a philosophical description. There is no complete discontinuity in human history so long as there are survivors. The discontinuity was of another nature. What we felt was that the Japanese tribal gods — the legion of them — could not save the people from the hands of the Americans this time.

Japan has twice in her long history been engaged in war with mighty nations, first with the Mongols in the thirteenth century and now with the United States in the twentieth century. The former was a war within Asia, a culturally local war, while the latter was between two very different cultures, religions, and civilizations. The military might of the Mongols was far superior to that of the Japanese when they invaded Japan in 1274 and 1281; but twice the invasion was frustrated by the sudden arrival of a strong typhoon, which from that time has been called the "Divine Wind" (*kamikaze*) by the Japanese. Japan was narrowly spared from the Mongols by sheer accidents in nature. The end of the war against the United States came with a far greater violence. The bombs blasted over inhabited cities. When these two interna-

6. According to the Information Center of the United Church of Christ in Japan (Bulletin issued on 20 June 1979), the officials of Yasukuni Shrine for the War Dead revealed that 1,005 war criminals have been added to the list of *kami* (gods) at the Shrine during the decade between 1969 and 1979. These new names include Tojo Hideki and other A Class war criminals. This was done secretly and only made public in 1979.

tional wars occurred, some 660 years apart, the government asked the people to pray at the shinto shrines and Buddhist temples for the "surrender of the enemy and victory of the Divine Land." In the thirteenth century it seemed that the nationwide prayer was answered. There was, as a matter of fact, a strong feeling of jealousy after the war on the part of the warriors against the gods and buddhas. The warriors felt that their sacrifice was not properly appreciated when the nation became so enthusiastically thankful to the Divine Wind. I think every war situation would produce this kind of tension between "warriors" and "gods." The nationwide prayer did not succeed in the case of war with the United States. The *kamikaze* did not blow. The spirits of the imperial ancestors were unable to protect the nation and the nation was destroyed. For the first time, in a serious manner, the Japanese people's faith in their own tribal gods was shaken.

What does this mean? It means that the national politics based on the ideological mythology of the solar goddess did not work. This was the message to the Japanese. But not to all the Japanese people. The great majority of the people never have believed in the imperial religion of ultranationalism. The imperial religion was a state ideology forced upon all the people without their willing consent. They were not surprised by the fact that the spirits of the imperial ancestors did not save Japan from the United States. They were, on the contrary, relieved from the spiritual and mental strain of their subordination to the power of the mythical state ideology. It had taken a great deal of national psychological energy to keep alive the impossible mythical ideology! The defeat of war showed the people that their gods were powerless and irrelevant to the challenges humankind faces in the twentieth century. Humor had disappeared from the nation. People became incapacitated to laugh about themselves. When idolatry intensified, humanity progressively disappeared. An old man came to me one day when I was a young boy and whispered to me that if Japan did win the war against the United States, she would lose it all the same since there is no way for Japan to govern the vast land and people of the United States beyond the great Pacific Ocean! Besides that, they speak a different language than Japanese and there will be thousands of snipers aimed at the "Japanese Occupational Force"! He continued and said that, of course, if Japan loses the war, it loses it! In both cases Japan is lost. Then he laughed heartily. This was my only humorous moment in the war time of idolatrous dead-seriousness.

The nation was paralyzed under the tyranny of the divine mythology. When the best of Japanese scholars were banned, the exercise of reason was condemned and the people were fed with unreasoned slogans which proclaimed that Japan was the righteous nation and her enemy was devilish. The world seemed divided into two camps, that of good people and that of the bad. The Japanese were good and the United States was the focus of all evil. Any attempt to reason about the validity of such a sweeping and unreasonable position was dealt with quickly by the mythology-committed government as coming from unpatriotic and dangerous elements of society. The identification of one's own country as a righteous nation is idolatry. The words of the apostle Paul sound sharply against national as well as personal self-righteousness.

> I have already charged that all men, both Jews and Greeks, are under the power of sin, as it is written: "None is righteous, no, not one, no one understands, no one seeks for God. All have turned aside, together they have gone wrong; no one does good, not even one." (Rom. 3:9-12)

The devastating effect of the edging out of reason by political mythology is that soon ethics will be ousted. Ethics arise from a human concern with understanding human conduct, individual as well as collective. To reflect critically on human conduct requires that the neighbor be taken seriously. Any ethics or human morality which ignores the presence of the other is a self-centered system which works against the common good of humanity. Human ethics must aim to achieve the broad, common good of humanity. The mythological ethics of Japan aimed only at the good of the Japanese nation, perhaps, in the final showdown, at the good of her leaders. This spelled the moral downfall of Japan. A self-centered ethics, if it can be called ethics, is idolatrous.

With reason and ethics out of the way, the stage was set for the worst kind of social manipulation. Political propaganda about the cult of the divine emperor made it possible for the leaders to take away from the people their right, even their ability, to protest. They were led as sheep to the slaughter. Families surrendered their young men to be sacrificed on beachheads, in the air, and on the sea. Food, freedom, and security were sacrificed on the altar of the imperial cult. Yet there were probably few, even among the leaders, who believed that the emperor was divine. After the war, government leaders, including the emperor himself, openly said that the idea of the divinity of the emperor was illusory.

The manipulation of the people receives its inspiration at the altar of idols. What, then, is idolatry?

But before we move on to the discussion of idolatry, we must make one more observation of the experience of Japanese people. The imperial cult did not save the nation from the attack by the United States. They prayed to their gods; the gods did not respond to their prayers. The classic image of the non-response of the idols is given in the story of Elijah as he battles against the prophets of Baal.

> "O Baal, answer us!" But there was no voice and no one answered. . . . And they cried aloud, and cut themselves after their custom with swords and lances, until the blood gushed out upon them. And as midday passed, they raved on until the time of the offering of the oblation, but there was no voice; no one answered, no one heeded. (I Kings 18:26, 28, 29)

The God of Elijah, however, answered Elijah's prayer. The people cried out, "the Lord, he is God; the Lord, he is God" (v. 39). The Elijah episode of Mount Carmel gives us a powerful paradigm for our theology of false gods and true God. The true God responds while the false gods do not and cannot. It may be said, however, that this is not necessarily what faith in God experiences all the time. It is possible that the true God does not respond to our prayer, and the false gods respond to the prayers of their believers. Perhaps the most agonizing of sayings in the whole Bible is the cry of Jesus on the cross: "My God, my God, why hast thou forsaken me?" (Mark 15:34), which points to the first possibility. The Japanese gods and buddhas responding to the prayer of Japanese people at the time of the Mongol invasion may illustrate the second possibility.

The religious experiences of humanity are extremely complex. We must take up the Elijah paradigm with our utmost theological perception so that we may hear from it its fundamental message. As we do so the concept of the holy comes into the background of our thought. If God is the holy One, then God is someone we cannot place under our control.

38 The Theological Implications of the Current Situation in the Holy Land: From the Point of View of a Christian Palestinian

Rafiq Khoury

In the second half of the nineteenth century, two kinds of nationalism arose: Jewish nationalism, which took on concrete forms in the Zionist organization; and the Palestinian, which was an integral element of the Palestinian-Arab nationalist movement. They opposed one another in Palestine, because both claimed this land as the territory for their own state — the one in the shape of a plan, the other on the basis of an obvious reality, which rests on a long history of at least thirteen hundred years. From this coexistence arose a painful conflict between the two kinds of nationalism, which is known as "the Israeli-Arab" or "Israeli-Palestinian" conflict.

This conflict has existed now for more than a century and has taken on various forms, among which was a series of bloody wars, one after another, in which much blood flowed and much wrong was done. The main victim of the conflict was the Palestinian people: a large portion of them was forcibly pushed to the margin of their homeland, while another remained in place, but was confronted there with a tense situation and robbed of their fundamental rights.

About ten years ago [ca. 1991] a peace process was initiated. Today, however, we know that this peace process had a bad beginning and developed in such a way that it had no chance of leading to a just and lasting peace. The second Intifada is simply the direct result of this development, which has been marked by insecurity and misunderstandings. We presently find ourselves in

---

Translated by Michael J. Hollerich.

an utterly absurd situation that cannot go on indefinitely and cannot leave us indifferent. For the Israeli-Palestinian conflict, the hour of truth is at hand. It is urgently necessary to become aware of this truth: it cannot be avoided, if we want to spare all concerned much suffering and innocent bloodshed.

Does theology have something to say to this conflict? In my contribution I would like to shed light on the theological implications which in one way or another have accompanied the conflict throughout the course of its history. Obviously the standpoint represented here is that of a Christian Palestinian. In the hour of truth all voices must be heard unconditionally if we are to create a just and peaceful future for a land that is in such tragic need of it. That holds for all of us, not just for the parties directly concerned.

1. Political Projects and Theological Justifications

It is indisputable that from the beginning the conflict has taken on a religious character, because the Zionist organization in both its secular and its religious branch justified on biblical grounds its claim to Palestine as state territory. Despite the highly diversified forms of Jewish thought in this area, it remains to be established that the foundation of the state of Israel is justified for most people by biblical texts that are treated either as expression of the divine will or as historical and cultural proof for the bond between the Jewish people and the land of Palestine. On the basis of this conviction, which in addition was buttressed by the celebrated (but false) Zionist slogan "A land without people for a people without land," the first "pioneers" embarked on the domination of Palestine — now by settlement (in the original sense of this word), now by force of arms.

Among Christians — especially of course in the West — such an attitude, which in the first instance rested on a fundamentalist interpretation of the Bible, could gain in power especially in certain Protestant circles. "The Christian Embassy in Jerusalem," which stands in solidarity with Israeli extremists, is today one of the unhappy and mistaken manifestations of this attitude. But especially after the Second World War, among Catholics engaged in Jewish-Christian dialogue, a specifically Catholic theology grew up which enjoys an ever wider acceptance in Catholic circles.

Naturally it is impossible here to explore in any detail the details and nuances of these biblical and theological visions. Despite the risk of over-schematizing, however, we can say that these visions in varying degree play out as a theological justification for the return of the Jews to the Promised

Land and the founding of the state of Israel. This leads partly to political positions that have taken root on the edge of rational thinking.

Obviously this theology — or better, these theologies — leave the Palestinians, at least, at a loss. In it they see:

- *The theological justification of a political process:* We know that theology, when it puts itself at the service of politics, can unleash tragic consequences, whether intended or not. It must be said that such an intellectual project is more ideological than theological, and it has already had many funerals. In the history of religions there are plenty of unhappy examples. In Palestine this way of thinking has led to the Palestinians' subjection to one of the most outrageous injustices of the previous century — a fact that we have to repeat at both convenient and inconvenient moments.

- *The advocacy of oppression:* After the Palestinian people became a victim of injustice, it was further exposed to various intolerable forms of oppression. Such a theology can only be a supportive instrument of oppression — whether unintentionally or unconsciously is no excuse. In every instance it subjects its adherents to a psychological state of mind that keeps it from being aware of the way things really are. For when one attributes a political project to God, the result is an a priori guarantee of its innocence. Doesn't this lead us to a theology that oppresses others?

- *A theology that stems more from the psychological than the strictly theological sphere:* We know that this theology has developed in a West that was truly traumatized by the phenomenon of anti-Semitism, the most demonic expression of which was the Shoah, with its unimaginable horrors. This phenomenon has enormously influenced theological reflection on Israel and the Israeli-Palestinian conflict. Anti-Semitism and its numerous ancient as well as modern forms of expression, which are totally irrational, have particularly in the West led to a guilt-complex regarding the Jewish people. Such a complex is not a healthy, dispassionate basis for developing a balanced theology that can deal with the questions posed by the conflict in the Holy Land. It is especially difficult in such a reflection to draw the boundaries between the psychological and the theological. May we suggest that both anti-Semitism and philo-Semitism can arise from an imbalanced mindset, one which in theology tries to find debatable justifications?

- *A selective theology:* A theology that depends on psychology and ideology cannot help but be reductionist and selective — reductionist both in what concerns the biblical revelation and the actual historical facts in Palestine. It not infrequently happens that such a theology appeals to one set of texts from biblical revelation (which are then taken out of context) while ignoring others that do not reinforce preconceived opinions. (In which case are we not faced with a misuse of the Bible?) Such a theology is similarly reductionist — and this at times in crass fashion — relative to the actual historical realities in Palestine (for example, when it denies to the Palestinians the designation as a "people") and to the concrete realities of the Holy Land. Are we not right to mistrust such a theology?

2. Theological Questions

The religious implications of the Israeli-Palestinian conflict force us to ask important and unavoidable theological questions. These questions are *of two types, one general and the other specific.*

A. Questions of a General Type

The questions of a general type fall into three categories: *Who is God? Who is the other? Who am I?*

Who is God? The question seems impertinent. But in the context of the Israeli-Palestinian conflict (and in the re-evaluation of religion that is occurring nearly everywhere) it becomes an urgent question which deserves a serious answer. The occupation of Palestine, with all the inequities that accompanied it, took place specifically in the name of God and of his promises. A Palestinian can't help asking the following burning, fearful questions: Who is this God in whose name we had to suffer such injustice? Is it a particularist, national God, a tribal deity, or a universal God, whose mercy and compassion include all peoples? Is it a God who stands against the oppressed and on the side of the oppressors? Is the state of Israel a "theocracy" that must be accepted on the basis of a divine *Diktat* that admits of no compromise? Is God a partitioner of land, who prefers the one and excludes the other? Is God an idol, in whose name it is permissible to commit injustice, or a mysterious God, who summons us to compassion and mercy?

Who is the other? In a historical context marked by changes in social mobility, transportation, migration, and communication that more and more bring peoples into contact with one another, "otherness" has become more than ever one of the great questions facing humanity. In the Holy Land, with all of its problems, this question takes on special color and urgency. The question of the relation between the state of Israel and the residents of the land stands in the middle of the discussion. Of what sort is the relationship of this state to the other residents of the land? What relationship do these residents have to the land? Are they merely "aliens" and "guests"? Do these biblical concepts suffice to define their identity and their equality with the Jews? Are the Palestinians in the occupied territories for their part simple residents, to whom only basic human rights apply? Or are they rather a people to whom fundamental international laws should apply? Does not the exclusive concept of the "Eretz-Israel," with its extremist applications, lead to an equally extremist reaction among some Palestinians who say "All of Palestine is ours" and thereby drive all of us into a blind alley and the spiral of violence? These are all questions of a far from academic kind. They touch the problem at its most sensitive points and confront Israeli society with choices that can fundamentally affect the whole conflict. They are therefore not of an exclusively political type: they also require a theological discussion.

Who am I? In the Holy Land we see two competing identities that both appeal to the same right to the land. Do they have to be exclusive ("him or me")? Does one have to exterminate the other in order to survive? Who is a Jew (if that as such is a theological question)? . . . We know that when the state of Israel was founded an intense debate broke out over this question, which to this day has yet to find a definitive resolution. But the concepts in which the debate is conducted concern only the Jews. Shouldn't the debate be widened in order to ask whether the non-Jews (in this case the Palestinians who live in the state of Israel) do not belong in a constitutive and organic way in the definition of the state of Israel? Does not the Palestinian element belong as an essential element in the discussion?

B. Questions of a Specific Kind

To the questions of a general type are added questions of a more specific kind. They concern biblical concepts that served as the theological basis of the justification of the state of Israel: the promises, the election, the land, the people. . . . In this connection numerous questions arise: Do the interpretations that are commonly and traditionally given to these realities suffice to deal with all the contemporary questions that the reality of the Holy Land poses? Is the land more important than the human person? Does not the danger exist that the celebrated concept of "Eretz-Israel" may usurp the place of God and humanity, to the point that it begins to function like an idol? How are promise and election supposed to be understood? In an exclusive or an inclusive sense, and in what way? Do they have to be taken in the sense of power and superiority, or in the sense of service and mission? And what do service and mission look like? We constantly hear about the faithfulness of God to his promises. What type of faithfulness is at work here? What does it really mean? What meaning does the election of a people have? What relationship is there between the universal (all peoples) and the particular (a specific people)? Do they include or exclude one another, and in what way? Why are such essential biblical concepts as the injustice and oppression that are the core of the prophets' proclamations left out of account? . . . What meaning do these concepts receive by virtue of Jesus Christ? Does not the proclamation of the Gospel bring out a deeper meaning in these concepts, by endowing them with a more inclusive and universal sense? The list of such questions could be extended indefinitely.

Clearly these questions are not mere intellectual speculation or simple mental games. They are questions of the highest importance, whose implications directly affect the fate of peoples. In the case of the Palestinian people, these one-sidedly and mistakenly interpreted biblical concepts form the basis for an ideology of expropriation and injustice under which this people does not cease to suffer grievously.

C. Questions of the Interpretation of the Bible

We see that the Bible stands right in the middle of the theological discussion. The Christian Palestinians have been accused of Marcionism, as if they were trying to reject the Old Testament. No one would dispute that reading the Bible may evoke a certain unease in the Christian Palestinian. He can't help referring what he reads there to the actual situation that he is living under. In that case his unease can turn into real anguish. The Palestinian asks himself whether salvation history is not perhaps a history that has developed at his cost. It must be stressed, however, that the Palestinian has no problem with the Bible in itself (Old and New Testament), in which he believes as an integral element in his apostolic faith, but with interpretations of it that operate too often in a selective, superficial, and ideological way. Who could blame him for that? When he sees how Jewish settlers with Bible in arm manage the occupied territories, and how in the name of God they arrogantly and forcibly confiscate land from Palestinian farmers, how can he help but ask himself such questions? Or when he reads in the *Jerusalem Post* letters from Christian readers who give a biblical justification for injustice and oppression, or when he sees that certain aspects, of the Old Testament at least, are offensively applied to him (Amalekites = Palestinians . . .), how is he likely to react to that? Or when he reads theological arguments over Israel (state, people, land . . .) without seeing his own drama mentioned at all, what is he then supposed to think? When the Palestinian sees himself betrayed by a certain one-sided theology and then feels that he has been led badly by his own church, how can he not be prey to anguish and confusion?

The interpretation of the Bible in these theological circles is mostly done in selective fashion. It is based on texts that could serve — consciously or unconsciously — the ideology that governs them, while leaving others unnoticed that could exert a disturbing or unsettling influence. The interpretation is superficial, for it readily limits itself to things that only support its ideological intentions and discredits others that are not amenable to their cause. All of this clearly falls into the realm of ideology, in the sense of a preconceived opinion that one tries to justify with theological flights of fancy, whose only purpose is to subject the word of God to the service of their ideology. Weren't there people — numerous Catholic enthusiasts among them — who, their good judgment impaired by elation over the June 1967 war, compared Moshe Dayan to Moses? One can imagine where such an ideology may lead and how suited it is to ease the way to oppressive policies, before which people close their eyes lest they find them disturbing.

All of which demands a biblical interpretation that takes into account the whole Bible and all the actual circumstances in the Holy Land.

3. Hermeneutical Reference Points

Everything that has been said to this point surely raises a hermeneutical question: How should the Bible be interpreted? It is neither our intention nor within our capability to present the kind of comprehensive biblical hermeneutics that would be appropriate. We will limit ourselves to offering some reference points for the discussion that could contribute to developing such a hermeneutic — one that could lead to a better understanding of the Bible (and consequently also to a more inclusive theology) and also shed more light on the situation in the Holy Land, which is more complex than people think.

A. The Hermeneutics of the Questions

Theology, like every intellectual endeavor, runs the risk of basing itself on fundamental and uncontested assumptions that no one dares to subject to questioning. Can one, for example, start from the solitary conviction that Palestine is a land that was promised unconditionally to the people of Israel, and build on that premise a whole theology which only considers this aspect of the problem and — intentionally or unintentionally — rules out other aspects (such as the reality of the Palestinian people) that could contribute nuances or even corrections that, in turn, would totally change elements of the original posing of the question? To cite another example: Is it likewise sufficient to develop a complete theology on the meaning of the state of Israel that rests on the firmly rooted and incontestable certitude that Israel is a special state for a special people in a special history? Do we not risk ending up asserting that the rules of universal justice have no relevance to this state? Does this not ultimately entail a form of concealed though real racism (election-elitism-racism)? It is easily recognized that in such a case the way is open to ignore or conceal the injustice that this state can commit, and even the injustice on which it itself is based.

Unfortunately, the modern history of the state of Israel, and the theology allied with it, is full of presuppositions that can't be discussed and that ultimately become myths and taboos, the consequences of which directly affect the fate of millions of men and women. It is time to force a breach in this way of thinking, but to do so in a sound and considered way that can promote the well-being of everyone involved. The hermeneutics of the questions consists in posing for oneself the questions — and even in putting *oneself* in question — in order to open the way towards a question that could not be more complex.

B. The Dynamic of Salvation History

Salvation has a history. Whoever says "history" means movement — and precisely movement forwards. Salvation history is not a static but a dynamic history, directed by a God of love, who prepares a way in the concrete history of human beings.

In this area *two* dangers are possible: The *first* consists of singling out a chapter of salvation history (e.g., regarding the land) and applying it univocally, just as it is, to a given situation. Does that not mean the hardening of salvation history at the cost of overlooking later developments (even within the Old Testament) and of turning the chief agent of this history — God himself — into an idol which suits our human plans? The *second* danger consists in dealing with a certain selection of biblical passages, and in paying attention only to those which tend towards one's own decisions, if not political and ideological presuppositions. Does that not lead to the distortion of salvation history and the setting of limits to its inner dynamic? I have the impression that the theology here described has in one way or another tended in both these directions.

Entering into the dynamic of salvation history means being integrated into the forward movement of a sacred history, in which one chapter sublates its predecessor and incorporates it into new horizons whose ultimate fulfillment is the kingdom of God. To be sure, the instrument of this dialectic is the word of God itself; but it is also the "signs of the times" that help to integrate the word of God into this movement. It seems to me that such an entering into salvation history can open domains that progressively widen and deepen, in ways that include and embrace, rather than exclude and isolate. God's ever new dimensions are thus always being inscribed in new dimensions of human history.

C. The Christological Angle

For a Christian, Jesus Christ is the central point of this dynamic of salvation history. Everything moves towards him and everything issues forth from him. Jesus Christ has transcended all the elements of salvation history from within, in order to endow them with a universal dimension, to be sure without neglecting the particular, which he rather incorporated within the dynamic of a humanity that is on its way towards the kingdom of God. For the Christian, God's faithfulness to his promises henceforth has a name that one cannot get around: *Jesus Christ.* For the Christian, he remains a way upon which every reflection on the realities of the Old Testament, such as the land, the promise, the people, etc., must travel. He it was who in his own body tore down the wall that separated the two communities, in order to make of them a unity and to establish peace between them (cf. Eph. 2:11-22).

Of course one may object that this holds only for Christians and is binding on no one else. In a certain sense that is true. But I think more can be said on this. In the center of human history, Jesus Christ has planted values that have gradually become the legacy of humanity. Can one not, for exam-

574

ple, say that today's universal recognition of human rights is the fruit of the gospel values that Christ brought us? In the case presently before us (the theological implications of the conflict in the Holy Land), we can say that it is no longer possible to think about the realities of the Old Testament (like land, people, etc.), without relating them to the progress in human thinking since the arrival of Jesus Christ. In this instance, can one really develop a theology of the land, limiting oneself strictly to the words of the Bible, with no reference to later developments and human values (such as human dignity) that — to say it again — have become reference points that can relativize the value of land (is land more important than people?)? To people today, God speaks too through these human values.

D. Historical Realities and Salvation History

Human and historical realities are an integral component of the mystery of salvation. They constitute an appeal and yet also conceal a mysterious divine presence, which requires consideration if its meaning and its summons are to be recognized. It would be stupid to think that the history of Palestine came to an end in the year 70 (with the destruction of Jerusalem by the Romans). It would be equally false to think that it came to a halt in 1948, and that there was a historical vacuum that was filled with the founding of the state of Israel (the slogan "A land without people for a people without land" is full of presuppositions) — as well as a suspension in salvation history that the founding of this state set in motion again.

History proceeds on its way, and God accompanies it with his mysterious presence. He invites human beings to participate in the dynamic of history, which continues on its way to its ultimate, salvation-bringing fulfillment. Unfortunately, theological thinking has often developed within the mental framework — perhaps more implicit than explicit — of this sort of vacuum and suspension. One insists, for example, on speaking of the Temple mount and completely forgets the reality of the al-Aqsa Mosque, as if it were located somewhere outside of human history. What do the historical realities that have overlain the Holy Land say to the theologian? Is it possible to take a theological look at these realities, and what kind of look might that be?

I have the feeling that these hermeneutical considerations are appropriate for freeing theology from its lack of transparency, in order to make of it a more inclusive and integrating theology. I am aware that this is difficult theological terrain, while at the same time I believe it is worth the effort to examine it with a keen eye, in order to derive from it all the possible theological conclusions.

4. The Palestinian People as a Question to Theology

The fact of the existence of the Palestinian people in the Holy Land is neither incidental nor peripheral nor secondary in its character. The Palestinian people are neither "aliens" nor "guests" in their land. The Palestinian people are an integral component of the identity of the Holy Land, and this in turn is an integral component of the identity of the Palestinians. Every failure to appreciate this truth leads in the political as well as the theological sphere to a reductive point of view whose practical consequences can't help but be unjust.

Unfortunately, this reality was almost totally ignored by theology, because it was seen as marginal and insignificant. Theology preferred to occupy itself with the meaning of the land and of the people, and with their relationship to one another. Such a partial point of view opens the door to the colonization of the occupied territories (which has been conducted with classic colonialist methods), which is commonly presented as a redemption (in the religious sense) of the land. The confiscation of Palestinian property through force and violence[1] is taking place in the name of this point of view (the appeal to "security" is merely a pretext).

It is true that some — through a misplaced even if authentic good intention — consider the Palestinians under the heading of "human rights." But they seem incapable of making the further leap towards considering them as a people whose reality warrants a theological reflection. It seems to me, however, that a theology of Israel in its present historical reality remains incomplete, if not actually distorted and repressive, so long as it does not include in its thinking the Palestinian people and their historical experience, whether present or past. Following the logic of the hermeneutic reference points discussed above, the Palestinian people are an important subject for theological reflection. They can even be a decisive condition for a balanced theology — without which it can't contribute to opening a path towards a just and genuine peace in the region.

In the Gospel of Mark (10:13-16), the disciples — along with their

---

1. Shouldn't this remind us of the story of Naboth, whose vineyard was unjustly seized by Ahab? Cf. on this Na'im Stifan 'Ateek, *Justice, Nothing but Justice! Towards a Palestinian-Christian Theology* (Fribourg/Brig, 1990), pp. 117-20.

mentality and their prejudices — were sitting with Jesus and taking in his divine teachings with keen delight, when children among the listeners started to act like irritating intruders. The disciples' spontaneous reaction was to shoo away these disturbers of the peace. But Jesus strongly objected to that and, taking the children lovingly in hand, he put them in the center of his attention and his teaching. In the Gospel it goes on to say: "And he took the children in his arms; then he laid his hands on them and blessed them" (Mark 10:16). This can show us that Jesus brought these "inconvenient ones" into salvation history, and thereby rebuked the narrow-mindedness of his disciples, whom he invited to have a broader and truer grasp of the kingdom of God. In this episode in the Gospel, we are confronted with a situation in which the forgotten, "the sick and the lowly," the marginalized persons in human history, become essential elements in the history of salvation. Doesn't salvation come most often to the benefit of those who stand on the margin?

In the current context, theology needs to pose a series of questions: What is the theological significance of the destruction of four hundred Palestinian towns and villages by the Israeli army during and after the war of 1948? What is the meaning of the expulsion at that time of nearly a million Palestinians (today they number more than three million) from their land, in favor of new Jewish immigrants? What is the meaning of the various types of repression imposed on the Palestinians in the occupied territories during the more than thirty years of the occupation? How should one evaluate the fact that Palestinian citizens of the state of Israel are treated as second-class citizens, and what kind of theological outlook is at the basis of such a reality? What are the results of an idolatrous attitude towards the land? Is the land more important than God and human beings? What does the Bible say about oppression? . . . One could extend the list of questions indefinitely.

In every instance, reflection on the theological significance of Israel and of the Israeli state is meaningless or at least incomplete if it does not include a profound reflection on the significance of the Palestinian people, without which theology can't help but succumb to ideology. This is a question of credibility and intellectual integrity, and a test of good will. The exodus of the Jewish people is not to be separated from the exodus of the Palestinian people: they mutually condition one another and also constitute one another's liberation. The way we regard the salvation of the Palestinian people is just the way we regard that of the Jewish people. All the more, therefore, does it seem to me that the substantive and morally compelling consideration of the Palestinian people can very likely mean the ultimate saving of the Jewish people in the Holy Land. Ultimately, the Jews in Israel must realize that only by attending to the salvation of the Palestinians can they themselves arrive at salvation (and also vice versa).

5. The Christian Community in Palestine

One is astonished to hear in our day someone like the prominent churchman Cardinal C. M. Martini, Archbishop of Milan, at a conference on the theme of "Jerusalem," mention the Hebrew-speaking Christian community, in order to ask "what theological significance the re-establishment of a community of Jewish Christians in Jerusalem"[2] could have — without at the same time feeling obliged to mention the two-thousand-year-old Palestinian Christian community, and to pose the question of *its* theological significance in Jerusalem. I would like to point out that the Christian community, just like the Palestinian people, is *the* underappreciated or ignored element, as though it were not part of salvation history as it continues in this world. The slight number[3] of its members does not excuse this neglect (do I need to repeat the point about the lowly and the forgotten?). It is time to bring an end to this omission — on the political as well as on the theological plane.

Everyone has their own take on the Christian community. The Israelis think about it in connection with the Shoah or with the fact that its adherents are Palestinians. It is also often regarded as a fossil community with little or no importance in the discussions that keep the region in turmoil. Their Muslim fellow-citizens often look at them through the lens of a Christian West which they see as the root of all evil. By their Christian brothers, especially in the West, they are unappreciated or scarcely known at all. And when these Christian brothers do come to know them, they are often disconcerted by the Christian Palestinians' diversity, without being able to recognize their richness. At times they are represented as victims caught between the hammer and the anvil, and they themselves can then succumb to a victim mentality and lament their uncertain destiny.

So how do the adherents of the Christian community see themselves in this distorting mirror? They know, despite everything, what they are: *Arabs, Palestinians, Christians.* They know too, like Palestinians in general, that the

2. Cf. C. M. Martini, *La parola nella città* (Bologna, 1982), p. 252.

3. In the occupied territories — including Jerusalem — and in the territories that are under Palestinian authority, there are about 50,000 believers (counting all the denominations).

Holy Land is an essential part of their identity, just as they in turn are an essential part of the identity of the Holy Land — that is, without them the Holy Land would not *be* the Holy Land. And from this standpoint they try, in spite of immense difficulties, to find their place under the sun, in the whirlwind of events that agitate the Holy Land. They continue to try situating themselves in a context which is more difficult than ever.

It must be emphasized that this little community is the one that has suffered the most under the theological deficiencies which we have tried to identify and explain. Naturally the Christian Palestinians were disturbed, if not indignant and angry, as the echo of this theology reached them by one means or another. They were poorly prepared for this theological discussion. But they had no way of answering, except to ask how such a theology can permit the suffering of this people to be forgotten and scant attention be paid to a Christian community that has experienced such a turbulent history. Do they stand on the margin of the history of the Holy Land? Do they constitute a superfluous element in the human and religious geography of Palestine? In the discussion that has concerned us, is there not also a word concerning them that is in danger of being lost? Do they themselves not have something to say as well? Their discontent, their indignation and anger, are all too understandable.

They were disturbed, indignant, and sickened, but they did not become immobilized. In the 1970s, years that were especially decisive for the history of the Near East in general and for the Holy Land in particular, they began to reflect seriously on their presence, their vocation, their witness, and their mission. They began to define and situate themselves, at first in small circles, then in more organized and systematic fashion. We do not intend to devote ourselves to the details of this reflection other than to say that these were years rich with ferment. In such an atmosphere, a Palestinian theology originated, piece by piece, that strove to root its reflection in the real, concrete context of the Holy Land. This reflection already possesses a rather significant theological substance.[4] It had to begin from scratch. In the several Christian churches of the Holy Land, above all in the Catholic and Protes-

---

4. For a detailed investigation of this theology, whose texts for the most part are written in Arabic, cf. Uwe Gräbe, *Kontextuelle palästinensischen Theologie* (Erlangen, 1999). For a comprehensive overview, also Rafiq Khoury, "Palästinensische kontextuelle Theologie: Entwicklung und Sendung" and "Die theologischen Implikationen der aktuellen Situation im Heiligen Land. Aus der Sicht eines christlichen Palästinensers," in Harald Suerman, ed., *Zwischen Halbmond und Davidstern: Christliche Theologie in Palästina Heute* (Freiburg: Herder, 2001), pp. 52-100.

tant ones, theologians have begun to get back on their feet and to search for what they alone could say from their actual situation. It is obvious that the theological questions evoked by Israel and the founding of the state of Israel stood in the center of this reflection.[5]

The question that concerns us in the present context is the following: What is the theological significance of this community in the midst of the various human and religious groupings in the Holy Land? Amidst the ruins of former churches in our land, one often finds baptisteries in which countless generations of Christians born in the land received the grace of baptism, through which they were assimilated into salvation history. This grace continues to be infused in our still living churches. What role does this small remnant play in the secular and religious history of the Holy Land? What is its calling, its mission, and of what type is its witness? What kind of salvific seed does this community bear within itself? . . . Such a reflection is being conducted in a very intensive way. It is not our intention to present all its elements. But it does exist, and it deserves the attention of all. The community needs to be consulted, if the theology that is being developed is supposed to deal with all the problems of the Holy Land. The community constitutes, then, a place for the word of God, the reading of and reflection on which is the necessary basis for understanding.

6. Jerusalem as Theological Challenge

It is not easy to talk about Jerusalem, for it is a city that lets itself be known reluctantly. Much time and a good measure of close-up scrutiny are necessary if one would like to crack the mystery of this city, or rather to let oneself be filled with it. Jerusalem is a city which hurts and heals, which provokes and calms. It is the "Easter city" par excellence. For a Christian — and especially for a Palestinian Christian — this means a great deal.

To speak on the Holy Land, in all its various aspects (political, religious, churchly . . .), without dwelling longer on the subject of Jerusalem, is in my view an inexcusable mistake. Unfortunately, this difficult problem in the political discussions was always deferred, for if it is true that it constitutes a problem, it is also true that it offers elements for a genuine solution of all the

---

5. It needs to be said that the first person who dared to raise these questions from a Palestinian perspective was the Palestinian Anglican pastor Na'im Stifan 'Ateek, in the book cited above.

problems of the Holy Land. Peace begins in Jerusalem. Of course the Holy City stirs up uncontrolled and uncontrollable emotions, and the current situation is not exactly conducive to calm reflection on the calling of this city and its prophetic mission. However, without forgetting what dangerous terrain we're entering, we must be ready for detailed investigation into the mystery of Jerusalem, if we are to understand the appeals and the possibilities that derive from it. In Jerusalem, history and the geography of salvation join hands and unite, in order to bring forth ever new forms of life.

Jerusalem is rich in theological possibilities, which we must be ready to exploit — for the benefit of everyone who lives in this city. Such a theology can be developed only on the basis of the concrete actualities in Jerusalem. Jerusalem must be saved from its myths, which obscure an examination of its actual circumstances. What are these concrete circumstances?

A. The Realities of Jerusalem

The realities of Jerusalem can be ordered in terms of the following slogan-like concepts:

- *Two peoples* (the Israeli and the Palestinian): The presence of both of these peoples in Jerusalem is hardly an illusion. Just going on foot through the Old City of Jerusalem is enough to discover the Arab and Palestinian character of the Holy City, with its typical oriental stamp (which invites comparison with Cairo, Damascus, Beirut, and other cities of the Arab world). And one need only travel the new streets of West Jerusalem in order to realize the Israeli reality in this part of the city, with all the variety that reflects and marks the diversity of the Jewish people. For both peoples, belonging to Jerusalem is something that is inseparable from their innermost national character.
- *Three monotheistic religions* (Judaism, Christianity, Islam): The three monotheistic religions come into contact with one another in Jerusalem. And each one of them is utterly convinced that Jerusalem belongs to its religious identity, to the extent that each believes that without this relationship to Jerusalem it can neither understand itself nor be understood. One can just as little understand Jerusalem apart from these three religions as one can understand them apart from Jerusalem. The symbols of this adhesion are the al-Aqsa Mosque for Muslims, the Wailing Wall for Jews, and the Anastasis basilica for Christians. And this pres-

ence is alive everywhere. Just visiting Jerusalem for the respective feasts of the three religions is enough to show this.

- *Different Christian churches:* Jerusalem is home to several Christian churches: the Orthodox community (Greek Orthodox), the community of the Oriental Orthodox (Armenians, Copts, Syrians), the Catholic community (six different Catholic churches), the Protestant community (primarily Anglicans and Lutherans).[6] Every one of these churches possesses its own history, memory, culture, language, liturgy, theology, spirituality, structure, in short its own heritage. . . . The presence of most of these churches under the cupola of the Anastasis basilica has a high symbolic value. They are different, but all are called to unity in Christ.
- *Two worlds* (East and West): Behind these two peoples, the Israeli and the Palestinian, two worlds face one another: the East and the West. We know that the juxtaposition of these two worlds in Jerusalem has not been simple (crusades, colonization, the problem of the Palestinians . . .). In Jerusalem the boundary between East and West is not a body of water (the Mediterranean Sea), but only a small street which separates East Jerusalem from West Jerusalem. Are both worlds there in order to speak with one another? In order to live together? In order to fight? To this one could also add the North-South dimension of Jerusalem. Does not all of this call for serious thinking?
- *All of humanity:* Because of the pilgrims from throughout the entire world, Jerusalem is a city with a universal appeal. It is not only of interest to its residents; on the contrary, it is a subject of concern for all of humanity. Therefore it cannot leave humanity indifferent.
- *God and humanity:* If we consider once more the realities of Jerusalem, we cannot remain satisfied with a horizontal dimension, above all because this particular dimension grows directly from the vertical dimension. Jerusalem is the city that God has chosen to enter, in his dialogue with humanity. Although it may not look this way, Jerusalem remains a city marked by this mystery.

On the basis of all these realities, a political solution must be sought. But politics is not our subject. We remain rather in the realm of theology.

6. We have adopted for this enumeration the categories of the Middle Eastern Church Council (MOCC).

B. Jerusalem, a Locus Theologicus

Jerusalem is no ordinary city, with problems with housing, traffic, or city planning. It is, rather, a unique city, in which a word was spoken and given. Without hesitation, one can say that Jerusalem is a *locus theologicus,* and in this respect, that this city is a site of revelation and a reference point for theological reflection (as the word of God, the living tradition . . .). From it, theological reflection draws an inspiration that enables it to enter into the mystery of God, of humanity in general, and of salvation history in particular. The realities of Jerusalem make it a theological research area of the first order. Precisely there the search for answers to the great questions that today preoccupy humanity finds its predetermined locus.

Without wanting to succumb to a fetishism of time and place, we can say that at *one* time God has revealed himself in order to make *the* time holy; and that he has revealed himself at *one* place in order to make *the* place holy, in order that from both he might make the time and the place of his revelation. "Take your shoes off; for the place where you stand is holy ground" (Exod. 3:5). In Jerusalem a divine word was spoken. This word is contemporary and addressed to all human beings alive today. Theological reflection on its mystery is done in the light of the Bible, of the living tradition, of the dynamic of salvation history, and also of the concrete realities as they confront us. We would like to focus on this last point.

There is reason to assume that the above-named realities of Jerusalem are not a historical accident. The facts of the presence of two peoples, of three monotheistic religions, of several Christian churches, of faithful from throughout the whole world, who come to Jerusalem as the deep source of their faith, as also the reality of God in his relationship to humanity, invite us to believe that God through all this wishes to say something unique to humanity, a message of which humanity, on the cusp of the third millennium, stands in deepest need. Is it bold to assert that these realities constitute a mysterious aspect of salvation history, one that opens a way forward through the concrete history of humanity? In that case it is urgently necessary to get the message that God is sending to the inhabitants of the city, and through them to all of humanity. The role of theology consists in devoting itself to this place of the word, in order to give shape to the appeals, dimensions, and requirements, beginning with the great questions of contemporary humanity and from the realities of Jerusalem. Theology has no loftier task than this.

Precisely in Jerusalem are found the great words that give voice to the yearnings of the human beings of this age, their deepest meaning and their most urgent requirements. Concepts like God, humanity, otherness, difference, justice, peace, truth, freedom, dialogue, reconciliation, pardon, mutual acceptance, etc., yield their most universal and concrete meanings. And therefore it is inadequate to repeat answers like some kind of prayer wheel; instead, we need to offer creative answers that in the light of the Easter mystery, which is stamped unmistakably with the character of the Holy City, reach down to the deepest level of things.

In this way we see that the solution to the problem of Jerusalem transcends its geographical and political boundaries. Every solution that is found for the problem of Jerusalem is of a typological sort, and serves as a model for the solution of great problems of our time. These problems are solved first in Jerusalem. A great deal is at stake and the responsibility is immense. The world waits in expectation.

One may rightly ask of which Jerusalem we are speaking. To gain access to the mystery of Jerusalem, it is not enough to repeat the commonplaces of political propaganda and to bow to the most primitive immediate interests. Jerusalem may not be defined on the basis of our passions but on the basis of its concealed spirit and the brilliance of its mystery. We must not drag Jerusalem down to the low levels of our spirit; rather, we need to raise ourselves to the high level of its mystery. Only under this condition will the city be able to share its gifts with all, magnanimously and in rich measure.

Concluding Remarks: Towards a Theology of Justice and Peace

In his famous encyclical *Pacem in Terris,* John XXIII grounded peace in "truth, justice, love, and freedom." This nearly forty-year-old vision is as relevant to the Holy Land as ever. It reminds us that these values are inseparable from one another. The current situation in the Holy Land obliges us in addition to deepen its meaning if we are to recognize its demands. This is as true for the future of the Palestinian and the Israeli people as it is for the future of the whole human race. Theology has the task of saying this again and again. In this way it can contribute to making of Jerusalem and the Holy Land not a cemetery but a place of life for all. We need to understand that, to hope against all hope.

39 Toward a Post-Colonial Feminist Interpretation of the Bible

Musa W. Dube

Introduction

To read the Bible as a Motswana African woman is to read a Western book. For many years, I have known that "biblical Christian believers" refers to the white Western believers while "pagans" refers to all non-Christian Africans.[1] I have related well to Matthew 23 and the "foolish Galatians" in Galatians 3:1, not reading Galatians and Pharisees as static historical persons but as a reference to all those who are not Christians. The rebuttal of the Pharisees in Matthew 23 has carried a painful fascination for me, for what I heard from this passage was not an old first-century story, but a familiar drama of nineteenth- to twentieth-century imperialist history upon all non-Christian Africans.

What may seem to be a gross misreading and mistaken identities of biblical characters can be contested. Some may link it to the orality of my background. Yet oral societies can read paintings. The image of Jesus was and still is a blue-eyed, blonde, white male, whose benevolent face, along with the likewise white faces of his disciples, still graces our churches today. The image of Mary the mother of Jesus was and is a white woman.[2] The devil was,

---

1. I do not consent to the use of "Africa" insofar as it implies a uniform people. My reading is representative of neither Africa nor of Botswana, my country. Africa is too large and diverse to be represented by one person's view. I am using this category insofar as I find it heavily imposed on me by the First World and because it has come to be representative of our common oppression.

2. As the new African American Bible highlights, these images are still being contested.

of course, a black, horned man (I do not know what color he is these days). Heaven was cast in the Western terrain, with a riotous fusion of all Western seasons in one painting. With all these images, my misreading and mistaken identities go beyond the orality of my African background. Undoubtedly, this reading grid has a historical base, which, to my surprise, has resisted erosion from my many years of biblical studies.

This exposition highlights that different readers act out the biblical story at different times in history. The Western imperial readers of the nineteenth and twentieth centuries wrote themselves into the text and characterized non-Christians as their pagan counterparts in order to validate the latter's subjugation. Recently, a wide range of readers, from textual ones to flesh-and-blood ones, have featured in biblical interpretation. However, biblical interpretation has yet to integrate various historical biblical readers from different points in the Christian history of the last nineteen hundred and ninety-six years. In short, the question of how different flesh-and-blood readers have acted out the biblical story in history, and how their act illumines some meaning of the text, needs to be integrated into the academic biblical studies.

The biblical story itself invites its readers to identify with it and to act it out in history. In John 20:21, for example, the resurrected Christ says, "As my Father sent me so I send you." Encapsulated in this sending is transference of power from Jesus to his disciples. The transference is a call to his hearers, readers, and believers to act out his story with almost the same authority that has characterized the Johannine Jesus. Furthermore, this transference of power, at least as it stands in the Gospels (Matt. 28:18-20/Luke 24:46-47) suggests that the biblical story is an unfinished story: it invites its own continuation in history; it resists the covers of our Bibles and writes itself on the pages of the earth. On these grounds, it is legitimate to hold that various biblical reader-actors, from different moments in history, should illumine the meaning and implications of the text for us.

Biblical scholars have in fact highlighted that the text, as we have it, already represents a drama of believers. What the narrative presents as Jesus speaking with his disciples represents the act of the first- and second-century believers. Analyzing John's text, J. Louis Martyn has termed this phenomenon a "two-level drama." Martyn points out that this drama did not end with Jesus' departure or composition of the texts; rather, it continues in the person of the Paraclete, operating through the believers. Martyn holds that "in order for the Paraclete to create the two-level drama, he must look not only like Jesus, but also like the Christian witness who is Jesus' 'double' in that drama."[3] Consequently, it seems to me that to insist on dwelling on one historical time in this biblical drama, ignoring the continuing character of the story, is to do injustice to that very text.

Given that I come from a historical experience of the Bible functioning as an imperialist text, I know that the biblical story is a story that is acted out in history. I have, therefore, journeyed with some sense of injustice and emptiness in my academic biblical studies, where the Bible became an antiqued text, firmly contextualized in ancient times. As a biblical student, I wrestled with issues behind or in front of the text, and, sometimes, I dealt with the first three centuries. In short, I found academic biblical interpretation divorced from its historical reader-actors of the nineteenth and twentieth centuries. The approach bracketed my questions and my experience.

To be sure, this approach of situating biblical studies in ancient times has facilitated many liberating and helpful discoveries for me. For a start, it was liberating to know that biblical texts are not Anglo-Saxon books, but Jewish texts. It was also helpful to know that far from being pure (as the modern colonial Christian agents claimed), early Christianity borrowed from the non-Christian cultures of its origin. Nevertheless, I have discovered that the privileging of the ancient historical setting in the academic interpretation of the Bible is a powerful tool that divorces my experience and my questions from the field. By privileging the ancient history in biblical interpretation, the biblical texts are perfectly shielded from its various historical reader-actors. The question of confronting the imperialist manifestation of the text is neatly bracketed. However, as Ulrich Luz points out, biblical "texts have power and cannot be separated from their consequences," and, as he further notes, "Christianity as we all know it is far from a history of loving your enemies."[4] For me to read the Bible as an African woman and from my experience, therefore, is to be inevitably involved with the historical events of imperialism. Indeed, to read the Bible as an African is to take a perilous journey, a sinister journey, that spins one back to connect with dangerous memories of slavery,[5] colonialism, apartheid, and neo-colonialism. To read the Bible as an African is to relive the painful equation of Christianity with civilization, paganism with savagery.

3. J. Louis Martyn, *History and Theology in the Fourth Gospel* (Nashville: Abingdon, 1979), p. 148.

4. Ulrich Luz (*Matthew in History: Interpretation, Influence, and Effects* [Minneapolis: Fortress, 1994], p. 33) points to such atrocities as the Holocaust and links it with the interpretation of the biblical text.

5. See Katie Cannon, "Slave Ideology and Biblical Interpretation," *Semeia* 47 (1987): 9-23, on the Christian justification of the enslavement of Africans.

Luckily, early feminist readers insisted on women's experience as a valid interpretive framework.[6] My African experience has taught me that the biblical characters shift and change with time so that what were "foolish Galatians" (Gal. 3:1) may be "Savage Africans," in one context and time, and something else in another; moreover, that such labels have adverse impact upon those tagged with them. My experience has taught me that a written book does not only belong to its authors — it also belongs to its readers and users;[7] and that the history of the biblical story is not limited to the first three centuries; hence, the selection of one particular historical period as the prime reference for determining textual meaning in biblical studies is not innocent.[8] I am historically situated within this framework of facts and experiences. I, therefore, read the Bible as a black Motswana woman from the region of Southern Africa, a student of religion, a survivor of colonialism, who lives in a *luta continua* (a continuous struggle) against neo-colonialism. The latter refers to "the creation of a single international (global) financial or capital market," which is impoverishing most Two-Thirds World countries with huge debts.[9] My analysis is both feminist and post-colonial.

Post-colonial, as used here, is a literary technical term defining the setting, the use, and the classification of texts.[10] In terms of setting, it covers the period beginning with the arrival and occupation of an imperial power, the struggle against it, independence, and post-independence — a continuity which remains valid with the persistence of imperial domination.[11] Further, as Homi Bhabha points out, post-colonial does not only define sequentiality or polarity between colonialism and independence; rather, it is a "gesture to the beyond" that seeks to "transform the present into an expanded and ex-

---

6. Although the category of feminist "experience" is being correctly problematized, it empowered many of us to voice our perspectives where the traditional approach insisted on neutral and disinterested methods of reading.

7. In fact, current reading theories that insist on the reader as the maker of meaning support my assertion.

8. Mary Ann Tolbert ("Protestant Feminists and the Bible: On the Horns of a Dilemma," in *The Pleasure of Her Text: Feminist Readings of Biblical and Historical Texts,* ed. Alice Bach [Philadelphia: Trinity, 1990], pp. 5-23) contests this dwelling on "purer origins" by pointing out that it treats those who do not share this history as somehow less important.

9. Christopher Lind, *Something's Wrong Somewhere: Globalization, Community, and the Moral Economy of the Farm Crisis* (Halifax: Fernwood, 1995), p. 31.

10. I am grateful to Fernando Segovia for introducing me to post-colonial theories.

11. Bill Ashcroft, Gareth Griffiths, and Helen Tiffin, *The Empire Writes Back: Theory and Practice in Post-colonial Literatures* (New York: Routledge, 1989), p. 2.

centric site of experience and empowerment."[12] Put differently, post-colonial is not a discourse of historical accusations, but a committed search and struggle for decolonization and liberation of the oppressed. In terms of classification, it refers to a complex collection of texts that are brought, born, and used in imperial settings, to legitimate, resist, or collaborate with imperialism. While this definition is an umbrella term that includes the texts of the colonizer and the colonized, the phrase "colonial discourse" is also used to distinguish the former from the latter.[13] As an umbrella term, a post-colonial approach is best understood as a complex myriad of methods and theories which study a wide range of texts and their participation in the making or subversion of imperialism.

Although colonizing texts are mainly written by the colonizer, they also rise from the colonized. Depending on different interest groups and stages of imperial domination, the colonized can condone its oppressors, cooperate with them, or totally reject them. Since imperialism actively adopts structural strategies of assimilation or colonizing the mind, collaboration among some circles of the colonized is unavoidable. The imperialist strategy of "control-at-a-distance,"[14] for instance, engages some local groups (usually the upper class) to become its ruling representatives, and this conceals the face of the imperial oppressor among the colonized. Revolting local groups, in turn, come to fight the collaborating group but, sometimes, they also come to compete for the attention of the oppressor amongst themselves. The enemy and its opponents are thus fully embodied within the colonized nation, a fact that is usually reflected in the wide range of texts produced in such settings.

Post-colonial theoretical frameworks were mainly developed from the analysis of nineteenth- and twentieth-century literature, upon the realization that texts were powerful tools for either buttressing or counteracting imperial powers. Given that imperialism has been a recurring phenomenon in the history of the world, post-colonial applicability to various other classical texts in the human history is legitimate. Its application should, indeed, open new ways to understand most of the canonized classical texts, as to how they may reflect imperial values of their origins, and how they have functioned in various empires that have risen and fallen in history.

12. Homi K. Bhabha, *The Location of Culture* (London: Routledge, 1995), p. 4.

13. Patrick Williams and Laura Chrisman, *Colonial Discourse and Post-colonial Theory: A Reader* (New York: Columbia University Press, 1994), p. 5.

14. James M. Blaut, *The Colonizer's Model of the World: Geographical Diffusionism and Eurocentric History* (New York: Guilford, 1993), p. 70.

Imperialism, as used here, describes the tendencies of metropolitan centers to impose their images, ideas, religions, economic structures, and political control in foreign lands.[15] Colonialism is a political manifestation of imperialism when it includes geographical control. Imperialism, however, does not always include colonialism, nor does it end with independence. The current neo-colonialism/globalization highlights that imperialism does not have to include geographical possession.

In view of the fact that Christian biblical religion has been "unique in its imperial sponsorship,"[16] in ancient and current times and over different people and different places, the Bible is also a colonizing text: it has repeatedly authorized the subjugation of foreign nations and lands. Further, in view of the fact that the New Testament and many other Hebrew Bible books were born in imperialist settings, they are post-colonial books. On these grounds, I shall briefly expound on reading the Bible from a post-colonial literary perspective. In particular, I read it from my historical background as an imperial/colonial text. Then, I shall explore the intersection and implications of post-colonial and feminist reading in biblical studies. In my conclusion, I shall propose that in the post-colonial era feminist biblical readers must also become decolonizing readers.

What Is a Post-Colonial Reading of Texts?

Amongst its many methods, a post-colonial reading may analyze the literary constructions of colonizing texts and how they function to justify imperialism. The analysis may focus on the construction of characters, geography, travelers, gender constructions, and unspoken intentions to highlight how these work in justifying the domination of one by another. Usually, these narrative texts construct both the colonizer and the colonized to accept the legitimacy of their respective positions. Post-colonial literary analysis, however, includes the works of decolonizing reader-writers who adopt various strategies to counteract the violence of imperialism.[17] The following exposition, however, only illustrates some of the literary constructions in coloniz-

---

15. Edward Said, *Culture and Imperialism* (New York: Alfred A. Knopf, 1993), pp. 9-13.

16. Wayne Meeks, *The First Urban Christians: The Social World of the Apostle Paul* (New Haven: Yale University Press, 1983), p. 1.

17. Barbara Harlow, *Resistance Literature* (New York: Methuen, 1987), pp. 1-75; Said, *Culture and Imperialism*, pp. 191-262.

ing texts, that is, texts designed to take possession of the minds and lands of those who are different.

To begin with characterizations, the colonized and colonizer are sharply contrasted in colonizing literature. The subjugated are depicted as helpless, evil, inarticulate, backward, disorganized, lazy, exotic, and babies in need of instruction.[18] Such characters are put side by side with those in control, civilized, Christian, teachers, articulate, literate, and cultivated. The contrast serves to validate the domination of the former by the latter.

Geographically, the setting of imperial narratives communicates the same ideology.[19] Some lands are depicted as empty, unoccupied, and waiting to be discovered. Some lands assume the symbol of light and holiness, while the others represent darkness, disease, and evil. The narratives also lead their readers to accept as normal the fact that someone (usually a white man) owns plantations, mines, or farms in other continents, populated and run by native servants. The geography of these narratives generally exhibits a universal and global outlook that invites expansion and relationships of domination and subjugation between nations.

Traveling is also central to colonial narratives. A few travelers,[20] mainly from the metropolitan centers, enter foreign lands. These travelers are notably authoritative strangers, who are not ignorant or dependent upon their hosts. Their authority is grounded on race, religion, technology, and knowledge. They are marked by their power to see deficiency everywhere and to right this deficiency by teaching or structurally developing the colonized people to depend on them. The subjugated may travel to the lands of their masters, but as powerless strangers, such as exiles, slaves, servants, students, or refugees, who depend on the benevolence of their masters.[21]

---

18. For examples of explicit literary colonizing constructions see Joseph Conrad, *Heart of Darkness, and The Secret Sharer* (1902; Bantam Classic, 1981) and Rudyard Kipling, "The White Man's Burden," in *The Imperialism Reader*, ed. Louis Snyder (New York: Van Nostrand, 1962), pp. 87-88.

19. Blaut, *The Colonizer's Model of the World*, pp. 69-90; Said, *Culture and Imperialism*, pp. 3-43.

20. The number of colonizing travelers is crucial for it can determine the type and intensity of colonialism experienced by the colonized. For example, in areas where colonizing travelers flooded a colony such as North America, South Africa, Canada, or Australia it led to settler colonialism, which tended to override the native groups.

21. See Fernando F. Segovia, "Towards a Hermeneutics of the Diaspora," in *Reading from This Place*, vol. 1, ed. Fernando F. Segovia and Mary Ann Tolbert (Minneapolis: Fortress, 1995), pp. 57-73, on the position of Hispanic-Americans in metropolitan centers of North America.

It is characteristic of colonizing texts to present an extremely gendered perspective of their subject.[22] The colonized lands are to be "entered," "penetrated," and subjugated. The colonized are symbolized by their indigenous women, who epitomize all backwardness, evil, and helplessness. The colonizer's civilization is symbolized by their women as well, who become the measure of their civilization.[23] The general picture is that imperialism is a male game with women characters articulating men's power positions in it.

It is also characteristic of colonizing texts to conceal their material interests. Nineteenth- and twentieth-century imperialism, for instance, was a power struggle of Western empires prompted by the need to create markets overseas and to import raw materials for their growing industries, but this factor was neatly wrapped in rhetorical terms such as "the duty to the natives." Imperialism was thus presented as a moral vocation to those in need of help; it hardly acknowledged its economic motivation. The hidden motives enable the subjugated to accept their positions to some extent and the colonizers to remain firmly convinced of their good intentions even in the face of overt violence.

In sum, post-colonial texts are born in settings of intense power struggle and they articulate that struggle. In particular, colonizing texts propound relationships of profound inequality, they are driven by expansionist aims, they exhibit fear of difference, they promote the authority of certain traveling strangers, and they have the tendency to disguise their economic interests under moral claims. As Jerry Phillips defines it:

> Imperialism — a system of economic, political, and cultural force that disavows borders in order to extract desirable resources and exploit an alien people — has never stayed away from a field of pedagogical imperatives, what might be called an ideology of instruction. Christianity, Progress, Democracy, or whatever is the prevailing imperialist version of history demands of certain cultures, nations, or chosen races that they subject those who fall radically short of the ideal state. Subject people are "savage," "infantile," "untutored," "backward," or simply "underdevel-

---

22. David Quint, *Epic and Empire* (Princeton: Princeton University Press, 1993), pp. 31-41; Rene Maunier, *The Sociology of Colonies: An Introduction to the Study of Colonies*, vol. 1 (London: Routledge, 1949), p. 70; Williams and Chrisman, *Colonial Discourse and Postcolonial Theory*, p. 194.

23. Margaret Strobel, *European Women and the Second British Empire* (Bloomington: Indiana University Press, 1991), pp. 1-15.

oped"; as the imperialist encounters them, a model of their "uplift" is always thus entailed.[24]

Given the global impact of imperialism and its persistence, post-colonial theorists argue that its models of relationships are among the many bedrocks of oppression in most canonized texts of literature. They point out that bracketing of imperialism as a category in Western academic schools serves to maintain the potency of these oppressive images in our thinking as well as to justify the subjugation of some nations and lands by the imperialistic metropolitan centers.[25] For this reason, I turn to arguing for the integration of post-colonial analysis into the liberationist vision of feminist biblical readers.

Intersecting Feminism and Post-Colonialism in Our Practice

With regard to white Western feminism and post-colonialism, it has been noted that the former often brackets imperialism in its analysis of male texts, or operates within imperialist frameworks of power.[26] In her book *Decolonizing Feminisms,* Laura Donaldson highlights that feminist readers use "anti-sexist rhetoric to displace questions of colonialism, racism, and their concomitant violence."[27] Donaldson points out that some feminists have theorized that man = colonizer and woman's body = colonized, a metaphorical articulation which, she notes, can be theoretically defended, but one which often fails to address colonialism as a form of oppression.[28] The latter position often obscures the fact that Western women were and are equally involved in and benefit from the imperialist oppression of Two-Thirds World women, a position that is still economically and politically in place.

The question for feminist biblical practitioners, therefore, is how to in-

---

24. Jerry Phillips, "Educating the Savages: Melville, Bloom, and the Rhetoric of Imperialist Tradition," in *Recasting the World: Writing after Colonialism,* ed. Jonathan White (Baltimore: The Johns Hopkins University Press, 1993), p. 26.

25. Chinua Achebe, *Hopes and Impediments: Selected Essays* (New York: Doubleday, 1989), pp. 1-20; Said, *Culture and Imperialism,* pp. 41-43, 60-61.

26. Audre Lorde, *Sister Outsider: Essays and Speeches* (Berkeley: Crossing, 1984), pp. 66-71; Chandra Mohanty, "Under Western Eyes: Feminist Scholarship and Colonial Discourses," in *Third World Women and the Politics of Feminism,* ed. Chandra Mohanty, Ann Russo, and Lourdes Torres (Bloomington: Indiana University Press, 1991), pp. 51-80.

27. Laura Donaldson, *Decolonizing Feminisms: Race, Gender, and Empire-building* (Chapel Hill: University of North Carolina Press, 1992), p. 62.

28. Donaldson, *Decolonizing Feminisms,* pp. 4-6.

tegrate post-colonial insights into their liberation discourse. Given the imperialist setting of the New Testament literature, I would propose that it is imperative for feminist inclusive readings to be more suspicious of imperialist legitimation. If, for example, Matthew characterizes Pilate's wife as a prophetic woman in the trial of Jesus, an inclusive reading must be wary that this positive construction may not necessarily articulate a liberative inclusion of an outsider woman; rather, it may serve to legitimate the imperialist presence by presenting it as holy and acceptable. Elaine Wainwright's feminist inclusive reading of Matthew, for example, demonstrates insufficient suspicion toward the implied author's motivations in constructing Pilate's wife as a divine agent.[29]

Paying attention to the imperialist setting of the New Testament will also necessitate a more careful assessment of inclusive versus exclusive traditions. In this setting of a struggle for power and survival against imperial forces, an "inclusive" impulse may signal an imperialist collaboration, while an "exclusive" approach may signal a strategic resistance of imperialist powers. For instance, interpretations of Matthew 10:5-6, 15:24, and 28:18-20 must weigh out these alternatives within a Roman setting of imperialist occupation and resistance. When post-colonial analysis is integrated, the celebration of "Christian inclusiveness" versus "Jewish exclusiveness" in an imperial setting may have to be re-evaluated.[30] A post-colonial analysis necessitates identifying the Roman Empire as the enemy and the Jewish emphasis on cultural boundaries as one of strategic resistance in the face of imposed political leadership, religion, images, languages, and taxes.[31] This framework immediately calls into question the vision of Matthew 28:18-20. That is, if the Jewish people of Matthew's time were struggling to maintain their cultural boundaries against the intrusion of the Roman Empire, does not Matthew's opening of boundaries, his agenda of discipling the whole world according to the commands of Christ, indicate a collaborative stance? Matthew's command to christianize the world ironically befriends the Roman Empire's political and cultural imposition of its structures on Jewish people and all its colonized subjects. It is when we re-

---

29. Elaine Wainwright, *Towards a Feminist Critical Reading of the Gospel according to Matthew* (Berlin: de Gruyter, 1991), pp. 285-86.

30. I am aware that rigid nationalism is oppressive even to its own people, but more especially to women. Nonetheless, nationalistic movements of the colonized must be seen within their contexts as a strategy of resisting the bigger enemy and as a temporary phase. Indeed, many colonized nations of the modern era adopted and used this strategy effectively.

31. Richard A. Horsley, *Jesus and the Spiral of Violence: Popular Jewish Resistance in Roman Palestine* (Minneapolis: Fortress, 1993), pp. 1-116.

mind ourselves that first-century Palestinian Jews were struggling to survive against the Roman Empire that Matthew's universal commission becomes a suspicious agenda — one which is driven by competition with other local groups for power and one which is consistent with the imperial ideology of disavowing boundaries and claiming cultural authority over foreign people and lands then resisting imperialism. In turn, the questioning of Matthew's worldwide agenda also helps us to understand why Christian missions (read reader-believer-actor of the Christian texts) have functioned compatibly with imperialist agendas of their countries. It also calls for a post-colonial feminist reimagining of Christian mission texts.

Similarly, the gendered construction of imperialist narratives is evident in the featuring of female characters of questionable morality and status in stories representing the penetration of other lands. A good example is Rahab, the prostitute, who becomes the point of contact in the possession of Jericho. Likewise, in both John and Matthew the Samaritan and Canaanite women are featured in stories foreshadowing the universal mission, that is, the penetration of other lands. Both these women are characterized as either helpless or immoral, symbolizing the status of their own people and thus authorizing the subjugation of their lands. Although these women are celebrated by feminists, a post-colonial analysis detects an ideology of subjugation that proceeds by negative labeling and the use of female gender to articulate relations of subordination and domination.

A post-colonial analysis also indicates that gender experiences in imperialist settings are different, depending on one's relation to the imperialist powers. Among the subjugated groups, women are burdened by two patriarchal systems, the national and the metropolitan one. As the national patriarchal system resists the intrusion of a foreign power, the call for protection of tradition intensifies gender constructions.[32] The enemy is the outsider and resistance calls women and men to remain faithful to national traditions. In inter-testamental times, both Essenes and Pharisees are representative of this type of resistance. However, the opposite response is also common. In various revolutions and in struggles against imperialism, gender roles are often relaxed for some time, until the groups are established. Thereafter women are put back to their original places. The Jesus movement and the early church represent this type of resistance.

While women on the side of the imperialist automatically belong to a higher class, race, and sometimes religion, they still remain male objects. As

32. Harlow, *Resistance Literature*, pp. 28-30.

attested by the biblical examples of Herod's and Pilate's wives, they are subject to male constructions in the maintenance of male power. Nonetheless, the issues of class, race, and religion are still factors of difference, among the colonized and the colonizer women. Thus a feminist inclusive reading cannot equate the experience of Pilate's wife with that of the mother of Andrew, the son of Zebedee, without taking into account the former's imperialist status of exploiter and oppressor.

This brings me to a crucial question: Which feminist should read from a post-colonial perspective? As the above comments indicate, imperialism has affected all of us and its narratives construct both the powerful and the powerless — all of those who pass through formal education are inducted to accept their positions. Therefore, imperialism involves both Western and Two-Thirds World women, women of color and white women, developed and the so-called underdeveloped countries, precisely because imperialism was and still is a global event and conception that has left little or no place untouched; hence, it informs our perception of the Other.

No doubt Two-Thirds World women suffer more from imperialist intrusion; hence, they are more conscious of it. Western feminist readers, on the other hand, benefit from their social location. They can, consciously or unconsciously, bracket out a post-colonial analysis. The bracketing, however, does not only speak of one's privileged position; it also plays into the maintenance of imperialist metropolitan centers' constructions, and, worse, it hinders building "political coalitions" of resistance among feminists of various cultural persuasions.[33]

Reading for Decolonization

Among biblical and theological feminist readers, the challenge to read post-colonially for decolonization, that is, the struggle to counter imperialist violence and to seek liberating ways of interdependence, is often presented by women from Two-Thirds World settings. Kwok Pui-lan, for instance, writes that "Christianity as it existed in the West had a right not only to conquer the world but to define reality for other peoples of the world."[34] Rosemary Edet

---

33. Mary Ann Tolbert, "Politics and the Poetics of Location," in *Reading from This Place*, vol. 1, *Social Location and Biblical Interpretation in the United States*, ed. Fernando F. Segovia and Mary Ann Tolbert (Minneapolis: Fortress, 1995), pp. 312-14.

34. Kwok Pui-lan, "Discovering the Bible in the Non-biblical World," in *Voices from the Margin: Interpreting the Bible in the Third World*, ed. R. S. Sugirtharajah (Maryknoll, NY:

and Bette Ekeya point out that among African people "there is alienation because evangelization has not been that of cultural exchange but of cultural domination and assimilation."[35] This challenge calls for a feminist reading that does not only recover or reconstruct women's participation in early church history, but also strives to re-envision the Christian mission. For instance, how do passages like Matthew 28:18-20, Luke 24:46-47, and John 20:21 construct the power relations in the encounter with the Other? Do they propose relationships of liberating interdependence[36] between races, genders, cultures, and nations, or do they propose a model of unequal inclusion? Kwok Pui-lan, grappling with the biblical models of international exchange, has suggested a "dialogical model of truth," whereby two different and equal subjects meet, and their word to each other is, "What treasures do you have to share?"[37] Such an invitation does not encounter the Other as a blank slate to be filled.

Therefore, conscious awareness of the fact that biblical texts were born in an imperialist setting and have been unique in sponsoring imperialist agendas over different times and people needs to be integrated in our feminist reading for liberation. This requires recognizing that many women in biblical religions also belong to Native American religions, African religions, and Asian religions; that this position is not only intricately related to imperialism, but must also inform our practice. This recognition implies that we are here as women in biblical religion together with our Other canons, written and unwritten, and they demand to be heard and read in their own right. I emphasize "Other canons" because imperialism proceeds by denying the validity of the narratives and values of its victims, while it imposes its own "master narratives" on them. Furthermore, most of us experienced the Christian mission not as a liberating egalitarian movement, but as a divinely authorized patriarchal and imperial program that subjugates all those who are not Christian. Consequently, unless feminist liberation readers want to stand in continuum with the imperialist "right" of the West "to define reality

---

Orbis, 1991), p. 303. Kwok quotes W. R. Hutchinson, "A Moral Equivalent for Imperialism: Americans and the Promotion of Christian Civilization, 1880-1910," in *Missionary Ideologies in the Imperialist Era: 1880-1920*, ed. T. Christensen and W. R. Hutchinson (Aarhus: Aros, 1982), p. 172.

35. Rosemary Edet and Bette Ekeya, "Church Women of Africa: A Theological Community," in *With Passion and Compassion: Third World Women Doing Theology: Reflections from the Women's Commission of the EATWT*, ed. Virginia Fabella and Mercy Amba Oduyoye (Maryknoll, NY: Orbis, 1988), p. 3.

36. See Said, *Culture and Imperialism*, pp. 3-43, 303-36.

37. Kwok, "Discovering the Bible in the Non-biblical World," p. 313.

for other people," the challenge is with us. It is imperative for the "women-church"[38] to become a post-colonial open-space and to read for decolonization — a practice that recognizes that we are already inscribed within an established tradition of imperial domination, collaboration, and resistance. To read for decolonization, therefore, is to consciously resist the exploitative forces of imperialism, to affirm the denied differences, and to seek liberating ways of interdependence in our multi-cultural and post-colonial world.

In this post-colonial interpretive open-space, feminist decolonizing readings should encourage "solidarity in multiplicity." Donaldson defines solidarity in multiplicity as a "story field" that affirms "stories" and "demands that each story negotiate its position in relation to all other stories included within the field, which in turn must recalculate their own position."[39] To translate the approach to feminist academic biblical studies, it calls for a practice of reading, imagining, and retelling biblical stories in negotiation with other religious stories in the post-colonial era. Anything short of this risks maintaining the "right" of the Christian biblical stories to remain at the highest peak of the hierarchy — a hierarchy sustained through the suppression of all other religious stories and the oppression of Two-Thirds World women.

How Can We Know and Respect the Other?[40]

Evidently, the main objective of a decolonizing reading is beyond just providing a deconstructive analysis that exposes the imperialist construction embedded in narratives. A decolonizing reading's main objective is liberation. It asks the question: "How can we know and respect the Other?" It is a struggle to conceive models that are not built along the lines of relegating all

---

38. Elisabeth Schüssler Fiorenza ("The Will to Choose or to Reject: Continuing Our Critical Work," in *Feminist Interpretation of the Bible*, ed. Letty Russell [Philadelphia: Westminster, 1985], pp. 126-27) uses the term "women-church" to describe a feminist hermeneutical center. I am extending the boundaries of this center because for survivors of imperialism the invitation to inhabit the "ekklesia," the white male, most hierarchical and exclusive of centers, dangerously befriends the ideology of imperialism that invites its subjects to yearn for their standards even as it structurally denies them access, while at the same time denying the colonized their difference. The colonized, in other words, can enter the "ekklesia" if they forego their cultures, pursue those of their masters, or agree that their cultural values are inferior.

39. Donaldson, *Decolonizing Feminisms*, p. 139.

40. See Williams and Chrisman, *Colonial Discourse and Post-colonial Theory*, p. 8. This is Edward Said's central question in his post-colonial work.

differences to deficiency. It is a struggle to build bridges for liberating inter-dependence cross-culturally. It is the desire to begin what have been termed "difficult dialogues,"[41] that is, to encounter and to dialogue with the different Other on a level of different and equal subjects.

At this level, a post-colonial feminist who reads for decolonization will ask how the Christian texts construct and legitimate encounter with people of different faith, race, gender, and sexuality. The phrase "difficult dialogues," indeed, accepts the fact that the construction of our narratives, hence, our thinking of the Other, has primarily operated on what Phillips has shown to be a denigrate and "uplift" model. In this imperialist model we have an aggressive inclusion but not equality. Consequently, to engage in cultivating "difficult dialogues," feminist readers must indeed become decolonizing readers: they must demonstrate awareness of imperialism as a persistent and exploitative force at a global scale, they must demonstrate a conscious adoption of resistance to imperialism, and they must struggle to map liberating ways of interdependence in our multi-cultural world. To bracket decolonizing is only to maintain the imperial strategies of exploitation and subjugation and to hinder building the necessary "political coalitions" among feminists of different cultures, nations, colors, classes, and sexuality.

Conclusion

In sum, the Bible as a Western book is bound to its imperialist history of subjugation and oppression. This imperialist history has constructed all of us, and its reality cannot be bracketed from our critical practice without perpetuating the history of unequal inclusion. The biblical story is at times a travel narrative; it commands its readers to travel. Consequently, the privileging of one historical time, the ancient times, in determining its meaning is ideologically suspect. Moreover, women in biblical religion also stand in other religions. The challenge, therefore, is to become decolonizing readers, who seek to build true conversations of equal subjects in our post-colonial and multi-cultural world. Without overlooking the differences of race, sexuality, religion, and class, I am proposing that our critical practice should be multi-cultural in a post-colonial open-space of women of the world as equal subjects.

41. Phillips, "Educating the Savages," pp. 40-41. Phillips traces this term to Johnella Butler ("Difficult Dialogues," *Women's Review of Books* 6, no. 5 [1989]: 16) who used it to describe "cultural negotiation between opposing ends of the earth," and Phillips uses it to point out that "for too long we have not listened to what others have to say."

40 Theology and Social Theory

Kwok Pui-lan

Long before the modern period, when the social sciences emerged as academic disciplines, theologians made efforts to connect themselves with the socio-political world of their times. Augustine's contrast of the two cities, Aquinas's just war theory, and Luther's view on church and state are examples that theologians in antiquity, the Middle Ages, and early modernity each had their own interpretations of society. With what Michel Foucault has called "the emergence of Man" in the human sciences since the Enlightenment,[1] theologians have had to converse with these critical new disciplines, in addition to philosophy, their customary dialogical partner.

Theologians have hotly contested the relationship between theology and social theory because of differing political commitments and divergent views of theology's concerns. On the one hand, political and liberation theologians have insisted that critical social theory is indispensable in theologizing. Political theologians have drawn insights from the Frankfurt School and the social theory of Jürgen Habermas.[2] From the beginning, Latin American liberation theologians, in particular Juan Luis Segundo, have famously argued that faith without ideology is dead. By ideology,

1. Michel Foucault, *The Order of Things: An Archaeology of the Human Sciences* (New York: Vintage Books, 1973).

2. See, for example, A. James Reimer, ed., *The Influence of the Frankfurt School on Contemporary Theology: Critical Theory and the Future of Religion* (Lewiston, NY: Edwin Mellen Press, 1992); Don S. Browning and Francis Schussler Fiorenza, eds., *Habermas, Modernity, and Public Theology* (New York: Crossroad, 1992); Paul Lakeland, *Theology and Critical Theory: The Discourse of the Church* (Nashville: Abingdon, 1990).

Segundo means the bridge between the "conception of God and the real-life problems of history."[3] On the other hand, theologians who continue to do theology out of a metaphysical framework chastise such heavy borrowing from social sciences as reductionistic and overlooking the unique contributions of the Christian tradition and the church.

Such debates intensified in the latter half of the twentieth century because of the proliferation of theological voices, particularly those emerging in connection with people from marginalized communities. These interlocutors have brought to bear on theological reflection not only neo-Marxist analysis and theories that pertain to gender, race, and ethnicity, but also queer studies and postcolonial and post-modern theories. They have challenged the ideological assumptions of theology, critiquing its gender, race, and class biases, along with the complicity of theologians with colonialism and other forms of oppression. In the globalized world, in which religion has increasingly played a significant role in politics, there has been a renewed interest of philosophers and social critics in religion and theology, thus opening new avenues for fruitful dialogues.[4]

Theology and the Social Sciences

Theologians have looked at the usefulness of social sciences from different vantage points. I would like to contrast two distinctly different approaches — liberation theology and radical orthodoxy — and point out their blind spots. Liberation theologians propose a theological methodology based on commitment to social praxis and the transformation of history. In contrast to theology as wisdom or theology as rational knowledge, liberation theology is defined by Gustavo Gutiérrez as a "critical reflection on praxis."[5] In order to carry out historical praxis in terms of the preferential option for the poor, theologians need to analyze the social situation aided by the tools of the social sciences. Gutiérrez's work has been much influenced by the theory of dependency of Latin American nations, which argues that the exploita-

3. Juan Luis Segundo, *The Liberation of Theology,* trans. John Drury (Maryknoll, NY: Orbis Books, 1976), p. 116.

4. Hent de Vries, *Philosophy and the Turn to Religion* (Baltimore: Johns Hopkins University Press, 1999); Creston Davis, John Milbank, and Slavoj Žižek, eds., *Theology and the Political* (Durham, NC: Duke University Press, 2005).

5. Gustavo Gutiérrez, *A Theology of Liberation: History, Politics, and Salvation,* rev. ed., trans. Sister Caridad Inda and John Eagleson (Maryknoll, NY: Orbis Books, 1988), p. 5.

tion of Latin America was exacerbated by its dependence on the more developed capitalist countries and by adopting their developmental model.

Gutiérrez says we need to maintain critical judgment in using social sciences because "to say that these disciplines are scientific does not mean that their findings are apodictic and beyond discussion."[6] Segundo also has consistently called attention to the dialogue between theology and social sciences because these disciplines can help to unmask unconscious or hidden "ideological infiltration of dogma."[7] However, Segundo is not blind to the fact that sociology has its ideological underpinnings as well, especially those types influenced by the United States, such as positivist or behaviorist sociology.[8]

Among the Latin American theologians, Clodovis Boff has presented a rigorous study on the epistemological foundations of liberation theology, including a detailed analysis of the relation between theology and the social sciences. If theology seeks to articulate praxis, Boff argues, it requires socio-analytical mediation, hermeneutical mediation, and dialectic of theory and praxis. He submits that social theories are not just tools for applying theology to concrete social circumstances, but are constitutive elements *of* theology:

> The sciences of the social enter into theology of the political as a *constitutive part.* . . . The text of a theological reading with respect to the political is prepared and furnished by the sciences of the social. Theology receives its text from these sciences, and practices upon its reading in conformity with its own proper code, in such a way as to extract from it a characteristically, properly, theological meaning.[9]

Theology, therefore, must be an interdisciplinary collaboration. Theologians have to respect that social sciences have their "scientificness," with their own methodologies, norms, and criteria. Boff is wary of the magisterium making pronouncements about the history and destiny of the world, often couched in religious terminologies, as if they were the authority on these matters. However, theologians must exercise their judgment and ethical choice in determining which social theory works best for liberation

---

6. Gustavo Gutiérrez, "Theology and the Social Sciences," in his *The Truth Shall Make You Free: Confrontations,* trans. Matthew J. O'Connell (Maryknoll, NY: Orbis Books, 1990), p. 58.

7. Segundo, *The Liberation of Theology,* p. 40.

8. Segundo, *The Liberation of Theology,* pp. 48-57.

9. Clodovis Boff, *Theology and Praxis: Epistemological Foundations,* trans. Robert R. Barr (Maryknoll, NY: Orbis Books, 1987), p. 31. Emphasis in original.

in a given situation.[10] He rejects the criticism that liberation theology is reductionistic, an "ideologization of faith," or a "socializing theology." While liberation theologians learn from Marxists' social theory to analyze the current socio-historical situation, they do not subscribe to its overall atheistic worldview.[11] Even as social sciences provide material raw data for theology, theology has its own proper subject, its own "theologicity," based on reflection on God as the object of faith and the praxis of the church.

Contrary to liberation theology's more positive assessment of the social sciences, radical orthodoxy, exemplified by the work of John Milbank, displays acute skepticism of modern, secular social theory. Milbank maintains that the "new science of politics" has its origin in theology and that "sociology is only able to explain, or even illuminate religion, to the extent that it conceals its own theological borrowings and its own quasi-religious status."[12] Even though sociologists reject the theological and the metaphysical and try to substitute supposedly "scientific" accounts of society, their secular theories leave much of the metaphysical framework intact. Sociologists have constructed the categories of "the social" or "social facts" as if they are more "real" than the religious, which is seen as arbitrary and irrational. Adopting a positivist stance, they commit the mistake of "socializing of the transcendental" (64) by reducing religious truth claims to statements about the social whole or the private life of an individual. Milbank therefore unveils sociology's theological presuppositions to show that "every secular positivism is revealed to be also a positivist theology" (143).

Milbank delineates the positive and negative contributions of Hegel and Marx. He finds Hegel's discussion of Christianity and his dialectics inadequate and Marx's anthropology and historical materialism wanting. Milbank suggests that only Christian socialism can offer the most incisive critique of the secular logic of capitalism (205). He criticizes the political and liberation theologians for relying on secular social theories for social mediation and thereby inheriting the shortcomings of those theories. The Latin American liberation theologians, in particular, have borrowed much from the humanist-Marxist tradition and erroneously equate liberation with salvation, he says. By doing so, they adopt a reductionist view of salvation that grounds ethics in the social and the political, separate from the reli-

10. Boff, *Theology and Praxis*, pp. 57-59.
11. Boff, *Theology and Praxis*, pp. 56-57.
12. John Milbank, *Theology and Social Theory: Beyond Secular Reason*, 2nd ed. (Malden, MA: Blackwell, 2006), p. 52. Hereafter page references will be given in parentheses in the text.

gious. By splitting salvation into a transcendental and "religious aspect," which is fundamentally an individual affair, and a "social" aspect that is purely secular, liberation theologians are too ready to accept modernity and its secularization process as positive (244).

Milbank may have created a false dichotomy between the individual and the social as well as between the religious and the political, and superimposed that dichotomy onto the work of the Latin American theologians. His claims that the latter have not dealt adequately with grace, forgiveness, and the sacraments offered by the church sound less than convincing. After pointing out the errors of secular reason associated with modernity, Milbank and his colleagues propose a return to pre-modern sources, especially the work of Augustine, for the development of an adequate Christian social and historical critique.

Milbank's dismissal of liberation theology has been vigorously contested, with Marcella Althaus-Reid calling it a "colonial theology."[13] Here I would like to pin-point some of the blind spots that both liberation theology and radical orthodoxy share. A critical blind spot is their Eurocentric bias in interpreting modernity and secularity. Philosophers and social theorists constructed secularity not only as a revolt against Christianity, but also as a demarcation of difference between Western societies and others. Richard King argues that "religion" is a category that plays a key role in the "imaginative cartography of western modernity."[14] The development of the secular West in modernity has been contrasted with the religious East, steeped in mysticism and traditional religions. In fact, much of modern social theorics has been developed based on data drawn from the so-called primitive or less advanced societies, interpreted through Eurocentric intelligibility. Social theorists then proceeded to develop their theories of the origin of religion (Durkheim), the evolutionary narrative of history (Hegel), and modernity as disenchantment of the world (Weber). Neither the liberation theologians nor radical orthodox theologians have attended to the colonial collusion of these so-called "scientific" social theories.

13. See the chapters by Elina Vuola, Mayra Rivera, and Mary Grey in *Interpreting the Postmodern: Responses to "Radical Orthodoxy,"* ed. Rosemary Radford Ruether and Marion Grau (New York: T. & T. Clark, 2006), and especially Marcella María Althaus-Reid, "A Saint and a Church for Twenty Dollars: Sending Radical Orthodoxy to Ayacucho," in *Interpreting the Postmodern,* pp. 107-18.

14. Richard King, "Cartographies of the Imagination, Legacies of Colonialism: The Discourse of Religion and the Mapping of Indic Traditions," *Evam: Forum on Indian Representations* 3 (2004): 273.

Both sides frame the questions surrounding theology and social theory with the assumption that Christianity is the dominant religion. The relationship between religion and society in non-Christian societies has not been taken into consideration. As Christian demographics have shifted to the South, many Christians are living in a religiously pluralistic world, having to negotiate theology and praxis amidst this pluralism. Focusing on Western social theories, both radical orthodoxy and liberation theology are oblivious to theories developed by scholars not working with Christian societies, such as Talal Asad, C. K. Yang, Rey Chow, Harry Harootunian, Ranajit Guha, and Achille Membe, to name just a few. If the works of these scholars are consulted, the parameters of the discussion will be greatly expanded, in recognition that the relation between theology and the social varies from culture to culture.

Finally, these male theologians show a lack of sensitivity to issues pertaining to race, gender, and sexuality. The liberation theologians regard the male peasant as paradigmatic of the poor,[15] while the radical orthodoxy theologians try to restore faith in the postmodern age for urban, white, middle-class men. Even though both have criticized the injustice of capitalism, neither has analyzed the mechanisms that place the burden of capitalism disproportionally on people of darker skin colors and on the majority of women and their children in the world.

Theology and Postcolonial Critique

Christian theology does not emerge out of a vacuum, but develops in constant negotiation with political and ecclesial empires and with other power dynamics throughout history. Postcolonial theory offers an invaluable vantage point on theology, because it interrogates how religious and cultural productions are enmeshed in the economic and political domination of colonialism and empire building. The postcolonial optic is quite different from that of the Latin American liberation theologies of an earlier era, which were keen on demystifying the ideological inscription in theology, seen variously as false consciousness, class interests, or the ideological apparatus of the state. Postcolonial critics, following Foucault, are concerned with how theological truth is made possible and how the regime of truth takes shape.

---

15. Marcella Althaus-Reid, *Indecent Theology: Theological Perversions in Sex, Gender and Politics* (London: Routledge, 2000), p. 30.

Moreover, contrary to the radical orthodox theologians, postcolonial critics insist that the return to the Christian metanarrative and the language of transcendence overlooks how Christianity has colluded with colonial interests and camouflages contradictions in the postmodern world.

If postcolonial critics have learned from Foucault about the relationship between power and knowledge, they have also gone beyond him, because Foucault's study of the "emergence of Man" never broached the dimensions of race and ethnicity. Rey Chow has argued that, "If Man is an historical invention, it is because he is a Western invention, which relies for its inventiveness — its originality, so to speak — on the debasement and exclusion of others."[16] The work of the Subaltern Studies Group and postcolonial studies from a wide range of cultural backgrounds have provided much new data and challenged the politics of representation, disciplinary boundaries, and the knowledge-production process. In the discipline of theology, postcolonial critics are interested in how the Other has been represented in theological discourse as a boundary marker to secure Christian identity and to stabilize the theological subject.[17] In this anthology [*Empire and the Christian Tradition: New Readings of Classical Theologians*], we can see that the description of the Other — Jews, Muslims, Natives, women, and other marginalized groups — occupies not a marginal but a central position in theological imagining throughout the centuries. For every Las Casas who defended the rights of the Natives, there were countless others who justified the interests of colonial empires, arguing in theological terms that the Natives were not fully human. For every Matteo Ricci who showed some respect for other peoples' culture, there were countless Hegels who could only see the development of the West as the fullest manifestation of the spirit and the culmination of universal history. In *Provincializing Europe*, Dipesh Chakrabarty argues that Europe has constructed itself as the center of the world from which all historical narratives evolve.[18] It seems to me that Christian theology has been part and parcel of the narratives of empire, and that it requires similar "provincializing" so that we can hear the pluriphonic voices coming out of the margins.

Postcolonial strategies of reading literary and cultural texts offer clues for

16. Rey Chow, *The Protestant Ethnic and the Spirit of Capitalism* (New York: Columbia University Press, 2002), p. 2.

17. Catherine Keller, Michael Nausner, and Mayra Rivera, eds., *Postcolonial Theologies: Divinity and Empire* (St. Louis: Chalice Press, 2005).

18. Dipesh Chakrabatry, *Provincializing Europe: Postcolonial Thought and Historical Difference* (Princeton, NJ: Princeton University Press, 2000).

developing critical theological hermeneutics. In *The World, the Text, and the Critic*, Edward W. Said discusses the "worldliness" or the circumstantial reality incorporated in the text, which forms "an infrangible part of its capacity for conveying and producing meaning!"[19] It would be reductionistic to explain a text in terms of its historical context; but to overlook the circumstantial reality — which calls the text into being and to which the text responds — also hinders our understanding a text on its multiple levels.[20]

Said also proposed a contrapuntal reading, which sees global histories as intertwined and overlapped. He demonstrates how the highly regarded novels of Jane Austen, Joseph Conrad, Rudyard Kipling, and Albert Camus, as well as the music of Verdi, inscribe empire. Said successfully shows that the justification of empire building was embedded in the cultural imagination of the age of empire.[21] Theologians were not immune to the ideas, thought patterns, and effects of the cultural productions of their time, and their respective responses were quite diverse.

Such a political reading of theological texts refuses to separate the center from the periphery and insists that the colonizers and colonized are mutually inscribed in the colonial process. It rejects a binary construction of center and margin, oppressors and victims, and the colonizers and their subjects. Using the theory of hybridity, which exposes the myth of cultural purity and colonialist disavowal,[22] postcolonial critics have shown how theologians from marginalized communities have creatively used elements from both the dominant and indigenous cultures in order to fashion their own theology. Korean American theologian Wonhee Anne Joh has said, "The power of hybridity is in the emergence of subjugated knowledge to enter into dominant discourses and thereby shift the basis of its authority."[23] Those situated closer to the center have often criticized these theological hybrids, but in fact there is no theology that does not borrow language, metaphors, and thought forms from its surrounding culture. When theologians use Plato or Aristotle, Heidegger or Derrida, they are touted as well-read and sophisticated, and if they dare to step outside the line laid down by the theo-

---

19. Edward W. Said, *The World, the Text, and the Critic* (Cambridge, MA: Harvard University Press, 1983), p. 39.

20. Nicholas Harrison discusses these issues with reference to Conrad's *Heart of Darkness* in his *Postcolonial Criticism* (Cambridge: Polity Press, 2003), pp. 22-61.

21. Edward W. Said, *Culture and Imperialism* (New York: Knopf, 1994).

22. Homi Bhabha, *The Location of Culture* (London: Routledge, 1994).

23. Wonhee Anne Joh, *Heart of the Cross: A Postcolonial Christology* (Louisville: Westminster John Knox Press, 2006), p. 54.

logical establishment and argue that Confucian teaching, African folktales, and slave narratives can provide theological data, they are considered less sophisticated or even accused of being syncretistic. Taiwanese theologian C. S. Song has said that resources for doing theology are unlimited: "What is limited is our theological imagination. Powerful is the voice crying out of the abyss of the Asian heart, but powerless is the power of our theological imaging."[24] This rings true for other contexts as well.

Postcolonial critics do not glorify the colonized, and speak of the collaboration of the colonized in the colonial regime and their divided and fragmented subjectivity. Theologians, as cultural and intellectual elites who have benefited from colonial education and enjoy the power and prestige provided by the church as a colonial artifact, must be vigilant about their own complacence. In the postcolonial period, theologians in many parts of the Third World have developed their indigenous or inculturated theologies. We must affirm the contributions of such theological movements to anti-imperialistic efforts by valuing the dignity and beauty of indigenous heritages and lifting up the voices of local leaders. However, we cannot be blind to the fact that there are shortcomings in these theologies as well, expressed for instance in the nationalistic fervor of some theologians, which has led some to construct theologies that dialogue only with elite culture, or which has presupposed a homogenous national culture that silences women, the dalits, and other marginalized groups. It has been shown repeatedly that after the colonizers were driven away they were replaced by a national bourgeoisie that was not sensitive to the plight of the masses. In addition, colonization and globalization processes have changed indigenous cultures so much that it becomes difficult to speak of a clear divide between the local and the global.

One of the leading postcolonial theorists, Gayatri Chakravorty Spivak, has constantly cautioned us of the ambiguities of speaking for or representing the subaltern. She reminds intellectuals of the gulf between them and the masses, the poor, or the subaltern, and of the difficulties of recovering the subjectivity of the subaltern and documenting subaltern consciousness, as if their consciousness were unambiguous and transparent.[25] The same can be said for liberation theologies and political theologies of all sorts, which seek to work in solidarity with the oppressed and downtrodden. Some liberation theologians

---

24. C. S. Song, *Theology from the Womb of Asia* (Maryknoll, NY: Orbis Books, 1986), p. 16.

25. Gayatri Chakravorty Spivak, "Subaltern Studies: Deconstructing Historiography," in her *In Other Worlds: Essays in Cultural Politics* (New York: Routledge, 1998), pp. 197-221.

are careful to point out that they cannot speak on behalf of the poor because of their own class or educational privileges. They are aware that theologians must be self-critical of their own position and responsive to their communities of accountability. In our commercialized world, when identity can be commodified and people of color are not just rewarded for imitating the whites, but also lured into playing their assigned roles as "protestant *ethnics*,"[26] theologians from these communities can easily be co-opted into the multicultural theological marketplace or the carnival of postmodern difference.

Theology, Empire, and Social Imaginary

In their book *Empire*, Michael Hardt and Antonio Negri argue that the old form of imperialism, defined by military and political control of foreign territories, has been replaced by Empire: "In contrast to imperialism, Empire establishes no territorial center of power and does not rely on fixed boundaries or barriers. It is a *decentered* and *deterritorializing* apparatus of rule that progressively incorporates the entire global realm within its open, expanding frontiers."[27] With the decline of colonial regimes since World War II and the increasingly global reach of the neo-liberal market economy, the nation-state is not as significant as before. The new Empire is defined more by economic power, secured and bolstered by military might; war becomes a continuation of politics by other means.

Hardt and Negri's theory has been criticized, because nation-states are reasserting themselves in global politics, in some cases to counteract globalizing forces, as in the Middle East and other Third World countries. Others have argued that territorial control is still important, as the United States seeks to exert its hegemony by using military force in its "grand imperial strategy."[28] However, Hardt and Negri's work is significant in calling our attention to reconceptualizing economics, the nation-state, and biopower in the age of globalization.

Another leading theorist of the cultural dimensions of globalization is Arjun Appadurai from India, whose work on "globalization from below" has

26. Chow, *The Protestant Ethnic*, pp. 103-8.

27. Michael Hardt and Antonio Negri, *Empire* (Cambridge, MA: Harvard University Press, 2000), p. xii. Emphasis in the original.

28. Noam Chomsky, *Hegemony or Survival: America's Quest for Global Dominance* (New York: Metropolitan Books, 2003), p. 11. See also David Harvey, *The New Imperialism* (Oxford: Oxford University Press, 2003).

captured the attention of both academics and social activists.[29] Globalization, he says, is characterized by disjunctive flows of people, capital, images and messages, technologies, and goods and services at enormous speed. Contrary to globalization from above, globalization from below depends on the coalition and collaboration of nongovernmental organizations, transnational advocacy networks, activists, public intellectuals, and socially concerned academics. He writes: "[O]ne positive force that encourages an emancipatory politics of globalization is the role of imagination in social life."[30] What can Christian theologians contribute to a social imaginary that will benefit the oppressed and marginalized?

In the Christian West, the ways people conceive human power, such as "will," "capacity," and "sovereign," are closely related to how divine power is imagined, as human beings are considered to be created in the image of God. As Milbank has argued, the "new sciences of politics" have their origins in theology, in that the basic characteristics of humanhood, such as private property, active rights, and absolute sovereignty, are rooted in Adam's *dominium*.[31] In past decades, the work of feminist theologians such as Carter Heyward has helped us to reimagine divine power not in terms of domination, but in terms of mutual relation.[32] Catherine Keller has linked the justification for preemptive force with the theologic of omnipotence that is influenced by Calvinism, an important component of the culture of Protestantism in the United States. Just as God, being omnipotent, does not need to wait to act, the United States, believing itself to be exceptional and innocent, can take preemptive action. Exposing such an imperial theologic, Keller calls for a new *theopoetics*, which reimagines and transcodes political power in terms of the *profundis* of creation and in service of counter-empire:

> God is called upon not as a unilateral superpower but as a relational force, not an omnipotent creator from nothing, imposing order upon chaos, but the lure to a self-organizing complexity, creation out of the chaos — the *tohuvabohu* of which Genesis 1 speaks.[33]

---

29. Arjun Appadurai, "Grassroots Globalization and the Research Imagination," in *Globalization,* ed. Arjun Appadurai (Durham, NC: Duke University Press, 2001), pp. 1-21.

30. Appadurai, "Grassroots Globalization and the Research Imagination," p. 6.

31. Milbank, *Theology and Social Theory,* p. 13.

32. Carter Heyward, *The Redemption of God: A Theology of Mutual Relation* (Washington, DC: University Press of America, 1982).

33. Catherine Keller, "Preemption and Omnipotence: A Niebuhrian Prophecy," in her *God and Power: Counter Apocalyptic Journeys* (Minneapolis: Fortress Press, 2005), p. 31.

The reconceptualization of divine power and sovereignty is closely related to violence in the Christian tradition. While some parts of the Bible depict God as merciful and compassionate, God has also been described as the one who commands the Israelites to kill their enemies, including their children and livestock. Jesus met his death with nonviolence, but he also said that he came not to bring peace but a sword (Matt. 10:34) and there are Zealots among his followers. While the early Christians adopted a pacifist approach in the first centuries, Ambrose and his student Augustine had begun to develop an ethic of war that considered war to be unavoidable because of fallen human nature and evil in the world. By the time of the crusades, Aquinas had developed a more detailed just war theory.[34] During the centuries of colonialism, violence and genocide were justified in the name of converting other peoples to Christ. Christianity both provided the religious sanction and justification of the colonial project and reaped the benefit. As political empires expanded, the ecclesial empire extended its global reach as well. After the September 11, 2001, incidents, some have sought to revive the just war tradition, though progressive Christian ethicists have strongly argued that the just war theory cannot be applied to our time. Because the technologies of war have changed so much and distinguishing between military and civilian persons and locations is so difficult, the ends can never justify the means.[35] At a time when violence and war are conducted in God's name, providing theological and moral imagination for building sustainable peace is a major challenge for theologians.

This theological rethinking has to start with none other than the central symbol of the cross. Feminist theologians have criticized classical atonement theories as "theological sadism" and divine child abuse.[36] Searching for a reinterpretation of the cross offers new possibilities for dialogue between theologians and critical theorists, since several of the latter have written explicitly on the cross. Julia Kristeva, for example, offers a psychoanalytical reading that the death of Christ expresses the melancholia of a subject rup-

---

34. See the discussion of violence in the Christian tradition in Oliver McTernan, *Violence in God's Name: Religion in an Age of Conflict* (Maryknoll, NY: Orbis Books, 2003), pp. 52-66.

35. Peter J. Haas, "The Just War Doctrine and Postmodern Warfare," in *Strike Terror No More: Theology, Ethics, and the New War*, ed. Jon L. Berquist (St. Louis: Chalice Press, 2002), pp. 236-44.

36. Dorothee Sölle, *Suffering*, trans. Everett R. Kalin (Philadelphia: Fortress Press, 1984); and Rita Nakashima Brock, *Journeys by Heart: A Christology of Erotic Power* (New York: Crossroad, 1988), p. 56.

tured from and longing for the maternal.[37] Slavoj Žižek reads the crucifixion through Lacanian lenses of a subject striking at himself to gain the space of free action.[38] A postcolonial perspective may find these theories unsettling as it is not clear how such psychoanalytical analyses will benefit those at the bottom of society.

Feminist theologians Rita Nakashima Brock and Rebecca Ann Parker take a different route and question if violence and redemptive suffering are key to salvation.[39] Their research has shown that in early Christian iconography and paintings, the dominant motifs had been on the resurrection, paradise, and fullness of life. The images of crucifixion appeared only after Christian violence erupted against the pagans. Anselm's satisfaction theory of atonement took shape during the First Crusade, when Jesus' death was seen as restoring God's honor. The symbol of crucifixion then becomes a justification for violence, which is remembered and re-enacted during Eucharist. Instead of glorifying suffering, Rita Nakashima Brock exhorts us to celebrate communal redemption: "Salvation comes from communal practices that affirm incarnation, the Spirit in life, and its ongoing promise of resurrection and paradise."[40]

Violence and salvation are closely related to the problem of evil. Womanist ethicist Emilie M. Townes breaks new ground in her exploration of race, gender, and the cultural production of evil. She is not satisfied with the objective and cool-headed studies of the "isms" which perpetuate oppression in society, and turns to narratives, especially those written by African-American writers, to probe "the deep interior material life of evil and its manifestations."[41] Building on and expanding Foucault and Gramsci's work, she elucidates how fantastic hegemonic imagination works to create caricatures and stereotypes of black people, especially black women, from the Black Matriarch to the Welfare Queen. She writes:

---

37. Julia Kristeva, "Holbein's Dead Christ," in her *Black Sun: Depression and Melancholia*, trans. Leon S. Roudiez (New York: Columbia University Press, 1989), pp. 105-38.

38. Slavoj Žižek, *The Fragile Absolute, or Why Is the Christian Legacy Worth Fighting For?* (London: Verso, 2000), pp. 157-60.

39. Rita Nakashima Brock and Rebecca Ann Parker, *Proverbs of Ashes: Violence, Redemptive Suffering and the Search for What Saves Us* (Boston: Beacon Press, 2001).

40. Rita Nakashima Brock, "The Cross of Resurrection and Communal Redemption," in *Cross-Examinations: Readings on the Meaning of the Cross Today,* ed. Marit Trelstad (Minneapolis: Fortress Press, 2006), p. 250.

41. Emilie M. Townes, *Womanist Ethics and the Cultural Production of Evil* (New York: Palgrave Macmillan, 2006), p. 5.

This imagination conjures up worlds and their social structures that are not based on supernatural powers and phantasms, but on the ordinariness of evil. It is this imagination, I argue, that helps to hold systematic, structural evil in place.[42]

To dismantle the cultural production of evil, Townes returns to H. Richard Niebuhr's notion of social solidarity in his responsibility ethics. Individuals must work with their communities and social worlds, and increasingly in a global context. People of faith must respond to God's call to respect others and all of creation and to construct a countermemory that proclaims hope in the midst of evil.

An insidious cultural production of evil — to maintain a particular quality of life for a privileged few — has subjected people to slavery, colonialism, and genocide. Twenty percent of the populations in developed nations consume 86 percent of the world's goods, while a huge population, mostly people of color, is condemned to living in abject poverty. Half of the world's population subsists on less than $2 a day. The poor nations spend $13 on debt repayment for every $1 they receive in grants. The lives of millions of children are needlessly lost annually because of world governments' failure to reduce poverty levels.[43] The conditions that set liberation theology into motion have not gone away, but have actually worsened. After the disintegration of the Soviet Union and the realignment of Eastern Europe, theologians who supported the neo-liberal economy, especially from the North, were quick to declare that liberation theology was dead, passé, because Marxism was outdated. They appear not to be cognizant of the fact that liberation philosophers and theologians such as Franz Hinkelammert and Enrique Dussel continue to be deeply engaged with issues of the globalized market and postmodernity.

Liberation theologians from the South have made further investigations regarding the relationship between class oppression and the degradation of the environment. Leonardo Boff has argued for a broader understanding of liberation to include the nonhuman realm. The option for the poor, he says, must include the most threatened beings in creation, and democracy must include socio-cosmic democracy. He envisages that the concern for a more integral liberation of human beings and the earth can open dialogues be-

42. Townes, *Womanist Ethics*, p. 21.
43. See the Global Issues that Affect Everyone website, http://www.globalissues.org//TradeRelated/Facts.asp#fact1.

tween the North and the South.[44] His colleague from Brazil, Ivone Gebara, has advanced an eco-feminist theology, which begins with criticizing the anthropocentric, patriarchal, and dualistic epistemology upon which traditional theology has been based. Instead of a salvation that focuses on humans, she argues for a biocentric understanding of salvation, which includes respect for the life of every being. Jesus does not possess a superior will, nor is he superior to other human beings. He is not the powerful "son of God" or the king who dominates. Rather, Jesus is reimagined as a symbol of our dream and our love, a model of communion with all things and of the vulnerability of love.[45]

Liberation theology meets postcolonialism and queer studies in the work of Marcella Althaus-Reid, born and raised in Argentina. By claiming that every theology is always a sexual theology, Althaus-Reid places sexuality firmly in a central position of the Christian imaginary. Contrasted with feminist theology's uncovering of the gender codes within Christian theology, Althaus-Reid's "indecent theology" reveals and undresses the sexual ideologies that pervade the assumptions and methodologies of theology. Sexuality is an integral part of liberation theology, she says, because there is no sexuality before society, and the poor are sexual beings as well as economic beings. She surmises:

> Sexual ideologies are foundational in economic and political structures of oppression, just as they remain foundational in our understanding of ourselves and ourselves in relation to God . . . only a political Feminist Theology has the capability of de-articulating the present gender ordering of the market system and liberating not only humanity but also God from the narrow sexual ideological confines in which God has been located.[46]

Shifting from gender to sexuality, with a perceptive understanding of the postcolonial condition, Althaus-Reid thus challenges both feminist theologians who dwell on gender and sexuality without talking about economics, and liberation theologians who dismiss women's and queer concerns as sidetracking from the "real" issues of liberation.

---

44. Leonardo Boff, *Cry of the Earth, Cry of the Poor* (Maryknoll, NY: Orbis Books, 1997), pp. 112-14.

45. Ivone Gebara, *Longing for Running Water: Ecofeminism and Liberation* (Minneapolis: Fortress Press, 1999), pp. 173-92.

46. Marcella Althaus-Reid, *From Feminist Theology to Indecent Theology* (London: SCM Press, 2004), p. 4.

Conclusion

Jesus said, "Render to Caesar what is Caesar's and to God what is God's" (Matt. 22:21). What is due to Caesar and to God has become a critical question for Christians living in the age of empire, when the United States has become a superpower the likes of which human history has never seen before. By learning how those theologians who have gone before us dealt with this question in their time, we gain critical insights for engaging with the empire of our time. One lesson is that we must see theology and politics not as two separate spheres, but as necessarily interacting with one another. The issues of race, class, gender, sexuality, and colonialism are not added on or tangential to theology, as if they can be separated from discourses on God, Christology, ecclesiology, etc. Every discussion about God is also a discussion about power, about human relations, about sexuality, about our being in the world.

The New Testament closes with a powerful social imaginary — that of the new heaven and the new earth (Rev. 21:1). Writing on the island of Patmos, the author of the Book of Revelation articulates a counterhegemonic theologic radically different from that of imperial Rome. Today, the vision of the new heaven and new earth continues to inspire us in search for justice, peace, and reconciliation for the whole world.

41 Spirit and Liberation: Achieving Postcolonial Theology in the United States

Mark Lewis Taylor

It was a fearful sight to see them thus frying in the fire and the streams of blood quenching the same, and horrible was the stink and scent thereof but the victory seemed a sweet sacrifice, and they gave the praise thereof to God, who had wrought so wonderfully for them, thus to enclose their enemies in their hands and give them so speedily a victory over so proud and insulting an enemy.[1]

Why do they hate us? The answer to that is that we're a Christian nation. . . . We are hated because we are a nation of believers. [Our] spiritual enemy will only be defeated if we come against them in the name of Jesus.[2]

Postcolonial theology becomes possible, thinkable — and then achievable — when and if it lives from communities of social practice that embody its viewpoints and values. Postcolonial theology in the United States, however, would seem to lack its social moorings because of U.S. Christian communities' explicit or *de facto* support of their nation's colonizing and imperial pursuits, from its founding to its present imperial wars.

1. William Bradford, 1867, cited in David E. Stannard, *American Holocaust: Columbus and the Conquest of the New World* (New York: Oxford University Press, 1992), p. 114.
2. William G. Boykin, Army Lt. Gen. and U.S. Deputy Undersecretary of Defense for Intelligence, lecturing in 2003 at U.S. churches about his foes in Somalia, Afghanistan, and North Korea, from William M. Arkin, "The Pentagon Unleashes a Holy Warrior," *Los Angeles Times*, 20 October 2003.

This chapter develops the problem of the socioreligious location of postcolonial theology in the United States. A first section notes U.S. Christian communities' widespread failure to resist U.S. imperial practice, their accommodating of empire. A second section constructs definitions of postcolonial theory and ethos. This is all preparatory to the heart of the essay, a third section, which shows how developments in postcolonial theory and also in the history of religious communities yield a notion of "postcolonial spirit" that can engender postcolonial theology. Achieving postcolonial theology today, however, will depend on postcolonial theologians' responding to certain contemporary practical crises that I treat in a final section.

Postcolonial Theology without a Church?

This chapter's epigraphs show the centuries of interplay between a twisted Christian piety and U.S. war-making against envisioned enemies. The mutual support that has flourished between Bush's neoconservative architects of a *Pax Americana* warrior-state, on the one hand, and the millions of nationalist evangelicals, on the other, is just one recent example of such cooperation in the long history of U.S. territorial expansion and acquisition, colonialism and slavery, neocolonialism and empire-building.

In spite of a broad literature on Christians' role in U.S. imperial and colonial expansionism, Christians, and also university students and scholars outside the church, remain ignorant or in denial of that legacy.[3] A heartless and contentious Christian triumphalism has been an enduring trait in U.S. history.

The dependence of any postcolonial theology on some corresponding community is not unlike the social dependency of nearly any theoretical position. Whether an intellectual position is a group ideology or a more institutionalized academic discipline, it is some sociohistorical community of flesh-and-blood interpreters/readers/believers that gives that intellectual position its life.

Any postcolonial theology will have a tough time finding an ecclesial or

---

3. Stannard, *American Holocaust*, and Richard Drinnon, *Facing West: The Metaphysics of Indian-Hating and Empire Building* (Minneapolis: University of Minnesota Press, 1980); Ward Churchill, *A Little Matter of Genocide: Holocaust and Denial in the Americas, 1492 to the Present* (San Francisco: City Lights, 1997).

religious group as its social mediator in the U.S. today. The present war in Iraq is but one more chapter in a history of Christian silence and support of U.S. policies of racist slavery, massacre, and genocide. Small numbers of U.S. Christians, even the leadership of large Protestant and Catholic churches, lifted their voices against the war in Iraq. But they could not rival the mix of nationalist evangelicalism and imperial politics that from William Bradford to William Boykin has left a history of destruction.

The festering wound of war and occupation in Iraq today focuses that history. Destruction abounds: in a Texas hospital a young female soldier crawls along a corridor with no legs, while her three-year-old son trails behind.[4] She is one of more than 7,000 U.S. soldiers maimed for life; more than 1,000 are dead in the Iraqi campaign.[5] These numbers are dwarfed by the thousands of Iraqi soldiers dead and wounded. Moreover, even by conservative estimates, some 7,000 to 10,000 Iraqi civilians were killed in the 2003 military assault, and the totals dying as a result of occupation and resistance are still mounting. Stories in the U.S. of parents, sons, and daughters maimed by war and occupation can be multiplied a thousand times over if we examine with equal care the plight of Iraqi families. The Bush regime worked this destruction as a unilateral and preemptive enactment of a long-planned invasion, ignoring or disdaining intelligence reports indicating that Iraq's weapons of mass destruction were not an immediate threat.[6] A wealthy President from a family that has long defended the nation's wealthiest classes is allowed to line the pockets of the corporate class with tax cuts and reconstruction contracts for his corporate colleagues.[7] Stoking citizen fear after 9/11, the Bush regime's surveillance state gobbles up civil liberties — first for groups long-stigmatized by racism, and then for nearly everyone.[8] Amid their nation's ever more militant and aggressive imperialism, U.S. Christian and religious communities seem toothless and compliant, if not outright supportive.

Is this what Christianity is, an ideology for reinforcing imperial war and

4. Jeffrey Gettleman, "A Soldier's Return to a Dark and Moody World," *New York Times,* 30 December 2003.

5. Alex Callinicos, *The New Mandarins of American Power: The Bush Administration's Plans for the World* (Cambridge: Polity Press, 2004; distributed in the U.S. by Blackwell).

6. Statistics taken in August 2004 from http://www.andwar.com/casatalties.

7. Kevin Phillips, *American Dynasty: Aristocracy, Fortune, and the Politics of Deceit in the House of Bush* (New York: Viking, 2004), pp. 21-22, 127-28, 149-77.

8. Christian Parenti, *The Soft Cage: Surveillance in America from Slavery to the War on Terror* (New York: Basic Books, 2003).

exploitation? Maybe, at best, it is a gentlemanly club espousing notions of "love" to teach empires some kinder and gentler ways. Against that conclusion, this chapter argues that there is failure here, indeed a betrayal of the Jewish and Christian prophetic impulses that developed within a religiopolitical resistance to the imperial ways of Roman power. It is against that past that Christianity's endorsement of empire today is seen as "failure." That past is one resource for theologians seeking common cause with antiimperial and anticolonialist efforts of postcolonial struggle.

But what *is* postcolonial theory such that we might find Christian communities at odds with it today, or such that we might propose that Christians make common cause with it? Some definitions are in order.

Postcolonial Theory — Terms, Tensions, Ethos

Overall, postcolonial theory is, in fact, a set of theories arising from and reflecting on anticolonial liberating struggle against, and within, geopolitical systems that generate large-scale human suffering. I identify, first, three closely related conceptual dyads that help organize the range of theoretical approaches postcolonial theorists take to understanding histories of global structures. These dyads, then, enable us to clarify postcolonial theory amid certain creative tensions that have become constitutive of postcolonial theorizing.

Colonialism/Imperialism

Postcolonial theory's primary focus is the modern colonial system, emerging with fifteenth-century Europeans' colonizing projects in the Americas, Africa, and Asia, as undertaken primarily by Spanish, British, and French imperial powers. "Colonialism" can be defined as the organized deployment of racialized and gendered constructs for practices of acquiring and maintaining political control over other social groups, settling their lands with new residents, and/or exploiting that land and its peoples through military and administrative occupiers.[9] A range of diverse practices was deployed toward

---

9. See Jürgen Osterhammel, *Colonialism: A Theoretical Overview* (Princeton, NJ: M. Wiener, 1996), pp. 22-25. See also Anne McClintock, *Imperial Leather: Race, Gender and Sexuality in the Colonial Contest* (New York: Routledge, 1995).

colonizing ends: forced removal of peoples from their lands, military or paramilitary slaughter, slavery, imprisonment, and more.

"Imperialism" shares with colonialism a tendency to subjugate other peoples, but it refers more to an organized power's drive to establish and expand its subjugating control. Indeed, the terms *colonialism* and *imperialism* often work together, so much so that they are at times used interchangeably; hence, I have interpreted them in dyadic relation to each other. Nevertheless, imperialism usually refers to the specific actions of colonizers to constitute their power as "a political machine that rules from the center, and extends its control to the furthest reaches of the peripheries."[10]

Decolonization/Recolonization

Postcolonial theory works also with a sense of a major transition: "decolonization." As a historical phenomenon, it began with the seventeenth- and eighteenth-century independence movements against Spain, producing new nations in Latin America. It continued in twentieth-century, anticolonial movements for liberation, often marked as beginning in 1947 with India's independence, but extending across Asia and Africa, with new nations carved from British, French, Dutch, and Portuguese domains.

But decolonization did not end colonial subjugation. Although certain opportunities came with independence, "recolonization" processes ran concurrently. The very terms of African independence, for example, were often established so as to preserve African countries' continuing political and economic subjugation to colonizing powers.[11] During the era of decolonization in Africa of the 1940s and 1950s, the U.S. became a key participant with European powers in crafting future modes of control over African regions.[12]

This notion of recolonization also reminds us that decolonizing independence movements often entailed processes of internal colonization of certain groups within the "independent" nations. The dispossession and disenfranchisement of indigenous and African peoples in the newly indepen-

10. Robert J. C. Young, *Postcolonialism: An Historical Introduction* (Oxford: Blackwell, 2001), p. 27.

11. Kwame Nkrumah, *Neo-colonialism: The Last Stage of Imperialism* (New York: International Publishers, 1966), p. x.

12. Amy Kaplan, "'Left Alone with America': The Absence of Empire in the Study of American Culture," in *Cultures of United States Imperialism,* ed. Amy Kaplan and Donald E. Pease (Durham, NC: Duke University Press, 1993), pp. 8, 20 n. 7.

dent United States is just one example. Again, decolonizing and recolonizing activities need to be thought in dyadic relation.

Neocolonialism/Imperialism

We obtain, then, a third dyad that is parallel to the first one. "Neocolonialism" is the name for the political and economic reconstitution of previous colonial subjugation. It is marked by new forms of political/economic dependency on particular European nations, or on multinational, corporately connected regimes such as the World Bank, the International Monetary Fund, or the World Trade Organization.[13]

Imperialism also is reconstituted, especially in the milieu of post–World War II neocolonialism, when the United States' new imperialist agenda becomes important to theorize: "Think of the Pentagon and the CIA in Washington, with their global strategy of controlling events in independent states all over the world in order to defeat communism or Islamic resistance and further US interests."[14] U.S. empire and imperialism were terms that once predominated largely among a marginalized left. Now they are commonly deployed by authors of various political approaches.[15]

Against the backdrop of these three dyadic relations, we may approach the notion of the *postcolonial*. The actual term stems from literary circles of the 1970s, amid the early intense decades of decolonization and recolonization, when writings from diverse colonial settings cross-pollinated with one another.[16] The postcolonial was a hybrid discourse, but increasingly also a discourse of resistance, especially because it was a discourse forged by colonized subjects' struggle. Those once rendered "native informants" now have emerged also "to resist a mere celebration of global hybridity" and to "anthropologize the heritage of the Euro–United States more deliberately."[17] In this way, postcolonial subjects become, in Spivak's language, "wild anthro-

---

13. Thandika Mkandawire and Charles Chukwuma Codesria Soludo, *African Voices on Structural Adjustment* (Trenton, NJ, and London: Africa World, Turnaround, 2003).

14. Young, *Postcolonialism*, p. 27.

15. Chalmers A. Johnson, *The Sorrows of Empire: Militarism, Secrecy, and the End of the Republic*, 1st ed. (New York: Metropolitan Books, 2004).

16. Bill Ashcroft, *Post-Colonial Transformation* (London and New York: Routledge, 2001), pp. 9-10.

17. Gayatri Chakravorty Spivak, *A Critique of Postcolonial Reason: Toward a History of the Vanishing Present* (Cambridge, MA: Harvard University Press, 1999), p. 157.

pologists"; in Mignolo's language, borrowing from Brazilian scholar Darcy Ribeiro, they are "anthropologians" *(anthrapolagadoros)* who, unlike First World anthropologists, belong to the worlds made "other" by colonizers.[18]

Postcolonial theorists, essayists, and others (poets, artists, writers, activists) were tossed about, and sometimes adrift, in the churning turbulence of decolonizing power meeting recolonizing power, of hopes raised and dashed. Like two rivers we might imagine colliding head on, the meeting of these two processes leaves a discourse fraught not just with hybridity, but with tumult, chaos, and also unexpected eddies and pools with hidden undercurrents and whirlpools. The second dyad of decolonization/recolonization, then, gives birth to ambiguities and ambivalences and to accompanying fruitful tensions in postcolonial theory.

A first such tension arises from the fact that *the "post-" is no longer "post-,"* or at least not in the sense of "after," for with neocolonialism and a strengthened militaristic imperialism so resurgent, there is no simple epoch "after colonialism." The "post-" comes now to signify not only a temporal "after" but also an always ongoing quality of being, a practice and struggle poised against and moving beyond colonial and neocolonial formations wherever those formations may be found. Postcolonial theory, then, displays a strange transtemporal frame: it traces history along a simplistic epochal road (pre-colonial/colonial/postcolonial), but within the turbulence of decolonization/recolonization it refigures that linearity as marking a quality of continuing and diverse struggle.

Postcolonial discourse wrestles with a second tension, *the near ubiquity of colonizing power.* The geohistorical subjugations attending "the historical fact" of European colonialism[19] interplay with a broad range of other subjugations, those that use constructs such as race, class, and gender. At times, these other subjugations may be theorized with so comprehensive a scope that they take on their own global meaningfulness, so that white racism, class exploitation, the oppression of women can each seem to be the geohistorical problematic. Postcolonial theory, however, usually reserves the geohistorical role to colonialism's historical fact and then studies colonialism as it is inscribed in other systemic violations.

The third tension is that of *diasporic tricontinentalism.* This concerns

---

18. Walter D. Mignolo, *Local Histories/Global Designs: Coloniality, Subaltern Knowledges, and Border Thinking* (Princeton, NJ: Princeton University Press, 2000), p. 20.

19. Bill Ashcroft, Gareth Griffiths, and Helen Triffin, eds., *The Post-colonial Studies Reader* (London and New York: Routledge, 1995), p. 2.

the way postcolonial studies locates the geopolitical sites of struggle. On the one hand, the basic tendency is to see (neo)colonial exploitation as occurring between Northern powers and tricontinental areas of "the South" (Latin America, Africa, Asia). Young points to the Havana Tricontinental of 1966, which united anticolonial activists from those continents and "initiated . . . the founding moment of postcolonial theory in its journal, the *Tricontinental.*"[20] On the other hand, postcolonial theory also reflects on (neo)colonizing exploitation occurring within Europe and the U.S., due especially to the diaspora of tricontinental peoples into imperialist nations, and due also to longstanding anticolonial struggles within those regions (especially by indigenous, African American, and Latino/a peoples in the U.S.).

Fourth, postcolonial studies features a tension termed *neocolonizing anticolonialism.* It is very difficult not to participate in neocolonizing formations when being a postcolonial or anticolonialist scholar. Because of this difficulty, Spivak has embraced a "deconstructive" approach, one that recognizes that the "no" uttered against (neo)colonialist structures comes often while also intimately inhabiting them.[21] Spivak thus focuses significant parts of her criticism on tensions and contradictions besetting "neocolonial anticolonialists," a category in which she, at times, also includes herself. It is precisely through this acknowledgment of complicity and this self-critique that postcolonial theory pursues some of its most critical tasks.

A final tension lies in postcolonial theorists' *struggle to relate hybridity to resistance.* Overall, we might say that this is an effort to balance "discourses of difference" with "discourses of liberation." It is an attempt to so craft hybridity's interstitial navigation of fluid worlds (differentiated one from another, changing into ever different forms) that the effects of that hybridity are resistant and liberatory. Or, beginning with liberation, it is a matter of so crafting a discourse of liberating resistance that simple binaries are transcended and the differentiated character of liberatory practice is attended to. In these ways, postcolonial theorists seek to nuance liberating anticolonialism without eviscerating their oppositional stances.

As I write, postcolonial studies in the United States is tempted to gloss its anticolonialist, liberating struggle, prone to morph into a ludic (playful) postmodernism in U.S. academies, which indulges ever-different reading and rereading of texts (usually in English), while losing along that way a politically liberating concern. In this way, scholars' discourses of difference

20. Young, *Postcolonialism*, p. 5.
21. Spivak, *Critique of Postcolonial Reason*, p. 191.

hide and sacrifice their discourses of liberation. This is unfortunate because the great formulators of poststructuralist and postmodern theory were never merely ludic. Their discourses of difference emerged out of the traumas of French colonialism and anticolonialist struggle and thus had liberating force.[22]

Today, though, after a number of U.S. scholars in postcolonial studies articulated critiques of U.S. policy, some conservative forces have responded by threatening to curtail federal funds for postcolonial and area studies programs.[23] Postcolonial studies programs are thus, occasionally, in an awkward position of going before U.S. political committees to assure them that they "actively collaborate with our national security and defense institutions."[24] If not striking such compliant postures, others in postcolonial studies may be tempted to deploy obscurantist poco/pomo-speak where the discourse of otherness (alterity) dulls the liberationist edge that cuts against present U.S. neocolonialism and imperialism.[25]

At its best, though, postcolonial theorists preserve the relation of the two discourses, holding together the discourses of difference (and all the interstitiality of hybrid states) with the discourses of liberating struggle. Working for this integral relation marks what I call an *ethos of postcolonial theory,* the thought-full participation in a practice of "differentiated liberating struggle." In this ethos the discourses of difference are taken up as intrinsic to, and facilitative of, liberating struggle.

As "liberating struggle" postcolonial theories' ethos is in continuity with anticolonialist struggles, especially seeking to move against and beyond current imperialist formations in today's U.S.-dominated neocolonizing milieu. Here persists that binary of colonized/colonizer so vividly struck by writers such as Frantz Fanon[26] and Albert Memmi,[27] which can-

22. Young, *Postcolonialism,* pp. 411-26.

23. See Zachary Lockman, "Behind the Battles over Middle East Studies," *Middle East Report Online* (January 2004), http://www.merip.orglinerolintersentions/iockmanainterv.html.

24. U.S. House Subcommittee on Select Education, Hearings on Reauthorization of Title ITT of the Higher Education Act, 108th Cong., 2003. Duke University's Gilbert W. Merkx testified before the subcommittee on June 19, 2003.

25. See also E. San Juan, "Establishment Postcolonialism and Its Alter/Native Others: Deciding to Be Accountable in a World of Permanent Emergency," in *Postcolonial America,* ed. C. Richard King (Urbana and Chicago: University of Illinois Press, 2000).

26. Frantz Fanon, *Toward the African Revolution: Political Essays* (New York: Grove Press, 1969), pp. 80-81.

27. Albert Memmi, *The Colonizer and the Colonized* (New York: Orion Press, 1965).

not be dissolved and which, in fact, is an essential part of effective anti-colonial resistance.[28]

But the ethos of postcolonial studies is also "differential," and as such its theories and practices always also depend on theorizing different sites of liberation, as well as different views of just what liberation is. This almost always complicates the necessary binary that is at the heart of liberatory struggle. But these differentiated complexities need not dissolve that binary. It is of the ethos of postcolonial studies, at its best, to take sides with the colonized against colonizing agents and powers, but in ways that do not exclude complexity and difference.

Postcolonial Theology and Postcolonial Spirit

When the postcolonial *ethos* of "differentiated liberating struggle" is discernible in religious communities, we can speak of those communities as manifesting postcolonial spirit.[29] These historical communities of spirit constitute necessary conditions for achieving a postcolonial theology. Before examining those dynamic communities, let us note a certain postcolonial "turn to spirit" among postcolonial theorists themselves.

Postcolonial Theory's Turn to Spirit

First, Tunisian philosopher and novelist Albert Memmi noted that although colonizers and churches often worked together to maintain the ruthless colonial relation, the conversionist agenda of the churches was often seen by colonial administrators as subversive of colonial hierarchical relations.[30]

This insight might direct us to the studies on missionary practice in colonialism as mixing blatant reinforcement of colonized peoples' subjugation with penchants for subverting that subjugation.[31] I make this point not to

28. Frances FitzGerald, *Fire in the Lake: The Vietnamese and the Americans in Vietnam*, 1st ed. (Boston: Little, Brown, 1972), pp. 168-75.

29. On the relationship of "spirit" and cultural ethos, see Mark Lewis Taylor, "Tracking Spirit: Theology as Cultural Critique in the Americas," in *Changing Conversations: Religious Reflection and Cultural Analysis*, ed. Sheila Greeve Davaney and Dwight N. Hopkins (New York: Routledge, 1997).

30. Memmi, *Colonizer and the Colonized*, pp. 72-73.

31. Jean Comaroff and John L. Comaroff, *Of Revelation and Revolution* (Chicago: University of Chicago Press, 1991), esp. pp. 78f.

argue for Christian missions. I only suggest that Memmi's point displays a consciousness among anticolonialist writings that the sheer presence of Christian communities — even in its conversionist modes — does not make them *eo ipso* only colonizing forces.

Second, some of the most recent expositions of postcolonialism show a penchant for considering spiritual communities as generating anticolonialist struggle. Robert Young, for example, emphasizes that very important modes of anticolonial resistance lie in "movements of religious revivalism: anti-colonial discontent articulated through religious movements that assert a traditional indigenous culture in the name of a utopic decolonized future."[32] He cites not only the study of the Comaroffs in South Africa but also analyses of Islamic and Hindu nationalism, the *Mahdi* movements in East Africa and South Asia, and diverse prophetic and messianic movements. Elsewhere, Young somewhat upbraids his postcolonial colleagues for an "unmediated secularism, opposed to and consistently excluding the religions that have taken on the political identity of providing alternative value-systems to those of the West. . . . Postcolonial theory, despite its espousal of subaltern resistance, scarcely values subaltern resistance that does not operate according to its own secular terms."[33]

Third, I point out Spivak's suggestions about the importance of certain theological tendencies in postcolonial reason itself. As Kant portrayed the human being as "programmed to supplement rational morality by the name God," so Spivak suggests that postcolonial rationality, especially when seeking to imagine the ethics of responsibility toward subaltern peoples, might consider the name "God" (after her thoroughgoing critique of the "axiomatics of imperialism" in Kant and others). To be sure, this would be a complex operation, one that she only limns:

> Working through the Kierkegaard-Levinas-Derrida rather than the Dewey-Rorty line, this name ["God"] may be seen as *a* name of the radical alterity that the self as "the narrative center of gravity" is programmed to imagine in an ethics of responsibility.[34]

There are other segments of *A Critique of Postcolonial Reason* in which she invites conversation with theologians, as when she admits to dreaming of "animist liberation theologies to girdle the perhaps impossible vision of

32. Young, *Postcolonialism*, p. 63.
33. Young, *Postcolonialism*, p. 338.
34. Young, *Postcolonialism*, p. 355 n. 59.

an ecologically just world." She quickly adds, though, "The name theology is alien to this thinking."[35]

The precise nature of this "theological" dreaming, and its implications, cannot be explored here. Her dreaming is enough, though, to suggest a certain openness of postcolonial theories, prompting mutual work between theology and postcolonial studies. But now, what of spiritual communities' openness to postcolonial ethos and study?

Religious and Spiritual Resources of Postcolonial Spirit

Are there communal conditions in religious and spiritual traditions that manifest a postcolonial ethos of differential liberatory struggle? Have these existed in ways that contest forces of colonialism, empire, and neocolonialism? I here turn briefly to four resources, beginning with a communal formation at the origins of Christianity. As will become evident with the fourth resource, however, any postcolonial theology will have to move beyond only being "Christian" and embrace new interreligious and intercultural modalities.

1. The first set of communal conditions is presented by the first-century Jesus movement, as rendered by recent historical research. No sweeping generalizations are possible here, nor should we idealize the origins as always counter-imperial. This literature does establish, though, that the early Christian and Jesus movements were profoundly counter-imperial in major ways. They were marked by a communal ethos that often resisted exploitative hierarchical power.[36] There was a restless political contentiousness, a series of large and small, daily resistances to oppressive powers, and a building of new communities against them.[37]

Centuries of Christian imperialist hermeneutics have obscured the counter-imperial elements of Christianity's own scriptural narratives: Jesus' contesting imperial corruption in the temple-state of his time; Gospel writer Mark's portraits of Jesus' actions in opposition to Roman occupying soldiers; Jesus' death by crucifixion, an execution usually for the seditious who threatened the religiously backed imperial order; the apostle Paul's money-

---

35. Young, *Postcolonialism*, p. 382.

36. Richard A. Horsley and Neil Asher Silberman, *The Message and the Kingdom: How Jesus and Paul Ignited a Revolution and Transformed the Ancient World* (New York: Grossett/Putnam, 1997).

37. Marianne Sawicki, *Crossing Galilee: Architectures of Contact in the Occupied Land of Jesus* (Harrisburg, PA: Trinity Press International, 2000).

raising and community-building activity that kept him quite literally on the run across imperial terrain until he was executed in the capital city, Rome.[38]

Again, none of this should lead us to deemphasize the centuries of Christianity's sanctioning of violence, war, repression, racism, and empire-building. Yet the diverse Jesus movement research in our period points to counter-imperial communal formations at the genesis of Christianity, making thinkable a contemporary theology that is politically liberationist and resistant to colonizing and imperial powers.

2. A second resource consists of those communities of liberation in the Americas that helped generate liberation theologies. I have in mind, primarily, the liberation theology from communities in Latin America, but also the movements and resistance of African Americans and women in North America and elsewhere, who generated, respectively, black and feminist liberation theologies. During the emergence of the present imperialist ideology in the U.S., there has been much talk about the "end" of liberation theology, this usually being associated with the collapse of state socialisms in Eastern Europe and the Soviet Union. Even *if* liberation theologies had ended, the fact of their vibrant presence from the 1950s to the 1980s would establish the presence of religious communities of anti-imperial resistance.

It must be stressed, though, that liberation theology is not dead, especially among Christians in Latin America and the Caribbean. There have been fundamental changes, to be sure,[39] but Latin American and Caribbean Christian communities still feature singers, preachers, liturgists, and theologians who cast their weekly worship, practice, and theological interpretations in ways that speak of political revolution against U.S. imperialism.

Moreover, the liberationist communal spirit is resident now, especially, in Protestant and neo-Pentecostal groups of Latin America. The majority of Protestant *evangélicos* in Latin America may often exhibit counter-liberationist rhetorics. But significant sectors *are* political and liberationist. All the leaders of one of the most important villages in the Zapatista movement of Chiapas, Mexico, are Presbyterians.[40] Protestants in Bolivia and Ec-

---

38. On adversarial politics in early Jesus movements, see Mark Lewis Taylor, *The Executed God: The Way of the Cross in Lockdown America* (Minneapolis: Fortress Press, 2001), pp. 79-98.

39. Michael Löwy, *The War of Gods: Religion and Politics in Latin America*, Critical Studies in Latin American and Iberian Cultures (London and New York: Verso, 1996), pp. 123-40.

40. Mark Lewis Taylor, "A Zapatista Church: Presbyterians in Chiapas," *Christian Century* 116 (27 Oct. 1999): 1028-31.

uador have had significant impact in the movements against corrupt governments backed by the U.S. and by G-7 economic powers. *Evangélicos* in Brazil, where once Catholic communities were the major source of liberation theology, have played a crucial role in bringing to power the Workers Party candidate, Luis Inacio Lula da Silva, whose Brazilian presidency often now challenges planners of U.S. hegemony.

3. One need not look only to the South for historical communities of postcolonial ethos, vibrant with "differentiated liberatory struggle."[41] There is also an often hidden religious revolutionary tradition in the North Atlantic. Historical studies such as Gilroy's *The Black Atlantic* and Linebaugh's and Rediker's *The Many-Headed Hydra* establish the presence of a centuries-long Christian liberatory social practice against European and North Atlantic capitalism, colonialism, and imperial power. Groups such as the Levellers and Diggers in England, through Christian thinkers and organizers such as Gerard Winstanley, and other activists such as the Jamaican Robert Wedderburn kept alive a Christian history of multireligious liberating struggle. In the seventeenth century, as the Levellers interacted with pirates, runaway slaves, migrants, and impressed seamen around the Atlantic, their spirit of resistance (informed by Christian thought) against English appropriation of commoners' lands became a political force to be reckoned with. Admirals, slave-ship captains, and U.S. "founding fathers" such as James Madison feared this "Levelling spirit."[42]

From the perspective of this history of the religious and revolutionary Atlantic, which faithfully continues the counter-imperial legacy of earlier Jesus movements,[43] the millions of U.S. evangelicals raising flags and Bibles today in obeisance to U.S. war and empire constitute a betrayal of Christian belief and spiritual character. Theologians seeking conversation with postcolonialism have a tradition of liberatory anti-imperial struggle, and they dare not allow that tradition to go without representation in this epoch of nationalistic evangelicalism in the U.S.

---

41. Paul Gilroy, *The Black Atlantic: Modernity and Double Consciousness* (Cambridge, MA: Harvard University Press, 1993).

42. Peter Linebaugh and Marcus Buford Rediker, *The Many-Headed Hydra: Sailors, Slaves, Commoners, and the Hidden History of the Revolutionary Atlantic* (Boston: Beacon Press, 2000), pp. 212-24. On Madison, p. 40. On liberating apocalyptic communities, see also Catherine Keller, *Apocalypse Now and Then: A Feminist Guide to the End of the World* (Boston: Beacon Press, 1996).

43. On this tradition, see Andrew Bradstock and Christopher Rowland, *Radical Christian Writings: A Reader* (Oxford, and Malden, MA: Blackwell, 2002).

4. A fourth resource for postcolonial ethos is offered by justice-oriented participants in loose-knit, interreligious coalitions. These persons may have memberships in relatively apolitical religious organizations, but their political force lies in the alliances for liberation they forge with other people of faith and conscience. Their groupings are usually ad hoc and at times fragmentary. They often gather in ceremonies attending major political mobilizations for justice. These are occasions when it is not unusual for Christians, Jews, Muslims, Buddhists, Hindus, and often spiritual representatives of Native American, African, and European (Celtic, Norse, et al.) traditions to come together to unite their interests in struggles for politically significant change.[44]

Even when their official religious orders are appallingly silent or immobilized in the face of repression, these communities have had a persistent presence. They were part of the resistance to the previous U.S.-backed regimes of repression in El Salvador, Nicaragua, and South Africa. They frequently mobilize against the U.S. death penalty. They have been a small but significant part of the alternative globalization movement. They contributed to the global mobilization against the Bush regime's war plans in Iraq.

These interreligious groups are essential for any postcolonial theology. Indeed, all the communal resources mentioned previously in this section were effective and vibrant not in the mode of any one religious order, but by being motley, ever-changing, multireligious political forces. Indeed, the Jesus movement, often portrayed as a very Christian social community, was in all probability more rife with other religious and cultural forms — and not just the obviously Jewish ones — than has yet been shown. R. S. Sugirtharajah has been especially vigorous in reminding Christians that the very teachings of Jesus, and the movement catalyzed around those teachings, were mediated also by Asian, particularly, Indian, religious and cultural ways.[45] The sociocultural site of the Jesus movement's historicality was an emergent "Christianity" that was Jewish, Hindu, and Buddhist, including elements Persian, Greek, and Roman, with key dimensions of Palestinian rural indigenous traditions, as well.[46]

---

44. For examples, see Roger S. Gottlieb, ed., *Liberating Faith: Religious Voices for Justice, Peace and Ecological Wisdom* (Lanham, MD: Rowman & Littlefield, 2003).

45. R. S. Sugirtharajah, *Asian Biblical Hermeneutics and Postcolonialism: Bible and Liberation* (Maryknoll, NY: Orbis Books, 1998), pp. 112-19.

46. On these religious and cultural elements, see John Dominic Crossan, *The Historical Jesus: The Life of a Mediterranean Jewish Peasant* (San Francisco: Harper San Francisco, 1991).

By Way of Conclusion — Practical Tests for a Postcolonial Theology

Postcolonial theologies can be achieved by keeping their moorings in communal resources of postcolonial spirit like those noted in the previous section. A postcolonial theology will still be insufficient, however, if it is not willing to venture, amid *Pax Americana*'s present nationalism and militarist imperialism, to stake out some politically challenging positions. If they are serious about postcolonial spirit, theologians and religious communities need to risk the opprobrium that will come to them when they take up four important, practical tasks. I offer these tasks as one test of the strength of any postcolonial theologies that would address current crises.

First, postcolonial religious communities and theology must begin by opening their eyes to what is occurring in the United States. What is taking place is a new, particularly vicious version of militarist exploitation that has been ongoing since the nation's founding. Whatever our allegiances to the people, to the land, to certain political traditions of the U.S. — opening our eyes today will mean experiencing and teaching a "great revulsion." I take the term from Paul Krugman's recent book, *The Great Unraveling.*[47]

Princeton economist and *New York Times* columnist Krugman tends to apply the phrase only to the shifts initiated by the neoconservative Bush regime: its subversion of economic futures for the U.S. middle class and poor, its protective policies for the wealthy corporate class, and its lying politics in the lead-up to the 2003 war in Iraq. Indeed, these recent shifts do call forth great revulsion, but so also does the treatment of many others in the history of U.S. colonialism and exploitation, extending from the wars against the Pequots to Pentagon warriors' death-dealing for thousands of Iraqi civilians.

Opening our eyes, experiencing "great revulsion," is part of the habitus of a theology that would be truly postcolonial, constitutionally unable to pursue a politics of denial regarding past and present consequences of U.S. imperial practice. We might hope for this as a kind of new "spiritual awakening" among U.S. theologians, so that they forge a counter-imperial critique in the U.S. that taps the postcolonial spirit that for decades — indeed centuries — has pulsed in the liberating struggle of indigenous, black, and worker groups across the tricontinental South, throughout the Americas, and also in U.S. radical movements. Theology rooted in something less risks creating "postcolonial theology" as only another vanguard among liberal theologies,

---

47. Paul R. Krugman, *The Great Unraveling: Losing Our Way in the New Century,* 1st ed. (New York: W. W. Norton, 2003), p. 20.

shoring up the present liberal hegemony of elite scholars in higher education who accommodate empire.

Second, there is a configuration of power at work in the U.S. that postcolonial theologians will need to address specifically. I have in mind the present alliance of many Christians (the so-called "Christian right"[48]) with a U.S. policy of nearly unqualified support for the repressive practices of Ariel Sharon in Israel.[49] Postcolonial theologians must speak vigorously against governing Israelis' repeated violation of Palestinian peoples' rights and lands. There is nothing like an even-handed policy by the U.S. on the Palestinian repression by contemporary Israeli leaders. Efforts of millions of U.S. Christians reinforce not only that present imbalance but also the institutionalized violence suffered by Palestinians. It also keeps Israeli citizens themselves exposed to the cycles of violence, as noted by many critics within Israel.[50] Grounded in the prophetic traditions of ancient Israel, as well as in Palestinian, Jewish, and others' resistance to Israeli policies, postcolonial theologians must deconstruct the Christian biblicist justification for a predominantly pro-Israel U.S. policy and must dare a theology of liberation for Palestinian peoples long repressed at the hands of British, Israeli, and U.S. powers.

Third, a postcolonial theology will need to relate to liberation movements in the Islamic community. At present, nearly all Islamic movements that understand themselves as resistant to U.S. colonialism and imperial power tend to be dismissed as Islamic fundamentalists or, worse, repressed as "terrorists." A postcolonial theology that theorizes U.S. imperial power, and knows that Muslim peoples have often been resisting it from greatly varying religious heritages, will not be afraid to seek out and support modes of Islamic resistance to neocolonialism that best embody the heritages of postcolonial spirit. This may be done by (a) engaging those who have written Islamic liberation theologies,[51] (b) thinking and working in solidarity with Islamic anti-imperialist groups in the United States and abroad working for justice and peace, and (c) taking up mutually critical dialogue with the black Muslim movements that are so strong in the United States.

---

48. Sara Diamond, *Not by Politics Alone: The Enduring Influence of the Christian Right* (New York: Guilford Press, 1998).

49. Baruch Kimmerling, *Politicide: Ariel Sharon's War Against the Palestinians* (London and New York: Verso, 2003).

50. Tom Segev, Roane Carey, and Jonathan Shainin, *The Other Israel: Voices of Refusal and Dissent* (New York: New Press, 2002).

51. Asgharali Engineer, *Islam and Liberation Theology: Essays on Liberative Elements in Islam* (New Delhi: Sterling, 1990).

Fourth, a truly postcolonial theology does well to position itself not only in relation to those suffering abroad from U.S. imperial adventures but also in relation to the two million-plus locked up in U.S. prisons today. This phenomenon as a whole is beginning to receive attention from postcolonial scholars,[52] especially because a significant number of the imprisoned — more than 70 percent of whom are people of color — are there due to direct or indirect forces of repression in the U.S.[53] Imperial repression abroad traditionally builds dominant coalitions at home,[54] and U.S. security and police-state powers today are targeting all racially stigmatized groups, but especially, now, Muslim, Arab, and South Asian immigrants.

Of note, too, are those activists being imprisoned for civil disobedience actions against U.S. military activity, covert and overt, in Latin America and Iraq. Christians and many others are serving stout sentences for peacefully contesting U.S. military policy.[55] A theology that truly wears the adjective "postcolonial" will not write theology while being silent about all political prisoners in the U.S., among whom must be counted those who resist U.S.-led military and paramilitary violence.

In sum, these four practical tests help mark out for contemporary theologians the religious and political positioning needed for achieving postcolonial theology. If this positioning risks opprobrium, cutting critically against the grain of past and present U.S. violence and imperialism, it may also invite theologians into new cadres of thought and action, into movements of differentiated liberating struggle, which are the manifold dwelling places of postcolonial spirit. As shown in this chapter's third section, postcolonial spirit has a long and rich history. Although U.S. churches rarely harbor postcolonial spirit today, their members, and theologians with them, might open up fresh spaces of postcolonial spirit's legacy by working today with people of spirit from diverse religious, moral, and political orientations. Postcolonial spirit is found in the turning toward ever-new hybrid spaces where the struggle for liberation is underway, and with that turning begins any achieving of postcolonial theology in the U.S.

52. Graeme Harper, *Colonial and Post-Colonial Incarceration* (New York: Continuum, 2001); and Taylor, *Executed God*.

53. On prisons and surveillance, see Christian Parenti, *Lockdown America: Police and Prisons in the Age of Crisis* (London and New York: Verso, 1999); and Parenti, *Soft Cage*.

54. Taylor, *Executed God*, pp. 48-67.

55. From http://www.soawne.org/.

IX. Church-Based Politics

Introduction

Nicholas Adams

The question as to what role the church should play in political life is especially hotly debated in the United States of America, perhaps because of its strong constitutional separation of church and state. The three authors presented here were working in American universities at the time their essays were published. All three essays converge on one point: the questions Christians tend to ask about the relationship between church and political life are often the wrong questions, guided by the wrong categories. Such questions include "What is the right relationship between liturgy and ethics?" (Yoder), "How can the church reconcile the demands of discipline with the demands of pastoral responsibility?" (Hauerwas), and "Should theology be accountable to the academy or to the church?" (Milbank). In each case the author shows that the questions need to be transformed, aided by an investigation to discover the right categories in which to pose them.

John Howard Yoder's "Sacrament as Social Process: Christ the Transformer of Culture" (1991) is short but dense. Its provocative title plays on H. Richard Niebuhr's *Christ and Culture* (1951). The latter, which is not explicitly named in the essay, lists five ways in which Jesus Christ and culture are related: Niebuhr's fifth way is called "Christ transforming culture." Yoder's essay — part of a symposium on rethinking liturgy — attempts to explore this relation in a fashion quite different from Niebuhr's. The text poses the initial question, "What is the right relationship between liturgy and ethics?" Its dominant categories are reconciliation and discernment, Zwinglian and sacramentalist sign-theory, sacramental realism, egalitarianism, democracy and socialism. Its shape is three sets of numbered lists (1-5, 1-5, 1-9) presented in a staccato style followed by a short epilogue.

Yoder finds the initial question to be the product of a bad habit: it treats liturgy and ethics as if they are two distinct things, and then mistakenly tries to build a bridge between them. The mistake is not the attempt to build a bridge, but the habit of thinking that liturgy and ethics are separate things that need a bridge at all. As so often in intellectual life, once a separation has been performed, it becomes formidably difficult to know how to relate the now-discrete entities. The deeper task is to diagnose and repair the cause of the separation. Instead of building (or refusing to build) a bridge, Yoder considers five practices which display features that cannot be described as *either* liturgical *or* ethical. These practices exemplify liturgical ethical life in their unseparated form. He goes on to investigate bad Catholic and Reformed habits that separate them.

The five practices are scriptural: fraternal admonition, the universality of charisma, the Spirit's freedom in the meeting, breaking bread, and induction into the new humanity. These descriptions are themselves noteworthy. They are primarily neither liturgical nor ethical in character, in the restricted senses these terms now have. They are practices of everyday life: reconciling those who have offended (Matt. 18:18), recognizing the value of each member (1 Cor. 12:7), permitting all to speak at meetings (1 Cor. 14:26-33; Yoder does not comment on verses 34-35, which exclude women), eating together (1 Cor. 11:23-24), and baptism (interpreted through Eph. 2:15). It is striking that even reconciliation, the breaking of bread, and baptism are regarded as not primarily liturgical. Yoder makes it explicit that the historically later narrowing of these practices to acts that are understood as specifically liturgical (in a sense that is contrasted with everyday action) robs them of their radical significance.

Baptism is a test case for Yoder: it displays the tendency to split liturgical from ethical categories. The "sacramentalist" tendency is to consider baptism in relation to original sin. The "Zwinglian" tendency is to consider baptism as an expression of an inward individual experience. By contrast a "sacramental realism" considers baptism as a practice that constitutes a new people and makes previous forms of hierarchy less absolute because of the new. This is a compressed diagnosis. Yoder suggests that the "sacramentalist" approach is realist, but its reality (original sin) is too distilled a description of the human condition. By contrast the "Zwinglian" approach is oriented to human experience, but the practice of baptism now "signifies" something rather than actually performing it: it is insufficiently realist. For Yoder, Scripture knows nothing of excessive distillation or mere signification: being baptized does not merely signify induction into the new humanity; being baptized is this induction.

It is noteworthy that Yoder identifies the tendency to split liturgical from ethical categories in both Roman Catholic and Reformed traditions. The one is too liturgical and the other too ethical. The solution is not to mediate liturgical and ethical categories (which already reproduces the original mistake of thinking them separate) but to refuse the split. "Sacramental realism" is Yoder's term for this repair. His nine "implications" spell this out in various ways; indeed, they help repair other false separations too, such as "reason and revelation," "Protestant and Catholic," and "radical and liberal."

Yoder takes a question that arises from a false separation. Instead of trying to answer the question directly, he attempts to repair the false separation that generates it. The question itself is transformed once the repair is complete.

Stanley Hauerwas's "How We Lay Bricks and Make Disciples," from *After Christendom?* (1991), poses an initial question: How can the church be a community of discipline if it understands itself (and is understood by others) to be a pastoral community? It appears that the requirements of "discipline" and "pastoral care" contradict each other. If one insists on discipline, one is not being pastoral; if one is pastoral, one cannot insist on discipline. The dominant categories are: care/discipline, voluntary/authoritative, friendly/witness, private/public, individual/community, pastoral/liturgical, formed/unformed, apprenticeship/common sense. The essay is structured into two broad sections. The first states a series of pairs in opposition to each other; the second calls into question these oppositions and produces different pairs. For example, the first part's opposition pastoral/disciplined is replaced by the opposition apprenticeship/common sense in the second part.

Hauerwas shows that, if a Christian thinker tries directly to resolve the contradictions expressed in the pairs individual/community, freedom/authority, care/discipline, this reproduces the error of assuming that they are, indeed, contradictions. Like Yoder, Hauerwas investigates the error that produces the false oppositions and tries to repair that more radical error.

The repair is an emphasis on training. Various words are used for this category: discipleship, apprenticeship, craftsmanship, tradition, authority. Modern persons, especially young people, are taught that they are already competent to judge, already sufficiently informed to decide, already free to choose for themselves. Instead, they need to be taught that they are incompetent to judge, are not yet formed in ways that enable them responsibly to take decisions, and as yet lack the capacity to make proper choices. Christians often mistakenly cast the key categories in opposing pairs because they wrongly consider issues of training irrelevant. Once one focuses appropriately on questions of training, the categories cease to oppose each other.

John Milbank's "The Last of the Last: Theology, Authority, and Democracy" (2002) poses an initial question: "Does theology answer to the academy or to the church?" The dominant categories are mostly pairs: faith/reason, solipsism/fiction, realist/nominalist, analogical/univocal, natural/supernatural, and finally participation (Greek: *methexis*). The shape is a set of three arguments that repair three false separations: between faith and reason, between ecclesial and academic authority, and between Scripture and tradition.

Milbank's argument is a historical narrative in which the key moment is the "crisis of 1300," when the pre-1300 synthesis, brought to a high point in the theology of the Dominican theologian Thomas Aquinas, was undone by a range of damaging innovations by the Franciscan theologians Duns Scotus and William of Ockham. The realist and analogical framework of Aquinas was dismantled in favor of the nominalist and univocalist structure of Scotus and his successors.

Asking what tasks these technical terms discharge in the text is more fruitful than trying to pin down definitions for them. The realist/analogical character of Aquinas's theology evokes, in Milbank's account, a world where humans are genuinely in relationship to each other and with their environment, where this is reflected in the kinds of knowledge they are taken to have, and where things and persons are different and have their own identity, yet are meaningfully related to each other and have a place in the world. The nominalist/univocalist character of Scotus's theology suggests a sphere where things are discrete and unrelated, except insofar as they appear in the same single space that extends infinitely on a single plane: they are just "there." Where in Aquinas there is excess, surplus, desire, and generative, inquiring ignorance, in Scotus there is precision, mere infinity, and cold bafflement. These are strong contrasts.

The principal argument is that many of the key oppositional pairs (e.g., faith versus reason, or Scripture versus tradition) are generated by the shift from realism to nominalism, and from analogy to univocity. Rather than trying to mediate faith and reason, or Scripture and tradition, Milbank investigates the shift that produces the oppositions.

The claims for the kind of repair needed are clearer than the actual repairs offered. For example, it is said that what is needed is a "'radical orthodoxy' that refuses the duality of reason and faith." The qualities of this refusal are outlined: there should be a beautiful mediation between invisible and visible; there should be openness towards that which lies beyond our capacity; it should be bodily and practical; it should embrace a desire that reaches into the unknown; it should display the theological virtues of faith, hope, and charity; it should be lodged in complex networks; its boundaries should be messy; it should respond to the supernatural. Most fundamentally, it should spell out a right relationship between supernatural and natural: what is wholly exceptional gives meaning to, and raises up, what is most ordinary. The shape of these prescriptions is noteworthy: it lists the problematic dualisms (e.g., bodily/intellectual, limited/unlimited, etc.) and declares that they are to be overcome. The demonstration of the repair is, however, deferred. More energy is put entirely into diagnosis ("the crisis of 1300") and into describing what qualities the cure must have, and rather less energy into the cure itself.

The opening question, "Does theology answer to the academy or to the church?" is broken down. Milbank attempts to repair the source of the opposition between autonomous reason and authoritative tradition rather than to side with one over the other, or to mediate between the two. His solution redescribes reason and tradition by relating both to the triune God. Theology's accountability to institutions is qualified by its participation in the mind of God; but the mind of God is only discerned in institutions. When the emphasis lies on institutions, God's transcendence is invoked; and when the emphasis lies on God's transcendence, institutions are invoked. Neither trumps the other or has the last word.

Each of these three texts considers a problematic opposition between key terms (worship/ethics, care/discipline, faith/reason) and then attempts, not to adjudicate between their claims, but to repair the causes of the oppositions. Yoder chooses biblical cases that resist being seen as either worship or ethics; Hauerwas argues that a focus on apprenticeship dissolves the opposition between care and discipline; Milbank attempts to repair the crisis of 1300 that produced the opposition between faith and reason. In each case the solution is a recovery of older models: crafts (Hauerwas), Dominican theology (Milbank), practices attested in Scripture (Yoder).

Yoder places "sacramental realism" in opposition to sacramentalism and Zwinglianism; Hauerwas places a model of apprenticeship where moral competence must be learned in opposition to a modernity that considers everybody morally competent; Milbank places realist analogy in opposition to nominalist univocity. These contemporary theological writings that relate politics and the church thus display four instructive tendencies: they (1) identify and overcome problematic oppositions, (2) redescribe problems, (3) investigate categories, and (4) institute new, more generative, oppositions. The results are visions of a church that itself heals divisions in society.

Three sets of questions might profitably be posed to these three authors. First, are their arguments equally anti-conservative and anti-liberal? Their arguments are taken — famously — to be anti-liberal. Yet both liberal and conservative arguments alike rely on false oppositions: each stresses one side of those oppositions. It seems that the way the arguments of Yoder, Hauerwas, and Milbank repair false oppositions is just as ruinous for conservative arguments as for liberal ones. Why are the theologians thought one-sidedly to be anti-liberal? Second, what are the significant differences between them? For example, how do they handle the relation between categories of thought that guide habits of action, and habits of action that generate categories of thought? Yoder points to habits of action in the church (admonishing, eating) and attempts to repair categories of thought in the light of those habits. Milbank points to categories of thought (analogy, realism) and suggests that habits of action would be repaired by them. Habits of action repair thinking and thinking repairs habits of action: there is a mutual relation between them. But where do the theologians' emphases lie, and what difference does it make? Third, how significant are their arguments for non-Christians? Their forms of argumentation are addressed, quite properly, to the church, and have only limited significance beyond this. They assume, quite reasonably, that most European and American atheists and agnostics inherit and distort Christian habits of action and thought; the theologians attempt to recover this inheritance and repair the distortions. But Jewish and Islamic habits of action and thought are not products of such inheritance and distortion. How should "church-based politics" orient itself to them, given the recognition that Christian theology should not be supersessionist in relation to Judaism, and given the importance of engaging positively with an Islam that never experienced the neglect of theology that modern European philosophy produced? Are there tendencies in these texts that explain why Hauerwas is so much more appreciative of Jewish thought than Milbank?

42 Sacrament as Social Process: Christ the Transformer of Culture

John Howard Yoder

Ever since Paul Ramsey spoke to the 1979 session of the Society of Christian Ethics on "Liturgy and Ethics,"[1] there has been within the ethicists' guild a rising awareness of the need to think more clearly about the interrelationship of worship and morality. For some it may even have displaced the earlier routine question of the relationship between Scripture and ethics. The connections between worship and ethics have been tested in various directions. Some say that what worship does is to form the character of the person or of the community, and then that character determines the style of moral discernment. For others worship contributes to ethics something less precise but more foundational: love or hope — what ordinary usage might call "motivation." What these varied efforts have in common is that they begin with the problem of a qualitative distance between the two realms of liturgy and ethics and maintain that a bridge of some kind needs to be built. With gratitude and great respect for those efforts, but not satisfied by them, I propose to set beside them a simpler account, one that at least complements them and might partially correct them.

I

Observe a commonality underlying five practices described in the New Testament, practices explicated mostly in the Pauline writings, but rooted as

1. *Journal of Religious Ethics* 7, no. 2 (1979): 139ff.

well in the Gospels and paralleled in the other epistles. What they have in common is that each of them concerns *both* the internal activities of the gathered Christian congregation *and* the ways the church interfaces with the world. Thus, each of the five practices described and mandated in the New Testament exemplifies a link between ecclesiastical practice and social ethics that is usually undervalued or ignored.[2] For each of them, I must dispense with detailed exegesis of the texts' linguistic and contextual dimensions, but not because more attention to the scholars' resources would not be corroborative.

(1) Fraternal Admonition

In a key passage of Matthew's Gospel, Jesus tells his disciples that, as they carry out a particular practice under his instructions, they do the activity of God: "What you bind on earth is bound in heaven," he says (Matt. 18:18). A specific human activity is mandated, and its form is prescribed in some detail. The context in Matthew, reinforced by the parallels in Luke and in John, makes it evident that one objective of the procedure is forgiveness, "remitting" an offense — that is, reconciliation, restoring to the community a person who had offended. Jesus' choice of a pair of rabbinic technical terms indicates, however, that more than that is involved: "To bind" is to respond to a question of ethical discernment (we still have the root in our word "obligate"), and to "loose" is to free from obligation (in the beginning of the Sermon on the Mount Jesus had warned that whoever does that with any commandment will be "the least in the Kingdom").

Into the interlocking of the dialog of reconciliation ("remitting") with the dialog of moral discernment ("binding" and "loosing"), Jesus inserts yet another element of classical due process: the participants who "harmonize" in this process (the verb is *symphōnein*, which we recognize in the noun form "symphony") are described in juridical terms as the "two or three witnesses" who according to Mosaic law[3] make a serious deliberation valid.

2. In grouping them in this way I am pursuing a suggestion made in the Stone Lectures at Princeton Theological Seminary in February 1980 and in my essay "The Kingdom as Social Ethic" in *The Priestly Kingdom* (Notre Dame: University of Notre Dame Press, 1984), p. 93. Earlier versions of this material were presented as lectures at Duke University, Loma Linda University, Boston University, Eden Theological Seminary, and Bangor Theological between February 1986 and February 1988.

3. Num. 35:30; Deut. 17:6, 19:15; John 8:17.

Paul referred to this process as "the law of Christ" (Gal. 6:2). The Reformers of the sixteenth century (Martin Luther, Martin Bucer, and some of the so-called Anabaptists) called it *Regnum Christi,* "the rule of Christ." They looked to this process to move the Reformation from the university lecture hall and the scholar's office to the life of the parish and the family.[4]

A process of human interchange combining the mode of reconciling dialogue, the substance of moral discernment, and the authority of divine empowerment deserves to be considered one of the sacramental works of the community. Only a few of the Reformation traditions came near to saying that, and the "Catholic" practices carried on under the rubric of "absolution" or "reconciliation" have long since come to have a much thinner meaning.

(2) The Universality of Charisma

The Paul of Ephesians uses the term "the fullness of Christ" to describe a new mode of group relationships in which every member of a body (it is to him that we owe the currency of the noun "body" to describe a social group) has a distinctly identifiable, divinely validated, and empowered role. The Paul of I Corinthians says literally that *every* member is the bearer of such a "manifestation of the Spirit for the common good," and he prescribes quite detailed counter-intuitive and counter-traditional guidelines for how this understanding leads to ascribing the greater value to the less honored members. The Paul of Romans instructs his readers about their ability and duty to think of themselves in such a way as to conform to "the grace that had been meted out" to each of them. He saw all this (there is Petrine corroboration which indicates that the entire thought pattern was not original or peculiar to Paul) as a specific working of God the Spirit, present in, with, and under a particular pattern of social process, profoundly different both from contemporarily available social models and from most of what later Christian history has done with the notions of "charisma" and "ministry."[5]

---

4. Cf. my review of the New Testament witness in "Binding and Loosing," pp. 211ff. in John White and Ken Blue, *Healing the Wounded* (Downers Grove, IL: InterVarsity Press, 1985). On the sixteenth-century place of this practice, see Ervin A. Schlabach, *The Rule of Christ among the Early Swiss Anabaptists* (Chicago: Chicago Theological Seminary PhD Thesis, 1977), and my "Hermeneutics of the Anabaptists," in W. Swartley, ed., *Essays on Biblical Interpretation* (Elkhart, IN: Institute of Mennonite Studies, 1984), pp. 24ff.

5. The apostolic testimony is summarized in my *The Fullness of Christ* (Elgin, IL: Brethren Press, 1987).

(3) The Spirit's Freedom in the Meeting

In the context of this already described vision of body process, yet distinguishable within it by its narrower focus, Paul instructs the Corinthians about how to hold a meeting in the power of the Spirit. Everyone who has something to say can have the floor, with only a relative priority being given to the mode of prophecy because it speaks "to improve, to encourage, and to console." The others "weigh" what the prophet has said.[6] The same assumptions were operative behind the narrative of Acts, where a foundational problem of missionary strategy yielded to a conversational process of whose conclusions the moderator could say that they had "seemed good to the Holy Spirit and to us."

I interrupt the listing to note that I began with these three specimens of apostolically prescribed social process[7] because they do *not* fall within what ordinarily is called "worship," even less "liturgy." Yet why should they not be so designated? Each speaks of practices carried out when believers gather, for reasons evidently derived from their faith and capable of being illuminated by doctrinal elaboration. These practices are described as involving both divine and human action and as mandatory. It makes a difference whether they are done rightly or wrongly. Are these not the characteristics of what we ordinarily call "worship"?

What New Testament believers were doing in these several practices — the three listed so far — can be spoken of in social process terms easily translated into nonreligious terms. The multiplicity of gifts is a model for the empowerment of the humble and the end of hierarchy in social process. Dialogue under the Holy Spirit is the ground floor of the notion of democracy. The admonition to bind or loose at the point of offense is the foundation for what now would be called conflict resolution and consciousness-raising.

The social-process meaning of the other two practices to which I now turn, more traditionally called "sacraments," has been less evident until recently. Part of the reason for not looking at them as social practices over the years may well be the special aura cast around them by the word "sacrament." Now, however, there is a veritable wave of writings connecting the

---

6. Cf. the section on "The Rule of Paul" in Yoder, "Hermeneutics of the Anabaptists."

7. I hesitate to use routinely and uniformly the term "practice," for fear that it be taken too technically as having a special meaning defined by ethicists. There are some who do this with the definition offered by Alasdair MacIntyre in his *After Virtue* (Notre Dame: University of Notre Dame Press, 1981), p. 175. There is nothing wrong with MacIntyre's description, but some take it as transforming a commonsensical meaning into a recondite one.

eucharist with economics; Orbis Press has several books making such a point. That this juxtaposition is now popular does not prove, of course, that it is exegetically warranted; many fads are not. In this case, though, others had been making this juxtaposition since long before the fad, but it was less noted because it was not in a Catholic frame of reference.[8]

(4) Breaking Bread

Fourth, then, the eucharist is an act of economic ethics. In the passages to which later generations gave the technical label "words of institution," Jesus says, "Whenever you do this, do it in my memory." Do *what* in his memory? It cannot mean "whenever you celebrate the Mass" because there was then no such thing as a Mass. He might mean "whenever you celebrate the Passover," but that is not what the hearers took him to mean. That would have called for an annual celebration. He must have meant (and the record indicates that they took him to mean) "whenever you have your common meal." The meal he blessed and claimed as his memorial was their ordinary partaking together of food for the body. Only because it was that communal meal of the disciples' fellowship could it provide the occasion for the reorganization of the ministering structures reported in Acts 6.

We commit the hermeneutical sin of anachronism when we look in the New Testament for any light on the much later eucharistic controversies. All of those later controversies were about something of which the apostolic generation had no notion, namely about the detailed theoretical definition of the meaning of specific actions and things ("sacraments") within the special set-apart world of the "religious" in a frame of reference that the later churches took over from paganism when the latter replaced Judaism as their cultural soil. What the New Testament is talking about in "breaking bread" is believers' actually sharing with one another their ordinary day-to-day material substance. It is not the case, as far as understanding the New Testament accounts is concerned, that, in an act of "institution" or symbol-making, God or the church would have said "let bread stand for daily sustenance." It is not even merely that, in many settings, as any cultural historian would have told us,

---

8. See Arthur Cochrane, *Eating and Drinking with Jesus* (Philadelphia: Westminster Press, 1974); Norman Fox, *Christ in the Daily Meal: The Ordinance of the Breaking of Bread* (New York: Fords, Howard and Hulbert, 1898); and William H. Willimon, *Sunday Dinner* (Nashville: The Upper Room, 1981).

eating together already stands for values of hospitality and community-formation, these values being distinguishable from the signs that refer to them. It is that bread *is* daily sustenance. Bread eaten together *is* economic sharing. Not merely symbolically, but in actual fact, it extends to a wider circle the economic solidarity that normally obtained in the family. When, in most of his post-Resurrection appearances, Jesus takes the role of the family head distributing bread (and fish) around his table, he projects into the post-Passion world the common purse of the wandering disciple band whose members had left their prior economic bases to join his movement.

A rationalistic or Zwinglian understanding of symbol says that a symbolic act has a "meaning" distinguishable from the act itself and that, for certain purposes, it is in fact helpful to disentangle the "meaning" from the act. This is in order to define it, to derive from it additional derivative meanings, and perhaps to resymbolize it into other forms in other settings. In this frame of reference, one can say (although no one did for a long time) that breaking bread together *means* economic solidarity, so that forms of social life that transcend individualism and share with larger communities are preferable to those that name as agents only independent individuals. But such an action of derivation is an intellectual operation, arbitrary and unaccountable. This we might call the "Zwinglian" way of access to an economic meaning of the eucharist.

At the other end of the scale, what we may call the "sacramentalist" view of a sign says that, by a distinct divine act of definition, a specific set of practices is pulled up out of daily life and given, by gracious decree, a distinctive meaning, one best served by accentuating the distance between the special meaning and the ordinary one. A separate "theology of sacraments" then develops a corpus of dogma about that special realm. The bread no longer looks or tastes like the bread one shares with children and guests or that is owed to cousins and to the beggar. It is not broken nor (classically) even put into the mouth the same way as ordinary real-world food. Its most important meaning is the one that forces us to debate in what sense the bread has now become the body of the Lord and in what sense our eating it mediates to us the grace of salvation. I submit (although this is no place to spread out the argument) there is no direct path from this point to economics. The Roman Catholic authors who establish such a connection have to start over again from somewhere else.[9]

9. Tissa Balasuriya, *The Eucharist and Human Liberation* (Maryknoll, NY: Orbis Press, 1979) makes the argument most directly. See also Geevarghese Osthathios, *Theology of a*

What I propose, for present purposes, to call the sacramental (as distinct from the sacramentalistic) view spares us those abstracted definitions and articulations of how the sign signifies. When the family head feeds you at his table, the bread for which he has given thanks, you are part of the family. The act does not merely *mean* that you are part of the family. To take the floor in a community dialogue does not mean that you are part of the group; it *is* operational group membership. To be immersed and to rise from the waters of the *mikvah* may be said to symbolize death and resurrection, but really it makes you a member of the historical community of the new age. This was the case, not only for Jesus, but also for John and for the other Jewish proselytizers and revivalists who used the baptism of repentance before him. This leads us to the fifth social-ethical ritual.

(5) Induction into the New Humanity

Baptism inducts persons into a new people, and one of the distinguishing marks of this new people is that all prior given or chosen definitions of identity are transcended. When Paul writes "if anyone is in Christ the whole world is new" so that "worldly standards have ceased to count in my estimate of a person" (II Cor. 5:16, 17), the concrete social-functional meaning of these statements is that social definitions based upon class and category are no longer basic. The phrase in Galatians, "neither slave nor free, neither male nor female . . . you are One in Christ Jesus" (Gal. 3:28), is explicitly a description of what baptism does, parallel to Ephesians 2 ("new humanity") or to II Corinthians 5 ("new creation") in its substance. The fundamental breakthrough at the point of the Jew-Gentile barrier, which generated these texts, demands and produces congruent breakthroughs where the barrier is slavery, gender, or class.[10]

There is of course a sacramentalist understanding of baptism, defining the salvation it mediates in terms of original sin. Egalitarianism or

---

Classless Society (Maryknoll, NY: Orbis Press, 1979); Rafael Avila, *Worship and Politics* (Maryknoll, NY: Orbis Press, 1981); Joseph A. Grassi, *Broken Bread and Broken Bodies* (Maryknoll, NY: Orbis Press, 1981); and, from another press, Monika Hellwig, *The Eucharist and the Hunger of the World* (New York: Paulist Press, 1976).

10. I have spelled out further the importance of the interethnic meaning of baptism in my "The Apostle's Apology Revisited," in William Klassen, ed., *The New Way of Jesus* (Newton, KS: Faith and Life Press, 1980), pp. 115-34, and in "The Social Shape of the Gospel," in Wilbert Shenk, ed., *Exploring Church Growth* (Grand Rapids: Eerdmans, 1983), pp. 277-84.

interethnic reconciliation cannot be part of its meaning. There is no clear reason not to do it to a newborn infant. There is no reason it was wrong to do it coercively in the Middle Ages.

Of course, there is also, at the other end of the scale, a Zwinglian understanding of what baptism properly "signifies." This is most widely represented today by Baptists, that is, by radicalized Zwinglians. If baptism signifies the new birth as an inward individual experience, it is obvious why we should disavow administering it coercively or to infants, but there is still no natural access to egalitarianism.

If, on the other hand, we can resurrect a sacramental realism, whereby baptism is the constitution of a new people whose newness and togetherness explicitly relativize prior stratifications and classification, then we need no path to get from there to egalitarianism. We start egalitarian, and the reasons to disavow any nonvoluntary practice of the act are built in.

II

We have now described five social practices, each with an underlying meaning given in the action itself:

(1) There is the interweaving of forgiveness and moral discernment, operative at the point of offense, driven by the intent to forgive, reflecting and also conditioning the reality of divine forgiveness. Jesus' word for this was "binding and loosing"; ours is sometimes "reconciliation," sometimes "discernment."

(2) There is the universalization of giftedness, with every member having his or her charismatic role, whose exercise the community helps define, celebrates, and monitors. It destroys patriarchalism, but not in the interest of anarchy or some other "-archalism." It equalizes, but it is the opposite of leveling. I am not sure we have a word for it. I am not sure we have ever seen it practiced with any approximation of the innovative depth and power that Paul was writing about, though several of our modern forms of social organization, role differentiation, and mutuality provide pale images of it.[11]

(3) There is decision-making by open dialogue and consensus; everyone can have the floor. Commonsense ground rules assure due process and con-

---

11. There are approximations of it in the Friends' rejection of a standard sacerdotal class, or in that of the ("Plymouth") Brethren, but in neither case is the affirmative notion of universal empowerment carried through.

tinuity with the rest of the church, past and present. I have described this process most sociologically in my essay "The Hermeneutics of People-hood."[12] I would call this "democracy," but with the recognition that that word has other definitions for some people.[13]

(4) There is the sharing of the simple wherewithal of human life, with the table as its instrument, a practice by its nature decentralized, particular, personal. The simplest word for this is family; another is socialism, although for some that has other meanings.

(5) There is status equality, acted out by baptism, defined as relativizing (not denying) social differences, rejecting their discriminatory impact.

My concern here is not to exposit further any one of these functions, either its "inner" meaning in the body of the community or its example for the world. My purpose in looking at the five specimens in parallel was to identify the lessons to be learned from their formal commonality, as they illuminate the way we see social ethics. Quite separate from one another with regard to subject matter, to where they appear in the New Testament, and to their respective agenda, vocabulary, and procedures, these five practices have much in common. The commonalities qualify my grouping them as an authentic induction.

III

What are the implications for ethics of these five practices? Each of them, first of all, is a wholly human, empirically accessible practice — nothing esoteric. Yet each is, according to the apostolic writers, an act of God. God does

---

12. John H. Yoder, *The Priestly Kingdom* (Notre Dame: University of Notre Dame Press, 1985), pp. 15-36. Reviewing its contribution to the development of democratic forms in the civil order would be a separate study. Specimens of the way "binding and loosing" and "everyone takes the floor" contribute to the origins of democracy would include (a) the way Calvin's vision of society is said to have had its roots in conciliarism; (b) A. D. Lindsay's rooting of the democracy of England and New England in the experience of the Puritan meeting; and (c) the fact that, even though Calvinist theory was at first elitist and in favor of government's repressing dissent, with time Reformed communities contributed in fact to the growth of civil rights, having found themselves in positions not of government but of dissent.

13. I shall return later to the notion that we should eschew the use of words that "might be misunderstood," i.e., that others would use differently. This concern is understandable, but if we took it seriously there would not be many words left. The meaning of incarnation hardly permits avoiding the ambivalence of all particular meanings.

not merely authorize or command them. *God* is *doing* them in, with, and under the human practice: "What you bind on earth is bound in heaven."

Second, all of them are practices that constitute the believing community as a social body. To see them in operation we need to do sociology, not semantics or philosophy. Together (though other dimensions could yet be added) they offer a well-rounded picture of the believing community, that is, of specific datable, nameable, local first-century messianic synagogues as a form of human life together demonstrating not only far-reaching continuities with earlier history and culture, but also foundational innovation.

Third, each of these practices can function as a paradigm for ways in which other social groups might operate. These forms are derived from and illuminated by reference to specific components of the faith stance of the first century's messianic synagogues, yet they are accessible to the public. People who do not share the faith or join the community can learn from them. "Binding and loosing" can provide models for conflict resolution, alternatives to litigation, and alternative perspectives on "corrections." Sharing bread is a paradigm, not only for soup kitchens and hospitality houses, but also for social security and negative income tax. "Every member of the body has a gift" is an immediate alternative to vertical "business" models of management. Paul's solidarity models of deliberation correlate with the reasons that the Japanese can make better cars than Detroit. It was not by accident or whim that I could use as labels the modern secular handles "egalitarianism," "democracy," and "socialism," although each of these terms needs to be taken in a way different from their secularistic and individualistic usages.

Some have warned me that it is dangerous to borrow such worldly words as "egalitarianism" or "freedom" since those concepts are not only hard to define but are the property of the liberal establishment, which is an oppressive elite. These friends are right in thus warning me. If I were to think that those contemporary terms have a univocal normative meaning, and if I were proposing that they simply be "baptized," I should have sold out. But those warning friends are wrong if they suggest that some other, less liberal words (for example "virtue," "narrative," "community") would be safer from abuse. The right corrective is not to seek fail-safe words never yet corrupted, but rather to renew daily the action of pre-empting the extant vocabulary, rendering every creature subject to God's rule in Christ. What is needed is to surface the criteria whereby we can tell whether, in the appropriation of each new language, the meaning of Jesus is authentically reenacted or abandoned.

Fourth, the reason for their paradigmatic accessibility to others and their translatability into other terms is that they are not "religious" or "ritual" activities at bottom. They are by nature "lay" or "public" phenomena. The two, from among the five, that did become "sacraments" in the later "Catholic" synthesis, after the divorce with Judaism and the remarriage with Constantine, had to change their basic meaning for that to be carried through.

Fifth, these practices are enabled and illuminated by Jesus of Nazareth, who is confessed as Messiah and as Lord. They are part of the order of redemption, not of creation. Hereby we loop back to the difference between the New Testament parallels and the standard account of the relations of particular and general truths, or of revelation and reason. The standard account of these matters had told us that in order for Christians to be able to speak to others we need to look less to redemption and more to creation, or less to revelation and more to nature and reason. In only slightly different ways, recent Reformed thinkers (for example Emil Brunner, Reinhold Niebuhr, and H. Richard Niebuhr[14]) play the Creator/Father off against the Redeemer/Son in such a way that the will of God as Father (known reliably by means of reason) counts for the social realm, as the words and example of the Son do not.

In the practices I am describing (and the thinking underlying them), the apostolic communities did it the other way around. The multiplicity of gifts is described in Ephesians 4 in analogy to the booty generously dispensed by a victorious champion (appropriating the military victory march hymn of Psalm 68). The ascended Lord Christ pours out the gifts. Binding and loosing makes us participants of the reconciling work of God in Christ. Egalitarianism is enabled by the "new creation," which baptism signs and seals.

In other words, all of these social/ethical/sacramental practices are formally rooted in the order of redemption. That by no means makes them less public. It makes them more realistic about sin and more hopeful about reconciliation than those approaches that trust the reason/nature/creation complex to derive our knowledge of what should be from what is.

Sixth, and also in contrast to the standard account, none of these practices makes the individual the pivot of change. The individual is in no way forgotten or relativized; nothing could be more particularly tailored to mea-

---

14. H. R. Niebuhr, "The Doctrine of the Trinity and the Unity of the Church," one of the few texts to be published twice in *Theology Today* in October 1946 and in July 1983. According to this modalistic trinitarianism, God the Father is more competent for ethical guidance in the realm of "culture" than is the Son.

sure than the notion of every member's possessing (or being possessed by) a distinctive charisma. Nothing empowers more potently than saying that in the meeting everyone can take the floor. But no trust is placed in the individual's changed insights (as liberalism does) or on the believer's changed insides (as does pietism) to change the world. The fulcrum for change and the forum for decision is the moral independence of the believing community as social body. The dignity of the individual is his or her uniqueness as specific member of that body.

Seventh, none of these five practices was revealed from above or created from scratch; each was derived from already existent cultural models. Table fellowship, baptism, and the open meeting were not new ideas, yet in the gospel setting they have taken on new meanings and a new empowerment.

Eighth, it is hard to link this picture with our guild's standard meta-ethical discussions of consistent moral discourse. Some ethicists believe that the most important, and the procedurally prior, task of the ethicist is to disentangle the varieties of modes of moral argument, and to argue that one of them is right. Do these apostolic models of social-ethical creativity reason consequentially or deontologically? Do they prefer the modes of story or of virtue? As far as I can tell, the questions are impertinent.[15] Not only would the apostolic writers not have understood what these questions mean, had they understood them, they would have refused to answer. They would have seen no reason to choose among those incommensurate kinds of resources; why not use them all? The originality and the specificity of their stance lie elsewhere than within the reach of that traditional but abstract methodology debate. Methodological analysis is helpful to illuminate problems of structure, but it is not the prerequisite for the community's right or capacity to reason morally.

Ninth, the apostolic model transcends some other dichotomies as well. It clearly assumes rootage in the normative events that some epistemological analysis calls "revelation," yet without selling reason short, contrary to those who play the orders of "redemption" and "reason" off against one another. Nothing could be more reasonable than the dialogue modes described in Acts 15 and I Corinthians 14. Were we to try to lay over it the Catholic/Protestant typological grid of James Gustafson, or the fivefold typology of his mentor H. Richard Niebuhr, it would fit nowhere. The apostolic model trusts a living magisterium more than does Rome and needs no special theo-

---

15. My doubts about the standard methodological disjunctions were already stated in my *Priestly Kingdom*, pp. 113ff.

ries about the epistemological status of its sources. In that way it is not "Protestant." It places little trust in non-congregational or supra-congregational office-bearers, and it has no place to locate the notion that there would be a body of "general" moral knowledge accessible without dialogue or context by means of "reason" or "nature." In that way it is not "Catholic." This is analogous to the way that, as I said, some have warned me of the danger of borrowing such worldly words as "egalitarianism" or "freedom" because those concepts are the property of the liberal establishment. The early communities do not let themselves be held at a distance by hermeneutic grids like "Protestant/Catholic" or "radical/liberal."

IV

The last few of these inductive observations have been polemic. I have identified some currently popular analytical perspectives that, while helpful for other purposes, cannot box in the apostolic experience. I also maintain that the apostolic model is "evangelical" in the functional sense. For some the label "evangelical" points to a checklist of traditional doctrines and for others to a key inner experience. I mean neither.

For a practice to qualify as "evangelical" in the functional sense means first of all that it communicates *news*. It says something particular that would not be known and could not be believed, were it not said. Second, it must mean functionally that this "news" is attested as *good;* it comes across to those whom it addresses as helping, as saving, and as *shalom*. It must be public, not esoteric, but the way for it to be public is not an *a priori* logical move that subtracts the particular. It is an *a posteriori* political practice that tells the world something it did not know and could not believe before. It tells the world what is the world's own calling and destiny, not by announcing either a Utopian or a realistic goal to be imposed on the whole society, but by pioneering a paradigmatic demonstration of both the power and the practices that define the shape of restored humanity. The confessing people of God is the new world on its way.

If the good is new, it will have to be said in new contexts, where there is no adequate language for it, until that language is crafted.[16] Since the new is

---

16. "To craft" is the fitting verb. We are not concerned with creation *ex nihilo;* language is not created that way. A craft works out of living familiarity with the material it transforms.

good, it will have to be said in such a creative, loving, and pertinent way that the hearers' acceptance of it is not obligatory, but the product of the fit between the news and the hearers' awareness of their lostness.

On the other hand, the search for a general language that people should have to believe does not want to have to depend upon faith or to avow lostness. Its wanting to avoid the risk of deniability is psychically coercive in intent. The credibility of that which is both "good" and "news" consists precisely in its vulnerability, its reusability. That weakness marks all five of the incarnational processes I have been describing. They are not ways to administer the world; they are modes of vulnerable, but also provocative, creative presence in its midst. That is the primordial way in which they transform culture.

43 The Politics of the Church: How We Lay Bricks and Make Disciples

Stanley Hauerwas

The church seems caught in an irresolvable tension today. Insofar as we are able to maintain any presence in modern society we do so by being communities of care. Pastors become primarily people who care. Any attempt in such a context for the church to be a disciplined and disciplining community seems antithetical to being a community of care. As a result the care the church gives, while often quite impressive and compassionate, lacks the rationale to build the church as a community capable of standing against the powers we confront.

That the church has difficulty being a disciplined community, or even cannot conceive what it would mean to be a disciplined community, is not surprising given the church's social position in developed economies. The church exists in a buyer's or consumer's market, so any suggestion that in order to be a member of a church you must be transformed by opening your life to certain kinds of discipline is almost impossible to maintain. The called church has become the voluntary church, whose primary characteristic is that the congregation is friendly. Of course, that is a kind of discipline, because you cannot belong to the church unless you are friendly, but it's very unclear how such friendliness contributes to the growth of God's church meant to witness to the kingdom of God.

This attitude about the church was nicely illustrated by a letter in *The Circuit Rider* about The United Methodist Church. It read:

> United Methodism has been criticized roundly and at length for what it is not — not liturgical enough, not theological enough, not scriptural enough, not congregational enough, etc.

I want to celebrate one ignored item not of United Methodism — namely, it is not harmful to religious people. In my work as a professor and parish minister, I have met all manner of people from other denominations whose minds and souls have been bent all out of shape by larger doses of rigor than many people can bear. Some folks have been given such high injections of some entities that their systems have developed a total immunity to the Christian religion.

By contrast, even many of the people who leave United Methodism because of what it is not go on to lead happy and productive Christian lives as clergy and members of other denominations. Whatever they did not get in United Methodism, they did not get a permanent hatred of the Christian church or of its God.

Wesley said it best. When asked what he intended to do with all those souls he was saving, he replied: "I would make them virtuous and happy, easy in themselves, and useful to others." Not a bad goal, Mr. Wesley! Not a bad record, United Methodism![1]

Such a letter no doubt describes not only United Methodism but the situation of many churches. As a result the church has increasingly found it difficult to maintain any kind of discipline that might make it identifiable as a distinct body of people with a mission to perform in the world. The church is very good at providing the kinds of services necessary to sustain people through the crises in their personal lives, but this simply reflects the fact that the church has become the privatized area of our culture. Of course this has had an effect on the very notion of the pastoral office because the ministers' authority is now primarily constituted by their ability to deliver pastoral services, rather than in liturgical leadership and the moral formation of the community.

The situation in which the church finds itself seems to make the activities of care and discipline incompatible. Care is identified with compassionate care of the individual and is now thought to be the first business of the church. Care requires understanding the particularities of the individual's situation so that the very idea of disciplining someone in a personal crisis is simply unthinkable. We seek to be understood and to understand — not to be judged.

In an attempt to respond to this set of circumstances, the primary strategy, at least for churches in the mainstream, has been to try to help people

1. *The Circuit Rider* 24 (March, 1989). The letter was signed by Dennis Groh of Evanston, Illinois.

come to a better understanding of what it means to be Christian. Such a strategy assumes that what makes a Christian a Christian is holding certain beliefs that help us better understand the human condition, to make sense of our experience.[2] Of course no one denies that those beliefs may have behavioral implications, but the assumption is that the beliefs must be in place in order for the behavior to be authentic. In this respect the individualism of modernity can be seen in quite a positive light. For the very fact that people are now free from the necessity of believing as Christians means that if they so decide to identify with Christianity, they can do so voluntarily.

When being Christian is construed in categories of self-understanding, with correlative senses of care, I fear that there is no way to recover a sense of the church as a community of discipline. Such an understanding of being Christian cannot help trying to cure our disease with more of the disease. The church cannot help become a life-style enclave and/or an umbrella institution where people are giving us the opportunity to associate with other people with their similar interests.[3] If we continue to follow the strategy that associates Christianity with certain beliefs or faith patterns, I cannot see how we will, in any fashion, avoid the trend so acutely described by Wuthnow in *The Restructuring of American Religion* of people being members of churches in order to be associated with people with similar interests that are not in any way shaped by Christian convictions.[4]

When Christianity is understood fundamentally as a belief system necessary for people to give meaning to their lives, we cannot but continue to reinforce the assumption that salvation is for the individual. It is one of the ironies of our time that many of those who are identified with urging Christians to engage in politics in the name of their Christian beliefs hold what are fundamentally individualistic accounts of Christian salvation. They assume that Christianity entails social engagement, but salvation was still

2. I think Lindbeck's account of the experiential expressivist model in his *The Nature of Doctrine: Religion and Theology in a Postliberal Age* (Philadelphia: Westminster Press, 1984) fails to give an adequate account of the material factors that make the experiential expressivist model so powerful. Experiential expressivism is almost required by the privatization of people's lives that goes hand in hand with political liberalism and capitalist economy. Even more conservative denominations, therefore, in spite of what they may hold explicitly, end up in some form of experiential expressivism.

3. The phrase *life-style enclave* I obviously have borrowed from Robert Bellah and his coauthors in their *Habits of the Heart: Individualism and Commitment in American Life* (Berkeley: University of California Press, 1985).

4. Robert Wuthnow, *The Restructuring of American Religion: Society and Faith Since World War II* (Princeton: Princeton University Press, 1988).

identified with the individual coming to a better self-understanding through the world view offered by Christianity. The even greater irony is that the very form of society that was assumed to be the ideal for which Christians ought to work, namely a liberal democratic society, entailed the very presupposition that could only undercut any genuine conception of the social character of Christian salvation.[5]

In short, the great problem of modernity for the church is how we are to survive as disciplined communities in democratic societies. For the fundamental presumption behind democratic societies is that the consciousness of something called the common citizen is privileged no matter what kind of formation it may or may not have had.[6] It is that presumption that gives rise to the very idea of ethics as an identifiable discipline within the modern university curriculum. Both Kant and utilitarians assumed that the task of the ethicist was to explicate the presuppositions shared by anyone. Ethics is the attempt at the systemization of what we all perhaps only inchoately know or which we have perhaps failed to make sufficiently explicit.

Such a view of ethics can appear quite anti-conventional, but even the

---

5. The originator of this peculiar blend of Christian social action with individualistic accounts of Christian salvation was, of course, Reinhold Niebuhr. In an odd way Niebuhr moved away from the social gospel exactly at the wrong point, as he gave what was an essentially Lutheran understanding of salvation in opposition to the more Calvinistic strains of the social gospel. Niebuhr, in effect, was the Lutheran law-gospel distinction in American pragmatic dress.

6. MacIntyre notes that the assumption of the eighteenth-century moralists was that there was a universality of moral agreement about fundamentals in ethics. They were not unaware, however, that often there were differences between cultures, but these differences were thought to derive from different application of the same set of moral rules in different circumstances. This was combined with a belief in progress, so that some societies were obviously further along than others concerning more appropriate application of the basic rules which all shared. The purpose of moral theory in such a world is not just recording and protecting the judgments of the plain person, but the constructive text "of organizing and harmonizing the moral beliefs of plain persons in the manner best calculated to secure a rational sense from the largest possible number of such persons, independently of their conflicting views upon other matters. The moral philosopher's aim, then, is, or ought to be, that of articulating a rational consensus out of the pre-theoretical beliefs and judgments of plain persons." *Three Rival Versions of Moral Inquiry: Encyclopedia, Genealogy and Tradition* (Notre Dame: University of Notre Dame Press, 1990), pp. 176-77. Modern moral philosophy from this perspective is a necessary correlative to the attempt to develop democratic societies that organize people irrespective of their moral training. I suspect that is the reason why some are beginning to see more commonality between Aristotelianism and Christianity, because in spite of their deep differences, they are both equally antidemocratic.

anti-conventional stance gains its power by appeal to what anyone would think upon reflection. This can be suitably illustrated in terms of the recent popular movie, *The Dead Poet's Society*. It is an entertaining, popular movie that appealed to our moral sensibilities. The movie depicts a young and creative teacher battling what appears to be the unthinking authoritarianism of the school in which he is teaching as well as his students', at first, uncomprehending resistance to his teaching method. The young teacher, whose subject is romantic poetry, which may or may not be all that important, takes as his primary pedagogical task to help his students think for themselves. Through great pedagogical sensitivity we watch him slowly awaken one student after another to the possibility of their own talents and potential. At the end, even though he has been fired by the school, we are thrilled as his students find ability to stand against authority, to think for themselves.

This movie seems to be a wonderful testimony to the independence of spirit that democracies putatively want to encourage. Yet I can think of no more conformist message in liberal societies than the idea that students should learn to think for themselves. What must be said is that most students in our society do not have minds well enough trained to be able to think — period. A central pedagogical task is to tell students that they do not yet have minds worth making up.[7] Thus training is so important, because training involves the formation of the self through submission to authority that will, if done well, provide people with the virtues necessary to be able to make reasoned judgment.

I cannot think of a more conformist and suicidal message in modernity than that we should encourage students to make up their own minds. That is simply to ensure that they will be good conformist consumers in a capitalist economy by assuming now that ideas are but another product that you get to choose on the basis of your arbitrary likes and dislikes. To encourage students to think for themselves is therefore a sure way to avoid any meaningful disagreement. That is the reason that I tell my students that my first object is to help them think just like me.[8]

The church's situation, I think, is not unlike the problems of what it

---

7. For a further development of this, see my "Honor in the University," *First Things* 10 (February, 1991): 26-31.

8. I am aware that such a claim appears authoritarian, but ironically I think it is just the opposite of authoritarianism. What does it mean to introduce students to think like me? It means I must introduce them to all the sources that think through me, and in the process they will obviously learn to think not only like me, but different from me as the different voices that think through me provide them with skills I have not appropriated sufficiently.

means to be a teacher in a society shaped by an ethos that produces movies like *The Dead Poet's Society*. Deterred by past presuppositions about the importance of commitment for the living of the Christian life, we have underwritten a voluntaristic conception of the Christian faith, which presupposes that one can become a Christian without training. The difficulty is that once such a position has been established, any alternative cannot help appearing as an authoritarian imposition.

In this respect it is interesting to note how we, that is those of us in mainstream traditions, tend to think about the loss of membership by mainstream churches and the growth of so-called conservative churches. Churches characterized by compassion and care no longer are able to sustain membership, particularly of our own children. Whereas conservative churches that make moral conformity and/or discipline their primary focus continue to grow. Those of us in liberal churches tend to explain this development by noting that people cannot stand freedom, and therefore, in a confusing world devoid of community, seek authority. Conservative churches are growing, but their growth is only a sign of pathology.

Yet this very analysis of "why conservative churches are growing" assumes the presumptions of liberal social theory and practice that I am suggesting are the source of our difficulty. The very way we have learned to state the problem is the problem. The very fact that we let the issue be framed by terms such as individual and community, freedom and authority, care versus discipline, is an indication of our loss of coherence and the survival of fragments necessary for Christians to make our disciplines the way we care.

For example, one of the great problems facing liberal and conservative churches alike is that their membership has been schooled on the distinction between public and private morality. Thus liberal and conservative alike assume that they have a right generally to do pretty much what they want, as long as what they do does not entail undue harm to others. The fact that such a distinction is incoherent even in the wider political society does little to help us challenge an even more problematic character in relationship to the church. Yet if salvation is genuinely social, then there can be no place for a distinction that invites us to assume, for example, that we have ownership over our bodies and possessions in a way that is not under the discipline of the whole church. For example, I was recently giving a lecture at a university that is identified with a very conservative Christian church. They were deeply concerned with the teaching of business ethics in their business school and had begun a lectureship to explore those issues. I was there giving a lecture called "Why Business Ethics Is a Bad Idea." I argued that business ethics was but a form of quandary ethics so characteristic of most so-called applied ethics. As a result, I suggested that business ethics could not help failing to raise the fundamental issues concerning why business was assumed to be a special area of moral analysis.

After I had finished a person who taught in their business school asked, "But what can the church do given this situation?" I suggested to her that if the church was going to begin seriously to reflect on these matters, it should start by requiring all those currently in the church, as well as anyone who wished to join the church, to declare what they earn in public. This suggestion was greeted with disbelief, for it was simply assumed that no one should be required to expose their income in public. After all, nothing is more private to us in our lives than what amount we earn. Insofar as that is the case, we see how far the church is incapable of being a disciplined community.

However, one cannot help feeling the agony behind the questioner's concern. For if the analysis I provided to this point is close to being right, then it seems we lack the conceptual resources to help us understand how the church can reclaim for itself what it means to be a community of care and discipline. Of course conceptual resources is far too weak a phrase, for if actual practices of care and discipline are absent, then our imaginations will be equally impoverished. What I propose, therefore, is to provide an account of what it means to learn a craft, to learn — for example — how to lay brick, in the hope that we may be able to claim forms of care and discipline unnoticed but nonetheless present in the church.

Teach People How to Lay a Brick

To help us get a better picture of what it means for the church to be a disciplined community, we ought to learn how to lay a brick. This discipline will help us think about what it means to be saved, what it means to be a Christian. To learn to lay brick, it is not sufficient for you to be told how to do it, but you must learn a multitude of skills that are coordinated into the activity of laying brick — that is why before you lay brick you must learn to mix the mortar, build scaffolds, joint, and so on. Moreover, it is not enough to be told how to hold a trowel, how to spread mortar, or how to frog the mortar, but in order to lay brick you must hour after hour, day after day, lay brick.

Of course, learning to lay brick involves not only learning myriad skills, but also a language that forms and is formed by those skills. Thus, for example, you have to become familiar with what a trowel is and how it is to be used, as well as mortar, which bricklayers usually call "mud." Thus "frogging mud" means creating a trench in the mortar so that when the brick is placed in the mortar, a vacuum is created that almost makes the brick lay itself. Such language is not just incidental to becoming a bricklayer but intrinsic to the practice. You cannot learn to lay brick without learning to talk "right."

The language embodies the history of the craft of bricklaying. So when you learn to be a bricklayer you are not learning a craft *de novo* but rather being initiated into a history. For example, bricks have different names — for example, klinkers — to denote different qualities that make a difference about how one lays them.[9] These differences are discovered often by apprentices being confronted with new challenges, making mistakes, and then being taught how to do it by the more experienced.

All of this indicates that to lay brick you must be initiated into the craft of bricklaying by a master craftsman. It is interesting in this respect to contrast this notion with modern democratic presuppositions. For as I noted above, the accounts of morality sponsored by democracy want to deny the necessity of a master. It is assumed we each in and of ourselves have all we need to be moral. No master is necessary for us to become moral, for being moral is a condition that does not require initiation or training. That is why I often suggest that the most determinative moral formation most people have in our society is when they learn to play baseball, basketball, quilt, cook, or learn to lay bricks. For such sports and crafts remain morally anti-democratic insofar as they require acknowledgment of authority based on a history of accomplishment.[10]

---

9. Klinkers were those bricks that were at the bottom of the kilns and they were therefore often overfired. They would sometimes have interesting projections that made quite beautiful walls. The difficulty with klinkers is they were extremely hard and therefore when you laid them, they could float on the mortar. Often bricklayers without much experience would find it very hard to lay klinkers because they were almost impossible to lay level over an entire course. The relationship between the consistency of the brick and the consistency of the mortar is a matter to which bricklayers constantly have to adjust. For example, how you lay brick at the midpoint of the day may be a bit different from how you lay brick early in the morning, as the sun is not out in full force and the mortar does not dry out as quickly. So in the morning you might be able to spread your mud further along the course than you can at midday.

10. George Will's *Men at Work: The Craft of Baseball* (New York: Macmillan Publishing Co., 1990) strikes me as a wonderful book in moral philosophy. The book really is about craft and how discipline is required to make the craft one's own. I must admit as I read through the book I thought I might catch Will distorting baseball by his own liberal presuppositions. The first chapters are primarily about individuals such as managers, pitchers, and

Of course, it is by no means clear how long we can rely on the existence of crafts for such moral formation. For example, bricklayers who are genuinely masters of their craft have become quite scarce. Those who remain command good money for their services. Moreover, the material necessary for laying brick has become increasingly expensive. It has therefore become the tendency of builders to try as much as possible to design around the necessity of using brick in building. As a result, we get ugly glass buildings.

The highly functional glass building that has become so prevalent is the architectural equivalent of our understanding of morality. Such buildings should be cheap, easily built, and efficient. They should be functional, which means they can have no purpose that might limit their multiple use. The more glass buildings we build, the fewer practitioners of crafts we have. The result is a self-fulfilling prophecy: the more buildings and/or morality we produce that eliminate the need for masters of crafts and/or morality, the less we are able to know that there is an alternative.

In his Gifford Lectures, *Three Rival Versions of Moral Inquiry: Encyclopedia, Genealogy and Tradition*, Alasdair MacIntyre develops an extensive account of the craftlike nature of morality. In contrast to modernity, MacIntyre argues that the moral good is not available to any intelligent person no matter what their point of view. Rather, in order to be moral, a person has to be made into a particular kind of person if he or she is to acquire knowledge about what is true and good. Therefore transformation is required if one is to be moral at all. In short, no account of the moral life is intelligible that does not involve some account of conversion. This is particularly true in our context, because to appreciate this point requires a conversion from our liberal convictions.

This transformation is like that of making oneself an apprentice to a master of a craft.[11] Through such an apprenticeship we seek to acquire the

---

hitters. However, Will clearly denotes the communitarian aspects of baseball in his chapter on the defense. It is a book well worth contemplating.

11. MacIntyre suggests "Moral inquiry moves toward arriving at theoretical and practical conclusions about [particular] virtues. But one cannot learn how to move toward such a conclusion without first having acquired some at least of those same virtues about which one is inquiring and without therefore having first been able to identify which virtues they are and, to at least some minimal extent, what it is about them which makes these particular habits virtues. So we are threatened by an apparent paradox and an understanding of moral inquiry as a type of craft: only insofar as we have already arrived at certain conclusions are we able to become the sort of person able to engage in such inquiry so as to reach sound conclusions. How was this threat a paradox — recognizably a version of that posed at the

intelligence and virtues necessary to become skilled practitioners. Indeed it is crucial to understand that intelligence and virtues cannot be separated as they require one another. Classically this was embodied in the emphasis that the virtue of prudence cannot be acquired without the virtues of courage and temperance, and courage and temperance require prudence. The circular or interdependent character of the relationship between prudence and courage suggests why it is impossible to become good without a master. We only learn how to be courageous, and thus how to judge what we must do, through imitation.[12] Apprentices have to learn two distinctions before they can learn anything else.

> The first is the distinction between what in particular situations it really is good to do and what only seems good to do to this particular apprentice, but is not in fact so. That is, the apprentice has to learn at first from his or her teachers and then his or her continuing self-education, how to identify mistakes made by him or herself in applying the acknowledged standard, the standard recognized to be the best available so far in the history of that particular craft. Secondly, the apprentice must learn the difference between what is good and what is best for them with their particular level of training and learning in this or that set of particular circumstances and what is the good or best thing to do unqualifiably. That is, the apprentice has to learn to distinguish between the kind of excellence which both others and he or she can expect of him or herself here and there, and the ultimate excellence which furnishes both the apprentice and the master craftsperson with their *telos*.[13]

---

outset by Plato and the *Meno* about learning in general — to be circumvented, dissolved, or otherwise met? The answer is in part that suggested by the *Meno*: unless we already have within ourselves potentiality for moving toward and achieving the relevant theoretical and practical conclusions, we shall be unable to learn. But we also need a teacher to enable us to actualize that potentiality, and we shall have to learn from that teacher and initially accept on the basis of his or her authority within the community of a craft precisely what intellectual and moral habits it is which we must cultivate and acquire if we are to become effective self-moved participants in such inquiries. Hence there emerges a conception of rational teaching authority internal to the practice of the craft of moral inquiry, as indeed such conceptions emerge in such other crafts as furniture making and fishing, where, just as in moral inquiry, they partially define relationships with master-craftsmen to apprentice." *Three Rival Versions of Moral Inquiry*, p. 63.

12. For my reflections on this circular account, see my "Happiness, the Life of Virtue, and Friendship: Theological Reflections on Aristotelian Themes," *Asbury Theological Journal* 45, no. 1 (Spring 1990): 21-35.

13. MacIntyre, *Three Rival Versions of Moral Inquiry*, pp. 61-62.

These distinctions are absolutely crucial if the teacher and apprentice are to be able to identify the defects and limitations of particular persons as they seek to achieve the *telos* of the craft. Habits of judgment and evaluation rooted in adequate and corrupt desires, taste, habits, and judgments must be transformed through being initiated into the craft. The apprentice must learn that there are some things that only the master can do, even though the apprentice might well accomplish what the master has done through luck. But luck or native talent is not sufficient to sustain the craft, so the apprentice must take the time to acquire the skills of judgment and accomplishment necessary for the achievement of the good.

So all crafts require that those who engage in the craft must come to terms with and make themselves adequate to the existence of some set of objects conceived to exist independent of their initial assumptions. Accordingly, there is a realist epistemological bias intrinsic to the crafts, but it is not the kind of correspondence theory that derives from the Enlightenment. The Enlightenment tried to show that the mind was immediately appropriate to a factual world without training. In contrast, our minds are adequate to that which we come to know only by being formed by the skills and practices of a tradition. Such training, of course, not only transforms us but transforms what it is that we think we need to know. That is why there can be no knowledge without appropriate authority.[14]

14. MacIntyre's epistemological views are more determinatively developed in the latter chapters of *Whose Justice? Which Rationality?* (Notre Dame: University of Notre Dame Press, 1988). There MacIntyre says, "The original and most elementary version of the correspondence theory of truth is one in which it is applied retrospectively in the form of a correspondence theory of falsity. The first question to be raised about it is: What is it precisely that corresponds or fails to correspond to what? Assertions in speech or writing, certainly, but these as secondary expressions of intelligent thought which is or is not adequate in its dealings with its objects, the realities of the social and rational world. This is a point at which it is important to remember that the presupposed conception of mind is not Cartesian. It is rather of mind as activity, of mind as engaging with the natural and social world in such activities as identification, reidentification, collecting, separating, classifying, and naming and all this by touching, grasping, pointing, breaking down, building up, calling to, answering to, and so on. The mind is adequate to its objects insofar as the expectations which it frames on the basis of these activities are not liable to disappointment and the remembering which it engages in enables it to return and to recover what it had encountered previously, whether the objects themselves are still present or not. The mind, being informed as a result of its engagements with objects, is informed by both images which are or are not adequate — for the mind's purposes — re-presentations of particular objects or sorts of objects and by concepts which are or are not adequate re-presentations of the forms in terms of which objects are grasped and classified. Representation is not as such picturing, but re-presentation. Pictures

When the moral life is viewed through the analogy of the craft, we see why we need a teacher to actualize our potential. The teacher's authority must be accepted on the basis of a community of a craft, which embodies the intellectual and moral habits we must acquire and cultivate if we are to become effective and creative participants in the craft. Such standards can only be justified historically as they emerge from criticisms of their predecessors. That we hold a trowel this way or spread mortar on tile differently than on brick is justified from attempts to transcend or improve upon limitations of our predecessors.

Of course, the teachers themselves derive their authority from a conception of perfected work that serves as the *telos* of that craft. Therefore, often the best teachers in a craft do not necessarily produce the best work, but they help us understand what kind of work is best. What is actually produced as best judgments or actions or objects within crafts are judged so because they stand in some determinative relation to what the craft is about. What the craft is about is determined historically within the context of particularistic communities.

MacIntyre points out that this temporal character of a craft stands in sharp tension with modernity's understandings of morality and truth. For it is modernity's presumption that any moral conviction or truth must be timeless. In contrast, the particular movement of rationality in a craft is justified by the history of the craft so far. "To share in the rationality of a craft

---

are only one mode of re-presenting, and their adequacy or inadequacy in functioning as such is always relative to some specific purpose of mind. One of the great originating insights of tradition-constituted enquiries is that false beliefs and false judgments represent a failure of the mind, not of its objects. . . . This falsity is recognized retrospectively as a past inadequacy when the . . . beliefs of an earlier stage of a tradition of enquiry are contrasted with the world of things and persons as it has come to be understood at some later stage. So correspondence or the lack of it becomes a feature of developing complex conception of truth. The relationship of correspondence or lack of correspondence which holds between the mind and objects is given expression in judgments, but it is not judgments themselves which correspond to objects or indeed to anything else" (pp. 356-57). Of course, the strength of MacIntyre's position is to deny the epistemological starting point of the Enlightenment tradition. That is why he must so starkly juxtapose traditions, as the Augustinian-Thomistic tradition does not assume it must secure a starting point epistemologically in order to begin reflection. Thus the very structure of the *Summa* as a disputation rightly indicates there is no place to start. This has deep implications for the style of philosophical and theological work since it becomes crucial that we find a form that unsettles the Enlightenment presumption that truth can be presented in a lecture and/or essay. Thus I must learn to write theology in a way that denies that theology can be systematic.

requires sharing in the contingencies of its history, understanding its story as one's own, and finding a place for oneself as a character in the enacted dramatic narrative, which is that story so far."[15]

A craft is never static. Thus masters are granted authority insofar as they exemplify in their work the best standards so far. What makes a master a master is that he or she knows how to go further, and especially how to direct others to go further, using what can be learned from tradition afforded by the past, so that he or she can move toward the *telos* of fully perfected works. The master knows how to link the past and the future, so that the *telos* of the craft becomes apparent in new and unexpected ways. Therefore, it is the ability to teach others how to learn this type of knowing these skills through which the power of the master within the community of the craft is legitimated as a rational authority.

For a craft to be in good condition, it has to be in a tradition in good order. To be initiated into a craft is to be initiated into that tradition. But as MacIntyre points out, such an initiation always involves at least two, if not more, histories. I come to the craft *qua* family member, *qua* community identity, *qua* training in other crafts. In order for my commitment to this craft to be intelligible, it must be understood in relationship to a hierarchy of crafts within a good community.[16]

I am not suggesting that we ought to think about becoming moral as an analogy to learning how to be a bricklayer, potter, or teacher. Rather I am suggesting that learning to lay brick or play basketball constitutes contexts in which we receive our most decisive moral training. As I argued in the second chapter [of *After Christendom*], it is only the prejudice of modernity that would create a realm of morality abstracted from determinative practices like bricklaying, quilting, or gardening.

Moreover, it is just such an abstraction that makes it so hard for us to rightly conceive of disciplined care. To be initiated into a craft by a master certainly requires discipline, but it is the nature of such discipline that it is hardly noticed as such. That does not mean we may not be asked at times to learn to do things that seem to have no point, but in the doing of them we discover the point. When a craft and a community are in good working or-

---

15. MacIntyre, *Three Rival Versions of Moral Inquiry*, pp. 64-65.

16. MacIntyre, *Three Rival Versions of Moral Inquiry*, p. 128. MacIntyre argues that philosophy necessarily must become the master craft if our hierarchies are to be rational. There I fear he and I may well be in disagreement, depending on what he means by philosophy, since I necessarily must argue that theology, not philosophy, is in service to a community that ultimately must claim philosophy as a servant.

der, discipline is quite literally a joy, as it provides one with power — and in particular a power for service — that is otherwise missing.

On Learning to Be a Disciple

But what does all this have to do with the church? First, it reminds us that Christianity is not beliefs about God plus behavior. We are not Christians because of what we believe, but because we have been called to be disciples of Jesus. To become a disciple is not a matter of a new or changed self-understanding, but rather to become part of a different community with a different set of practices.

For example, I am sometimes confronted by people who are not Christians but who say they want to know about Christianity. This is a particular occupational hazard for theologians around a university, because it is assumed that we are smart or at least have a Ph.D., so we must really know something about Christianity. After many years of vain attempts to "explain" God as Trinity, I now say, "Well, to begin with we Christians have been taught to pray, Our Father, who art in heaven . . .'" I then suggest that a good place to begin to understand what we Christians are about is to join me in that prayer.

For to learn to pray is no easy matter but requires much training, not unlike learning to lay brick. It does no one any good to believe in God, at least the God we find in Jesus of Nazareth, if they have not learned to pray. To learn to pray means we must acquire humility not as something we try to do, but as commensurate with the practice of prayer. In short, we do not believe in God, become humble, and then learn to pray, but in learning to pray we humbly discover we cannot do other than believe in God.

But, of course, to learn to pray requires we learn to pray with other Christians. It means we must learn the disciplines necessary to worship God. Worship, at least for Christians, is the activity to which all our skills are ordered. That is why there can be no separation of Christian morality from Christian worship. As Christians, our worship is our morality, for it is in worship we find ourselves engrafted into the story of God. It is in worship that we acquire the skills to acknowledge who we are — sinners.

This is but a reminder that we must be trained to be a sinner. To confess our sin, after all, is a theological and moral accomplishment. Perhaps nowhere is the contrast between the account of the Christian life I am trying to develop and most modern theology clearer than on this issue. In an odd manner Christian theologians in modernity, whether they are liberals or conservatives, have assumed that sin is a universal category available to anyone.[17] People might not believe in God, but they will confess their sin. As a result, sin becomes an unavoidable aspect of the human condition. This is odd for a people who have been taught that we must confess our sin by being trained by a community that has learned how to name those aspects of our lives that stand in the way of our being Jesus' disciples.

For example, as Christians we cannot learn to confess our sins unless we are forgiven. Indeed, as has often been stressed, prior to forgiveness we cannot know we are sinners. For it is our tendency to want to be forgivers such that we remain basically in a power relation to those we have forgiven. But it is the great message of the gospel that we will only find our lives in that of Jesus to the extent that we are capable of accepting forgiveness. But accepting forgiveness does not come easily, because it puts us literally out of control.

In like manner we must learn to be a creature. To confess that we are finite is not equivalent to the recognition that we are creatures. For creaturehood draws on a determinative narrative of God as creator that re-

17. Again, Reinhold Niebuhr is the great representative of this tendency in modern theology. There is no question, moreover, it was a powerful apologetic strategy as long as one could presume the lingering habits of a Christian civilization. However, those habits now seem to me to be gone for good and with good riddance. This issue again is nicely illustrated by Martha Nussbaum's review of MacIntyre's *Whose Justice? Which Rationality?* titled "Recoiling from Reason," *New York Review of Books* 36, no. 19 (December 7, 1989): 36-41. In that review she accuses MacIntyre of introducing the concept of sin to underwrite an authoritarian politics, and in this case a church, that cannot but offend any rational account of human existence. In contrast, Nussbaum argues that we must recover Aristotle without Christian eyes because only then are we capable of securing the kind of rational agreement necessary to sustain modern liberal society. Thus she says, "This is not to minimize the difficulty of going beyond recognition of common experience in problems to construct common norms. With each step such an inquiry should balance the concrete experience of particular groups with an interest in what is common to all. How one might do this remains an immensely challenging question, but I see no reason to suppose that it cannot be done. If the doctrine of original sin, as MacIntyre interprets it, were true, the obstacles in the way of carrying out such a project would be formidable, since presumably original sin impedes the reasoning of each reasoner, as well as making it difficult for a reasoned view to win acceptance. But MacIntyre has given us no good reason to believe that doctrine is true. And unless and until we accept some such idea we do not have reason to relax our demands for good reasons, deferring to authority" (p. 41). Though I think Nussbaum is wrong to assume that an account of sin is meant to underwrite an authoritarian politics, she is surely right to argue that those committed to the grand liberal project should reject any notion of sin. For a more extended discussion of Nussbaum see my "Can Aristotle Be a Liberal? Nussbaum on Luck," *Soundings* 72, no. 4 (Winter 1989): 675-92.

quires more significant knowledge of our humanity than simply that we are finite. For both the notions of creature and sinner require that we find ourselves constituted by narratives that we did not create.

As I indicated earlier, that is to put us at deep odds with modernity. For the very notion that our lives can be recognized as lives only as we find ourselves constituted by a more determinative narrative that has been given to us rather than created by us, is antithetical to the very spirit of modernity. But that is but an indication of why it is necessary that this narrative be carried by a body of people who have the skills to give them critical distance to those of the world.

In some ways all of this remains quite abstract because the notions of sinner and creature still sound more like self-understanding rather than characteristics of a craft. That is why we cannot learn to be a sinner separate from concrete acts of confession. Thus in the letter of James we are told, "Are any among you sick? They should call for the elders of the church and have them pray over them, anointing them with oil in the name of the Lord. The prayer of faith will save the sick, and the Lord will raise them up; and anyone who has committed sins will be forgiven. Therefore confess your sins to one another, and pray for one another, so that you may be healed. The prayer of the righteous is powerful and effective" (James 5:14-16). Such practice, I suspect, is no less important now as it was then. We cannot learn that we are sinners unless we are forced to confess our sins to other people in the church. Indeed it is not possible to learn to be a sinner without a confession and reconciliation. For it is one thing to confess our sin in general, but it is quite another to confess our sin to one in the church whom we may well have wronged and to seek reconciliation. Without such confessions, however, I suspect we cannot be church at all.[18]

For example, when Bill Moyers did his public broadcast series on religion in America, the taping on fundamentalism was quite striking. He showed a fundamentalist pastor in Boston discussing a pastoral problem with one of his parishioners. The parishioner's wife had committed adultery

---

18. One of the great problems after Protestantism lost the confessional was any ability to know how to name sins as sins. It is one of the great riches of the Catholic tradition that it is able to locate avarice, greed, lust, theft, adultery, and murder in a tradition that gives them a rational display as sin. As Protestants we have lost the ability to name our sins and thus lack the kind of discerning practices to have our lives located within the narrative of the church. For further reflections in this respect see my "Casuistry in Context," *Experience in Medicine,* ed. by Warren Reich [published as chapter 11 of Stanley Hauerwas, *In Good Company: The Church as Polis* (Notre Dame: University of Notre Dame Press, 1995)].

and had confessed it to the church. After much searching and discussion, the church had received her back after appropriate penitential discipline. However, her husband was not ready to be so forgiving and did not wish to receive her back.

The fundamentalist pastor said, "You do not have the right to reject her, for as a member of our church you too must hold out the same forgiveness that we as a church hold out. Therefore I'm not asking you to take her back, I am telling you to take her back."

I anticipate that such an example strikes fear in most of our liberal hearts, but it is also a paradigmatic form of what I take forgiveness to be about. In Boston one with authority spoke to another on behalf of the central skills of the church that draw their intelligibility from the gospel. There we have an example of congregational care and discipline that joins together for the upbuilding of the Christian community.

Of course if the church lacks masters who have undergone the discipline of being forgiven, then indeed we cannot expect that such discipline will be intelligible. But I do not believe that we are so far gone to lack such masters. Indeed they are the ones who continue to carry the history to help us learn from our past so that our future will not be determined by the temptation to live unforgiven and thus unskillful lives.

44 The Last of the Last:
Theology, Authority, and Democracy

John Milbank

I

Should theology owe its prime allegiance to the academic community or to the Church? Should it be, as David Tracy advocates, primarily a "public discourse" answerable to the critical norms and liberal values, or should it be the faith of the Church seeking understanding according to a logic inseparable from this faith, as encouraged by Joseph Ratzinger?

Faced with such a stark alternative, the tendency is to propose a compromise. Given that the notion of a contextless reason without presuppositions and practical commitments is a fiction (as recent philosophy has come to conclude), then it is not contrary to reason to suggest that a well-established community may undertake to articulate its own implicit reasonings. However, if this reflection is not to be merely self-regarding, then it must also be subject to critical reflections from external sources, sources such as the diagnosis of "ideologies."

Yet, the problem with any mere compromise is that it produces a double problem and compounds it with contradiction. One is still left with the question of an uncritical solipsism and of the fictional perspective from nowhere. If the two are combined, then one is trying to believe at once that reason founds itself and that this is impossible. At this point, some theologians have had recourse to semi-Hegelian solutions, often inspired by Jürgen Habermas. Critique is imminent: one must begin with traditions and assumptions, but a negative process of unravelling contradictions gradually drives toward a universal *logos*.

This solution is no better. Traditions unfold by acts of hermeneutic discrimination as well as by overcoming contradictions. Something inherently subjective and imbued with feeling is just as involved in development as in inheritance, continuation, and origin. However long the process of formally objective logical negation, this cannot alter the positive status of the beginnings. One remains entirely inside a tradition. Conversely, if a logical process is still the only criterion for socially acceptable truth, then one is persisting with placeless, formal, and self-founded criteria for reason. The idea that a tradition will edge toward the universal through the working out of contradiction, or conversely, that a foundation will finally emerge at the conclusion, is contradictory. So one still has to compromise between two perhaps unsatisfactory positions, which sustains the unsatisfactoriness of both and adds to this the unacceptability of downright incoherence.

Is it possible to do any better? Very often, documents issued in the name of joint doctrinal statements among various churches produce their results by toning down given differences or by glossing over their ineluctable historical reality. For example, one could say that Aquinas and Luther have "essentially the same" doctrine of justification. There can be much truth in this sort of conclusion, given that by Luther's day the nature of Aquinas' account of salvation had been obscured, and that thereafter the views of both in this area have been further obscured. Yet, in the end, an irremovable difference significantly linked with their exceedingly different ontologies (realist/analogical versus nominalist/univocalist) tends to be ignored. Luther's nominalism will not really admit the Thomist paradox of an entirely supernatural righteousness. Instead, the younger, more "participatory" Luther is actually developing the consequences of an almost Monophysite (well, actually *more* Monophysite than the formal monophysitism of the Monophysites — although John Philoponus at least seems already to have been a sort of nominalist) Ockhamist Christology, which can neither think two universal "natures" in a single personal reality nor think this reality other than on the model of a single finite thing "within which" God has somehow entered.[1] Within such a perspective, the participation in Christ by which one is justified edges too closely toward mere identity and subsumption. Actually, Aquinas' apparently similar Cyrilline tendencies have a totally different realist logic. Luther's nominalist

---

1. See Graham White, *Luther as Nominalist* (Helsinki: Luther-Agricola-Society 1994), pp. 231-99; Henry Chadwick, "Philoponus the Christian Theologian," in Richard Sorabji, ed., *Philoponus and the Rejection of Aristotelian Science* (London: Duckworth, 1987); and William of Ockham, *Quodlibetal Questions,* 5.10.

univocalism finds another solution in his later extrinsicist, imputational account of grace, which is more obviously alien to that of Aquinas.

This upshot in ecumenical documents does a disservice to the cause of truth and, from an academic perspective, runs the risk of making theology look biased. What seems crucial here is that, while ecumenical reflection makes some use of historical research to upset prejudices about what different communities have believed from their outsets, it does not take this process far enough. At bottom, it is a matter of developing mutual respect between different ecclesial bodies, not of questioning their character. In this respect, ecumenics is very much conducted on a basis internal to received variants of the faith. Yet, here a more external, objective approach might be more inclined to ask questions about the common intellectual assumptions of both the post-Reformation and the post-Tridentine faiths, and the possible deviation of these from earlier Christian views.

There seems to be an increasing consensus among historians that neither the Reformation nor the somewhat elusive "Renaissance," nor even the later "Enlightenment" was anything like such crucial shifts in Western theory and practice as the multiple changes which took place before and after the year 1300.[2] At that time, a far greater gap between specialists and non-specialists in all fields became evident; administration became more technical and distant; clerical control over the laity increased; sharper differentiations were made between academic disciplines; theology assumed a far more technical character; the traditional centrality in theology of participation, deification, apophaticism, allegory, and the church as engendered by the Eucharist were all abruptly challenged in a fashion that proved epochally successful. Meanwhile, ecclesial authorities declared unacceptable much that had been taken for granted in the Aristotelian/Neoplatonic synthesis and had been shared with Byzantine, Jewish, and Islamic cultures. Many historians claim that the later breakup of Christendom was in large measure the upshot of these changes, and that the same changes ushered in a drift toward "secularity." This has implications both for ecumenism and for the debate about the relation of theology and secular culture. Sometimes, great faith is invested in the possible upshot of Christian reunion, particularly within the Yale School of American theologians: secularization is seen as a negative reaction to Christian disunity; re-unification, as the key to renewed mission.

---

2. See Michel de Certeau, *The Mystic Fable,* trans. Michael B. Smith (Chicago: University of Chicago Press, 1992), pp. 79-113; and Eric Alliez, *Capital Times: Tales from the Conquest of Time,* trans. Georges Van Den Abbeele (Minneapolis: University of Minnesota Press, 1996).

However, if the new emerging historical consensus is correct, then it is rather the case that secularization, not ecumenism, is the prior problem. It might be that Christian division was an outcome of a severe weakening of the Christian vision, and that the key to ecumenical discussion would be a far more drastic critique of existing ecclesial bodies.

However, this may appear to impose too much duality between theology and history. It cannot be an accident that much of the new picture of the history of ideas and of the Church is inspired by theologians prepared to be critical of the contemporary norms of the ecclesial body to which they belong (overwhelmingly, this body is the Roman Catholic Church).

The sources of intellection in theology are often taken to be scripture, tradition, and reason, and all too often the Anglican community has claimed to have a uniquely balanced orientation toward all three loci. This way of understanding the grounds for theologizing is, however, unsatisfactory — in fact, it is ultimately an upshot of the "crisis of 1300." It tends to result in arguments for the predominance of one of these elements, or else for compromise between their respective sways. But the problem with "tradition" seems to be solipsism; the problem with "reason" seems to be its unreal and impotent abstraction; the problem with "scripture" is its magical positivity. Compromise among these three again compounds problems and adds to these contradictions, since replete positivity does not need the supplement of community in time or of neutral reason, and tradition cannot admit a positive foundation that would render it redundant.

To overcome this *impasse,* one needs to understand that scripture, tradition, and reason were *not* seen as separate sources prior to 1300. Throughout these considerations, questions arise: first, should one want to *return* to this earlier perspective, or must one return with difference, given a certain validity to some post-1300 considerations? Second, how should one handle a situation in which there is a real secular sphere, as there was not in the Middle Ages? Can a certain pre-1300 fluidity between faith and reason be helpful in the modern predicament?

The transformation of theology from before 1300 to today will now be considered under three categories: the supernatural, the *corpus mysticum,* and allegory. Through all these categories runs a fourth, which will not be considered explicitly on its own: participation. The first three categories derive mostly from the work of Henri de Lubac, especially as re-interpreted by Michel de Certeau, Jean-Yves Lacoste, and Olivier Boulnois. The fourth category derives in part from Erich Przywara, Sergei Bulgakov, Hans Urs von Balthasar, and again Boulnois. What is at issue in the first category is theology between faith and reason; in the second, theology under ecclesial authority; and in the third, theology between scripture and tradition.

II

A correct Roman Catholic view, proclaimed since the time of the Church under persecution, is that truth should be freely pursued, since all knowledge points toward God. Coercion into understanding defeats its own object, since the divine truth freely shines out everywhere. There is no question, then, but that the Church is on the side of free scientific enquiry.

Since at least the Counter-Reformation, however, the Catholic Church has tended to construe its support of science in terms of a duality of reason and faith. In the thought of Cardinal Cajetan, the Thomistic paradox of a natural desire for the supernatural — a desire which must be already the lure of grace, since humanity cannot raise itself to God of its own accord — is occluded.[3] Instead, Cajetan underwrites the late medieval and non-Thomistic espousal of a purely "natural beatitude" accessible by philosophy, according to which the latter is supposed to be able to attain by natural powers of intellect and will to some sort of positive knowledge and contemplation of the divine. By comparison, Aquinas had spoken of a philosophic reach to a negatively defined first cause, and in other statements indicated that even this reach is inseparable from a divine drawing forth by grace, which defines humanity as such.[4] Cajetan instead espoused in effect a "closed humanism," with its own transcendental reach, that essentially was unrelated to the arrival of revelation. Since there was no longer any natural anticipation of grace, faith was now construed in very "extrinsicist" terms as assent to a series of revealed propositions; gradually, in a process culminating in Suárez, revelation also lost its integration of inner experience with interpretation of outward sign, and was bifurcated between one and the other.[5] The realm of grace now

3. Henri de Lubac, *Surnaturel* (Paris: Aubier, 1946); *The Mystery of the Supernatural*, trans. Rosemary Sheed (London: Geoffrey Chapman, 1967). See also Jean-Yves Lacoste, "Le désir et l'inéxigible: préambules à une lecture," in *Les Etudes Philosophiques* 2 (1995): 223-46; and Olivier Boulnois, "Les deux fins de l'homme," in the same issue, pp. 205-22.

4. See John Milbank and Catherine Pickstock, *Truth in Aquinas* (London: Routledge 2001), Ch. 2, "Truth and Vision," pp. 19-26.

5. See John Montag, S.J., "Revelation: The False Legacy of Suárez," in *Radical Orthodoxy: A New Theology*, ed. John Milbank, Catherine Pickstock, and Graham Ward (London: Routledge, 1999), pp. 38-64.

concerned external positive data superadded to the conclusions of reason, or else an ineffable realm of inner "mystical" experience, equally positive and equally subject to experimental testing for the reality of "presence."[6]

As both Lacoste and Boulnois argue, modern "philosophy" does not simply emancipate itself from theology, but arises in a space that theology has carved out for it: pure nature.[7] To be sure, "natural beatitude" was supposed to correspond roughly to the pagan *theoria* achieved by Plato and Aristotle. But this was a delusion: pagan *physis* was not Christian *natura*, since the latter exists only in paired contrast with the supernatural. It would be true to say that the Platonic and Peripatetic philosophies contain some rough anticipation of the Christian supernatural, as much as they do of the Christian natural, since they both understand wisdom to be primarily the prerogative of the divine, and human wisdom to be sharing in this replete wisdom to some degree.

Boulnois correctly radicalizes Lubac's reading of Aquinas to show that the paradox of natural orientation to the supernatural in Aquinas is in fact in continuity with a cosmology and ontology that adopts themes from the Graeco-Arabic legacy, even though it transforms them in terms of a much stronger grasp of the idea of divine creation.[8] Thus, it is not simply that one naturally desires the supernatural; it is also that intellect modeled on the angelic intellect which moves the celestial spheres, drawn in ceaseless perfect motion by the immovable, only exists in the space of this paradox. Indeed, while all finite motions are proper to specific natures, nature as a whole is only in motion because it is drawn by higher powers toward a stilling of motion. The motion of human intellect is like a more intense and reflexive influx and concentration of natural motion, while the celestial spheres combine the inwardness of the intellect of the separate substances which move them with the totality of circulating finite motion. In this way, the natural human destiny toward the vision of God is only the outworking of a knowingly and willingly created nature of the paradox of creation; of itself, it is nothing, and only exists by participation. (For this reason creation requires a purer sense of *methexis*, as grasped by the biblical teaching of the presence of wisdom and glory in the cosmos; thus, St. Paul, with self-conscious irony, proclaimed *methexis* to the Athenians: "God, in whom we live and move and have our being.") Therefore, everything — not just humanity — is already

6. Certeau, *The Mystic Fable*.
7. Lacoste, "Le désir et l'inéxigible"; and Boulnois, "Les deux fins de l'homme."
8. Boulnois, "Les deux fins de l'homme."

more than itself, and this more is in some sense a portion of divinity. It is not that something "more" is added to the natural human soul, but rather that the psychic is the conscious concentration of the paradoxical nature of every *ens*. Even though Aquinas rejects the Arabic doctrine of a single superhuman intellect, he nevertheless adopts their concern to attend to the phenomenology of thinking, which presupposes that one is never in charge of thought: thought occurs, so thinking is something occurring within one, as well as something that one thinks.

The collapse of the paradox of the natural orientation to the supernatural was an aspect of the collapse of this entire cosmology and ontology. Aquinas had sought a cause for finite being: *esse commune*. But in the later Middle Ages — beginning, ironically, with Siger of Brabant — this was deemed to be a question that made little sense, since *esse* no longer was thought of as something superadded to essence, thereby rendering an arriving accident paradoxically more fundamental than the essential in the constitution of the creature.[9] Instead, one could now ask only for the final cause of finite being in its given finite circumstances. But something finite as existing — the dog in its existing dogness, rather than the why of there being a dog, for example — was now regarded as making full sense in its own finite terms. To know that a truth was from God was no longer, as it was for Aquinas, thought to change the very character of the truth. This new space of univocal existence, of sheer "thereness," quickly became as much thereness for mere entertained thought as for ontic reality. Indeed, the emergence of this space was encouraged inversely by a parallel drift, ever since Roger Bacon, away from the Aristotelian view that knowledge is the realization of migrating species as pure form in one's mind, toward knowledge as representational mirroring of a reality having no essential orientation toward understanding. Ideas and fictions now started to acquire ontological equality with real being as all equally "things."[10]

The new univocalist/representational space was one that could be explored as the realm of pure nature. It extended beyond the finite: indeed, as Boulnois points out, Duns Scotus found it contradictory that Aquinas had combined the view that the primary object of the human intellect is sensory with the view that every act of understanding is orientated toward the supernatural.[11] Instead of Thomas' aporias and conundra, he substituted the view

9. See Olivier Boulnois, *Etre et Représentation: Une généalogie de la Metaphysique Moderne à L'Epoque de Duns Scot (xiii-xiv siècle)* (Paris: PUF, 1999).

10. Boulnois, *Etre et Représentation.*

11. Boulnois, "Les deux fins de l'homme."

that the human intellect, in its pure prelapsarian essence, is naturally capable of the grasp of non-material essences: this (already, following Karl Rahner, one wants to say "transcendentalist") reaches the intellect and is then the natural base for the reception of positive supernatural information.

The combination of a univocalist and representational concept of understanding — intellect represents "things" simply there in their differential exemplifying of a bare "presence" outside participation — with the idea of a natural beatitude permitted theology to encourage the emergence of independent philosophy faculties in the early modern period (the diverse presence of philosophy in mediaeval arts and theology faculties represented a totally different intellectual economy). Where previously philosophy had survived as a kind of pagan "moment" within Christian theology, which was linked with the necessary discursiveness of our finitude, there were now professional "philosophers." Ironically, the new division of powers had emerged in part to counter the threat of Latin Averroism, which was thought (probably erroneously) to pursue a philosophy altogether independent of theology. The only drastic way to achieve institutional control over such tendencies was to purge theology of an essential metaphysical detour through a vision of the participatory reflection of the divine essence in the cosmos, and to insist that it is rather a purely positive discourse founded upon the divine *potentia absoluta*, now regarded as a real unknown reserve of limitless options. In this way, there can be a final court of appeal against wayward reason, whose procedures are not so much guaranteed by partial illuminatory intuition and dialectical discursiveness as by recourse to positive sources and to methods for discriminating among and ordering those sources. Actually, this new positive approach was only perfected in the sixteenth century with the new insistence on theological loci, especially in the work of Melchior Cano.

What is important to grasp here is what appears to be the counter-intuitive link between a new autonomy for philosophy and an increased censorship of, or aspiration to censor, philosophy by theology. This remains crucial for understanding the situation even today. But, as Lacoste has noted, this had ludicrous consequences. Granted autonomy to explore pure nature, philosophers did not find what they were supposed to find, but were announcing materialisms, pantheisms, idealisms, etc. Shortly thereafter, they were disconnecting natural beatitude from any contemplation of the divine. This meant that the only "true" philosophy was mostly done by the theologians' left hand. Philosophy was supposed to be able to reach natural truth solely by reason. But since faith knew that the higher truth of revelation overrides apparently sound reasonings, every philosophy conflicting with faith had to be denied twice over: first, on positive grounds of faith; and second, in terms of a better reasoning which then must be sought out.

Such convolutions surely have helped to bring Christianity into disrepute. Yet, they are entirely remote from the real outlook of the High Middle Ages. What is more, the "bad" philosophers of modernity have always been more truly theological than the "sound" ones, since they have refused to conclude to God from uninflected objective reason, and thereby have in some measure avoided idolatry. All this has been set out in detail, though from very different if complementary perspectives, by Michael Buckley and Jean-Luc Marion.[12]

But are the same mistakes still being perpetuated today? Roman Catholic culture finds it very difficult, for institutional reasons, to deny a false Tridentine legacy altogether, and to pursue all the consequences of Lubac's theological revolution (a subversion as real as it was stealthy). An enterprise of "natural theology," which historians have now shown dates back no further than to Duns Scotus, is perpetuated, along with a non-Thomist "natural law," i.e., apart from the law of charity. This perpetuation is common to both "conservatives" and "liberals." Indeed, it is that secret common ground upon which they are distributed as conservatives and liberals, stressing respectively either faith or reason, but both assuming a two-tier economy. Even someone as influenced by Lubac as Balthasar still pursues, unlike Lubac, a "metaphysical" prolegomenon to *sacra doctrina*. When discussing Martin Heidegger, he falls into exactly the same trap as Étienne Gilson: Heidegger has recovered the ontological difference already known to Thomas, yet does not "pursue questioning far enough," thereby perpetuating as a pure mystery the non-necessity of the ontic and the excess of the ontological shown through this contingency. Further questioning is supposed to give rise ineluctably to the thought of being as a personal donor.[13] But, of course, it does not: such a recourse remains also a "mystery." Heidegger has his own resolution of the mystery: being is also nothing, but is the continual presencing of absence in time.

In purely rational terms, Heidegger appears to be the more rigorous of the two, if by "rational" one means the exploration of pure given nature as

---

12. Michael Buckley, *At the Origins of Modern Atheism* (New Haven: Yale University Press, 1987); Jean-Luc Marion, *L'Idole et La Distance* (Paris: Grasset et Fasqueile, 1977).

13. Hans Urs von Balthasar, *The Glory of the Lord: A Theological Aesthetics,* vol. 5: *The Realm of Metaphysics in the Modern Age,* trans. Brian McNeil et al. (San Francisco: Ignatius, 1989), pp. 635-65.

representable by finite intellect and subject to the maneuvering of finite will. As Lacoste contends, the space of pure nature must confine the human essence to what the human being is capable of, and must equally confine true human understanding to this capacity in its cognitive aspect.[14] Within such a confinement, the world will be defined by technological capacity, by an empty reach toward a sublime unknown, and by systematic indeterminacy, since limits turn out to be the perpetual anarchic transgression of limits (the inevitable postmodern turn of modernity), as well as by the horizon of death. As Lacoste points out, even the later Heidegger's exceeding of these options in terms of a symbolic dwelling within the cosmos remains a resignation to the impersonal, without hope beyond death, and thus subordinate to the desires and aspirations of the body.

It would seem, then, that the history of modern ideas negatively bears out the view that no natural beatitude will be concluded to, save under the promptings of an explicit orientation to the supernatural. This situation is half-recognized in the papal encyclical *Fides et Ratio*,[15] where philosophy is exhorted to be "wisdom" rather than merely "reason," and this means to take account of right desiring, of the link between thought and life, and to be open to receive something beyond the grasp of reason. This is all well and good, but needs further defining. The "autonomy" of rational enquiry is still advocated, and not merely in terms of legal freedom (which one should, of course, endorse, in keeping with the early Christian view that truth can only be freely accepted), but also in terms of some essential good proceeding from such autonomy. However, if right desiring and openness to revelation have entered the picture, then, according to post-Lubac logic, this is already a work of grace, and already exists in some sort of typological, i.e., historical, relation to scripture and tradition. All the traces of "wisdom" on which philosophy might build in the modern world do not stand simply "outside" Christian tradition, as far as this tradition is concerned. Thus, all ethical topics are marked by the passage of the gospel through the world, and even when philosophy appeals to the Greeks, it appeals to a legacy which is taken up, in part and in places, in the New Testament, and is thereby a constituent element of Christianity.

However, the exaggerated and somewhat naive opposition of the encyclical to "relativism," which militates against attention to historicity, means that the pursuit of wisdom cannot be pursued in this fashion. Instead, *Fides*

14. Lacoste, "Le désir et l'inéxigible."
15. John Paul II, *Faith and Reason* (London: Catholic Truth Society, 1998).

et Ratio seems at times to insist on a reason that is the same in all times and places, and is an autonomous natural faculty without presuppositions. In that case, this is a return to all the old post-Tridentine absurdities: the world is granted leave to think autonomously; yet, left to itself, it turns out that it cannot do this. So, the Church ends up teaching the contradiction that autonomy needs assistance.

Given this situation, one natural reaction is fideistic. It tells a story: once upon a time, it seemed as if the Church could rely on metaphysical cosmology; then, it seemed as if it could rely upon a metaphysical ethics; but now, it must learn to cling to the Cross alone — perhaps construing even this as the tragic presence of God in his secular absence. It is the story told by Dietrich Bonhoeffer, and also in large measure by Balthasar, although the latter still adds to revelation the (essentially Kantian) props of a phenomenological aesthetic and personalistic ethics taken as prolegomena, if only in part.[16] However, this is not to suggest a critique of Balthasar in the manner of Karl Barth and in a purely fideistic recourse.

The alleged profundity of the fideistic grand narrative turns out to be adolescent. What has been outgrown is not a natural childhood, but a childhood of error without innocence that need never have happened, which is not *at all* to say that mankind should have remained forever in the culture of the twelfth and thirteenth centuries; no, it is an *unknown* future that mankind has missed and must seek to rejoin. Historical research since the 1960s makes it abundantly clear that the metaphysical cosmology of the High Middle Ages was thoroughly informed by and transformed through the biblical legacy. When this metaphysics was lost with the nominalists, it was not on the basis of a rediscovery of a biblical God of will, law, and covenant, etc., but rather as the consequence of a catastrophic invasion of the West by ultimately Islamic norms (which are now turned back on Islam, imagining them to be the "other"). The very 1277 condemnations by the Archbishops of Paris and of Canterbury, which swept away a cultural legacy shared with Islam (as well as with Judaism and Byzantium), also repeated within the West a gesture of Islamic orthodoxy: banish and regulate philosophy; impose instead a positivistic order based on literal punctiliar revelation underwritten by absolute sovereignty, which is now the only trace on earth of an inscrutable deity. Caliphization of the West: the Bible is now read as if it were the Koran, with Calvin's *asharia* looming on the horizon.

---

16. See especially Hans Urs von Balthasar, *Love Alone: The Way of Revelation,* ed. Alexander Dru (London: Sheed and Ward, 1977).

In light of these developments, it proved extremely difficult to think through the central Christian doctrines that depend on the realism of universals, reality of relation, and the truth of *methexis* — all denied by the terminists. Thus, Ockham's Trinity becomes three ontic persons within one unity of an individual; his Christology appears Monophysite, because he cannot think the divine hypostasis relationally; transubstantiation is trivialized into bilocation and extrinsicist miracle, and the Creation starts to acquire such autonomy that, for Ockham, there is no longer any "reason" to ascribe its origin to God, rather than to the intelligences. Consequently, all these doctrines become lifeless: no longer informing reason, they are rather matters merely to be believed on pain of death in this world or the next. They are now left to the Church as a huge pile of nakedly ideological resources.

The cosmos of participation was never "argued against" in some unanswerable fashion. There was simply an epistemic switch, complexly linked with social transformations to representation and univocity. Certain tenets of natural philosophy may have been disproved, but even here one can exaggerate: Thomas Torrance has rightly pointed out how much nearer Robert Grosseteste's Christian/Neoplatonic cosmology of light, with its "Cantorian" sets of nested differentiated infinities (and actually no celestial/terrestrial duality), was to modern physics than that of the Later Middle Ages or of Newton.[17]

The point then is not that one must now cling to faith in ascetic nakedness. Instead, one must pass beyond the still all-too-modern fideism of neo-orthodoxy, and move toward a "radical orthodoxy" that refuses the duality of reason and faith. The issue is that what has recently passed for reason is not, as far as Catholic faith is concerned, the work of the *logos* at all, or only jaggedly and intermittently so. Recent reason shows this to be the case negatively, since the strict rigorous upshot of its objective, representing concern is to discover the rule of unreason beyond reason, and the founding of sense in nonsense. Reason's domain is nihilism; whereas the discovery of a meaningful world governed by a *logos* can be made only by faith. This is perhaps the nearest one can get to an apologetic gesture (echoing Jacobi's thought), but it still does not decide the issue ineluctably.[18]

As Lacoste suggests, what has passed for reason is a mere decision to see

---

17. Thomas Torrance, "Creation and Science," in *The Ground and Grammar of Theology* (Charlottesville, VA: University of Virginia Press, 1980), pp. 144-75; "The Theology of Light," in *Christian Theology and Scientific Culture* (New York: Oxford University Press, 1981). Here, one must admit Grosseteste's Neoplatonism and escape his straining at the limits of Calvinism.

18. See John Milbank, "Knowledge: The Theological Critique of Philosophy in Jacobi and Hamann," in *Radical Orthodoxy*, pp. 21-38.

that which is, in a Promethean sense, within one's capacity as the key to human nature and the secrets of the world, or else the key to a knowable world limited to the truth that arises for human purposes. This has often been seen as a pious gesture: confine reason and nature within their limits, thereby letting the gratuity of grace in its glory shine all the more. Even in the case of Kant, a true reading shows that he is trying to protect a rarefied and anti-liturgical pietistic faith from contamination by limited images, much more than to protect reason from contamination by religion — Kant, the last Scotist, Ockhamist, Suarezian, as he has been variously described.

The Kantian attempt to acknowledge limits self-deconstructs, since they will appear only if one claims to surmount them absolutely. Thus, one gets Kant's dogmatic hierarchy of practically perceived *noumena* above theoretically perceived phenomena. Yet, even a postmodern, deconstructed Kant, where the sublime overflows every temporary restraint, still erects a shrine to pure nature and the confines of reason: its mark is now the hypostatization of the unknown only as an empty void, and refusal of any possibility of "beautiful" mediation between the invisible and the visible.

However, this worship of limits that constructs pure reason is only a *decision* without reasons. As Lacoste has explained, such a decision adopts a hermeneutic of human essence and of nature, which makes that which lies within perceived capacity fundamental. But, suppose that the human aspiration or even openness to that which lies beyond its capacity were taken instead to be the hermeneutic key. Lacoste here puts in a sharper light the insistence of many twentieth-century Christians — Charles Peguy supremely — on the virtue of hope. Reason orientated only to a beatitude supposedly within its grasp dispenses with hope, only to end up without hope, and at best resigned to this condition. Likewise, if such a reason is taken to be hermeneutically decisive, it must downgrade the promptings, urgings, and longings of the body. The supernatural in one may be intelligence as such, intelligence thinking through one, but it is also always conjoined with sensation, as Aquinas taught. Therefore, intelligence begins as a bodily exercise, accompanied by desire that reaches into the unknown. Only by the exercise of an artificial abstraction can one prise reason apart from desire, which reaches beyond one's capacity. This prised-apart "pure reason" is also a totally individualistic reason, whether on the level of the single person or of collective humanity. For such a *logos*, one cannot be completed by the other, and so others cannot mediate to one the lure of a wholly other who is also "not other" as *intimo interior meo*, according to the creationist logic of paradoxical priority of supplementation.

What *faith* proposes as *reason,* then, is taking as hermeneutic keys to reality, first *hope,* and then *charity,* which is the erotic lure of the other and one's giving oneself over to the other.

How does such a perspective impact upon the task of theology today? Primarily, it absolutely forbids mankind to baptize the secular desert as the realm of pure reason, pure nature, natural law or natural rights, etc., since this is not at all to acknowledge this sphere in its integrity, but rather to define it in terms of an impoverished baroque theology, even though it still defines itself in this way, as if everyone were really a headless theologian. Rather, what one sees is a postmodern simultaneity of remote times, places, and cultures. It cannot be dealt with in terms of a single Western liberal narrative of pure nature, because this will only issue in bombs and destruction of the other. And none of this complex confusion is exactly "outside" the Church! The Church reads it all in terms of multiple, but converging narratives of typological anticipation, unrecognized scattering of the seeds sown by the incarnate *logos,* and various fallings-away and partial survivals of Christian norms.

So, the answer cannot be the one Tracy offers, i.e., responsibility before a uniform liberal court. This court is a fiction, and one whose dark inner secret is constituted by a voluntarist theology securing order through the formal regulation of chaos from a single sovereign center. Such a liberal option in theology remains confined within a logic constructed by extrinsicism. Its essentially authoritarian character is revealed when it stamps philosophical conclusions already reached with a theological seal of approval derived from doctrines that extrinsically symbolize supposedly universal truths.

But the answer cannot be fideistic, and it cannot even be that of Ratzinger — to the extent that this is not entirely self-consistent, and still preserves, like Balthasar, traces of a metaphysical prolegomenon, even for Christians, and of a somewhat still-too-positivistic account of revealed truth. Revelation is not in any sense a layer added to reason. It arrives as the augmentation of illumination, and faith is found only in the highly complex and tortuous course of a reason that is hopeful and charitable. It is lodged in all the complex networks of human practices, and its boundaries are as messy as those of the Church. Lubac's paradox forbids one to privilege either a human above or a human below. Rather, what has real priority in his scheme is the supernatural, which so exceeds human hierarchies that it includes every degree of them equally, and is as near to the below as to the above. So, although the lure of the supernatural takes precedence over nature that is drawn toward it (and this cannot be perverted into Rahner's transcendentalist terms), this lure is only acknowledged by aspiring nature in all her lowly variety. Theological truth abides, first of all, in the body of the faithful. Yet, where are their bodies, especially today? Not neatly gathered in, but disseminated outwards in complex minglings and associations. A faith obedient to the Church is protected from solipsism precisely at the point where one recognizes that the Church always has been, as John Henry Newman recognized, the taking-up and inter-mingling of many traditions. It even consists from the outset in seeing how the diverse might cohere, and continues to enact this analogical mingling.

Therefore, the plural spaces of the academy, as perhaps *best* symbolized by religious studies departments, where alone *alternative* traditions of reason are sometimes recognized, are not totally other to the space of the Church, which is also pluralistic and also construes its truth, as does the Bible, to be, in one of its aspects, a certain narration of "the history of religions." The difference is that the Church has a project of integration, to which the theologian is bound.[19] Within both the academy and the Church, the task of theology is to foreground Christian difference and non-difference — to think through the Christian *logos* as something entirely exceptional, which also continues and elevates what is most usual to humanity.

III

How is the nature of ecclesial authority and its bearing on theology to be understood? Marion has said that the key is to realize that the bishop is the true theologian.[20] He is right, but his point has usually been misunderstood (especially in the U.S.). What he invokes is a vital link between theology and the eucharist. The bishop is the original president at the eucharist; he is also the prime preacher of the word, a function which he performs only in conjunction with his representing of the body and blood of Christ.

The idea that all theologians must derive their authority from the bishop is only authoritarian under an erroneous understanding of the relation of the bishop to the eucharist, to the word of God, and to his *cathedra*, which is at once his teaching office and the place where he presides — usu-

19. It is much easier to operate within this kind of department, rather than in a traditional theology department, where Christian liberals always seem to bring to a high point of refinement the paradox of liberal nontolerance and manipulation.

20. Jean-Luc Marion, *God Without Being*, trans. Thomas A. Carlson (Chicago: University of Chicago Press, 1991), pp. 139-61.

ally a city of long standing. However, such an erroneous understanding was already encouraged by shifts in the concept of the Church and its relation to the eucharist in the late mediaeval and early modern periods. As Lubac describes these transformations, roughly after the middle of the twelfth century, the term *corpus verum* ceased to be applied to the Church, and was transferred to the body of Christ in the eucharist. Inversely, the term *corpus mysticum* migrated from the eucharist to the Church.[21] Gradually, the latter was drained of physical solidity, which was transferred to the transubstantiated elements. "Mystical" slowly ceased to mean "to do with the liturgical mysteries of initiatory passage, participation, and ascent," and came to mean secrecy, absence, and symbolism. Accompanying this transformation was a change in the relation of both bodies to the historical body of Christ. Earlier, the sacramental and ecclesial bodies stood near each other, and both represented the historical body. But, in the new scheme, the historical and sacramental bodies start to stand near each other as alien sources of authority over against the Church, which, as Certeau stresses in his brilliant commentary on Lubac's *Corpus Mysticum* and *Medieval Exegeses*, increasingly comes to be seen as an ideal space to be constructed in order to realize the dicta of authority, or else to make manifest a new inner "mystical" experience, which is the residue of liturgical ascent that finds no place in a more legal and less liturgical construal of the public sphere.[22]

As long as an essential relation between the three bodies remained, however, strong traces of the older view persisted, e.g., in the thought of Bonaventure or Aquinas. The historical body was mediated to the Church by the sacramental body. The eucharist still "gave" the Church in such a fashion that, as Pickstock puts it, the Church was not a closed self-governing entity, like most political bodies (whether hierarchic or democratic), but rather received its very social embodiment from outside itself.[23] At every eucharist it had, as it were, to begin again, to receive itself anew from outside, from the past and from the angelic Church above. Inversely, the transubstantiation of the bread and wine into the body and blood of Christ was seen as a dynamic action of divine self-giving inseparable from the bringing about and consolidating of the body of the faithful. (Incidentally, the term "transubstantiation" is much older than the term "real presence," which perhaps originated

---

21. Henri de Lubac, *Corpus Mysticum: L'Eucharistie et L'Eglise au Moyen Age* (Paris: Aubier-Montaigne, 1949). See also Catherine Pickstock, *After Writing: On the Liturgical Consummation of Philosophy* (Oxford: Blackwell, 1998), pp. 121-67.

22. Certeau, *The Mystic Fable*, pp. 79-113.

23. Pickstock, *After Writing*, pp. 158-66.

with Latimer and Cranmer; *praesentia corporalis* was used in the Middle Ages, but shied away from by Aquinas[24] — and is dubiously linked with a static sense of local presence that is also "over-against" the congregation).

The really drastic change came when, as Certeau, following Lubac, stresses, the sacramental body ceased to perform this mediating function. Then, instead of a triad, one had alternating dyads: a direct relation of either the absent historical body as testified to by scripture to the Church, or else of the sacramental body to the Church, now taken to be a source of authority *independent* of scripture and deriving from a hierarchic transmission of ecclesial orders. As Certeau concludes, this eventually brings about a total shift from a priority of the diachronic to a priority of the synchronic and functional. Previously, the past really had been made present again through the eucharist, and the Church had re-emerged through its sustaining of a bond to the past and the projection forward to the future by the re-offering of the sacraments and the re-interpretation of the *sacra scriptura*. Now, instead, the past started to seem like a remote lost source of authority that historical detective work must flesh out (thus, the rise of humanist concern with "historicity"). As remote, it stood apart from and over against the Church, which no longer re-presented it. Its relation to the other sacramental source of authority was bound now to be disputed, since the sacramental body was no longer seen to be an essential way in which the lost historical body as traced out by the scriptures was "performed" again in the present. Either sacraments as validated by tradition were seen to be an essential supplement to the now remote scriptures, as in the late mediaeval and Tridentine views, or else the need for this supplement was rejected and one was left with the Protestant *sola scriptura*. But Certeau's drastic conclusion here is both rigorous and undeniable: the crucial shift was certainly not the Reformation; rather, Protestantism and Tridentine Catholicism represented two alternative versions of "reformation," which should be defined as the switch from the triadic to the dyadic account of the relation of the various bodies of Christ. This is the sort of realization that could be the ground for a more honest and self-critical ecumenism. (Protestants need to see that the Reformation was mostly a perpetuation of error, while Catholics need to see that much of what they have taken to be Catholic is not authentic.)

Under the new perspective, the power of clerical authority was necessarily increased. When the historical body was again made present in the eucha-

24. See Jean Yves Lacoste, "Etre [c]," in *Dictionnaire Critique de Theologie*, ed. Jean Yves Lacoste (Paris: PUF, 1998).

rist, and the eucharistic body was only fully realized in the congregation, primary authority was both symbolic and collective, and initially bypassed vertical hierarchy. Only by a sort of reflex was episcopal authority constituted. The bishop was, first of all, powerful to the extent that he was identified with a particular *cathedra*. This was a specific intersection of time and place that recorded a particular Christian fulfillment of a particular local legacy. Thus, nearly all churches were built on earlier sacred sites, not primarily as a matter of propaganda, but of vital continuity in and through a surpassing. As president at the eucharist and teacher, the bishop enacted once again the essence of a certain place (usually, the abode of sacred relics) and perpetuated the stream of glory refracted through it in a specific way. The bishop held authority, from Ignatius of Antioch onward, as symbolizing in his singleness the unity of the Church in a single *civitas*. Of course, the bishop was also the guardian and guarantor of correct transmission, and, of course, his exercise of these powers might often overstep the mark of his representational and dramatic function. Nevertheless, up to the middle of the thirteenth century or so, that clerical sacramental and preaching authority was much more "mingled" with lay participation than it later became (although, at first, in the Late Middle Ages, the laity defended itself with the increased activity of semi-independent lay fraternities).[25] But during this period the techniques of remote, secret, and invasive clerical control, as deployed through auricular confession, exorcism, and staged miracles, first mooted in the twelfth century and promulgated through the Lateran Councils, were vastly extended. The "gothic" realm of complex overlapping spaces and social participations started to give way to the "gothick" realm of systematic terror through surveillance. It is no accident that one of the great "gothick" novels of the eighteenth century, Charles Maturin's *Melmoth the Wanderer*, deploys a critique of the Spanish Inquisition also as a critique of Calvinist predestinarianism and modernity.

This increased clerical control was inseparable from the new economy of the three bodies. No longer was the transmission of authority carried

---

25. This is how some of Eamon Duffy's evidence should be interpreted. Duffy takes less account than Bossy and Scarisbrick of a late medieval decadence inaugurating tendencies that early modernity will intensify, because he wishes to argue that Catholicism was in good shape on the eve of the Reformation. In this respect, his position is less complex than that of the two other writers. See Eamon Duffy, *The Stripping of the Traditional Religion in England 1400-1580* (New Haven, CT: Yale University Press, 1992); John Bossy, *Christianity in the West 1400-1700* (Oxford: Oxford University Press, 1985); J. J. Scarisbrick, *The Reformation and the English People* (Oxford: Blackwell, 1984).

through in a superhuman "angelic" fashion by liturgical action. No longer did the historical body pass via the bishop into the mouths of communicants or (more often) the eyes of witnesses, who then "performed" what the liturgical script suggested. Instead, the historical and sacramental bodies were now more like inert objects in need of human subjective assistance. For the magisterial Reformation, the ordained clergy were the privileged interpreters of the Word, who quickly established "orthodox" parameters within which it could be read, thus neutralizing its supposedly self-interpreting authority, as Catholic critics swiftly pointed out. For Tridentine Catholicism, the ordained hierarchy was the guarantee of a eucharistic miracle now seen as a spectacle quite apart from its dynamic action of "giving" the body of the Church.

Thus, one cannot possibly speak of an increased lay influence in Protestantism over against a Catholic clericalist reaction. Rather, in either case, there is a substantial loss of mediaeval lay participation (as the British Catholic historians John Bossy, John Scarisbrick, and Eamon Duffy have all argued),[26] while in either case there is also a significant rise in compensating lay pieties and mysticisms that try to colonize the no man's land that had arisen in the gap between a closed humanism, on the one hand, and an extrinsicist system of dogma, on the other. As Certeau argues, a "mystic" discourse arises with a redoubling of the sense of the absence of a true ecclesial body, although it is often recruited into the machinations of ecclesiastical discipline and the attempts to verify abstractions with experience and to build a new future on the basis of formal method.

It would seem, then, that the earlier, high mediaeval model offers a much better understanding of the relation of the bishop to teaching and so to theological reflection. Theology is answerable to the bishop as the occupant of the *cathedra* and as the president at the eucharist. But this means that the theologian is primarily answerable, not so much to a Church hierarchy in its synchronic spatiality — this is all too modern — but rather to a hierarchical, educative *manuductio* of the faith down through the ages. Equally, he is answerable to a specific locality or very often multiple specific localities, such that his sense of perpetuating a history must be combined with his sense of pursuing an archeology and mapping a geography. Finally, he is also answerable to the mode of the reception of the Sacrament and the Word by the congregation, even if in the early twenty-first century this is often impossible, and the theologian must exercise what is an excessively critical function by ideal standards.

26. For a summary of their views, see Pickstock, *After Writing.*

But this sounds rather abstract. Who really constrains the theologian and to what degree? The bishop? The congregation? And how is one to understand the workings of ecclesiastical hierarchy today in the realm of knowledge, given the great approval that the Church appears to extend to democracy in the secular sphere?

IV

To try to answer these questions, it is helpful to go back to Nicholas de Cusa's early work, *De Concordantia Catholica*.[27] While this was a conciliarist treatise, Cusanus' later papalist position did not abandon its essential conclusions. This is interesting, because it almost uniquely preserves at a late date a much earlier perspective on the mediating role of sacramental signs, between historical and ecclesial bodies. At the same time, it also shows traces of more modern elements that are perhaps inescapable today: a new stress on mass assembled participation in the present, and on historical variation due to the cultural variety of human imagining. In addition, following Augustine, Cusanus and other patristic sources anticipate an apocalyptic time when the Church is in terminal decline, which may be the situation today. Perhaps, Cusanus provides some keys not merely to recovering the lost pre-1300 world, but also to going forward to the future one might always have had, yet never had.

Cusanus claims that the eucharist generates the Church. What stands uppermost in the Church hierarchy is not a *de jure* legal power, but rather sacramental signs. In this way, in the Dionysian tradition, the ecclesial and the experiential are still fused through liturgical mysteries. For Cusanus, the sacramental signs correspond at a lower level of the cosmic hierarchy with the Triune God at the top of the hierarchy. God is said to know fully the members of the Church in love, and they are orientated to the Trinity through a desire that exceeds their intellection — a very "Eastern" element here. The next rank within the heavenly *ecclesia*, eternal Jerusalem (wherein God "is" through all perpetuity, as in later Russian sophiology), below God, is the angelic. The angels, in a rather Arabic fashion, see into all human intellects, and human thought puts one in contact with the separate intelligences. Within the ecclesial hierarchy the priesthood is linked to the angelic in terms

27. Nicholas of Cusa, *The Catholic Concordance*, trans. Paul E. Sigmund (Cambridge: Cambridge University Press, 1995), especially Book I, § 1-68.

of its teaching function, and its occupancy of *cathedrae,* since the *Apocalypse* says that angels are guardians of ecclesial places. In the third rank comes the blessed in heaven, who link to humanity on earth through the body, and who correspond to the body of the faithful within the Church Militant here below.

There are certain complications within this scheme in relation. To bridge their orders the clergy correspond to the first sacramental rank, but this seals the priority of their sacramental, transmissive function over their authoritative, teaching one. In fact, the clergy span all three degrees, because, in terms of their participation with the laity in intercessory offices, they belong to the lowest level, which simply praises and does not mediate. In addition, there seems to be a certain lack of consistency: the laity are the most bodily, and yet their function of praise is also a spiritual synthesis of sacramental sign and physically situated *cathedra.* The same lack of clarity pertains in the heavenly Church: the resurrected faithful are the most corporeal, and yet their third psychic position (in keeping with the Neoplatonic hierarchy of the One, *nous,* and *psyche*) also synthetizes through desire the origin that is God and the intellection that belongs to the angels. Perhaps, the confusion has its source in the blending of Proclus with Trinitarian theology, since for Cusanus all these degrees also correspond to the respective persons of the Trinity, and though the Son as *logos* is intellectual, as *imago* he is also somewhat "corporeal," compared with the unity in desire shown by the Spirit.

The presence of the Trinity at the top of the hierarchy has a deconstructive effect at every level, although Cusanus also inherits the deconstructions inherent in Proclean Neoplatonism. Yet, here he offers the fullest exhibition ever of the multiple paradoxes of hierarchy. Out of them he generates an early democratic theory. The idea that he simply "mixes" mediaeval hierarchy with proto-modern democracy, as Paul Sigmund says, is simply not the case; instead, he returns to earlier high mediaeval mystical and educative notions of hierarchy, and out of these notions generates new democratic theses.[28] This gives a basis for conciliarism and consensus other than William of Ockham's constructualism, which blasphemously reduces Church government to a balance of power between formally considered individual forces.

The place to begin is with the paradoxes already glimpsed by Neoplatonism. Paradox one: for a hierarchy to be a hierarchy, it requires stages, or else it would be a flux without quality. But then, a stage can be distinguished

28. Paul E. Sigmund, "Introduction" to Cusa, *The Catholic Concordance,* pp. xxxvii-ix.

within a flux only if it marks out a level, which will be a field of equality. To sustain the ontological primacy of hierarchy — every emanation from on high is continuously diminishing — the level must be broken up as a hierarchy within a hierarchy. This, of course, threatens a *mise en abyme,* indicated in Cusanus' text by a slightly insane process of triadic sub-dividing by an author who knew that finitude was subject to infinite division. A consequence of this logic of levels is that the subordinate within a certain stage is nonetheless equal — with its subordinateness entirely cancelled — to all members of that stage, if one rises to a more fundamental hierarchical viewpoint.

This is what provides Cusanus with his fundamental conciliarist principle. From the *highest* perspective, all that is created is on a level; within the Church Militant, all its members are on a level, just as the sacramental and ecclesial bodies are on a level. Since the true ontological character of the Church, following Augustine, is peace and harmony, which for Cusanus is extended into *discors concordia,* the first ruling principle within the Church is consensus. Not, of course, majority rule, but absolute consensus, since the Church is not a vehicle of correct teaching, but the *event* of *concordantia.* Doctrine is about nothing but the giving of divine *concordantia* in the Creation, and its restoration through the Incarnation and the Church. Thus, there cannot be true teaching without consensus — even if this consensus and the key to harmony can dwindle to being present only in a few. Augustine anticipates that this will eventually happen only when the "last of the last" will remain.[29] This is why teaching is inseparable from the guarantee of the Holy Spirit's presence in the Church. In the long run and for the most part, the members of the Church will be reliable, because otherwise there could be no true doctrine. In fact, doctrine is first of all a body and not simply words; Christ was the supreme teacher as the event of the return of *concordantia* to the world. For truth, there must be democratic consent, although this must also be a uniting in "the right way," according to the true measure of harmony. If "democracy" failed, the Church would cease to be; however, much of the time the keys to democratic consensus must be safeguarded by an ecclesiastical elite, gathered round the bishops.

At this point, the significance of the nested hierarchy within each level comes to the fore. It is not really a principle in opposition to "democracy." That is only the case where, within a closed immanent circle based on a balance of interests between forces, a sovereign center is granted *de facto* power.

---

29. Augustine, *Ad Hesychium* (PL 33, p. 913), cited by Cusanus, *The Catholic Concordance,* Book I, §14.

This is why liberalism always generates terrifying hierarchies not linked to the transmission of values: hierarchies of money, bureaucratic organization, and policing. Here, one has the necessary authoritarian counterpart to the mitigated anarchy of market society. By contrast, the power Cusanus invests in the *cathedra* is a salve against the closure that the emerging sovereign state and later liberal democracy would soon place around a specific, often "national" community. In fact, even a global community is closed against a wider democracy, if it is only "in the present." This is the point of Edmund Burke's appeal to the votes of all the ages: the bishop and those gathered round him must sustain the *concordantia* with the past, and preserve its resources for the future against the likely ravages of the present. Thus, the bishop is poised between the always arriving order of signs and the people's consensus, which alone can fulfill that order. His authority derives from both. Ultimately, of course, he must appeal to the widest democracy of all, i.e., the original *concordantia* of the whole cosmos, grounded in the consensus of the Trinity, which Cusanus already presents as the coincidence of the opposites of the one and the many.

Cusanus' ecclesiology results constitute the interplay between democratic and aristocratic principles, combined with a monarchial principle in terms of the papacy. But even in the latter case, the stress is on *cathedra*: the pope's authority is that of an ancestral place,[30] which has been the focal intersection of so much for so long, evil as well as good, and is likely to have priority in terms of the persistence of the rhythms of truth. This is how Cusanus sees it. To a lesser degree, the same applies to every episcopal seat. Thus, a single principle legitimates both the democratic and the aristocratic aspects. This principle is "for the most part." Applied synchronically, one gets democracy; the consensus of the entire laity and clergy is the most reliable guide — a Newman-like principle. Applied diachronically, one gets aristocracy: the longest persisting locations and their representatives will be the least likely to err. Yet, the entire diachrony merges with an eternal synchrony: the voices of all times and places are the final court of appeal, insofar as they sing with one true voice of praise.

Thus, for Cusanus, speaking *ex cathedra*, true infallibility resides in the whole Church because of the hypostatic presence of the Holy Spirit, without which human salvation would be null and void. It resides in the conciliar assembly of the bishops and, finally, in the supreme *cathedra* of Rome — the longest abiding seat of sacred legitimacy. The pope is the supreme guardian:

---

30. Cusa, *The Catholic Concordance*, Book I, § 56-59.

he has the right to summon a general council. But the consensus of the council is a more reliable locus of infallibility than the pope, since it is weaker than the entire ecclesia. A council has the right to depose a false pope. Cusanus holds this view even in his later papalist phase.[31]

Throughout these considerations, which owed much to Cyprian as well as to Augustine, Cusanus never lost sight of his sense of the primacy of the sacramental. This primacy, as Augustine saw against the Donatists, ensures that even erring clergy can be true ministers, since belief in the infallibility of the Church is not a peculiar superstition, but resides ultimately in one's trust in certain signs. Since one cannot command the meaning of any sign, true signs will always outwit one's worst intentions, and will inhabit one promisingly, despite oneself. This is how the Holy Spirit is hypostatically present in the Church.

A second paradox of hierarchy is that the higher element within a lower stage must always be more akin to the lower than to the higher stages. This is aporetic, because stages involve not just a smooth descent, but a regular folding back of the whole process upon itself to produce the instance of stages. Thus, the high element within each stage re-invokes the summit *out of series;* while the lower one anticipates the nethermost base, also out of series. Thus, e.g., if the hierarchy runs throughout from spirit to body, the higher elements in lower stages will be more spiritual than the lower elements within that stage, but more bodily than everything higher up, so that these elements shift undecidably between "more spirit" and "more body." There will also be an increasing tendency as one descends the hierarchy to perceive even the uppermost stages as "more bodily," and thus an asymptotic tendency *to reverse* the hierarchy in the lower stages altogether. Ethnographers have discovered that many local tribes with symbolic hierarchies actually carry this through this reversal, so that, e.g., "male" will be on top in the higher realm, but "female" in the lower.

This second paradox can combine with a third to produce an interesting effect. The third paradox, of which Neoplatonism was fully aware, is to produce a distinct new level that must "hold back" the free fall of emanation: a new charge from the original source must somehow flow down the chain and to a degree interrupt the process of diminution. Or, to put this the other way around, a distinct new phase must somehow override the immediately higher intermediaries and re-invoke the origin directly.

When combined, these two paradoxes tend to produce explicit reversal

31. Sigmund, "Introduction," p. xxxiii.

in the lower realm, and parallel orders of hierarchy, albeit hierarchically arranged. In the case of Cusanus, this happens with the body of the faithful. Insofar as concerns are more fleshly, they assume priority. The laity of the Church are governed by the Emperor within a separate hierarchy that owes direct responsibility to the Trinity.[32] Cusanus denies the authenticity of the donation of Constantine, and the crowning of the emperor is seen as confirmation of an already proclaimed power, as applies also to the coronation of the pope. Yet, the realm of the emperor still belongs to *ecclesia*. Unlike his contemporaries, Cusanus does not speak of "the state." Ultimately, concerns of the flesh remain subordinate to those of the spirit, and the emperor, like the pope, is still answerable to the infallibility of the entire body of the Church. Insofar as this is concentrated and focused in the pope, in some sense he remains answerable to Rome. Indeed, he is the Holy Roman Emperor. (Cusanus' perspective is naturally Germanic.)

A fourth paradox of hierarchy is much accentuated by Trinitarian theology. The origin of a hierarchy cannot merely be the highest rung: as the source of every stage, it must transcend hierarchy and even equalize within itself all stages of the hierarchy, negating their differentiation. This is the Neoplatonic doctrine of the mystical One. However, the Trinity tends to turn this non-differentiation into the preservation as much as obliteration of the many, as Cusanus stresses. But this increases the sense that, at the top, there are no longer any degrees. Furthermore, hierarchy requires distinguished stages, and in fact a minimum of three stages, since if there were only two there would not be mediation and interval and thus no stages at all. So Cusanus, like Neoplatonism in general, posits three main stages, and also subdivides his stages into three. But the Trinity teaches that the One is also Three, and that it "complicates" what hierarchy "explicates," to use Cusanus' terminology. Within every stage, the totality of the stage ranks above the uppermost rank, so that the bishop is above the laity, but the whole Church is above the bishop. The invocation of the Trinity, however, makes this principle apply to the totality of everything that is created and not Creator. Because in God the second and the third stage are equal and co-original, this means that the totality of the cosmos really comes next after God, since at the summit of the created hierarchy all the lower degrees are fully equalized: body is restored to parity with spirit, as occurs in the resurrection of the dead.

The cosmos, however, is really the totality of the restored cosmos con-

---

32. Cusa, *The Catholic Concordance,* Book III, § 294-312.

centrated in the heavenly Jerusalem. In his glorious presence, this is God plus the angels, plus the resurrected faithful.[33] At this highest level, one can infer that the laity and the emperor are equalized with the bishop, while the latter's *cathedra* is equalized with sacramental signs now fully released. Indeed, via the resurrected body of the Lamb in the heart of the eternal city, the Bride Jerusalem is equalized with God and drawn through deification entirely into the life of the Trinity.

Thus, the principle of hierarchical ascension guards truth against democracy, but the more ascension is enacted, the more is democracy implemented in the truth. It is not that democracy is a compromise for the here and now: it can only arrive in the perfection of *concordantia* as deification. To eternalize democracy and to maintain its link with excellence, rather than with the mutual concessions of baseness, requires deification as the doctrine of the offer of equality with God.

Such divine democracy is approximated to here below in the processes of historical *traditio*. For Cusanus, as a "Renaissance" thinker, these now include a passage through the cultural relativity of different human fictions: different sacraments and sacrifices in all human cultures, which all really indicate the one sign of Christ and his sacrifice.[34] It is here that a "modern" factor enters the picture: a new sense that institutions really do spring from collective "makings." This sense is also what pushes Cusanus toward revealing the latent democratic implications of an inherited and highly traditional — in his day, totally out of date — Trinitarian and liturgical hierarchical vision. Even hierarchical structures are erected by fashioned consensus, beginning with God himself. Cusanus was truly "radically orthodox."

For Cusanus, as for Augustine, the ontological diminution through emanation worked also downwards through time. For Augustine, the sixth age of the world inaugurated by Christ is human old age, marked by decline and a worsening of the effects of the Fall. Yet, here also, the paradoxes kick in, reinforced by Trinitarian theology: direct contact with the Origin can be established even in senescence. Almost at the end, there is absolute rejuvenation. Thus, for Augustine, "progress" becomes possible for the first time in the era of ultimate degeneration. Here is an absolute duality: as W. H. Auden understood in his libretto for the Christmas Oratorio, "For the Time Being,"

---

33. This is the Sophia that is also the ground of the procession of the Son and the Spirit in the Trinity for the Russians, or the primal "outgoing" that Gregory of Nyssa named *dynamis*, and Dionysius *dynameis*.

34. Cusa, *The Catholic Concordance*, Book I, § 4.

the Incarnation institutes a time of dread when one must live in the partial meaninglessness of an aftermath to the appearance of the ultimate — live in absolute waiting for the consummation of what was begun and yet is, "for the time being," suspended.[35] It is also the time of terrible demand for bodily perfection and, therefore, the time when this absolute demand for goodness will be rejected. In Augustinian terms, evil will appear in its nakedness as the Antichrist. Confronted with this terror, the faithful are likely to be fewer and fewer, until the "last of the last." Cusanus agreed and thought he had reached that point. Writing in the *De Concordantia* in 1433, he gave the world 600 more years, until Europe had been destroyed, although Christ would be preached throughout the world. Therefore, he anticipated both globalization and the end of Christendom. Yet, this disastrous era is also the time in which at last a conciliar and democratic ideal that will truly reflect the Trinity can be achieved on earth.

In a sense, it is comforting to realize that mankind's predicament was foreseen from the outset — Augustine and Cusanus only build on Christ's warnings and promises in the gospels. This is neither triumphalism nor celebration of secular autonomy, but a catastrophic refusal of charity. However, the hypostatic presence of the Holy Spirit on earth will not fail, and thus the "time being" will still prove to be a time of meaningful realization of deified democracy: especially in the darkening period toward the end. There will be decline, and yet there will be progress.

V

Therefore, theology is answerable to reason precisely insofar as it is answerable to the Church. In the latter domain, it is first of all answerable to the Triune God, since theology is participation in the mind of God before it is obedience to any authority, whether scriptural or hierarchical. As such, it is equally a participation in the whole deified Church as in the heavenly Jerusalem. The latter is only encountered through earthly mediation, and here theology is first answerable to the whole Church Militant. This involves a certain answerability to the bishop. But in what way is theology also answerable to scripture? Here, once again, clarity is possible only if one rejects post-1300 dualities.

---

35. W. H. Auden, "For the Time Being: A Christmas Oratorio," in *Collected Longer Poems* (London: Faber and Faber, 1968).

Protestantism privileged the historical body of Christ; Trent, the sacramental body. This meant a preference either for scripture or tradition, respectively. Before Henry of Ghent, there had been no such juxtaposition. For the first time, he asked which had priority, thereby revealing that something had already changed. Now, scripture appeared as a closed book in the past that needed supplementing by a separate oral command. Basil had spoken of written and unwritten traditions, but the latter were seen by him and by later theologians as consisting in the "performance" of the text. Tradition was the handing over of the text into practice. Thus, Aquinas speaks of *sacra scriptura* as the sole authority for *sacra doctrina,* in a way that sounds "Protestant" by later Tridentine standards. But he is not speaking of the Protestant Bible. There was, as yet, no single printed book, but many manuscripts of different books of the Bible — usually surrounded by patristic commentary. Gregory the Great claimed that when he read and commented on the Bible, the text expanded.[36] It was up to the commentator to go on trying to achieve the Bible as the infinite "Borgesian" library spoken of at the end of St. John's Gospel, as it was equally up to the painter and producer of miracle plays. Such a Novalis-like or "Mallarmean" perspective was also presupposed by the entire practice of allegorical exegesis.

This rendered theology possible by showing how Christological and ecclesial restoration of the world depended on the assumption of a divine "rhetoric of things." Things referred to in the Old Testament were already redeemed, since they pointed forward allegorically to Christ: in the "time being" after Christ, one could be redeemed because one's deeds indicated and made possible one's anagogical performances. As Certeau put it, all this depended on a sense that there were "essential" shared universal meanings between things; consequently, nominalism ensured the collapse of allegory as the real divine rhetoric and thus of the true inner basis of Christian theology. Without real intrinsic aesthetic connections, the ways of God in history became indecipherable, and one was left with a series of positive institutions, only linked as logically possible manifestations of the divine absolute power. Logical reflection on this situation was now divorced from ontology, and the rhetorical dimension of scripture and preaching was thereafter somewhat confined to mere words. The "treatise on sacred rhetoric" emerged within both a Reformation and a Counter Reformation ambience.

Certeau, however, exaggerates. His own theology seems to require the

---

36. See Certeau, *The Mystic Fable,* p. 222, citing the work of Pier Cesari Bori on Gregory the Great's reading of Ezekiel's vision.

later decadent situation of bodily absence to be normative. He exaggerates the negativity of the "time being." The Church is not, as he claims, just a mystical substitute for the lost real Israel and living body of Christ. In all its physicality and placement in *cathedrae,* it is also exactly both. It only lost this positivity through the processes traced by Lubac and Certeau. Moreover, is the work of the univocalist/nominalist Antichrist within the Church to be perceived only negatively? Without lapsing into Hegelian dialectic, it can be acknowledged that catastrophe may help to see more clearly, and that the nominalist critique exposes certain faults. In the face of nominalism and univocity, Cusanus argued that both realism about universals and analogical participation require one to see the limited scope of the law of identity. For Ockham, a common essence would be in the same respect both particular and universal and an analogous *esse* in the same respect both shared and proper.[37] Cusanus also claimed that universals are constructed through language, but that "fictionalized" universals may still exhibit something that holds in reality, albeit in a more "conjectural" fashion than hitherto acknowledged.[38] In this way, Cusanus opened new spaces for rhetoric, poetics, and the construction of history. If Boulnois is right that the Thomist paradox of the supernatural is partly inspired by the Aristotelian maxim "art imitates nature" (which is also paradoxical, because here an observation of nature also exceeds and completes it), then Cusanus' new space suggests a more explicit coincidence of grace with the art that is intellect.

Despite Certeau, such a coincidence is also found in certain exponents of sacred rhetoric. Thus, in the work of the Lutheran Mathias Flaccius Illyricus rhetoric is not reduced to ornament and propagandistic manipulation, and traditional fourfold exegesis is not totally abandoned. Instead, here one finds a fusion of a rhetoric that sustains a Longinian interest in the ways words can both reveal and enact the real through performance (Longinus

---

37. William of Ockham, *Quodlibetal Questions* 5.12 and 14. Nicholas de Cusa's interest in human participation in divine creative power can also be related to Scotus and Ockham. Given univocity, unlike Aquinas, they tend to say that creatures can fully bring about being. Thus, Ockham says that, in a sense, human beings create (QQ 2.9). Cusanus says this too, but he restores the bringing about of being in a finite thing to the context of participation and mediation that still sees being as really the effect of God alone. However, he still talks explicitly of human creation in a way Aquinas and Bonaventure did not.

38. As Libera notes, Dietrich of Freibourg and Ulrich of Strasbourg sought to save the Dominican realist legacy instead by speaking of a purely internal mental construction of the universal, thus at once returning to Plotinus and anticipating idealism. See Libera, *Introduction à la Mystique Rhenane* (Paris: O.E.I.L., 1984).

may have been close to theurgic Neoplatonism), with a continued acknowledgement of the divine real rhetoric in allegory.[39] Here, the anagogic continues to "produce" the past in the older sense of "lead forth," but this production now also includes a moment of the creative "production" of truth in words. Through a blending of Longinus with Augustine's rhetorical writings often repeated by both Protestant and Catholic writers, the indwelling of the Spirit is re-thought in terms of a doctrine of poetic inspiration. Biblical writings are considered by Flaccius Illyricus in terms of a human rhetorical construction as well as a divine allegory of the real. This was possible in terms of a Longinian perspective that saw style with the most sublimely persuasive "coiled force" to be a "brief," albeit figurative one full of *res* and a minimum of *verba*. Such a fusion of human and divine rhetoric carries right through to the Anglicans John Dennis and Robert Lowth in the seventeenth and eighteenth centuries, and thus to Hamann, and to many in the nineteenth century, both Catholic and Protestant, influenced by him.[40]

All such people indicate how, in times of diminution, one's task is not only to recover the pre-1300 vision, but also to acknowledge human consensus, co-operation, and varied free poetic power in a way this vision did not fully envisage. Theologians, who may be the last of the last, still have a task before them.

39. See Debora Shuger, *Sacred Rhetoric: The Christian Grand Style in the English Renaissance* (Princeton: Princeton University Press, 1988), pp. 73-76ff.

40. See John Milbank, "Pleonasm, Speech and Writing," in John Milbank, *The Word Made Strange: Theology, Language, Culture* (Oxford Blackwell, 1997), pp. 55-84.

X. Christendom Reconsidered

Introduction

Graham Ward

Both of the essays that follow, the first by Oliver O'Donovan examining the relationship between the legislative process and the judiciary, and the second by Rowan Williams examining the relationship between the Christian and the secular city, articulate political theologies around the notion of "sovereignty" — the one who is to pass judgment. For both theology is inextricably political because the need to pass judgment is a divinely ordained matter, subject to the sovereignty of God and the reign of Christ. Each theologian, in propounding their arguments and employing their distinctive analyses, reminds the reader not only of a theological heritage with respect to reflections upon sovereignty, but also of the continuing relevance of such reflections with respect to the contemporary situation. If O'Donovan wishes to offer the present crisis of sovereignty (precipitated by early modern notions of popular sovereignty that led to a conflation in parliament between government and governed and the rise of "competing jurisdictions") a genealogy of its predicament, then Williams wishes to recover Augustine's theological engagement with *res publica* from apolitical readings such that the Christian ruler is presented with her or his "insoluble dilemma" and potential tragedy: between the integrity of the *civitas* in its maintenance of pastoral justice whose *telos* lies in the city of God and the security and longevity of the *civitas* against all its enemies. Both essays then seek to return to the reader what Williams describes as "the true *ordo* of sovereignty," though each sets about doing this in quite distinctive ways and with quite different results.

O'Donovan's essay is wide-ranging insofar as it attempts to sketch an epic landscape within which the present crisis sits. The essay opens with the current situation in all its contingent messiness: the problem of coherence between constitutional form, human rights, and law-making by courts that lack democratic accountability. As things stand there is an ambiguity between the legislative and the judicial arms of a government that is meant to judge. O'Donovan does not suggest a return to early modern political theory that distinguished among those who legislate, the people or their representatives for whom the legislation provides an overall framework for social organization, and the courts that implement the legislation; for there is no consensus on how these three branches of government related to one another. Rather, O'Donovan wishes to return us to the pre-modern Christian account, rooted in both the Hebrew Bible and the New Testament, in which the legislator has authority over the courts, and a primacy in just judgment. The law in accordance with which judgment was handed out was established by God as law-maker; hence human "rights" as established by human laws were considered doubtful additions. Furthermore, although O'Donovan does not make anything of this, human law-making or rights — as, for example, those created under Roman law — were based on the owning of property; it was private, not public law. Law-making was understood to be a divine activity and earthly government, even when an analogy was drawn between Christ as Logos and earthly rulers. Earthly rulers, too, were subject to the law. By the high Middle Ages this conception of law-making had changed, but subtly. Now the sovereign prince had the right to legislate, but his laws were still subject to, and had to be in accord with, natural or revealed law. With Marsiglio of Padua that, too, changed in favor of the people as legislator and legislation not as one of the things government does but as "the constitutive act that lies behind all government." If this governing was still subject to God's law in Marsiglio's time, this subjection was viewed as irrelevant from the seventeenth century on, and so legislature becomes a branch of government and the rule of law becomes the rule of the people. Each successive government is involved then in an endless process of lawmaking because such lawmaking is now viewed as the foundation for political viability and social rationality.

It is in this context that the current crisis of sovereignty arises: the tensions between the rejection of positive legislation in favor of human freedom and the advocacy of an anthropological, pre-political ground for law in natural rights that the courts struggle to clarify. But the crisis can be resolved to some extent by returning to the earlier Christian model of sovereignty in which the "defining role of secular government is to exercise judgment."

This judgment is exercised through the executive founding of a judiciary, a differentiation in roles between the head of a government responsible for policy making and the courts that treat particular cases. The trouble with the modern tradition is that it puts the legislature first, whereas in the Judeo-Christian tradition all human beings stand before a law that pre-exists them — and so the judiciary comes first. Furthermore, in order to legislate well there needs to be consultation, for the consequences are far-reaching when a law is made or changed. The consultation goes on in parliament, but parliament today is itself another branch of government, and so there have been an "implosion of government and parliament upon each other" and a mutual dependence that compromises the ability of the politicians to respond to the petitions of the people. In frustration at the deadlock in sovereignty, the courts themselves begin to review legislation; but in doing so they are no longer subject to external control. Hence it is that the separation of legislature from judiciary leads to competing jurisdictions, a situation that cannot resolve conflicts because there is a crisis of sovereignty, the source of governmental authority. Where the courts engage in a flurry of law-making with the collusion of politicians and a government that should be answerable for the consequences, then there is a cheapening of the law. The genealogy O'Donovan provides offers a Judeo-Christian reminder of how the legislature and the judiciary need to respect each other's jurisdictions and exercise self-discipline both in law-making and in its subsequent interpretation in the courts.

The essay requires a detailed exposition of its argument not only because that argument is nuanced and covers a number of issues — positive law, natural law, human rights — and the historical changes marking any institution, but also because only a detailed exposition allows us to appreciate the role Christian theology is playing here. At stake is the question of what kind of political theology, if any, is being articulated through this historical method. The theological is not normative; rather, it exemplifies the best practice in the past for the exercise of earthly sovereignty in passing judgment. The passing of judgment is a God-given task, viewed from a Judeo-Christian perspective, although God now is an optional part of the picture and no longer the basis for the practice. The political as it presents itself today is viewed, by O'Donovan, in terms of the autonomous realm it has become; theology provides a model for secular sovereignty to emulate so that the effects of its own crisis might be somewhat mitigated and better government might ensue. As a mode of doing political theology, both disciplines maintain their separate jurisdictions, but because they share a common history the former can be reminded of lessons learned by the latter — and in this limited way they can remain in critical dialogue.

This approach to the relationship between religion and politics is quite different from that in Rowan Williams's essay. Williams's focus is more specific: an interpretation and defense of Augustine's theology and its political implications. But while the analysis is limited mainly to *De Civitate Dei*, Williams evidently has his eye on the contemporary situation; for while his argument will be a refutation of Hannah Arendt's critique of Augustine's conception of the city of God as non-worldly society, he wishes to endorse Arendt's attention to the need for some form of participation in the public world. If such participation is necessary for the disruption of mindless and idolatrous "mass society," then the question behind the analysis of Augustine's work concerns the extent to which his political theology can indeed help "the subversion of the public" and fashion a new form of citizenship.

Williams argues that Augustine's theology totally disrupts the orders and priorities of the social realm, not by offering an alternative politics as such, but by returning human beings to the goal of their existence — the enjoyment of God — and the virtuous behavior practiced in public by those oriented toward such a goal. Any public realm that forgets this human telos fails to be truly human and therefore fails to be "truly public, authentically political." It is not simply a matter of forgetting; for the desire for the infinite remains a human characteristic, though in the *civitas terrena* this desire is now directed toward finite goods and finite satisfactions. The justice wielded in such a public domain cannot be just, because if God the creator of the world cannot be given his due, then neither can the citizens who comprise the *res publica*. Without the grounding of a state's common goals and values in the *lex aeterna* of this theological anthropology, then any stability it might attain is transitory and fragile; such states cannot become genuine commonwealths, for their sovereignty is not based upon true order. The classical republic is founded upon a *libido dominandi*, a lust for glory and a preoccupation with achievement, each of which is ultimately an exhortation to the sin of pride. Any unity such a state might have has to be imposed externally. For Augustine, sovereignty has to begin with the prioritizing of the spiritual over the material, the submission of all desire to God's desire for us, and the bonds of love that share the common good. This prioritizing implies hierarchy and so cuts across modern notions of the liberal state — although before God there is some measure of equality among all human beings. Hierarchy requires the exercise of power, the imposition of law, and the possible use of coercion, even by those in the *civitas Dei* such as a Christian emperor. But the exercise of power has to be in accord with the end for which human beings were created: the peace in the human soul that is concordant with the peace of God. Beginning with headship in the family, this *civitas* is then a pastoral community with a care for the soul.

It is at this point in his essay that Williams emphasizes the dilemmas that must surface for a Christian prince when God's *ordo* cannot be strictly identified with the rule of any state. Put pithily: "*good* government" may not "necessarily [be] *successful* government in the world's sense." As a pastor of souls, the goal of the Christian prince cannot be worldly triumph and the extension of national power. (A pertinent reminder at a time when there is a British investigation into why we declared war on Iraq — and as with O'Donovan, Williams is keen to make such pertinent reminders!) Only God can defend or extend the City of God. But this principle is not an axiom for withdrawal from the social and political, for the Christian ruler knows the right ordering of God's sovereignty. The exercise of official power must be maintained by such a ruler, even where a certain indifference to the future of the state is necessary. Augustine is not then sympathetic to the kind of involvement in the public realm that Arendt advocates, but then the involvement Arendt seeks is wedded to gaining a secular reputation that stands above the restlessness "*constitutive* of our human creaturehood" and the vulnerability that comes with accepting the vicissitudes of time. For Augustine the future is not nearly as guaranteeable as it is for Arendt; he can then provide no final form for our political life.

Distinct from O'Donovan's approach (at least in this essay), which views the early Judeo-Christian tradition as a past that might still serve as a lesson for today, Williams's approach is far more theological — that is, returning us to the sovereignty of God and his eternal *ordo* irrespective of where we are in history. Hence Williams can employ Augustine's theological anthropology to point up the perennial consequences of human fallenness as they manifest themselves in the public domain of late Antiquity, Arendt's "public realm," and liberal governments more generally. If O'Donovan is acting as a good Christian citizen of a liberal democracy, reminding the state of the forgotten sovereignty of God, then Williams (on the basis of Augustine's theology) is being far more evangelical, and disruptive, in calling for nothing less than a change of heart and a reorientation of a very human desire for God's sovereignty. For both, the pursuit of human rights in and for themselves, which are either pre-political (O'Donovan) or not authentically political (Williams), will not assuage the crisis of sovereignty, only exacerbate it.

45 Government as Judgment

Oliver O'Donovan

The democracies that emerged victorious from the Second World War, in undertaking to entrench human rights against the cruel politics of power, left themselves with a major problem of self-understanding, a cleft running deep through the heart of democratic theory. The terms "democracy" and "human rights" do not mean the same thing, and they do not refer to the same thing. Whether democracy is compatible with human rights depends on two contingent factors: how the democratic societies conduct themselves, and what rights human beings assert. One cannot champion "democracy and human rights" without quite quickly having to decide which takes precedence between them, a question to which there is no formally and universally correct answer; since either of those terms, and not just one of them, may from time to time be used as a cloak for self-interest and tyranny, there is no universally correct answer. That is the underlying problem of coherence in contemporary Western ideology.

My interest here, however, lies not with that problem, but with one deriving from it, a constitutional problem about the judicial review of legislation: "legislation by courts" as it is often alleged to be, which in the service of human or civil rights deprives lawmaking of democratic accountability. This problem has often been addressed as a question for U.S. constitutional theory, in terms of a shift in the traditional relation between the legislative and judicial branches of government. But this is not the only possible constitutional form that the problem may take. Similar difficulties confront European societies with other constitutional traditions. The constitution of the Republic of Ireland, for example, has acquired the shape of a baggy Aran sweater, full of detailed amendments that would never belong in such a document had not the Supreme Court at some point in time maintained the opposite. Even the constitution of the United Kingdom, boasting a radical centralization of authority in parliament, meets the same problem through its adherence to the European Convention of Human Rights, with its attendant Commission and Court.[1]

It is natural to suppose that the solution lies in recovering early-modern doctrines about the separation of three powers of government. These doctrines derive originally from the fourteenth-century Italian thinker, Marsiglio of Padua, who distinguished the "legislator," the people itself or its representatives, from those who implemented the laws, in domestic adjudication on the one hand and against external threats on the other. Yet there is a difficulty with this approach: on the all-important question early-modern thinkers achieved no stable consensus to which we may appeal. We may compare two forms in which the separation of powers was argued, with contradictory emphases, within a fifty-year period at the turn of the eighteenth century. Locke and Montesquieu both claimed to base their observations on the best English practice; both affirmed three distinct powers of government (though only Montesquieu used their modern names, and only Locke used the word "separate"); and yet they are very different. In Locke's theory the greatest point of "separation" is still between the originating legislature and the two consequential branches of government. The consequential branches are not so distinct from one another, since they must, Locke thought, rest in the same hands — so saving the face of the British monarchy.[2] But Montesquieu articulated something resembling the familiar three-leaved shamrock pattern, an equal distance separating each of the branches. He required also that the separation be concrete, with the different branches of government in the hands of different people. From these two perspectives, which provided matrices for later British and U.S. constitutional practice respectively, the causes of our current problem and its likely solution appear quite different.

Moreover, Christian thinkers have their own reasons for not being content with a return to early-modern sources, for they have a long theological tradition in which judicial and legislative activities are related quite differently. This should raise the question, at least, whether the root of the prob-

1. The European Convention on Human Rights and Its Five Protocols, in I. Brownlie, ed., *Basic Documents on Human Rights,* 2nd ed. (Oxford: Oxford University Press, 1981), pp. 242-65.

2. *Two Treatises* 2.13.151. Having "a share in the legislative," the executive was "in a very tolerable sense . . . supreme."

lem lies not in recent neglect of early-modern theory, but in early-modern neglect of the yet earlier Christian understanding. What the Christian tradition maintained, and the early-modern thinkers denied, was *the primacy of the act of judgment.* And this primacy entailed a distinctive understanding of the task of legislation, which explains more satisfactorily the nature and scope of the legislator's authority over courts. In what follows, I shall first sketch the history of pre-modern Christian thought on the subject; second, suggest how it supports a superior account of the branches of government; and finally, return briefly to our problem, the right and limits of judicial review of legislation.

I

Jesus has ascended in triumph to God's right hand; yet the subdued "authorities" of this age, St. Paul maintained, "persist."[3] This, he said, was to approve good conduct and "to execute God's wrath on the wrongdoer." The reign of Christ in heaven has left *judgment* as the single remaining political need. We should remark that this was an unprecedentedly lean doctrine of civil government. Judgment alone never comprised the whole of what ancient peoples, least of all the Jews, thought government was about. Paul's conception stripped government of its representative, identity-conferring functions, and said nothing about law. He conceded, as it were, the least possible function that would account for its place within God's plan. The secular princes of this earth, shorn of pretensions to our loyalty and worship, are left with the sole function of judging between innocent and guilty.

1. In later centuries it was Latin-speaking Western Christendom that adhered most fully to Paul's conception. "Jurisdiction" was the term that came to define that ever-fascinating and difficult relation between church and state. Courts were the central locus of government, for church as for kingdom. Human government was understood to differ from that of God, notably (for our purposes) in that God is a legislator as well as judge. His law provides human judges with a sufficient basis for their judgments; and the Latin Church Fathers were frankly suspicious of human attempts to add to it. "The term 'rights,'" says Augustine, "cannot be applied to the inequitable

---

3. Rom. 13:6: εἰς αὐτὸ τοῦτο προσκαρτεροῦντες, "persisting for this very purpose," or perhaps, "to this very day," not, as contemporary translators prefer, "attending to this very thing" (RSV).

constitutions of men."[4] What rulers do when they act obediently to their vocation is to apply divine law to the infinite possibilities of human wrongdoing. Still in the later Middle Ages, an Augustinian idealist, John Wyclif, harked back to this suspicion, representing the ideal judge in his court with "no law but natural law. . . . It would be the best form of government for a people to be ruled solely through the law of God by judges."[5]

In Eastern Christendom a difference of emphasis is noticeable. Here the way was beaten for the church by the greatest Jewish thinker of the classical world, Philo of Alexandria (ca. 20 B.C.–A.D. 50). Philo conceived Jewish social existence partly in contrast with, partly in correspondence to, the political experience of a Greek city-state, constituted by the work of a "legislator" *(nomothetēs)*. Lawgiving in the Hellenistic world was thought of as *foundation*, the creation of a polis by the creation of a distinctive corpus of law. As Lycurgus was to Sparta and Solon to Athens, so, according to Philo, was Moses to the Jewish *politeia*, though he was unique in that he was directly inspired by the Logos or Reason of God. Also taken over from a Hellenistic commonplace about government was the conception that Moses was *empsychos nomos*, a "living law."[6] The Christian Clement, a fellow-citizen of Alexandria, followed Philo's lead gladly. Now the lawgiver was Christ, the Logos himself, whom Moses had uniquely anticipated and represented.[7]

Yet this did not really lead Greek-speaking Christians in a different direction from the Latin-speaking West. The tendency of Hellenistic Christendom to allow a direct analogy between Christ the Logos and earthly rulers is notorious. But even when that analogy was most developed, as in Eusebius's panegyric on Constantine, there was no hint that Christ's role as lawgiver could be transferred to the earthly ruler. Law was a feature of all earthly government, but law-keeping rather than lawmaking was its characteristic activity; there was simply "*lawful* government."[8] In the East, too, the subject of *human* lawmaking is still passed over in silence. The term *nomothetēs* and its cognates is hardly ever applied to the emperor by theologians, though in secular writing it was common. And in 530 when Justinian acceded to the impe-

---

4. *City of God* 19.21. Cf. also Ambrose's words to the Emperor Valentinian: "The law of God has taught us what to follow; human laws cannot teach us this" (*Ep.* 75.10).

5. *Civil Dominion* 1.27 (62d).

6. *Life of Moses* 2.1.3f.

7. *Stromateis* 1.24-7. Oliver O'Donovan and Joan Lockwood O'Donovan, eds., *From Irenaeus to Grotius: A Sourcebook in Christian Political Thought* (Grand Rapids: Eerdmans, 1999), pp. 30-38 (hereafter *IG*).

8. *Speech on the Anniversary of Constantine's Accession* 4. *IG*, pp. 56-65.

rial throne in Byzantium, a work of exhortation addressed to him by a theologian insisted, among other things, on his being subject to law, but contained virtually no acknowledgment that the task of this most famous imperial jurist would include *making* law.[9]

2. That this is not at all the situation among the thinkers of the high Middle Ages is due to two influences, of whom Justinian himself, at a remove, was one. Through the growth of Western jurisprudence out of the legacy of his *Corpus of Civil Law,* Justinian came to be regarded as a model for the Christian lawmaker, and the description of human government came to include lawmaking as a dimension. But lawmaking was not understood simply as legal innovation. Justinian's influence served to dignify, above all, the task of codification; and the term *legis lator,* when it appears in the twelfth century, refers primarily to the early jurists who ordered and systematized the Roman law. The other influence was that of Aristotle, with whom the classical conception of legal foundation reenters the stream of Western thought. In the *Politics* and *Ethics* the term *nomothetēs* is applied not only to the legal founders of city-states, Lycurgus and Solon, but also to political theorists who advanced overarching proposals for social organization. Plato is one of Aristotle's *nomothetai,* and democracy and oligarchy are among his instances of *nomothesia.*

The Justinianic conception can be seen at its most persuasive in St. Thomas's great treatise on law in the *Summa Theologiae.*[10] The structuring of a social order requires, Thomas thinks, not merely the *application* of divine law, natural or revealed, but a *lex humana,* a "positive law" which is to *determine* matters otherwise left unresolved. The *ius ponendi leges,* the "right of making law," was the mark of a sovereign prince. Still, the authority of human lawmakers reposes on divine law, to which human law may never stand in contradiction. So the positive aspect of human lawmaking is safeguarded by a negative proposition: that a law defying natural or revealed law has no standing at all.[11] The influence of Aristotle, however, is particularly strong in another work attributed to Thomas (falsely, I am inclined to think), the variously named *On Kingship, to the King of Cyprus* or *On Princely Rule.* "We must first and principally expound the king's duty," the author tells us, "from the institution of the state or kingdom. . . . The name of Romulus

---

9. Agapetos, *Heads of Advice. IG,* pp. 180-88.

10. *ST* 1a2ae. 90-108. For what follows cf. especially questions 95-96. *IG,* pp. 342-54.

11. This proposition has been vigorously reasserted by Pope John Paul II, *Evangelium Vitae,* pp. 68-74.

would be unknown today, had he not founded Rome."[12] Those words, startling to ears attuned to early medieval political reflections, announce the reappearance of legislation as foundation, the concept which the early church had in effect neutralized by confining legislation to Moses and Christ. They attest a situation in which there is interest in how new political communities may be brought into being. At this point, the line between the Aristotelian revival and the early Renaissance seems very thin.

This is the context in which the modern theory of popular sovereignty first saw the light of day. The role of Marsiglio of Padua's *Defensor pacis* (1325) in articulating the new departure is commonly acknowledged, as is the fact that he drew both on Aristotle and on Roman law in articulating it. Less commented on is Marsiglio's startling use of the *term* "legislator," applying it to the whole in the sense of "founding lawgiver." As originating legislator the populace is the primary authorization for any subsequent form or act of government. Legislation is not one of the things that government does; it is the constitutive act that lies behind all government. Even so conceived, however, legislation is ventured only *under God*, who is the author and vindicator of all law. The tradition of "constitutionalism" which arose from Marsiglio's new departure understood the founding legislative act as a response to a divinely given law of nature defining the possibilities of political society. It can arise only as it is authorized by what Wyclif called the *primum ius*, the First Right, i.e., God's. So what now comes to be said about legislation as constitutional foundation is formally parallel to what is said about judgment: as we may judge subject to God's judgment, so we may found lawful societies under God's law.

3. A decisive shift of perspective occurred in the seventeenth century. This was not the result of atheism, for atheism, by and large, came later. But its effect was to make divine law irrelevant to the foundations of political order. The nature and causes of this shift can be described in many ways. It is enough for our purposes to say that the *primum ius* vanished from consideration, so that the act of human foundation ceased to depend on divine foundation, and began to look like a repetition of it. The sovereign arbitrariness of God's creative decree was taken into the human act of founding a society, so that it appeared rather like a creation *ex nihilo*, presupposing no prior law, no pre-existing social rationality, a new beginning not merely relatively and politically but absolutely and metaphysically. Legislation thereby became the *foundation of a social reality*.

12. *De regno* 2.1 (alternatively, 2.5). *IG*, pp. 330-41.

In setting out to radicalize the act of human foundation, this change actually destroyed it. The contractarians attempted to answer, without invoking God, the constitutionalists' question about how a civil society could begin. But they could not for long conceal a guilty secret: in reproducing the divine legislative act they had abolished the moment of beginning altogether. Since it seemed *possible* for human society to replicate the original *fiat lux* of God in constituting itself as a sphere of order, it was *necessary* for it to do so; and if it was necessary once, it was necessary again and again. The "beginning" was constantly reenacted, the drama of bringing order out of chaos as the perpetual law, of every society's being; and the language of a primitive social contract was unveiled as what on contractarian terms it always had to be, a mere thought experiment to show how society works. With the progress of the early-modern era we see a waning of the Renaissance interest in genuinely new foundations (the North Americans were the last people, perhaps, in a position to draw on that legacy); in its place we find an interest in the possibilities of dissolution and reconstruction within existing societies, an interest in *revolution,* a word that enters the common currency of the West with the events of 1688 in Britain.

This explains the quite innovative place accorded to the legislators by early-modern constitutional theories. As in the Renaissance, legislation is foundational; but foundation is no longer *origin,* but a continuous spring of rationality that sustains the political society in being. In place of the originating assembly that first constituted the political society, the legislature is now a standing branch of government that lays claim to the sovereignty hitherto held by the Head of Government. In this way early-modern theory fulfills the aspirations of ancient democracy; but it does so only indirectly and covertly, since the whole point is (as it never ceases to insist) not the rule of the people but the rule of law. Political society is a lived rationality, of which lawmaking is the source and spring. And as, when government was seen as judgment, God, the supreme judge, was known to be "angry every day," i.e., to hold daily assizes,[13] so now the legislative branch, standing in for the rationality of divine providence, had better not slumber or sleep. An incessant stream of lawmaking is the fundamental proof of political viability.

Against this background we understand our own late-modern crisis. It is, first of all, born of a reaction against this notion of positively legislated rationality, of a desire for freedom to assert right prior to and independent of the "unequal constitutions of men." It responds to a Judeo-Christian im-

---

13. Ps. 7:11.

pulse. In the postwar documents that express the late-modern faith in human rights, the use of quasi-religious concepts is decisive, as in the UN Declaration of Human Rights, which speaks in its preamble of the "recognition of the inherent dignity and of the equal and inalienable rights of all members of the human family."[14] That the problem of autonomous courts should have come to the fore in *this* period, and in the nations most involved with *those* documents, attests the twentieth-century search for a prepolitical moral ground of law. The distinctive features of the U.S. Constitution merely served as a channel for an anti-positivist reaction common to our civilization. It is, of course, profoundly disappointing that no better alternative should have been found than the fragmented and antisocial notion of "human rights"; but the impulse deserves, for all that, its due recognition and acknowledgment. Our crisis, however, also attests that we have *not* in fact succeeded in breaking with the early-modern concept of positively legislated government. Neither we nor our courts have proved capable of forming a clear idea of what it is to recognize a claim of natural right without erecting the courts as counter-legislature, an equal and opposite imitation, and so precipitating the crisis over sovereignty.

II

Let us attempt, then, to reconstruct, starting from the Pauline premise that the defining role of secular government is to exercise judgment. In this case, the *court* is the central paradigm of government *in all its branches*.

1. In the simplest model, such as we find in the political pedagogic of Ancient Israel, in the narratives of David and Solomon, and in the Psalms, the monarch is a judge who sits in court. "Morning by morning I will destroy all the wicked in the land," he declares in what is probably a kind of oath of office.[15] Daily assizes are the proof of a just king. Ancient Israel also knew, however, that the task of judgment required not only that the monarch sit in court, but that he also found courts. Three separate Pentateuchal narratives, each with a slightly differing emphasis, explore the logic of this move in relation to Moses. In Exodus 18, the first of these narratives in order of canonical appearance (I imply no conclusions about historical sources),

14. I. Browlie, ed., *Basic Documents in International Law* (Oxford: Clarendon, 1953), p. 250.

15. Ps. 101:8.

Jethro persuades Moses of the simple fact that the business pressing on any court is far too great for only one judge to deal with. A unified system of justice, then, requires a tiered system of courts in which the ruler hears a case only as the last resort. In the second narrative (Numbers 11) it is recognized that the community possesses a variety of local, family, and tribal loyalties which need to be harnessed to the task of judgment, since without their cooperation the ruler cannot achieve his purpose. The third, combining elements of these two, stands in a programmatic place at the opening of that highly programmatic book, Deuteronomy, and employs the concept of law to conflate the monarchical emphasis of the one with the tribal emphasis of the other. The various courts based on tribal identities are held together by the authority of one law, authenticated by the monarch.

Looked at from one angle, this development logically presages the exclusion of the monarch from the judiciary; for as the court of last resort, the monarch should never sit, but rather so act through ministers as to retain one last throw, should it be needed. Yet it also presages a sphere of administrative government in which the monarch *still* exercises judgment, though not in court. For to provide a court in which a judge sits is no less an act of judgment than to sit in court himself. The monarch considers the situation in which those who are wronged lack access to public interest and vindication, finds it wanting, and redresses it by inaugurating courts. The monarch does not found the judiciary *from outside*, as it were, like a businessman founding a University Chair without himself being a man of learning. The founding of the judiciary is precisely the founding judicial act; it gives judgment in favor of the oppressed. Not in favor of one particular oppressed person in this case, but in favor of the oppressed as a class; yet not a universal class (for the ruler does not undertake to remedy the wrongs of all oppressed people everywhere in every age), but a concrete historical class, the oppressed of *this* kingdom at *this* juncture of history. What can be said about the foundation of courts applies equally to the *maintenance* of courts: the monarch's duty is to keep the courts open. To let "judgment flow like a torrent and vindication like a river in flood," as Amos picturesquely put it,[16] is quite simply a responsibility to exercise conscientious judgment.

What early-modern theorists speak of as "the separation of executive and judiciary" is a distinction *within the single task* of giving judgment, between the originating judgment that founds courts and the dependent judgments that take place in the courts. If we are to express this in other than a

---

16. Amos 5:24.

monarchical context, we shall need to find some other term than "executive." I shall employ "the Head of Government" to refer to that locus of government to which responsibility for maintaining justice ultimately reverts. For "executive" has built into it the suggestion of a role that is both dependent and non-judicial. When we think in such ways, we run into the troubling modern cleavage between government and justice, the idea that there are excellences attainable in government which are only contingently related to justice. The amoralism of this conception of the executive generates an equal and opposite moralism about the judicial task. A justice pursued by courts without prudence is purely formal, and no more satisfying than prudence pursued by executives without justice. Prudence, the provision of what people need, integrally belongs to justice, as justice belongs to prudence.

At the same time, however, as we stress the juridical matrix of all government, the differentiation of roles must be allowed due space. And not only for the practical reasons that Jethro gave Moses, but because any given instance of wrong may be examined in more than one perspective, more broadly or more narrowly. Faced with a social crisis over drug abuse, for example, we must attend practically to the pressing problem of protecting young people against the influence of drug dealers; but we must also attend with impartial minds to the charges of drug dealing brought against *this* person at *this* time and place. We cannot attend to the second, more focused matter if we are preoccupied by the first. ("If this man is acquitted, what sort of message will it send out to drug dealers everywhere?") *Both* ways of practically attending are acts of judgment: *both* are particular, i.e., belonging to a definite time and place and situation; but the second way is more limited in scope, because injustice may be committed on a narrow front when we try to do justice on a broad front. The public interest in justice is an interest in both levels of judgment being pursued, each on its own proper terms. So the government confines itself to policy making, the court excludes policy making. The *sub judice* rule, which is the essential element of truth in the differentiation, protects the examination of narrow questions about individual cases.

But the policy which is the Head of Government's business is not other than *judicial* policy. We depend on rulers keeping an eye on courts, just as we depend on their keeping their hands off cases. If over a significant period courts prove incapable of convicting terrorist offenders, they, or the law they administer, must be reformed. The Head of Government must ensure not only that courts exist, but that they function, those two responsibilities being in fact one and the same. Reasonable expedition of legal process, reasonable restraint of legal fees, reasonable rules of procedure over such matters as the admissibility of evidence, use of juries, and so on — all these are the proper concerns of the Head of Government, who is charged with ensuring that justice, not arbitrary whim, prevails in social relations. Legislation is one form that the discharge of this responsibility takes.

2. In the unfolding of the different moments of human government, the judicial moment comes first, the administrative moment second, and the legislative third. The mistake in the modern tradition was to place legislation first, following the Hellenistic association of legislation and founding. This supposed that law and legislation, *nomos* and *nomothesia,* were coextensive; that without the framework of founding legislation there was no law. The Christian assertion, on the contrary, was that no human creation was ever prior to law, that lawful government never depended upon prior legislation as a precondition. "If 'laws are silent among arms,'" says Hugo Grotius, "it is the *civil* laws that are so . . . not those other laws that are perpetually in force and appropriate for each and every season."[17]

In Hebrew the most general word for law, *tôrah,* meant simply "a decision." It referred to the "ruling" that a priest would give when consulted.[18] In the same way we say that the judge "declares the law" in relation to a case, meaning not that he quotes from law books, but that he announces a decision. "The law of the case" is simply the generic principle applied in the particular judgment. But since judgment is not merely a series of separate and discrete divisions but a continuous activity, the law of each case is discerned in relation to the law of preceding cases; if it is to be justly proportioned, it cannot be wildly out of line with previous decisions. No act of judgment, then, simply invents law *de novo,* for that would defeat one of the purposes of judging, which is to determine what is proportionate. Each judgment depends on a law derived from many cases, a law of precedent that stands over and behind the present decision and can be appealed to in support or in criticism of it. But a law of precedent requires no distinct human legislator. Divine law, natural or revealed, when mediated through traditions of right innate in the society, is sufficient to allow courts to develop a law by way of their own judgments, a conception which our shared English legal tradition names the "common law."

But when the authority of courts is undermined because they operate on principles repugnant to the community's conscience or because their or-

---

17. *The Right of War and Peace.* Proleg. 26. Translation from *IG,* p. 797.
18. Exod. 18:16, 20; Deut.17:11.

ders are impossible to implement, the responsibility for correcting their law lies with the Head of Government. The legal tradition needs correction. The obligation of the courts to maintain self-consistency makes them reluctant to innovate. But innovation may sometimes be required, and that for two causes: first, where tradition has deviated from natural right; secondly, where it is ill-adapted to the practical possibilities within society. These two concerns are often confused, but they are in principle quite different, moving, as it were, in opposite directions, the one bringing law closer to the moral norm, the other removing it further from it. There are idealistic reforms, attempting to correct our vices; there are compromise reforms, making some kind of settlement with them. Either kind of reform may be necessary at one or another juncture, since acts of judgment have to be at once truthful and effective. Every change in law aims to squeeze out, as it were, the maximum yield of public truthfulness available within the practical constraints of the times. Sometimes it does this by attempting more, sometimes by attempting less.

The Christian legal tradition took over, gingerly enough, the Hellenistic commonplace which saw the ruler as the *empsychos nomos,* the "living law." Whereas this had meant originally to identify the ruler as the source of law, in Christian use it was combined with the assertion that the ruler was under the law, charged, like anyone else, with keeping it. But the *way* in which the ruler "keeps" the law is different from others: he keeps it by ensuring that it is applied and upheld in courts. Furthermore, when the fluid character of the practice of law is recognized, its tendency to fall into disuse and neglect, it is added that the ruler "keeps" it by intervening, where necessary, into the legal tradition, safeguarding it from degeneration.

The paradigm instance in the traditions common to the U.S. and Great Britain was the invention of the Court of Chancery in fifteenth-century England and Wales. The common-law courts being widely perceived to have become ineffective on many fronts, the government responded by developing a new court, derived from royal council and under the supervision of the Lord Chancellor, a minister who to that date had had no special connection with the operation of law. Chancery devised rules for its own operation superior to those prevailing in the common-law courts, and took over areas of litigation where those courts had seemed peculiarly incompetent. This illustrates on a large scale what happens in fact in any act of legislation: some element in the existing tradition of the court's law is corrected or adjusted from the source of government. But it also illustrates a precise danger, which required further correction at a later stage: the setting up of conflicting jurisdictions within a single system. This has a bearing on our contemporary problem, as we shall see.

Yet one more dialectical distinction arises between this act of government and other acts. Legislation is *generic,* which is what distinguishes it from acts that concern bare particulars. When the Head of Government appoints a chief justice or supplies a sum of money to create new courts, he decides only who is to be the Lord Chief Justice *next,* or where the money is to come from *now.* When a law is passed, on the other hand, it concerns what is *always* to be done in such cases as it specifies. Imagine two supposed miscarriages of justice, both uncorrected by the courts themselves, which provoke public anxiety and demands for government action. In the one case there is public doubt about the evidence for identification on which a conviction was secured. In the other case there is a judicial ruling that evidence important to the defense is technically inadmissible. Both are assumed miscarriages, but for different reasons. The first related to a particular, "*This* is the man who was observed at the scene of the crime"; the second related to a generic principle, "*This kind* of evidence is not admissible in defense." The two miscarriages must be addressed quite differently. In the one case the Home Secretary reviews the case, and if it seems warranted, instructs the Court of Appeal to look at it again. In the second case the Lord Chancellor prepares new legislation to amend the law of evidence.

Now, these two different kinds of corrective action require a different measure of public support. If the Home Secretary refers the first case back, or simply issues a pardon, not much is needed by way of public consent. We understand that the minister has these powers, and we require only that he use them reasonably. It is not possible to settle the validity of any verdict by public consensus. Nor does it matter to the public very much in the long run if the minister actually reaches the wrong answer, provided that he is seen to reach it reasonably, conscientiously, and without prejudice. In the second case, though, where legislation is in question, it is a far different matter. Hundreds of cases yet undreamed of will be affected. So something more than bare consent is needed to validate a legislative act. There must be a positive assent to the principles on which reform is proposed. No deep cleavage can be allowed to develop between the general sense of what is right and what the law exacts. So the two kinds of governmental act proceed in quite different ways. Proposals for legislation need examination, both to explore unforeseen implications and to test them against the moral attitudes and convictions of those who will be governed by them and may ultimately be tempted to find them tyrannous.

Hence the British constitutional doctrine, maintained by Locke despite his advocacy of "separation," that the legislature in a government is *the monarch in parliament*. That is to say: not some *other* agent than the Head of Government, but the Head of Government as engaged in a process of consultation. But what is the status of parliament as a consultation partner? Among the radical constitutionalists of the later sixteenth century, Parliament (or, in other European traditions, the Estates or the Diets) underwent a change of status, from a body that existed to represent popular concerns *to* government, to become a *branch* of government. It drew to itself the role of the founding people covenanting with God and monarch to establish government, but also, in Reformed thought especially, the role of a distinct magistracy charged with protecting the state against abuses practiced by the sovereign. In this development its true significance was lost sight of. In England parliament began life as a *court of common pleas,* a means by which the governed spoke to government about their frustrations, an organic line of communication between the two that served to legitimate government as pursuit of the common good. The extension of parliament's role to that of a deliberative forum, first for the authorizing of taxation and then for the formation of legislation, recognized the need for government to listen to the *vox populi,* to respect its deeply held convictions, and to take stock of its anxieties.

In this context we may see a point in Montesquieu's anxiety: "When the legislative and executive powers are united in the same person, or in the same body of magistrates, there can be no liberty; because apprehensions may arise, lest the same monarch or senate should enact tyrannical laws, to execute them in a tyrannical manner."[19] It is at first sight puzzlingly expressed. What other than tyrannical manner could there be, we might ask, of enacting tyrannical laws? And given the lamentable hypothesis that a legislature will legislate tyrannically, does not the separation of powers merely entrench the legislature against correction? We can understand the point of the remark, however, as being that when a certain *dialogue* fails to accompany the formation of a law, its enactment simply becomes another form of executive action. It loses its distinctive law-like character. But Montesquieu mislocated the dialogue required, and so underestimated it. What is needed is not simply a dialogue between departments of government, but a dialogue between government and people.

By converting parliament into a branch of government, modern constitutional theory lost a vital sense of the dialogue between government and

---

19. *The Spirit of the Laws* 11.6, trans. Thomas Nugent (New York: Hafner, 1949), p. 151.

governed as the heart of the legislative process. This, I believe, lies at the root of the perceived problems of the British constitution in our century. Many contemporary critics have identified the difficulty simply in terms of the excessive power of the executive. But this analysis is one-sided, since the source of the current imbalance was parliament's absorbing, one by one, all the powers of sovereignty that used to belong to the monarch's ministers. The sheer success of parliament in taming the willfulness of monarchy led to an implosion of government and parliament upon each other, leaving unhealthy mutual dependence. Parliament (in effect, one chamber of Parliament) wrested effective control over ministerial appointments, so that ministers depended on it for continuance in office. Ministers forced parliament to agree to their legislative proposals with the threats of resignation or dissolution, for which Members of Parliament would have to answer at the polls. The sense of dialogue was lost. Ministers and Parliament gained, and still have, too much power over each other, too little authority on their own ground. The stranglehold exercised by the party system, effectively controlling the terms of all political debate, is the worst symptom of the stasis. But the long-term cost of co-opting parliament into government has been a loss of belief in the capacity of "politicians" — the term is an expressive one, bundling ministers and popular representatives together in one homogeneous class — to respond to what actually moves the people. "Politicians" argue energetically with one another about "the issues." But what the issues are to be, they have settled among themselves.

III

We return at last to judicial review of legislation, which we may understand as a reaction against the paradoxical dominance of parliamentary government and the positivism of legislative supremacy. The turn to the courts expresses frustration with legislative parliaments that claim to be the sovereign government and fail in any meaningful sense to be a court of common pleas.

We have said that there is nothing impossible in the idea that law may be made by courts. Indeed, if we understand the work of courts correctly, the making of law is an essential part of it: they must declare the principles on which they have decided cases, and those principles must in some measure be a law for subsequent courts. The question, then, is not whether courts shall make law, but how. Are they to be autonomous, or under correction from some other locus than a higher court? When we contemplate the sight of military leaders ruling by decree, we may wish to concede that there can be worse forms of autocratic rule than that which judges exercise. Nevertheless, there are reasons, which I will not now explore, why autocratic government is not good government; and there are also, as I have tried to show, three good reasons why good government requires courts to be subject to external correction: (a) good court practice requires concentration on the particular case, but good lawmaking requires attention to general policy (the *sub judice* principle); (b) good court practice requires insulation from pressures of public concern, but good lawmaking requires exposure through consultation to public concern (the democratic principle); (c) good court practice requires a conservative approach to legal tradition, but good lawmaking needs a measure of critical distance on tradition (the natural law principle).

As I have reflected on this problem, I have come to the conclusion that the root of the matter lies in the faulty early-modern articulation, which, lacking a sense of the judicial character of all branches of government, allowed separation to create *competing jurisdictions.* This is a situation which political authority cannot endure. The multiple variation of functions within a complex government allows for an extensive plurality of function and decision, but the plurality rests on the hypothesis of a *summa potestas,* a source of governmental authority, to which in the last analysis the resolution of conflicts must return. That is the heart of the matter.

There is an alternative analysis of the problem, frequently argued in Canada at the time of the introduction of the Bill of Rights in 1982, and often urged by British opponents of a Bill of Rights: that the root of the problem lies in assigning legal status to a *philosophical document,* whether a Bill of Rights or a *Grundrecht* or whatever else it may be, that is *too underdetermined* in legal terms, and so undercuts the concrete determinations of ordinary legislation. This is not the root of the problem, because if an underdetermined document has the status of law, it is easy enough in principle to provide it with determinations. A problem arises only when there is competition between *rival* determinations.

This is illustrated by a famous controversy between the European Court of Human Rights and the British government, which turned precisely on such an underdetermined expression, and led to Great Britain's only derogation from the Convention. Article 5(3) of the European Convention on Human Rights requires that an arrested person must be "brought promptly before a judge."[20] In British anti-terrorist legislation the time lapse between

20. Brownlie, *Basic Documents,* p. 323.

arrest and appearance in court was, in exceptional circumstances, allowed to be as long as seven days; the Court of Human Rights insisted on a limit of three days. Now, either three days or seven days will plausibly serve as a determination of the word "promptly." Which is the *better* determination will depend on the circumstances in which one has to be prompt, which is why alternative determinations for differing circumstances are conceivable, even desirable. The controversy, then, did not follow from the bare possibility of differing determinations, nor from the fact that the phrase was, as it stood, underdetermined. It was simply born of a failure to achieve a workable conception of the way in which the jurisdiction of the court related to that of the government of the United Kingdom.

Unlike most other signatory countries, Britain regarded the Convention simply as a treaty, without any direct force in domestic law. The Strasbourg court thought it had no reason to attribute to the British courts and legislation the intention of enforcing the Convention and applying it appropriately. In relation to Great Britain it seemed to enjoy a monopoly on interpreting human rights, standing over against a civil society in which both legislature and courts apparently ignored them. This was not *concretely* the case, of course; but *formally* the matter so appeared. One can hardly blame the European court for acting out a legally subversive role. But that role was simply the result of allowing competition to arise between jurisdictions: on the one side, a court with a document all of its own; on the other side, national government and courts, obliged to respect the document but with no share in interpreting it.

It was understandable, therefore, that the British Government should recently have incorporated the European Convention of Human Rights within English and Scottish law, in a way that, it was hoped, would overcome the existing liability to generate conflicts, while also protecting the legislative supremacy of the Queen in Parliament. The Human Rights Act allows the Convention to be interpreted as British law in British courts, and so allows British statute law to be applied within the interpretative context of the Convention. It will have the effect of presenting the Strasbourg court with interpretative decisions on the Convention reached under British law by British courts, and so do something to reconcile the jurisdictions. While stopping short of according Strasbourg rulings *ipso facto* force in British law, it requires British courts to take those rulings into account, thereby allowing a serious contribution to the interpretation of British law from outside Great Britain. But by depriving the Strasbourg court of its interpretative monopoly, it ensures that the interpretation of the Convention begins to reflect British legal realities.[21]

One might say that this measure attempts to do *institutionally* what still remains to be done *conceptually*, which is to reintegrate the falsely polarized conceptions of positive law and human rights, the one supposedly enjoying immunity from moral criteria, the other supposedly enjoying natural-law supremacy over positive law. The truth of the natural-law principle, that for law to be valid it must be morally tolerable, must apply across the whole range of legislative endeavor, not merely to claims of individuals against governments. The truth of the principle behind positive law, on the other hand, must also be maintained: the rights of individuals cannot be given proper effect simply by letting them cut across legal traditions, invading, as it were, by sudden irruptions of court judgment at unpredictable moments; they must be an essential aspect of the spirit of a well-tempered law, a "Right" in the singular, which government takes responsibility for sustaining and correcting.

We return to the respective roles of courts and legislators. The essence of the courts' task, in the first place, is to apply statute law intelligently in the light of natural law, to make good moral and social sense of a body of legislation that may sometimes have been incoherently or inconsiderately compiled. In handling this body of law we should not require that the courts be slavish. There should be no prejudice in favor of "strict construction," except where that has become the only acknowledged alternative to sheer willfulness. What we should require of courts is a due acknowledgment of the authority of government in providing law, and a commitment to giving it the best interpretation to which it is susceptible, according to the most consistent interpretative principles (not necessarily the most literalistic) that can be developed. The possibility of absolutely rejecting some legal provision as inconsistent with divine and natural right cannot be ruled out *a priori*, since we cannot *a priori* exclude the possibility of tyrannous law, which requires the performance of wicked actions or forbids the performance of obligations. Such an event, however, needs to be seen as a last resort, implying the invocation of an emergency procedure — our new British legislation envisages a formal declaration — which will bring the legislators urgently to the

---

21. The tackling of the problem of monopoly may be the key to the very different constitutional context of the U.S., as one recent contribution to the debate suggested: "The Founders never intended to give the federal courts a monopoly over the interpretation of the Constitution. . . . Courts must apply the Constitution . . . other branches must do the same according to their own best lights." Robert George and Ramesh Ponnuru, "Courting Trouble" in *National Review,* August 1998.

point, and cause bad statutes to be remade, but by parliament, not by the courts. The procedure of "striking down" was rejected by the British Government, and rightly, since it is precisely that procedure that produces the situation in which legislative responsibility slips away from parliament.

But here we must recall the main point of our analysis: that the problem arose in the first place because populist constitutional doctrine asserted an idolatrously inflated conception of legislative power. The aggrandizement of positive legislation has resulted in a cheapening of law and a general contempt for legislative process: too much law made too fast and too carelessly. Law, as Montesquieu feared, has turned into a form of executive action, as parties compete at elections with their rival legislative programs, which they promise to ram through within one parliamentary term (or, even worse, within the first hundred days). In this ethos the shifting of real responsibility to the courts by no means occurred without the collusion of politicians. It enabled them to sustain a flurry of lawmaking without being ultimately answerable for its consequences. (I recall, with a shudder of despair, one Premier of Ontario, who, promoting a controversial and wide-ranging amendment to the Province's Bill of Rights, answered all questions about what it would mean with the simple formula: "We don't know. The courts will decide!") In consequence, the forms for sanctioning legislation came to be seen as merely provisional, and in some places new law was hardly thought authoritative until it had been challenged at least once through the court system.

No solution of the problem can be imagined which does not involve an address to the process of legislation. What our democracies most need is not judicial review of law after the event, but a high standard of preparatory scrutiny before laws are entered in the statute book. One of the most positive aspects of the new British law is that new legislation must come before Parliament accompanied by a statement assuring its compatibility with the provisions of the Convention. The courts are not bound to agree with the statement, of course, should it be challenged. But the practice requires legislators to respect the Convention in their legislative endeavors, and to heed the advice of jurists on the matter *ab initio*. Yet something will be required of the courts in turn: to recognize the implications of this legislative process, to acknowledge the intent of a law to insert itself into a natural-law-governed practice, and to interpret it in good faith. In this way real understanding between lawmakers and courts may be developed, and the burden against impugning a law which has had a clean bill of health will be a greater one. Self-discipline in legislative quarters and self-discipline in judicial quarters must go hand in hand.

46 Politics and the Soul: A Reading of the *City of God*

Rowan Williams

"Augustine seems to have been the last to know at least what it once meant to be a citizen."[1] Hannah Arendt's judgment is all the more interesting because she clearly considered Augustine to be the single thinker most responsible for the Christian repudiation of the "public realm" — a repudiation which she regarded as, in its modern guise, one of the major threats to the security, peace, and sanity of the human world. The "public realm" is seen by Arendt as the world we consciously have in common, to paraphrase her rather condensed exposition.[2] We could say that the common world is what provides us with an identity in terms of language; it is the possibility of securing what I have been and done and said as an individual by locating it in a *tradition* of speech and recollection. It is what makes it possible for me to be remembered, for me to be part of the conversation of a future generation. Thus it is the sign of a *common humanity,* existing independently of my will or imagination: to engage in "public" life is to accept that I am finite and time-bound, born *into* a continuum of language and interaction I did not choose or invent, and yet also to transcend my finitude in the only way I can, by striving to contribute to the language and interaction of the group some new qualification or nuance that can reasonably and properly become part of a tradition, a heritage. Our goal should be to make our lives "a symbol perfected in death."[3] Without this, we are doomed to the futile insignificance of

1. H. Arendt, *The Human Condition* (Chicago, 1958), p. 14.
2. Arendt, *The Human Condition*, pp. 50-58.
3. T. S. Eliot, *Little Gidding* III.

purely private and individual life, futile insofar as its value is perceptible only to my subjectivity and the subjectivities of those I am immediately in contact with, and because its conduct is likely to be constrained and dominated by my need to survive and meet my necessities and those of my dependents. In this sense, says Arendt,[4] classical thought considered the public realm to be the sphere of true freedom: rule, coercive power, even violence, belong in the household, since they are the means of mastering necessity, organizing the threatening incipient chaos of daily life. Without the patterns of dominance securely fixed in the domestic order, no one would be able to go out into the *polis* among equals, freed from private need so as to engage in the creative, intelligible work of constructing shared meanings and shared futures, in action worthy of remembrance, action establishing a human continuity that transcends the immediate and the local. The private has no history, because the struggle for survival and the meeting of needs has no history. And without this public realm of active, creative persons taking responsibility for the integrity and continuation of a form of talking and understanding, we are condemned either to the animal pointlessness of the mere effort to subsist, or to the more typically modern unfreedom of "mass society," in which financial achievement and reward or security replaces glory and repute, the notion of worthiness to be remembered, and the quality of public action as creative, as formative of a "conversation" extending beyond individual death, is undermined. Society becomes increasingly incapable of intelligent speech, common imagination, increasingly enslaved to idolatrous objectifications, fetishes, and slogans.[5]

How then does Christianity — or Augustinian Christianity in particular — carry forward this subversion of the public? The early Church, Arendt suggests,[6] is a community of people more or less marginalized by their refusal of Roman imperial authority and their anticipation of the end of the world: humanly speaking, the "conversation" is simply not going to continue. What then can "replace the world" as a bond between such persons? The sense of belonging to a community which is in important respects more like a kindred, a family, than a *polis,* a community in which achievement, excellence, and creativity are irrelevant to membership, even damaging. It is a

---

4. Arendt, *The Human Condition,* pp. 28-30. See also the excellent article by Paul A. Rahe, "The Primacy of Politics in Classical Greece," *The American Historical Review* 89 (1984): 265-93.

5. Arendt's analysis here should be compared with that of Adorno on objectification and the menace of the "totally administered society."

6. Arendt, *The Human Condition,* pp. 53-54.

body held together by love, *caritas:* "The bond of charity between people, while it is incapable of founding a public realm of its own, . . . is admirably fit to carry a group of essentially wordless people through the world."[7] *Caritas* is, in the Augustinian system, a love which is indifferent to merit and achievement: it sees the bonds between persons as resting simply on their common createdness and equal sinfulness, and thus operates impartially and, in a sense, impersonally. In her doctoral thesis of 1929, *Der Liebesbegriff bei Augustin,*[8] Arendt had argued that *caritas* means "loving the eternal" in ourselves and others, and that this is the essence of Christian neighborly love: we see in one another tokens of both the creative and the redemptive work of God. As creatures, we love still at a distance, we "coexist"; but as sinful objects of the saving work of Christ, we are brought together in communion. A non-worldly society is thus created, the "City of God."[9] By the time she came to write *The Human Condition* in the 1950s, Arendt was far more openly hostile to the idea of non-worldly community than she had been in 1929 (that, as she would no doubt have said, is what the twentieth century does to you); but the analysis of Augustine and the principle of "worldless" love remains much the same. The *civitas Dei* is a substitute for the public realm, and thus its enemy.

Yet Augustine knew "at least what it once meant to be a citizen." This is a remark made in passing, puzzling in the light of the conclusion that it is Augustine who makes it more or less impossible for a Christian to *be* a citizen. In this paper, I want to explore precisely why Augustine might be said to understand what is involved in citizenship, and how far he may at the same time be rightly seen as a subverter of the values of the classical public and political realm. Hannah Arendt is, I believe, right, though not perhaps for the right reasons. And on the other hand, a recent defense of Augustine as fundamentally political educator — Peter Bathory's *Political Theory as Public Confession*[10] — seeks to correct the imbalance that prompts the notion

---

7. Arendt, *The Human Condition,* p. 53. Note that Arendt, in alluding to the Augustinian ascription of some kind of "political" virtue to even the robber band (*De civ. Dei* XIX, 12), misses Augustine's point. There is no assimilation of the "worldlessness" of the saint and the criminal to each other: Augustine is making a general observation on the universality of the desire for peace, without which no corporate life or action can exist.

8. Berlin, 1929; see esp. pp. 62-68 (there is a good summary of this rather rare and inaccessible work on pp. 490-500 of Elizabeth Young-Bruehl's fine biography, *Hannah Arendt: For Love of the World* (New Haven and London, 1982).

9. *Der Liebesbegriff bei Augustin,* pp. 75-90; Young-Bruehl, *Hannah Arendt,* pp. 496-97.

10. New Brunswick and London, 1981.

that Augustine commended passivity or disengagement, yet does so at the expense of any analysis of the saint's radical assault on the conventionally political as such. Both Arendt and Bathory, in fact, seem to resolve what many readers of Augustine have found to be an irresoluble set of tensions. As will appear, I do not believe Augustine is guilty simply of flat contradictions; but I see little value in trying to extract a wholly consistent program from the *City of God*. We should look less for a systematic account of "church" and "world" (let alone church and state), more for a scheme for reflecting on the nature of social virtue.

Robert Markus, in what remains probably the finest survey of Augustine's political thinking in English, argues for a tendency in the *De civitate* to "atomistic personalism" where Augustine is reflecting on what we should call state power. Augustine may write of a *civitas terrena;* yet his discussion deals not with anything that could be called an institution, but rather with persons and processes.[11] Thus we cannot really say that he has a theory of *the* state at all (even in the attenuated sense discussed by Figgis, who is careful to warn against the translation of *civitas* by any strictly political term).[12] Augustine does not think — or at least does not consistently think — of two distinct kinds of human association, the sacred and the secular, or even the private and the public. His concern is with the goal of human life as such. Thus, at the end of Book XVIII of the *De civitate*, we read that both cities, of God and of this world, experience the same vicissitudes of earthly life and make use of the same temporal goods, but *diversa fide, diversa spe, diverso amore:* their goals are distinct, and so will be their eternal rewards.[13] Book XIX then opens the discussion of the end of human existence; and the "political" debate of this book must be read in this light. Augustine is not here seeking to pronounce on what might be an appropriate relationship between the two cities; he has just completed[14] a fairly full account of the history of

11. *Saeculum: History and Society in the Theology of St Augustine* (Cambridge, 1970), pp. 149-52.

12. J. N. Figgis, *The Political Aspects of Saint Augustine's 'City of God'* (London, 1921), pp. 51ff.

13. *De civ. Dei* XVIII, 54; cf. XIX, 17 for the distinction between *communis usus* and the diversity in *finis utendi* as between the city of God and the city of the world. It is important to recognize that the common use/diverse ends model has nothing to do with pluralism *within* a society; this clarification is forcefully made in an unpublished paper on Augustine's *City of God* XIX and Western political thought by my colleague, Oliver O'Donovan, and I am much indebted to him for allowing me to read and discuss this essay with him.

14. *De civ. Dei* XVIII, 49-53.

persecution, and concluded firmly that there can be no guarantee of persecution ever being a thing of the past. The last thing he is likely to wish to do is to draft a concordat between the city of God and its avowed enemies. His question in Book XIX is, rather, about the optimal form of corporate human life in the light of what is understood to be its last end. At this level, the *De civitate* is not at all a work of political theory in the usual sense, but sketches for a theological anthropology and a corporate spirituality. The political and the spiritual are not separate concerns: Book XIX seeks to show that the spiritual is the *authentically* political. Although it is in one sense quite true to say, with Markus,[15] that Augustine abandons the classical idea of "creative politics," of life in the empirical city as the sphere of the free development of moral persons towards the human goal, this does *not* mean that the saint repudiates the public realm for something else, or even that his perspective is "atomistic" in quite Markus' sense. Rather he is engaged in a *redefinition* of the public itself, designed to show that it is life outside the Christian community which fails to be truly public, authentically political. The opposition is not between public and private, church and world, but between political virtue and political vice. At the end of the day, it is the secular order that will be shown to be "atomistic" in its foundations.

In both Books II and XIX, Augustine refers us to Cicero's *De re publica* for a definition of "the public realm" or the "commonwealth," as Healey accurately renders it. A *populus* is not just any contingent gathering of persons, but a group bound together *juris consensu et utilitatis communione*.[16] This, then, is where discussion of the properly political, consciously and articulately shared life, must begin: in agreement over what are and are not legitimate moves within the social grouping, and in some sort of guaranteed common access to the things that sustain life (not too far from access to the "means of production," perhaps; there are worse translations of *utilitas*!). In a celebrated polemical section,[17] Augustine demolishes the claim of pagan Rome to be a "commonwealth" on the grounds of what seems to be a piece of lexical sleight of hand: *jus* gives to each his or her due; but pagan society cannot give *God* his due. It offers sacrifice to demons; only the Christian community offers sacrifice to the true God, and, what is more, the only acceptable sacrifice, itself as a totality redeemed in Christ.[18]

---

15. *Saeculum*, ch. 4, esp. pp. 94-95.

16. *De civ. Dei* II, 21; XIX, 21.

17. *De civ. Dei* XIX, 21-23.

18. *De civ. Dei* XIX, 23; cf. XVIII, 54; X 4, 5, 19, and 20. Markus (*Saeculum*, pp. 64-65) rather misleads the reader by eliding most of the detail of Augustine's argument, when he

This is not, however, quite as disingenuous as it sounds. A social practice which impedes human beings from offering themselves to God in fact denies that central impulse in human nature which Augustine defined as the unquenchable desire for God and his truth.[19] It provides *ersatz* gratifications, finite substitutes for the infinite. And as such it diminishes humanity itself, in that it takes away the one principle that can rightly order our wills and affections. *Quando quidem Deo non serviens nullo modo potest juste animus corpori aut humana ratio vitiis imperare.*[20] There are, indeed, other factors which may regulate the passions; but the supposed virtue resulting from this kind of control is really vice — pride and vainglory — insofar as it is not referred to God.[21] So *beate vivere* is made impossible for us when society directs us to goals other than the glory of our maker. Thus if the pagan *res publica* is deficient as a commonwealth, it is not because Augustine polemically sets a standard of unattainably high righteousness or religious probity, but because a society incapable of giving God his due fails to give its citizens their due — as human beings made for the quest and the enjoyment of God. Where there is no *jus* towards God, there is no common sense of what is due to human beings, no *juris consensus*. And this theme proves to be the main burden of the *De civitate's* vision of political virtue.

If this reading of XIX, 21-23 is correct, then the argument about true and false commonwealths cannot be resolved by appealing to Augustine's allegedly more pragmatic definition of the *res publica* in XIX, 24. Normally[22] this has been seen as indicating that Augustine has exhausted his polemic, and is now attempting to work a more constructive vein. The definition of a *populus* as united by *jus* has been shown to be inapplicable to any but the people of God; is the Roman republic then no more than an arbitrary *coetus*? No, for there are other possible definitions; let us try one. We might define

---

says that the saint identifies Ciceronian *jus* with Christian righteousness; this would make the argument about sacrifice redundant.

19. *Conf.* I,1.1, etc. On the vast subject of desire as a theological theme in Augustine, see recently Isabelle Bodset, *Saint Augustin et le désir de Dieu* (Paris, 1982).

20. *De civ. Dei*, XIX, 21.

21. *De civ. Dei*, XIX, 25.

22. As, e.g., by Figgis (*Political Aspects*, pp. 61-64), Ernest Banker, in his introduction to the Everyman printing of Healey's translation of *De civ. Dei* (Lofoten, 1945), pp. xxxi-xxxii, Markus (*Saeculum*, pp. 65-66, 69ff., where he speaks of the "neutral, positivistic terms" of Augustine's definition), and others. Markus' identification of the concept of a neutral secular realm in *De civ. Dei* was challenged by Gerald Bonner, "*Quid imperatori cum ecclesia?* St Augustine on History and Society," *Augustinian Studies* 2 (1971): 231-51, esp. pp. 244-47; see also, more recently, J. van Oort, *Jeruzalem en Babylon* ('s-Gravenhage, 1986), pp. 127-29.

the commonwealth as unified *rerum quas diligit concordi communione* — by harmony as regards the things it loves or values.[23] On this showing, of course, there is a sense in which Rome counts as a commonwealth; so would *any* empirical political unit (we may as well say "state" from now on, misleading as the term is in many respects). But what is often missed in this chapter is the note of *irony:* in the catalogue of nations thus admitted under the definition of a *res publica,* Athens begins the list, and Babylon ends it. There is a continuum between the ideal of classical politics and its antithesis, the tyrannies of the Orient; for without God's justice, the one is merely on the way to becoming the other. *Justitiae veritas* is by no means secured by this putative harmony about values. In this chapter, Augustine recalls the arguments of earlier books to the effect that, while Rome may once have been in principle committed to a genuinely common harmony, it has long since become an empty word. A state may claim to possess the necessary concord as regards the objects of its *delectio;* but what degree of stability can such a society possess? It is doomed to vice (XIX, 25) and its security is transitory (XIX, 26). In short, while it may be empirically an intelligibly unified body, it is constantly undermining its own communal character, since its common goals are not and cannot be those abiding values which answer to the truest human needs.

So far from XIX, 24 representing a shift in Augustine's analysis towards a more pragmatic and positive view of the state, it is in its context a final stage in the argument begun in XIX, 21. Take even the most minimal and trivial definition of a political body — the unity of common aims — so that you include tyrannies as well as the classical *polis,*[24] and you will still have a picture of societies that cannot *cohere,* that are their own worst enemies, condemning themselves to abiding insecurity. We may call them commonwealths if we will, since there is no doubt that they exist as identifiable social units, but their character and structure are inimical to the very nature of an ordered unity in plurality, a genuine *res publica.*

To understand this more fully, we must refer back to earlier books of the *City of God,* those more directly formed by controversial interest. Book II, 21, in its summary of the argument attributed in Cicero's *De re publica* to Scipio, lays great stress on justice and harmony as the conditions of unity in the state: the various orders of society collaborate rationally, each contributing

---

23. Cf. *De civ. Dei,* II, 21.

24. Augustine has already noted in *De civ. Dei* XVIII, 2, 22, and 27 that Rome is to be seen, both chronologically and spiritually, as the heir of Assyria or Babylon.

its own particular note to the harmony. This, of course, assumes that the function of each person or rank in the *civitas* is uncontroversial. And if any class or functionary acquires disproportionate power, "injustice" is created, and the *res publica* therewith ceases to exist.[25] Thus all members of a society must know their place in a universal *ordo,* they must know how to live in accord with natural law. But, Book II argues, how are they to know this? Chapters 4 to 7, 14 to 16, and 22 to 26 in particular demonstrate that neither the pagan gods, nor the antique philosophers (for all their achievements) enable citizens to live well, in accord with a *lex aeterna.* A poet like Persius may exhort men and women to learn *ordo,* the bounds of aspiration, the will of God;[26] but he writes as a private individual. Such are not the values celebrated in the public worship and festival of antiquity: how then are such values to be established as the common human heritage?

The classical world is thus shown to be without any authentic conception of public virtue. Book V takes this still further in its treatment of the motivation of virtue in Roman society. We have noted that in XIX, 25 it is admitted that virtue of a sort is possible where vice is restrained from motives other than the fear of God; that brief aside is meant to recall the bleak reductionism of V, 12-20. The longing for public praise, for glory and good name, controls that *libido dominandi* which so ruins the unity of any state.[27] In this way (under the providence of God) a specious unity is given to the existing order, even a measure of stability. A small number of persons taking a leading role in the state, obsessed with their desire for glory, are enabled — one would almost think, supernaturally — to resist the greater power of other nations. The remarkable successes of the early Roman republic are not due to the favor of the Roman gods (we have already seen in Books II and III that they show little sign of being concerned for the welfare of their worshippers),[28] nor simply to immanent causes like the extraordinary power of disinterested virtue. Augustine's explanation is at once cynical and theological: the lust for glory restrains the more obvious factors making for disintegration in the state; and God elects to raise up a new empire over against the an-

---

25. *Sic ex summis et infimis et mediis interjectis ordinibus, ut sonis, moderata ratione civitatem consensu dissimillimorum concinere, et qua harmonia a musicis dicitur in cantu, eam esse in civitate concordiam, artissimum atque optimum omni in re publica vinculum incolumitatis, eamque sine justitia nullo pacto esse posse.*

26. II.6.

27. E.g., *De civ. Dei* I, 21; II, 20; V, 12-13, etc., as well as V, 19.

28. *De civ. Dei* II, 16, 22ff.; cf. VI, 1.

cient tyrannies of the East, one which at least represents some kind of judgment upon the unbridled *libido dominandi* of those older systems.

Yet the Roman polity is still vacuous at its core. Cicero recommends that the ruler of a city should be educated in the longing for glory;[29] thus the rebellious impulses to tyranny, prodigality, or whatever are governed and ordered by one supreme sin, pride. This means that the classical republic is shut out from *ordo* and *lex aeterna:* it is built on disorder, in that what should restrain passion is itself replaced by a passion. That sovereignty of spiritual over material interest which is the essence of *ordo*[30] is parodied by the elevation to supreme status of a material or worldly interest capable of masquerading as spiritual. But this is not the only problem about a glory-dominated public ethic. "Glory" is of its very nature an individual matter, won by competition, not open to all. Augustine mentions without stressing it in V, 12 that the classical Roman story is of the achievements and virtues of the few;[31] and while this is, in the context, part of a testimony to the striking nature of the republic's triumphs, it is also made clear that the majority of the population, politically inactive, are kept united only by fear of external enemies.[32] The desire for glory is not a universal moral instructor or preserver of social order: it can assist the unity of a society only negatively, as we have seen, by restraining tyranny. And in Book XV, Augustine has still harsher things to say. Romulus and Remus are alike prompted by the desire for glory in their work in founding the Roman state: but glory is not easily shared. *Qui enim volebat dominando gloriari, minus utique dominaretur, si ejus potestas vivo consorte minueretur.*[33] Preoccupation with achievement brings in its wake a preoccupation with power and pre-eminence: the whole point of the quest for glory lies in the urge to gain advantage over another. In contrast, the love and longing for goodness which marks the city of God is of its essence a desire which seeks to share its object: *tanto eam reperiet ampliorem, quanto amplius ibi potuerit amare consortem* — more is gained by the love of those others who share the quest and the goal. But the search for glory means that the *civitas terrena* is torn by constant strife. The very thing which can in certain circumstances save a society from total dissolution is also potentially a murderous and divisive force.

29. *De civ. Dei* V, 13.

30. E.g., *De civ. Dei*, XIX, 13.

31. *De civ. Dei* V, 12 repeats several times *pauci . . . paucorum.*

32. Cf. *De civ. Dei* V, 12; I, 29, on the effects of the destruction of Carthage upon the internal affairs of Rome.

33. *De civ. Dei* XV, 5.

The conclusion is clear enough: classical society and classical political thought provide ideals for the corporate life of humanity which they cannot provide the means to realize. Already, in the *Confessions*,[34] Augustine had had much to say about those (in that case the Platonists) who offered the possibility of vision without transformation: here, in the *De civitate*, the same complaint can be heard. It is all very well to talk about the public realm, about justice and commonalty; but, empirically speaking, the means employed to make a *coetus* of persons more than a chance aggregate consistently subvert true common life. It does not greatly matter whether or not we decide to accord the *name* of *res publica* to this or that political order: the reality of common or public life is not there. Unity will always be something imposed from outside rather than growing from within; and so it comes about that states need enemies. As Augustine observes in Book I, Carthage played a highly significant role in securing order and justice in Rome. The destruction of the Republic's great rival meant that the *libido dominandi* hitherto checked by the need for discipline and unity and to some extent exercised in defense against an external aggressor came to be exercised within the state, producing gross inequality and injustice.[35] Aggression not dealt with in the inner ecology of social beings seeks outlets — if not against a stranger, then by making strangers of fellow-citizens. Fear, hatred, and the struggle to survive become characteristic of relations between those orders of society which, for Augustine as for Cicero, ought to live in interdependent harmony. But such a vision of interdependence is empty without the undergirding of a vision of humanity in the purposes of its maker.

This interdependence, and the critique of internal social aggression must not be misconstrued; it is nothing to do (as a modern liberal might hope) with collaboration and exchange between equals. Augustine believed that we enjoyed a measure of equality as God's creatures;[36] but his universe, including his social world, is unmistakably hierarchical. The subordination of the less rational to the more is certainly part of the *ordo* spelled out in

---

34. E.g. *Conf.* VII, 17-21.

35. *Delata quippe Carthagine magno scilicet terrore Romanae rei publicae depulso et extincto tanta de rebus prosperis orta mala continuo subsecuta sunt, ut corrupta disruptaque concordia prius saevis cruentisque seditionibus, deinde mox malarum conexione causarum bellis etiam civilibus tantae strages ederentur . . . ut Romani illi, qui vita integriore mala metuebant ab hostibus, perdita integritate vitae crudeliora paterentur a civibus* (*De civ. Dei* I, 29).

36. The image of God is equally in all, irrespective of the differentiation of more and less rational; cf. the discussion of the *imago* in women, *De Trin*, XII, 7, 9.

Book XIX, and the authority of the Roman *paterfamilias* over family and slaves is accepted and defended as a model.[37] Slavery as such is a punishment for sin,[38] the way in which God conserves the *ordo* menaced by Adam's transgression. Yet the implication of much of what Augustine says, here and elsewhere,[39] is that, although it may be a decline from primitive liberties that some human beings are so drastically at the disposal of others, it is servitude, not subordination, that is the new thing. That subordination needs reinforcement by mechanisms of compulsion is the consequence of our fallenness; and that compulsion so readily converts itself into a tool for selfish interest, a means of exercising the *libido dominandi*, is the sign of how far fallen we are. Markus argues persuasively that the origin of strictly political rule, like the origin of slavery, lies in the necessities of our fallenness; and that therefore (on Augustinian principles) the empirical state will be distinguished from the city of God insofar as it is always characterized by the exercise of coercive power.[40] Eschatologically this holds true: there will be no compulsion in heaven.[41] But meanwhile the citizens of the heavenly city certainly do exercise coercion,[42] nor are they necessarily compromising with the *civitas terrena* when they do so. They are merely working within the inescapable constraints of fallen finitude. No, the city of God is not set over against "the state" as a body which invariably exercises its power in a different manner from the secular arm (Augustine is emphatically not a

37. *De civ. Dei* XIX, 16 on the *paterfamilias;* the theme is not unfamiliar from Augustine's correspondence.

38. *De civ. Dei* XIX, 15.

39. *De civ. Dei* XIX, 13 on the natural hierarchy in creation; the discussion of woman's post-lapsarian subjection to man in *De Gen. ad litt.*, XI, 37, 1 brings out the distinction he wishes to make between natural subordination experienced as joy and fulfillment and the (necessarily) enforced domination of the status quo. It is kindest to say that Augustine is seldom at his best in passages like this. Figgis (*Political Aspects*, pp. 52-54) draws a helpful distinction between natural power over the inferior being and "dominion" in the strict classical sense of absolute right, almost possession, exercised by master over slave, and suggests that this is the distinction Augustine has in mind in the relevant portions of *De civ. Dei* XIX.

40. Markus, *Saeculum*, p. 95 and ch. 6; naturally he observes that Augustine himself cannot be made to say that coercion is alien to the Church's life, but the point is that his principles ought to move him in this direction.

41. *De civ. Dei* XIX, 16: . . . *caelestem domum, ubi necessarium non sit officium imperandi mortalibus.*

42. The anti-Donatist literature is clear enough on the rights of the Church to coerce recalcitrant members back into the fold, though there is no suggestion that it can use force against non-members; see the texts quoted by Markus, *Saeculum*, pp. 148-49, esp. from pp. 173 and 185.

Tolstoyan); the difference is, as we should expect, in the ends for which power is exercised, and the spirit in which it is exercised. While it is true that the hierarchy of command in the *res publica* does not have to correspond to any natural hierarchy,[43] the purpose under God of the former is, so far as possible, to restore the rebellious wills of human beings to some approximation to the divine *ordo* — which, as Augustine repeatedly reminds us, is also the right ordering of our internal lives, the dominance of soul over body, reason over passion. In household and society, coercion is properly aimed at restoring the offender *paci unde desiluerat*,[44] and as we have been told by Augustine in XIX, 13 that "peace is indivisible," so to speak, that the *pax* of the individual soul and the *pax* of the universe are parts of a single continuum, so that attempts at peace on the lower levels without regard to the higher are doomed to disaster, it is clear enough that just rule (including, where necessary, the use of force) must aim at peace which is not restricted only to temporary adjustments or passing convenience.

Hence the significance of the link which Augustine makes between *imperare* and *consulere: imperant enim, qui consulunt.*[45] *Consulere* is spiritual nurturing. Because it is itself an activity based on a lively apprehension of the true meaning of *ordo* and of the indivisibility of peace (as XIX, 14 explains at length), it does not run the risk of slipping over into *libido dominandi*. The exercise in authority as *consulere* takes it for granted that the body's peace must serve the soul's, and that the soul's peace is in the love of God and neighbor. The natural order of family life — with the not-quite-so-natural appendage of the household slaves — is the primary locus for the exercise of such an office: a dramatic reversal of what Hannah Arendt saw as the classical set of priorities. So far from being the sphere of bondage and necessity, the household has become a "laboratory of the spirit," a place for the maturation of souls (the soul of the ruler as well as the ruled). This may sound like a privatizing strategy — creativity being shifted into the domestic sphere. Yet Augustine makes it plain in what follows in the same discussion (two chapters later) that the *pax* of the household is to be "referred" *ad pacem civicam*,[46] even that the *paterfamilias* should derive his standards from the law of the city. The implication seems to be that the *civitas* is itself, like the household, ideally a creative and pastoral community, educating the *paterfamilias* as to

---

43. This is implicit in *De civ. Dei* XIX, 15, 17, and 26; cf. IV, 33.
44. *De civ. Dei* XIX, 16.
45. *De civ. Dei* XIX, 14.
46. *De civ. Dei* XIX, 16.

his priorities as he educates his own subjects. The family has become, in some sense, the paradigm political community; but instead of this meaning either that family is opposed to large-scale *civitas* (as in certain sorts of bourgeois politics) or that the *polis* is conceived in organic and "totalizing" ways, the implication here is that both the small and the large-scale community are essentially *purposive*, existing so as to nurture a particular kind of human life: in both, authority is determined in relation to a specific goal.

This is not spelled out in any detail; but it helps us to see why Augustine, despite his distaste for blandly triumphalist ideologies of the Christian empire, can wax so lyrical in Book V[47] about the virtues of the Christian emperor, who is not afraid of sharing or delegating authority, who uses his power to point to the majesty of God, whose primary longing is to possess and rule his own soul in *ordo,* and whose motive in all he does is love and not the lust for glory. Theodosius I is regarded (V, 26) as a ruler well on his way towards this ideal. We should not read this as any kind of uncritical eulogy for a despot, however: Augustine is not doing for Theodosius what Eusebius did for Constantine, but depicting those features of Theodosius' reign least congenial to an ideology of the emperor's sole authority and unlimited right. He does not cling to undivided supremacy; he is not swayed by private grudges; when (as a result of sharing his responsibilities and being influenced by counsel?) he makes mistakes such as the Thessalonian massacre, he accepts the role of penitent. We may be more suspicious of Theodosius than was Augustine, but we should note what exactly it is that Augustine picks out as the marks of good government — law and coercion employed for the sake of the subject by one who is manifestly not in thrall to *libido dominandi* or vainglory, because he is capable of sharing power and accepting humiliation.

This is good government, but it is not, Augustine is careful to tell us, necessarily successful government in the world's sense. The well-governed state is not automatically the victorious state; God gives or withholds extensiveness and duration of dominion as he pleases. The government of the commonwealth by the redeemed rationality of a Christian prince is precisely a government whose policy is not determined by considerations of worldly triumph. And this leads us to consider a final and very searching paradox in Augustine's reflections on power and rule. The commonwealth is, ideally, a

---

47. 24-26. On the portrait of Theodosius, see Y. M. Duval, "L'éloge de Théodose dans la 'Cité de Dieu' v. 26," *Recherches Augustiniennes* 4 (1966): 135-79. Markus' comment (*Saeculum,* p. 149, n. 2) that Augustine's picture emphasizes the "private" virtues of Theodosius is odd; he is commended, after all, for ruling in a specific way.

pastoral reality, its ruler a director of souls. Thus it is understandable that Augustine is happiest with the idea of a world composed of small states, comparable to the households of a city:[48] only so are the *pax* and *ordo* of the individual city truly related to the *pax* of the whole world as it should be. "He favoured," wrote Figgis, poignantly, at the end of the Great War, "a League of Nations"[49] — though for theological reasons rather than pragmatic ones. Augustine's devastating critique of imperialism in Books III and IV of the *De civitate* displays the impossibility of an expansionist state doing the proper job of a *civitas:* imperial adventures, arising out of the *libido dominandi,* are always a distraction from the real problems of a community, an attempt, conscious or not, to create an *ersatz* unity in a fundamentally fragmented and disordered group. Occasionally, Augustine grants, there is a case for a war waged to subdue an enemy whose aggression directly menaces your own survival; but he has severe words for those who seek, in effect, to provoke another's aggression, to harden attitudes, to provide themselves with an object of hatred and fear, with the goal of reinforcing or extending a nation's power (words not without some contemporary pertinence). And he adds, wryly, that the Romans have been fortunate in being confronted with enemies sufficiently unjust and unpleasant to give their own cause some semblance of righteousness.[50]

However, to go to war is to enter the arena of historical risk and uncertainty in a most dramatic way; the just community is *not* guaranteed protection in such a conflict. In a not very much discussed passage in Book XXII,[51] Augustine takes the issue a little further. Cicero considers that state to be just which goes to war only in self-defense or for the sake of its *fides* — its honour, in particular its treaty obligations; and the obligation of self-defense rests, for him, on the fact that the perishing of a *civitas* is the perishing of a whole "world." Death for the individual may be a happy release; "death" for the state is the dissolution of those bonds of speech and meaning which make the world rational and properly human (hence the connection of its fate with the preservation of *fides,* covenanted loyal mutuality). But, Augustine responds, the city of God as such *never* goes to war even in self-defense: for to go to war is for it to lose its integrity, its *fides.* In this case, *fides* and security are one and the same, for the *fides* of the Church (there is an obvious

---

48. *De civ. Dei* IV, 15.
49. Figgis, *Political Aspects,* p. 58.
50. *De civ. Dei* IV, 15.
51. *De civ. Dei* XXII, 6: cf. III, 20 on the incident in question.

but nuanced play on the word) is its trust in the abiding city of God, which is not found on earth. Ultimately, the true bonds of human speech and meaning, the sense of the human world, are preserved in God's eternal will and in the *ordo* of the universe as a whole. It is not contingent upon the survival of any human system of meaning. To defend the city of God would thus be a sign of unfaith, an abandonment of the Church's integrity.

Cicero's picture is, in fact, Augustine implies, a naive one. What of those tragic circumstances in which a *civitas* seems to be faced with the choice between integrity or loyalty and security (as in the well-known case of the Saguntines in the Second Punic War)? The secular politician has no means of deciding here; the city of God has no need to decide. This poses a considerable problem for the interpreter. There are, it seems, legitimate — if risky — defensive wars which may be waged in self-defense; yet such wars cannot be waged in defense of the city of God. The wise ruler will refrain from conquest and aggression, and will only reluctantly and even penitently take up arms to pacify an aggressive neighbor: it is not recommended that he abstain entirely from defense. But what it seems he must beware of is supposing that what he is defending is the city of God. Insofar as the commonwealth is just and orderly, it is worth preserving, and its ruler will take steps to preserve it; that is, insofar as it is *imperfectly* just and orderly, it justifies defensive action. True justice and orderliness cannot be defended by such means, because they participate in the city of God, which depends upon defenseless trust in the continuance of God's *ordo*.

The Christian ruler is thus left with a stark and more or less theoretically insoluble dilemma: if he makes the state's earthly triumph or survival his over-riding goal, he betrays any real "justice" in the *civitas* he seeks to defend. There can be no crusades, no victory at any price: he has the alarming task of discerning the point at which what he is defending has ceased to be defensible because the means of defense beyond this point undermine the real justice in the state by implicitly treating it as an absolute, to be preserved at all costs. No particular *ordo* is identical with the order of God's city, and so no state can rightly be defended as an absolute "value" in itself; the potential tragedy of the ruler is in his responsibility to determine the moment at which he must condemn his *civitas* to defeat.

At first sight, this seems to confirm Markus' conclusion that Augustine points towards a "secular" neutral space for the state; no political system can be regarded as sacred, as having final legitimacy in itself. But the conclusion is not in fact quite so clear. All this is true; but, for Augustine, there is only one person who can be trusted to perform the task of the ruler in such circumstances — the detached and mature believer, who in his own soul knows the true nature and the true *ordo* of sovereignty. In such a situation, what will the unbeliever do but yield to the *libido dominandi*, with all its ruinous consequences for the genuinely common or public character of the commonwealth? So we arrive at the paradox that the only reliable political leader, the only ruler who can be guaranteed to safeguard authentically *political* values (order, equity, and the nurture of souls in these things) is the man[52] who is, at the end of the day, indifferent to their survival in the relative shapes of the existing order, because he knows them to be safeguarded at the level of God's eternal and immutable providence, vindicated in the eternal *civitas dei*. Politics and the art of government take on the Socratic coloring of a discipline of dying; and only so do they avoid the corruption of the *civitas terrena*, the anti-city, the realm of what Bathory aptly calls "anti-politics,"[53] in which value and unity rest on essentially divisive and contingent factors and yet are bitterly and unscrupulously fought for.

This is not precisely to say that only the saint should be "allowed" to govern. Augustine does not envisage a situation in which anyone is able to *decide* about the structures of governmental authority, nor does he ever provide any basis for an abstract discussion of what might be the best form of government, or who the best persons to administer it. In this, he is conspicuously a man of the *bas-empire*, assuming, unclassically, the givenness of the existing order. Indeed, the most disturbing and uncongenial feature of this analysis for most modern students is probably the absence of any idea that the actual structures of government and society are answerable to some critical principle. Christians are to be indifferent to the *mores* of the nations among whom they live[54] — and the word is wide enough to include many of the institutions of public or civil life. It is demonstrably *good* that the state should be ruled by persons aware of the right order of sovereignty because of their own spiritual maturity; and insofar as anyone has the choice of assuming or rejecting the exercise of official power, it is good for them to accept, however reluctantly;[55] but he is not interested in reinventing the inherited forms of power or guaranteeing a succession of saints in office (a form, surely, of defending the city of God by worldly means). Here lies Augustine's great difference from all sides in the mediaeval debates about sovereignty —

52. I use the masculine advisedly.

53. E.g., *Political Theory as Public Confession*, p. 165.

54. *De civ. Dei* XIX, 17 (cf. 19).

55. See Augustine's correspondence with Marcellinus (e.g., *Ep.* 138) and Boniface (*Ep.* 220) on the duties of public involvement; cf. Markus, *Saeculum*, p. 94.

from the ardent defenders of papal hegemony to Thomist rationalists. However, we should also remember that he is not a Luther, for whom the Law of God in the earthly kingdom can be dispensed equally well by Duke Frederick or Sultan Suleiman. The Christian has — at least — the authority and the duty to point out what will happen in the land whose king is a moral and spiritual child, incapable of unifying his people through the evangelical exercise of command as nurture.

Where, then, are we left as regards Hannah Arendt's strictures on Augustine as the great enemy of the public realm? In one obvious sense, her criticism is well-directed: Augustine is profoundly at odds with anything resembling Arendt's notion of public involvement (and its motivation, which is so precisely what he castigates in Book II). Yet it is not right to see him as replacing it with a more "private" love ethic. Two points need to be remembered: first, that Augustine's condemnation of "public" life in the classical world is, consistently, that it is not public enough, that it is incapable of grounding a stable sense of commonalty because of its pervasive implicit élitism, its divisiveness, its lack of a common human *project;* and second, that the member of the city of God is committed *ex professo* to exercising power when called upon to do so, and, in responding to such a call, does not move from a "church" to a "state" sphere of activity, but continues in a practice of nurturing souls already learned in more limited settings. Bathory considerably overstates his case in arguing that Augustine provides a universal political *paideia* for all believers, fostering in them the spirit of authentic public responsibility: such a picture of an Augustine devoted to the cause of "community politics" over against late Roman bureaucratic centralism is seductive but anachronistic. It is true, however, that Augustine assumes that a person nurtured in the Church and in the ordered *caritas*[56] it inculcates is uniquely qualified to take responsibility for wielding political power.

Arendt's further gravamen, that Augustine's model of community relationships represents a flight from *time*,[57] is a weighty one. For Arendt, we are summoned to join a conversation that was begun before our birth and will

---

56. A notion excessively personalized and psychologized in Arendt's earlier discussion, and to some extent in *The Human Condition* also. We must bear in mind that it is more than a sensation for Augustine, more even than the fact of mutual acceptance for God's sake, but is ultimately the activation of what is ontologically basic in us, our humanness itself, and expresses itself in firm institutional ways, as the Holy Spirit binds us to Christ in the Church.

57. This is implied in the opposition sketched out between the Christian view and Arendt's own analysis of our involvement in *the human conversation;* see pp. 54ff. in *The Human Condition*.

continue after we die, accepting, as we do so, precisely the fact that our participation is temporary, bounded by mortality and "natality": this is the conversation that constitutes rationality, and, frail as it is, can and must be celebrated as we join in it. But Augustine would have replied[58] that the decision to
"inscribe" ourselves within the human conversation in the terms described by
Hannah Arendt is bound to that quest for reputation and secular immortality
that actually itself represents a deep denial of the temporal. The guarantee of
a place in the human story, gained by active participation in the public realm,
seeks to assuage the fundamental restlessness that is constitutive of our human creaturehood by offering us the glamour of an assured historical future.
For our souls' sake, we need to know that there is no guaranteeable future
such as Arendt's neo-classical vision might suggest: real temporality is more
vulnerable, and so also more open to radical hope (hope in God). It is the
awkwardness and provisionality, the endlessly *revisable* character (morally
speaking) of our social and political relationships,[59] that, in the Augustinian
world, keeps us faithful to the insight of humility — that we are timebound in
everything here below, that our love is an unceasing search.

In this dimension of the political vision of the *De civitate,* the deep skepticism about a human future and a continuing memory, we see not a further
sign of "Augustinian pessimism," so called, but, more subtly, a corollary of
Augustine's pervasive hostility to two things: an élitist concept of human
commonality (immortality as the acquisition of a remembered name) and a
nostalgia for some escape from the shapelessness and uncertainty of temporal existence as such (the Manichaean isolation of a pure and inviolate,
ahistorical soul in us, the Platonist promise of ecstasy, the Donatist quest for
absolute institutional purity, the Pelagian hope to achieve purity of will, un-
conditioned moral liberty). For Augustine, the problem of the life of the two
cities is, like every other question presented to the theologian, inextricably
linked with the fundamental issue of what it is to be a creature animated by
desire, whose characteristic marks are lack and hunger, who is made to be
this kind of creature by a central and unforgettable absence, by lack and
hunger. On such a basis there is no possibility of building a theory that
would allow final security and "finishedness" to any form of political life.
The claims of such a theory would be, ultimately, anti-political because anti-
human: denials of death.

---

58. In the terms especially of *De civ. Dei* books IV and V.

59. As indicated, Augustine does not think in terms of structural revisability; this is not
within his political horizon.

XI. After 9/11

Introduction

Jean Bethke Elshtain

Moral clarity in time of war is hard to come by, as the tightly argued and conceptually sophisticated exchange between George Weigel and Archbishop of Canterbury, Rowan Williams, demonstrates. In a time of conflict, one often finds oneself wading through dense layers of misunderstanding, ideological fervor, fear and confusion, and mischievous misstatement of fact. In the West, we are fortunate to have sustained over centuries a habit of self-criticism. As philosopher Charles Taylor and others have pointed out in volume after volume, self-criticism in the West helped to constitute the Western tradition over time. This habit manifests itself in the just or justified war tradition, a form of critical reflection on occasions for the use of force and whether or not the type of force being brought to bear is consistent with two main principles: discrimination and proportionality.

Discrimination means, simply, that those deploying force must do their level best to distinguish combatants from non-combatants. Proportionality requires that the level of force being brought to bear is measured, does not use more force than is necessary to "do the job" militarily speaking. Some armies are deeply imbued with these norms as part of their rules of engagement. This is undeniably true of the United States military, where training regimens, rituals, and requirements put discrimination up front as an often overriding consideration. Soldiers are instructed frequently — depending on the situation, of course — to retreat rather than engage where civilians would, even if unintentionally, be the primary victims of an attack.

Now, this is quite simply a fact about the modern U.S. military. Anyone who investigates how training is done, who interviews soldiers and chaplains, and who pays close attention, comes to this recognition soon enough. Unfortunately, many there are who make pronouncements, especially those of a highly indignant, that is to say, moralistic nature, who do not regard themselves as under any obligation to "get it straight." Rather, they proceed as if the facts of the matter do not, in fact, matter. Such commentators will insist, against all the evidence, that an air campaign is indiscriminate by definition rather than investigating the question. Cranked-up statistics about damage can always be found on activist and advocacy websites, while the soberer efforts compiled by a variety of serious sources are ignored.

This is a problem the so-called Christian realists, of whom Reinhold Niebuhr is often pointed to as a prime example, grappled with by insisting that moral evaluation, especially in time of crisis, must begin with the most complete and accurate description of the actual situation it is possible to construct, rather than with an abstract, ideologically driven "imagined" scene. In this, Christian realism and the just war tradition are compatriots, for just war thinking proceeds concretely as well.

Just war thinkers are enjoined not to join in unsubstantiated claims and rumors, such as, for example, Elsa Tamez's claim that the United States' war of self-defense against the Taliban regime in Afghanistan proceeded under the name "Infinite Justice." This is simply not true. The name was suggested — and *rejected* — as an instance of overreach. President Bush made this clear, and anyone interested in the facts can check it out. This may seem a rather trivial matter but, of course, it is not, for Tamez builds her entire essay on a mischaracterization of a fundamental fact.

She further assumes that violence has an "unlimited nature," when we know that this, too, is false to the evidence, historic and current. She states that terrorists "will never admit that the objective of the airplanes was to kill innocent victims," but, of course, they do. This is made clear again and again in bin Laden's multiple fatwas where he disdains any distinction between combatant and non-combatant, calling for all "infidels, Americans, and Jews" to be killed whenever and wherever one can find them. Particularly noxious, for bin Ladenism, are homosexuals and free women.

She continues that, even as terrorists won't admit that they really aim to kill civilians, so President Bush would not admit that "his objective is to kill the Afghan people." This flies in the face of all stated war objectives — by contrast to the stated objectives of bin Laden. Whatever one thought of former President Bush, he made it clear from the first moments after 9/11 that the conflict was not with Islam in general or with the Afghan people in general but with a murderous regime that tormented its own people in ways documented by all international agencies and the United Nations; that was, in fact, denied international legitimacy measured by *de jure* status (being recognized only by Pakistan); and that harbored terrorists and terrorist training camps.

What would be the reason for any American president to want to kill all the Afghan people? One crude measure would be this: given the American arsenal of weapons, if the aim had been to slaughter Afghanis, why didn't we simply use massive indiscriminate weaponry against all Afghan cities, getting maximum civilian "kill" in this way, go on to raze the entire countryside, and then just salt the whole place over as the Romans did Carthage?

The *casus belli* for the United States was not per se to protect the human rights of Afghan women, indeed all Afghanis, but this is certainly a secondary benefit. No, the primary reason the war was waged, as one of the leading just war thinkers and himself a democratic socialist, Michael Walzer, insists, was self-defense. There was nothing to prevent future attacks aimed at maximum kill of non-combatants unless the ability to mount such attacks was destroyed. Given that the Taliban were not prepared to send al-Qaeda packing and, indeed, reveled in 3,000 civilian deaths, a measured use of force was decided upon. This decision belongs within one of the major categories of just war, namely, *jus ad bellum,* assessing whether or not the resort to force is justified.

At this point, we bring Weigel and Williams onto the stage. The exchange begins with Weigel's essay "Moral Clarity in a Time of War," a piece Williams describes as "formidable and sophisticated." That it is. The gravamen of Weigel's piece is to note the lamentable "forgetting" of the just war tradition among those who were, historically, its "keepers," especially religious leaders and moral theologians. And he does mean "forgetting" rather than explicit and reasoned rejection. People act as if the tradition is not there or they offer back-handed rejections of it or radical misstatements of its requirements. If just war thinking is kept alive anywhere, it is in our military academies: here, too, Weigel is simply noting a feature of our contemporary world.

Because so much of the commentary of late from the moral philosophers and religious elites consists of what might be called "functional pacifism," other commentators, despairing of such opinion, insist that only a resolute warrior ethos, drawn from pagan antiquity, can do the job that needs to be done. So the map they draw up is hard-core "realpolitik" against functional pacifism. The upshot is an impoverished discourse as neither side confronts the rich complexities of just war thinking.

After taking the temperature of the moment, Weigel argues that the just war tradition is "best understood as a sustained and disciplined intellectual attempt to relate the morally legitimate use of proportionate and discriminate military force to morally worthy political ends." This is a tradition of statecraft, "not simply a method of casuistry"; it is a tradition that can shape an authentic "public moral culture" of some depth; and it is crucial that the tradition's distinction between *bellum* and *duellum* be consistently lifted up. The latter is a duel, the use of force for private ends. The former is the use of force enjoined by public authority, and it begins with a presumption *for* justice rather than against violence, as some insist.

The justice of which the justified use of force is the goal is a "right order" of things, a world in which civic peace and a measure of justice pertain. For Weigel, Tamez's privileging of a "God of mercy" to the nigh exclusion of a God of justice distorts radically the Christian tradition. Weigel's essay concludes with a response to those who claim the just war tradition is defunct. To suggest that, he insists, "is to suggest that politics — the organization of human life into purposeful political communities — is obsolete."

The exchange between Williams and Weigel follows on the heels of "Moral Clarity in a Time of War." Williams finds numerous points of agreement between him and Weigel. War and statecraft must be within the purview of morality, must not be construed as "unrestrained" or "infinite," as both functional pacifists and, oddly enough, theorists of total war insist. War is an activity that can have, and should have, a moral structure. With all this Williams concurs as he does with Weigel's overall characterization of terrorist networks as having as their primary aim "the slaughter of innocents for ignoble political ends." But — and it is a major *but* — there is one area where they part company, namely, in Weigel's denial of "any presumption against violence in the tradition."

To the contrary, Williams finds in St. Thomas Aquinas's discussion of violence in his *Summa Theologiae* a presumption against war. At the same time, the ruler has the duty to preserve peace internally and externally and this sometimes calls for use of the sword. All private use of violence is wrong — on this he and Weigel agree; but force under public authority may or may not be wrong. The occasions for its use must be investigated. Minimally, then, Williams insists, Weigel's "claim that there is no presumption against violence in classical just war theory needs a good deal of refining." Surely it is the case that violence "is essentially anomalous because the essence of healthy social life is the voluntary restriction of any one agent's liberty in the corporate act of social life."

754

On one other matter, Williams challenges Weigel. To be sure, the "terrorist is objectively wicked, no dispute about that, in exercising the most appalling form of blackmail by menacing the lives of the innocent. Nothing should qualify this judgment. But this does not mean the terrorist has no serious moral goals." If the goal of self-criticism is to be kept alive, and the just war tradition has been one way of doing that, one should be very cautious about a blanket claim that a terrorist's stated ends, in addition to killing as many civilians as possible, which is both end and means, should not be voided in advance because of his objectively wicked means. Here some sort of international entity might be helpful to consult, perhaps a Standing Commission on Security within the UN structure. Given our world of interdependence, should any state simply act in its own behalf at every point, or claim it is acting in behalf of the international common good (understood as right order) without serious input from other sources? Williams concludes by fretting that portions of Weigel's essay may, in fact, weaken the "freedom of moral theology to sustain the self-critical habit in a nation and its political classes."

Weigel responds by defending his argument that the just war tradition does not *begin* with a presumption against the use of force; rather, it begins somewhere else. Where is that somewhere else and why does it matter anyway?

Given that just war thinking is an account of statecraft, it begins with the "obligation of public authority to pursue the peace of right order. . . . That, and nothing other than that, is the 'starting point' for just war thinking." All the questions we now associate with the just war tradition emerge over time, but, in the beginning, a sovereign can certainly override any prima facie case against war because of his (or her) responsibility to "defend the peace of right order."

Where does this leave us here and now? Sadly, the presumption against war has undermined the authority that we lodge in public officials to defend the polity, and it has rendered armed force as per se an "inherently suspect" moral category. This is a "smuggled pacifist premise," and it inverts the tradition: thus Weigel. On this point, he and Williams will disagree.

One way to negotiate this disagreement might be to share Weigel's account of the historic origins of just war thinking but to insist that Williams's observation concerning an emerging presumption "against violence" over time must also be taken into account. There are dangers in going either direction without nuance. Weigel is clear about the problems of "the presumption against force" turning moral theologians into functional pacifists who distort or are ignorant of just war thinking. It would be interesting for Williams to spell out where he finds weaknesses or any troubling implications in his "presumption against violence" claim, if indeed he believes such exist.

Finally, is it possible to approach terrorist goals sympathetically given their objectively wicked means? Weigel doubts it; Williams grants it. Weigel points out that the most often stated overarching goal is the restoration of an Islamic caliphate and the utter elimination of all "infidels." Other stated goals, for example, to destroy the "Zionist entity" or, in bin Laden's most recently released tape, the risible charge that "global warming" is another reason to kill civilians, are not the stuff of serious politics. Williams's case would be much, much stronger had he offered examples of terrorist goals that should be the occasion for thought on the part of those whom terrorists are trying to kill.

47 Infinite Justice, Injustice without End

Elsa Tamez

In his second message to the nation after the attacks on the World Trade Center and the Pentagon, the president of the United States, George Bush, named "Infinite Justice" the military operation that he planned to carry out as a reprisal against the guilty parties hiding in Afghanistan. The bombing started days later and is still going on now, November of 2001. The spokespersons of the White House and Pentagon insist that the American people, like the whole world, understand that this war — different from the rest because it is against international terrorism — is going to be long-term. There is no end in sight.

Osama bin Laden's address broadcast over television signaled that the United States, in the attack on the twin towers, was tasting what the Muslims had suffered for many years at the hands of the U.S. With this it was also made clear that the attack of September 11 was an act of revenge, as was Bush's response to the attack. Bin Laden also threatened that there would be no security in the U.S. while there was none in the Middle East. With these words bin Laden too is shouting "infinite justice!"

The purpose of this article is to give a theological reading and my interpretation of these events. A theological reading is an exposition of how, from the logic of the faith (in my case Christian), I understand the advent of this war that is introducing us to the third millennium, and where, interpreted by faith, we can find new paths to follow.

Translated by William T. Cavanaugh.

Every major act of history reveals the state of humanity: who we are and where we are going. At the same time, from the historical specificity of the event a "who's who" among humanity comes to light, revealing their interests or dreams. But history is one, if viewed from the outside, and what affects one part of humanity affects the whole. Not only that, but what affects the natural world, where people dwell, affects humans and vice versa. Different civilizations share the world and at the same time we are experiencing a globalized civilization. This is felt above all when we are faced with events of such breadth.

1. Infinite Justice and the Violence at the Heart of Civilizations

The attacks on the towers of the World Trade Center in New York and on the Pentagon in Washington that occurred on September 11 — and the subsequent reprisal against the Taliban regime in Afghanistan — make the reality of humanity come to the surface. Civilizations are perceived as violent on a grand scale. It is a matter of an "unredeemed humanity," seen by some myths as belonging to the very foundation of human civilization. I am not alluding to the pessimistic anthropology of certain theological currents in the history of Christian thought, as in Saint Augustine and Luther, but rather to those wise men who observed the development of violence in their civilization and could not find a better explanation than to attribute the existence of the crime to civilization itself from its very origins.

I have two myths in mind. One comes from the Mexican cultural heritage, the other from the Judeo-Christian faith. Both myths reflect the violence of their civilizations.

I will begin with the Mexican myth. I will take the myth as narrated by Roldán Peniche, who in turn takes it from the chroniclers of the sixteenth century and calls it "The Abominable Goddess Tlatecutli." The storyteller describes the goddess negatively. She was a sacred monster who had many repugnant eyes issuing from every part of her immense body. She also had an infinite number of mouths that bit with tremendous fury. There were also two gods, Tezcaltipoca and Quetzalcóatl, described as restless. They seized the goddess from the sky and allowed her to walk on the waters. They watched her from afar. These masculine gods understood then that from this sacred being, who was venerated as chaos, the earth would be founded. So these gods transformed themselves into gigantic serpents and fell on her with violence, splitting her in two. They founded the earth with one part of the goddess' body, and the sky with the other part. The old gods were horrified at such a ghastly and violent outrage committed against the goddess Tlatecutli, and they decided, as a way of compensating for the pain of the goddess, that all good would germinate from her head, so that human beings could live on earth. Thus "from her hair they made trees and flowers and plants; from her skin plants very slender and flowery; from her eyes, deep wells and fountains and little caves; from her mouth, rivers and great caverns; from her nose, valleys and mountains." But the tale does not end here. According to the myth, the goddess would cry inconsolably at night, and so, to silence her terrible wailing, the priests, "in their great compassion," gave the goddess human hearts to eat.[1]

This mythical tale could be an etiology, that is, a story which attempts to explain a custom, an institution, a rite, a phenomenon, etc. whose original significance has been lost. The myth I have laid out here is complex, and gives reasons for various things: the creation of the cosmos, the imposition of order, the domination of men over women, the relations of humans to nature, the suffering of the earth, and the existence of human sacrifice. One way to decode the myth could be as follows. The goddess Tlatecutli is chaos. What the masculine gods fear is her infinity of eyes with which she can dominate all that happens with her gaze. Nothing can appear unperceived by her eyes; what one eye fails to see in some corner, the others capture. Likewise, she possesses innumerable mouths, and with them she can speak without tiring, and attack where no one expects. No one can silence her, for while one mouth is shut, another speaks, and if both are shut the others speak, and so on, without end. According to the myth, chaos is gendered female, perhaps because the feminine in the majority of patriarchal cultures has been seen as mysterious, incapable of being encompassed by the dominant masculine parameters of reasoning. In an ordered society, chaos has no place. It is unmanageable. Therefore it must be eternally repressed. The creation of the cosmos is based on the repression of chaos. This is the founding act of the universe and of human civilization. Violent repression marks the beginning of the world. Order and law are charged with carrying on cosmic creation and civilization. Order also has a gender, which is masculine, and to do away with chaos once and for all a power superior to chaos is needed. Thus are the two male gods charged with cutting Tlatecutli into pieces. Tezcaltipoca and Quetzalcóatl are rival gods in other myths, but in this one they unite against chaos to impose order. They violently seize the goddess from the sky and lower her down to walk on

---

1. Roldán Peniche B., *Mitología mexicana* (México: Panorama Editorial, 1995), pp. 1-2.

the waters. They watch her from afar and plan the creation. Creation, or the new order of things, will put an end to chaos. They have to fight against her, "Blessed Chaos," and sacrifice her in order to achieve their objective, since order and chaos cannot exist in the same space. The gods must mutate into giant monsters, like her, and they do so by transforming themselves into two giant serpents. And so, from the severed body parts of the goddess arise the sky on one side and the earth on the other. But despite their separation, both parts of creation remain united as witnesses to a crime regarded as necessary to give birth to the universe. The suffering of the goddess will be infinite, because she will never disappear.

The founding crime of creation is not something covered up; conscience eternally brings it to light. The old gods, perhaps accustomed to the existence of Tlatecutli, could not forget. Horrified by the abuse, the myth says, they decide to render justice for the pain of the goddess. They want to ensure that her sacrifice was worth it, was for something good, so from her head will issue incomparable blessings so that the earth will be inhabited and civilized by humans. They venerate her for her prodigal goodness.

Nevertheless, the rectifying of the crime was not sufficient for the goddess, because it did not ease her pain. More sacrifices were necessary. At night her mournful cries broke the silence, demanding justice. It was the priests, the ministers of the gods, who took pity on her. To silence her cry, caused by the crime, they showed their compassion for her by sacrificing human beings every night. Humans needed to be sacrificed to calm the cry of someone — Chaos — who needed to be sacrificed to create the world. The male gods, order, and the priests felt obliged to sacrifice the goddess and humans, first to do away with chaos and create the world, and second for compassionate and humanitarian — or rather "divinitarian" — reasons; that is, because of the pain of the goddess.

The original crime demanded other crimes and justifications. Even the narrator of the myth renders his value judgment: Tlatecutli is the abominable goddess, Quetzalcóatl and Tezcaltipoca are the restless gods, and the priests who cut out hearts are the compassionate ones. The definite losers in the myth are the goddess and the humans. The justification for the sacrifices of the goddess and humans is the welfare of humans — to enjoy nature — and the goddess — to calm her cries.

It is very probable that this myth has been categorized as "barbarous," but it isn't, or if it is, it is so not only at the level of the myths of all cultures; it plainly demonstrates how all civilizations are no matter how much they boast of being cultured. The current acts of war signal this barbarous human attitude, as much the terrorists as the governments behind the war, who represent another form of terrorism.

This Mexican myth calls to mind the biblical myth of Cain and his descendents, especially Lamech. Cain was building a city when he begat Enoch. Enoch was the name of the world's first city. There is nothing wrong with this if one does not associate Cain, the murderer of his brother Abel, with cities or civilization. For the Bible the murder of Cain is the first crime of humanity, and the first city with its civilization was founded by a criminal. Crime is the basis of civilization. Cain is from the country and he was expelled from there for committing murder. He had no alternative but to build a city so he would not have to wander and risk attack from anyone and everyone. Cain was pardoned for his crime. This had been the perfect solution to avoid more crimes. Nevertheless the tale intends to demonstrate something else, as if it were something intrinsic in all civilizations: ancestral violence. In response to Cain's fear of being hurt, God promises him that he will be avenged sevenfold if anyone hurts or kills him. The sign that God puts on Cain is the law that forbids killing him; even more, if anyone dares to do it he will know, through the law, that he will be avenged sevenfold. This reflects a conception of violence internal to civilization, if order is transgressed. The law instituted by the sign says "do not kill Cain," and the condemnation appears immediately if the law is transgressed: "If you kill Cain, you will be killed seven times over." The function of the law is here, therefore, to make the violence worse.

The myth comes to its climax when one of the descendents of Cain named Lamech — whose children by his two wives Zillah and Adah would be the inventors of culture (zither and flute) and industry (forges of copper and iron) — sings to his wives the following verse: "I killed a man for wounding me, and a boy for striking me; Cain will be avenged sevenfold, but Lamech seventy-sevenfold" (Gen. 4:23-24). The myth appears to reflect the fact that the more civilization advances and progresses, the more vengeful violence appears. Lamech kills for a wound, and it does not matter if the one he kills is old or young. Lamech does not alter either the *lex talionis* or the prohibition on killing. But he does adapt to the inherent logic of revenge, and augments it. He appropriates the sign of vengeance from his ancestor Cain, humanity's first murderer according to the biblical myth, and takes it to infinity. Lamech boasts of being infinitely avenged, even more than his ancestor Cain. Lamech here is a symbol of power. It is not by accident that the verse is sung to his wives Zillah and Adah. For Lamech, to be avenged seventy-sevenfold means doing "infinite justice."

To repeat, the two myths do not seek to consecrate and legitimate the violence of civilizations, although they can be used to reinforce or justify it. These myths, insofar as they are etiological tales, reflect lived realities; they are not to be understood on their own terms, but as attempts to explain why these realities exist. In this case, they explain ever-present violence and the origins of its unlimited nature. In essence these two myths, by revealing violence without ideological drapery, are converted into critical voices against this unlimited violence. Curiously, myths about the foundation of the Greek *polis* do not have this critical function. In Greek myths the gods appear as founders of the *polis*. The city left behind human underdevelopment and uncertainty to clear the way for the fullness of civilization with all its virtues. Perhaps this is why Western civilization is not accustomed to self-criticism.

Now, to affirm that civilizations as such, by their laws, institutions, customs, etc., have a tendency to criminality and a spiral of sacrifices means that we need to take a close look at the particularities of these criminal acts. That is, we need to distinguish murderers from victims, but more than the subjects themselves, the constants and mechanisms visible in their acts, since the concrete subjects will be victims in some circumstances and killers in others.

In the Mexican myth, the conditions of the subjects are clear. The powerful allied gods kill the goddess, the Other; and the priests, who control the power of religion, kill humans to silence the consciousness of the first murder. Both crimes are called sacrifices for the common good. The masculine gods have the power to kill the goddess Tlatecutli. The fact that the butchers are male is not a coincidence. It alludes to the idea that the society is violent because it is patriarchal. Nevertheless, we also have to understand the genders symbolically and see in the feminine gender the fear of the other, the unknown, the different, seen as chaos because it does not fit into a familiar framework of reasoning. Human history is full of examples of this type, above all in imperial conquests.

In the biblical myth, those who can kill with impunity, like Lamech, and at the same time be infinitely avenged (seventy-seven times), are those who control culture and industry, the city bosses. Insofar as it is possible to speak of an "original sin" of civilizations in the functional mechanisms of laws, institutions, and customs, as shown in the above myths, we would need also to speak of the sin of infinite violence that belongs to those who control those mechanisms.

The myths help to read the current realities in which the war was unleashed. We can read reality in the light of these myths, but now with proper names. Some crazy fundamentalists wounded the U.S., causing terror in innocent victims, and Bush sings like Lamech: "infinite justice!" that is, revenge seventy-sevenfold. Terrorism is chaos for the West, so it must be exterminated wherever it is, and to do so we must sacrifice innocent victims, the unintended effects of war, in this case, the residents of Afghanistan. But as the media cannot hide from public opinion the ridiculous mismatch of forces or the misery and terror of Afghani civilians before the American missiles, there has to be a minimum of compassion for these people; therefore many bombs and a few packets of food fall from the sky as humanitarian aid. The justification: to save the world from terrorism and save Afghanis from hunger. There is no difference between the frightening images of the commercial airplanes exploding into the towers and the images of warplanes dropping bombs on the prostrate country of Afghanistan. The terrorists will never admit that the objective of the airplanes was to kill innocent victims. Their objectives were clear: the World Trade Center and the Pentagon. The innocent victims that by chance were on the airplane or in the towers or in the Pentagon are, for the terrorists, the necessary sacrifices to achieve their objective, the unintended effects of their attacks. Likewise, Bush of course will never admit that his objective is to kill the Afghan people. It is rather to eliminate military bases and other dangerous institutions, including schools for religious training. The innocent victims of the bombs are the unavoidable sacrifices to achieve the goal. No one is in favor of attacking innocent victims, but all do it without wanting to, some legally and some illegally. "Infinite justice" is in reality infinite injustice.

Lamech is truly incarnated in Bush and bin Laden, not to mention the fundamentalist Taliban that are the protectors of bin Laden. They assumed power "to save" the people from the "perdition of the West"; well-known are the letters of Afghan women about the miserable situation they suffered day after day when the Taliban took power. The Mexican myth is repeated with some variations: the male gods kill the goddess to give order to the world, the women cry their own outrage without ceasing. The priests sacrifice the women's freedom to save them from what does not suit them according to tradition.

The spiral of violence is unleashed in a globalized world. Bush attacks the Taliban for not handing over bin Laden, who resides in Afghanistan. And Afghanistan is converted into a place where the "saviors" on each side meet to kill each other. Afghan women, victims of the Taliban regime and of Western bombs, are the chief victims in that place of infinite justice. I hope that their cries do not prompt the compassionate priests to offer them human hearts. Or did hearts already arrive together with the missiles? Yes, like magic, they are the hearts of dead civilians and soldiers. Where they come from does not matter.

The "original sin" of violence generated by infinite vengeance comes to light at the beginning of the Third Millennium. The unintended sacrifices are the victims of the two sides. The American people are as terrorized by a possible terrorist attack or a biological war as are the miserable Afghani people that anxiously await the end of the "infinite justice" of globalized civilization.

When the facts are seen in this way, it appears that there are two antagonists blessed by their respective gods. But it is not so. Even though the myths can be applied as much to the Taliban as to the United States government or to other cultures, what is being experienced today is a globalized world, whose absurd economic rationality tends toward self-destruction. Human history is one, manifested in the diversity of civilizations, but unified by the politics of globalization, in which the economic interests of rich nations take priority. For this reason there is nothing unusual about the fact that Europe, led by England and France, has rapidly allied itself with the U.S. to fight Afghanistan and possibly other countries that are considered dangerous to the interests of globalization. The U.S., England, and France are, in that order, the countries that most benefit from the arms business. It all occurs within globalization: bin Laden, it is said, is a product of the Central Intelligence Agency of the U.S., as are the Taliban.[2] So the denunciation of myths applies as much to particular civilizations as to the human civilization realized today in globalization, in which the West calls the shots and makes the rules.

2. The Justice of God — Infinite Mercy

A theological reading of the problems of history also requires pointing toward possible solutions. As I am a Christian theologian, I speak from my location in that faith. And because in this war "justice" is frequently invoked, the logical question is "What does the justice of God mean today?" The question is difficult because theological words are being co-opted for the ideology of war. To speak of "lasting freedom" or "infinite justice" in the

---

2. Just before the assault on the statues of the Buddha in Bamyan, Selig Harrison, an American expert on South Asia, confirmed this at a conference entitled "Terrorism and Regional Security: Confronting the Challenges of Asia" in front of other experts on security in London. This is taken from a circular letter of Noam Chomsky I received via the Internet.

midst of the discourse of war is to trash some very valued concepts of the Christian tradition. We can say the same thing of the term "holy war," in which the gods appear to be invited to participate in the slaughter.

Nevertheless, insofar as we are Christians, it is important that we view the events of today in the light of the biblical meaning of the justice of God, in the first place because it is opposed to the justice called "infinite" which seeks to avenge crimes, and in the second place because it offers ways to alter the destructive trajectory of globalized civilization.

The key to enter into the concept is contained in the brief dialogue between Peter and Jesus that appears in Matthew 18:21-22. "Peter then approached him and said: 'Lord, how many times do I have to forgive my brother who sins against me? As many as seven times?' Jesus answered him: 'Not seven, I tell you, but seventy-seven times.'" Surely Jesus had in mind the story of Cain and his descendent Lamech. Faced with infinite vengeance, the Christian faith proposes infinite forgiveness. To forgive seventy-seven times means to forgive infinitely.

For particular civilizations and globalized civilization, this proposal is very difficult to accept, because it touches the very heart of their operation. Besides, on the one hand, crimes cannot remain unpunished, or the injustice and oppression of peoples would never end. On the other hand, infinite vengeance inevitably is converted into justified crimes, and eventually the dividing line between injustice and justice, truth and lies, disappears. For that reason, it is the truth of deeds, not of words, that should guide us to rethink events in order to assume other attitudes, new discourses and commitments. Innocent victims are the plain truth of deeds done before the eyes of the entire world, and those victims are generally the poorest, both men and women, those considered negligible because of their gender or color, excluded, insignificant, the weakest, young boys and girls, elderly men and women. Likewise are those victims of terrorism who, while having no part in the conflicts, are sacrificed for an objective. All are victims, regardless of race, culture, or religion. These deaths have no price, or should not have one. The American victim is worth the same as the Afghani or Latin American.

Some of the wisest words during recent events were those of a couple who lost their son on September 11th of this year. In the name of their son, victim of the attack on the Twin Towers, they begged that war not be waged, to avoid more victims.[3] This is how people ought to carry themselves; re-

---

3. The letter is entitled "Not in Our Son's Name" and was written by Phyllis and Orlando Rodríguez, parents of Greg, the victim. Letter received via the Internet.

spect for the lives of all human beings is the white flag that asks for peace or the scarecrow that drives away the missiles.[4]

The justice of God is defined within the semantic field of forgiveness. We are aware that it sounds quite cheap to say it so plainly, especially for us Latin Americans, frequent witnesses to impunity. So we need to make distinctions or determine precisely the different levels of forgiveness. It is the apostle Paul, in his letter to the Romans, who explicitly discusses the justice of God. Let us dedicate a few paragraphs to this theme following the thought of the apostle.

In the theological discourse of Paul, the justice of God appears opposed to human justice; in historical terms, the author opposes it specifically to the Roman Empire, something like the "globalized ancient world" of Greco-Roman culture and the interests of the empire. Also in the ancient world one would need to consider the fact of victims and excluded ones, to clear away the smoke of imperial ideology, to push aside the common slogans of the age, such as "peace and security," "peace and concord," or the titles of Caesar such as "savior," "liberator," "peacemaker," "divine Caesar," and so on. We should note that much Pauline theological language is the political language of the age as applied to Caesar.[5] Paul speaks of "another gospel," opposed to the imperial system. We know that the decrees or notices of the emperor about military triumphs, births, or anniversaries were called "gospels."[6] For Paul, of course, these were not gospels or good news. He opposes them to another: the gospel of Jesus Christ, in which God's justice is revealed (Rom. 1:17). This sounds very strange for those who are not familiar with theology and perhaps even sounds stupid for those who are so familiar with dogmas that they are not able to see beyond empty terms. In reality, the phrase is dense and should be analyzed slowly.

"Gospel" means good news, so we must ask "What is there in the gospel that can be good news and reveal the justice of God?" Paul tells his communities that the true gospel lies in believing that the crucified Messiah was resurrected. This is the content of his gospel. The question remains "Why is this the justice of God?" To answer this we should refer to the very marrow of the

---

4. I take this image from a cartoon that appeared in the Costa Rican newspaper *La Nación,* October 2001.

5. Cf. Richard A. Horsley, ed., *Paul and Empire* (Harrisburg, PA: Trinity Press International, 1997).

6. Cf. the famous Priene inscription from 9 B.C. that praises the emperor who ended the war and brought peace. For the world of that time, the birth of the divine Augustus is the beginning of the gospel of peace.

gospel: the crucifixion and resurrection of Jesus, the awaited Messiah. Let us analyze, then, the significance of the Messiah, the cross, and the resurrection.

The Messiah, we know, was the person awaited by Israel to liberate the people from the Roman Empire. This was understood to occur by means of military triumph. However, the movement of the Galilean Messiah took another path. In announcing the Kingdom of God, it included not only love for the neighbor, but love for the enemy. Surely many were greatly disappointed. The fact that the Messiah was crucified was a scandal for all, as much for the Jews as for the Romans. For the former, the Messiah could not have been hung on a tree, and for the latter it was ridiculous to speak of a crucified God. Roman law stipulated crucifixion as capital punishment for slaves and subversives.

Let us pause to consider the fact of the cross and Jesus as victim of Roman justice. Crucifixion was the terrorist arm of the Roman state, and it was used as a warning to those who would revolt. For this reason they would crucify people on main thoroughfares in plain sight of the people, and they would leave their bodies exposed, to be eaten by scavenger birds or dogs. Few were the bodies buried after having been crucified. Cases of crucifixion were abundant in Palestine. Historians of antiquity tell how the Jews were witnesses to innumerable crucifixions in various anti-imperialist rebellions. It is said that during the conquest of Jerusalem in 70 A.D. there were 500 crucifixions each day and there was no room for more crosses.[7] This, we could say, was the "infinite justice" of the Roman Empire, used to prevent new rebellions.

Jesus of Nazareth, considered Messiah by his followers, was crucified as an innocent man. For the Christian faith, that God emerges in history through a crucified man is a fact of supreme significance. This Crucified One is the innocent victim *par excellence,* or as 1 Peter 2:7 says, the stone rejected by the builders. In this event of the cross, considered central for the faith, two facts are in evidence. On the one hand, insofar as he is innocent, the Crucified One is the representative of all innocent victims before God and humans. And on the other hand, insofar as he is the Son of God for Christian faith, he is likewise the representative of God in those events of human history. In the center of Christian theology there appears, then, a God who is in solidarity with victims. Thus, a theological reading sees in this divine act his maximum solidarity with the excluded and the innocent victims of history. Here we perceive something of the significance of the justice of God.

7. Cf. Neil Elliott, *Liberating Paul: The Justice of God and the Politics of the Apostle* (Maryknoll, NY: Orbis Books, 1994), pp. 93-99.

Already Jesus of Nazareth, born in a manger, showed part of the significance of this justice of God in his practice of justice and proclamation of the Kingdom. This justice of God is partial, marked by mercy for those who are excluded.

Let us move now to the event of the resurrection. Paul, in his theological reading of the reality of his time, as we said above, affirms that God's justice is revealed to all those that believe that the crucified Messiah or liberator, condemned by Roman justice, is vindicated and resurrected by God. In other words, the crucified one is the resurrected one, or as the Salvadoran theologian Jon Sobrino says, the resurrected one is none other than the crucified one. Again: what do these words, so familiar to our ears, mean in light of the facts?

Let us return to the original event of Golgotha. If the Messiah was condemned by Roman justice and resurrected by God, we would have to see that his resurrection is a product of God's justice, it is the judgment of God, and from there analyze where this justice is to be found, how it is achieved, and why it is gospel, that is, good news for all men and women.

Looking at the simple facts, this justice that comes from God and that, in rendering the verdict of the resurrection, puts God on the side of the victims, contradicts the systematic imperial legality that kills innocents and shows its intolerance of those who oppose it or challenge its interests. This is seen clearly in confirming that this justice of God is absolutely disinterested, realized in pure love for his creatures, and is fruit of his mercy. For this reason we affirm that this justice does not require any antecedent merit for God to demonstrate his love in revealing his justice. God is grace because he acts via mercy. One could say that ultimately it is God's mercy that is at the center of the crucifixion-resurrection event. And so the unquestionable distinguishing mark of being Christian is mercy; only in this way is God imitated. According to Sobrino, in Jesus and in God this dimension is given more as a principle than as a virtue. Mercy, he says, "is at the origin of the divine and the human. God is guided by this principle and humans should be guided by it, and to this principle all others are subordinated."[8] This is so much the case that a world without mercy bespeaks the absence of God and questions the attitude of those of us who call ourselves Christians.

Paul does not explicitly mention the Roman Empire in opposing the two justices, that of the Romans and that of God, but only alludes to it by the language he uses. The Roman Empire is a specific name of a particular story;

8. Jon Sobrino, *El principio de misericordia* (San Salvador: UCA, 1992), p. 38.

there were other empires before it and others would come after. Paul's analysis transcends the proper name of the Roman system because he applies it to all systems — imperial or not — that blindly follow the institutional arrangements that are essential to their functioning. This is why Paul locates the justice of God in the ambit of faith, independent of the law (in its generic sense). To locate justice in the ambit of faith and not the law, as we have written elsewhere, means to opt for a different way of living, free and mature with respect to the relations between subjects and the logic of all law that is intrinsic to institutions, the laws themselves, customs, traditions, etc. Subjects subordinated without discernment to the Law (capitalized) — that is, all law that is legal, cultural, religious, or institutional — go from being subjects to being objects. Their acts are conditioned by norms and, as Paul says, they are converted into slaves of the law. The Mexican and biblical myths manifest this logic of the law in which blindly following produces death. In the case of the Mexican myth, sacrifices, product of the first sacrifice, are unstoppable until someone intervenes and breaks the circle of sacrificial violence; in the Cain-Lamech myth, the logic of infinite vengeance likewise will not stop until it is interrupted by a new consciousness.

And finally we enter into a fundamental and surprising aspect of the justice of God. Although it is true that this justice has its starting point in solidarity with victims, victims are not the only beneficiaries of this justice. In affirming that God acts through mercy, we affirm that this mercy reaches out to all humans, victims, victimizers, and accomplices. Even though in various biblical texts we read of the punishment of evildoers with the phrase "Vengeance is mine, says the Lord," in practice mercy abides for all men and women. If the Bible reiterates that vengeance is of God and not of humans, it is in order to break the cycle of infinite vengeance experienced in particular civilizations and in globalized civilization.

God's justice is strange because it does not condemn the murderer. It is difficult to understand this in concrete terms when one is walking among the corpses of innocent victims, like the victims of New York or Afghanistan. Nevertheless, if we penetrate the logic of civilizations projected by the myths analyzed above, there is no better way out than to interrupt and break once and for all the circle of sacrifice or infinite vengeance by means of infinite forgiveness: "seventy-seven times." Concrete beings are victims of a system whose logic demands war or revenge to do justice or to bring "peace and salvation." This is what Paul calls "structural sin," and he proposes the justice of God to save us from the logic of the law, from sin and from death. God's justice does not justify crimes but proposes another logic by which, through forgiveness, humans are transformed and reconciled among themselves. And all this is done for the love of the victims, so that there are no more crimes. The forgiveness of God's justice is free but not cheap, for there is a plan for humanity behind it. The primary motivation of forgiveness is not to overlook the crimes but to do away with the system of infinite vengeful justice and create a new humanity, merciful, just, and living in solidarity.

It is time to establish an "international truth commission" of human civilization to write a book that narrates the horrors of civilizations with proper names. A book of life that bears the title Never Again!

48 Moral Clarity in a Time of War

George Weigel

In Book Three of Tolstoy's epic, *War and Peace,* the hero, Pierre Bezukhov, arrives at the battlefield of Borodino to find that the fog of war has descended, obscuring everything he had expected to be clear. There is no order, there are no familiar patterns of action, all is contingency. He could not, Count Bezukhov admits, "even distinguish our troops from the enemy's." And the worst is yet to come, for once the real fighting begins, chaos takes over in full.

From the *Iliad* to Tolstoy and beyond, that familiar trope, "the fog of war," has been used to evoke the millennia-old experience of the radical uncertainty of combat. The gut-wrenching opening scenes of *Saving Private Ryan* brought this ancient truth home to a new generation of Americans: in even the most brilliantly planned military campaign, such as the Allied invasion of Normandy, contingency is soon king, and overcoming it draws on a man's deepest reserves of courage and wit.

Some analysts, however, take the trope of "the fog of war" a philosophical step further and suggest that warfare takes place beyond the reach of moral reason, in a realm of interest and necessity where moral argument is a pious diversion at best and, at worst, a lethal distraction from the deadly serious business at hand.

To which men and women formed by biblical religion, by the great tradition of Western moral philosophy, or by the encounter between biblical religion and moral philosophy that we call moral theology must say: "No, that is a serious mistake." Nothing human takes place outside the realm or beyond the reach of moral reason. Every human action takes place within the purview of moral judgment.

Thus moral muteness in a time of war *is* a moral stance: it can be a stance born of fear; it can be a stance born of indifference; it can be a stance born of cynicism about the human capacity to promote justice, freedom, and order, all of which are moral goods. But whatever its psychological, spiritual, or intellectual origins, moral muteness in wartime is a form of moral judgment — a deficient and dangerous form of moral judgment.

That is why the venerable just war tradition — a form of moral reasoning that traces its origins to St. Augustine in fifth-century North Africa — is such an important *public* resource. For fifteen hundred years, as it has been developed amidst the historical white water of political, technological, and military change, the just war tradition has allowed men and women to avoid the trap of moral muteness, to think through the tangle of problems involved in the decision to go to war and in the conduct of war itself — and to do all that in a way that recognizes the distinctive realities of war. Indeed, in the national debate launched by the war against terrorism and the threat of outlaw states armed with weapons of mass destruction, we can hear echoes of the moral reasoning of Augustine and his successors:

What is the just cause that would justify putting our armed forces, and the American homeland, in harm's way?

Who has the authority to wage war? The President? The President and Congress? The United States acting alone? The United States with a sufficient number of allies? The United Nations?

Is it ever right to use armed force first? Can going first ever be, not just morally permissible, but morally imperative?

How can the use of armed force contribute to the pursuit of justice, freedom, and order in world affairs?

That these are the questions that instinctively emerge in the American national debate suggests that the just war tradition remains alive in our national cultural memory. And that is a very good thing. But it is also a somewhat surprising thing, for the past thirty years have witnessed a great forgetting of the classic just war tradition among those who had long been assumed to be its primary intellectual custodians: the nation's religious leaders, moral philosophers, and moral theologians. That forgetting has been painfully evident in much of the recent commentary from religious leaders in the matter of U.S. policy toward Iraq, commentary that is often far more dependent on political and strategic intuitions of dubious merit than on solid moral reasoning. The fact of the matter today is that the just war tradition, as a historically informed method of rigorous moral reasoning, is far more alive in our service academies than in our divinity schools and faculties of theology; the just war tradition "lives" more vigorously in the officer corps, in the Uniform Code of Military Justice, and at the higher levels of the Pentagon than it does at the National Council of Churches, in certain offices at the United States Conference of Catholic Bishops, or on the Princeton faculty. (There are different degrees of forgetfulness here, of course, and recent statements by the U.S. Catholic bishops on the question of Iraq were of a higher degree of intellectual seriousness than the effusions of other national religious bodies. But the bishops' statements did, I would argue, continue a pattern of just war forgetfulness whose origins I shall discuss below.)

This "forgetting" in the places where the just war tradition has been nurtured for centuries has led to confusions about the tradition itself. Those confusions have, in turn, led to distorted and, in some cases, irresponsible analyses from the quarters to which Americans usually look for moral guidance. That is why it is imperative that the just war tradition be retrieved and developed in these first perilous years of the twenty-first century. At issue is the public moral hygiene of the Republic — and our national capacity to think with moral rigor about some very threatening realities of today's world.

In one of last year's most celebrated books, *Warrior Politics,* veteran foreign correspondent Robert Kaplan suggested that only a "pagan ethos" can provide us with the kind of leadership capable of safely traversing the global disorder of the twenty-first century. Kaplan's "pagan ethos" has several interlocking parts. It is shaped by a tragic sense of life, one that recognizes the ubiquity, indeed inevitability, of conflict. It teaches a heroic concept of history: fate is not all, and wise statecraft can lead to better futures. It promotes a realistic appreciation of the boundaries of the possible. It celebrates patriotism as a virtue. And it is shaped by a grim determination to avoid "moralism," which Kaplan (following Machiavelli, the Chinese sage Sun-Tzu, and Max Weber) identifies with a morality of intentions, oblivious to the peril of unintended or unanticipated consequences. For Kaplan, exemplars of this "pagan ethos" in the past century include Theodore Roosevelt, Winston Churchill, and Franklin Roosevelt.

Reading *Warrior Politics,* and reflecting on the concept of morality that informs it, reminded me of an old story related by Father John Courtney Murray, S.J. During the Korean War, the proudly Protestant Henry Luce, son of China missionaries, found himself confused by the debate over "morality and foreign policy" that Harry Truman's "police action" had stirred up. What, Luce asked Fr. Murray, did foreign policy have to do with the Sermon on the Mount? "What," Fr. Murray replied, "makes you think that morality is identical with the Sermon on the Mount?" Kaplan, a contemporary exponent of foreign policy realism, seems to share Henry Luce's misimpression that in the classic tradition of the West the moral life is reducible to the ethics of personal probity and interpersonal relationships, the implication being that issues of statecraft exist somewhere "outside" the moral universe. The just war tradition takes a very different view.

As indicated above, the classic tradition insists that no aspect of the human condition falls outside the purview of moral reasoning and judgment — including politics. Politics is a human enterprise. Because human beings are creatures of intelligence and free will — because human beings are inescapably *moral* actors — every human activity, including politics, is subject to moral scrutiny. There is no Archimedean point outside the moral universe from which even the wisest "pagan" statesman can leverage world politics.

Indeed, what Kaplan proposes as a "pagan ethos" is a form of moral reasoning that would be enriched by a serious encounter with the classic just war tradition. One need not be a "pagan," as Kaplan proposes, to understand the enduring impact of original sin on the world and its affairs; Genesis 1–3 and a good dose of Augustine's *City of God* will do the job just as well, and arguably better. One need not be a "pagan" to be persuaded that moral conviction, human ingenuity, and wise statecraft can bend history's course in a more humane direction; one need only reflect on the achievement of Pope John Paul II and the church-based human rights resistance in Central and Eastern Europe in helping rid the world of the plague of communism.

A realistic sense of the boundaries of the humanly possible in given situations is not foreign to the classic moral tradition of the West; prudence, after all, is one of the cardinal virtues. Nor is patriotism necessarily "pagan"; indeed, in a country culturally configured like the United States, patriotism is far more likely to be sustained by biblical rather than "pagan" moral warrants. As for "moralism" and its emphasis on good intentions, I hope I shall not be thought unecumenical if I observe that that is a Protestant problem, and that Catholic moral theology in the Thomistic stream is very dubious about voluntaristic theories of the moral life and their reduction of morality to a contest between the divine will and my will.

Kaplan notwithstanding, we can get to an ethic appropriate for leadership in world politics without declaring ourselves "pagans." And, as Brian Anderson has argued in a thoughtful review of Kaplan's book in *National Review*, we can get there while retaining "a crucial place for a transcendent *ought* that limits the evil governments can do." An ethic for world politics can be built against an ampler moral horizon than Kaplan suggests.

As a tradition of statecraft, the just war argument recognizes that there are circumstances in which the first and most urgent obligation in the face of evil is to stop it. Which means that there are times when waging war is morally necessary to defend the innocent and to promote the minimum conditions of international order. This, I suggest, is one of those times. Grasping that does not require us to be "pagans." It only requires us to be morally serious and politically responsible. Moral seriousness and political responsibility require us to make the effort to "connect the dots" between means and ends.

Thus the just war tradition is best understood as a sustained and disciplined intellectual attempt to relate the morally legitimate use of proportionate and discriminate military force to morally worthy political ends. In this sense, the just war tradition shares Clausewitz's view of the relationship between war and politics: unless war is an extension of politics, it is simply wickedness. For Robert Kaplan, Clausewitz may be an archetypal "pagan." But on this crucial point, at least, Clausewitz was articulating a thoroughly classic just war view of the matter. Good ends do not justify any means. But as Fr. Murray liked to say, in his gently provocative way, "If the end doesn't justify the means, what does?" In the classic just war tradition of statecraft, what "justifies" the resort to proportionate and discriminate armed force — what makes war make moral sense — is precisely the morally worthy political ends being defended and/or advanced.

That is why the just war tradition is a theory of statecraft, not simply a method of casuistry. And that intellectual fact is the first thing about the just war tradition that must be retrieved today if we seek a public moral culture capable of informing the national and international debate about war, peace, and international order.

The second crucial idea to be retrieved in the contemporary renewal of the just war tradition is the distinction between *bellum* and *duellum*, between warring and "dueling," so to speak. As intellectual historian and just war theorist James Turner Johnson has demonstrated in a number of seminal works, this distinction is the crux of the matter in moral analysis. *Bellum* is the use of armed force for *public* ends by *public* authorities who have an *obligation* to defend the security of those for whom they have assumed responsibility. *Duellum*, on the other hand, is the use of armed force for *private* ends by *private* individuals. To grasp this essential distinction is to understand that, in the just war tradition, "war" is a moral category. Moreover, in the classic just war tradition, armed force is not inherently suspect morally. Rather, as Johnson insists, the classic tradition views armed force as something that can be used for good or evil, depending on who is using it, why, to what ends, and how.

Thus those scholars, activists, and religious leaders who claim that the just war tradition "begins" with a "presumption against war" or a "presumption against violence" are quite simply mistaken. It does not begin there, and it never did begin there. To suggest otherwise is not merely a matter of misreading intellectual history (although it is surely that). To suggest that the just war tradition begins with a "presumption against violence" inverts the structure of moral analysis in ways that inevitably lead to dubious moral judgments and distorted perceptions of political reality.

The classic tradition, as I have indicated, begins with the presumption — better, the moral judgment — that rightly constituted public authority is under a strict moral obligation to defend the security of those for whom it has assumed responsibility, even if this puts the magistrate's own life in jeopardy. That is why Thomas Aquinas locates his discussion of *bellum iustum* within the treatise on charity in the *Summa Theologiae* (II-II, 40.1). That is why the late Paul Ramsey, who revivified Protestant just war thinking in America after World War II, described the just war tradition as an explication of the public implications of the Great Commandment of love-of-neighbor (even as he argued that the commandment sets limits to the use of armed force).

If the just war tradition is a theory of statecraft, to reduce it to a casuistry of means-tests that begins with a "presumption against violence" is to begin at the wrong place. The just war tradition begins by defining the moral responsibilities of governments, continues with the definition of morally appropriate political ends, and only then takes up the question of means. By reversing the analysis of means and ends, the "presumption against violence" starting point collapses *bellum* into *duellum* and ends up conflating the ideas of "violence" and "war." The net result is that warfare is stripped of its distinctive moral texture. Indeed, among many American religious leaders today, the very notion of warfare as having a "moral texture" seems to have been forgotten.

The "presumption against violence" starting point is not only fraught with historical and methodological difficulties. It is also theologically dubious. Its effect in moral analysis is to turn the tradition inside-out, such that war-conduct *(in bello)* questions of proportionality and discrimination take theological precedence over what were traditionally assumed to be the prior war-decision *(ad bellum)* questions: just cause, right intention, competent authority, reasonable chance of success, proportionality of ends, and last resort. This inversion explains why, in much of the religious commentary after the terrorist attacks of September 11, 2001, considerable attention was paid to the necessity of avoiding indiscriminate noncombatant casualties in the war against terrorism, while little attention was paid to the prior question of the moral obligation of government to pursue national security and world order, both of which were directly threatened by the terrorist networks.

This inversion is also theologically problematic because it places the heaviest burden of moral analysis on what are inevitably contingent judgments. There is nothing wrong, per se, with contingent judgments; but they are *contingent*. In the nature of the case, we can have less surety about *in bello* proportion and discrimination than we can about the *ad bellum* questions. As I hope I have shown above, the tradition logically starts with *ad bellum* questions because the just war tradition is a tradition of statecraft: a tradition that attempts to define morally worthy political ends. But there is also a theo-logic — a theological logic — that gives priority to the *ad bellum* questions, for these are the questions on which we can have some measure of moral clarity.

The "presumption against violence" and its distortion of the just war way of thinking can also lead to serious misreadings of world politics. One such misreading, precisely from this intellectual source, may be found in the 1983 U.S. bishops' pastoral letter, "The Challenge of Peace" (TCOP). TCOP was deeply influenced by the emphasis laid on questions of *in bello* proportionality and discrimination because of the threat of nuclear war. No doubt these were important issues. But when that emphasis drove the moral analysis, as it did in TCOP, the result was a distorted picture of reality and a set of moral judgments that contributed little to wise statecraft. Rather than recognizing that nuclear weapons were one (extremely dangerous) manifestation of a prior conflict with profound moral roots, the bishops' letter seemed to suggest that nuclear weapons could, somehow, be factored out of the conflict between the West and the Soviet Union by arms control. And in order to achieve arms control agreements with a nervous, even paranoid, foe like the Soviet Union, it might be necessary to downplay the moral and ideological dimensions of the Cold War. That, at least, was the policy implication of the claim that the greatest threat to peace (identified as such because *in bello* considerations and the "presumption against violence" trumped everything else) was the mere possession of nuclear weapons.

The opposite, of course, turned out to be true. Nuclear weapons were not the primary threat to peace; communism was. When communism went, so did the threat posed by the weapons. As the human rights resistance in Central and Eastern Europe brought massive regime change inside the Warsaw Pact, creating dynamics that eventually led to the demise of the USSR itself, the risks of nuclear war were greatly diminished and real disarmament (not "arms control") began. The "presumption against violence" starting point, as manifest in TCOP, produced a serious misreading of the political realities and possibilities.

The claim that a "presumption against violence" is at the root of the just war tradition cannot be sustained historically, methodologically, or theologically. If the just war tradition is a tradition of statecraft, and if the crucial distinction that undergirds it is the distinction between *bellum* and *duellum*, then the just war tradition cannot be reduced, as too many religious leaders reduce it today, to a series of means tests that begins with a "presumption against violence." To begin here — to imagine that the role of moral reason is to set a series of hurdles (primarily having to do with *in bello* questions of proportionality and discrimination) that statesmen must overcome before the resort to armed force is given moral sanction — is to begin at the wrong place. And beginning at the wrong place almost always means arriving at the wrong destination.

Fifteen years ago, before I had learned something about literary marketing, I published a book entitled *Tranquillitas Ordinis: The Present Failure and Future Promise of American Catholic Thought on War and Peace*. There I argued that, as a theory of statecraft, the just war tradition contained within itself a *ius ad pacem*, in addition to the classic *ius ad bellum* (the moral rules governing the decision to go to war) and *ius in bello* (the rules governing the use of armed force in combat). By coining the phrase *ius ad pacem*, I was trying to prise out of the just war way of thinking a concept of the peace that could and should be sought through the instruments of politics — including, if necessary, the use of armed force. Like the just war tradition itself, this concept of peace finds its roots in Augustine: in *The City of God*, peace is *tranquillitas ordinis*, the "tranquillity of order," or as I preferred to render it in more contemporary terms, the peace of "dynamic and rightly ordered political community."

In Augustine's discussion of peace as a *public* or political issue, "peace" is not a matter of the individual's right relationship with God, nor is it a matter of seeking a world without conflict. The former is a question of interior conversion (which by definition has nothing to do with politics), and the latter is impossible in a world forever marked, even after its redemption, by the *mysterium iniquitatis*. In the appropriate *political* sense of the term, peace is, rather, *tranquillitas ordinis:* the order created by just political community and mediated through law.

This is, admittedly, a humbler sort of peace. It coexists with broken hearts and wounded souls. It is to be built in a world in which swords have not been beaten into plowshares, but remain swords: sheathed, but ready to be unsheathed in the defense of innocents. Its advantage, as Augustine understood, is that it is the form of peace that can be built through the instruments of politics.

This peace of *tranquillitas ordinis,* this peace of order, is composed of justice and freedom. The peace of order is not the eerily quiet and sullen "peace" of a well-run authoritarian regime; it is a peace built on foundations of constitutional, commutative, and social justice. It is a peace in which freedom, especially religious freedom, flourishes. The defense of basic human rights is thus an integral component of "work for peace."

This is the peace that has been achieved in and among the developed democracies. It is the peace that has been built in recent decades between such traditional antagonists as France and Germany. It is the peace that we defend within the richly diverse political community of the United States, and between ourselves and our neighbors and allies. It is the peace that we are now defending in the war against global terrorism and against aggressor states seeking weapons of mass destruction.

International terrorism of the sort we have seen since the late 1960s, and of which we had a direct national experience on September 11, 2001, is a deliberate assault, through the murder of innocents, on the very possibility of order in world affairs. That is why the terror networks must be dismantled or destroyed. The peace of order is also under grave threat when vicious, aggressive regimes acquire weapons of mass destruction — weapons that we must assume, on the basis of their treatment of their own citizens, these regimes will not hesitate to use against others. That is why there is a moral *obligation* to ensure that this lethal combination of irrational and aggressive regimes, weapons of mass destruction, and credible delivery systems does not go unchallenged. That is why there is a moral *obligation* to rid the world of this threat to the peace and security of all. Peace, rightly understood, demands it.

This concept of peace-as-order can also enrich our understanding of that much-bruited term, the "national interest." The irreducible core of the "national interest" is composed of those basic security concerns to which any responsible democratic statesman must attend. But those security concerns are related to a larger sense of national purpose and international responsibility: we defend America because America is worth defending, on its own terms and because of what it means for the world. Thus the security concerns that make up the core of the "national interest" should be understood as the necessary inner dynamic of the exercise of America's international responsibilities. And those responsibilities include the obligation to contribute, as best we can, to the long, hard, never-to-be-finally-accomplished "domestication" of international public life: to the quest for ordered liberty in an evolving structure of international public life capable of advancing the classic goals of politics — justice, freedom, order, the general welfare, and peace. Empirically and morally, the United States cannot adequately defend its "national interest" without concurrently seeking to advance those goals in the world. Empirically and morally, those goals will not be advanced if they are pursued in ways that gravely threaten the basic security of the United States.

In eradicating global terrorism and denying aggressive regimes weapons of mass destruction, the United States and those who walk this road with us are addressing the most threatening problems of global *dis*order that must be resolved if the peace of order, the peace of *tranquillitas ordinis,* is to be secured in as wide a part of the world as possible in the twenty-first century. Here, national interest and international responsibility coincide.

Moral clarity in a time of war requires us to retrieve the idea of the just war tradition as a tradition of statecraft, the classic structure of just war analysis, and the concept of peace as *tranquillitas ordinis.* Moral clarity in *this* time of war also requires us to develop and extend the just war tradition to meet the political exigencies of a new century, and to address the international security issues posed by new weapons technologies. Permit me to sketch briefly three areas in which the *ad bellum* ("war-decision") criteria of the just war tradition require development, even as I suggest what the policy implications of these developments might be in today's circumstances.

Just Cause

In the classic just war tradition, "just cause" was understood as defense against aggression, the recovery of something wrongfully taken, or the punishment of evil. As the tradition has developed since World War II, the latter two notions have been largely displaced, and "defense against aggression" has become the primary, even sole, meaning of "just cause." This theological evolution has parallels in international law: the "defense against aggression" concept of just cause shapes Articles 2 and 51 of the Charter of the United Nations. In light of twenty-first-century international security realities, it is imperative to reopen this discussion and to develop the concept of just cause.

As recently as the Korean War (and, some would argue, the Vietnam War), "defense against aggression" could reasonably be taken to mean a defensive military response to a cross-border military aggression already underway. New weapons capabilities and outlaw or "rogue" states require a development of the concept of "defense against aggression." To take an obvious current example: it makes little moral sense to suggest that the United States must wait until a North Korea or Iraq or Iran actually launches a ballistic missile tipped with a nuclear, biological, or chemical weapon of mass destruction before we can legitimately do something about it. Can we not say that, in the hands of certain kinds of states, the mere possession of weapons of mass destruction constitutes an aggression — or, at the very least, an aggression waiting to happen?

This "regime factor" is crucial in the moral analysis, for weapons of mass destruction are clearly not aggressions waiting to happen when they are possessed by stable, law-abiding states. No Frenchman goes to bed nervous about Great Britain's nuclear weapons, and no sane Mexican or Canadian worries about a preemptive nuclear attack from the United States. Every sane Israeli, Turk, or Bahraini, on the other hand, is deeply concerned about the possibility of an Iraq or Iran with nuclear weapons and medium-range ballistic missiles. If the "regime factor" is crucial in the moral analysis, then preemptive military action to deny the rogue state that kind of destructive capacity would not, in my judgment, contravene the "defense against aggression" concept of just cause. Indeed, it would do precisely the opposite, by giving the concept of "defense against aggression" real traction in the world we must live in, and transform.

Some will argue that this violates the principle of sovereignty and risks a global descent into chaos. To that, I would reply that the post-Westphalian notions of state equality and sovereign immunity assume at least a minimum of acquiescence to minimal international norms of order. Today's rogue states cannot, on the basis of their behavior, be granted that assumption. Therefore, they have forfeited that immunity. The "regime factor" is determinative, in these extreme instances.

To deny rogue states the capacity to create lethal disorder, precisely because their possession of weapons of mass destruction threatens the minimum conditions of order in international public life, strengthens the cause of world order; it does not undermine it. Surely the lessons of the 1930s are pertinent here.

On the matter of just cause, the tradition also needs development in terms of its concept of the relevant actors in world politics. Since September

11, some analysts have objected to describing our response to the international terrorist networks as "war" because, they argue, al-Qaeda and similar networks are not states, and only states can, or should, wage "war," properly understood. There is an important point at stake here, but the critics misapply it.

Limiting the legitimate use of armed force to those international actors who are recognized in international law and custom as exercising "sovereignty" has been one of the principal accomplishments of just war thinking as it has shaped world political culture and law; over a period of centuries, the classic distinction between *bellum* and *duellum* has been established in international law. At the same time, however, it does not fudge or blur this crucial distinction to recognize that al-Qaeda and similar networks function like states, even if they lack certain of the attributes and trappings of sovereignty traditionally understood. Indeed, terrorist organizations provide a less ambiguous example of a legitimate military target, because, unlike conventional states (which are always admixtures of good and evil, against whom military action sometimes threatens the good as well as the evil), the "parasite states" that are international terrorist organizations are unmitigated evils whose only purpose is wickedness — the slaughter of innocents for ignoble political ends. Thus the exigencies of the current situation require us to think outside the Westphalian box, so to speak, but to do so in such a way as to avoid dismantling de facto the distinction between *bellum* and *duellum*.

Competent Authority

Two questions involving the *ad bellum* criterion of "competent authority" have been raised since September 11: the question of the relationship between a government's domestic and foreign policy and its legitimacy as a belligerent, and the question of whether "competent authority" now resides in the United Nations only.

One of the more distasteful forms of post–September 11 commentary can be found in suggestions that there were "root causes" to terrorism — root causes that not only explained the resort to mass violence against innocents, but made the use of such violence humanly plausible, if not morally justifiable. The corollary to this was the suggestion that the United States had somehow brought the attacks on itself, by reasons of its dominant economic and cultural position in the world, its Middle East policy, or some combination thereof. The moral-political implication was that such a misguided government lacked the moral authority to respond to terrorism through the use of armed force.

The root causes school blithely ignores the extant literature on the phenomenon of contemporary terrorism, which is emphatically not a case of the wretched of the earth rising up to throw off their chains. But it is the moral-political implication the root causes school draws that I want to address. Here, Lutheran scholar David Yeago has been a wise guide. Writing in the ecumenical journal *Pro Ecclesia*, Yeago clarified an essential point:

> The authority of the government to protect the law-abiding and impose penalties on evildoers is not a reward for the government's virtue or good conduct. . . . The protection of citizens and the execution of penalty on peace-breakers is the commission which constitutes government, not a contingent right which it must somehow earn. In the mystery of God's providence, many or indeed most of the institutional bearers of governmental authority are unworthy of it, often flagrantly so, themselves stained with crime. But this does not make it any less the vocation of government to protect the innocent and punish evildoers. A government which refused to safeguard citizens and exercise judgment on wrong out of a sense of the guilt of past crime would only add the further crime of dereliction of duty to its catalog of offenses.

The question of alliances and international organizations must also be addressed in the development of just war thinking about competent authority. Must any legitimate military action be sanctioned by the UN Security Council? Or, if not that, then is the United States obliged, not simply as a matter of political prudence but as a matter of moral principle, to gain the agreement of allies (or, more broadly, "coalition partners") to any use of armed force in response to terrorism, or any military action against aggressive regimes with weapons of mass destruction?

That the UN Charter itself recognizes an inalienable national right to self-defense suggests that the Charter does not claim sole authority to legitimate the use of armed force for the Security Council; if you are under attack, according to the Charter, you don't have to wait for the permission of China, France, Russia, or others of the veto-wielding powers to defend yourself. Moreover, the manifest inability of the UN to handle large-scale international security questions suggests that assigning a moral veto over U.S. military action on these fronts to the Security Council would be a mistake. Then there is the question of what we might call "the neighborhood" on the Security Council: What kind of moral logic is it to claim that the U.S. government must assuage the interests of the French foreign ministry and the strategic aims of the repressive Chinese government — both of which are in full play in the Security Council — in order to gain international moral authority for the war against terrorism and the defense of world order against outlaw states with weapons of mass destruction? A very peculiar moral logic, indeed, I should think.

Building coalitions of support for dismantling the international terror networks and denying rogue states lethal weapons capacities is politically desirable (and in some instances militarily essential). But I very much doubt that it is morally imperative from a classic just war point of view. The United States has a unique responsibility for leadership in the war against terrorism and the struggle for world order; that is not a statement of hubris but of empirical fact. That responsibility may have to be exercised unilaterally on occasion. Defining the boundaries of unilateral action while defending its legitimacy under certain circumstances is one crucial task for a developing just war tradition.

Last Resort

Among those who have forgotten the just war tradition while retaining its language, the classic *ad bellum* criterion of last resort is usually understood in simplistically mathematical terms: the use of proportionate and discriminate armed force is the last point in a series of options, and prior, nonmilitary options (legal, diplomatic, economic, etc.) must be serially exhausted before the criterion of last resort is satisfied. This is both an excessively mechanistic understanding of last resort and a prescription for danger.

The case of international terrorism again compels a development of this *ad bellum* criterion. For what does it mean to say that all nonmilitary options have been tried and found wanting when we are confronted with a new and lethal type of international actor, one that recognizes no other form of power except the use of violence and that is largely immune (unlike a conventional state) to international legal, diplomatic, or economic pressures? The charge that U.S. military action after September 11 was morally dubious because all other possible means of redress had not been tried and found wanting misreads the nature of terrorist organizations and networks. The "last" in last resort can mean "only," in circumstances where there is plausible reason to believe that nonmilitary actions are unavailable or unavailing.

As for rogue states developing or deploying weapons of mass destruction, a developed just war tradition would recognize that here, too, last resort cannot be understood mathematically, as the terminal point of a lengthy series of nonmilitary alternatives. Can we not say that last resort has been satisfied in those cases when a rogue state has made plain, by its conduct, that it holds international law in contempt and that no diplomatic solution to the threat it poses is likely, and when it can be demonstrated that the threat the rogue state poses is intensifying? I think we can. Indeed, I think we must.

Some states, because of the regime's aggressive intent and the lack of effective internal political controls on giving lethal effect to that intent, cannot be permitted to acquire weapons of mass destruction. Denying them those weapons through proportionate and discriminate armed force — even displacing those regimes — can be an exercise in the defense of the peace of order, within the boundaries of a developed just war tradition. Until such point as the international political community has evolved to the degree that international organizations can effectively disarm such regimes, the responsibility for the defense of order in these extreme circumstances will lie elsewhere.

Finally, moral clarity in this time of war requires a developed understanding of the "location" of the just war tradition in our public discourse and in responsible governance.

If the just war tradition is indeed a tradition of statecraft, then the proper role of religious leaders and public intellectuals is to do everything possible to clarify the moral issues at stake in a time of war, while recognizing that what we might call the "charism of responsibility" lies elsewhere — with duly constituted public authorities, who are more fully informed about the relevant facts and who must bear the weight of responsible decision-making and governance. It is simply clericalism to suggest that religious leaders and public intellectuals "own" the just war tradition in a singular way.

As I have argued above, many of today's religious leaders and public intellectuals have suffered severe amnesia about core components of the tradition, and can hardly be said to own it in any serious intellectual sense of ownership. But even if today's religious leaders and public intellectuals were fully in possession of the tradition, the burden of decision-making would still lie elsewhere. Religious leaders and public intellectuals are called to nurture and develop the moral-philosophical riches of the just war tradition. The tradition itself, however, exists to serve statesmen.

There is a charism of political discernment that is unique to the vocation of public service. That charism is not shared by bishops, stated clerks, rabbis, imams, or ecumenical and interreligious agencies. Moral clarity in a time of war demands moral seriousness from public officials. It also demands a measure of political modesty from religious leaders and public intellectuals, in the give-and-take of democratic deliberation.

Some have suggested, in recent months, that the just war tradition is obsolete. To which I would reply: to suggest that the just war tradition is obsolete is to suggest that politics — the organization of human life into purposeful political communities — is obsolete. To reduce the just war tradition to an algebraic casuistry is to deny the tradition its capacity to shed light on the irreducible moral component of all political action. What we must do, in this generation, is to retrieve and develop the just war tradition to take account of the new political and technological realities of the twenty-first century. September 11, what has followed, and what lies ahead, have demonstrated just how urgent that task is.

49 War and Statecraft: An Exchange

Rowan Williams and George Weigel

Rowan Williams

In October 2002, George Weigel of the Ethics and Public Policy Center in Washington, D.C., delivered a lecture on "Moral Clarity in a Time of War." The lecture was a response to various statements from religious leaders in the run-up to the conflict in Iraq, most of which, in Weigel's judgment, exhibited a deplorable ignorance or misunderstanding of the just war tradition. Weigel sets out not only to dust off what he believes is the authentic heart of the tradition, but also to defend a reading of that tradition which would offer secure moral grounding for a preemptive U.S. action against Iraq, or any comparable "rogue state."

It is a formidable and sophisticated essay, building upon the author's earlier work on the theological definitions of peace and order and upon the extensive work over several decades of James Turner Johnson on just war in the modern age. With much of Weigel's critique I am in sympathy. I believe, however, that his account of the tradition is in one respect seriously questionable, and that his defense of preemptive action cannot be accommodated as easily as he thinks within the terms of classical just war theory.

First, though, my points of agreement. Weigel refers to recent work in the U.S. on the need for a "warrior" ethos of a fundamentally pagan kind to sustain us through the trials of late modern international politics; we need — so this style of argument maintains — heroism, ruthlessness, patriotic fervor, and a profound suspicion of moralistic or idealistic rhetoric that clouds our sense of what is possible in tragically constrained circumstances. As Weigel

787

notes, this is effectively to say that morality has no public voice, that what he calls "statecraft" is beyond the reach of moral, especially religiously moral, principle; and he rightly rejects this as an unsustainable view for any religious person. Just war theory is a form of statecraft (i.e., it is an aspect of political ethics, which concerns how to do right in the conduct of ordered community life); it is a way of saying that war is not some monstrous aberration in human life, for which all standing orders are suspended, but is a set of actions requiring the same virtues as political life in general. As Weigel writes, "The just war tradition is best understood as a sustained and disciplined intellectual attempt to relate the morally legitimate use of proportionate and discriminate military force to morally worthy political ends." Interestingly, Weigel here echoes, without mentioning, the argument of Oliver O'Donovan in *Peace and Certainty* (1989) about certain justifications of nuclear deterrence — that the Cold War advocates of massive deterrence involving indiscriminate targeting were, like pacifists, refusing to see war as an activity among others with a possible ethical structure. The apologist for deterrence of this kind assumes a sort of Manichaean view that war is of its nature irrational and apocalyptic, avoidable only by threats of total annihilation.

Against this mythology, Weigel rightly claims that we must think about war in moral categories and treat it as essentially a *public* enterprise, as opposed to private violence. But here my doubts begin. Weigel accuses recent writers on the subject of presenting the tradition as having a "presumption against violence" and thus making it a "casuistry of means-tests," a set of hoops to be jumped through; and he says that one result of this is to focus attention unduly on what are usually called the *ius in bello* issues of restraint on the methods to be used in conflict. He claims that, in fact, the tradition has no such presumption and must be understood as beginning from questions about just cause, which are directly related to the defense of the political good of a society against aggression, the punishment of aggression against another, or of some other flagrant evil. Such aggression, Weigel suggests, doesn't have to be an actual event of military violence: the mere possession of weapons of mass destruction by a state whose regime may properly be mistrusted as an enemy of justice constitutes some sort of sufficient cause for intervention. Weigel finds terrorist networks to be enough like states to present even more obviously legitimate targets for preemptive action. At the same time, such networks are unlike states (even very bad states) in being not a mixture of good and bad, but "unmitigated evils whose only purpose is wickedness — the slaughter of innocents for ignoble political ends."

So to my first caveat. Weigel denies any presumption against violence in the tradition. But this is an odd reading of, say, St. Thomas Aquinas' discussion in the *Summa Theologiae* (II-II.40). Formally, this is a consideration of those conditions under which what would otherwise be gravely sinful would not be so. It is true to say that there is no specific discussion here of violence (to which I shall return in a moment); the focus is on the scriptural warnings about warfare, the sinfulness of disturbing peace, and so on. But it would be quite fair to say that St. Thomas is granting that there is a prima facie case against war, which is only resolved by appeal to the duty of the ruler to preserve peace internally and externally by the literal use of the sword (something explicitly allowed in Scripture). Private use of violence is wrong because a private person always has the alternative of resorting to law to seek redress; but if (as we might say) law itself is threatened, and the public good undermined, there is no higher court to look to.

Some of this is illuminated if we turn to Aquinas' discussions of violence (I-II.6.4; II-II.66.8 and 175.1). Violence is an external force compelling certain sorts of action; as such, it is bound to appear as against nature or against justice (since it takes from someone or some group what is theirs, intrudes on their territory, restricts the exercise of their freedom of choice, and so on). External acts may be subject to violence, though the freedom of the will can never be affected in itself. There is, however, a recognition that external force is sometimes used to accelerate a natural movement; in which case it is not exactly violence in the pure sense. The implication is that action which intends what is natural to human beings, even if formally coercive, is legitimate; so that action which employs violence of some sort for the restoration of a broken or threatened social order does not have the nature of sin. This is the basis on which a large part of Aquinas' discussion of legal penalties rests (II-II.64-65).

Public good is what is natural to human beings, the context in which they may exercise their freedom to realize the image of God. Confronted with action that is inimical to order, action that is "inordinate" in respect of public goods, the restraint on the freedom of others, the intrusion into what is theirs, and the privation of their personal resources, what we normally call violence is not sinful. But in the nature of the case, only those charged with preserving the public good are competent and legitimate judges of the public good. An act of private redress, private vengeance, vigilantism, or whatever, may purport to punish inordinate behavior but it only deals with the offense to the individual, not the offense to the social body; thus it fails to heal the social body and even makes the wound worse. The private person must never use the violence that the ruler can rightly use, as a private person has the right of redress by legal due process.

The point of this long excursus into somewhat technical matters is to establish that Weigel's claim that there is no presumption against violence in classical just war theory needs a good deal of refining. The ruler who administers the law may use coercion for the sake of the common good in domestic policing and in international affairs. But such coercion will always need publicly available justification in terms of the common good, since otherwise it will appear as an arbitrary infringement of natural justice. The whole point is that there is precisely a presumption against violence, which can be overcome only by a very clear account of the needs of the common good and of what constitutes a "natural" life for human beings.

Now Weigel is clear about some of these wider considerations: he writes of "the long, hard, never-to-be-finally-accomplished 'domestication' of international public life." Likewise, he states that "the quest for ordered liberty in an evolving structure of international public life capable of advancing the classic goals of politics — justice, freedom, order, the general welfare, and peace" must serve as the "inner dynamic" of any pursuit of the national interest by the U.S. in order for it to be described as "just." My problem is that by denying that there is a presumption against violence in the tradition, Weigel denies himself the most significant touchstone in the tradition for discerning the rationale of using force: external constraint on human liberty is normally a bad thing, but it is not so when human liberty is exercised against the liberty of others or indeed against one's own dignity as a social and moral being. The point is that coercion is simply not to be justified unless it is answerable to a clear account of common *human* good. Even the security of a specific state has to be seen in the light of this broader framework. So to provide an account of coercion as a moral tool, we need to have a robust account of the balance of liberties in an ordered society, just as Weigel wants — but one, I suggest, in which it is understood that violence, as an external limit on the freedom of another, is essentially anomalous because the essence of healthy social life is the *voluntary* restriction of any one agent's liberty in the corporate act of social life. More specifically still, Christian doctrine, in describing the optimal human community as the Body of Christ, with all its biblical associations, considers the social unit as an exchange of free gift before it is a community ruled by coercion. If and when coercion is exercised, it is in response to situations in which certain citizens or subgroups are prevented from proper social action by the arbitrary violence of others. This is intrinsic to the exercise of law in our world, where voluntary self-gift is not exactly automatic.

This begins to suggest that the active reconstruction of justice in a society is not an optional extra to military engagement; but it also reinforces the point about which I agree most earnestly with Weigel, that war as a moral option is a tool for the promotion of specific social goods. As such, however, it is subject to the usual criteria by which means towards an end are to be judged — to considerations of "prudence." In the language of scholastic ethics, we must judge the fitness of means to ends. Or, more plainly, military options have to be weighed against other ways of securing or restoring justice. Weigel seems to assume that we have already gotten to the point where such a discernment has happened; not only coercion in general but military coercion has emerged as the only possible course. In what he says about terrorism, Weigel makes this assumption explicit: there is no point in asking what responses are appropriate to terrorism. "In circumstances where there is plausible reason to believe that nonmilitary actions are unavailable or unavailing," Weigel claims, "the 'last' in 'last resort' can mean 'only.'"

This suggests, uncomfortably, that there are circumstances in which you will know almost automatically when it is a waste of time to consider nonmilitary options; and the implication of earlier comments is that where terrorism is concerned this can be taken for granted, since terrorists have no recognizable political aims, or are devoid of political rationality. The assumption that an enemy can be regarded as devoid of political rationality is briefly but effectively discussed by Oliver O'Donovan in the essay mentioned above. There he argues that the principle of "total" deterrence (the nuclear threat) is presented as the only realistic option by assuming "an enemy . . . who cannot be made susceptible to the codes of honor and rational political interest"; but this, he points out, is to locate original sin or radical evil outside oneself (corporate or individual) — to assume that it is unproblematic to identify political rationality with one's own agenda. But such a view is the opposite of "realism."

Which brings us to an awkwardness in Weigel's position. The terrorist, he says, has no aims that can be taken seriously as political or moral. But this is a sweeping statement, instantly challengeable. The terrorist is objectively wicked, no dispute about that, in exercising the most appalling form of blackmail by menacing the lives of the innocent. Nothing should qualify this judgment. But this does not mean that the terrorist has no serious moral goals. It is possible to use unspeakably wicked means to pursue an aim that is shared by those who would not dream of acting in the same way, an aim that is intelligible or desirable. The risk in claiming so unproblematic a right to define what counts as politics and so to dismiss certain sorts of political calculation in combating terrorism is that the threatened state (the U.S. in this instance) loses the power of self-criticism and becomes trapped in a self-referential morality which creates even deeper difficulties in the application of just war theory.

I noted earlier the need for a ruler or government to be exposed to assessment by larger standards of the human good than national interest. Weigel is clear that the U.S. is de facto the only power capable of taking the lead in the struggle for world order, and he is skeptical of an international tribunal in which "the interests of the French foreign ministry and the strategic aims of the repressive Chinese government" dictate the determinations of the Security Council. The point is not without substance; but who is to adjudicate the interests of the U.S. government and its strategic aims, which cannot automatically be assumed to be identical with the detached promotion of "world order"?

This is by no means an anti-American argument, as the same could be said about any specific government assuming the identity of its interests with "world order." Weigel is unconvinced that any kind of international consensus is imperative for just war theory to be applicable to a U.S. intervention against rogue states or terrorist networks. But, granting the weakness of international legal institutions and the practical difficulties entailed in activating them credibly, it is important to allow that no government can simply be a judge in its own case in this respect. Indeed, this issue takes us back to one of the absolute fundamentals of just war theory: violence is not to be undertaken by private persons. If a state or administration acts without due and visible attention to agreed international process, it acts in a way analogous to a private person.

The private person has redress in a higher court; do states? Aquinas and later just war theorists were writing in a context where what we understand as international legal structures did not exist (outside the Church, whose standing in such matters was a matter of complex dispute in the Middle Ages). There is a principle which allows the lower jurisdiction to act if the higher is absent or negligent. Does this apply in the modern context? I do not seek to settle these questions here, only to note that their significance for restating anything like a just war theory seems to be underrated by Weigel. Even if the international structures do not exist or lack credibility, the challenge remains as to how any one nation can express its accountability to the substantial concerns of international law.

As to the appropriate structures for this in the middle- to long-term, that too is a question I cannot seek to settle here. But if I may make a suggestion which I have outlined elsewhere, there is surely a case for a Standing Commission on Security within the UN structure, incorporating legal and other professionals, capable of taking expert evidence, which could advise on these questions and recommend UN intervention where necessary — instead of complete reliance on the present Security Council framework, which suffers from all the problems Weigel and others have identified. This is one way of recognizing that in the present world of global economic interdependence, colonial and postcolonial relationships, instant communications, and so forth, it is more essential than ever to have institutions that express and activate some commitment to a common good that is not nationally defined. A significant part of what I have been arguing is that the just war tradition in fact demands this kind of internationalism, in the sense that it makes a strong challenge to violence as the tool of private interest or private redress; and "privacy" of this kind is most definitely something that can be ascribed to states as well as individuals.

Weigel concludes his argument by appealing for a recognition of where just war theory should fit into the processes of democratic decision making. He rightly says that it represents an ethic designed to serve statesmen; but then he proposes a really startling theological novelty. He writes that "a charism of political discernment is unique to the vocation of public service," and he claims that this is a gift denied to church leaders and other religious spokespersons, so that a measure of modesty is appropriate in such persons when they participate in public argument.

This is related to, though not identical with, the more prosaic point that religious leaders don't know what governments know and therefore have no privileged extra information that would enable them to make more morally secure judgments than their rulers. But this requires further thought. First of all, there is no such thing in moral theology as a "charism of political discernment." A charism is a gift of the Holy Spirit bestowed for the building up of the Body of Christ, and wisdom is undoubtedly a gift of the Holy Spirit. But there is no charism that goes automatically with political leadership. A political leader may or may not be open to the gifts of the Spirit; democracy itself assumes, though, that the professed wisdom of any leader or any party is challengeable.

What we can properly expect in political leaders is not charism but virtue — the virtue of political prudence, which involves, once again, understanding what means are appropriate to agreed ends. Like all virtues, this one requires good habits that are formed by appropriate teaching and learning and that do not simply reach a plateau of excellence but need daily renewal and exercise. Of course governments know things that citizens don't (it would be a bit worrying if they didn't); but it needs to be said, with appropriate modesty, that others know things that the government sometimes does not. Lawyers, NGOs, linguists, anthropologists, religious communities, journalists, strategists, military and diplomatic historians — all know some things that may not instantly appear on the radar screen of any government, and the democratic process is about making sure that government hears what it may not know. This is not a claim to superior expertise overall, but simply to a voice in the debate and a freedom to exercise discernment on the basis of what is publicly available for judgment. Any appeal to universally superior knowledge, let alone some sort of charism of office, risks preempting real political or, indeed, theological debate in this area.

In the end, my unease with Weigel's otherwise welcome and excellent essay is that it encourages a weakening of the freedom of moral theology to sustain the self-critical habit in a nation and its political classes. By sidestepping the subtleties of the analysis of violence in the traditional theory it ends by leaving the solitary nation-state battling terror or aggression morally exposed to an uncomfortable degree; and it attempts to avoid this problem by appealing to a not-very-plausible theological innovation in the shape of the "charism of responsibility." If the just war theory is to be properly reconsidered — not as a checklist of moral requirements but as part of a wide-ranging theory of political good and political coercion — it needs to be re-planted in a greater depth of soil. And it needs to see itself, as Weigel correctly says, as part of a protracted argument about statecraft. In that argument, many voices have a proper place, more at times than governments might find comfortable.

George Weigel

Rowan Williams' lecture makes abundantly clear that a formidable theological intelligence is now resident at Lambeth Palace. That is a development of prime importance in refining the public moral debate in this time of war, and I welcome it wholeheartedly. I am also grateful to the Archbishop for identifying the significant points of agreement between us — although, as I hope to demonstrate, I have a rather different reading of the implications of several of those agreements.

In order to foster the further clarification of thought for which Dr. Williams calls, let me begin with some context-setting. In writing "Moral Clarity in a Time of War," my first intention was not to promote a reading of the just war tradition that would provide a secure moral rationale for preemptive U.S.-led military action against the regime of Saddam Hussein, similar outlaw states, or international terrorism; it was to propose a revitalization of the just war way of thinking as the basis of morally serious statecraft in the Western democracies in the circumstances of a post–September 11 world. To be sure, Iraq was an urgent test case for the just war tradition in this new and dangerous situation; and it is no secret that, in my judgment, a just war case for military action against the Saddam Hussein regime could be mounted. Still, I trust that my essay did not put the policy cart before the theological horse.

For the essay's first purpose was to address a grave theological and ecclesial problem: over more than a quarter century, religious intellectuals and pastoral leaders had distorted, and were continuing to distort, the just war tradition by disengaging it from its proper context within a theory of statecraft. And it seemed to me that the only way to bring the tools of moral reasoning to bear on the distinctive circumstances of this particular time of war, this post–September 11 world, was to restore just war thinking to its proper location within Christian moral reflection on the distinctive ends of public life. Thus I take it as a very good sign for the future of the discussion that Dr. Williams agrees with me on four crucial points: that the just war tradition is not a free-floating casuistry of means tests; that just war thinking must function within a normative understanding of the political task; that, in this very specific sense, "war" is a moral category — it is the use of proportionate and discriminate armed force for public ends by publicly accountable public authorities who have a moral obligation to defend those for whom they have assumed responsibility; and that "war" *(bellum)* must be rigorously distinguished from brigandage, piracy, terrorism, and other forms of *duellum,* the use of armed force by private persons for private ends.

These points of agreement bring us to the first significant disagreement — one that involves the starting point for just war reflection. Does the just war way of thinking begin with a "presumption against war," or does it begin elsewhere?

This entire discussion has been confused by the tendency of "presumption against war" proponents to fudge the language, so that in some instances we are told that the tradition begins with a presumption against war, whereas on other occasions the tradition is said to begin with a presumption against violence. While I quoted both these formulations in "Moral Clarity," the real issue is the so-called presumption against war, as the *terminus a quo* for just war thinking. Thus the Archbishop's interesting observations on the Aristotelian-Thomistic understanding of "violence" do not quite get us to the heart of the argument.

In thinking about these matters, I rely on the historical research of James Turner Johnson, who insists that there is simply no warrant in the tradition — in its Augustinian, medieval, or early modern forms — for starting just war thinking with a presumption against war. Rather, as I wrote with emphasis in my essay, the tradition "begins somewhere else." If the just war tradition is theologically and historically embedded within a more comprehensive theory of statecraft — a theory which stresses the prior obligation of public authority to advance and defend the peace of right order *(tranquillitas ordinis),* which is composed of freedom, justice, and security — then just war thinking "begins" not with presumptions for or against war but with a context-setting moral judgment about the obligation of public authority to pursue the peace of right order — which includes the obligation of providing for the security of one's people against aggression. That, and nothing other than that, is the "starting point" for just war thinking. Questions of how — can the peace of right order be defended and advanced through nonmilitary means, or must proportionate and discriminate armed force be deployed? — come into focus only when the what and the why of morally defensible political ends have been established. Dr. Williams' reference to Aquinas' discussion of just war in the *Summa* demonstrates this (even as it undermines his historically and theologically questionable claim that Aquinas, too, shares the presumption against war). Why can a sovereign ruler override what Dr. Williams calls Aquinas' "prima facie case against war"? Because, I suggest, the ruler is under a prior moral obligation, a responsibility to defend the peace of right order. That prior obligation is the beginning of all morally serious thinking about the use of armed force for morally serious ends.

Thus just war thinking, in Aquinas and elsewhere, has to be located within a given theologian's more comprehensive understanding of the normative character of statecraft, its ends, and the means appropriate to securing those ends — a point I could have made clearer in my essay.

What does this have to do with today's arguments? A lot, actually. For the net result of the presumption against war has not been to reinforce the obvious — namely, that public authority has to make a moral case that the use of armed force in defending the peace of right order is the only responsible option in this instance, because other nonmilitary means have failed or have been reasonably judged to be unavailing, given the threat and the aggressor. Rather, the presumption against war has smuggled into the just war discussion a pacifist premise — armed force is wicked — that classic just war thinking rejects. As I suggested in "Moral Clarity," the classic just war tradition does not regard armed force as inherently suspect morally; rather, classic just war thinking treats armed force as an instrument that can be used for good or for evil, depending on who is using it, for what ends, and how.

That smuggled pacifist premise has made a hash of theological method, inverting the tradition by putting *ius in bello* questions ahead of the determinations that give those questions moral sense — the determinations of the *ius ad bellum*. It has also distorted the prudential judgments of many religious leaders as they have tried to read the signs of the times through the filter of the presumption against war. Time and again in recent years religious leaders have been proven wrong in their predictions about the likely consequences of various uses of armed force. There is certainly an ideological element to these failures of prognostication, as more and more of the world's established Christian leadership has adopted, from the international left, a functional pacifism whose primary objection to the use of armed force has to do with who is using it — that is, the West, understood as an oppressor culture. But ideological predispositions don't explain every facet of this global clerical lurch *à gauche;* something else is also going on here. And that something else is, I think, the presumption against war, which functions like a badly manufactured pair of eyeglasses, distorting the vision of the observer. To return, once again, to the most obvious example of this artificial myopia: in their 1983 pastoral letter, "The Challenge of Peace," the Catholic bishops of the United States seriously misread the moral and political dynamics of the last decade of the Cold War (insisting that nuclear arms control was the key to peace, not regime change in the Soviet Union and its satellites), not because the (complex) facts of the case were not there to be seen and understood, but because the presumption against war blurred their perception of what they were seeing. The same, I suggest, holds true for the many warnings of catastrophe from religious leaders that preceded the Gulf War of 1991 and the most recent Iraq War.

Dr. Williams once jocularly referred to himself as a "hairy lefty," and while his article here rises far above the standards of analysis and judgment typically found in religious activist circles, there are several points in his essay at which, I respectfully suggest, portside-tilting politics are getting the better of empirically informed theological analysis.

The first of these has to do with terrorism and outlaw states. The Archbishop's claim that today's terror networks are motivated by some form of political rationality is, at the very least, misleading, for it seems to ignore the powerful currents of nihilism at work in the Taliban, al-Qaeda, and other contemporary terrorist organizations and networks. Anarchic nihilism has been a prominent feature of modern terrorism since its origins in nineteenth-century Russia. When that form of nihilism is married to a distorted conception of monotheism, it yields a goal that I am sure Dr. Williams rejects on moral grounds (i.e., the coercive imposition of politicized Islam on a national and international scale) and a method — mass murder — that he rightly deplores. As for outlaw states, it would strain credulity to suggest that Kim Jong Il's aims for North Korea are either "intelligible" or "desirable," so I cannot imagine that the Archbishop's (entirely appropriate) counsel to be careful in defining "what counts as politics" applies here. Moreover, to deny that a rogue state or terrorist organization lacks morally defensible goals is not to conclude, without further analytic ado, that military action is the most appropriate means for dealing with the threat posed by, say, North Korea. As classic just war thinking would affirm, there is no one-size-fits-all strategic prescription for dealing with the world's madmen.

The Archbishop is right to caution against nations acting as judges in their own cases. But is that really what happened in the U.S. government's decision making prior to the recent Iraq War? The U.S.-led action in Iraq was supported by allies, most notably the government of Dr. Williams' own country. After strenuous efforts to secure Security Council approval for the use of armed force to vindicate Security Council resolutions, the Bush administration, its judgment confirmed by the governments involved in a coalition of the willing, did not decide to act as its own judge; it decided, again with allies, that some of the judges in this instance — in particular, France, Germany, and Russia — could not be taken seriously as moral or political arbiters of the case in question. The administration's judgment, supported by Great Britain, Spain, Italy, Poland, Australia, and others, was not unilateralist; and that judgment was reached after vigorous public and governmental debate within the states involved in the U.S.-led coalition. For that reason (and many others), the suggestion that the United States government was acting, in the case of Saddam Hussein's regime, as a "private person" strikes me as unpersuasive.

The Archbishop is quite right in arguing that the just war tradition demands a form of internationalism. The question for prudential judgment is whether the current UN system is in fact a form of internationalism that commands moral respect. Dr. Williams and I are quite agreed that the UN is in need of serious reform. The difference between us seems to involve a disagreement about whether the present UN is in fact a political and moral entity independent of states and a genuinely disinterested internationalist force in world politics. In my view, the recent debacle in the Security Council with respect to Iraq demonstrates that, in dealing with international security issues, today's UN is entirely the tool of states, many of the most important of which — again, France, Germany, and Russia — are certainly not making their policy calculations on genuinely internationalist grounds, or on grounds of moral reason rightly understood. Perhaps this could change; but until it does, the moral obligations of national leaders will remain what they have always been.

This fact of life leads to the important question of the international accountability of a powerful country such as the United States. Serious moral reasoning about that question does not begin by assuming that the present UN system is the only, or perhaps even the primary, locus for measuring that accountability. The development of morally and politically worthy international institutions of conflict resolution — which is demanded both by the just war tradition (as the Archbishop suggests) and by Catholic social doctrine from Pius XII through John Paul II — must begin with a frank assessment of the corruptions of the present UN system, not with the assumption that the UN has achieved any sort of monopoly on the moral legitimation of the use of armed force in defense of the peace of right order.

I gladly accept Dr. Williams' proposal that "virtue" (with specific reference to the virtue of prudence) is the apt word for getting at the distinctive *habitus* to be desired in public authorities, while assuring him that, in using "charism," I was not suggesting that the presidential oath of office (or its British parliamentary equivalent) involves an infusion of any particular gift of the Holy Spirit. And we are quite agreed that public authorities ought to consult widely in developing their own moral clarity in this time of war. It is certainly true that those outside the halls of power can sometimes see things that those inside have difficulty discerning. From my own experience with the present U.S. administration, I can say with some assurance that this point is well understood in the White House, the National Security Council, and the Department of Defense.

These things happen differently in the United States than in Great Britain, where the policy debate (at least as I observe it) is conducted within far more confined circles; the Archbishop rightly cautions against drawing that circle of consultation too narrowly. By the same token, as a distinguished theologian, he surely agrees that public authorities will be more willing to learn from theology's distinctive perspective on national and international security issues when theologians and clergymen demonstrate that their perceptions are informed by a clear view of the just war tradition as part of a responsible Christian theory of statecraft.

Having written early and at length that a revolution of conscience preceded and made possible the Revolution of 1989 in Central and Eastern Europe, I am not unaware of the imperative of sustaining what Dr. Williams nicely describes as "the freedom of moral theology to sustain the self-critical habit in a nation and its political classes." Perhaps the aforementioned difference between the United States and Great Britain as political cultures leads me to be somewhat less concerned about the possibility of a weakening of theology's critical voice in the foreign policy debates of the early twenty-first century. My confidence that the debate will continue to be morally informed here in America may also have something to do with the relative culture-forming capacities of Christian communities here and in Britain. (It would be interesting, for example, to learn if the just war tradition is as alive in the British defense and military establishment, or at Sandhurst and Dartmouth, as it is in the American officer corps, and at West Point and Annapolis.)

In any event, and to return to the beginning, I take Dr. Williams' lecture — and our basic agreement on the intrinsic relationship of the just war tradition to a morally informed Christian theory of statecraft — as a hopeful sign that what I termed the "forgetting" of the just war tradition may be remedied by the kind of forthright, critical, and ecumenical conversation to which the Archbishop and I are both committed.

Index

as body and bride of Christ, 98, 103-4, 126-29, 135, 151-52, 219, 689, 702, 793; as bride of Christ, 306, 344; and colonialism, 608, 616-18, 625, 633; and infallibility, 152, 696-98; and the Kingdom of God, 99, 161, 165-70, 172-73, 195-97, 209, 377, 393; as political, 340, 363-64, 518, 520-24, 637-42, 657-73, 674-702; polity as democratic, 152, 651, 694-95; and the poor, 7, 9, 15-16, 18-19, 21-26, 64, 133, 135, 137, 162-63, 174-76, 179-81, 185, 189-93, 212, 397, 539-40; and race, 421, 431-34, 439-43, 445-53, 466-68, 482, 497-98, 585; and reconciliation, 300, 303-6, 308-9, 314, 452, 477, 486, 490, 493, 497, 642, 644, 672; and the sacraments, 98, 102-13, 116, 118, 119-38, 135, 212, 580, 604, 647-50, 653; in the third world, 323-26; and unity, 122, 132-34, 137, 240, 296, 311, 314, 486, 582-83, 691, 744; visibility, xxiii, 135, 170n.2, 234, 303-4, 306-8, 314, 641; and women, 394-96, 400, 595, 597. *See also* Authority: of the church; Baptism; Base Communities; Church and state; Eucharist; Hierarchy

Church and state, xvii, xxii, 34, 37, 218-22, 272-74, 286-302, 303-15, 320, 600, 698, 714, 734, 747

Church-world distinction, 36-37, 110, 112, 116, 118, 119, 127, 136, 190, 222, 301, 306, 344, 393, 644, 651, 658, 672, 684, 734-35

Cicero, 227-28, 236n.18, 735, 737, 739-40, 744-45

Civil religion, 217, 321

Civil rights, 247, 374, 379-80, 385, 405, 408-9, 443, 449, 450, 453, 651n.12, 712

Class struggle, 133, 233, 471. *See also* Equality and inequality

Clausewitz, Carl von, 458, 775

Cold War, 219, 338, 777, 788, 797

Colonization/colonialism, xxii, 6, 21, 38, 376, 378, 395, 446-47, 475-81, 483, 523n.46, 587, 589, 601, 604-15, 616-33,

793; in Africa, 447, 483, 504n.1, 508n.13, 588; and interpretation of the Bible, 588-99; in Korea, 525, 532; in Palestine, 576, 582. *See also* Imperialism; Post-colonialism

Comaroff, Jean, 523n.46, 626

Comaroff, John, 523n.46, 626

Common good, 103, 173, 219, 246, 420, 564, 710, 725, 755, 790, 793

Communism, 101, 217, 237, 256-57, 343, 528, 533-34, 621, 774, 777

Cone, James, 372, 374-75

Conflict resolution, 646, 652, 727, 799

Confucius/Confucianism, 528, 530, 532, 608

Conrad, Joseph, 503-4, 591n.18, 607

Constantine, 31, 133, 653, 698, 715, 743

Constitution: of the Indian Republic, 545; of Japan, 561; of the United States, 240-45, 248-50, 379, 637, 712, 719, 729n.21

Constitutionalism, 712, 717-18, 725, 730, 779

Cortes, Donosoc, 276, 285

Counterhistory, 375, 458-59, 462, 466-69

Cox, Harvey, 111, 119, 129

Creation, 38, 42-43, 110, 114, 117, 211, 229, 287, 290, 295-96, 333, 356, 365, 367-68, 376, 396, 487, 610, 613, 679, 685-86, 759-60; *ex nihilo*, 655n.16, 717; hierarchy in, 741n.39; new, 108, 133, 397, 649, 653; order of, 133, 289, 305, 308, 312, 377-78, 653

Crucifixion, 535, 361, 612, 627, 767-68

Cuban revolution, 62

Dalits, 8, 78-86, 477, 537-52, 608

Daly, Mary, 390, 403

Davis, Angela, 399-401, 407, 411

Day, Dorothy, 337-38, 341

Death of God, 7, 445

Debt, 69, 132, 513, 588, 613

Decolonization, 478, 589, 596, 598-99, 620-22

Democracy, xxi, 37, 62, 68, 151-52, 168, 176, 217-20, 227, 247, 252, 279, 281,